BARRON'S

6 SAT*

PRACTICE TESTS

Ira K. Wolf, Ph.D.
President, PowerPrep, Inc.
Former High School Teacher, College Professor,
and University Director of Teacher Preparation

Philip Geer, Ed.M.
Director, Mentaurs Educational Consultants
Former College English Instructor
and Department Chairman

BARRON'S

*SAT is a registered trademark of the College Board, which was not involved in the production of, and does not endorse, this product.

DEDICATION

To Elaine Wolf, my wife, my best friend and fellow author, for all of your love and support throughout the years.

I.K.W.

To my English teacher colleagues in Singapore, America, Britain, Hong Kong, and Australia, particularly Dr. Peter Saunders and Dr. Robert Wilks, with whom I enjoyed many interesting discussions about the English language and other subjects over the years. And, as always, to my wife, Susan, for all her love and support.

P.M.G.

ACKNOWLEDGMENTS

The authors would like to acknowledge their great team at Barron's: Wayne Barr and Bob O'Sullivan for their decision to publish this book; Linda Turner for her expertise and conscientious hard work in editing the book; and Erica Wong for her assistance with permissions for passages.

ABOUT THE AUTHORS

Dr. Ira Wolf has had a long career in math education. In addition to teaching math at the high school level for several years, he was a professor of mathematics at Brooklyn College and the Director of the Mathematics Teacher Preparation program at SUNY Stony Brook. Dr. Wolf has been helping students prepare for the PSAT, SAT, and SAT Subject Tests in Math for 35 years. He is the founder and president of PowerPrep, a test preparation company on Long Island that currently works with more than 1,000 high school students each year.

Philip Geer (Ed.M.) has been teaching English and preparing students for the SAT and GRE for over 30 years in high schools and colleges in the United States and abroad. He is the author of a number of test-preparation books and the founder of Mentaurs Educational Consultants, which helps students around the world through Internet instruction. If you need assistance with the scoring or evaluation of your SAT essay, you can send an e-mail to essay@mentaurs.com.

All inquiries should be addressed to:
Barron's Educational Series, Inc.
250 Wireless Boulevard
Hauppauge, New York 11788
www.barronseduc.com

ISBN: 978-0-7641-4723-4
ISSN: 2166-5834

PRINTED IN THE UNITED STATES OF AMERICA
9 8 7 6 5 4 3 2 1

10%
POST-CONSUMER
WASTE
Paper contains a minimum
of 10% post-consumer
waste (PCW). Paper used
in this book was derived
from certified, sustainable
forestlands.

CONTENTS

Sat Format

Sample SAT Format

Total Time: 4 Hours and 5 Minutes (including two breaks)	
Section 1: Essay *Time—25 minutes*	
Section 2: Critical Reading— **24 Questions** *Time—25 minutes*	8 Sentence Completion 4 Reading Comprehension (2 short passages) 12 Reading Comprehension (1 long passage)
Section 3: Mathematics—20 Questions *Time—25 minutes*	20 Standard Multiple-Choice
Break *Time—10 minutes*	
Section 4: Writing Skills—35 Questions *Time—25 minutes*	11 Improving Sentences 18 Identifying Sentence Errors 6 Improving Paragraphs
Section 5: Experimental *Time—25 minutes*	This section can be Critical Reading, Mathematics, or Writing Skills
Section 6: Critical Reading— **24 Questions** *Time—25 minutes*	5 Sentence Completion 4 Reading Comprehension (paired short passages) 15 Reading Comprehension (2 long passages)
Break *Time—10 minutes*	
Section 7: Mathematics—18 Questions *Time—25 minutes*	8 Standard Multiple-Choice 10 Student-Produced Response (Grid-in)
Section 8: Critical Reading— **19 Questions** *Time—20 minutes*	6 Sentence Completion 13 Reading Comprehension (paired long passages)
Section 9: Mathematics—16 Questions *Time—20 minutes*	16 Standard Multiple-Choice
Section 10: Writing Skills— **14 Questions** *Time—10 minutes*	14 Improving Sentences

Note: As stated above, the "experimental" section can be an extra 25-minute Critical Reading, Mathematics, or Writing Skills section. This section, which permits the test-makers to try out new questions, does not count in your score; but because there is no way to know which section is the experimental one, you must do your best on every section.

Section 1 is *always* the essay. Sections 2–7, which are each 25-minutes long, can come *in any order*. In particular, the experimental section is <u>not necessarily</u> Section 5—it can be any of Sections 2–7. Sections 8 and 9 are *always* a 20-minute Mathematics section and a 20-minute Critical Reading section—*in either order*. Section 10 is *always* the 10-minute Writing Skills section.

Because the tests in this book don't have an experimental section, they take 25 minutes less than an actual SAT.

Countdown to the SAT

The day before you take the test, don't do practice tests. Do look over all the tactics listed below so they will be fresh in your mind.

BEFORE THE TEST

If the test location is unfamiliar to you, drive there before the test day so that you will know exactly where you're going on the day you take the test.

Set out your test kit the night before. You will need your admission ticket, a photo ID (a driver's license or a non-driver picture ID, a passport, or a school ID), your calculator (the same one you used on all your practice tests), four or five sharpened No. 2 pencils (with erasers), plus a map or directions showing how to get to the test center.

Get a good night's sleep so you are well rested and alert.

Wear comfortable clothes. Dress in layers. Bring a sweater in case the room is cold.

Bring an accurate watch—not one that beeps—in case the room has no clock. **Note:** you may *not* use a cell phone to check the time.

Bring a small snack for quick energy.

Don't be late. Allow plenty of time for getting to the test site. You want to be in your seat, relaxed, before the test begins.

DURING THE TEST

First answer all the easy questions; then tackle the hard ones if you have time.

Remember which sorts of questions you do well on. Aim for them.

Pace yourself. Don't work so fast that you start making careless errors. On the other hand, don't get bogged down on any one question.

Feel free to skip back and forth between questions within a section.

Play the percentages: guess whenever you can eliminate one or more of the answers.

Make educated guesses, not random ones. As a rule, don't fill in answers when you haven't even looked at the questions.

Watch out for eye-catchers, answer choices that are designed to tempt you into guessing wrong.

Change answers only if you have a reason for doing so; don't change them on a last-minute hunch or whim.

Check your assumptions. Make sure you are answering the question asked and not the one you *thought* was going to be asked.

Remember that you are allowed to write anything you want in your test booklet:

- Do math calculations and draw diagrams.
- Underline key words in reading passages and sentence completions.
- Cross out answer choices you are *sure* are wrong.
- Circle questions you want to come back to.

Be careful not to make any stray marks on your answer sheet. The test is graded by a machine, and a machine cannot always tell the difference between an accidental mark and an intentionally filled-in answer.

Check frequently to make sure you are answering the questions in the right spots.

Remember that you don't have to answer every question to do well.

TIPS FOR THE CRITICAL READING QUESTIONS

Read all the answer choices before you decide which is best.

Think of a context for an unfamiliar word; the context may help you come up with the word's meaning.

Break down unfamiliar words into recognizable parts—prefixes, suffixes, roots.

Consider secondary meanings of words. If none of the answer choices seems right to you, take another look. A word may have more than one meaning.

Sentence Completion Questions

First, read the sentence carefully to get a feel for its meaning.

Before you look at the choices, think of a word that makes sense.

Watch for words that signal a contrast (*but, although, however*) or indicate the continuation of a thought (*also, additionally, besides, furthermore*). These signal words are clues that can help you figure out what a sentence actually means.

Look for words that signal the unexpected, such as *abnormal, illogical,* and *ironic.* These words indicate that something unexpected, possibly even unwanted, exists or has occurred.

In double-blank sentences, test one blank at a time, not two.

Passage-Based Reading Questions

When you have a choice, tackle reading passages with familiar subjects before passages with unfamiliar ones.

Make use of the introductions to acquaint yourself with the text.

Read as rapidly as you can with understanding, but do not force yourself.

As you read the opening sentence, try to predict what the passage is about.

When you tackle the questions, use the line references to help you answer them.

Base your answer only on what is written in the passage, not on what you know from other books or courses.

In answering questions on the long paired reading passages, first read one passage and answer the questions based on it; then read the second passage and tackle the remaining questions.

Try to answer *all* the questions on a particular passage.

TIPS FOR THE MATHEMATICS QUESTIONS

Whenever you know how to answer a question directly, just do it. The tactics that are reviewed below should be used only when you need them.

Memorize all the formulas you need to know. Even though some of them are printed on the first page of each math section, during the test you do not want to waste any time referring to that reference material.

Be sure to bring a calculator, but use it only when you need it. Don't use it for simple arithmetic that you can easily do in your head.

Remember that no problem requires lengthy or difficult computations. If you find yourself doing a lot of arithmetic, stop and reread the question. You are probably not answering the question asked.

Answer every question you attempt. Even if you can't solve it, you can almost always eliminate two or more choices. Often you know that an answer must be negative, but two or three of the choices are positive, or an answer must be even, and some of the choices are odd.

Unless a diagram is labeled "<u>Note</u>: Figure not drawn to scale," it is perfectly accurate, and you can trust it in making an estimate.

When a diagram has not been provided, draw one, especially on a geometry problem.

If a diagram has been provided, feel free to label it, and mark it up in any way, including adding line segments, if necessary.

Answer any question for which you can estimate the answer, even if you are not sure you are correct.

Don't panic when you see a strange symbol in a question; it will always be defined. Getting the correct answer just involves using the information given in the definition.

When a question involves two equations, either add them or subtract them. If there are three or more, just add them.

Never make unwarranted assumptions. Do not assume numbers are positive or integers. If a question refers to two numbers, do not assume that they have to be different. If you know a figure has four sides, do not assume that it is a rectangle.

Be sure to work in consistent units. If the width and length of a rectangle are 8 inches and 2 feet, respectively, either convert the 2 feet to 24 inches or the 8 inches to two-thirds of a foot before calculating the area or perimeter.

Standard Multiple-Choice Questions

Whenever you answer a question by backsolving, start with Choice C.

When you replace variables with numbers, choose easy-to-use numbers, whether or not they are realistic.

Choose appropriate numbers. The best number to use in percent problems is 100. In problems involving fractions, the best number to use is the least common denominator.

When you have no idea how to solve a problem, eliminate all of the absurd choices and guess.

Student-Produced Response (Grid-in) Questions

Write your answer in the four spaces at the top of the grid, and *carefully* grid in your answer below. No credit is given for a correct answer if it has been gridded improperly.

Remember that the answer to a grid-in question can never be negative.

You can never grid in a mixed number—you must convert it to an improper fraction or a decimal.

Never round off your answers. If a fraction can fit in the four spaces of the grid, enter it. If not, use your calculator to convert it to a decimal (by dividing) and enter a decimal point followed by the first three decimal digits.

When gridding a decimal, do not write a zero before the decimal point.

If a question has more than one possible answer, grid in only one of them.

There is no penalty for wrong answers on grid-in questions, so you should grid in anything that seems reasonable, rather than omit a question.

TIPS FOR THE WRITING SKILLS QUESTIONS

Read all the answer choices before you decide which is correct.

Use your ear for the language to help you decide whether something is wrong.

Pay particular attention to the shorter answer choices. Good prose is economical. Often the correct answer choice will be the shortest, most direct way of making a point.

Remember that not every sentence contains an error or needs to be improved.

Identifying Sentence Errors Questions

First read the sentence to get a feel for its structure and sense.

Remember that the error, if there is one, must be in an underlined part of the sentence.

Look first for the most common errors (lack of subject–verb agreement, pronoun–antecedent problems, faulty diction, incorrect verb tense).

Improving Sentences Questions

If you immediately spot an error in the underlined section, eliminate any answer choice that also contains the error.

If you don't spot an error in the underlined section, look at the answer choices to see what is changed in each one. The nature of the changes may reveal what kind of error is present.

Make sure that all parts of the sentence are logically connected.

Make sure that all sentence parts arranged as a series are similar in form. If they are not, the sentence suffers from a lack of parallel structure.

Improving Paragraphs Questions

First read the passage; then read the questions.

First tackle the questions that ask you to improve individual sentences; then tackle the ones that ask you to strengthen the passage as a whole.

Consider whether the addition of signal words or phrases—transitions—would strengthen the passage or particular sentences within it.

When you tackle the questions, *go back to the passage* to verify each answer choice.

Tips for the Essay

First, read and re-read the prompt with care. Be sure you understand the topic.

Decide on your thesis, the main point you want to make.

Pace yourself: keep to your essay-writing plan.

Allow yourself 4 minutes *at most* for pre-writing and outlining.

Keep careful track of your time. Allow yourself time to come to a conclusion.

Write as legibly as you can.

Length counts: write as much as you can (while still making sense) within the allotted time.

Follow traditional essay-writing conventions. Write 4 to 5 paragraphs. Indent them. Use transitions.

Upgrade your vocabulary judiciously. Avoid throwing in big words that you don't understand.

Acknowledgments

Page 41: From "On Humanitarianism; Is Helping Others Charity, or Duty, or Both?" by Michael Walzer. Reprinted by permission of *Foreign Affairs*, July/August 2011. Copyright 2011 by the Council on Foreign Relations, Inc. www.foreignaffairs.com

Page 42: From "Defending Democracy in Cote d'Ivoire: Africa Takes a Stand: A New African Diplomacy" by Thomas J. Bassett and Scott Straus. Reprinted by permission of *Foreign Affairs*, July/August 2011. Copyright 2011 by the Council on Foreign Relations, Inc. www. foreignaffairs.com

Page 43: "Mesas," from *Indian Country* by Peter Matthiessen. Copyright © 1979, 1980, 1981, 1984 by Peter Matthiessen. Used by permission of Viking Penguin, a division of Penguin Group (USA), Inc.

Page 45: From *Flappers and Philosophers* by F. Scott Fitzgerald, C. Scribner's Sons, New York,1920.

Page 45: From *Flappers and Philosophers* by F. Scott Fitzgerald, C. Scribner's Sons, New York, 1920.

Page 53: From *On the Origin of Species or the Preservation of Favoured Races in the Struggle for Life* by Charles Darwin, 1859.

Page 53: Excerpt from *Pilgrim at Tinker Creek* by Annie Dillard, page 175. Copyright © 1974 by Annie Dillard. Used by permission of HarperCollins Publishers.

Pages 54–55: From "Hiroshima: A Soldier's View" by Paul Fussell. Reprinted by permission of *The New Republic*, © 1981.

Pages 73–74: From "The Professionalization of Poetry" in *Heavy Lifting* by David Alpaugh. Copyright © 2007 Alehouse Press. Reprinted by permission of the author.

Page 118: From *From Slavery to Freedom, 8th Ed.* by J. Franklin and E. Higginbotham. Copyright © 2000 by the McGraw-Hill Companies.

Page 118: From *Out of America* by Keith B. Richburg. Copyright © 2009 Keith B. Richburg. Reprinted by permission of Basic Books, a member of the Perseus Books Group.

Pages 119–120: From *Balzac and the Little Chinese Seamstress* by Dai Sijie. Published by Alfred A. Knopf, 2001. English translation Copyright © 2001 by Ina Rilke.

Page 134: From *A Crude Predicament: The Era of Volatile Oil Prices* by Robert McNally and Michael Levi. Reprinted by permission of *Foreign Affairs*, July/August 2011. Copyright 2011 by the Council on Foreign Relations, Inc. www.foreignaffairs.com

Page 134: From "Near-Earth Object Survey and Deflection Analysis of Alternatives" in the *National Aeronautics and Space Administration Report to Congress*, NASA, March 2007.

Pages 135–136: From *Lord Jim* by Joseph Conrad, J.M. Dent and Sons, London, 1917.

Pages 136–137: From *Reflections of a Neoconservative* by Irving Kristol. Copyright © 1983 Irving Kristol. Reprinted by permission of Basic Books, a member of the Perseus Books Group.

Pages 145–146: From "The Clash of Civilizations?" by Samuel P. Huntington. Reprinted by permission of *Foreign Affairs*, Summer 1993. Copyright 1993 by the Council on Foreign Relations, Inc. www.foreignaffairs. com

Page 146: From "Do Civilizations Hold?" by Albert L. Weeks in *The Clash of Civilizations: The Debate* published by the Council on Foreign Relations, 2010. Copyright © 1993 by Albert L. Weeks. Reprinted by permission of the author.

Page 182: From "Next Generation Nuclear Power" by James A. Lake, Ralph G. Bennett, and John F. Kotek in

Scientific American, January 2002. Reproduced by permission. Copyright © 2002 Scientific American, Inc. All rights reserved.

Page 182: From "Nuclear Power and Global Warming" in *Public Citizens' Energy Program*, Public Citizen, June 2007.

Pages 183–185: From *The Great Boer War* by Arthur Conan Doyle, Thomas Nelson and Sons, London, 1902.

Page 199: From *A Text-Book of the History of Painting* by John C. Van Dyke, L.H.D. Published by Longmans, Green, and Co., 1894.

Pages 199–200: From *A Text-Book of the History of Architecture* by A.D.F. Hamlin, A.M. Published by Longmans, Green, and Company, 1909.

Pages 200–201: From *Fermat's Enigma* by Simon Singh. Published by Doubleday, a division of Bantam Doubleday Dell Publishing Group, Inc., 1998. Copyright © 1997 by Simon Singh.

Page 202: OECD/ Nuclear Energy Agency (2000), "Nuclear Energy in a Sustainable Development Perspective," www.oecd-nea.org/sd

Pages 202–203: From "Sustainability and Renewable Resources" by Steven Hayward, Ph.D., Elizabeth Fowler, and Laura Steadman. Copyright © 2000 by the Mackinac Center for Public Policy, Midland, Michigan.

Pages 211–212: From "What Poets Can Learn from Songwriters" by David Alpaugh in the October 2011 issue of *Scene4 Magazine*. Copyright © 2011 by David Alpaugh, © 2011 *Scene4 Magazine*. Reprinted by permission of the author.

Page 249: From *Manual of Egyptian Archaeology and Guide to the Study of Antiquities in Egypt* by G. Maspero, D.C.L., Oxon, 1895.

Page 249: From the Federal Research Division, Library of Congress, *Country Studies: India*, 1996.

Pages 250–251: From *I Know Why the Caged Bird Sings* by Maya Angelou. Published by Random House, Inc. (Ballantine Books), 2009. Copyright © 1969 by Maya Angelou.

Pages 251–252: From *The Souls of Black Folk* by W.E.B. Du Bois, John Wilson and Son, Cambridge, Mass., 1903.

Page 259: From *A Text-Book of the History of Painting* by John C. Van Dyke, L.H.D. Copyright © 1894, Longmans, Green, and Co.

Page 259: From *Renaissance in Italy: The Fine Arts* by John Addington Symonds. Published by Smith, Elder & Co, London, 1899.

Pages 260–261: From *No-No Boy* by John Okada. Published by the University of Washington Press, copyright © 2001. Reprinted by permission of the University of Washington Press.

Pages 262–263: From *Disturbing the Universe* by Freeman Dyson. Published by Basic Books, 1981. Copyright © 1979 by Freeman J. Dyson. Reprinted by permission of Basic Books, a member of the Perseus Books Group.

Pages 276–277: "Medical Lessons From History," from *The Medusa and the Snail* by Lewis Thomas, copyright © 1974, 1975, 1976, 1977, 1978, 1979 by Lewis Thomas. Used by permission of Viking Penguin, a division of Penguin Group (USA) Inc.

Page 319: From the Federal Research Division, Library of Congress, *Country Studies: Jordan*, 1989.

Page 319: From the Federal Research Division, Library of Congress, *Country Studies: Japan*, 1994.

Pages 320–321: From *The Americanism of Washington* by Henry Van Dyke, Harper and Brothers, New York, 1906.

Pages 322–323: From *Pragmatism: A New Name for Some Old Ways of Thinking* by William James, Longman, Green, and Co., London, 1907.

Page 338: From "How Health Care Can Save or Sink America: The Case for Reform and Fiscal Sustainability: Moving To Quality" by Peter Orszag. Reprinted by permission of *Foreign Affairs*, July/August 2011. Copyright 2011 by the Council on Foreign Relations, Inc. *www.foreignaffairs.com*

Page 338: From Department of Health and Human Services, Centers for Medicare & Medicaid Services, 2011.

Page 339: From Suparna Choudhury, "Culturing the adolescent brain: What can neuroscience learn from anthropology?" *Social Cognitive and Affective Neuroscience*, 2010, 5(2–3), 159–167, by permission of Oxford University Press.

Pages 339–340: Excerpt from *Patterns of Culture* by Ruth Benedict. Copyright 1934 by Ruth Benedict, © renewed 1961 by Ruth Valentine. Reprinted by permission of Houghton Mifflin Harcourt Publishing Company. All rights reserved.

Pages 347–348: From *The Art of Teaching* by Gilbert Highet, copyright 1950, copyright renewed 1977 by Gilbert Highet. Used by permission of Alfred A. Knopf, a division of Random House, Inc.

Page 385: From a letter written by Susan B. Anthony to Friends of Human Progress, 1859.

Page 385: From an editorial in *The Hartford Post*, October 29, 1869.

Page 386: From *From Slavery to Freedom*, 8th Ed. by J. Franklin and E. Higginbotham. Copyright © 2000 by the McGraw-Hill Companies.

Pages 388–389: From *The Life and Letters of Charles Darwin*, John Murray, London, 1887.

Page 404: From *Caesar: A Sketch* by James Anthony Froude, M.A., Longman, Green, and Co., London, 1879.

Page 404: From *Japan* by David Murray, Ph.D., LLD, G.P. Putnam's Sons, New York, 1894.

Page 405: From "Hotspots: Mantle thermal plumes" in *This Dynamic Earth: The Story of Plate Tectonics* by Jacquelyne Kious and Robert I. Tilling, U.S. Geological Survey, 1996.

Pages 405–406: From "Scientists Locate Deep Origins of Hawaiian Hotspot" press release 09–232, December 3, 2009, National Science Foundation.

Pages 413–414: Excerpt from *Ex Libris: Confessions of a Common Reader* by Anne Fadiman. Copyright © 1998 by Anne Fadiman. Reprinted by permission of Farrar, Straus and Giroux, LLC.

Introduction:

Let's Look at the SAT

WHAT IS THE SAT?

The SAT is a standardized exam that most high school students take before applying for college. Generally, students take the SAT for the first time as high school juniors. If they do very well, they are through. If they want to try to boost their scores, they can take the test a second or even a third time.

The SAT tests you in three areas: reading, writing, and mathematical reasoning. As a result, each time you take the test you get three separate scores: a critical reading score, a writing score, and a math score. Each of these scores will fall somewhere between 200 and 800. For each of the three parts of the test, the median score is approximately 500: about 50 percent of all students score below 500 and about 50 percent score 500 or above. In talking about their results, students often add the three scores and say, "Ron got a 1560," or "Hermione got a 2400." (Total scores range from 600 to 2400, with a median of about 1500.)

WHAT IS SCORE CHOICE?

In 2009, the College Board instituted a Score Choice policy for the SAT. Now, you may take the SAT as many times as you want, receive your scores, and then choose which scores the colleges to which you eventually apply will see. In fact, you don't have to make that choice until your senior year when you actually send in your college applications.

HOW DO I SIGN UP TO TAKE THE SAT?

Online: Go to *www.collegeboard.org*
Have available your social security number and/or date of birth.
Pay with a major credit card.
Note: If you are signing up for Sunday testing, or if you have a visual, hearing, or learning disability and plan to sign up for the Services for Students with Disabilities Program, you *cannot* register online. You must register by mail well in advance.
By mail: Get a copy of the SAT Program Registration Bulletin from your high school guidance office or from the College Board. (Write to College Board SAT Program, P.O. Box 025505, Miami, FL 33102, or phone the College Board at 866-756-7346.)
Pay by check, money order, fee waiver, or credit card.

CAUTION

Most colleges allow you to use Score Choice; some do not. Some want to see all of your scores. Be sure to go to *http://sat.collegeboard. org/register/sat-score-choice* to check the score-choice policy of the colleges to which you wish to apply.

Here's How Score Choice Works

Suppose you take the SAT in May of your junior year and again in October of your senior year, and your October scores are higher than your May scores. Through Score Choice you can send the colleges only your October scores; not only will the colleges *not* see your May scores, they won't even know that you took the test in May. The importance of the Score Choice policy is that it can significantly lessen your anxiety anytime you take the SAT. If you have a bad day when you take the SAT for the first time, and your scores aren't as high as you had hoped, relax: you can retake it at a later date, and if your scores improve, you will never have to report the lower scores. Even if you do very well the first time you take the SAT, you can still retake it in an attempt to earn even higher scores. If your scores do improve, terrific—-those are the scores you will report. If your scores happen to go down, don't worry—-you can send only your original scores to the colleges and they will never even know that you retook the test. In fact, you can take the test more than twice. No matter how many times you take the SAT, because of Score Choice, you can send in only the scores that you want the colleges to see.

CHECKLIST: WHAT SHOULD I BRING TO THE TEST CENTER?

☐ admission ticket

☐ photo ID (driver's license, passport, official school photo ID)

☐ calculator (*Note*: Check the batteries the day before!)

☐ 4 or 5 sharpened No. 2 pencils (with erasers)

☐ wristwatch or small clock (*not* one that beeps!)

☐ map and directions to the test center

☐ sweater

☐ a drink and a small snack for quick energy

WHAT IS THE FORMAT OF THE SAT?

The SAT is a 4-hour plus exam divided into ten sections; but because you should arrive a little early and because time is required to pass out materials, read instructions, collect the test, and give you two 10-minute breaks between sections, you should assume that you will be in the testing room for 4½ to 5 hours.

Although the SAT contains ten sections, your scores will be based on only nine of them: five 25-minute multiple-choice sections (two math, two critical reading, and one writing skills); two 20-minute multiple-choice sections (one math and one critical reading); one 10-minute multiple-choice section (writing skills); and one 25-minute essay-writing section. The tenth section is an additional 25-minute multiple-choice section that may be on math, critical reading, or writing skills. It is what the Educational Testing Service (ETS) calls an "equating" section, but most people refer to it as the "experimental" section. ETS uses it to test new questions for use on future exams. However, because this section typically is identical in format to one of the other sections, you have no way of knowing which section is the experimental one, and so you must do your best on all ten sections.

THE CRITICAL READING SECTIONS

There are two types of questions on the critical reading portion of the SAT: sentence completion questions and passage-based reading questions.

Examples of each type appear in this introduction to the test. The 67 sentence completion and passage-based reading questions are divided into three sections, each of which has its own format. Below is one typical format for the SAT. You should expect to see something like the following on your test, although not necessarily in this order:

24-Question Critical Reading Section (25 minutes)

Questions 1–8   sentence completion

Questions 9–12   passage-based reading
                            (short passages)

Questions 13–24   passage-based reading
                            (long passages)

24-Question Critical Reading Section (25 minutes)

Questions 1–5   sentence completion

Questions 6–9   passage-based reading
                            (short passages)

Questions 10–24   passage-based reading
                            (long passages)

19-Question Critical Reading Section (20 minutes)

Questions 1–6   sentence completion

Questions 7–19   passage-based reading (long passages)

> **NOTE**
>
> If the 25-minute experimental section on your SAT is a critical reading section, it will follow exactly the same format as one of the two 25-minute sections described above. Since, however, there will be no way for you to know which one of the 25-minute critical reading sections on your test is experimental, *you must do your best on each one.*

As you see, most of the critical reading questions on the SAT directly test your reading skills.

Pay particular attention to how the sections described above are organized. These sections contain groups of sentence completion questions arranged roughly in order of difficulty: they start out with easy warm-up questions and get more difficult as they go along. The passage-based reading questions, however, are not arranged in order of difficulty. Instead, they follow the organization of the passage on which they are based: questions about material found early in the passage precede questions about material occurring later. This information can help you pace yourself during the test.

Here are examples of the specific types of critical reading questions you can expect.

Sentence Completions

Sentence completion questions ask you to fill in the blanks. In each case, your job is to find the word or phrase that best completes the sentence and conveys its meaning.

> **Directions:** Choose the word or set of words that, when inserted in the sentence, best fits the meaning of the sentence as a whole.
>
> Records of colonization can be found as far back as the Phoenicians, but colonization became a major force in world history only when European countries began, in the fifteenth century, to make ---- Asia, the Americas, and Africa.
>
> (A) queries about   (B) incursions into   (C) tirades against
>
>   (D) enemies in   (E) amends for

The words "colonization became a major force" signal that European countries made successful colonization efforts in Asia, the Americas, and Africa. Choice B, *incursions into,* is a very good choice because *incursions* means *unwelcome intrusions*, which could be the beginnings of colonization. It is wise to check the other choices to make sure that there is not another answer that also might make good sense. Choice A makes little sense because making *queries about* (questions about) does not suggest the beginning of colonization. Choice C, *tirades against* (long angry speeches against), makes some sense, but like Choice A does not necessarily suggest the beginning of colonization. Similarly, Choice D makes some sense, but is not as good of a choice as Choice B because *making enemies* is not necessarily related to the beginning of colonization. Choice E does not make sense because *amends* are *things given in compensation for a wrong*. Thus, Choice B is clearly the correct answer.

Some sentence completion questions require you to select an answer for two blanks rather than one blank. When answering these double-blank questions, make sure that *both* of your answers make good sense in the original sentence.

Passage-Based Reading

Passage-based reading questions ask about a passage's main idea or specific details, the author's attitude to the subject, the author's logic and techniques, the implications of the discussion, or the meaning of specific words.

> **Directions:** The passage below is followed by questions based on its content. Answer the questions on the basis of what is *stated* or *implied* in that passage.

The history of money-getting, which is commerce, is a history of civilization, and wherever trade has flourished most, there, too, have art and science produced the noblest fruits. In fact, as a general thing,
Line money-getters are the benefactors of our race. To them, in a great
(5) measure, are we indebted for our institutions of learning and of art, our academies, colleges and churches. It is no argument against the desire for, or the possession of wealth, to say that there are sometimes misers who hoard money only for the sake of hoarding and who have no higher aspiration than to grasp everything which comes within
(10) their reach. As we have sometimes hypocrites in religion, and demagogues in politics, so there are occasionally misers among money-getters. These, however, are only exceptions to the general rule. But when, in this country, we find such a nuisance and stumbling block as a miser, we remember with gratitude that in America we have
(15) no laws giving the eldest child the right to inherit his parents' property, and that in the due course of nature the time will come when the hoarded dust will be scattered for the benefit of mankind. To all men and women, therefore, do I conscientiously say, make money honestly, and not otherwise, for Shakespeare has truly said, "He that
(20) wants money, means, and content, is without three good friends."

1. In line 20, "wants" most nearly means

   (A) desires
   (B) requires
   (C) lacks
   (D) seeks with intent to gain
   (E) ridicules

The first question asks you the meaning of a word in context. The most common meaning of the verb "wants" is *desires*, which is the answer for Choice A. However, this meaning does not make sense in context because the author is quoting Shakespeare to support his view that men and women should strive to make money. Choice C, *lacks*, is the only choice that makes good sense in context.

2. The author believes that the fact that there are people who care only about acquiring money for its own sake

   (A) shows that most people are misers
   (B) shows that both money and the desire to make money are bad
   (C) does not prove that the desire to make money is bad
   (D) proves that money, on balance, does more harm than good to mankind
   (E) shows that misers are the greatest benefactors of mankind

The second question asks you to figure out what the author believes based on what is stated in the passage. The author's main argument is that, generally speaking, the pursuit of wealth has been beneficial to humanity. He says, "It is no argument against the desire for, or the possession of wealth, to say that there are sometimes misers who hoard money only for the sake of hoarding and who have no higher aspiration than to grasp everything which comes within their reach" (lines 6–10). He adds that misers "are only exceptions to the general rule" (line 12). The author is suggesting that misers are an unusual case and that, therefore, the existence of misers does not mean that the desire to make money is bad in the case of most people. Choice C is, therefore, the correct answer.

3. Based on what he says in the passage, which of the following statements would the author be most likely to agree with?

   (A) Money is intrinsically evil.
   (B) Money itself is not bad; only the desire to make it is bad.
   (C) Few people aspire to anything more than building up their bank account.
   (D) Civilization would be more advanced if so much human energy were not devoted to commerce.
   (E) Without a widespread desire to make money, civilization would not have reached an advanced state.

The third question asks you to make an inference (that is, a conclusion reached on the basis of given information). As seen in the discussion of the previous question, the author's main argument is that the pursuit of money has generally been very good for humanity. There is nothing to suggest that the author would agree with Choices A, B, or C. Choice D might appear at first look to make sense. However, the author argues that "wherever trade has flourished most, there too, have art and science produced the noblest fruits" (lines 2–3). It can be inferred from this that the author believes that the great effort expended to conduct commerce has been essential for the creation of advanced civilization. Choice E is the correct answer because, based on his argument, it is reasonable to infer that the author would agree that a widespread desire to make money was necessary for the creation of advanced civilization.

THE MATHEMATICS SECTIONS

There are two types of questions on the mathematics portion of the SAT: multiple-choice questions and grid-in questions.

There are 54 math questions in all, divided into three sections, each of which has its own format. You should expect to see, although not necessarily in this order, the following:

- a 25-minute section with 20 multiple-choice questions
- a 25-minute section with 8 multiple-choice questions followed by 10 student-produced response questions (grid-ins)
- a 20-minute section with 16 multiple-choice questions

Within each of the three math sections, the questions are arranged in order of increasing difficulty. The first few multiple-choice questions are quite easy; they are followed by several of medium difficulty; and the last few are considered hard. The grid-ins also proceed from easy to difficult. As a result, the amount of time you spend on any one question will vary greatly.

Note that, in the section that contains eight multiple-choice questions followed by ten grid-in questions, questions 7 and 8 are hard multiple-choice questions, whereas questions 9–11 and 12–15 are easy and medium grid-in questions, respectively. Therefore, for many students, it is advisable to skip questions 7 and 8 and to move on to the easy and medium grid-in questions.

Multiple-Choice Questions

On the SAT, all but 10 of the questions are multiple-choice questions. Although you have certainly taken multiple-choice tests before, the SAT uses a few different types of questions, and you must become familiar with all of them. By far, the most common type of question is one in which you are asked to solve a problem. The straightforward way to answer such a question is to do the necessary work, get the solution, look at the five choices, and choose the one that corresponds to your answer. Let's look at a couple of examples.

EXAMPLE 1

What is the average (arithmetic mean) of all the even integers between −5 and 7?

(A) 0

(B) $\dfrac{5}{6}$

(C) 1

(D) $\dfrac{6}{5}$

(E) 3

To solve this problem requires only that you know how to find the average of a set of numbers. Ignore the fact that this is a multiple-choice question. *Don't even look at the choices.*

- List the even integers whose average you need: −4, −2, 0, 2, 4, 6. (Be careful not to leave out 0, which *is* an even integer.)
- Calculate the average by adding the six integers and dividing by 6.

$$\frac{(-4)+(-2)+0+2+4+6}{6} = \frac{6}{6} = 1.$$

- Having found the average to be 1, look at the five choices, see that 1 is Choice C, and blacken **C** on your answer sheet.

EXAMPLE 2

A necklace is formed by stringing 133 colored beads on a thin wire in the following order: red, orange, yellow, green, blue, indigo, violet; red, orange, yellow, green, blue, indigo, violet. If this pattern continues, what will be the color of the 101st bead on the string?

(A) Orange
(B) Yellow
(C) Green
(D) Blue
(E) Indigo

Again, you are not helped by the fact that the question, which is less a test of your arithmetic skills than of your ability to reason, is a multiple-choice question. You need to determine the color of the 101st bead, and then select the choice that matches your answer.

The seven colors keep repeating in exactly the same order.

Color:	red	orange	yellow	green	blue	indigo	violet
Bead number:	1	2	3	4	5	6	7
	8	9	10	11	12	13	14	etc.

- The violet beads are in positions 7, 14, 21, . . . , 70, . . . , that is, the multiples of 7.
- If 101 were a multiple of 7, the 101st bead would be violet.
- But when 101 is divided by 7, the quotient is 14 and the remainder is 3.
- Since $14 \times 7 = 98$, the 98th bead completes the 14th cycle, and hence is violet.
- The 99th bead starts the next cycle; it is red. The 100th bead is orange, and the 101st bead is yellow.
- The answer is **B.**

NOTE

Did you notice that the solution didn't use the fact that the necklace consisted of 133 beads? This is unusual; occasionally, but not often, a problem contains information you don't need.

In contrast to Examples 1 and 2, some questions *require* you to look at all five choices in order to find the answer. Consider Example 3.

EXAMPLE 3

If *a* and *b* are both odd integers, which of the following could be an odd integer?

(A) $a + b$

(B) $a^2 + b^2$

(C) $(a + 1)^2 + (b - 1)^2$

(D) $(a + 1)(b - 1)$

(E) $\dfrac{a+1}{b-1}$

The words *which of the following* alert you to the fact that you will have to examine each of the five choices to determine which one satisfies the stated condition, in this case that the quantity *could* be odd. Check each choice.

- The sum of two odd integers is always even. Eliminate A.
- The square of an odd integer is odd; so a^2 and b^2 are each odd, and their sum is even. Eliminate B.
- Since *a* and *b* are odd, $(a + 1)$ and $(b - 1)$ are even; so $(a + 1)^2$ and $(b - 1)^2$ are also even, as is their sum. Eliminate C.
- The product of two even integers is even. Eliminate D.
- Having eliminated A, B, C, and D, you know that *the answer must be* E. Check to be sure: $\dfrac{a+1}{b-1}$ need not even be an integer (e.g., if $a = 1$ and $b = 5$), but it *could be*. For example, if $a = 3$ and $b = 5$, then

$$\frac{a+1}{b-1} = \frac{3+1}{5-1} = \frac{4}{4} = 1,$$

which *is* an odd integer. The answer is **E.**

Another kind of multiple-choice question that appears on the SAT is the Roman numeral-type question. These questions actually consist of three statements labeled I, II, and III. The five answer choices give various possibilities for which statement or statements are true. Here is a typical example.

EXAMPLE 4

If x is negative, which of the following *must* be true?

I. $x^3 < x^2$

II. $x + \dfrac{1}{x} < 0$

III. $x = \sqrt{x^2}$

(A) I only
(B) II only
(C) I and II only
(D) II and III only
(E) I, II, and III

- To solve this problem, examine each statement independently to determine if it is true or false.
  - I. If x is negative, then x^3 is negative and so must be less than x^2, which is positive. (I is true.)
  - II. If x is negative, so is $\dfrac{1}{x}$, and the sum of two negative numbers is negative. (II is true.)
  - III. The square root of a number is *never* negative, and so $\sqrt{x^2}$ could not possibly equal x. (III is false.)
- Only I and II are true. The answer is **C.**

Grid-in Questions

Ten of the mathematics questions on the SAT are what the College Board calls student-produced response questions. Since the answers to these questions are entered on a special grid, they are usually referred to as *grid-in* questions. Except for the method of entering your answer, this type of question is probably the one with which you are most familiar. In your math class, most of your homework problems and test questions require you to determine an answer and write it down, and this is what you will do on the grid-in problems. The only difference is that, once you have figured out an answer, it must be recorded on a special grid, such as the one shown at the right, so that it can be read by a computer. Here is a typical grid-in question.

NOTE

You should almost never leave out a Roman numeral-type question. Even if you can't solve the problem completely, there should be *at least one* of the three Roman numeral statements that you *know* to be true or false. On the basis of that information, you should be able to eliminate two or three of the answer choices. For instance, in Example 4, if all you know for sure is that statement I is true, you can eliminate choices B and D. Similarly, if all you know is that statement III is false, you can eliminate choices D and E. Then, as you will learn, you *must* guess between the remaining choices.

EXAMPLE 5

At the diner, John ordered a sandwich for $3.95 and a soda for 85¢. A sales tax of 5% was added to his bill, and he left the waitress a $1 tip. What was the total cost, in dollars, of John's lunch?

- Calculate the cost of the food: $3.95 + $0.85 = $4.80
- Calculate the tax (5% of $4.80): .05 × $4.80 = $0.24
- Add the cost of the food, tax, and tip: $4.80 + $0.24 + $1.00 = $6.04

To enter this answer, you write 6.04 (*without* the dollar sign) in the four spaces at the top of the grid, and blacken the appropriate oval under each space. In the first column, under the 6, you blacken the oval marked 6; in the second column, under the decimal point, you blacken the oval with the decimal point; in the third column, under the 0, you blacken the oval marked 0; and, finally, in the fourth column, under the 4, you blacken the oval marked 4.

Always read each grid-in question very carefully. Example 5 might have asked for the total cost of John's lunch *in cents*. In that case, the correct answer would have been 604, which would be gridded in, without a decimal point, using only three of the four columns, as shown in the grid above.

Gridding in your answers is not difficult, but there are some special rules concerning the types of numbers that can be the answer to a grid-in question and the proper way to enter them. Read the following rules carefully, because the worst thing that could happen would be to solve a problem correctly but not get credit for it because you entered in incorrectly.

Entering Your Answers on the Answer Sheet

Indicate your answers to math multiple-choice questions on your answer sheet exactly as you do for critical reading and writing skills questions. Once you determine which answer choice you believe is correct, blacken the corresponding oval on the answer sheet. For grid-in questions the situation is a little more complicated.

The answer sheet for the section containing grid-in questions will have one blank grid for each question. Each one will look exactly like the grid on the left. After solving a problem, the first step is to write the answer in the four boxes at the top of the grid. You then blacken the appropriate oval under each box. For example, if your answer to a question is 2450, you write 2450 at the top of the grid, one digit in each box, and then in each column blacken the oval that contains the number you wrote at the top of the column. (See the grid on the right.) This is not difficult; but there are some special rules concerning grid-in questions, so let's go over them before you practice gridding-in some numbers.

> **NOTE**
>
> Any multiple-choice question whose answer is a positive number less than 10,000 could be a grid-in question. If Example 1 had been a grid-in question, you would have solved it in exactly the same way: you would have determined that the average of the six numbers is 1; but then, instead of looking for 1 among the five choices, you would have entered the number 1 on a grid. The mathematics is no harder on grid-in questions than on multiple-choice questions. However, if you don't know how to solve a problem correctly, it is harder to guess at the right answer, since there are no choices to eliminate.

> **Helpful Hint**
>
> As you prepare for this test, memorize the directions for each section. *When you take the SAT, do not waste even one second reading directions.*

1. The only symbols that appear in the grid are the digits 0 to 9, a decimal point, and a slash (/), used to write fractions. Keep in mind that, since there is no negative sign, **the answer to every grid-in question is a positive number or zero**.

2. Be aware that you will receive credit for a correct answer no matter where you grid it. For example, the answer 17 could be gridded in any of three positions:

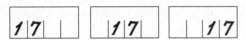

   Neverthelesss, try to consistently **write all your answers** the way numbers are usually displayed—**to the right, with blank spaces at the left**.

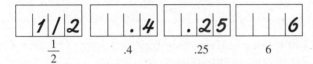

3. **Never round off your answers**. If a decimal answer will fit in the grid and you round it off, your answer will be marked wrong. For example, if the answer is .148 and you correctly round it off to the nearest hundredth and enter .15, you will receive *no credit*. If a decimal answer will not fit in the grid, enter a decimal point in the first column, followed by the first three digits. For example, if your answer is 0.454545 . . . , enter it as .454. You would receive credit if you rounded it to .455—but don't do this. You might occasionally make a mistake in rounding, whereas you'll *never* make a mistake if you just copy the first three digits. *Note:* If the correct answer has more than two decimal digits, *you must use all four columns of the grid*. You will receive *no credit* for .4 or .5 or .45. (These answers are not accurate enough.)

4. **Never write a 0 before the decimal point**. The first column of the grid doesn't even have a 0 in it. If the correct answer is 0.3333 . . . , you must grid it as .333. You can't grid 0.33, and 0.3 is not accurate enough.

5. **Never reduce fractions**.

   • If your answer is a fraction that will fit in the grid, such as $\frac{2}{3}$ or $\frac{4}{18}$ or $\frac{6}{34}$, *just enter it*. Don't waste time reducing it or converting it to a decimal.

   • If your answer is a fraction that won't fit in the grid, do not attempt to reduce it; use your calculator to *convert it to a decimal*. For example, $\frac{24}{65}$ won't fit in a grid—it would require five spaces: 2 4 / 6 5. Don't waste even a few seconds trying to reduce it; just divide on your calculator, and enter .369.

   Unlike $\frac{24}{65}$, the fraction $\frac{24}{64}$ can be reduced—to $\frac{12}{32}$, which doesn't help, or to $\frac{6}{16}$ or $\frac{3}{8}$, either of which could be entered. *Don't do it!* Reducing a fraction takes time, and you might make a mistake. You won't make a mistake if you just use your calculator: $24 \div 64 = .375$.

6. ***Be aware that you can never enter a mixed number***. If your answer is $2\frac{1}{2}$, you *cannot* leave a space and enter your answer as 2 1/2. Also, if you enter $\boxed{2\,1\,/\,2}$, the machine will read it as $\frac{21}{2}$ and mark it wrong. You must enter $2\frac{1}{2}$ as the improper fraction $\frac{5}{2}$ or as the decimal 2.5.

7. Since full credit is given for any equivalent answer, use these guidelines to ***enter your answer in the simplest way***. If your answer is $\frac{6}{9}$, you should enter 6/9. (However, credit would be given for any of the following: 2/3, 4/6, 8/12, .666, .667.)

8. Sometimes grid-in questions have more than one correct answer. On these questions, ***grid in only one of the acceptable answers***. For example, if a question asked for a positive number less than 100 that was divisible by both 5 and 7, you could enter *either* 35 *or* 70, but not both. Similarly, if a question asked for a number between $\frac{3}{7}$ and $\frac{5}{9}$, you could enter any *one* of more than 100 possibilities: fractions such as $\frac{1}{2}$ and $\frac{4}{9}$ or *any* decimal between .429 and .554—.43 or .499 or .52, for example.

9. ***Keep in mind that there is no penalty for a wrong answer to a grid-in question***. Therefore, you might as well guess, even if you have no idea what to do.

10. Be sure to ***grid every answer very carefully***. The computer does not read what you have written in the boxes; it reads only the answer in the grid. If the correct answer to a question is 100 and you write 100 in the boxes, but accidentally grid in 200, you get *no* credit.

11. If you know that the answer to a question is 100, can you just grid it in and not bother writing it on top? Yes, you will get full credit, and so some SAT guides recommend that you don't waste time writing the answer. This is terrible advice. Instead, ***write each answer in the boxes***. It takes less than 2 seconds per answer to do this, and it definitely cuts down on careless errors in gridding. More important, if you go back to check your work, it is much easier to read what's in the boxes on top than what's in the grid.

12. Be aware that the smallest number that can be gridded is 0; the largest is 9999. No number greater than 100 can have a decimal point. The largest number less than 100 that can be gridded is 99.9; the smallest number greater than 100 that can be gridded is 101.

CALCULATOR TIPS

- Bring a calculator to the test: it's not required, but it sometimes can help.
- *Don't* buy a new calculator the night before the SAT. If you need one, *buy one now* and become familiar with it. Do all the practice exams in this book with the calculator you plan to take to the test—probably the same calculator you use in school.
- The College Board recommends a scientific calculator with parentheses keys, ( ); a reciprocal key, $\frac{1}{x}$; and an exponent key, y or$^\wedge$.
- Use your calculator when you *need* to; ignore it when you don't. Most students use calculators more than they should. You can solve many problems without doing *any* calculations—mental, written, or calculator-assisted.
- Throughout this book, the icon will be placed next to a problem where the use of a calculator is recommended. As you will see, this judgment is subjective. Sometimes a question can be answered in a few seconds, with no calculations whatsoever, *if* you see the best approach. In that case, the use of a calculator is not recommended. If you don't see the easy way, however, and have to do some arithmetic, you may prefer to use a calculator.
- No SAT problem ever requires a lot of tedious calculation. However, if you don't see how to avoid calculating, just do it—*don't spend a <u>lot</u> of time looking for a shortcut that will save you a <u>little</u> time!*

THE WRITING SKILLS SECTIONS

There are three types of questions on the writing skills section of the SAT:

1. Improving sentences
2. Identifying sentence errors
3. Improving paragraphs

Examples of each type of question appear in this section.

The writing skills section on your test will contain 49 questions. The two sections break down as follows:

35-Question Writing Skills Section (25 minutes)
Questions 1–11   Improving sentences
Questions 12–29   Identifying sentence errors
Questions 30–35   Improving paragraphs

14-Question Writing Skills Section (10 minutes)
Questions 1–14   Improving sentences

Here are examples of the specific types of writing skills questions you can expect.

Improving Sentences

Improving sentences questions ask you to spot the form of a sentence that works best. Your job is to select the most effective version of a sentence.

> **Directions:** Some or all parts of the following sentences are under-lined. The first answer choice, (A), simply repeats the underlined part of the sentence. The other four choices present four alternative ways to phrase the underlined part. Select the answer choice that produces the most effective sentence, one that is clear and exact.

Example

In her comments after the debate, the judge said that she had been impressed by the ability of both teams to exploit logical weaknesses and <u>in citing relevant examples</u>.

(A) in citing relevant examples
(B) in that relevant examples had been cited
(C) in the citing of relevant examples
(D) to cite relevant examples
(E) to be able to cite relevant examples

The sentence contains an error in parallelism. The phrase *to exploit logical weaknesses* is an infinitive phrase referring to the noun *ability*. The phrase *in citing relevant examples* also refers to *ability*. However, it is not in the same form (infinitive phrase) as *to exploit logical weaknesses*, as required for correct parallelism. Choice D changes the phrase to an infinitive phrase, making the structure parallel. Note that the meaning remains the same, as required for an answer to be correct. Sentence improvement questions sometimes contain grammatical errors similar to those that appear on sentence error questions, but more often contain awkward, ambiguous, or wordy language.

Identifying Sentence Errors

Identifying sentence errors questions ask you to spot something wrong. Your job is to find the error in the sentence, not to fix it.

> **Directions:** These sentences may contain errors in grammar, usage, choice of words, or idioms. Either there is just one error in a sentence or the sentence is correct. Some words or phrases are underlined and lettered; everything else in the sentence is correct.
> If an underlined word or phrase is incorrect, choose that letter; if the sentence is correct, select <u>No error</u>.

Example

The number of stars <u>visible in</u> the sky on any <u>given</u> night <u>vary</u>, mainly
 A B C
<u>because of</u> changes in atmospheric conditions and in the phases of the Moon.
 D
<u>No Error</u>
 E

This sentence contains an error in subject–verb agreement. The simple subject of the independent clause *The number of stars visible in the sky on any given night vary* is the noun *number*, which is singular. Therefore, the main verb *vary*, which is plural, must be changed to the singular *varies* to agree with *number*. Thus, the correct answer is Choice C. It is important to identify the simple subject so that you are not distracted by words that appear between the simple subject and the main verb. In this example, three prepositional phrases come between the simple subject and the main verb.

Improving Paragraphs

Improving paragraphs questions require you to correct the flaws in a student essay. Some questions involve rewriting or combining separate sentences to come up with a more effective wording. Other questions involve reordering sentences to produce a better organized argument.

> **Directions:** The passage below is the unedited draft of a student's essay. Parts of the essay need to be rewritten to improve sentence structure, choice of words, clarity of expression, organization, and development.
>
> After reading the draft, answer each question below it, choosing the answer that best conforms to the requirements of standard written English.

(1) One of the beauties of English prose is its flexibility. (2) One writer can write effectively by taking a logical and sober approach—Charles Darwin, say, in his *The Voyage of The Beagle*. (3) Another writer can succeed with the opposite approach—John Kennedy Toole's zany approach in *A Confederacy Of Dunces*, for example. (4) Even within one work, a writer can be by turns serious, mocking, ironic, satirical, admiring—just about anything—and write good prose. (5) That is, if he or she has the skill to carry it off.

(6) Good writing can turn up just about anywhere. (7) For many years, Lewis Thomas' elegant prose graced the pages of *The New England Journal of Medicine*—an august journal, to be sure—but not one particularly associated with good writing. (8) It might even turn up in a government report. (9) And yet, judging from the extracts printed recently in this newspaper from the U.S. National Commission on Terrorism, that committee managed to produce a considerable amount of lucid and engaging prose.

NOTE

Remember, this essay is a rough draft. It is likely to contain grammatical errors and awkward phrasing. Do not assume it is exemplary prose.

1. Which of the following sentences would be the best sentence to insert between sentence 8 and sentence 9?

   (A) Generally, an essay should take a balanced approach so that the topic is discussed in a fair and objective way.

   (B) Good writers often use rhetorical devices intuitively, knowing that effective communication depends on a range of techniques that must be adapted to each situation.

   (C) Writing that is full of clichés is generally insipid.

   (D) The English author George Orwell said, "In our time it is broadly true that political writing is bad writing."

   (E) The Russian writer Aleksandr Solzhenitsyn said, "I refuse to see literature as amusement, as a game."

The correct answer is Choice D. This is the best choice because sentence 8 says that good writing might "even" turn up in a government report, suggesting that good writing is not common in the kind of political writing found in government reports. The sentence in Choice D elaborates on this idea, quoting a famous writer. Sentence 9 logically follows because it gives an exception to the generalization that political writing is bad writing.

WINNING TACTICS FOR THE SAT

You now know the basic framework of the SAT. It's time for the big question: How can you become a winner on the SAT?

- First, you have to decide just what winning is for you. For one student, winning means breaking 1500; for another, only a total score of 2100 will do. Therefore, the first thing you have to do is set *your* goal.

- Second, you must learn to pace yourself during the test. You need to know how many questions to attempt to answer, how many to spend a little extra time on, and how many simply to skip.

- Third, you need to understand the rewards of guessing—how *educated guesses* can boost your scores dramatically. Educated guessing is a key strategy in helping you to reach your goal.

Here are your winning tactics for the SAT.

TACTIC

Set your goal.

Before you begin studying for the SAT, you need to set a realistic goal for yourself. Here's what to do.

1. Establish your **baseline score**. You need to know your math, critical reading, and writing scores on one actual PSAT or SAT to use as your starting point.
   - If you have already taken an SAT, use your actual scores from that test.
   - If you have already taken the PSAT but have not yet taken the SAT, use your most recent actual PSAT scores, adding a zero to the end of each score (55 on the PSAT = 550 on the SAT).

- If you have not yet taken an actual PSAT or SAT, do the following:
  - □ Go to: *http://www.collegeboard.org/student/testing/sat/prep_one/prep_one.html* and click on the link to the Official SAT Practice Test. Print a copy.

    OR

    Get a hard copy of the College Board's SAT preparation booklet from your school guidance office. (The online practice test and the test in the preparation booklet are the same.)
  - □ Find a quiet place where you can work for $3^3/_4$ hours without interruptions.

  - □ Take the SAT under true exam conditions:

    Time yourself on each section.

    Take no more than a 2-minute break between sections.

    After finishing three sections, take a 10-minute break.

    Take another 10-minute break after section 7.
  - □ Follow the instructions to grade the test and convert your total raw scores on each part to a scaled score.
  - □ Use these scores as your baseline.

2. Look up the average SAT scores for the most recent freshman class at each of the colleges to which you're applying. This information can be found online on the colleges' websites or in a college guide, such as Barron's *Profiles of American Colleges*. You want to beat that average, if you can.

3. Now **set your goals**. Challenge yourself, but be realistic. If you earned 470 on the critical reading portion of the PSAT, for example, you might like to get 700 on the SAT, but that's unrealistic. On the other hand, don't wimp out. Aim for 550, not 490.

General Guidelines for Setting Your Initial Goals on Each Part of the SAT

Current Score	Goal (change in score)	Current Score	Goal (change in score)
Less than 400	+100	550–590	+60
400–440	+90	600–640	+50
450–490	+80	650–690	+40
500–540	+70	700 or more	+30

TACTIC

2

Know how many questions you should try to answer.

Why is it so important to set a goal? Why not just try to get the highest score you can by correctly answering as many questions as possible? The answer is that *your goal tells you how many questions you should try to answer*. The most common tactical error that students make is trying to answer too many questions. Therefore, surprising as it may be, the following statement is true for almost all students:

THE BEST WAY TO INCREASE YOUR SCORE ON THE SAT
IS TO ANSWER FEWER QUESTIONS.

Why is slowing down and answering fewer questions the best way to increase your score on the SAT? To understand this, you first need to know how the SAT is scored. There are two types of scores associated with the SAT: raw scores and scaled scores. First, three raw scores are calculated—one for each part of the test. Each raw score is then converted to a scaled score between 200 and 800. On the SAT, every question is worth exactly the same amount: 1 raw score point. You get no more credit for a correct answer to the hardest math question than you do for the easiest. For each question that you answer correctly, you receive 1 raw score point. For each multiple-choice question that you answer incorrectly, you lose $\frac{1}{4}$ point.

Questions that you leave out and grid-in questions you miss have no effect on your score. On each of the SAT's three parts—Critical Reading, Math, and Writing Skills—the raw score is calculated as follows:

$$\text{\# of correct answers} - \frac{\text{\# of incorrect multiple-choice answers}}{4} = \text{Raw Score}$$

On every SAT, one math section has 20 multiple-choice questions. The questions in this section are presented in order of difficulty. Although this varies slightly from test to test, typically questions 1–6 are considered easy, questions 7–14 are considered medium, and questions 15–20 are considered hard. Even within the groups, the questions increase in difficulty: questions 7 and 14, for example, may both be ranked medium, but question 14 will definitely be harder than question 7. Of course, this depends slightly on each student's math skills. Some students might find question 8 or 9 or even 10 to be easier than question 7, but everyone will find questions 11 and 12 to be harder than questions 1 and 2, and questions 19 and 20 to be harder than questions 13 and 14.

However, all questions have the same value: 1 raw score point. You earn 1 point for a correct answer to question 1, which might take you only 15 seconds to solve, and 1 point for a correct answer to question 20, which might take 2 or 3 minutes to solve. Knowing that it will probably take at least 10 minutes to answer the last 5 questions, many students try to race through the first 15 questions in 15 minutes or less and, as a result, miss many questions that they could have answered correctly, had they slowed down.

Suppose a student rushed through questions 1–15 and got 9 right answers and 6 wrong ones and then worked on the 5 hardest questions and answered 2 more correctly and 3 more incorrectly. His raw score would be $8\frac{3}{4}$: 11 points for the 11 correct answers minus $2\frac{1}{4}$ points for the 9 wrong answers. Had he gone slowly and carefully, and not made any careless errors on the easy and medium questions, he might have run out of time and not even answered any of the 5 hardest questions at the end. But if spending all 25 minutes on the first 15 questions meant that he answered 13 correctly, 2 incorrectly, and omitted 5, his raw score would have been $12\frac{1}{2}$. If he had a similar improvement on the other math sections, his raw score would have been about 10 points higher, an increase of approximately 80 SAT points.

In this hypothetical scenario, a student increased his score significantly by answering fewer questions, but eliminating careless errors.

Now, let's see how slowing down improved the scores of two actual students.

Student 1: John

Class standing: mid-range
Grade point average: low 80s
Junior year SAT math score: 500
Goal: 570

Here's how John did on the 25-minute math section with 20 questions.

Time Spent	Questions Answered	# Right	# Wrong
13 minutes	1–13	9	4
12 minutes	14–20	2	5

Total: 11 right, 9 wrong

Raw score: $11 - 2\dfrac{1}{4} = 8\dfrac{3}{4}$

OUR ADVICE TO JOHN: **Slow down. Don't even try the hard problems at the end of the section. Spend all 25 minutes on the first 13 questions so that you** *avoid all careless mistakes.*

John then took a practice SAT. On the 20-question math section, this is what happened:

Time Spent	Questions Answered	# Right	# Wrong
25 minutes	1–13	12	1

Total: 12 right, 1 wrong

Raw score: $12 - \dfrac{1}{4} = 11\dfrac{3}{4}$

John's raw score went up 3 points on just one section. He made similar improvements in the other two math sections, which resulted in a total increase of 8 raw score points, which raised his math scaled score by 70 points.

OUTCOME: With practice, John learned he could get the first 13 questions right in about 20 minutes, rather than 25. He used his extra 5 minutes to work on just two of the remaining questions in the section, selecting questions he had the best chance of answering correctly. As a result, his math score improved by more than 100 points!

Student 2: Mary

Class standing: top 10–15%
Grade point average: low 90s
Junior year SAT math score: 710
Junior year SAT reading score: 620
Goal: 1400 total in reading and math

PROBLEMS:

• slow reader
• raced through sentence completions to have more time for reading passages
• skimmed some reading passages instead of reading them

> OUR ADVICE TO MARY: Slow down. On the reading section with two long passages, skip the 5-question passage and focus on reading the 10-question passage slowly and carefully.
>
> OUTCOME: At first, Mary strongly resisted the idea of leaving out questions on the SAT, but she agreed to take our advice. When she retook the SAT her senior year, she answered just 59 reading questions and left out 8. Mary's senior year reading score: 700.

What did John and Mary learn?

THE BEST WAY TO INCREASE YOUR SCORE ON THE SAT
IS TO ANSWER FEWER QUESTIONS.

Many students prefer to think about the statement above paraphrased as follows:

THE BIGGEST MISTAKE MOST STUDENTS MAKE
IS TRYING TO ANSWER TOO MANY QUESTIONS.

So, how many questions should *you* try to answer?

First, set your goal based on your original scores. For example, using the table on page 17, if your original reading score was 540, your goal should be 610.

Next, look at the SAT score conversion table on the College Board's website or on page 84 in this book, reproduced, in part, below. Find the raw scores that correspond to your scaled score goals.

CRITICAL READING CONVERSION TABLE

Raw Score	Scaled Score
51	650
50	640
49	630
48	620
47	610
46	610
45	600
44	590
43	590
42	580

You need a raw score of about 46 to reach your goal of 610 in critical reading. One way to do that would be to get 46 questions correct and no questions wrong. But probably, even going slowly, you'll miss a few, so answer about 6 more.

How many reading questions should you answer?

$46 + 6 = 52$

Remember, since you lose $\frac{1}{4}$ point for each question you answer incorrectly, you should answer 52 questions (omitting 15) so that, even if you miss 5, your raw score will still be 46.

$$47 - \frac{5}{4} = 45\frac{3}{4} = 46 \,(\text{rounded raw score})$$

How does that work out for each of the three reading sections?
On each 24-question critical reading section, aim to answer 19 questions and omit 5.
On the 19-question critical reading section, answer 14 questions and omit 5.

$$19 + 19 + 14 = 52$$

TACTIC

Know how to pace yourself, section by section. Never get bogged down on any one question, and never rush.

Go quickly but carefully through the easy questions, slowly but steadily through the harder ones. Always keep moving.

Here is one pattern to follow:

20-Question Math Section (25 minutes total)

Questions 1–5	1 minute each
Questions 6–10	2 minutes each
Questions 11–14	$2\frac{1}{2}$ minutes each
Questions 15–20	Don't even read them!

Unless you are consistently getting at least 12 of the first 14 questions right, *do not go any faster.*

What if you finish all 14 questions in 22 or 23 minutes, and still have 2 or 3 minutes left? Here's what to do. Take 30 seconds to read questions 15 and 16. Quickly decide which one you have the better chance of getting right or making an educated guess on. Use your remaining time on that one question.

What if you finish all 14 questions in just 20 minutes, and have 5 minutes left? You have time to answer two more questions at most. Do *not* automatically try to answer questions 15 and 16. Take a quick look at the remaining questions and pick the 2 questions that *you* like best. It's like cherry-picking: pick the questions that look good to you. If you like geometry questions, try those. If you like algebra questions, try those instead. Skip around. Just be sure to mark your answer choices in the correct spots.

Of course, if you are very good at math and can consistently answer almost all of the questions correctly, your strategy might be to answer 18 of the 20 questions, or maybe even all 20. You shouldn't, however, be answering all the questions if you are getting more than two or three incorrect; in that case, you should slow down and answer fewer questions and make fewer mistakes.

TACTIC

Know how to guess, and when.

The rule is, if you have worked on a problem and have eliminated even one of the choices, you *must* guess. This is what is called an *educated* guess. You are not guessing wildly, marking answers at random. You are working on the problem, ruling out answers that make no sense. The more choices you can rule out, the better your chance is of picking the right answer and earning one more point.

You should almost always be able to rule out some answer choices. Most math questions contain at least one or two answer choices that are absurd (for example, negative choices when you know the answer must be positive). In the critical reading section, once you have read a passage, you can always eliminate some of the answer choices. Cross out any choices that you *know* are incorrect, and go for that educated guess.

Unconvinced? If you are still not persuaded that educated guessing will work for you, turn to the end of this introduction for a detailed analysis of guessing on the SAT.

TACTIC

Keep careful track of your time.

Bring a watch. Even if there is a clock in the room, it is better for you to have a watch on your desk. Before you start each section, set your watch to 12:00. It is easier to know that a section will be over when your watch reads 12:25 than to have a section start at 9:37 and have to remember that it will be over at 10:02. Your job will be even easier if you have a digital stopwatch that you start at the beginning of each section; either let it count down to zero, or start it at zero and know that your time will be up after the allotted number of minutes.

TACTIC

Don't read the directions or look at the sample questions.

For each section of the SAT, the directions given in this book are identical to the directions you will see on your actual exam. Learn them now. Do not waste even a few seconds of your valuable test time reading them.

TACTIC

Remember, each question, easy or hard, is worth just 1 point.

Concentrate on questions that don't take you tons of time to answer.

TACTIC

Answer the easy questions first; then tackle the hard ones.

Because the questions in each section (except the critical reading questions) proceed from easy to hard, usually you should answer the questions in the order in which they appear.

TACTIC

Be aware of the difficulty level of each question.

Easy questions (the first few in each section or group) can usually be answered very quickly. Don't read too much into them. On these questions, your first hunch is probably right. Difficult questions (the last few in a section or group) usually require a bit of thought. On these questions, be wary of an answer that strikes you immediately. You may have made an incorrect assumption or fallen into a trap. Reread the question and check the other choices before answering too quickly.

TACTIC

10

Feel free to skip back and forth between questions within a section or group.

Remember that you're in charge. You don't have to answer everything in order. You should skip the hard sentence completions at the end and go straight to the reading questions on the next page. You can temporarily skip a question that's taking you too long and come back to it if you have time. Just be sure to mark your answers in the correct spot on the answer sheet.

TACTIC

11

In the critical reading and writing sections, read each choice before choosing your answer.

In comparison to math questions, which always have exactly one correct answer, critical reading questions are more subjective. You are looking for the *best* choice. Even if A or B looks good, check out the others; D or E may be better.

TACTIC

Make sure that you answer the question asked.

Sometimes a math question requires you to solve an equation, but instead of asking for the value of x, the question asks for the value of x^2 or $x - 5$. Similarly, sometimes a critical reading question requires you to determine the LEAST likely outcome of an action; still another may ask you to find the exception to something, as in "The author uses all of the following EXCEPT." To avoid answering the wrong question, circle or underline what you have been asked for.

TACTIC

13

Base your answers only on the information provided— never on what you think you already know.

On critical reading questions, base your answers only on the material in the passage, not on what you think you know about the subject matter. On data interpretation questions, base your answers only on the information given in the chart or table.

TACTIC

Remember that you are allowed to write anything you want in your test booklet.

Circle questions you skip, and put big question marks next to questions you answer but are unsure about. If you have time left at the end, you want to be able to locate those questions quickly to go over them. In sentence completion questions, circle or underline key words such as *although, therefore,* and *not.* In reading passages, underline or put a mark in the margin next to any important point. On math questions, mark up diagrams, adding lines when necessary. And, of course, use all the space provided to solve the problem. In every section, math, reading, and writing, cross out every choice that you *know* is wrong. In short, write anything that will help you, using whatever symbols you like. But remember: the only thing that counts is what you enter on your answer sheet. No one but you will ever see anything that you write in your booklet.

TACTIC

Be careful not to make any stray pencil marks on your answer sheet.

The SAT is scored by a computer that cannot distinguish between an accidental mark and a filled-in answer. If the computer registers two answers where there should be only one, it will mark that question wrong.

TACTIC

Don't change answers capriciously.

If you have time to return to a question and realize that you made a mistake, by all means correct it, making sure you *completely* erase the first mark you made. However, don't change answers on a last-minute hunch or whim, or for fear you have chosen too many A's and not enough B's. In such cases, more often than not, students change right answers to wrong ones.

TACTIC

17

Use your calculator only when you need to.

Many students actually waste time using their calculators on questions that do not require them. Use your calculator whenever you feel it will help, but don't overuse it. And remember: no problem on the SAT requires lengthy, tedious calculations.

TACTIC

18

When you use your calculator, don't go too quickly.

Your calculator leaves no trail. If you accidentally hit the wrong button and get a wrong answer, you have no way to look at your work and find your mistake. You just have to do it all over.

TACTIC

Remember that you don't have to answer every question to do well.

You have learned about setting goals and pacing. You know you don't have to answer all the questions to do well. It is possible to omit more than half of the questions and still be in the top half of all students taking the test; similarly, you can omit more than 40 questions and earn a top score. After you set your final goal, pace yourself to reach it.

TACTIC

20
Don't be nervous: if your scores aren't as high as you would like, you can always take the SAT again.

Relax. The biggest reason that some students do worse on the actual SAT than they did on their practice tests is that they are nervous. You can't do your best if your hands are shaking and you're worried that your whole future is riding on this one test. First of all, your SAT scores are only one of many factors that influence the admissions process, and many students are accepted at their first-choice colleges even if their SAT scores are lower than they had expected. But more important, because of Score Choice, you can always retake the SAT if you don't do well enough the first or second time. So, give yourself the best chance for success: prepare conscientiously and then stay calm while actually taking the test.

AN AFTERWORD: MORE ON GUESSING

Are you still worried about whether you should guess on the SAT? If so, read through the following analysis of how guessing affects your scores. The bottom line is, even if you don't know the answer to a question, whenever you can eliminate one or more answer choices, you *must* guess.

In general, it pays to guess. To understand why this is so and why so many people are confused about guessing, you must consider what you know about how the SAT is scored.

Consider the following scenario. Suppose you work very slowly and carefully, answer only 32 of the critical reading questions (omitting 35), and get each of them correct. Your raw score of 32 will be converted to a scaled score of about 510. If that were the whole story, you should use the last minute of the test to quickly fill in an answer to each of the other questions. Because each question has 5 choices, you should get about one-fifth of them right. Surely, you would get *some* of them right—most likely about 7. If you did that, your raw score would go up 7 points, and your scaled score would then be about 560. Your critical reading score would increase 50 points because of 1 minute of wild guessing! Clearly, this is not what the College Board wants to happen. To counter this possibility, there is a so-called *guessing penalty,* which adjusts your scores for wrong answers and makes it unlikely that you will profit from wild guessing.

The penalty for each incorrect answer on the critical reasoning sections is a reduction of $\frac{1}{4}$ point of raw score. What effect would this penalty have in the example just discussed? Say that by wildly guessing you got 7 right and 28 wrong. Those 7 extra right answers caused your raw score to go up by 7 points. But now you lose $\frac{1}{4}$ point for each of the 28 problems you missed—a total reduction of $\frac{28}{4}$ or 7 points. As a result, you broke even: you gained 7 points and lost 7 points. Your raw score, and hence your scaled score, didn't change at all.

Notice that the guessing *penalty* didn't actually penalize you. It prevented you from making a big gain that you didn't deserve, but it didn't punish you by lowering your score. It's not a very harsh penalty after all. In fairness, however, it should be pointed out that wild guessing *could* have lowered your score. It is possible that, instead of getting 7 correct answers, you were unlucky and got only 5 or 6, and as a result, your scaled score dropped from 510 to 500. On the other hand, it is equally likely that you would have been lucky and gotten 8 or 9 rather than 7 right, and that your scaled score would have increased from 510 to 520 or 530.

> **NOTE**
>
> On everage, *wild guessing does not affect your score on the SAT.*

Educated guessing, on the other hand, can have an enormous effect on your score: it can increase it dramatically! Let's look at what is meant by educated guessing and see how it can improve your score on the SAT.

Consider the following sentence completion question.

> In Victorian times, countless Egyptian mummies were ground up to produce dried mummy powder, hailed by quacks as a near-magical ----, able to cure a wide variety of ailments.
>
> (A) toxin
> (B) diagnosis
> (C) symptom
> (D) panacea
> (E) placebo

Clearly, what is needed is a word such as *medicine*—something capable of curing ailments. Let's assume that you know that *toxin* means poison, so you immediately eliminate Choice A. You also know that, although *diagnosis* and *symptom* are medical terms, neither means a medicine or a cure, so you eliminate Choices B and C. You now know that the correct answer must be Choice D or E, but unfortunately you have no idea what either *panacea* or *placebo* means.

You *could* guess, but you don't want to be wrong; after all, there's that penalty for incorrect answers. Then should you leave the question out? Absolutely not! *You must guess!* We'll explain why and how in a moment, but first let's look at one more example, this time a math question.

> What is the slope of line ℓ in the figure to the right?
>
> (A) $-\dfrac{2}{3}$
>
> (B) $-\dfrac{3}{2}$
>
> (C) 0
>
> (D) $\dfrac{2}{3}$
>
> (E) $\dfrac{3}{2}$

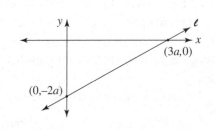

Suppose that you have completely forgotten how to calculate the slope of a line, but you do remember that lines that go up (↗) have positive slopes and that lines that go down (↘) have negative slopes. Then you know the answer must be Choice D or E. What do you do? Do you guess and risk incurring the guessing penalty, or do you omit the question because you're not sure which answer is correct? *You must guess!*

Suppose that you are still working slowly and carefully on the critical reading sections, and that you are sure of the answers to 32 questions. Of the 35 questions you planned to omit, there are 15 in which you are able to eliminate 3 of the choices, but you have no idea which of the remaining 2 choices is correct; and the remaining 20 questions you don't even look at. You already know what would happen if you guessed wildly on those 20 questions—you would probably break even. But what about the 15 questions you narrowed down to 2 choices? If you guess on those, you should get about half right and half wrong. Is that good or bad? *It's very good!* Assume you got 7 right and 8 wrong. For the 7 correct answers, you would receive 7 points, and for the 8 incorrect answers, you would lose $\frac{8}{4}=2$ points. This is a net gain of 5 raw score points, raising your critical reading SAT score from 510 to 540. It would be a shame to throw away those 30 points just because you were afraid of the guessing penalty.

At this point, many students protest that they are unlucky and that they never guess right. They are wrong. *There is no such thing as a poor guesser,* as we'll prove in a minute. For the sake of argument, however, suppose you were a poor guesser, and that when you guessed on those 15 questions, you got twice as many wrong (10) as you got right (5). In that case you would have received 5 points for the correct ones and lost $\frac{10}{4}=2\frac{1}{2}$ points for the incorrect ones. Your raw score would have increased by $2\frac{1}{2}$ points, which would be rounded up to 3, and your scaled score would still have increased: from 510 to 530. Therefore, even if you think you're a poor guesser, you should guess.

Actually, the real guessing penalty is not the one that the College Board uses to prevent you from profiting from wild guesses. **The real guessing penalty is the one you impose on yourself by not guessing when you should.**

Occasionally, you can even eliminate 4 of the 5 choices! Suppose that in the sentence completion question given above, you realize that you do know what *placebo* means, and that it can't be the answer. You still have no idea about *panacea,* and you may be hesitant to answer a question with a word you never heard of; but you must. If, in the preceding math question, only one of the choices were positive, it would have to be correct. In that case, don't omit the question because you can't verify the answer by calculating the slope yourself. Choose the only answer you haven't eliminated.

What if you can't eliminate 3 or 4 of the choices? You should guess if you can eliminate even 1 choice. Assume that there are 20 questions whose answers you are unsure of. The following table indicates the most likely outcome if you guess at each of them.

On an actual test, there would be some questions on which you could eliminate 1 or 2 choices and others where you could eliminate 3 or even 4. No matter what the mix, guessing pays. Of course, if you can eliminate 4 choices, the other choice must be correct; it's not a guess.

Number of choices eliminated	Most Likely Effect				
	Number correct	Number wrong	Raw score	Scaled Score	
				Verbal	Math
0	4	16	+0	+0	+0
1	5	15	+1.25	+10	+15
2	7	13	+3.75	+30	+40
3	10	10	+7.50	+50	+70
4	20	0	+20	+120	+150

The scoring of the math sections is somewhat different from the scoring of the critical reading. The multiple-choice math questions have the same $\frac{1}{4}$-point penalty for incorrect answers as do all the critical reading and writing skills questions. There is *no penalty*, however, on grid-in questions, so you can surely guess on those. Of course, because you can grid in any number from .001 to 9999, it is very unlikely that a wild guess will be correct. But, as you will see, sometimes a grid-in question will ask for the smallest integer that satisfies a certain property (the length of the side of a particular triangle, for example), and you know that the answer must be greater than 1 and less than 10. Then guess.

It's time to prove to you that you are not a poor guesser; in fact, no one is. Take out a sheet of paper and number from 1 to 20. This is your answer sheet. Assume that for each of 20 questions you have eliminated three of the five choices (B, C, and E), so you know that the correct answer is either A or D. Now close this book and guess. Next to each number write either A or D. When you are done, turn to page 29. Tests 1, 2, and 3 list the order in which the first 20 A's and D's appeared on three actual SATs. Check to see how many right answers you would have had. On each test, if you got 10 out of 20 correct, your SAT score would have risen by about 60 points as a result of your guessing. If you had more than 10 right, add an additional 10 points for each extra question you got correct; if you had fewer than 10 right, subtract 10 points from 60 for each extra one you missed. If you had 13 right, your SAT score increased by 90 points; if you got only 7 right, it still increased by 30 points. Probably, for the three tests, your average number of correct answers was very close to 10. You couldn't have missed all of the questions if you wanted to. You simply cannot afford not to guess.

You can repeat this experiment as often as you like. Ask a friend to write down a list of 20 A's and D's, and then compare your list and his. Or just go to the answer keys for the model tests in the back of the book, and read down any column, ignoring the B's, C's, and E's.

Would you like to see how well you do if you can eliminate only two choices? Do the same thing, except this time eliminate B and D and choose A, C, or E. Check your answers against the answer keys for Tests 4, 5, and 6 on page 29. Give yourself 1 raw score point for each correct answer and deduct $\frac{1}{4}$ point for each wrong answer. Multiply your raw score by 8 to learn approximately how many points you gained by guessing.

A few final comments about guessing are in order.

- If it is really a guess, don't agonize over it. Don't spend 30 seconds thinking, "Should I pick A? The last time I guessed, I chose A; maybe this time I should pick D. I'm really not sure. But I haven't had too many A answers lately; so, maybe it's time." STOP! A guess is just that—a guess.

- You can decide right now how you are going to guess on the actual SAT you take. For example, you could just always guess the letter closest to A: if A is in the running, choose it; if not, pick B, and so on. If you'd rather start with E, that's OK, too.

- If you are down to two choices and you have a hunch, play it. But if you have no idea and it is truly a guess, do not take more than two seconds to choose. Then move on to the next question.

ANSWER KEY
For Guessing

TEST 1		TEST 2		TEST 3	
1. A	11. D	1. D	11. D	1. A	11. D
2. D	12. D	2. A	12. A	2. D	12. D
3. D	13. A	3. D	13. D	3. D	13. D
4. A	14. D	4. A	14. D	4. A	14. A
5. A	15. A	5. D	15. A	5. D	15. A
6. D	16. D	6. A	16. A	6. D	16. D
7. D	17. A	7. A	17. D	7. D	17. A
8. A	18. D	8. D	18. D	8. A	18. A
9. A	19. A	9. A	19. D	9. A	19. D
10. A	20. D	10. A	20. A	10. D	20. D

TEST 4		TEST 5		TEST 6	
1. A	11. E	1. C	11. C	1. C	11. C
2. C	12. A	2. A	12. E	2. C	12. E
3. A	13. E	3. A	13. E	3. E	13. A
4. C	14. E	4. A	14. E	4. E	14. C
5. E	15. C	5. C	15. A	5. A	15. A
6. E	16. C	6. E	16. E	6. A	16. A
7. C	17. C	7. A	17. C	7. C	17. A
8. A	18. E	8. C	18. C	8. E	18. C
9. E	19. E	9. C	19. C	9. E	19. E
10. C	20. A	10. C	20. E	10. A	20. E

Advice on Taking the 6 Practice SAT Tests in This Book

This book contains six practice SAT tests, each of which resembles an actual SAT in format, in difficulty, and in content.

For optimal results, you should use this book in conjunction with the latest edition of Barron's *SAT*, the leading test-prep book for over 50 years. Of course, this book of practice tests provides complete solutions and answer explanations for all of the questions on each of the exams. But, whenever you miss a question or leave one out and you want more information than is provided in the explanation, you can find it in Barron's *SAT*—whether it's a more complete analysis of a grammar rule or a fuller review of a particular math concept. Barron's *SAT* also includes dozens of test-taking tactics that can help you earn higher scores on the tests in this book, as well as on the actual SAT that you eventually take.

If you have not yet taken any practice SATs, you should take the first test in this book without timing yourself, just to get used to the types of questions that are on the test. During this first test you can carefully read the directions for each section and look at the sample questions. Later, when you take the other tests in this book, and especially when you take your actual SAT, you should *never* spend even one second reading directions. When the proctor says, for example, "Open your booklets to Section 2 and begin work," the first word you should read is the first word of Question 1—you shouldn't look at the directions, because you will already know them.

As mentioned above, if, after taking the first test and reading the solutions for all of the questions you missed or left out, you find that there are math topics that you don't understand and/or grammar rules that aren't clear, you should try to learn them by reading the relevant sections of Barron's *SAT* before tackling the other tests in this book.

Finally, it is very important to set a realistic goal for yourself, based on the information on pages 16–17 in this book. If you haven't yet done that, do it now. Once you have done that, you should then start taking the other tests in this book at a rate of about one per week.

Before the date of your actual SAT, you should take at least two or three of the exams in this book under true exam conditions. *You should take the entire test in a single sitting adhering to the following suggestions:*

- **TAKE THE TEST IN A QUIET SPOT.** Try to complete the entire test in a place where you won't be distracted or interrupted.
- **TIME YOURSELF ON EACH SECTION.** Allow *precisely* 25 minutes for each of Sections 1 through 7, 20 minutes for each of Section 8 and 9, and 10 minutes for Section 10. Recall that on a real SAT one of the six 25-minute sections from Section 2 through Section 7 is an "experimental" section that does not count in your score. The Practice Tests in this book do

not have experimental sections; so when you finish Section 7, you will have completed six sections and have three more sections to do.

- **TAKE BREAKS.** Take two 10-minute breaks—the first after completing the first three sections and the second after completing the next three sections. During those breaks you may go to the bathroom, walk around, and/or have a snack. Between all other sections take a one-minute break to relax and take a few deep breaths.
- **PACE YOURSELF.** Concentrate and work carefully, without going too fast. Remember, it is better to answer fewer questions and avoid making careless mistakes than to race through trying to answer all the questions.
- **TAKE EDUCATED GUESSES.** If you read a question and don't know the correct answer, always try to eliminate some choices and guess. *Never omit a question if you can eliminate any of the choices.*

If you use the guidelines listed above, you will be making the best use of the time you devote to preparing for the SAT. When you finally take the SAT for real, you will know exactly what to expect. GOOD LUCK!

AN IMPORTANT SYMBOL

Throughout the answer explanations for the tests in this book, the symbol "$\Rightarrow$" is used to indicate that one step in the solution of a problem follows *immediately* from the preceding one, and that no explanation is necessary. You should read:

$$2x = 12 \Rightarrow x = 6$$

as $2x = 12$ *implies* (or *which implies*) *that* $x = 6$, or, *since* $2x = 12$, then $x = 6$.

The Practice Tests

Answer Sheet—Practice Test 1

Section 1   ESSAY

Essay (continued)

If a section has fewer questions than answer spaces, leave the extra spaces blank.

Section 2

1 Ⓐ Ⓑ Ⓒ Ⓓ Ⓔ	8 Ⓐ Ⓑ Ⓒ Ⓓ Ⓔ	15 Ⓐ Ⓑ Ⓒ Ⓓ Ⓔ	22 Ⓐ Ⓑ Ⓒ Ⓓ Ⓔ	29 Ⓐ Ⓑ Ⓒ Ⓓ Ⓔ
2 Ⓐ Ⓑ Ⓒ Ⓓ Ⓔ	9 Ⓐ Ⓑ Ⓒ Ⓓ Ⓔ	16 Ⓐ Ⓑ Ⓒ Ⓓ Ⓔ	23 Ⓐ Ⓑ Ⓒ Ⓓ Ⓔ	30 Ⓐ Ⓑ Ⓒ Ⓓ Ⓔ
3 Ⓐ Ⓑ Ⓒ Ⓓ Ⓔ	10 Ⓐ Ⓑ Ⓒ Ⓓ Ⓔ	17 Ⓐ Ⓑ Ⓒ Ⓓ Ⓔ	24 Ⓐ Ⓑ Ⓒ Ⓓ Ⓔ	31 Ⓐ Ⓑ Ⓒ Ⓓ Ⓔ
4 Ⓐ Ⓑ Ⓒ Ⓓ Ⓔ	11 Ⓐ Ⓑ Ⓒ Ⓓ Ⓔ	18 Ⓐ Ⓑ Ⓒ Ⓓ Ⓔ	25 Ⓐ Ⓑ Ⓒ Ⓓ Ⓔ	32 Ⓐ Ⓑ Ⓒ Ⓓ Ⓔ
5 Ⓐ Ⓑ Ⓒ Ⓓ Ⓔ	12 Ⓐ Ⓑ Ⓒ Ⓓ Ⓔ	19 Ⓐ Ⓑ Ⓒ Ⓓ Ⓔ	26 Ⓐ Ⓑ Ⓒ Ⓓ Ⓔ	33 Ⓐ Ⓑ Ⓒ Ⓓ Ⓔ
6 Ⓐ Ⓑ Ⓒ Ⓓ Ⓔ	13 Ⓐ Ⓑ Ⓒ Ⓓ Ⓔ	20 Ⓐ Ⓑ Ⓒ Ⓓ Ⓔ	27 Ⓐ Ⓑ Ⓒ Ⓓ Ⓔ	34 Ⓐ Ⓑ Ⓒ Ⓓ Ⓔ
7 Ⓐ Ⓑ Ⓒ Ⓓ Ⓔ	14 Ⓐ Ⓑ Ⓒ Ⓓ Ⓔ	21 Ⓐ Ⓑ Ⓒ Ⓓ Ⓔ	28 Ⓐ Ⓑ Ⓒ Ⓓ Ⓔ	35 Ⓐ Ⓑ Ⓒ Ⓓ Ⓔ

Section 3

1 Ⓐ Ⓑ Ⓒ Ⓓ Ⓔ	8 Ⓐ Ⓑ Ⓒ Ⓓ Ⓔ	15 Ⓐ Ⓑ Ⓒ Ⓓ Ⓔ	22 Ⓐ Ⓑ Ⓒ Ⓓ Ⓔ	29 Ⓐ Ⓑ Ⓒ Ⓓ Ⓔ
2 Ⓐ Ⓑ Ⓒ Ⓓ Ⓔ	9 Ⓐ Ⓑ Ⓒ Ⓓ Ⓔ	16 Ⓐ Ⓑ Ⓒ Ⓓ Ⓔ	23 Ⓐ Ⓑ Ⓒ Ⓓ Ⓔ	30 Ⓐ Ⓑ Ⓒ Ⓓ Ⓔ
3 Ⓐ Ⓑ Ⓒ Ⓓ Ⓔ	10 Ⓐ Ⓑ Ⓒ Ⓓ Ⓔ	17 Ⓐ Ⓑ Ⓒ Ⓓ Ⓔ	24 Ⓐ Ⓑ Ⓒ Ⓓ Ⓔ	31 Ⓐ Ⓑ Ⓒ Ⓓ Ⓔ
4 Ⓐ Ⓑ Ⓒ Ⓓ Ⓔ	11 Ⓐ Ⓑ Ⓒ Ⓓ Ⓔ	18 Ⓐ Ⓑ Ⓒ Ⓓ Ⓔ	25 Ⓐ Ⓑ Ⓒ Ⓓ Ⓔ	32 Ⓐ Ⓑ Ⓒ Ⓓ Ⓔ
5 Ⓐ Ⓑ Ⓒ Ⓓ Ⓔ	12 Ⓐ Ⓑ Ⓒ Ⓓ Ⓔ	19 Ⓐ Ⓑ Ⓒ Ⓓ Ⓔ	26 Ⓐ Ⓑ Ⓒ Ⓓ Ⓔ	33 Ⓐ Ⓑ Ⓒ Ⓓ Ⓔ
6 Ⓐ Ⓑ Ⓒ Ⓓ Ⓔ	13 Ⓐ Ⓑ Ⓒ Ⓓ Ⓔ	20 Ⓐ Ⓑ Ⓒ Ⓓ Ⓔ	27 Ⓐ Ⓑ Ⓒ Ⓓ Ⓔ	34 Ⓐ Ⓑ Ⓒ Ⓓ Ⓔ
7 Ⓐ Ⓑ Ⓒ Ⓓ Ⓔ	14 Ⓐ Ⓑ Ⓒ Ⓓ Ⓔ	21 Ⓐ Ⓑ Ⓒ Ⓓ Ⓔ	28 Ⓐ Ⓑ Ⓒ Ⓓ Ⓔ	35 Ⓐ Ⓑ Ⓒ Ⓓ Ⓔ

Section 5

1 Ⓐ Ⓑ Ⓒ Ⓓ Ⓔ	8 Ⓐ Ⓑ Ⓒ Ⓓ Ⓔ	15 Ⓐ Ⓑ Ⓒ Ⓓ Ⓔ	22 Ⓐ Ⓑ Ⓒ Ⓓ Ⓔ	29 Ⓐ Ⓑ Ⓒ Ⓓ Ⓔ
2 Ⓐ Ⓑ Ⓒ Ⓓ Ⓔ	9 Ⓐ Ⓑ Ⓒ Ⓓ Ⓔ	16 Ⓐ Ⓑ Ⓒ Ⓓ Ⓔ	23 Ⓐ Ⓑ Ⓒ Ⓓ Ⓔ	30 Ⓐ Ⓑ Ⓒ Ⓓ Ⓔ
3 Ⓐ Ⓑ Ⓒ Ⓓ Ⓔ	10 Ⓐ Ⓑ Ⓒ Ⓓ Ⓔ	17 Ⓐ Ⓑ Ⓒ Ⓓ Ⓔ	24 Ⓐ Ⓑ Ⓒ Ⓓ Ⓔ	31 Ⓐ Ⓑ Ⓒ Ⓓ Ⓔ
4 Ⓐ Ⓑ Ⓒ Ⓓ Ⓔ	11 Ⓐ Ⓑ Ⓒ Ⓓ Ⓔ	18 Ⓐ Ⓑ Ⓒ Ⓓ Ⓔ	25 Ⓐ Ⓑ Ⓒ Ⓓ Ⓔ	32 Ⓐ Ⓑ Ⓒ Ⓓ Ⓔ
5 Ⓐ Ⓑ Ⓒ Ⓓ Ⓔ	12 Ⓐ Ⓑ Ⓒ Ⓓ Ⓔ	19 Ⓐ Ⓑ Ⓒ Ⓓ Ⓔ	26 Ⓐ Ⓑ Ⓒ Ⓓ Ⓔ	33 Ⓐ Ⓑ Ⓒ Ⓓ Ⓔ
6 Ⓐ Ⓑ Ⓒ Ⓓ Ⓔ	13 Ⓐ Ⓑ Ⓒ Ⓓ Ⓔ	20 Ⓐ Ⓑ Ⓒ Ⓓ Ⓔ	27 Ⓐ Ⓑ Ⓒ Ⓓ Ⓔ	34 Ⓐ Ⓑ Ⓒ Ⓓ Ⓔ
7 Ⓐ Ⓑ Ⓒ Ⓓ Ⓔ	14 Ⓐ Ⓑ Ⓒ Ⓓ Ⓔ	21 Ⓐ Ⓑ Ⓒ Ⓓ Ⓔ	28 Ⓐ Ⓑ Ⓒ Ⓓ Ⓔ	35 Ⓐ Ⓑ Ⓒ Ⓓ Ⓔ

Section 6

1 Ⓐ Ⓑ Ⓒ Ⓓ Ⓔ	8 Ⓐ Ⓑ Ⓒ Ⓓ Ⓔ	15 Ⓐ Ⓑ Ⓒ Ⓓ Ⓔ	22 Ⓐ Ⓑ Ⓒ Ⓓ Ⓔ	29 Ⓐ Ⓑ Ⓒ Ⓓ Ⓔ
2 Ⓐ Ⓑ Ⓒ Ⓓ Ⓔ	9 Ⓐ Ⓑ Ⓒ Ⓓ Ⓔ	16 Ⓐ Ⓑ Ⓒ Ⓓ Ⓔ	23 Ⓐ Ⓑ Ⓒ Ⓓ Ⓔ	30 Ⓐ Ⓑ Ⓒ Ⓓ Ⓔ
3 Ⓐ Ⓑ Ⓒ Ⓓ Ⓔ	10 Ⓐ Ⓑ Ⓒ Ⓓ Ⓔ	17 Ⓐ Ⓑ Ⓒ Ⓓ Ⓔ	24 Ⓐ Ⓑ Ⓒ Ⓓ Ⓔ	31 Ⓐ Ⓑ Ⓒ Ⓓ Ⓔ
4 Ⓐ Ⓑ Ⓒ Ⓓ Ⓔ	11 Ⓐ Ⓑ Ⓒ Ⓓ Ⓔ	18 Ⓐ Ⓑ Ⓒ Ⓓ Ⓔ	25 Ⓐ Ⓑ Ⓒ Ⓓ Ⓔ	32 Ⓐ Ⓑ Ⓒ Ⓓ Ⓔ
5 Ⓐ Ⓑ Ⓒ Ⓓ Ⓔ	12 Ⓐ Ⓑ Ⓒ Ⓓ Ⓔ	19 Ⓐ Ⓑ Ⓒ Ⓓ Ⓔ	26 Ⓐ Ⓑ Ⓒ Ⓓ Ⓔ	33 Ⓐ Ⓑ Ⓒ Ⓓ Ⓔ
6 Ⓐ Ⓑ Ⓒ Ⓓ Ⓔ	13 Ⓐ Ⓑ Ⓒ Ⓓ Ⓔ	20 Ⓐ Ⓑ Ⓒ Ⓓ Ⓔ	27 Ⓐ Ⓑ Ⓒ Ⓓ Ⓔ	34 Ⓐ Ⓑ Ⓒ Ⓓ Ⓔ
7 Ⓐ Ⓑ Ⓒ Ⓓ Ⓔ	14 Ⓐ Ⓑ Ⓒ Ⓓ Ⓔ	21 Ⓐ Ⓑ Ⓒ Ⓓ Ⓔ	28 Ⓐ Ⓑ Ⓒ Ⓓ Ⓔ	35 Ⓐ Ⓑ Ⓒ Ⓓ Ⓔ

Practice Test 1

Section 7

1 Ⓐ Ⓑ Ⓒ Ⓓ Ⓔ   3 Ⓐ Ⓑ Ⓒ Ⓓ Ⓔ   5 Ⓐ Ⓑ Ⓒ Ⓓ Ⓔ   7 Ⓐ Ⓑ Ⓒ Ⓓ Ⓔ
2 Ⓐ Ⓑ Ⓒ Ⓓ Ⓔ   4 Ⓐ Ⓑ Ⓒ Ⓓ Ⓔ   6 Ⓐ Ⓑ Ⓒ Ⓓ Ⓔ   8 Ⓐ Ⓑ Ⓒ Ⓓ Ⓔ

9   10   11   12   13

14   15   16   17   18

Section 8

1 Ⓐ Ⓑ Ⓒ Ⓓ Ⓔ   5 Ⓐ Ⓑ Ⓒ Ⓓ Ⓔ   9 Ⓐ Ⓑ Ⓒ Ⓓ Ⓔ   13 Ⓐ Ⓑ Ⓒ Ⓓ Ⓔ   17 Ⓐ Ⓑ Ⓒ Ⓓ Ⓔ
2 Ⓐ Ⓑ Ⓒ Ⓓ Ⓔ   6 Ⓐ Ⓑ Ⓒ Ⓓ Ⓔ   10 Ⓐ Ⓑ Ⓒ Ⓓ Ⓔ   14 Ⓐ Ⓑ Ⓒ Ⓓ Ⓔ   18 Ⓐ Ⓑ Ⓒ Ⓓ Ⓔ
3 Ⓐ Ⓑ Ⓒ Ⓓ Ⓔ   7 Ⓐ Ⓑ Ⓒ Ⓓ Ⓔ   11 Ⓐ Ⓑ Ⓒ Ⓓ Ⓔ   15 Ⓐ Ⓑ Ⓒ Ⓓ Ⓔ   19 Ⓐ Ⓑ Ⓒ Ⓓ Ⓔ
4 Ⓐ Ⓑ Ⓒ Ⓓ Ⓔ   8 Ⓐ Ⓑ Ⓒ Ⓓ Ⓔ   12 Ⓐ Ⓑ Ⓒ Ⓓ Ⓔ   16 Ⓐ Ⓑ Ⓒ Ⓓ Ⓔ   20 Ⓐ Ⓑ Ⓒ Ⓓ Ⓔ

Section 9

1 Ⓐ Ⓑ Ⓒ Ⓓ Ⓔ   5 Ⓐ Ⓑ Ⓒ Ⓓ Ⓔ   9 Ⓐ Ⓑ Ⓒ Ⓓ Ⓔ   13 Ⓐ Ⓑ Ⓒ Ⓓ Ⓔ   17 Ⓐ Ⓑ Ⓒ Ⓓ Ⓔ
2 Ⓐ Ⓑ Ⓒ Ⓓ Ⓔ   6 Ⓐ Ⓑ Ⓒ Ⓓ Ⓔ   10 Ⓐ Ⓑ Ⓒ Ⓓ Ⓔ   14 Ⓐ Ⓑ Ⓒ Ⓓ Ⓔ   18 Ⓐ Ⓑ Ⓒ Ⓓ Ⓔ
3 Ⓐ Ⓑ Ⓒ Ⓓ Ⓔ   7 Ⓐ Ⓑ Ⓒ Ⓓ Ⓔ   11 Ⓐ Ⓑ Ⓒ Ⓓ Ⓔ   15 Ⓐ Ⓑ Ⓒ Ⓓ Ⓔ   19 Ⓐ Ⓑ Ⓒ Ⓓ Ⓔ
4 Ⓐ Ⓑ Ⓒ Ⓓ Ⓔ   8 Ⓐ Ⓑ Ⓒ Ⓓ Ⓔ   12 Ⓐ Ⓑ Ⓒ Ⓓ Ⓔ   16 Ⓐ Ⓑ Ⓒ Ⓓ Ⓔ   20 Ⓐ Ⓑ Ⓒ Ⓓ Ⓔ

Section 10

1 Ⓐ Ⓑ Ⓒ Ⓓ Ⓔ   5 Ⓐ Ⓑ Ⓒ Ⓓ Ⓔ   9 Ⓐ Ⓑ Ⓒ Ⓓ Ⓔ   13 Ⓐ Ⓑ Ⓒ Ⓓ Ⓔ   17 Ⓐ Ⓑ Ⓒ Ⓓ Ⓔ
2 Ⓐ Ⓑ Ⓒ Ⓓ Ⓔ   6 Ⓐ Ⓑ Ⓒ Ⓓ Ⓔ   10 Ⓐ Ⓑ Ⓒ Ⓓ Ⓔ   14 Ⓐ Ⓑ Ⓒ Ⓓ Ⓔ   18 Ⓐ Ⓑ Ⓒ Ⓓ Ⓔ
3 Ⓐ Ⓑ Ⓒ Ⓓ Ⓔ   7 Ⓐ Ⓑ Ⓒ Ⓓ Ⓔ   11 Ⓐ Ⓑ Ⓒ Ⓓ Ⓔ   15 Ⓐ Ⓑ Ⓒ Ⓓ Ⓔ   19 Ⓐ Ⓑ Ⓒ Ⓓ Ⓔ
4 Ⓐ Ⓑ Ⓒ Ⓓ Ⓔ   8 Ⓐ Ⓑ Ⓒ Ⓓ Ⓔ   12 Ⓐ Ⓑ Ⓒ Ⓓ Ⓔ   16 Ⓐ Ⓑ Ⓒ Ⓓ Ⓔ   20 Ⓐ Ⓑ Ⓒ Ⓓ Ⓔ

Practice Test 1 $\quad$ 1 $\quad$ 1 $\quad$ 1 $\quad$ 1 $\quad$ 1 $\quad$ 1 $\qquad$ 1

SECTION **1** $\qquad$ **Time—25 Minutes** $\qquad$ **ESSAY**

Write your essay on the lines provided on the answer sheet on pages 35–36. Be careful to write legibly. Write on the topic, carefully presenting your point of view. Your essay will be scored on the basis of the ideas it contains and its effectiveness in expressing these ideas. Pay special attention to logic, clarity, and the accurate use of language.

Think about the topic presented in the following excerpt and in the assignment below it.

The young people of today think of nothing but themselves. They have no reverence for parents or old age. They are impatient of all restraint. They talk as if they alone know anything.

— Peter the Hermit, eleventh century A.D.

ASSIGNMENT: Have young people today lost traditional values such as respect for elders and concern for others? Plan and write an essay in which you develop your point of view on this question. Support your position with reasoning and examples taken from your experience, reading, or observations.

Practice Test 1

2   2   2   2   2   2   2   2   2   2   2

SECTION 2   Time—25 Minutes   **Choose the best answer to each of the following questions in this section. Then blacken the appropriate space on your answer sheet.**
24 Questions

Each of the following sentences contains one or two blanks, indicating that a word or set of words has been omitted. Beneath each sentence there are five answer choices labeled A to E from which you must select the word or set of words that best fits the meaning of the sentence as a whole.

Example:

Records of colonization can be found as far back as the Phoenicians, but colonization became a major force in world history only when European countries began, in the fifteenth century, to make ---- Asia, the Americas, and Africa.

(A) queries about   (B) incursions into
   (C) tirades against   (D) enemies in
    (E) amends for

Ⓐ ● Ⓒ Ⓓ Ⓔ

---

1. The modern computer looks ---- in the room decorated in an ornate, old-fashioned style.

   (A) ornamental   (B) incongruous
      (C) unwarranted   (D) splendid
       (E) antiquated

2. Scientific and technical terms have become ----, and so a great deal of jargon has passed into everyday language (*feedback*, *fine tune*, and *filter*, for example).

   (A) difficult   (B) suggestive   (C) rare
       (D) elusive   (E) ubiquitous

3. The book is an anthology of stories dealing with the theme of ----; ----, however, the person who collected the stories is known for his inability to understand the feelings of others.

   (A) misogyny . . inexplicably
   (B) misanthropy . . paradoxically
   (C) empathy . . ironically
   (D) altruism . . fortunately
   (E) love . . parenthetically

4. Sherlock Holmes, with his amazing powers of observation and deduction, is often called the ---- private detective.

   (A) articulate   (B) archetypal   (C) subdued
       (D) laconic   (E) somber

5. In her article the art critic draws ---- between how the universe is ---- by modern physics and by the popular modern art form, Cubism.

   (A) analogies . . impaired
   (B) disparities . . articulated
   (C) inferences . . repudiated
   (D) parallels . . depicted
   (E) conclusions . . ratified

GO ON TO THE NEXT PAGE

2   2   2   2   2   2   2   2   2   2   2

Below are passages followed by questions on them. Questions on a pair of related passages may be about the relationship between the two passages. For each question, select the best answer based on what is stated or implied in the passage (or passages).

Questions 6–7 are based on the following passage.

Humanitarianism is probably the most important "ism" in the world today, given the collapse of communism, the discrediting of
Line neoliberalism, and the general distrust of large-
(5) scale political ideologies. Its activists often claim to escape or transcend partisan politics. We think of humanitarian aid, for example, first of all as a form of philanthropy—a response to an earthquake in Haiti or a tsunami in Asia, which is
(10) obviously a good thing, an effort to relieve human suffering and save lives, an act of international benevolence. But there is a puzzle here, for helping people in desperate need is something that we ought to do; it would be
(15) wrong not to do it—in which case it is more like justice than benevolence. Words such as "charity" and "philanthropy" describe a voluntary act, a matter of kindness rather than duty. But international humanitarianism seems more like
(20) duty than kindness, or maybe it is a combination: two in one, a gift that we have to give.

6. Which of the following would the author be most likely to discuss in the paragraph following this one?
   (A) Why people have lost their trust in "large-scale political ideologies"
   (B) Should the international community provide more help to people in urgent need
   (C) The nature and extent of the duties owed by one person to another
   (D) The distinctions that can usefully be made between benevolence, humanitarianism, and philanthropy
   (E) Why neoliberalism has failed to provide a moral underpinning for humanitarianism

7. The author of the passage apparently believes that
   (A) in some cases benevolence is a duty
   (B) most people contribute to international aid as a result of a conscious sense of duty to others, rather than as a result of a feeling that others need their help
   (C) communism, though in decline, is the only ideology that places a high priority on international humanitarianism
   (D) there is no longer a place in the world for large-scale political ideologies
   (E) disaster relief is the most important contribution made by international humanitarianism

GO ON TO THE NEXT PAGE

2   2   2   2   2   2   2   2   2   2   2

Questions 8–9 are based on the following passage.

For many years, "African solutions to African problems" has been a catchall slogan promoted by donor countries and African leaders alike. At
Line the most general level, the maxim implies that
(5) Africans will take more responsibility for the multiple challenges they face. But critics have worried that the phrase could become an excuse for powerful states in the West to neglect Africa or for authoritarian leaders, such as Robert
(10) Mugabe in Zimbabwe, to reject criticisms of human rights abuses. Côte d'Ivoire showed that neither scenario is necessarily the case. African leaders repeatedly condemned Gbagbo's flagrant violation of democratic norms, and France and
(15) the UN intervened militarily when it counted. What happened in Côte d'Ivoire is thus consistent with an emergent, pro-democracy policy in which African heads of state are taking on significant roles in conflict resolution.

8. The passage offers the most support for the idea that
   (A) Africans are incapable of solving African problems without help from Western countries
   (B) human rights should be restricted in African countries until more mature democracies emerge there
   (C) Africans should continue to take more responsibility for solving problems in African countries
   (D) authoritarian regimes offer African countries the only realistic way to solve their problems without Western assistance
   (E) Western states are increasingly neglecting Africa and its problems

9. Which best describes the structure of the passage?
   (A) Criticism of a widely accepted principle; description of problems that often arise when that principle is put into practice; discussion of cases in which such problems do not arise; recommendations for future policy
   (B) Description of problems in Africa suggesting solutions to those problems; providing examples where such problems were solved; reaching a conclusion that will be the basis of further action
   (C) Description of a guiding principle; description of cases in which the principle works and does not work in practice; recommendations for future action
   (D) Description of a widely accepted guiding principle; discussion of possible problems of that principle; providing evidence that these problems do not necessarily arise; reaching a general conclusion
   (E) Description of a widely accepted principle; discussion of cases in which the principle is inappropriately applied, discussion of how the principle can be better applied; recommendations for future policy

GO ON TO THE NEXT PAGE

2 **2** **2** **2** **2** **2** **2** **2** **2** **2** **2** **2**

Questions 10–15 are based on the following passage.

The traditionals have always been wary of the white man's consumer mentality, and now they were worried about what could happen when the Black Mesa mine was dead, when a dependent
(5) and poverty stricken people, having been left with waste and desecration where a sacred mountain had once stood, found themselves forced to accept more leases and more desolation. This threat was increased by the prospect of legal
(10) "termination," or dissolution of a people as a cultural unit, with which Indians are threatened every other year. Termination legislation, which had already wiped out a number of small tribes, not only withdraws all federal aid, but turns the
(15) Indians over to the mercies of state jurisdiction and property taxation, forcing a people with no other recourse to put their last resource—land— upon the market. ("That is all we have. When the land is gone, we will walk away from our homes
(20) with our beds upon our backs.") By eliminating an Indian nation, termination quiets Indian claims to tribal lands that were never ceded to the U.S. government by treaty, which happens to describe almost all the "federal" land in the Far West;
(25) instead, the people must accept whatever monetary settlement has been bestowed upon them by the Court of Claims, which was set up not to administer justice but to expedite adjudication of land titles and head off any future
(30) claims that Indians might make on lands already coveted by the white economy.

The Hopi chairman's brother, Wayne, a prosperous Mormon, proprietor of a thriving Hopi craft shop, with holdings in the family
(35) ranch and a construction company, complains in his progressive newspaper, *Qua Toqti*, of the poor attitude of the traditionals toward "their fellow tribesmen in business," and criticizes white supporters of the traditionals for "wanting to keep
(40) us in our 'primitive' state." He has declared, "We will never go back to our cornfields and orchards unless we are forced to." In another column in

the newspaper, Wayne Sekaquaptewa inquires, "When will someone come along to convince us
(45) that we are squabbling like untrained children over everything in the name of our useless religion?" (Sekaquaptewa believes that the true story of the Hopi may be found in the Book of Mormon.) Not surprisingly, *Qua Toqti*
(50) vociferously supports the eviction of the "enemy Navajo" from Hopi land.

The progressives feel that there is no place for old, slow Hopi ways in a world that is going on without them; they look down on the traditionals,
(55) with their wood stoves and kerosene lamps and outhouses, their "useless religion." (I notice, however, that outhouses in Oraibi and Hotevilla are not locked to keep out witches, as are the Christian outhouses of Walpi.) The traditionals
(60) know that those who follow the lead of the progressives will be assimilated—that is, swept away into a competitive economy for which they have no training. So long as the Hopi hold their land, those still able to make corn grow in the
(65) slow, patient techniques of dry farming will survive even when all help has been taken away, proceeding as best as they can according to their sacred instructions until the Day of Purification restores harmony and balance to all land and life,
(70) until the bad road taken by the white man comes to its inevitable end, as foretold in the stark etching on the Life Plan Rock.

10. According to the author, the Court of Claims referred to in line 27
   (A) adjudicates cases fairly
   (B) almost always favors Indian claims to land over white claims to land
   (C) has little real effect on Indian affairs
   (D) is biased toward white people in its judgments
   (E) is responsible for deciding which Indians receive monetary assistance from the U.S. government

GO ON TO THE NEXT PAGE

11. The author says, "I notice, however, that outhouses in Oraibi and Hotevilla are not locked to keep out witches, as are the Christian outhouses of Walpi" (lines 56–59). What does the author probably intend the reader to infer from this observation?

    (A) That traditional Hopi religion has not developed even to the point at which it believes in witches

    (B) That followers of traditional Hopi religion are careless in the practice of their religion compared to the progressives, who scrupulously follow the teachings of Christianity

    (C) That followers of traditional Hopi religion might be less superstitious than the Hopi followers of the white man's predominant religion, Christianity

    (D) That there is one case in which the traditionals are right and the progressives are wrong

    (E) That progressive Indians are, sensibly, aware of the danger presented by witches

12. The traditionals believe that

    (A) the only way in which the Hopi can survive as a distinct culture is to follow the lead of the progressives and adapt to the white man's ways

    (B) Hopi religion is based on a misplaced faith that balance will eventually be restored in the world

    (C) it is very possible that the truth about the origin and destiny of the Hopi is to be found in the Book of Mormon

    (D) the U.S. government has, by and large, been fair in its dealings with Indians

    (E) the only chance that the Hopi have to survive as a cultural unit is to cling to their traditional ways

13. The author's main purpose in citing the views of Wayne Sekaquaptewa is to help

    (A) present the views of the progressives in the Hopi nation

    (B) show that progressive Hopis are more realistic than traditional Hopis

    (C) illustrate the influence of Mormonism on Hopi society

    (D) show that Indians, if given the opportunity, can be as successful in business as whites

    (E) illustrate the contradictory attitudes held by progressive Hopis

14. Which of the following statements best describes the author's view of the "Day of Purification" referred to in line 68?

    (A) He believes it will come as long as enough Hopis abandon their traditional culture and adopt the ways of the white man.

    (B) He is certain that it will come one day, precisely as predicted in Hopi teaching.

    (C) He believes that it represents the time when the sun dies, ending life on earth.

    (D) He thinks that it is a myth believed by a primitive culture that contains no truth, even on a symbolic level.

    (E) He respects it as an important Hopi belief and sees it as symbolic of a future time that may very possibly come to pass.

15. Which word or phrase would traditional Hopi be most likely to use to describe the white man?

    (A) Articulate
    (B) Trustworthy
    (C) Altruistic
    (D) Materialistic
    (E) Respectful of nature

GO ON TO THE NEXT PAGE ⟶

2 2 2 2 2 2 2 2 2 2 2

Questions 16–24 are based on the following passages.
Each of the following passages is from the beginning of a short story.

Passage 1

This unlikely story begins on a sea that was a
blue dream, as colorful as blue-silk stockings,
and beneath a sky as blue as the irises of
Line children's eyes. From the western half of the sky
(5) the sun was shying little golden disks at the
sea—if you gazed intently enough you could see
them skip from wave tip to wave tip until they
joined a broad collar of golden coin that was
collecting half a mile out and would eventually
(10) be a dazzling sunset. About half-way between the
Florida shore and the golden collar a white
steam-yacht, very young and graceful, was riding
at anchor and under a blue-and-white awning aft
a yellow-haired girl reclined in a wicker settee
(15) reading *The Revolt of the Angels*, by Anatole
France. She was about nineteen, slender and
supple, with a spoiled alluring mouth and quick
gray eyes full of a radiant curiosity. Her feet,
stockingless, and adorned rather than clad in
(20) blue-satin slippers which swung nonchalantly
from her toes, were perched on the arm of a
settee adjoining the one she occupied. And as she
read she intermittently regaled herself by a faint
application to her tongue of a half-lemon that she
(25) held in her hand. The other half, sucked dry, lay
on the deck at her feet and rocked very gently to
and fro at the almost imperceptible motion of
the tide.

The second half-lemon was well-nigh pulpless
(30) and the golden collar had grown astonishing in
width, when suddenly the drowsy silence which
enveloped the yacht was broken by the sound of
heavy footsteps and an elderly man topped with
orderly gray hair and clad in a white-flannel suit
(35) appeared at the head of the companionway. There
he paused for a moment until his eyes became
accustomed to the sun, and then seeing the girl
under the awning he uttered a long even grunt of
disapproval. If he had intended thereby to obtain
(40) a rise of any sort he was doomed to
disappointment. The girl calmly turned over two
pages, turned back one, raised the lemon
mechanically to tasting distance, and then very
faintly but quite unmistakably yawned.

Passage 2

(45) The sunlight dripped over the house like
golden paint over an art jar, and the freckling
shadows here and there only intensified the rigor
of the bath of light. The Butterworth and Larkin
houses flanking were entrenched behind great
(50) stodgy trees; only the Happer house took the full
sun, and all day long faced the dusty road-street
with a tolerant kindly patience. This was the city
of Tarleton in southernmost Georgia, September
afternoon.

(55) Up in her bedroom window Sally Carrol
Happer rested her nineteen-year-old chin on a
fifty-two-year-old sill and watched Clark
Darrow's ancient Ford turn the corner. The car
was hot—being partly metallic it retained all the
(60) heat it absorbed or evolved—and Clark Darrow
sitting bolt upright at the wheel wore a pained,
strained expression as though he considered
himself a spare part, and rather likely to break.
He laboriously crossed two dust ruts, the wheels
(65) squeaking indignantly at the encounter, and then
with a terrifying expression he gave the steering-
gear a final wrench and deposited self and car
approximately in front of the Happer steps. There
was a heaving sound, a death-rattle, followed by
(70) a short silence; and then the air was rent by a
startling whistle. Sally Carrol gazed down
sleepily. She started to yawn, but finding this
quite impossible unless she raised her chin from
the window-sill, changed her mind and continued
(75) silently to regard the car, whose owner sat
brilliantly if perfunctorily at attention as he
waited for an answer to his signal. After a
moment the whistle once more split the dusty air.

16. The phrase "quick gray eyes" (lines 17–18) is most
likely used to suggest that the girl portrayed in
Passage 1 is

(A) afraid
(B) alert
(C) nervous
(D) shifty
(E) distracted

GO ON TO THE NEXT PAGE ⟶

2 2 2 2 2 2 2 2 2 2 2

17. The phrase "adorned rather than clad" (line 19) suggests that the girl described in Passage 1

   (A) is indifferent to how her feet look
   (B) likes to make herself attractive
   (C) is wearing slippers because they are the most practical footwear for a passenger on a yacht
   (D) tends to be forgetful, as shown by the fact that she is not wearing stockings
   (E) does not know much about fashion

18. In line 40, "rise" most nearly means

   (A) reply
   (B) increase
   (C) greeting
   (D) reaction
   (E) wave

19. What can most reasonably be inferred about the man portrayed in Passage 1?

   (A) He is the girl's father.
   (B) He is the girl's grandfather.
   (C) He does not enjoy being on a yacht.
   (D) He does not often come on deck because his illness confines him to bed below deck.
   (E) He does not approve of the girl's spending so much of her time reading.

20. In Passage 2 the author uses the words and phrases "tolerant kindly patience" (line 52), "indignantly" (line 65), and "death-rattle" (line 69) mainly to

   (A) portray inanimate objects as having human emotions
   (B) help the reader imagine what is being described
   (C) exaggerate and distort reality to give the reader a fresh perspective
   (D) make an ironic comment on the events described
   (E) create humor

21. The whistle mentioned in line 71 of Passage 2 was most likely produced by

   (A) a passerby
   (B) Clark Darrow's car
   (C) Sally Happer
   (D) Clark Darrow
   (E) a policeman

22. One can reasonably infer that the words "sat brilliantly if perfunctorily at attention" in Passage 2 (lines 75–76) suggest that Clark Darrow regards his visit to the Happer house largely as

   (A) a dramatic way to demonstrate his romantic interest in Sally Happer
   (B) a great honor
   (C) one of the most embarrassing things he has ever had to do
   (D) an uninteresting routine duty to be performed, albeit in a somewhat showy manner
   (E) an exciting change from his regular activities

23. Which of the following words best describes both of the girls as they are portrayed in Passage 1 and Passage 2?

   (A) Pretty
   (B) Relaxed
   (C) Intelligent
   (D) Indolent
   (E) Voluble

24. In both Passage 1 and Passage 2 the arrival of a male character

   (A) primarily helps to create humor
   (B) is followed by a condemnation of self-indulgence
   (C) interrupts a tranquil mood
   (D) suggests that the male characters dominate the female characters
   (E) establishes a serious atmosphere

STOP

IN ANY REMAINING TIME YOU MAY REVIEW THE ANSWERS YOU CHOSE IN THIS SECTION. DO NOT WORK ON ANY OTHER SECTION OF THE TEST DURING THIS TIME.

3 3 3 3 3 3 3 3 3 3 3 3

SECTION **3**

Time—25 Minutes
20 Questions

For each problem in this section determine which of the five choices is correct and blacken the corresponding choice on your answer sheet. You may use any blank space on the page for your work.

Notes:

- You may use a calculator whenever you think it will be helpful.
- Only real numbers are used. No question or answer on this test involves a complex or imaginary number.
- Use the diagrams provided to help you solve the problems. Unless you see the words "Note: Figure not drawn to scale" under a diagram, it has been drawn as accurately as possible. Unless it is stated that a figure is three-dimensional, you may assume it lies in a plane.
- For any function, f, the domain, unless specifically restricted, is the set of all real numbers for which $f(x)$ is also a real number.

Reference Information

Area Facts

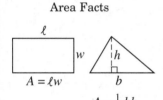

$A = \ell w$

$A = \frac{1}{2} bh$

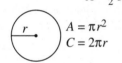

$A = \pi r^2$
$C = 2\pi r$

Volume Facts

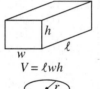

$V = \ell w h$

$V = \pi r^2 h$

Triangle Facts

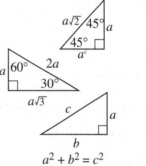

$a^2 + b^2 = c^2$

Angle Facts

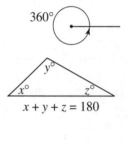

$x + y + z = 180$

1. In a class, the ratio of the number of boys to the number of girls is 3:7. What fraction of the students in the class are girls?

(A) $\dfrac{3}{7}$

(B) $\dfrac{4}{7}$

(C) $\dfrac{3}{10}$

(D) $\dfrac{4}{10}$

(E) $\dfrac{7}{10}$

2. When they went to the store, Maryline, Sandrine, and Nicholas noticed that Maryline had twice as much money as Sandrine, and Nicholas had five times as much money as Maryline. If Sandrine had $10, how much money did the three of them have altogether?

(A) $50
(B) $80
(C) $100
(D) $130
(E) $160

GO ON TO THE NEXT PAGE

Practice Test 1

3. Penny and Olive went into Frank's Fast Food. Penny ordered 2 hamburgers and 1 side of fries; Olive ordered 1 hamburger and 2 sides of fries. If Penny's order cost $7.25 and Olive's order cost $5.50, what is the price of a hamburger?

(A) $1.25
(B) $2.00
(C) $2.50
(D) $3.00
(E) $3.25

4. If the vertices of triangle ABC are the points $A(-7, -2)$, $B(-1, 1)$, and $C(-1, -2)$, what is the area of $\triangle ABC$?

(A) 6
(B) 9
(C) 10
(D) 12
(E) 18

5. How many positive multiples of 4 less than 100 are NOT multiples of 6?

(A) 8
(B) 12
(C) 16
(D) 20
(E) 24

6. If $a^2 + 2ab + b^2 = 4$, what is the value of $(a + b)^6$?

(A) 8
(B) 16
(C) 24
(D) 32
(E) 64

7. If the average of a, a, b, and b is $a + 1$, which of the following must be true?

(A) $b = a + \dfrac{1}{2}$

(B) $b = a + 1$
(C) $b = a + 2$
(D) $a = b + 1$
(E) $a = b + 2$

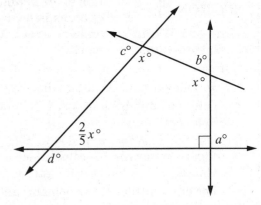

8. In the figure above, four lines intersect as shown. What is the value of $a + b + c + d$?

(A) 180
(B) 225
(C) 270
(D) 300
(E) 360

9. If a month has 5 Sundays, which of the following is a list of all the possible days that could be the 10th of that month?

(A) Sunday, Monday
(B) Sunday, Monday, Tuesday
(C) Friday, Saturday
(D) Saturday, Sunday
(E) Friday, Saturday, Sunday

10. Mr. Baldwin gave 500 raffle tickets to the 282 people who attended a charity banquet. Each person received at least one ticket, and no one received more than three. If 108 people received exactly two tickets, how many people received exactly three tickets?

(A) 55
(B) 70
(C) 110
(D) 119
(E) 174

GO ON TO THE NEXT PAGE

3   3   3   3   3   3   3   3   3   3   3   3

11. If x is inversely proportional to y^2, and if $y = 4$ when $x = 5$, what is the value of x when $y = 6$?

   (A) $\dfrac{9}{20}$

   (B) $\dfrac{20}{9}$

   (C) $\dfrac{24}{5}$

   (D) $\dfrac{15}{2}$

   (E) $\dfrac{45}{4}$

Questions 12–13 refer to the graph below.

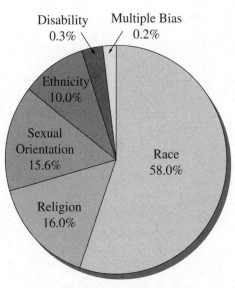

Disability
0.3%

Multiple Bias
0.2%

Ethnicity
10.0%

Sexual Orientation
15.6%

Religion
16.0%

Race
58.0%

Bias-Motivated Offenses 2000
Percent Distribution

12. If in 2000 there were 10,000 bias-motivated offenses based on ethnicity, how many more offenses were based on religion than on sexual orientation?

   (A)   4
   (B)   40
   (C)   400
   (D) 4,000
   (E) 40,000

13. If it was later determined that between 25 percent and 50 percent of the offenses included under Religion were, in fact, not bias-motivated, and those offenses were removed from the study, which of the following could be the percentage of bias-motivated offenses based on race?

   (A) 58%
   (B) 60%
   (C) 62%
   (D) 64%
   (E) 66%

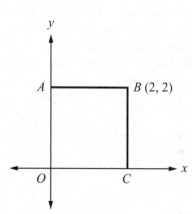

14. In square *OABC*, *D* and *E* (not shown) are the midpoints of sides $\overline{OA}$ and $\overline{BC}$, respectively, and *M* and *N* (not shown) are the midpoints of $\overline{BD}$ and $\overline{OE}$, respectively. What is the perimeter of quadrilateral *DMEN*?

   (A) 1
   (B) 2
   (C) $2\sqrt{5}$
   (D) 4
   (E) $4\sqrt{5}$

GO ON TO THE NEXT PAGE

3   3 3 3 3 3 3 3 3 3 3   3

15. Lines ℓ_1, ℓ_2, and ℓ_3 all have a *y*-intercept of 4. If ℓ_1 passes through (3, 3), ℓ_2 passes through (3, 4), and ℓ_3 passes through (3, 5), and if m_1, m_2, and m_3 represent the slopes of ℓ_1, ℓ_2, and ℓ_3, respectively, which of the following is true?

(A) $m_1 < m_2 < m_3$
(B) $m_1 < m_3 < m_2$
(C) $m_2 < m_1 < m_3$
(D) $m_2 < m_3 < m_1$
(E) $m_3 < m_2 < m_1$

16. John is a member of a baseball card collector's club. The number of cards that John has is 60% of the total number of cards that everyone else in the club has. What fraction of the total number of cards of everyone in the club belongs to John?

(A) $\dfrac{1}{4}$

(B) $\dfrac{3}{8}$

(C) $\dfrac{2}{5}$

(D) $\dfrac{1}{2}$

(E) $\dfrac{3}{5}$

17. In the sequence a_1, a_2, a_3, a_4, a_5, . . . , each number after the first is 3 times the preceding number. If $a_5 - a_1 = 100$, what is the value of a_2?

(A) $\dfrac{5}{4}$

(B) $\dfrac{5}{2}$

(C) 3

(D) $\dfrac{15}{4}$

(E) 9

18. At Central High School, $\dfrac{2}{3}$ of the 825 students take a Spanish course and 460 students play on a team. Of the students who play on a team, 310 take Spanish. How many students do not take Spanish and do not play on a team?

(A) 125
(B) 150
(C) 240
(D) 275
(E) 390

19. The decimal expansion of $\dfrac{3}{7}$ is the repeating decimal 0.428571428571. . . . What is the sum of the first 100 digits to the right of the decimal point?

(A) 432
(B) 446
(C) 451
(D) 453
(E) 458

20. What is the area of a regular hexagon whose perimeter is 24?

(A) 24
(B) 36
(C) 48
(D) $24\sqrt{3}$
(E) $48\sqrt{3}$

STOP

IN ANY REMAINING TIME YOU MAY REVIEW THE
ANSWERS YOU CHOSE IN THIS SECTION. DO NOT WORK
ON ANY OTHER SECTION OF THE TEST DURING THIS TIME.

5 5 5 5 5 5 5

SECTION 5 | Time—25 Minutes
24 Questions | Choose the best answer to each of the following questions in this section. Then blacken the appropriate space on your answer sheet.

Each of the following sentences contains one or two blanks, indicating that a word or set of words has been omitted. Beneath each sentence there are five answer choices labeled A to E from which you must select the word or set of words that best fits the meaning of the sentence as a whole.

Example:

Records of colonization can be found as far back as the Phoenicians, but colonization became a major force in world history only when European countries began, in the fifteenth century, to make ---- Asia, the Americas, and Africa.

(A) queries about
(B) incursions into
(C) tirades against
(D) enemics in
(E) amends for

1. The court accepted the medical evidence on the authoritative testimony of the ---- doctor.

(A) excitable   (B) young   (C) docile
(D) eminent   (E) distraught

2. Some ecosystems are ----, whereas others are fragile, susceptible to small changes in conditions.

(A) self-sufficient   (B) scanty   (C) robust
(D) tenacious   (E) stable

3. In the fifth century B.C.E, the Greek philosopher Democritus ---- that matter must be composed of tiny particles composed of a material that makes up the fundamental quality of substances in nature.

(A) speculated   (B) sanctioned
(C) resolved   (D) admonished
(E) dictated

4. The process of finding a middle ground in a controversy is difficult in the case of ---- issues on which views are ----.

(A) political . . homogenous
(B) social . . congruent
(C) contentious . . polarized
(D) ambiguous . . unwarranted
(E) controversial . . current

GO ON TO THE NEXT PAGE

5   5   5   5   5   5   5

5. Geologists believe that ice ages are caused by small changes in Earth's orbit around the Sun and in Earth's tilt on its axis which—although not of great ---- —have a considerable ---- effect.

   (A) precision . . retroactive
   (B) magnitude . . cumulative
   (C) acuity . . sharpening
   (D) balance . . retrograde
   (E) size . . correlative

6. The theory that companies in the consumer products industry practice planned ---- is a plausible idea to someone who has suffered repeated breakdowns of a recently purchased appliance.

   (A) anachronism   (B) bankruptcy
    (C) serendipity   (D) efficiency
     (E) obsolescence

7. The etymology of "OK," that ---- American expression that has been widely adopted around the world, is uncertain; however, it seems clear that unlike most other fashionable abbreviations, it was not consigned to ---- because it attained prominence in political campaigns in the early nineteenth century.

   (A) quintessentially . . oblivion
   (B) overtly . . lassitude
   (C) useful . . anachronism
   (D) essentially . . ambivalence
   (E) jingoistic . . the future

8. Gravity appears to be rather ----: Scientists who study it describe it as both elusive and as having ubiquitous effects.

   (A) sinister   (B) strong   (C) paradoxical
    (D) feckless   (E) peripheral

GO ON TO THE NEXT PAGE ⇨

5 5 5 5 5 5 5

Below are passages followed by questions on them. Questions on a pair of related passages may be about the relationship between the two passages. For each question, select the best answer based on what is stated or implied in the passage (or passages).

Questions 9–12 are based on the following passages.

Passage 1

It is interesting to contemplate an entangled bank, clothed with many plants of many kinds, with birds singing on the bushes, with various
Line insects flitting about, and with worms crawling
(5) through the damp earth, and to reflect that these elaborately constructed forms, so different from each other, and dependent on each other in so complex a manner, have all been produced by laws acting around us. These laws, taken in the
(10) largest sense, being growth with reproduction; inheritance, which is almost implied by reproduction; variability from the indirect and direct action of the external conditions of life, and from use and disuse; a ratio of increase so
(15) high as to lead to a struggle for life, and as a consequence to natural selection, entailing divergence of character and the extinction of less-improved forms. Thus, from the war of nature, from famine and death, the most exalted object
(20) which we are capable of conceiving, namely, the production of the higher animals, directly follows. There is grandeur in this view of life, with its several powers, having been originally breathed into a few forms or into one; and that,
(25) whilst this planet has gone cycling on according to the fixed law of gravity, from so simple a beginning, endless forms, most beautiful and most wonderful, have been, and are being, evolved.

Passage 2

(30)   The faster death goes, the faster evolution goes. If an aphid lays a million eggs, several might survive. Now, my right hand, in all its human cunning, could not make one aphid in a thousand years. But these aphid eggs—which run
(35) less than a dime a dozen, which run absolutely free—can make aphids as effortlessly as the sea makes waves. Wonderful things, wasted. It's a wretched system. . . . Arthur Stanley Eddington, the British physicist and astronomer who died in

(40) 1944, suggested that all of "Nature" could conceivably run on the same deranged scheme. "If indeed she has no greater aim than to provide a home for her greatest experiment, Man, it would be just like her methods to scatter a
(45) million stars whereof one might haply achieve her purpose." I doubt very much that this is the aim, but it seems clear on all fronts that this is the method.

9. What paradox does the author of Passage 1 see in the process of the production of the higher animals?

(A) That the law of gravity produced such diversity of life on Earth
(B) That war ultimately gives rise to more life than death
(C) That advanced life arose from famine and death
(D) That such varied life produced such advanced life
(E) That the struggle for life leads to natural selection

10. The primary purpose of the author of Passage 2 in saying, "Now, my right hand, in all its human cunning, could not make one aphid in a thousand years" (lines 32–34) is most likely to

(A) illustrate with an example the limited abilities of human beings
(B) show that the process of evolution takes thousands of years
(C) explain that she is not responsible for all the aphids that die because she did not create them in the first place
(D) show that only God has the ability to create complex life forms like aphids
(E) show the unique power of evolution to create complex life forms

GO ON TO THE NEXT PAGE ⟶

5   5   5   5   5   5   5

11. Which of the following statements would the author of both passages be likely to agree with?

   (A) The main reason that nature was created was to produce human beings.

   (B) Death is an unfortunate part of the evolutionary process.

   (C) The fact that nature is so profligate is deeply disturbing.

   (D) Consideration of the process of evolution primarily fills one with awe and wonder.

   (E) More evidence is needed before evolution can be accepted as scientific fact.

12. The author of Passage 1 would be most likely to respond to the observations made in Passage 2 by saying that

   (A) the author of Passage 2 is exaggerating the amount of waste created in nature

   (B) although it is true that the process of evolution relies on death, that does not mean it is "deranged," considering the fact that so much awe-inspiring life has been created by that process

   (C) the author of Passage 2 does not demonstrate a sound understanding of the process of evolution

   (D) it is irrelevant to quote the view of an astronomer in a discussion of evolution

   (E) although nature has in the past been wasteful, evolution has achieved its aim and so the wastage has ceased

Questions 13–24 are based on the following passage.

    In an exchange of views not long ago in *The New York Review of Books*, Joseph Alsop and David Joravky set forth the by now familiar
Line argument on both sides of the debate about the
(5) "ethics" of the bomb. It's not hard to guess which side each chose once you know that Alsop experienced capture by the Japanese at Hong Kong early in 1942, while Joravsky came into no deadly contact with the Japanese: a young,
(10) combat-innocent soldier, he was on his way to the Pacific when the war ended. The editors of *The New York Review of Books* gave the debate the tendentious title "Was the Hiroshima Bomb Necessary?" surely an unanswerable question
(15) (unlike "Was It Effective?") and one precisely

indicating the intellectual difficulties involved in imposing *ex post facto* a rational and even a genteel ethics on this event. In arguing the acceptability of the bomb, Alsop focuses on the
(20) power and fanaticism of War Minister Anami, who insisted that Japan fight to the bitter end, defending the main islands with the same techniques and tenacity employed at Iwo Jima and Okinawa. Alsop concludes: "Japanese
(25) surrender could never have been obtained, at any rate without the honor-satisfying bloodbath envisioned by . . . Anami, if the hideous destruction of Hiroshima and Nagasaki had not finally galvanized the peace advocates into
(30) tearing up the entire Japanese book of rules." The Japanese plan to deploy the undefeated bulk of their ground forces, over two million men, plus 10,000 kamikaze planes, plus the elderly and all the women and children with sharpened spears
(35) they could muster in a suicidal defense makes it absurd, says Alsop, to "hold the common view, by now hardly challenged by anyone, that the decision to drop the two bombs on Japan was wicked in itself, and that President Truman and
(40) all others who joined in making or who (like Robert Oppenheimer) assented to this decision shared in the wickedness." And in explanation of "the two bombs," Alsop adds: "The true, climactic, and successful effort of the Japanese
(45) peace advocates . . . did not begin in deadly earnest until *after* the second bomb had destroyed Nagasaki. The Nagasaki bomb was thus the trigger to all the developments that led to peace." At this time the army was so unready for
(50) surrender that most looked forward to the forthcoming invasion as an indispensable opportunity to show their mettle, enthusiastically agreeing with the army spokesman who reasoned early in 1945, "Since the retreat from
(55) Guadalcanal, the Army has had little opportunity to engage the enemy in land battles. But when we meet in Japan proper, our Army will demonstrate its invincible superiority." This possibility foreclosed by the Emperor's post-A-bomb

GO ON TO THE NEXT PAGE →

5   5   5   5   5   5   5

(60) surrender broadcast, the shocked, disappointed officers of one infantry battalion, anticipating a professionally impressive defense of the beaches, killed themselves in the following numbers: one major, three captains, ten first lieutenants, and *(65)* twelve second lieutenants.

David Joravsky, now a professor of history at Northwestern, argued on the other hand that those who decided to use the A-bombs on cities betray defects of "reason and self-restraint." It all *(70)* needn't have happened, he says, "if the U.S. government had been willing to take a few more days and to be a bit more thoughtful in opening up the age of nuclear warfare." I've already noted what "a few more days" would mean to the *(75)* luckless troops and sailors on the spot, and as to being thoughtful when "opening up the age of nuclear warfare," of course no one was focusing on anything as portentous as that, which reflects a historian's tidy hind-sight. The U.S. government *(80)* was engaged not in that sort of momentous thing but in ending the war conclusively, as well as irrationally Remembering Pearl Harbor with a vengeance. It didn't know then what everyone knows now about leukemia and various kinds of *(85)* carcinoma and birth defects. Truman was not being sly or coy when he insisted that the bomb was "only another weapon." History, as Eliot's "Gerontion" notes,

    . . . has many cunning passages, contrived *(90)*   corridors
    And issues, deceives with whispering ambitions,
    Guides us by vanities . . .
                            Think
    Neither fear not courage saves us.
(95)   Unnatural vices
    Are fathered by our heroism. Virtues
    Are forced upon us by our impudent crimes.

   Understanding the past requires pretending that you don't know the present. It requires *(100)* feeling its own pressure on your pulses without any *ex post facto* illumination. That's a harder thing to do than Joravsky seems to think.

13. In the opening lines of the passage ("In an exchange . . . . the war ended.") (lines 1–11), what assumption does the author appear to be making?

  (A) The reader is familiar with the military careers of Joseph Alsop and David Joravsky.
  (B) A soldier who is captured by the enemy will always feel hatred toward the enemy that will distort that person's judgment about the enemy.
  (C) A person's opinions are determined to a large extent by his or her experiences.
  (D) The views of a soldier who has not experienced combat about the enemy cannot be taken seriously.
  (E) It is not possible for anyone to reach an objective judgment about an emotional topic like the ethics of the dropping of A-bombs on Hiroshima.

14. Why does the author say that the question "Was the Hiroshima Bomb Necessary?" is unanswerable?

  (A) Necessity is not something that can be determined.
  (B) Americans are still so deeply divided about this event that no definitive answer can yet be given.
  (C) The word "necessary" in the question requires that the answer to the question be "no," because the Japanese could have been defeated without the use of the atomic bomb, albeit at the cost of great loss of life.
  (D) Ethical issues can never be conclusively decided.
  (E) Questions about the past are meaningless because the past remains the past no' matter what is decided about it in retrospect.

GO ON TO THE NEXT PAGE ⇨

5 5 5 5 5 5 5

15. What does the "Japanese book of rules" mentioned in line 30 refer to?

(A) The guidelines Japanese peace advocates had been following before the destruction of Hiroshima and Nagasaki

(B) The deeply held values governing Japanese conduct, especially in regard to national pride, individual honor, and conduct in war

(C) The plan devised at the highest levels of Japanese government to defend the homeland against invasion at all costs

(D) The code of conduct of Japanese soldiers

(E) The compromise reached between militarists and peace advocates in Japan agreeing to negotiate a peace settlement with the Americans

16. What information, if it came to light, would support Joseph Alsop's contention, cited by the author in lines 24–30, that the only way Japan could have been induced to surrender other than by the dropping of the atomic bomb would have been an "honor-satisfying bloodbath"?

(A) Documents showing that a month before the first bomb was dropped Japanese leaders had been briefed thoroughly by U.S. military officials on its destructive power

(B) Sociological studies suggesting that Japanese people place less value on honor than is generally thought

(C) Evidence that the case being made by peace advocates in Japan was being received with increasing interest by the Japanese populace

(D) Surveys of public opinion in Japan near the end of the war suggesting that the vast majority of the population would fight to the death to defend Japan

(E) Documents showing that the civilian population was poorly organized and unmotivated to fight trained Allied soldiers to defend Japan

17. Which of the following statements would the author be most likely to agree with?

(A) There is little chance that Kamikaze planes would have been used by the Japanese military against a U.S. led invasion.

(B) In considering the morality of the atom bombing of Japan, Americans tend to ignore the fact that Japanese culture places great stress on honor, even if it requires great sacrifice.

(C) There is little reason to think that Japanese civilians would defend their country as ferociously as Japanese soldiers.

(D) The ferocity of the fighting at Iwo Jima and Okinawa has been greatly exaggerated by Hollywood movies.

(E) If U.S. leaders had shown greater understanding of Japanese culture, the Japanese would have surrendered without the need for either the invasion of the home islands or the dropping of the atomic bomb.

18. What phrase best expresses what the author means by "a genteel ethics" in line 18?

(A) A flexible value system

(B) Middle class values

(C) Religious morals

(D) Generally accepted social norms

(E) The morality of polite society

19. In line 17, "*ex post facto*" most nearly means

(A) willy-nilly

(B) as a result of past events

(C) retroactively

(D) arbitrarily

(E) without considering all the facts

GO ON TO THE NEXT PAGE ⇒

5 5 5 5 5 5 5

20. What information, if discovered, would support the argument made by Joseph Alsop, cited in lines 43–48 ("The true, climactic . . . led to peace."), that the dropping of an atomic bomb on Nagasaki was morally justifiable?

(A) Evidence that a secret offer of unconditional surrender by the Japanese emperor had been received one day after the atom bomb was dropped on Hiroshima

(B) Studies by the U.S. military arguing persuasively that Japanese civilians would not make an effective fighting force

(C) Information showing that the Japanese military had nearly run out of fuel at the time the A-bomb was dropped on Nagasaki

(D) Documents showing that the Japanese leaders possessed secret information that led them to believe (incorrectly) after the atomic bomb was dropped on Hiroshima that the Americans did not possess another atomic bomb that was ready for use, and it would be several months before another one would be ready

(E) Evidence showing that the will to fight of the average Japanese soldier greatly decreased after the atomic bombing of Hiroshima

21. In line 79, "tidy" most nearly means

(A) neat
(B) clean
(C) orderly
(D) substantial
(E) satisfactory

22. The phrase "as well as irrationally Remembering Pearl Harbor with a vengeance" (lines 81–83) suggests that the author believes that

(A) in deciding to drop atomic bombs on Hiroshima and Nagasaki, officials in the U.S. government were partly motivated by a desire for revenge against the Japanese

(B) U.S. government officials were not acting at all rationally in deciding to drop atomic bombs on Japanese cities

(C) in their desire to drop atomic bombs on Japanese cities, the U.S. government was motivated entirely by the memory of the surprise Japanese attack on Pearl Harbor

(D) in using atomic bombs on Japanese cities, the U.S. government intended primarily to rally a war-weary nation

(E) the U.S. government allowed itself to be distracted from the main business of decisively and expeditiously ending the war by a desire for vengeance for Japan's surprise attack on Pearl Harbor

23. In line 101, "illumination" most nearly means

(A) clarification
(B) intellectual enlightenment
(C) pressure to condemn
(D) pretension to knowledge
(E) spiritual enlightenment

24. The lines from T.S. Eliot's poem "Gerontion" serve mainly to

(A) remind historians that to understand an event in the past they must imagine that they are ignorant of what the consequences of the event were

(B) make the point that a heroic action might result in evil, and a cowardly action might result in good

(C) provide another example of how different the view of an event is at the time of the event as opposed to long after the event

(D) encourage the reader to investigate what great poets have written about both the heroism war inspires and the horrors it entails

(E) reinforce the point that the consequences of an action (for good or ill) are not known by those who decide to take the action at the time of their decision

IN ANY REMAINING TIME YOU MAY REVIEW THE
ANSWERS YOU CHOSE IN THIS SECTION. DO NOT WORK
ON ANY OTHER SECTION OF THE TEST DURING THIS TIME.

Practice Test 1

6   6 6 6 6 6 6 6 6 6 6 6   6

SECTION **6**   Time—25 Minutes
35 Questions   Choose the best answer to each of the following questions in this section. Then blacken the appropriate space on your answer sheet.

Each sentence below may or may not employ correct or effective expression. If you think that the underlined phrasing makes the most clear and precise sentence, select choice A. If, however, you think that the underlined phrasing makes the meaning of the sentence unclear or awkward, or that it is grammatically incorrect, select another answer from choices B to E.

In choosing your answers, follow the conventions of English as it is used by educated writers. Consider sentence structure, grammar, word choice, and punctuation. Choose the answer that produces the sentence that is the most clear and effective.

Example:

In her comments after the debate the judge said that she had been impressed by the ability of both teams to exploit logical weaknesses and in citing relevant examples.

(A) in citing relevant examples
(B) in that relevant examples had been cited
(C) in the citing of relevant examples
(D) to cite relevant examples
(E) to be able to cite relevant examples

Ⓐ Ⓑ Ⓒ ● Ⓔ

1. As editor of the influential journal *Foreign Issues*, Mr. Hamilton's readers regard him as an expert in the field of international affairs.

(A) Mr. Hamilton's readers regard him as an expert in the field of international affairs
(B) Mr. Hamilton's readers regard him to be an expert in the field of international affairs
(C) Mr. Hamilton is regarded an expert in the field of international affairs
(D) his readers regard Mr. Hamilton as an expert in the field of international affairs
(E) Mr. Hamilton is regarded as an expert in the field of international affairs by his readers

2. For as many as thirty years and more Dr. Smith practiced medicine in the state of New Jersey.

(A) as many as thirty years and more
(B) thirty years, and more than that,
(C) more than thirty years
(D) as many as thirty years and over
(E) thirty years, and more,

3. Myths, often providing people with a plausible explanation for bemusing things, such as the apparent capriciousness of nature.

(A) Myths, often providing people with a plausible explanation for bemusing things,
(B) Myths, they often provide people with a plausible explanation for bemusing things,
(C) Myths often provide people with a plausible explanation for bemusing things,
(D) Often providing people with a plausible explanation for bemusing things, it is myths,
(E) It is myths providing people with a plausible explanation for bemusing things,

4. The minister of the recently established church in town, together with his wife and three young children, are taking a vacation in the south of France this year.

(A) together with his wife and three young children, are
(B) with his wife and three young children, are
(C) and his wife and three young children, are
(D) his wife and three young children, is
(E) together with his wife and three young children, is

GO ON TO THE NEXT PAGE

6 6 6 6 6 6 6 6 6 6 6 6 6 6

5. Modern societies must find a healthy balance between excessive conformity and excessive <u>individualism; the former stifles</u> individual expression, and the latter alienates people from one another, making social life difficult.

    (A) individualism; the former stifles
    (B) individualism. The former, stifling
    (C) individualism, the former stifles
    (D) individualism, the former, stifling
    (E) individualism, the former stifling

6. Iconography is a set of specified or traditional symbolic <u>forms associating with the subject or theme of a stylized work of art.</u>

    (A) forms associating with the subject or theme of a stylized work of art
    (B) forms that the subject or theme of a stylized work of art is associating with
    (C) forms; associated with the subject or theme of a stylized work of art
    (D) forms associated with the subject or theme of a stylized work of art
    (E) forms, they are associated with the subject of theme of a stylized work of art

7. Most astronomers searching for asteroids that come close to Earth work in the United <u>States; however, humanity is</u> essentially oblivious to asteroids that are visible when the United States is in daylight, or that are visible only from the Southern Hemisphere.

    (A) States; however, humanity is
    (B) States; nevertheless, humanity is
    (C) States, humanity being
    (D) States, yet humanity is
    (E) States; thus, humanity is

8. It is conceivable that Mars colonists could synthesize their electronic devices from indigenous elements, such as zinc, lead, and potassium, and some day perhaps even conduct a flourishing trade with <u>Earth, for an exchange of their plentiful minerals for the minerals that they lack.</u>

    (A) Earth, for an exchange of their plentiful minerals for the minerals they lack.
    (B) Earth, whereby making an exchange of minerals they lack for their plentiful minerals.
    (C) Earth, at the same time exchanging their plentiful minerals for those they lack.
    (D) Earth, in effecting a trade of their plentiful minerals for those they lack.
    (E) Earth, exchanging their plentiful minerals for those they lack.

9. <u>He discovered, too late, that it would have been</u> more worth his while to have worked for the mining company than for the telecommunications company.

    (A) He discovered, too late, that it would have been
    (B) He discovered, too late, that it had been
    (C) It was too late when he had discovered that it would have been
    (D) It had been too late when he discovered that it would be
    (E) It was too late that he discovered it had been

10. When the student was about to begin the mathematics exam, <u>she realized, discontented</u> that she had forgotten her calculator.

    (A) she realized, discontented
    (B) she realized discontent
    (C) she realized, discontentedly,
    (D) she, realizing discontent,
    (E) she realized, discontentedly then,

11. The framers of the U.S. Constitution were aware that the system of government that they had created was predisposed toward the formation of <u>factions, and each supporting</u> its special interest.

    (A) factions, and each supporting
    (B) factions, each supporting
    (C) factions, and each was supporting
    (D) factions, and each supported
    (E) factions where each supported

GO ON TO THE NEXT PAGE

6   6 6 6 6 6 6 6 6 6 6 6   **6**

Each of the sentences below contains either one error or no error in grammar or usage. If there is an error, it will be underlined. If the sentence contains an error, indicate this by selecting the letter for the one under-lined part that should be changed to make the sen-tence correct. Follow the requirements of standard written English in choosing answers. If the sentence is already correct, select choice E.

Example:

The number of stars <u>visible in</u> the sky on any
                          A

<u>given</u> night <u>vary</u>, mainly <u>because of</u> changes in
  B   C   D

atmospheric conditions and in the phases of the

Moon. <u>No Error</u>
          E

12. Lobby groups are groups <u>whose</u> members share
                                A
    certain goals and work <u>to bring about</u> the passage,
                              B
    modification or <u>repealing</u> of laws that <u>affect</u> these
                       C   D
    goals. <u>No Error</u>
              E

13. George Highet, <u>a junior</u> at Western States
                      A
    <u>University, he is</u> a member of the college tennis
           B
    and debating teams, and <u>writes</u> for the <u>literary</u>
                               C   D
    magazine and the college newspaper. <u>No Error</u>
                                            E

14. A problem <u>faced by</u> China in <u>its</u> economic
                 A   B
    development is the <u>rapid</u> increasing gap between
                          C
    <u>the affluent</u> and the poor. <u>No Error</u>
         D   E

15. Many years <u>after writing</u> *Brave New World*, Aldous
                   A
    Huxley <u>had written</u> *Island*, a novel in which he
              B
    <u>depicts</u> a utopian society <u>based on</u> Hindu and
       C   D
    Buddhist teachings. <u>No Error</u>
                            E

16. As he <u>frantically</u> searched the house for his
             A
    missing car keys, Raj thought it wise <u>calling</u> his
                                             B
    girlfriend for a ride to college so that he
    <u>wouldn't be</u> late for his history exam <u>in</u>
         C   D
    Livingston Hall that morning. <u>No Error</u>
                                      E

17. These techniques help the authors <u>give us</u> the
                                         A
    information we need clearly and concisely and
    <u>allows</u> them to comment <u>succinctly on</u> the points
       B   C
    <u>put forward</u> by John Anthony. <u>No Error</u>
       D   E

18. After <u>passing through</u> immigration, visitors can
             A
    collect <u>his or her</u> luggage from the belts <u>located</u> in
               B   C
    the <u>airport's</u> baggage collection area. <u>No Error</u>
           D   E

19. Even though the new resident of the seaside villa
    was <u>totally</u> aware <u>to be watched</u> by the villagers
           A   B
    <u>as he walked</u> along the beach, he ignored their
       C
    curious stares and gave his full attention <u>to</u> the
                                                  D
    fleet of fishing boats out near the horizon.
    <u>No Error</u>
       E

GO ON TO THE NEXT PAGE →

6   6 6 6 6 6 6 6 6 6 6 6   6

20. The article <u>claims that</u> during the 1960s the music
           A
of The Rolling Stones and The Beatles was more
<u>widely heard</u> around the world and <u>more popular</u>
   B   C
with rock 'n' roll fans <u>than The Beach Boys</u>.
                              D
<u>No Error</u>
   E

21. <u>Culinary</u> herbs can be divided into three <u>groups:</u>
   A   B
those whose foliage <u>furnish</u> the flavor, those whose
               C
seeds are used, and <u>those few</u> whose roots are
                     D
prepared. <u>No Error</u>
       E

22. <u>In order for</u> the public to believe that cigarette
   A
smoking causes lung cancer <u>they</u> must be
                       B
convinced by epidemiological studies <u>that smoking</u>
                             C
is the decisive causative factor
<u>in the development of</u> lung cancer. <u>No Error</u>
      D   E

23. <u>Because</u> his parents <u>usually</u> leave very early for
   A   B
work each day, Mark <u>was served</u> breakfast by
                C
<u>one of</u> his brothers or his sister on weekday
   D
mornings. <u>No Error</u>
       E

24. A "poverty trap" is a situation <u>in which</u> one is
                         A
unable to escape poverty because one is
<u>dependent on</u> state benefits, <u>which</u> are reduced by
   B   C
the same amount <u>as</u> any extra income gained.
              D
<u>No Error</u>
   E

25. Some psychologists believe <u>that</u> the spectacular
                      A
economic success of countries such as Singapore
and Japan is <u>at least partially</u> attributable <u>with</u> the
            B   C
willingness of <u>their</u> citizens to work hard.
            D
<u>No Error</u>
   E

26. Mr. Green's <u>wide</u> teaching experience enables him
           A
to effectively teach <u>a range of</u> age and ability
                B
levels <u>and a variety of</u> subjects in <u>the humanities</u>
          C   D
and social sciences. <u>No Error</u>
             E

27. A famous American writer who reads what he
<u>has written</u> to his wife every evening <u>says</u> that
   A   B
without his wife's criticism his writing <u>wouldn't be</u>
                              C
nearly <u>as good</u>. <u>No Error</u>
      D   E

28. Scientists may be able to gain an understanding of
the <u>implications</u> of the greenhouse effect <u>for</u>
      A   B
Earth's climate by studying <u>the global warming</u>
                          C
that Mars <u>underwent</u> millions of years ago. <u>No Error</u>
        D   E

29. Their <u>leisurely</u> camping trip around Australia <u>had</u>
      A   B
two purposes: a much needed period of relaxation
after a hectic year of teaching and lecturing <u>with</u>
                              C
the opportunity <u>to collect</u> important information
               D
for their upcoming travel book. <u>No Error</u>
                    E

GO ON TO THE NEXT PAGE ⇨

6　　6　6　6　6　6　6　6　6　6　6　　6

The following early draft of an essay needs to be rewritten to improve sentence structure, choice of words, clarity of expression, organization, and development. After reading the draft, answer each question below it, choosing the answer that best conforms to the requirements of standard written English.

(1) According to sociologists, every modern industrial society has some form of social stratification. (2) Sociologists disagree on exactly how these factors should be defined and how they relate to each other, but all agree that they are the decisive determinants in deciding where a person ranks in the social hierarchy.
(3) Class can be defined as a person's economic position in society. (4) A well-known and commonly used classification is lower class, middle class, and upper class. (5) One sociologist says that 53% of Americans belong to the lower class, 46% belong to the middle class, and 1% belong to the upper class. (6) Interestingly, according to sociologists, 45% of Americans identify themselves as belonging to the middle class. (7) A surgeon earning $500,000 a year and a bus driver earning $50,000 a year both identify themselves as middle class!
(8) Power refers to the amount of power a person has over other people. (9) Obviously, people in positions of great power, such as governors and senators, they are people who exercise considerable power, whereas people who take orders from others (in a company, for example), have less power. (10) Power and class do not always coincide, however. (11) For example, the governor of a state has great power, but he or she may not belong to a corresponding economic class. (12) Generally, however, there is a correlation between power and class. (13) There aren't too many people who aren't millionaires in the U.S. Senate, for example!
(14) Status refers to the honor or prestige attached to a person's position in society. (15) Like power and class, status can be affected by other determinants. (16) For example, a university professor may have a high status but not belong to a high social class or wield a lot of power over others.

30. Which of the following would most improve the first paragraph (sentences 1 and 2)?

(A) Insert a sentence after sentence 2 giving examples of famous sociologists.

(B) Insert a sentence between sentence 1 and sentence 2 defining what is meant by "modern industrial society."

(C) Insert a sentence between sentence 1 and sentence 2 giving a fuller explanation of "social stratification."

(D) Insert a sentence after sentence 2 describing one major disagreement among sociologists about social stratification.

(E) Insert a sentence before sentence 1 explaining what sociology is.

31. Which of the following sentences, if inserted immediately after sentence 4, would most effectively link sentences 4 and 5?

(A) Interestingly, people in both the high class and the lower class tend to see themselves as middle class.

(B) Such classifications are regarded as almost meaningless by some sociologists.

(C) Again, there is disagreement about how these terms should be defined, but they do describe societies like the United States quite well.

(D) According to sociologists, people in the lower class tend to exaggerate their chances of becoming middle class.

(E) As is generally known, there are many more people in the lower class than in the middle class

GO ON TO THE NEXT PAGE

6   6 6 6 6 6 6 6 6 6 6   6

32. Which of the following is the best version of the underlined portion of sentence 9 (reproduced below)?

Obviously, people in positions of great power, such as governors and senators, they are people who exercise considerable power, whereas people who take orders from others (in a company, for example), have less power.

(A) (As it is now)
(B) senators, exercise
(C) senators who are people exercising
(D) senators are people who exercise
(E) senators; these are people who exercise

33. Which of the following should be done with sentence 13 (reproduced below)?

There aren't too many people who aren't millionaires in the U.S. Senate, for example!

(A) Delete the sentence.
(B) Change it to "There are many people who aren't millionaires in the U.S. Senate, for example!"
(C) Add "However," at the beginning of the sentence and delete "for example" at the end of the sentence.
(D) Change the sentence to "There are too many people who are millionaires in the U.S. Senate, for example!"
(E) Leave it as it is.

34. All of the following strategies are used by the writer of the passage EXCEPT

(A) exaggeration for effect
(B) citing the findings of an authority
(C) providing examples of general assertions
(D) assertion of fact
(E) providing definitions of key terms

35. In context, what is the best way to revise sentence 15 (reproduced below)?

Like power and class, status can be affected by other determinants.

(A) Add "but not necessarily so." to the end.
(B) Add "a number of" after "by."
(C) Delete "Like" and replace it with "Likewise."
(D) Change the sentence to "Status, like power and class, can be affected by other determinants."
(E) Change "affected" to "effected."

STOP

IN ANY REMAINING TIME YOU MAY REVIEW THE
ANSWERS YOU CHOSE IN THIS SECTION. DO NOT WORK
ON ANY OTHER SECTION OF THE TEST DURING THIS TIME.

7

SECTION 7

Time—25 Minutes
18 Questions

You have 25 minutes to answer the 8 multiple-choice questions and 10 student-produced response questions in this section. For each multiple-choice question, determine which of the five choices is correct and blacken the corresponding choice on your answer sheet. You may use any blank space on the page for your work.

Notes:
- You may use a calculator whenever you think it will be helpful.
- Only real numbers are used. No question or answer on this test involves a complex or imaginary number.
- Use the diagrams provided to help you solve the problems. Unless you see the words "Note: Figure not drawn to scale" under a diagram, it has been drawn as accurately as possible. Unless it is stated that a figure is three-dimensional, you may assume it lies in a plane.
- For any function, *f*, the domain, unless specifically restricted, is the set of all real numbers for which $f(x)$ is also a real number.

Reference Information

Area Facts

$A = \ell w$

$A = \frac{1}{2} bh$

$A = \pi r^2$

$C = 2\pi r$

Volume Facts

$V = \ell w h$

$V = \pi r^2 h$

Triangle Facts

$a^2 + b^2 = c^2$

Angle Facts

$x + y + z = 180$

---

1. If Roseanne can address 40 packages per hour, how many minutes will it take her to address 150 packages?

   (A) 3.75
   (B) 75
   (C) 100
   (D) 225
   (E) 6,000

2. What number is halfway between $-\frac{3}{4}$ and $\frac{7}{8}$?

   (A) $-\frac{1}{16}$

   (B) $\frac{1}{16}$

   (C) $\frac{1}{8}$

   (D) $\frac{3}{8}$

   (E) $\frac{13}{16}$

GO ON TO THE NEXT PAGE

3. If the average (arithmetic mean) of c and d is A, which of the following is the value of d in terms of c and A?

(A) $2A - c$
(B) $2(A - c)$
(C) $A - c$
(D) $A - 2c$
(E) $A + c$

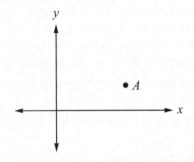

4. In the figure above, for how many points in Quadrant II is the distance from the point to the origin the same as the distance from point A to the origin?

(A) 0
(B) 1
(C) 2
(D) 4
(E) More than 4

5. If $f(x) = 3x + 2$, for what value of c is $f(2c) = 4c$?

(A) -2
(B) -1
(C) 0
(D) 1
(E) 2

6. Line ℓ passes through points $(-4, 1)$, $(4, 3)$, and (a, b). If $a = 5$, what is the value of b?

(A) 3.2
(B) 3.25
(C) 3.5
(D) 3.75
(E) 3.8

7. Dan and Laurel each drew a triangle. Both triangles have two sides whose lengths are 10, and the length of the third side of each triangle is an integer. What is the greatest possible difference between the perimeters of the two triangles?

(A) 18
(B) 19
(C) 20
(D) 38
(E) 50

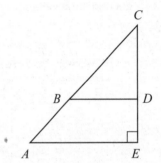

8. In the figure above, $\overline{BD} \parallel \overline{AE}$ and $\triangle ACE$ is isosceles. If the ratio of BD to AC is 1 to 2, what is the ratio of the area of $\triangle BCD$ to the area of trapezoid $ABDE$?

(A) $\dfrac{1}{2}$

(B) $\dfrac{1}{\sqrt{2}}$

(C) $\dfrac{1}{1}$

(D) $\dfrac{\sqrt{2}}{1}$

(E) $\dfrac{2}{1}$

GO ON TO THE NEXT PAGE

7

Directions for Student-Produced Response Questions (Grid-ins)

In questions 9–18, first solve the problem, and then enter your answer on the grid provided on the answer sheet. The instructions for entering your answers are as follows:

- First, write your answer in the boxes at the top of the grid.
- Second, grid your answer in the columns below the boxes.
- Use the fraction bar in the first row or the decimal point in the second row to enter fractions and decimal answers.

- Grid only one space in each column.
- Entering the answer in the boxes is recommended as an aid in gridding, but is not required.
- The machine scoring your exam can read only what you grid, so you **must grid in your answers correctly to get credit.**
- If a question has more than one correct answer, grid in only one of these answers.
- The grid does not have a minus sign, so no answer can be negative.
- A mixed number *must* be converted to an improper fraction or a decimal before it is gridded. Enter $1\frac{1}{4}$ as 5/4 or 1.25; the machine will interpret 1 1/4 as $\frac{11}{4}$ and mark it wrong.
- **All decimals must be entered as accurately as possible.** Here are the three acceptable ways of gridding

$$\frac{3}{11} = 0.272727\ldots$$

Answer: $\frac{8}{15}$ Answer: 1.75

Write your → answer in the boxes.

Grid in → your answer.

Answer: 100

Either position is acceptable

3/11   .272   .273

- Note that rounding to .273 is acceptable, because you are using the full grid, but you would receive **no credit** for .3 or .27, because these answers are less accurate.

7

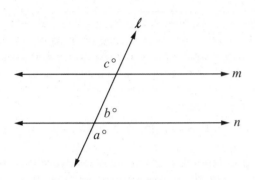

Note: Figure not drawn to scale.

9. In the figure above, lines m and n are parallel. If $c = b$, what is the value of a?

10. If Kathy's salary is 50 percent greater than Leah's salary and 40 percent less than Bruce's salary, then Leah's salary is what percent of Bruce's salary?

11. Let A be the set of all numbers of the form $\dfrac{n}{n+2}$, where n is a positive odd integer less than 50. What is the product of all the numbers in A?

12. If $\dfrac{4}{5}$ the perimeter of a square is 11.2, what is $\dfrac{4}{5}$ the area of that square?

13. If $y = f(x)$ is the equation of a straight line, and if $f(1) = 5$ and $f(2) = 13$, what is $f(4)$?

14. From a group of 3 boys and 3 girls, three children are chosen at random. What is the probability that all three children are of the same gender?

15. For any real number, $a \neq 0$, the equation $|5 - 2x| = a$ has two solutions. What is their sum?

16. If O represents the number of integers between 10,000 and 100,000 all of whose digits are odd, and E represents the number of integers between 10,000 and 100,000 all of whose digits are even, what is the value of $O - E$?

17. If the graph of $y = |-5x - 3|$ intersects the x-axis at $(a, 0)$ and intersects the y-axis at $(0, b)$, what is the value of $a + b$?

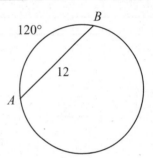

Note: Figure not drawn to scale.

18. In the circle above, the measure of arc AB is 120° and the length of chord $\overline{AB}$ is 12. If the area of the circle is $k\pi$, what is the value of k?

IN ANY REMAINING TIME YOU MAY REVIEW THE ANSWERS YOU CHOSE IN THIS SECTION. DO NOT WORK ON ANY OTHER SECTION OF THE TEST DURING THIS TIME.

8 8 8 8 8 8 8 8 8 8 8

SECTION 8

Time—20 Minutes
16 Questions

For each problem in this section determine which of the five choices is correct and blacken the corresponding choice on your answer sheet. You may use any blank space on the page for your work.

Notes:

- You may use a calculator whenever you think it will be helpful.

- Only real numbers are used. No question or answer on this test involves a complex or imaginary number.

- Use the diagrams provided to help you solve the problems. Unless you see the words "Note: Figure not drawn to scale" under a diagram, it has been drawn as accurately as possible. Unless it is stated that a figure is three-dimensional, you may assume it lies in a plane.

- For any function, f, the domain, unless specifically restricted, is the set of all real numbers for which $f(x)$ is also a real number.

Reference Information

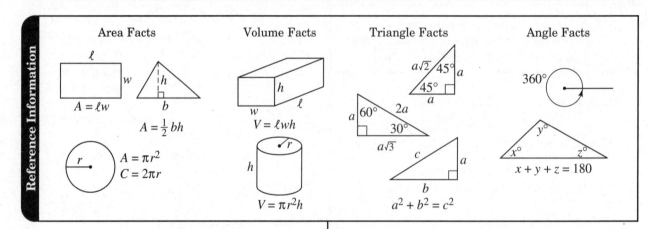

1. In the figure above, what is the value of a?

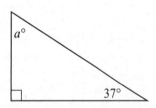

(A)   37
(B)   53
(C)   63
(D)   127
(E)   143

2. At Sam's Superette, boxes of corn flakes that normally sell for $2.75 each are on sale at 30% off. If a customer buys 6 boxes of those corn flakes at the sale price, how much money will she save?

(A) $ 0.83
(B) $ 1.80
(C) $ 4.95
(D) $ 5.50
(E) $11.55

List I: 50, 48, 72, 50, 86, 90
List II: 72, 48, 72, 80, 28, 91, 78

3. The median of the numbers in List II, above, is how much greater than the median of the numbers in List I, above?

   (A) 0
   (B) 1
   (C) 11
   (D) 14
   (E) 22

4. The sum of the positive even integers less than or equal to 50 is how much greater than the sum of the positive odd integers less than 50?

   (F)   1
   (G)   5
   (H)   25
   (I)   50
   (J)   100

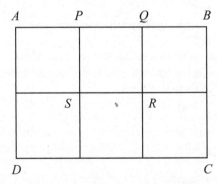

5. Rectangle *ABCD*, above, is divided into six congruent squares. If the perimeter of rectangle *ABCD* is 1, what is the perimeter of square *PQRS*?

   (A) $\dfrac{1}{100}$

   (B) $\dfrac{1}{36}$

   (C) $\dfrac{1}{10}$

   (D) $\dfrac{1}{6}$

   (E) $\dfrac{2}{5}$

6. There are more than twice as many girls as boys in Central High School's chorus. The average (arithmetic mean) GPA is 3.5 for the girls in the chorus and 3.0 for the boys in the chorus. Which of the following could be the GPA of all the students in the chorus?

   I.   3.25
   II. 3.35
   III. 3.45

   (A) I only
   (B) II only
   (C) I and II only
   (D) II and III only
   (E) I, II, and III

7. The lengths of the sides of $\triangle ABC$ are 5, 5, and 6, and the lengths of the sides of $\triangle PQR$ are 3, 4, and 5. What is the ratio of the area of $\triangle ABC$ to the area of $\triangle PQR$?

   (A) 2:1
   (B) 4:3
   (C) 1:1
   (D) 5:2
   (E) 3:1

8. The remainder when the positive integer n is divided by 17 is 10. What is the remainder when $n + 10$ is divided by 17?

   (A)   3
   (B)   7
   (C)   10
   (D)   17
   (E)   20

GO ON TO THE NEXT PAGE

8   **8**   **8** **8** **8** **8** **8** **8** **8** **8**   **8**

Questions 9 and 10 refer to the following definition.

For any numbers x and y, let $x \odot y$ be defined as
$$xy - (x + y).$$

9. For what value of x does $5 \odot x = 10 \odot x$?

(A) −5
(B) −1
(C) 0
(D) 1
(E) 5

10. How many positive numbers are solutions of the equation $y \odot y = y$?

(A) None
(B) 1
(C) 2
(D) 3
(E) More than 3

11. If, for all numbers x, $f(x) = x^2 + 1$, then which of the following is equivalent to $f(x^2 + 1)$?

(A) $x^2 + 2$
(B) $x^4 + 1$
(C) $x^4 + 2$
(D) $x^4 + 2x^2 + 1$
(E) $x^4 + 2x^2 + 2$

12. A group of students met in the lobby of their school. First, $\frac{1}{3}$ of the students were sent to the gym. Then $\frac{1}{3}$ of the remaining students were sent to the cafeteria. Finally, $\frac{1}{3}$ of the students still in the lobby were sent to the auditorium, and all the remaining students were sent home. Which of the following could NOT have been the number of students who originally met in the school lobby?

(A) 81
(B) 135
(C) 162
(D) 207
(E) 243

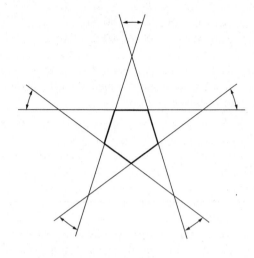

13. In the figure above, five lines intersect as shown, forming a regular pentagon and five triangles. What is the sum of the measures of the five marked angles?

(A) 90°
(B) 180°
(C) 270°
(D) 360°
(E) 540°

14. What is the greatest number in a set of 10 consecutive odd integers, if the sum of the first five of them is S?

(A) $\dfrac{S - 20}{5}$

(B) $\dfrac{S + 5}{5}$

(C) $\dfrac{S + 30}{5}$

(D) $\dfrac{S + 50}{5}$

(E) $\dfrac{S + 70}{5}$

GO ON TO THE NEXT PAGE

8   8   8   8   8   8   8   8   8   8   8

15. If p and q are prime numbers, which of the following could be the value of $p - q$?

   I. 5
  II. 6
 III. 7

(A) I only
(B) II only
(C) I and II only
(D) II and III only
(E) I, II, and III

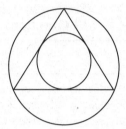

16. In the figure above, the two circles are concentric; the smaller one is inscribed in an equilateral triangle, which is inscribed in the larger circle. What is the ratio of the area of the large circle to the area of the small circle?

(A) $\sqrt{2}$:1
(B) $\sqrt{3}$:1
(C) 2:1
(D) 4:1
(E) It cannot be determined from the information given.

STOP

IN ANY REMAINING TIME YOU MAY REVIEW THE
ANSWERS YOU CHOSE IN THIS SECTION. DO NOT WORK
ON ANY OTHER SECTION OF THE TEST DURING THIS TIME.

Practice Test 1

9   9   9   9   9   9   9

| SECTION 9 | Time—20 Minutes 19 Questions | Choose the best answer to each of the following questions in this section. Then blacken the appropriate space on your answer sheet. |

Each of the following sentences contains one or two blanks, indicating that a word or set of words has been omitted. Beneath each sentence there are five answer choices labeled A to E from which you must select the word or set of words that best fits the meaning of the sentence as a whole.

Example:

Records of colonization can be found as far back as the Phoenicians, but colonization became a major force in world history only when European countries began, in the fifteenth century, to make ---- Asia, the Americas, and Africa.

(A) queries about   (B) incursions into
    (C) tirades against   (D) enemies in
      (E) amends for

1. Five of the Supreme Court justices ---- their colleague's opinion, while three dissented.

(A) objected to   (B) disagreed with
    (C) concurred with   (D) questioned
      (E) protested against

2. The American businessman prides himself on being ----; he feels as comfortable in Tokyo, Paris, Singapore, and Rio de Janeiro as he does in Atlanta.

(A) cosmopolitan   (B) efficient
    (C) urbane   (D) solvent
      (E) diligent

3. Noticing a lack of ---- in his students' writing, the English teacher ---- the traditional approach that he had been using in his teaching and adopted one that encouraged creativity.

(A) discipline . . disagreed with
(B) originality . . continued with
(C) irony . . criticized
(D) spontaneity . . abandoned
(E) clarity . . changed from

4. In the vast majority of cases, a competent doctor can accurately ---- the future course of a person's illness because his or her predecessors have built up, through ---- observation, a record of the course of similar illnesses in the past.

(A) foretell . . prescient
(B) preempt . . meticulous
(C) diagnose . . personal
(D) prognosticate . . methodical
(E) reiterate . . careful

5. For some people language has ---- interest; different language systems, their history and relationships, are considered worth investigating in themselves.

(A) a pragmatic   (B) an anachronistic
    (C) an intrinsic   (D) a theological
      (E) a utilitarian

6. The South African ---- of apartheid* assigned to the African ethnic groups approximately fourteen percent of the country's land; in this assigned area ("homelands"), Africans possessed specified rights, but in the rest of the country their rights were severely ----.

(A) policy . . circumscribed
(B) legacy . . emboldened
(C) etymology . . censured
(D) scourge . . castigated
(E) dirge . . disenfranchised

---

*Apartheid was officially sanctioned racial discrimination formerly practiced in South Africa.

GO ON TO THE NEXT PAGE →

9　　　9　　　9　　　9　　　9　　　9　　　9

Below are passages followed by questions on them. Questions on a pair of related passages may be about the relationship between the two passages. For each question, select the best answer based on what is stated or implied in the passage (or passages).

Questions 7–19 are based on the following passage.

As colleges and universities increasingly make the education, publication, sustenance, and honoring of American poets their business,
Line writing program professionals have assumed a
(5) number of nonpoetic responsibilities. It has become part of their business to attract students and sponsor an ever-growing body of work produced by graduates and colleagues. Such practical concerns have led professionals to
(10) tolerate aesthetic trends designed not so much to make poetry better as to make it easier to produce and publish.

Most obvious is the "prosification" of poetry—the publication of flat, pedestrian prose
(15) with the assurance, explicit or implied, that it is the real thing. The notion that lineation is a magic wand that can turn prose into poetry has been uncritically accepted by too many literary editors. So many poets publish lineated prose today that it
(20) would be unfair to single out one or two. In "On the Prosing of Poetry," an installment of the Boston Comment published on Web del Sol, poet and columnist Joan Houlihan makes a similar argument, providing poems by writers such as
(25) Donald Hall, John Balaban, John Brehm, and Robert Creeley as examples. She writes, "We have reached the point [where] we are being asked to believe that a text bloc, chopped randomly into flat, declarative lines, is a poem."
(30) If the profusion of prose made to look like poetry is disconcerting, it is equally annoying when similar fare is dished up under the faddish moniker "prose poem," a form in which text is set like prose in ragged or justified type, line
(35) breaks thereby losing significance. The "poem" part of the equation promises greater density and compression than we normally expect from prose, achieved through poetic devices such as rhythm, imagery, metaphor, simile, and figures of speech.
(40) William Blake and Christopher Smart wrote prose poems long before the term was invented. Poe and Baudelaire more consciously a century later. In our own time Russell Edson has written

brilliantly in this genre, producing a body of
(45) original work that can hold its own with the best poetry of our time.

The current popularity of the genre is attested to by Peter Johnson, editor of *The Best of the Prose Poem: An International Journal*. "I have
(50) read so many prose poems," he complains, "that I feel as if a large gray eraser is squatting in the hollow of my head. I am not even sure what my criteria are, anymore." At least one prestigious graduate writing program understands the genre
(55) well enough to offer students an entire course in "The Prose Poem."

The jury is still out on definitions. Some critics deny that the term has any meaning at all. Others concede that the term is muddied, since it
(60) is difficult to define the genre without opening the door to the heightened prose of many a novelist and short story writer. Still, the term leads us to expect a combination of and tension between prose and poetic elements.
(65) Unfortunately, these expectations aren't always met.

Examples abound. Here are two excerpts from "Doubt," by Fanny Howe, which appeared in *The Best American Poetry: 2001*, edited by David
(70) Lehman and Robert Hass, both long associated with writing programs:

Virginia Woolf committed suicide in 1941 when the German bombing campaign against England was at its peak and when she was reading Freud
(75) whom she had staved off until then.

Edith Stein, recently and controversially beatified by the Pope, who had successfully worked to transform an existential vocabulary into a theological one, was taken to Auschwitz in August 1942.

GO ON TO THE NEXT PAGE

9   9   9   9   9   9   9

(80) These excerpts from what appears to be a paracritical* essay on Virginia Woolf and other writers (the author is a writing professor at the University of California, San Diego) are part of a "prose poem" that goes on for four pages. Howe (85) offers interesting insights in a style appropriate for a scholarly or critical journal. But it's hard to find any definition from Aristotle to the present that would admit such writing as poetry, certainly not under the term free verse or open form; for it (90) has been the concern of responsible poets in those movements to find non-traditional, personalized strategies for making poetry musical. "Poetry atrophies, when it gets too far from music," Ezra Pound observes in his *ABC of* (95) *Reading*. Howe's piece lacks the rhythmical, metaphorical texture needed to fulfill the poetry part of the prose-poem equation. In her author's note, Howe explains that she "can no longer make distinctions" between poetry and prose. It is (100) unfortunate that the editors of an anthology entitled *The Best American Poetry* are equally unable to make a distinction that readers who buy a book with that title have a right to expect.

Even more unfortunate (for what it implies (105) about the future of poetry) is *The Spoon River Poetry Review*'s award of its $1,000 Editors' Prize for 2002 to "Departing Iceland" by Suzette Bishop. Written by a creative writing instructor at Texas A&M University, it's a "prose poem"— (110) chock-full of technical data-sheet jargon like the following:

The EC2001 Panther is a fiber optic system that transmits information over SONET (Synchronous Optical NETwork), video, voice, (115) and low speed data. . . .

For instance with Intelligent Vehicle Highway Systems (IVHS), if an accident or blockage occurs, remote detectors activate video cameras and relay live video feeds of the (120) occurrence back to the maintenance position. . . .

The ever-increasing prosification of poetry assures prospective students that they needn't employ meter or rhyme or cadence or figurative (125) language, or any of the devices, for that matter, in a standard poet's dictionary; that the drabbest encyclopedia prose, even technical jargon, can be hailed as "poetry" of the highest order. It's the profession's way of redefining the art downward (130) to accommodate its talent pool.

7. The phrase "aesthetic trends" in line 10 most nearly means
   (A) movements in the arts designed to challenge conventional notions of artistic beauty
   (B) literary theories about what makes one text "better" than another
   (C) fashions in what is regarded as worthwhile in the arts and literature
   (D) changes in people's attitudes to poetry away from regarding it as separate from economic reality to regarding it as a commodity like anything else
   (E) the increasing tendency of poetry to be like prose

8. In line 14, "pedestrian" most nearly means
   (A) pedantic
   (B) undistinguished
   (C) prose-like
   (D) popular
   (E) static

Paracritical refers to literary criticism that itself aspires to be literature.

GO ON TO THE NEXT PAGE →

9 9 9 9 9 9 9

9. Based on what he says in the first paragraph of the passage, the author would probably agree that

(A) quite a few people involved in teaching the writing of poetry at American colleges and universities care more about making their programs popular than encouraging the writing and publication of good poetry

(B) most of the people involved in teaching the writing of poetry in American colleges and universities care more about maintaining a high standard of poetry than they do about encouraging the production of poetry, regardless of its quality

(C) many of those who teach the writing of poetry in American colleges and universities do so because they are unable to write good poetry themselves

(D) most teachers of the writing of poetry in American colleges and universities are, as a rule, unable to distinguish good poetry from bad poetry

(E) writing programs in American universities have become almost wholly concerned with attracting students in order to counteract declining enrollments

10. The "real thing" in line 16 refers to

(A) traditional "great" poets
(B) prose poems
(C) good prose
(D) poetry
(E) original writing of any type

11. It is most likely that the author used the phrase "dished up" rather than the word "published" in line 32 in order to

(A) subtly suggest a relationship between the consumption of food and the reading of prose poetry

(B) suggest that prose poetry is, in many ways, like fast food

(C) colorfully emphasize his dislike for currently fashionable prose poetry

(D) create the impression in the reader's mind that he is not above using colloquial language

(E) demonstrate that he is capable of poetic expression as well as critical analysis

12. In line 36, "equation" most nearly means

(A) the combination of poetic elements with elements from prose to create prose poetry

(B) the use of poetic devices in prose to create poetic prose

(C) tacit agreement on the part of poets to use poetic devices responsibly when producing prose poetry

(D) the poetic elements in prose poetry that can be quantified

(E) the widespread but incorrect belief that the production of good poetry (of any sort) is, like everything, governed by precise, definable laws

13. According to the author, William Blake and Christopher Smart

(A) were not aware that some of their work was prose

(B) worked primarily in the genre of prose poetry

(C) did not consciously set out to write work that would later come to be called prose poetry

(D) were largely responsible for the creation of the literary genre now known as prose poetry

(E) came to regret writing poetry that spurred the creation of the genre now known as prose poetry

14. The author's tone in lines 53–56 ("At least one . . . 'The Prose Poem.' ") is most accurately described as

(A) hopeful
(B) sarcastic
(C) self-deprecating
(D) ambivalent
(E) hopeful

GO ON TO THE NEXT PAGE

9   9   9   9   9   9   9

15. In line 57, "The jury is still out" most nearly means

   (A) the board of leading poets and literary scholars convened to decide what prose poetry is has not yet come to a decision

   (B) a legal case prohibiting the publication of prose poetry is still pending

   (C) poets and scholars have not yet reached a consensus (on the definition of the term "prose poem")

   (D) the term "prose poem" will never be satisfactorily defined

   (E) poets are still working to write prose poems that succeed as poems

16. The phrase "heightened prose" in line 61 refers to

   (A) poetic prose

   (B) the prose of poets

   (C) pretentious writing

   (D) spiritually elevating writing

   (E) profoundly meaningful prose

17. Which of the following statements would the author of this passage be likely to agree with?

   (A) Prose poetry never succeeds as poetry.

   (B) Writing free verse frees a poet from having to follow the conventions of poetry as a genre.

   (C) Any distinction between poetic prose and prose poetry is meaningless.

   (D) To be considered poetry a piece of writing must make significant use of rhythm and metaphor.

   (E) Deciding what constitutes good poetry is a subjective matter.

18. The author includes the two excerpts from "Doubt" (lines 72–82) primarily to

   (A) provide examples to support his contention that many prose poems being written do not successfully combine prose elements and poetic elements

   (B) show that editors of poetry anthologies who are associated with college writing programs are able to identify poetry of a high order

   (C) provide support for the view that prose poetry is a legitimate genre

   (D) demonstrate that prose poems can make effective use of traditional poetic devices

   (E) show that prose poems are uniquely suited for literary criticism because they combine the analytic precision of prose with the intuitive insight of poetry

19. In line 131, "redefining the art downward" most nearly means

   (A) defining true poetry by reference to the most talented poets writing at a particular time

   (B) lowering the minimum academic credentials required for a person to have his or her poetry accepted by a reputable poetry magazine

   (C) "rebranding" poetry to make it more appealing to a mass market

   (D) describing the process of writing poetry in vague terms so that prospective students in poetry-writing classes are not discouraged from applying for such classes

   (E) changing the definition of poetry so that writing it requires less talent and effort

STOP

IN ANY REMAINING TIME YOU MAY REVIEW THE ANSWERS YOU CHOSE IN THIS SECTION. DO NOT WORK ON ANY OTHER SECTION OF THE TEST DURING THIS TIME.

10   10   10   10   10   10   10

SECTION 10   Time—10 Minutes
14 Questions

Choose the best answer to each of the following questions in this section. Then blacken the appropriate space on your answer sheet.

Each sentence below may or may not employ correct or effective expression. If you think that the underlined phrasing makes the most clear and precise sentence, select choice A. If, however, you think that the underlined phrasing makes the meaning of the sentence unclear or awkward, or that it is grammatically incorrect, select another answer from choices B to E.

In choosing your answers, follow the conventions of English as it is used by educated writers. Consider sentence structure, grammar, word choice, and punctuation. Choose the answer that produces the sentence that is the most clear and effective.

Example:

In her comments after the debate the judge said that she had been impressed by the ability of both teams to exploit logical weaknesses and in citing relevant examples.

(A) in citing relevant examples
(B) in that relevant examples had been cited
(C) in the citing of relevant examples
(D) to cite relevant examples
(E) to be able to cite relevant examples

1. Each of these vocabulary books are excellent, but students should also look up words they do not know in a dictionary when they are reading.

(A) are excellent, but
(B) is excellent, but
(C) is excellent, except
(D) are excellent, although
(E) are excellent, and

2. With modern transportation, no matter the state you live in you can enjoy fresh produce such as pineapples from Hawaii and avocados from Mexico all year round.

(A) transportation, no matter the state you live in you can
(B) transportation it doesn't matter which state you live in you can
(C) transportation you can live in any state but
(D) transportation, no matter what state you live in you can
(E) transportation, no matter which is the state you live in you can

3. Although Bob has long expressed a great interest in Chinese culture, he rarely watches Chinese films and had never enrolled in a Chinese language class.

(A) he rarely watches Chinese films and had never enrolled
(B) it is rare for him to watch Chinese films and never to enroll
(C) it is rare that he watches Chinese films or never enrolls
(D) he will rarely watch Chinese films and had never enrolled
(E) he rarely watches Chinese films and has never enrolled

4. As he lectured his students on the oeuvre of the German composer Ludwig van Beethoven, the music instructor felt it important stressing that most critics regard Beethoven's works as the culmination of the classical period in music and the beginning of the romantic period.

(A) it important stressing
(B) that it was important stressing
(C) the importance of stressing
(D) it important to stress
(E) the importance to stress

GO ON TO THE NEXT PAGE

10   10   10   10   10   10   10

5. Regarded as one of the greatest players in tennis history, John McEnroe combined subtlety and <u>power more effectively than the play of perhaps</u> any other player in tennis history.

   (A) power more effectively than the play of perhaps

   (B) power more effective than the play of perhaps

   (C) power more effectively than was the play, perhaps, of

   (D) power more effectively, perhaps, than

   (E) power, and more effective than perhaps

6. One of the most demanding pursuits in the world, world class tournament chess <u>has even more demands, more preparation and mental stamina than fields such as</u> organic chemistry.

   (A) has even more demands, more preparation, and mental stamina than fields such as

   (B) has even more demands, more preparation and mental stamina than do fields such as

   (C) is even more demanding, requiring more preparation and mental stamina, than fields such as

   (D) is even more demanding, and has more preparation and mental stamina than does

   (E) has even more demands, and more preparation and mental stamina than fields such as

7. Although Thomas Hardy is better known for his novels, such as *The Mayor of Casterbridge* and *Tess of the D'Urbervilles*, <u>both of which they were making</u> into feature films, many critics consider his poetry to be his greatest achievement.

   (A) both of which they were making

   (B) which both having been made

   (C) these both have been made

   (D) both of which have been made

   (E) and both of these made

8. The noted author described writing as a process of making thousands of small <u>decisions and you hope</u> more of them are correct than incorrect.

   (A) decisions and you hope

   (B) decisions, and you hope

   (C) decisions and hoping that

   (D) decisions in hoping that

   (E) decisions where you hope that

9. Two of the greatest chess players of all time, Anatoly Karpov and Gary Kasparov, tended to play very different styles of <u>chess; Kasparov preferring a sharp, tactical style, Karpov preferring</u> a patient, positional style.

   (A) chess; Kasparov preferring a sharp, tactical style, Karpov preferred

   (B) chess. Kasparov preferring a sharp, tactical style, yet Karpov preferred

   (C) chess where Kasparov was preferring a sharp. tactical style, Karpov preferring

   (D) chess, Kasparov preferring a sharp, tactical style, although Karpov preferring

   (E) chess, Kasparov preferring a sharp, tactical style, and Karpov preferring

10. After reading the essay, we understand better why the author is so impressed with the young assistant <u>professor: he believes her</u> approach to teaching language skills through the use of material found in contemporary culture is an excellent one.

   (A) professor: he believes her

   (B) professor. It is his belief that her

   (C) professor, believing her

   (D) professor. He believes she has an

   (E) professor and believes an

11. The phrase "save your skin" means "save your <u>life," with the suggestion that a person doing so is</u> not concerned with anything except preserving his or her own life.

   (A) life," with the suggestion that a person doing so is

   (B) life," in suggesting that a person doing so is

   (C) life," by the suggestion that a person is doing so

   (D) life," and suggesting that a person doing so is

   (E) life," and this is suggesting that a person doing so is

GO ON TO THE NEXT PAGE ▷

10   10   10   10   10   10   10

12. A number of companies are adopting flexible working hour policies, <u>something many experts say will benefit both companies and workers</u>.

   (A) something many experts say will benefit both companies and workers
   (B) many experts say it will benefit both companies and workers
   (C) it is something many experts say will benefit both companies and workers
   (D) something, according to experts, that will benefit both companies and workers
   (E) it's a benefit for both companies and workers, according to many experts

13. <u>Contrasting the deviousness and self-interest of the clergy, Trollope also describes</u> the kindness of the farmer who gives Mrs. Quiverful a ride to Barchester.

   (A) Contrasting the deviousness and self-interest of the clergy, Trollope also describes
   (B) Not only does Trollope contrast the deviousness and self-interest of the clergy, he describes, too,
   (C) In order to contrast the deviousness and self-interest of the clergy, Trollope also describes
   (D) Trollope contrasts the deviousness and self-interest of the clergy and then
   (E) As a contrast to the deviousness and self-interest of the clergy, Trollope also describes

14. Some books, like Richard Adam's modern classic *Watership Down* and the more recent *The Curious Incident of the Dog in the Night-time* by Mark Hadden, can be appreciated by both young people and <u>adults, whereas only adults can really appreciate some books, such as Joseph Conrad's Nostromo</u>.

   (A) adults, whereas only adults can really appreciate some books, such as Joseph Conrad's *Nostromo*
   (B) adults, whereas adults, they only can really appreciate some books, such as Joseph Conrad's *Nostromo*
   (C) adults; whereas only adults can really appreciate some books, such as Joseph Conrad's *Nostromo*
   (D) adults: whereas only adults can really appreciate some books, such as Joseph Conrad's *Nostromo*
   (E) adults, whereas some books, such as Joseph Conrad's *Nostromo*, can only really be appreciated by adults

STOP

IN ANY REMAINING TIME YOU MAY REVIEW THE ANSWERS YOU CHOSE IN THIS SECTION. DO NOT WORK ON ANY OTHER SECTION OF THE TEST DURING THIS TIME.

Answer Key

CRITICAL READING

	Section 2				Section 5				Section 9		
Ans.	Level of Diff.	Ans.	Level of Diff.	Ans.	Level of Diff.	Ans.	Level of Diff.	Ans.	Level of Diff.	Ans.	Level of Diff.
1. B	2	13. A	3	1. D	1	13. C	3	1. C	1	11. C	4
2. E	2	14. E	4	2. C	2	14. C	5	2. A	2	12. A	3
3. C	3	15. D	4	3. A	3	15. B	5	3. D	3	13. C	3
4. B	3	16. B	1	4. C	3	16. D	3	4. D	3	14. B	4
5. D	4	17. B	2	5. B	3	17. B	4	5. C	4	15. C	3
6. C	3	18. D	3	6. E	4	18. E	5	6. A	5	16. A	5
7. A	2	19. E	4	7. A	4	19. C	3	7. C	3	17. D	4
8. C	3	20. B	5	8. C	5	20. D	4	8. B	4	18. A	3
9. D	4	21. D	3	9. C	2	21. C	3	9. A	3	19. E	3
10. D	1	22. D	5	10. E	4	22. A	2	10. D	2		
11. C	2	23. B	4	11. B	3	23. B	3				
12. E	3	24. C	4	12. B	3	24. E	4				

MATH

	Section 3				Section 7				Section 8		
Ans.	Level of Diff.	Ans.	Level of Diff.	Ans.	Level of Diff.	Ans.	Level of Diff.	Ans.	Level of Diff.	Ans.	Level of Diff.
1. E	1	11. B	3	1. D	1	10. 16	1	1. B	1	9. D	3
2. D	1	12. C	3	2. B	1	11. 1/51	2	2. C	1	10. B	4
3. D	1	13. C	3	3. A	2	12. 9.8	3	3. C	2	11. E	3
4. B	2	14. C	4	4. E	2	13. 29	3	4. C	2	12. D	3
5. C	1	15. A	3	5. B	3	14. 1/10 or 0.1	3	5. E	2	13. B	3
6. E	2	16. B	3	6. B	3	15. 5	4	6. D	3	14. E	3
7. C	3	17. D	4	7. A	4	16. 625	4	7. A	3	15. C	4
8. E	2	18. A	4	8. C	4	17. 12/5 or 2.4	5	8. A	3	16. D	5
9. B	3	19. C	5	9. 90	1	18. 48	5				
10. A	3	20. D	5								

WRITING

	Section 6								Section 10		
Ans.	Level of Diff.	Ans.	Level of Diff.	Ans.	Level of Diff.	Ans.	Level of Diff.	Ans.	Level of Diff.	Ans.	Level of Diff.
1. E	1	10. C	4	19. B	2	28. E	5	1. B	1	9. E	3
2. C	1	11. B	4	20. D	3	29. C	5	2. D	1	10. A	3
3. C	1	12. C	1	21. C	3	30. C	3	3. E	2	11. A	4
4. E	2	13. B	1	22. B	3	31. C	2	4. D	2	12. A	4
5. A	2	14. C	2	23. C	3	32. B	1	5. D	3	13. E	4
6. D	3	15. B	2	24. E	3	33. E	3	6. C	3	14. E	5
7. E	3	16. B	2	25. C	3	34. A	4	7. D	3		
8. E	3	17. B	2	26. E	3	35. A	4	8. C	3		
9. A	3	18. B	2	27. E	3						

Score Your Own SAT Essay

Use this table as you rate your performance on the essay-writing section of this Practice Test. Circle the phrase that most accurately describes your work. Enter the numbers in the scoring chart below. Add the numbers together and divide by 6 to determine your total score. The higher your total score, the better you are likely to do on the essay section of the SAT.

Note that on the actual SAT two readers will rate your essay; your essay score will be the sum of their two ratings and could range from 12 (highest) to 2 (lowest). Also, they will grade your essay holistically, rating it on the basis of their overall impression of its effectiveness. They will *not* analyze it piece by piece, giving separate grades for grammar, vocabulary level, and so on. Therefore, you cannot expect the score you give yourself on this Practice Test to predict your eventual score on the SAT with any great degree of accuracy. Use this scoring guide instead to help you assess your writing strengths and weaknesses, so that you can decide which areas to focus on as you prepare for the SAT.

Like most people, you may find it difficult to rate your own writing objectively. Ask a teacher or fellow student to score your essay as well. With his or her help you should gain added insights into writing your 25-minute essay.

	6	5	4	3	2	1
POSITION ON THE TOPIC	Clear, convincing, & insightful	Fundamentally clear & coherent	Fairly clear & coherent	Insufficiently clear	Largely unclear	Extremely unclear
ORGANIZATION OF EVIDENCE	Well organized, with strong, relevant examples	Generally well organized, with apt examples	Adequately organized, with some examples	Sketchily developed, with weak examples	Lacking focus and evidence	Unfocused and disorganized
SENTENCE STRUCTURE	Varied, appealing sentences	Reasonably varied sentences	Some variety in sentences	Little variety in sentences	Errors in sentence structure	Severe errors in sentence structure
LEVEL OF VOCABULARY	Mature & apt word choice	Competent word choice	Adequate word choice	Inappropriate or weak vocabulary	Highly limited vocabulary	Rudimentary
GRAMMAR AND USAGE	Almost entirely free of errors	Relatively free of errors	Some technical errors	Minor errors, and some major ones	Numerous major errors	Extensive severe errors
OVERALL EFFECT	Outstanding	Effective	Adequately competent	Inadequate, but shows some potential	Seriously flawed	Fundamentally deficient

Self-Scoring Chart

For each of the following categories, rate the essay from 1 (lowest) to 6 (highest)

Position on the Topic _____

Organization of Evidence _____

Sentence Structure _____

Level of Vocabulary _____

Grammar and Usage _____

Overall Effect _____

TOTAL _____

(To get a score, divide the total by 6) _____

Scoring Chart (Second Reader)

For each of the following categories, rate the essay from 1 (lowest) to 6 (highest)

Position on the Topic _____

Organization of Evidence _____

Sentence Structure _____

Level of Vocabulary _____

Grammar and Usage _____

Overall Effect _____

TOTAL _____

(To get a score, divide the total by 6) _____

Scoring Practice Test 1

Refer to the answer key for Practice Test 1 on page 80. Then use the Scoring Worksheet below to determine your raw scores for Critical Reading, Mathematics, and Writing. For each section, give yourself one point for each answer that is correct. Your total raw score is the total number of correct answer points minus $\frac{1}{4}$ of the total number of incorrect answer points. Round off the total raw score to the nearest whole number to get your Rounded Raw Score. Convert your raw scores to scaled scores using the Conversion Tables on pages 84–85.

SCORING WORKSHEET

Critical Reading

Section 2 $\underline{\hspace{2cm}}_{\text{number correct}} - \frac{1}{4}\left(\underline{\hspace{2cm}}_{\text{number incorrect}} \right) = \underline{\hspace{2cm}}$ (A)

Section 5 $\underline{\hspace{2cm}}_{\text{number correct}} - \frac{1}{4}\left(\underline{\hspace{2cm}}_{\text{number incorrect}} \right) = \underline{\hspace{2cm}}$ (B)

Section 9 $\underline{\hspace{2cm}}_{\text{number correct}} - \frac{1}{4}\left(\underline{\hspace{2cm}}_{\text{number incorrect}} \right) = \underline{\hspace{2cm}}$ (C)

Critical Reading Raw Score = (A) + (B) + (C) = $\underline{\hspace{2cm}}$

Critical Reading Scaled Score (see Table 1) = $\underline{\hspace{2cm}}$

Mathematics

Section 3 $\underline{\hspace{2cm}}_{\text{number correct}} - \frac{1}{4}\left(\underline{\hspace{2cm}}_{\text{number incorrect}} \right) = \underline{\hspace{2cm}}$ (D)

Section 7
Part I
(1–8) $\underline{\hspace{2cm}}_{\text{number correct}} - \frac{1}{4}\left(\underline{\hspace{2cm}}_{\text{number incorrect}} \right) = \underline{\hspace{2cm}}$ (E)

Part II
(9–18) $\underline{\hspace{2cm}}_{\text{number correct}}$ $= \underline{\hspace{2cm}}$ (F)

Section 8 $\underline{\hspace{2cm}}_{\text{number correct}} - \frac{1}{4}\left(\underline{\hspace{2cm}}_{\text{number incorrect}} \right) = \underline{\hspace{2cm}}$ (G)

Mathematics Raw Score = (D) + (E) + (F) + (G) = $\underline{\hspace{2cm}}$

Mathematics Scaled Score (see Table 2) = $\underline{\hspace{2cm}}$

Writing

Essay $\dfrac{\rule{2.5cm}{0.4pt}}{\text{score 1}} + \dfrac{\rule{2.5cm}{0.4pt}}{\text{score 2}}$ $= \rule{3cm}{0.4pt}$ (H)

Section 6 $\dfrac{\rule{2.5cm}{0.4pt}}{\text{number correct}} - \dfrac{1}{4}\left(\dfrac{\rule{2.5cm}{0.4pt}}{\text{number incorrect}}\right) = \rule{3cm}{0.4pt}$ (I)

Section 10 $\dfrac{\rule{2.5cm}{0.4pt}}{\text{number correct}} - \dfrac{1}{4}\left(\dfrac{\rule{2.5cm}{0.4pt}}{\text{number incorrect}}\right) = \rule{3cm}{0.4pt}$ (J)

Writing Raw Score = I + J (H is a separate subscore) = $\rule{3cm}{0.4pt}$

Writing Scaled Score (see Table 3)   = $\rule{3cm}{0.4pt}$

TABLE 1: CRITICAL READING CONVERSION TABLE

Raw Score	Scaled Score	Raw Score	Scaled Score	Raw Score	Scaled Score	Raw Score	Scaled Score
67	800	49	630	31	510	14	400
66	790	48	620	30	510	13	400
65	790	47	610	29	500	12	390
64	780	46	610	28	490	11	380
63	770	45	600	27	490	10	370
62	760	44	590	26	480	9	360
61	750	43	590	25	480	8	350
60	740	42	580	24	470	7	340
59	730	41	570	23	460	6	330
58	720	40	570	22	460	5	320
57	710	39	560	21	450	4	310
56	700	38	550	20	440	3	300
55	690	37	550	19	440	2	280
54	680	36	540	18	430	1	270
53	670	35	540	17	420	0	260
52	660	34	530	16	420	−1	230
51	650	33	520	15	410	−2 and below	210
50	640	32	520				

TABLE 2: MATH CONVERSION TABLE

Math Raw Score	Math Scaled Score	Math Raw Score	Math Scaled Score	Math Raw Score	Math Scaled Score	Math Raw Score	Math Scaled Score
54	800	40	630	26	500	12	390
53	790	39	620	25	500	11	380
52	770	38	610	24	490	10	370
51	750	37	600	23	480	9	360
50	730	36	590	22	470	8	340
49	710	35	580	21	460	7	330
48	700	34	570	20	450	6	320
47	690	33	560	19	450	5	300
46	680	32	560	18	440	4	290
45	670	31	550	17	430	3	270
44	660	30	540	16	420	2	250
43	650	29	530	15	410	1	240
42	640	28	520	14	410	0	230
41	640	27	510	13	400	−1 and below	200

TABLE 3: WRITING CONVERSION TABLE

Writing Raw Score	Essay Score					
	6	5	4	3	2	1
49	800	800	770	740	710	680
48	800	790	750	710	680	650
47	790	760	720	690	660	630
46	770	740	700	670	640	610
45	760	730	690	650	620	590
44	740	710	670	640	610	580
43	730	700	660	620	600	570
42	720	690	650	610	580	550
41	710	670	630	600	570	540
40	690	660	620	590	560	530
39	680	650	610	580	550	520
38	670	640	600	570	540	510
37	670	630	590	560	530	500
36	660	630	590	550	520	490
35	650	620	580	540	510	480
34	640	610	570	530	510	480
33	630	600	560	530	500	470
32	620	590	550	520	490	460
31	620	590	550	510	480	450
30	610	580	540	500	480	450
29	600	570	530	500	470	440
28	590	560	520	490	460	430
27	590	560	520	480	450	430
26	580	550	510	480	450	420
25	570	540	500	470	440	410
24	570	540	500	460	440	410
23	560	530	490	460	430	400
22	560	520	480	450	420	390
21	550	520	480	440	420	390
20	540	510	470	440	410	380
19	540	510	470	430	400	370
18	530	500	460	430	400	370
17	520	490	450	420	390	360
16	520	490	450	410	380	350
15	510	480	440	410	380	350
14	500	470	430	400	370	340
13	500	470	430	390	370	340
12	490	460	420	390	360	330
11	480	450	410	380	350	320
10	480	450	410	370	350	320
9	470	440	400	370	340	310
8	460	430	390	360	330	300
7	460	420	390	350	320	290
6	450	420	380	340	310	280
5	440	410	370	330	310	280
4	430	400	360	320	300	270
3	420	390	350	310	280	250
2	400	360	330	300	270	240
1	390	360	320	290	260	230
0	370	340	300	270	240	210

ANSWERS EXPLAINED
Section 2 Critical Reading

1. **B** A modern computer would look *incongruous* (not fitting) in a room decorated in an ornate (elaborately decorated), old-fashioned style.

2. **E** If scientific and technical terms have become *ubiquitous* (widespread), it makes sense that a lot of this *jargon* (specialized language) has become part of everyday language.

3. **C** The word "however" in the sentence signals that the word in the first blank will contrast with "known for his inability to understand the feelings of others." *Empathy* (putting oneself in another's place) is thus the best choice for the first blank.
    Ironically is the best choice for the second blank because it is *ironic* (resulting in an unexpected or contrary outcome) that a person known for his inability to understand the feelings of others would collect stories for an anthology with the theme of empathy.

4. **B** Sherlock Holmes has "amazing powers of observation and deduction," so it makes sense that he is called the *archetypal* (related to an *archetype*, the original type that others are based on) private detective.

5. **D** The art critic draws *parallels* (comparisons indicating likenesses) between how the universe is *depicted* (represented) by modern physics and by Cubism.

6. **C** The author says that "humanitarian aid . . . is obviously a good thing" (lines 7–10) and "something we ought to do" (line 14), so we can conclude that he believes that we have a duty to do good. Also, in the final sentence he says that international humanitarianism might be a combination of duty and kindness: "a gift that we *have to give*" (line 21; italics mine). Since the author has asserted that the people of one country have a duty to help people of other countries in "desperate need," it would be reasonable to expect him to next discuss the nature and extent of these duties. He might, for example, define "desperate need" and say how much of a country's resources should be allocated to international foreign aid.

7. **A** As mentioned above, the author says that international humanitarianism might be a combination of duty and kindness: "a gift that we have to give" (line 21). The author says that "we think of humanitarian aid . . . first of all as a form of philanthropy" (lines 6–8).

8. **C** The author says critics are wrong that the slogan "African solutions to African problems" could be used as an excuse for authoritarian African leaders to "reject criticisms of human rights abuses" (lines 10–11). In the case of Cote d'Ivoire, "African leaders repeatedly condemned Gbagbo's flagrant violations of democratic norms" (lines 12–14). The author concludes "what happened in Cote d'Ivoire is thus consistent with [a] policy in which African heads of state are taking on significant roles in conflict resolution" (lines 16–19).

9. **D** The passage first describes (lines 1–2) the maxim (concise formulation of a guiding principle) "African solutions to African problems." Next (lines 6–11), it discusses concerns that the maxim could be used as an excuse for the West to neglect Africa or African leaders to reject criticisms of human rights abuses. Next (lines 11–12), the example of Cote d'Ivoire is cited to show that in this case neither problem arose. Finally (lines 16–19), a general conclusion is reached about the implications of what happened in Cote d'Ivoire for a pro-democracy policy in Africa and the role of African heads of state in furthering that policy.

10. **D** The author says "the Court of Claims . . . was set up not to administer justice but to expedite adjudication of land titles and head off any future claims that Indians might make on lands already coveted by the white economy" (lines 27–31).

11. **C** In the sentence preceding the one cited in the question, the author describes the attitude of the progressives toward the traditionals and their "useless religion" (line 56) as one of scorn for outdated beliefs and practices. The observation that it is the progressives rather than the traditionals who feel it necessary to keep witches out of outhouses suggests that the author believes that it is the progressives rather than the traditionals who are superstitious.

12. **E** This is the only statement about the traditionals supported by the passage: "The traditionals know . . . been taken away" (lines 59–66).

13. **A** The first paragraph of the passage describes the bleak future the Hopi face, focusing on the views of the traditionals. The second paragraph describes what Wayne Sekaquaptewa, a leading progressive, thinks about the views of the traditionals.

14. **E** Although the author does not say that he agrees with the traditionals, he takes a sympathetic view of them and their beliefs throughout the passage. Also, he shows respect for Hopi beliefs in general. In lines 59–72 ("The traditionals know . . . Life Plan Rock.") he describes the views of the traditionals very sympathetically, suggesting strongly that he agrees with them that their only chance of survival as a distinct culture is to cling to their traditional beliefs and practices. We can infer, however, that because he is not a Hopi he does not agree with the literal meaning of the Day of Purification, but rather that he sees it as symbolic of a future that may come to pass in which the Hopi survive amid the ruins of the white man's world.

15. **D** The author says, "The traditionals have always been wary of the white man's consumer mentality" (lines 1–2). (A) *articulate* (clear and effective in speech) makes little sense. (B) and (C) can be eliminated because the author describes the duplicitous dealings of the U.S. government toward the Hopi, views which we can infer that the traditionals hold. (E) can be eliminated because the whites are described as always wanting land to use for mining, leaving "waste and desecration" (line 6).

16. **B** The girl's eyes are also described as "full of radiant curiosity" (line 18), so it makes sense that the phrase "quick gray eyes" is used to suggest that the girl is alert.

17. **B** The word "clad" means *clothed*, whereas the word *adorned* means *made attractive*, suggesting the girl likes to make herself attractive.

18. **D** Immediately before the word "rise" is used, the old man is described as grunting: "There he paused . . . grunt of disapproval" (lines 35–39), suggesting that he intended to communicate something to the girl. Thus, in context, *rise* means *reaction*.

19. **E** The elderly man is described as "utter[ing] a long even grunt of disapproval" (lines 38–39) when he sees the girl sitting and reading a book. It cannot be conclusively inferred that he is disapproving of her reading a novel, but the fact that the grunt is described as one of "disapproval" means that he does not approve of something. There is some evidence for (A), (B), (C), and (D), but none of it is as strong as the evidence for (E). Thus, (E) is the best choice.

20. **B** The author appears to be mainly concerned with vividly describing the scene. He uses these words and phrases to *personify* (portray inanimate objects as having human emotions) the house and the car in Passage 2 to help the reader to imagine the scene. (A) Although the writer uses these words and phrases to portray inanimate objects as having human emotions, he is not using personification as an end in itself. He uses personification to describe the scene vividly. (C) There is an element of exaggeration and distortion of reality in the author's use of these words and phrases. However, the main purpose is not to use exaggeration or distortion of reality to give the reader a fresh perspective. Rather, it is to describe the scene. (D) There is no suggestion of irony (use of words conveying a meaning opposite to the literal meaning) in the use of any of these words and phrases. (E) The phrase "tolerant kindly patience" does not primarily create humor. Rather, it helps portray the house as a welcoming and friendly place. The other two phrases do add an element of humor to the scene, describing the car as an indignant and dying person; however, their main purpose is to describe the scene vividly.

21. **D** It is not stated who or what produced the whistle mentioned in line 71, but it is reasonable to infer that the "signal" referred to in line 77 was the whistle mentioned in line 71. Choices (A), (C), and (E) are all possible, but there is no evidence for them. Choice (B) makes some sense because sounds are described as coming from the car, but it is more reasonable to infer that the whistle was a signal.

22. **D** Choice (D) is the best answer because "perfunctorily" means *done routinely and with little interest*. The fact that Clark Darrow is sitting in this way suggests that visiting the Happer house is probably part of his routine. "Sat brilliantly . . . at attention" suggests that he regards the visit as something to be done in a somewhat showy manner. (A) Although "sat brilliantly . . . at attention" suggests that Clark Darrow regards the visit as something to be done dramatically, the word *perfunctorily* suggests that he regards the visit as something done as a duty, and which he has little interest in. If Clark Darrow were visiting the Happer house to show his romantic interest in Sally he would probably not be sitting *perfunctorily*. (B) Although the words "sat brilliantly . . . at attention"

suggest that he could regard his visit as an honor, one would not normally respond to a great honor by sitting *perfunctorily* (in a manner suggesting that one regards it as a duty). (C) There is nothing to suggest that Clark Darrow is embarrassed. (E) The fact that Clark Darrow sits *perfunctorily* shows that he regards the visit as a routine duty, not as an exciting change from his regular activities.

23. **B** Both of the girls are depicted as being *relaxed*. The girl in Passage 1 is sitting in a wicker settee, very relaxed, reading a book, and Sally Happer in Passage 2 is resting her chin on a window sill, gazing down sleepily at the car. (A) *Pretty* is not the correct choice because, although there is some suggestion that the girl in Passage 1 is pretty ("slender and supple . . . alluring mouth," lines 16–17), nothing is suggested about Sally Happer's appearance. (C) There is a suggestion that the girl in Passage 1 is *intelligent* ("quick grey eyes full of radiant curiosity," lines 17–18), but there is nothing to suggest that Sally is intelligent. (D) Neither girl can be described as *indolent* (habitually lazy) because not enough information is provided to show whether they are frequently lazy, and there is nothing in the passages to suggest that either girl is (E) *voluble* (talkative).

24. **C** In Passage 1 "the drowsy silence" (line 31) is broken by the "heavy footsteps" of the elderly man. In Passage 2 Sally Happer looks down "sleepily" (line 72) at Clark Darrow's noisy arrival in his old Ford. (A) In Passage 1 the arrival of the elderly man does not mainly create humor. In Passage 2 there is a stronger suggestion than there is in Passage 1 that the arrival of the male character is intended, at least in part, to be humorous. However, in neither passage does the male character's arrival mainly serve to create humor. (B) It is possible that the elderly man grunts because he condemns the girl's self-indulgence, but there is nothing to suggest a condemnation of self-indulgence in Passage 2. (D) In Passage 1 the girl ignores the elderly man, and in Passage 2 Sally Happer appears in no hurry to acknowledge Clark Darrow's signal. Their behavior does not show that males are dominant in the story. (E) In Passage 1 the elderly man interrupts the mood briefly but does not really change the atmosphere. The girl ignores him and continues reading and eating a lemon. In Passage 2 Clark Darrow's arrival does not create a serious atmosphere. On the contrary, it creates a somewhat comical atmosphere.

Section 3 Mathematics

<u>Note</u>:

1. See page 32 for an explanation of the symbol ⇒ that is used in some answer explanations.

2. A calculator icon, 🖩, is placed next to the answer explanation of any question for which a calculator *could* be useful. Almost always, the question can be answered easily without using a calculator.

3. If you are unfamiliar with any of the math facts used in the following answer explanations, refer to Barron's *SAT*, which, in addition to having practice tests, has a full review of all the math you need to know.

1. **E** Since there are 3 boys for every 7 girls, for every 10 students there are 3 boys and 7 girls. So $\frac{3}{10}$ of the students are boys and $\frac{7}{10}$ of the students are girls.

2. **D** There is no need for algebra here. If Sandrine had $10, then Maryline had twice as much, $20, and Nicholas had 5 × $20 = $100. In total, they had $130.

3. **D** Let h = price of a hamburger and f = price of a side of fries, both in dollars. Then, $2h + f = 7.25$ and $h + 2f = 5.50$.
   There are several ways to solve this system of equations. One easy way is to add the equations:

   $$3h + 3f = 12.75 \Rightarrow h + f = 4.25.$$

   Since 1 hamburger and 1 side of fries cost $4.25, Penny's second hamburger cost $7.25 − $4.25 = $3.00.

4. **B** Sketch the triangle.

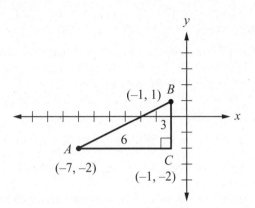

$$AC = -7 - (-1) = 6, BC = 1 - (-2) = 3, \text{ and } m\angle C = 90°.$$

So the area of $\triangle ABC$ is $\frac{1}{2}(6)(3) = 9$.

5. **C** There are 24 positive multiples of 4 less than 100:

$$1 \times 4 = 4, 2 \times 4 = 8, \ldots, 24 \times 4 = 96.$$

Of these multiples of 4, 8 of them (every third one) are multiples of 6:

$$4, 8, \cancel{12}, 16, 20, \cancel{24}, \ldots, \cancel{84}, 88, 92, \cancel{96}.$$

So, there are $24 - 8 = 16$ positive multiples of 4 less than 100 that are not multiples of 6.

6. **E** Since $a^2 + 2ab + b^2 = (a + b)^2$, $(a + b)^2 = 4$, and so $(a + b)^6 = [(a + b)^2]^3 = 4^3 = 64$.

7. **C** **Solution 1.** If the average of a, a, b, and b, is $a + 1$, then $\frac{a+a+b+b}{4} = a+1$.

So $2a + 2b = 4(a + 1) = 4a + 4$. Subtracting $2a$ from each side, we get $2b = 2a + 4$ and, dividing by 2 yields $b = a + 2$.

Solution 2. Since the average is $a + 1$, each of the two a's are 1 less than the average, and so each of the two b's must be 1 more than the average.

8. **E** **Solution 1.** You don't have to solve for x, if you know that the sum of the exterior angles, taking one at each vertex, is *always* 360°.

Solution 2. The sum of the measures of the four angles in *any* quadrilateral is 360°. Therefore,

$$\frac{2}{5}x+x+x+90 = 360 \Rightarrow \frac{12}{5}x = 270 \Rightarrow 12x = 1350 \Rightarrow x = 112.5, \text{ and } \frac{2}{5}x = 45. \text{ So, } a = 90, b = c = 67.5, \text{ and}$$
$$d = 135, \text{ and their sum is 360.}$$

9. **B**
- If the first Sunday of the month is the 1st day of the month, then the dates of the five Sundays are: 1, 8, 15, 22, and 29, in which case the 10th is Tuesday.
- STOP. If you are alert, you will see that only answer choice (B) includes Tuesday, so that must be the correct answer. If you didn't notice that, just continue.
- If the first Sunday is the 2nd day of the month, then the five Sundays are: 2, 9, 16, 23, and 30, in which case the 10th is on Monday.
- If the first Sunday is the 3rd day of the month, then the five Sundays are: 3, 10, 17, 24, and 31, in which case the 10th is on Sunday.
Since no month has more than 31 days, these are all the possibilities.

10. **A** **Solution 1.** The 108 people who received 2 tickets each got a total of 216 tickets. The remaining $500 - 216 = 284$ tickets were given to the other $282 - 108 = 174$ people. After each of those people received a ticket, there were still $284 - 174 = 110$ tickets left, enough for 55 people to get two additional tickets.

Solution 2. Assume one ticket was given to each of the 282 people. Then there would be $500 - 282 = 218$ tickets left. Of these, one each was given to the 108 people who wound up with two tickets. As for the remaining 110 tickets, two each were given to 55 people, who now had three tickets each.

Solution 3. Solve the problem algebraically. Let a, b, and c represent the number of people with 1, 2, and 3 tickets, respectively. Then $a + b + c = 282$. Also, the total number of tickets sold was $a + 2b + 3c = 500$. Since it is given that $b = 108$, we have that $a + 108 + c = 282 \Rightarrow a + c = 174$, and $a + 2(108) + 3c = 500 \Rightarrow a + 216 + 3c = 500 \Rightarrow a + 3c = 284$. Subtracting $a + c = 174$ from $a + 3c = 284$, we get that $2c = 110$ and so $c = 55$.

11. **B** If x is inversely proportional to y^2, then the product xy^2 is constant. Since $y = 4$ when $x = 5$, that constant is

$5 \times 4^2 = 5 \times 16 = 80$. Then, if $y = 6$, we have that $x(6^2) = 36x = 80$. So, $x = \dfrac{80}{36} = \dfrac{20}{9}$.

12. **C** Since there were 10,000 bias-motivated offenses based on ethnicity, and that represents 10% of the total, there were 100,000 bias-motivated offenses in total. Of these, 16,000 (16% of 100,000) were based on religion, and 15,600 (15.6% of 100,000) were based on sexual orientation. The difference is 400.

13. **C** Since this is a question about percentages, assume that the total number of bias-motivated offenses in 2000 listed in the circle graph was 100, of which 16 were based on religion and 58 were based on race.

- If 8 of the religion-based offenses (50% of 16) were deleted, then there would have been 92 offenses in all, of which 58 were based on race. $\dfrac{58}{92} = 0.6304 = 63.04\%$

- If 4 of the religion-based offenses (25% of 16) were deleted, then there would have been 96 offenses in all, of which 58 were based on race. $\dfrac{58}{96} = 0.6041 = 60.41\%$

Only choice (C) lies between 60.41% and 63.04%.

14. **C** Draw in the missing line segments and label the diagram.

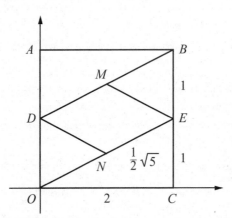

By the Pythagorean theorem: $(OE)^2 = 1^2 + 2^2 = 5 \Rightarrow OE = \sqrt{5}$ and $NE = \dfrac{1}{2}\sqrt{5}$

Similarly, $DM = \dfrac{1}{2}\sqrt{5}$, and by symmetry, or using the distance formula, $DN = ME = \dfrac{1}{2}\sqrt{5}$. So, the perimeter of $DMEN$ is $4 \times \left(\dfrac{1}{2}\sqrt{5}\right) = 2\sqrt{5}$.

15. **A Solution 1.** If you make a quick sketch, you won't have to calculate any slopes.

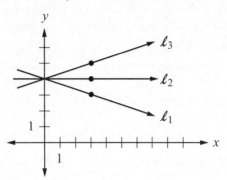

From the sketch it is clear that m_1 is negative, $m_2 = 0$, and m_3 is positive. So, $m_1 < m_2 < m_3$.

Solution 2. Of course, you *can* calculate the slopes:

$$m_1 = \frac{3-4}{3-0} = -\frac{1}{3}; \qquad m_2 = \frac{4-4}{3-0} = 0; \qquad m_3 = \frac{5-4}{3-0} = \frac{1}{3}.$$

16. **B Solution 1.** Let J represent the number of cards that John has and let T represent the total number of cards owned by everyone in the club, including John. Then $T - J$ is the number of cards owned by everyone else.

Since $60\% = \frac{3}{5}$, $J = \frac{3}{5}(T - J)$. So $5J = 3T - 3J$, and $8J = 3T$. Therefore, $J = \frac{3}{8}T$.

Solution 2. Since this is a problem involving percents, assume that everyone other than John had a total of 100 cards and that John had 60 cards (60% of 100). Then the total number of cards of everyone, including John, is

160 and $\frac{60}{160} = \frac{6}{16} = \frac{3}{8}$.

17. **D** Since each number is 3 times the preceding number, the first five numbers are: a_1, $3a_1$, $9a_1$, $27a_1$, and $81a_1$. So, $a_5 = 81a_1$, and $100 = a_5 - a_1 = 81a_1 - a_1 = 80a_1$.

Therefore, $80a_1 = 100$, and $a_1 = \frac{100}{80} = \frac{5}{4}$.

Finally, $a_2 = 3(a_1) = 3 \times \frac{5}{4} = \frac{15}{4}$.

18. **A** First, $\frac{2}{3}(825) = 550$, so 550 students take Spanish. Now draw a Venn diagram.

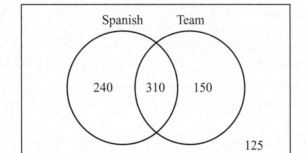

Since 310 team members take Spanish, $460 - 310 = 150$ team members do not take Spanish, and $550 - 310 = 240$ students who take Spanish are not on a team. Finally, $240 + 310 + 150 = 700$ students either are on a team or take Spanish (or both), so $825 - 700 = 125$ neither take Spanish nor play on a team.

19. **C** In the decimal expansion of $\frac{3}{7}$ the six digits 4, 2, 8, 5, 7, and 1 repeat indefinitely in that order. The largest

multiple of 6 less than 100 is $16 \times 6 = 96$. So the first 96 digits constitute 16 sets of the digits 4, 2, 8, 5, 7, and 1, whose sum is 27. Therefore, the sum of the first 96 digits is $16 \times 27 = 432$. The 97th, 98th, 99th, and 100th digits are 4, 2, 8, and 5, respectively, and their sum is 19. So the sum of the first 100 digits is $432 + 19 = 451$.

Practice Test 1

20.   **D**   Since a hexagon has 6 sides, and since in a regular hexagon all the sides are congruent, the length of each side is 24 ÷ 6 = 4. Now sketch the hexagon, and since there is no general formula for the area of a hexagon, divide it into pieces whose areas you can determine.

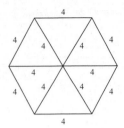

Option 1. Draw in three diagonals, dividing the hexagon into 6 equilateral triangles.

The formula for the area of an equilateral triangle of side s is $A = \dfrac{s^2\sqrt{3}}{4}$. So the area

of each triangle is $\dfrac{4^2\sqrt{3}}{4} = 4\sqrt{3}$, and the area of the hexagon is $6 \times 4\sqrt{3} = 24\sqrt{3}$.

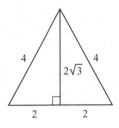

If you don't know the formula for the area of an equilateral triangle, just use $A = \dfrac{1}{2}bh$.

So $A = \dfrac{1}{2}(4)(2\sqrt{3}) = 4\sqrt{3}$.

Option 2. Draw in the diagonals that divide the hexagon into a rectangle and two triangles.

Altitude $\overline{FG}$ divides $\triangle AFG$ into two 30-60-90 right triangles. So the areas

of $\triangle AFE$ and $\triangle BCD$ are each $\dfrac{1}{2}(4\sqrt{3})(2) = 4\sqrt{3}$, and the area of rectangle

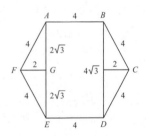

$ABDE = 4 \times 4\sqrt{3} = 16\sqrt{3}$. So the area of the hexagon is

$4\sqrt{3} + 4\sqrt{3} + 16\sqrt{3} = 24\sqrt{3}.$

Section 5 Critical Reading

1.   **D**   It makes sense that "authoritative testimony" would be given to the court by an *eminent* (distinguished) doctor.

2.   **C**   The word "whereas" in the sentence signals a contrast to "fragile," so *robust* (strongly constructed) makes good sense.

3.   **A**   *Speculated* (inferred from inconclusive evidence) is the only appropriate choice.

4.   **C**   Finding a *middle ground* (point of view between two extremes) is difficult in the case of *contentious* (controversial; causing quarrels) issues on which views are *polarized* (concentrated around two conflicting positions). These are the only two choices that make sense together.

5.   **B**   "Small changes" signals that the changes in the Earth's orbit around the Sun and in its tilt on its axis are not of great size. Thus, changes that are not of great *magnitude* (of great size) and *size* are both good choices. *Cumulative* (increasing by successive addition) is the best choice for the second blank because, despite the fact that the changes are not large, their effects build up steadily over time. *Correlative* (corresponding), the second word in choice (E), makes little sense because there is nothing to suggest a correspondence between two things.

6.   **E**   The word *plausible* (credible) in the sentence suggests that the word must have something to do with making appliances that break down regularly. Planned *obsolescence* (the process of becoming obsolete) thus makes good sense.

7.   **A**   *Quintessentially* (most typically) is a good choice. The other four choices in the first column all make sense. However, in the second column only *oblivion* (the state of being completely forgotten) makes sense.

8.   **C**   Scientists describe gravity as having two characteristics that seem somewhat *paradoxical* (seemingly contradictory). It is *elusive* (difficult to perceive) yet its effects are *ubiquitous* (being everywhere at the same time).

9. **C** The author says, "Thus, from the war of nature, from famine and death, the most exalted objects which we are capable of conceiving, namely, the production of higher animals, directly follows" (lines 18–22). Although the author does not use the word "paradox" it is reasonable to apply this word to the process of the production of the higher animals because there is a *paradox* (contradiction or apparent contradiction) in such advanced "exalted" (elevated) life being produced through such unexalted means.

10. **E** In this sentence the author notes that a person could not make an aphid, and in the sentence immediately following, she contrasts this inability of human beings to make aphids with the ability of aphid eggs to make aphids "effortlessly." Thus, it is likely she wrote the sentence to show the unique power of evolution to create life forms.

11. **B** Passage 1 stresses the "grandeur" (line 22) of the evolutionary process. However, the author notes that evolution proceeds "from the war of nature, from famine and death" (lines 18–19). It is reasonable to infer from this that she regards death as an unfortunate part of the evolutionary process. The author of Passage 1 would also be likely to agree with (D). Since her main point is the waste in the evolutionary process, the author of Passage 2 would certainly agree with both (B) and (C). Thus, the best choice is (B).

12. **B** The author of Passage 1 says that evolution proceeds "from famine and death" (line 22), but his focus in the passage is on "the grandeur in this view of life" (line 19) and how evolution has produced "forms most beautiful and wonderful" (lines 27–28). Therefore, he would be very unlikely to agree with the author of Passage 2 that the process of evolution is "deranged."

13. **C** The author says in the first few lines of the passage, "It's not hard to guess which side [of the debate about the ethics of using the atomic bomb] each chose once you know that Alsop experienced capture by the Japanese at Hong Kong early in 1942, while Joravsky came into no deadly contact with the Japanese" (lines 5–9). This statement makes the assumption that Alsop's and Joravsky's opinions about whether the use of the atomic bomb was ethical are determined by their experience in the war.

14. **C** The author's point is that the question does not fairly and objectively present the crucial issue for debate because it can only be answered "no." A person, such as the author, who on balance favored the use of the atomic bomb, is forced to answer "no" because, strictly speaking, dropping the atomic bomb was not really necessary because the war could have been ended by other means.

15. **B** From the context it can be inferred that the atomic bombing of Hiroshima and Nagasaki prompted peace advocates in Japan to call into serious question deeply held Japanese values about national pride and individual honor because the atomic bombing radically changed their significance. A short-hand term for these values is "the Japanese book of rules."

16. **D** Such opinion surveys would support Joseph Alsop's contention that a blood bath would have been inevitable without the use of the atomic bomb because they show that most Japanese would have joined the fight against the invaders and fought fiercely.

17. **B** The author quotes Joseph Alsop: "It [is] absurd . . . to hold the common view . . . that the decision to drop the two bombs on Japan was wicked in itself" (lines 35–39). We can see from this that the author agrees with Mr. Alsop's view that most Americans mistakenly condemn the dropping of the atomic bombs on Japan. It is reasonable to infer that one of the reasons the author believes that they make this mistake is that they tend to ignore the great stress placed on honor in Japanese culture, leading them to believe that the Japanese would not have fought an invasion fiercely. The author quotes Joseph Alsop's conclusion: "Japanese surrender could never have been obtained, at any rate without the honor-satisfying bloodbath envisioned by . . . Anami" (lines 24–27) without the dropping of the atomic bombs on Japan.

18. **E** The word "genteel" means "belonging to polite society," so "genteel ethics" are the ethics, or moral values, of polite society. The term suggests that such morality is removed from the harsh realities faced by ordinary people, and is able to stand apart and make fine moral judgments free of involvement in the events that are judged.

19. **C** "Ex post facto" means "retroactively." The author is discussing the intellectual problems that arise when the ethics of an event is judged by the application of information that was not known at the time by the people involved in the event.

20. **D** The discovery of documents showing that the Japanese leadership possessed information leading them to (incorrectly) believe that the Americans would not have a second atomic bomb ready for use for several months would suggest Joseph Alsop's argument that dropping an atomic bomb on Nagasaki was morally justifiable because it would strengthen the likelihood that the Japanese would have fought to the death to defend their country, even if it meant a "bloodbath" (line 26).

21. **C** In context the word "tidy" means "orderly." The author is saying that the historian can use hindsight to analyze events of the past in an orderly manner. An example of this is that they know the implications (such as "opening up the age of nuclear warfare") of events, whereas the people involved in them could not know such implications. Thus, the historian, using hindsight, can fit everything into an orderly view of what happened.

22. **A** The words "as well as" signal that, in dropping atomic bombs on Japan, U.S. government officials were motivated not only by a desire to end the war but also by a desire for revenge against the Japanese for attacking Pearl Harbor and starting the war in the Pacific.

23. **B** In context the word "illumination" means *intellectual enlightenment*. The author is saying that to understand the past one must put aside one's knowledge of subsequent events and not consider any intellectual enlightenment that comes with considering these later events.

24. **E** The lines from the poem "Gerontion" suggest that when a person acts it is difficult for the person to know the consequences of those actions, and that acting neither from fear nor from courage ensures that history will judge the person's acts as being virtuous. In the context of the passage these lines are appropriate because the author is arguing that the people who decided to drop atomic bombs on Japan could not know the full implications of their decision. Perhaps "unnatural vices" (the consequences of the atomic bombings) were "fathered by [their] heroism" (lines 95–96) in their deciding to drop the bombs, or perhaps their "impudent crimes" (dropping the bombs) resulted in their being considered virtuous.

Section 6 Writing

1. **E** This corrects the dangling participle "As editor of the influential journal Foreign Issues," which refers to Mr. Hamilton.

2. **C** This corrects the idiom error "for as many as thirty years and more."

3. **C** The given sentence is incomplete because "often providing people with a plausible explanation for bemusing things is a participial phrase referring to the subject, "myths." The verb "provide" creates a complete sentence.

4. **E** This corrects the error in subject–verb agreement. The singular *is* must be used to agree with the subject *minister* rather than the plural *are*.

5. **A** The given sentence is correct because a semicolon links two independent clauses. The second clause elaborates on what is said in the first clause, which is correct usage.

6. **D** This corrects *associating with*, which is a passive participle rather than an active participle required by the structure of the sentence.

7. **E** *However* is not a suitable transitional word because it is a contrastive term, and there is no contrast between the two main parts of the sentence. *Thus* is the best transitional word because the fact that most astronomers searching for meteors that come close to Earth work in the United States. is the reason humanity is oblivious to the asteroids mentioned in the second part of the sentence.

8. **E** The given sentence is not correct because "for an exchange" cannot be used in this sentence structure. The verb *exchanging* corrects this error by creating a participial phrase referring to "trade."

9. **A** The sentence is clear and grammatical.

10. **C** An adjective, *discontented*, cannot be used to modify a verb (*realized*). This uses the correct part of speech (adverb) to modify the verb *realized*. *Discontentedly* describes how the student realized that she had forgotten her calculator. The adverb is correctly set off by commas, making the meaning clear.

11. **B** The phrase "and each supporting its special interests" is not grammatical in this sentence structure. The phrase beginning "each supporting" is a participial phrase referring to *factions*, so the word *and* is not necessary.

12. **C** Faulty parallelism. *Repealing* must be changed to *repeal* so that it is the same form as *passage* and *modification*.

13. **B** Run-on sentence. Omit the pronoun *he*.

14. **C** Incorrect part of speech. *Rapid* modifies the verb *increasing*, so it must be an adverb. Use *rapidly*.

15. **B** Verb tense error. We are told that Aldous Huxley wrote *Island* after writing *Brave New World*. The use of the past perfect *had written* is incorrect because the past perfect should be used to refer to an action that took place previous to another action in the past. Therefore, *had written* should be changed to *wrote*, the simple past tense form of the verb.

16. **B** The gerund *calling* cannot be used after the phrase "thought it wise." Change *calling* to *to call*, an infinitive phrase used as an adjective to modify the noun *wise*.

17. **B** Subject–verb agreement. The verb *allows* must agree with its subject, *techniques*. Change *allows* to *allow*. The structure of the sentence is a bit confusing. *Techniques* is the subject and the two main verbs are *help* and *allow*.

18. **B** Pronoun–antecedent agreement. The antecedent *visitors* is plural, so the pronoun must be plural. *His* or *her* is singular. Use the plural pronoun *their*.

19. **B** Error in idiom. The adjective *aware* cannot be followed by an infinitive. Change *to be watched* to *of being watched*.

20. **D** Faulty comparison. (D) should be changed to *than the music of The Beach Boys* or *than that of The Beach Boys* because the music of The Beach Boys is being compared to the music of The Rolling Stones and The Beatles.

21. **C** Subject–verb agreement. The subject *foliage* is singular, so the verb *furnish* must also be singular. Use *furnishes*.

22. **B** Pronoun–antecedent agreement. The pronoun *they* refers to the *public*, a collective noun. In this context, the noun *public* is considered as one group, making it singular. Therefore, the pronoun *they*, which is plural, must be changed to the singular pronoun *it* so that it agrees with the noun *public*.

23. **C** Tense error. The simple present tense rather than the past tense should be used to make a generalization.

24. **E** No error.

25. **C** Wrong preposition. The adjective *attributable* can only be followed by the preposition *to*. Change *with* to *to*.

26. **E** No error.

27. **E** No error.

28. **E** No error.

29. **C** Incorrect part of speech. The "two purposes" are *a period* and *the opportunity*. Change the preposition *with* to the conjunction *and* so that the two are correctly linked.

30. **C** A fuller explanation of the term social stratification would be helpful because it is the main topic of the passage. Also, it would help the reader understand what is meant by "these factors" referred to in sentence 2. (A) This is not relevant to the main topic. (B) This makes some sense, but it would digress from the main topic. Digression should be avoided, especially in an introductory paragraph. (D) Like B, this is a digression. (E) Again, this is a digression.

31. **C** This makes good sense because it provides an explanation for the classification described in the preceding sentence (sentence 4). Also, the reference to the United States helps introduce the following two sentences, which describe class in America. In addition, the word "again" links the sentence to the disagreement among

sociologists mentioned in sentence 2. (A) This makes little sense here and does not link sentence 4 and sentence 5. (B) This is a digression and does not link sentence 4 and sentence 5. (D) This makes little sense here and does not link sentence 4 and sentence 5. (E) This is too specific, makes little sense here, and does not link sentence 4 and sentence 5.

32.   **B**   This creates a grammatically correct sentence that clearly and succinctly gives an example of people in positions of great power. (A) This is not a grammatical sentence because of the phrase "they are people." (C) This does not create a grammatical sentence. (D) This does not create a grammatical sentence. (E) This is not grammatical because the first part of the sentence (before the semicolon, that is) is not an independent clause.

33.   **E**   The sentence gives a relevant example of the point made in sentence 12. (A) The paragraph is not as effective without this supporting example. (B) This changes the meaning. (C) Adding "However" at the beginning of the sentence creates a sentence that makes no sense placed after sentence 12. (D) This changes the meaning so that it does not make sense in the passage.

34.   **A**   Exaggeration for effect is not used. (B) "One sociologist"—an authority—is cited in sentence 5. (C) A number of examples of general assertions are given; for example, sentence 11. (D) An example of an assertion of fact is sentence 1, in which the fact that sociologists say that every modern industrial society has some form of social stratification is asserted. (E) Several definitions of key terms are provided, for example, sentence 3.

35.   **A**   The words "but not necessarily so" help link sentence 15 and sentence 16 because sentence 16 provides an example in which status is not affected by other determinants. This is the best choice. (B) The phrase "a number of" does not provide any more information than the word "other" alone. (C) This makes no sense and is not grammatical. (D) This has the same meaning and is as clear as the original. However, it is not as good of a choice as choice (A) because it lacks the phrase "but not necessarily so." (E) "Affected" is the correct verb in context.

Section 7 Mathematics

Note:

1.   See page 32 for an explanation of the symbol ⇒ that is used in some answer explanations.

2.   A calculator icon, , is placed next to the answer explanation of any question for which a calculator *could* be useful. Almost always, the question can be answered easily without using a calculator.

3.   If you are unfamiliar with any of the math facts used in the following answer explanations, refer to Barron's *SAT*, which, in addition to having practice tests, has a full review of all the math you need to know.

1.   **D**   Set up a proportion, reducing if you like, and then cross-multiply.

$$\frac{40 \text{ packages}}{1 \text{ hour}} = \frac{40 \text{ packages}}{60 \text{ minutes}} = \frac{4 \text{ packages}}{6 \text{ minutes}} = \frac{2 \text{ packages}}{3 \text{ minutes}}$$

Then, $\dfrac{2 \text{ packages}}{3 \text{ minutes}} = \dfrac{150 \text{ packages}}{x \text{ minutes}}$. So $2x = (3)(150) = 450$, and $x = 225$.

2.   **B**   The number halfway between two numbers is their average:

$$\frac{-\frac{3}{4} + \frac{7}{8}}{2} = \frac{\frac{1}{8}}{2} = \frac{1}{16}$$

3.   **A**   By the definition of average: $A = \dfrac{c+d}{2}$. So $2A = c + d$, and, therefore, $d = 2A - c$.

4. **E** If the distance from A to the origin is r, then *every* point that is on the circle whose center is at the origin and whose radius is r and that lies in Quadrant II satisfies the condition. There are infinitely many such points.

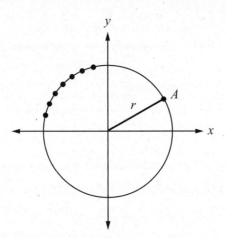

5. **B** **Solution 1.** Since $f(x) = 3x + 2$, we have $f(2c) = 3(2c) + 2 = 6c + 2$. So, if $f(2c) = 4c$, then $6c + 2 = 4c$, and so $2c = -2$ and $c = -1$.

Solution 2. Test the choices. For example, if $c = 0$, then $2c = 0$, and $f(2c) = f(0) = 3(0) + 2 = 2$, which is not equal to $4(0) = 0$. But if $c = -1$, then $2c = -2$, and $f(2c) = f(-2) = 3(-2) + 2 = -6 + 2 = -4$, which *does* equal $4(-1)$.

6. **B** Even though you should almost always sketch a figure on geometry problems, here, because the answer choices are so close to one another, it won't help. Since l passes through $(-4, 1)$ and $(4, 3)$, the slope of l is
$$\frac{y_2 - y_1}{x_2 - x_1} = \frac{3 - 1}{4 - (-4)} = \frac{2}{8} = \frac{1}{4}.$$

But l passes through $(4, 3)$ and $(5, b)$, so $\dfrac{1}{4} = \dfrac{b - 3}{5 - 4} = \dfrac{b - 3}{1}$.

Therefore, $1 = 4(b - 3) = 4b - 12$. So, $4b = 13$ and $b = \dfrac{13}{4} = 3.25$.

7. **A** Assume the lengths of the three sides of a triangle are 10, 10, and x. By the triangle inequality, the sums of the lengths of any two sides must be greater than the length of the third side. So,

$$10 + 10 > x, \text{ which means that } 20 > x, \text{ and}$$
$$10 + x > 10, \text{ which means that } x > 0.$$

Since in this question, x must be an integer, the least possible value of x is 1, in which case the perimeter of the triangle would be 21, and the greatest possible value of x is 19, in which case the perimeter of the triangle would be 39. The greatest possible difference, then, is $39 - 21 = 18$.

8. **C** You could let $BD = x$ and $AC = 2x$, but since this is a question about ratios, it is easier to plug in a number. Let $BD = 1$ and $AC = 2$. Since $\triangle ACE$ is isosceles, $\text{m}\angle A = 45°$, and since $\overline{BD} \parallel \overline{AE}$, $\text{m}\angle B = 45°$ and $\text{m}\angle D = 90°$. So $\triangle BCD$ is also isosceles.

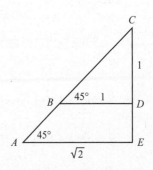

*   The area of $\triangle BCD = \dfrac{1}{2}(1)(1) = \dfrac{1}{2}$.

*   Since $AC = 2$, AE and CE are each $\dfrac{2}{\sqrt{2}} = \sqrt{2}$, and the area of $\triangle ACE$

    is $\dfrac{1}{2}(\sqrt{2})(\sqrt{2}) = 1$.

*   The area of trapezoid $ABDE$ = area of $\triangle ACE$ − area of $\triangle BCD = 1 - \dfrac{1}{2} = \dfrac{1}{2}$

So the area of trapezoid $ABDE$ and $\triangle BCD$ are equal. The ratio is 1:1.

9.   **90**   In the diagram below, because lines m and n are parallel, $b = d$ and $c + d = 180$.

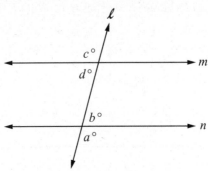

Since $c = b$, $c = d$, and since $c + d = 180$, c and d are each 90, as are a and b.

10.   **40**   **Solution 1.** Let B, K, and L represent Bruce's, Kathy's, and Leah's salaries, respectively.

Then $K = L + .50L = 1.5L$ and $K = B - .40B = .60B$. So, $.60B = 1.5L \Rightarrow L = \dfrac{.60}{1.5}B = \dfrac{6}{15}B = \dfrac{2}{5}B = 40\%B$.

Solution 2. Assume Bruce's salary is \$100. Then since 40% of \$100 is \$40, Kathy's salary is \$40 less, namely \$60. Since Kathy's salary is 50 percent greater than Leah's salary, Leah's salary is \$40 (50% of \$40 is \$20, and \$20 + \$40 = \$60), which is 40% of \$100.

11. $\dfrac{1}{51}$ $A = \left\{\dfrac{1}{3}, \dfrac{3}{5}, \dfrac{5}{7}, \ldots, \dfrac{47}{49}, \dfrac{49}{51}\right\}$. So the product of all the numbers in A is $\dfrac{1}{\cancel{3}} \times \dfrac{\cancel{3}}{\cancel{5}} \times \dfrac{\cancel{5}}{\cancel{7}} \times \ldots \times \dfrac{\cancel{47}}{\cancel{49}} \times \dfrac{\cancel{49}}{51} = \dfrac{1}{51}$.

12.   **9.8**   Let P and A represent the perimeter and area of the square, respectively.

Then $\dfrac{4}{5}P = 11.2 \Rightarrow 4P = 5 \times 11.2 = 56 \Rightarrow P = 14$. So, each side of the square is $14 \div 4 = 3.5$,

and $A = (3.5)^2 = 12.25$. Finally, $\dfrac{4}{5}(12.25) = 9.8$.

13.   **29**   **Solution 1.** As x increases from 1 to 2, $f(x)$, or y, increases from 5 to 13, an increase of 8. Since $y = f(x)$ is a linear function, y will continue to increase by 8, whenever x increases by 1. So $f(3) = 13 + 8 = 21$, and $f(4) = 21 + 8 = 29$.

Solution 2. Since $(1, 5)$ and $(2, 13)$ are each points on the line $y = f(x)$, the slope of the line is $\dfrac{13-5}{2-1} = 8$. So if

$(4, c)$ is a point on the line, then $8 = \dfrac{c-5}{4-1} = \dfrac{c-5}{3}$.

Cross-multiply: $8 \times 3 = 24 = c - 5 \Rightarrow c = 29$.

Solution 3. Since, as we saw above, the slope of the line is 8, the equation of the line is $y = 8x + b$. Then, since $(1, 5)$ is a point of the line, we have $5 = 8(1) + b$, and so $b = -3$. Finally, since $f(x) = y = 8x - 3$, then $f(4) = 8(4) - 3 = 32 - 3 = 29$.

14. $\dfrac{1}{10}$ or **0.1**   **Solution 1.** Regardless of who is chosen first, 2 of the 5 remaining children are of the same gender as the first one chosen, and then if the first two children chosen are of the same gender, 1 of the remaining 4 children is of that gender.

So, P(all 3 the same gender) $= \dfrac{2}{5} \times \dfrac{1}{4} = \dfrac{2}{20} = \dfrac{1}{10}$.

Solution 2. P(3 boys) $= \dfrac{3}{6} \times \dfrac{2}{5} \times \dfrac{1}{4} = \dfrac{6}{120} = \dfrac{1}{20}$.

Similarly, P(3 girls) $= \dfrac{1}{20}$. So,

P(3 boys or 3 girls) $= \dfrac{1}{20} + \dfrac{1}{20} = \dfrac{2}{20} = \dfrac{1}{10}$.

15. **5**   **Solution 1.** If $|5 - 2x| = a$, then

$$
\begin{aligned}
5 - 2x &= a &\text{or}& & 5 - 2x &= -a \\
-2x &= a - 5 &\text{or}& & -2x &= -a - 5 \\
2x &= 5 - a &\text{or}& & 2x &= 5 + a \\
x &= \frac{5 - a}{2} &\text{or}& & x &= \frac{5 + a}{2}.
\end{aligned}
$$

So the sum of the two solutions is $\dfrac{5 - a}{2} + \dfrac{5 + a}{2} = \dfrac{10}{2} = 5$.

Solution 2. The question implies that the sum is independent of a. So, pick an easy-to-use number for a, say $a = 1$. To solve $|5 - 2x| = 1$, either do exactly what was done above, (except that it is easier using 1 than a), or by inspection, see that the two solutions are $x = 2$ and $x = 3$. Finally, $2 + 3 = 5$.

16. **625**   Use the counting principle to evaluate O and E. Every integer between 10,000 and 100,000 has five digits. If each digit is to be odd, there are 5 possibilities (1, 3, 5, 7, and 9) for each digit. So $O = 5 \times 5 \times 5 \times 5 \times 5 = 3{,}125$. If each digit is to be even, there are 4 possibilities for the first digit (2, 4, 6, and 8) and 5 possibilities for each of the other 4 digits (0, 2, 4, 6, and 8). So $E = 4 \times 5 \times 5 \times 5 \times 5 = 2{,}500$. Then $O - E = 3{,}125 - 2{,}500 = 625$.

17. $\dfrac{12}{5}$ or **2.4**   **Solution 1.**

- If $(a, 0)$ is a point on the graph, then $0 = |-5a - 3|$.

  So, $-5a - 3 = 0 \Rightarrow -5a = 3 \Rightarrow a = -\dfrac{3}{5}$.

- If $(0, b)$ is a point on the graph, then $b = |0 - 3| = 3$.

  So $a + b = -\dfrac{3}{5} + 3 = 2\dfrac{2}{5} = \dfrac{12}{5} = 2.4$.

Solution 2. The graph of $y = -5x - 3$ is below at the left and the graph of $y = |-5x - 3|$ is below at the right. Note that the graph of $y = |-5x - 3|$ is obtained by reflecting in the x-axis the portion of the graph of $y = -5x - 3$ that lies below the x-axis.

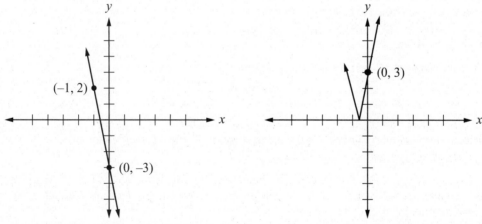

Since the y-intercept of the graph on the left is -3, then b, the y-intercept of the graph on the right is 3. The two graphs cross the x-axis at the same point: $(a, 0)$. So, $0 = -5a - 3 \Rightarrow a = -\dfrac{3}{5}$. Finally, $-\dfrac{3}{5} + 3 = 2\dfrac{2}{5} = \dfrac{12}{5} = 2.4$.

18. **48** Draw the circle with center O and radii $\overline{OA}$ and $\overline{OB}$.

Since $OA = OB$, $\triangle OAB$ is isosceles, and m$\angle A =$ m$\angle B$.

Since the measure of a central angle equals the measure of its intercepted arc, m$\angle O = 120°$, and so m$\angle A =$ m$\angle B = 30°$. Altitude $\overline{OC}$ is also a median,

so $AC = CB = 6$. Since $\triangle OAC$ is a 30-60-90 right triangle, $OC = \dfrac{6}{\sqrt{3}}$

and $OA = 2\left(\dfrac{6}{\sqrt{3}}\right) = \dfrac{12}{\sqrt{3}}$.

Finally, the area of the circle is $\pi\left(\dfrac{12}{\sqrt{3}}\right)^2 = \dfrac{144}{3}\pi = 48\pi$, so $k = 48$.

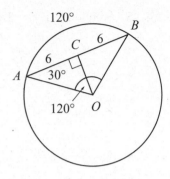

Section 8 Mathematics

Note:

1. See page 32 for an explanation of the symbol $\Rightarrow$ that is used in some answer explanations.

2. A calculator icon, , is placed next to the answer explanation of any question for which a calculator *could* be useful. Almost always, the question can be answered easily without using a calculator.

3. If you are unfamiliar with any of the math facts used in the following answer explanations, refer to Barron's *SAT*, which, in addition to having practice tests, has a full review of all the math you need to know.

1. **B** **Solution 1.** The sum of the measures of the two acute angles in any right triangle is 90°. So, $a + 37 = 90$, and $a = 53$.

   Solution 2: The sum of the measures of the three angles in any triangle is 180°. So $a + 37 + 90 = 180 \Rightarrow a + 127 = 180$, and so $a = 53$.

2. **C** **Solution 1.** The regular price for 6 boxes of corn flakes is $6 \times \$2.75 = \$16.50$. So the customer saves $30\%(\$16.50) = 0.3 \times \$16.50 = \$4.95$.

   Solution 2. On each box, the customer saves $30\%(\$2.75) = 0.3 \times \$2.75 = \$0.825$. So on 6 boxes, she saves $6 \times (\$0.825) = \$4.95$.

3. **C** Write the numbers in each list in increasing order.

   List I: 48, 50, 50, 72, 86, 90
   List II: 28, 48, 72, 72, 78, 80, 91

   The median of the numbers in List II is 72, the middle number.
   The median of the numbers in List I is 61, the average of 50 and 72, the two middle numbers.
   So the difference between the two medians is $72 - 61 = 11$.

4. **C** The set $\{1, 2, 3, \ldots, 49, 50\}$ contains 50 integers, 25 of which are odd and 25 of which are even. Each of the 25 even integers is 1 more than the odd integer that precedes it. So the sum of the 25 even integers is 25 more than the sum of the 25 odd integers.

5. **E** Let $PQ = s$. Then, since all the small squares are the same size, $AB = 3s$, $BC = 2s$, and the perimeter of rectangle $ABCD$ is $10s$. So $10s = 1$, and $s = \dfrac{1}{10}$. Since the perimeter of square $PQRS$ is $4s$, the perimeter is

   $4 \times \dfrac{1}{10} = \dfrac{4}{10} = \dfrac{2}{5}$.

6. **D** If there were exactly twice as many girls as boys in the chorus, then the average GPA would be the weighted average:

$$\frac{2(3.5)+1(3.0)}{3} = \frac{10}{3} = 3.33$$

Since there are more than twice as many girls than boys, the average must be more than 3.33. I is false. Any number greater than 3.33 but less than 3.5 is possible. For example, if there were 9 girls and 1 boy in the chorus, the average would be

$$\frac{9(3.5)+1(3.0)}{10} = \frac{34.5}{10} = 3.45$$

II and III are true.

7. **A** **Solution 1.** Sketch the two triangles, noting that $\triangle ABC$ is isosceles and $\triangle PQR$ is a 3-4-5 right triangle.

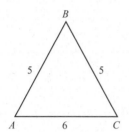 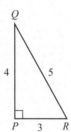 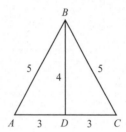

Altitude $\overline{BD}$ in $\triangle ABC$ divides the triangle into two 3-4-5 right triangles.
So the area of $\triangle ABC$ is twice the area of $\triangle PQR$, and the ratio of their areas is 2:1.

Solution 2. Calculate the area of the two triangles. From the diagrams above, we see that the area of $\triangle PQR$ is $\frac{1}{2}(3)(4)=6$, and the area of $\triangle ABC$ is $\frac{1}{2}(6)(4)=12$.

8. **A** **Solution 1.** If the remainder when n is divided by 17 is 10, then n is 10 more than a multiple of 17, which means that for some positive integer q: $n = 17q + 10$.
Therefore, $n + 10 = 17q + 20 = 17q + 17 + 3 = 17(q + 1) + 3$, and so $n + 10$ is 3 more than a multiple of 17.

Solution 2. Choose a small value for n that is 10 more than a multiple of 17, say $n = 27$.
Then $n + 10 = 37$, and $37 = 2 \times 17 + 3$.

Note: Even if you don't remember how to do remainder problems, the remainder, when you divide by 17, must be less than 17, so eliminate choices D and E and guess.

9. **D** If $5 ❂ x = 10 ❂ x$, then $5x - (5 + x) = 10x - (10 + x)$. Therefore,

$$5x - 5 - x = 10x - 10 - x \Rightarrow 4x - 5 = 9x - 10$$

So, $5x = 5$, and $x = 1$.

10. **B** If $y ❂ y = y$, then $yy - (y + y) = y$. So, $y^2 - 2y = y$. Therefore,

$$y^2 - 3y = 0 \Rightarrow y(y - 3) = 0 \Rightarrow y = 0 \text{ or } y = 3$$

So the equation has two solutions, one of which is positive.

11. **E** **Solution 1.** $f(x) = x^2 + 1$ means that $f(\text{anything}) = (\text{that thing})^2 + 1$.
So, $f(x^2 + 1) = (x^2 + 1)^2 + 1 = x^4 + 2x^2 + 1 + 1 = x^4 + 2x^2 + 2$.

Solution 2. Pick a simple number for x, say $x = 1$. Then

$$f(x^2 + 1) = f(1^2 + 1) = f(2) = 2^2 + 1 = 5$$

Which of the answer choices is equal to 5 when $x = 1$? Only choice (E):

$$1^4 + 2(1)^2 + 2 = 1 + 2 + 2 = 5.$$

12. **D** Assume that there were x students in the lobby. Then the number of students sent to the gym was $\frac{1}{3}x$ and twice that many, $\frac{2}{3}x$, remained. The number of students sent to the cafeteria was $\frac{1}{3}\left(\frac{2}{3}x\right) = \frac{2}{9}x$, and twice that many, $\frac{4}{9}x$, still remained. Finally, $\frac{1}{3}\left(\frac{4}{9}x\right) = \frac{4}{27}x$ students were sent to the auditorium. Since $\frac{4}{27}x$ must be a whole number, x must be divisible by 27. Of the five choices, only choice (D), 207, is not divisible by 27.

13. **B** The sum of the measures of the five interior angles of a pentagon is $(5 - 2) \times 180° = 3 \times 180° = 540°$.

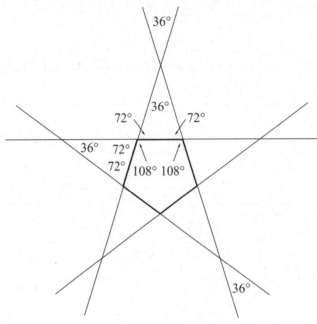

Since the pentagon is regular, the measure of each of its five interior angles is $\frac{540°}{5} = 108°$, and the measure of each of its exterior angles is $180° - 108° = 72°$. So each of the five triangles is isosceles with two base angles of 72°. So each triangle has a vertex angle of $180° - (72° + 72°) = 36°$. Therefore, each of the five marked angles also measures 36°, and so their sum is $5 \times 36° = 180°$.

14. **E** The obvious way to attack this problem is algebraically. However, the easier solution is to avoid the algebra.

Solution 1 (the algebraic way): If the smallest of the odd integers is n,

then $n + (n + 2) + (n + 4) + (n + 6) + (n + 8) = S \Rightarrow 5n + 20 = S$. So $n = \dfrac{S - 20}{5}$.

The tenth number in the set is $(n + 18)$, and $n + 18 = \dfrac{S - 20}{5} + \dfrac{90}{5} = \dfrac{S + 70}{5}$.

Solution 2 (an easier way): If S is the sum of the first five numbers, then $\dfrac{S}{5}$ is their average. But the average of five consecutive odd integers is the middle one, namely the third one. The tenth number in the set is 14 more than the third one: $\dfrac{S}{5} + 14 = \dfrac{S}{5} + \dfrac{70}{5} = \dfrac{S + 70}{5}$.

Solution 3 (the easiest way): Pick 10 consecutive odd integers, say 1, 3, 5, 7, 9, 11, 13, 15, 17, and 19. The sum, S, of the first five integers is 25. Only choice (E), $\dfrac{S + 70}{5}$, is equal to 19 when $S = 25$: $\dfrac{25 + 70}{5} = \dfrac{95}{5} = 19$.

15. **C** Since the difference between two odd numbers is even, in order for $p - question$ to be odd, one of them must be even, and the only even prime is 2.
   - Since 7 is a prime, and $7 - 2 = 5$, I is true.
   - Since $p - 2 = 7 \Rightarrow p = 9$, and 9 is not prime, III is false.
   - There are many examples to show that $p - q$ could be 6: $6 = 13 - 7 = 17 - 11 = 19 - 13 = 47 - 41$, etc. So II is true.

16. **D** Let r and R be the radii of the two circles. In the diagram at the right, r and R are the smaller leg and hypotenuse, respectively, of a 30-60-90 right triangle. So $R = 2r$. The area of the small circle is πr^2 and the area of the large circle is $\pi R^2 = \pi (2r)^2 = 4\pi r^2$. So the ratio of their areas is 4:1.

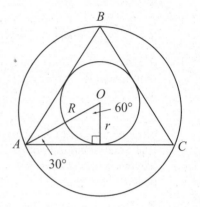

Section 9 Critical Reading

1. **C** *Concurred with* (agreed with) contrasts with the *dissented* (disagreed) in the sentence.

2. **A** A businessman who feels comfortable all over the world can be described as *cosmopolitan* (so sophisticated as to be at home all over the world). (C) *Urbane* (sophisticated) makes some sense, but a person could be urbane but not feel comfortable in many different cities of the world.

3. **D** Because the sentence says that the teacher noticed a lack of something in his students' writing and as a result "abandoned one that encouraged creativity," (B) *originality* and (D) *spontaneity* are both good choices. However, (B) *continued with* makes no sense, whereas (D) *adopted* makes good sense because the teacher changed to a new approach.

4. **D** (A) *Foretell* and (D) *prognosticate* (predict based on present indicators) both make sense because of the phrase "the future course of a person's illness." However, (D) is a better choice than (A) because it makes sense that *methodical* (systematic) observation was necessary to create this record, whereas it makes little sense to describe observation as *prescient* (showing foresight).

5. **C** The phrase "in themselves" in the sentence signals that the best word to describe such a person's interest in language is an *intrinsic* (relating to the essential nature of a thing) one.

6. **A** *Policy* is the appropriate word to refer to "apartheid," which was an officially sanctioned practice. The word *but* signals that although Africans "possessed specified rights" in an assigned area, these rights were severely *circumscribed* (limited) elsewhere in the country.

7. **C** The word "aesthetic" means *concerning the appreciation of beauty or good taste*. In context, it refers to what is regarded as worthwhile aesthetically in the arts and literature. The word "trends" refers to changes in what is regarded as worthwhile over time (fashions).

8. **B** The word "pedestrian" is used to describe prose. In context it means *ordinary, undistinguished*. The word "flat" (line 14) provides a clue to the meaning of "pedestrian."

9. **A** The author says that writing professionals have made it their business to attract students to their poetry writing programs, and that in so doing have assessed the value of poetry more on the basis of "practical concerns" (line 9) than on its aesthetic merit. It is reasonable to infer from this that quite a few of these writing program professionals care more about making their programs popular than they do about encouraging the production of good poetry.

10. **D** In lines 13–16 ("Most obvious is . . . the real thing.") the author discusses the phenomenon of poetry becoming more like prose. The "real thing" refers to writing that has not lost the essential character of poetry—that is, *poetry*.

11. **C** In lines 30–35 ("If the profusion . . . thereby losing significance") the author expresses his dislike for prose poetry. Using the informal expression "dished up" helps him to express this dislike colorfully.

12. **A** In lines 35–36 the author refers to the "'poem' part of the equation." From this we can infer that to create a prose poem it is necessary to add poetic elements to prose elements. (Prose elements + poetic elements = prose poem.)

13. **C** In lines 42–43 ("Poe and Baudelaire . . . a century later") the author says that Poe and Baudelaire wrote prose poems "more consciously" than Blake and Smart before them. This suggests that the author is saying that Blake and Smart did not consciously decide to write work that would come to be called prose poetry; rather, they wrote in this style because it was one of a number of forms they used in the course of composing their poems.

14. **B** The author makes the comment in lines 53–56 immediately after citing Peter Johnson, who says, "I am not even sure what my criteria [for deciding what a prose poem is] are, anymore" (lines 52–53) Thus, we can infer that the author is being sarcastic in saying that one graduate writing program understands the genre well enough to offer an entire course in it. Also, in the paragraph after this comment, the author says that the definition of the genre of prose poetry is still very controversial.

15. **C** "The jury is still out" is an informal expression that means an issue has not yet been decided. In context, it refers to the fact that scholars and poets are still in the process of deciding the definition of "prose poem."

16. **A** In lines 59–62 ("Others concede that . . . short story writer") the author says that some critics believe that it is difficult to exclude "the heightened prose of many a novelist and short story writer" from the genre of prose poetry. Since the definition of prose poetry is being discussed, it can be inferred that "heightened prose" refers to prose that has characteristics of poetry.

17. **D** Throughout the passage the author describes distinctions between poetry and prose. In lines 35–39 ("The 'poem' part . . . figures of speech") he says that a prose poem is made poetic by the use of poetic devices such as rhythm and metaphor. In lines 91–95 ("for it has . . . making poetry musical") he mentions the importance of music in even free and open verse. In lines 97–99 ("Howe's piece lacks . . . prose-poem equation") he stresses that rhythm and metaphor are essential to poetry.

18. **A** In the paragraph immediately preceding the one in which he cites the two excerpts from "Doubt," the author says that the term prose poem leads one to expect a work designated as such to be comprised of "a combination of and tension between prose and poetic elements" (lines 63–64), but that "these expectations aren't always met" (lines 65–66) The sentence "Examples abound" (line 67) signals that the two excerpts from "Doubt" are examples in which prose poetry does not meet these expectations.

19. **E** In the final paragraph of the passage the author says that the increasing "prosification" of poetry means that students planning to take courses in the writing of poetry need not be concerned with any of the devices of the "standard" poet. This "prosification," says the author, changes the definition of poetry so that it can be written by people with less talent than the talent needed to write poetry that is not prose-like.

Section 10 Writing

1. **B** Subject–verb agreement. The subject *each* is singular, so *are* should be changed to the singular *is*.

2. **D** This corrects the idiom error in the given sentence by deleting the word *the* before the word *state* and replacing it with the word *what*.

3. **E** This corrects the tense error in the given sentence by changing the past perfect *had never enrolled* to the present perfect *has never enrolled*. The independent clause beginning with "He" has the verb *watches*, which is in the present tense and states a generalization about what Bob does. The present perfect tense makes good sense because it describes Bob's activities in the past and in the present, and suggests that they will be the same in the future.

4. **D** This corrects the grammar error in the given sentence by changing *stressing* to the infinitive phrase *to stress*, which modifies *important*.

5. **D** Faulty comparison. *John McEnroe* cannot be compared to *play*. This corrects the error by comparing John McEnroe to *any other player*.

6. **C** The given sentence contains an idiom error. Choice (C) corrects the error.

7. **D** The given sentence is not grammatically correct. Choice (D) creates a grammatical sentence that makes good sense. The present perfect *have been made* is a good choice in this sentence because it makes sense that Hardy's novels were made into films in the past and that this process is likely to continue.

8. **C** There is an unnecessary shift in the given sentence, resulting in faulty parallelism. The word *making* is a gerund and the object of a prepositional phrase (*of making thousands of small decisions*) referring to *process*. By continuing this structure, *hoping* becomes the second object of the prepositional phrase, thus maintaining parallelism.

9. **E** The given sentence is not grammatical because the part of the sentence after the semicolon is not an independent clause. Rather, it is a participial phrase, which cannot be linked to a clause by a semicolon. This corrects the error because a comma can link an independent clause and a participial phrase.

10. **A** The sentence is clear and grammatical. The colon is used correctly: The part of the sentence after the colon explains the point made in the first part of the sentence.

11. **A** The given sentence is clear and grammatical.

12. **A** This is a clear and grammatical sentence.

13. **E** The given sentence is grammatical but awkward. Placing the phrase "as a contrast to" at the beginning of the sentence helps make clear that Trollope contrasts the kindness of the farmer with the deviousness and self-interest of the clergy.

14. **E** The given sentence is grammatical, but it does not have correct parallel structure because the second part of the sentence is unnecessarily cast in the active voice rather than in the passive voice. Choice (E) maintains the passive structure used in the first part of the sentence.

Answer Sheet—Practice Test 2

Section 1 ESSAY

Essay (continued)

Practice Test 2

Remove answer sheet by cutting on dotted line

If a section has fewer questions than answer spaces, leave the extra spaces blank.

Section 2

1 Ⓐ Ⓑ Ⓒ Ⓓ Ⓔ
2 Ⓐ Ⓑ Ⓒ Ⓓ Ⓔ
3 Ⓐ Ⓑ Ⓒ Ⓓ Ⓔ
4 Ⓐ Ⓑ Ⓒ Ⓓ Ⓔ
5 Ⓐ Ⓑ Ⓒ Ⓓ Ⓔ
6 Ⓐ Ⓑ Ⓒ Ⓓ Ⓔ
7 Ⓐ Ⓑ Ⓒ Ⓓ Ⓔ
8 Ⓐ Ⓑ Ⓒ Ⓓ Ⓔ
9 Ⓐ Ⓑ Ⓒ Ⓓ Ⓔ
10 Ⓐ Ⓑ Ⓒ Ⓓ Ⓔ
11 Ⓐ Ⓑ Ⓒ Ⓓ Ⓔ
12 Ⓐ Ⓑ Ⓒ Ⓓ Ⓔ
13 Ⓐ Ⓑ Ⓒ Ⓓ Ⓔ
14 Ⓐ Ⓑ Ⓒ Ⓓ Ⓔ
15 Ⓐ Ⓑ Ⓒ Ⓓ Ⓔ
16 Ⓐ Ⓑ Ⓒ Ⓓ Ⓔ
17 Ⓐ Ⓑ Ⓒ Ⓓ Ⓔ
18 Ⓐ Ⓑ Ⓒ Ⓓ Ⓔ
19 Ⓐ Ⓑ Ⓒ Ⓓ Ⓔ
20 Ⓐ Ⓑ Ⓒ Ⓓ Ⓔ
21 Ⓐ Ⓑ Ⓒ Ⓓ Ⓔ
22 Ⓐ Ⓑ Ⓒ Ⓓ Ⓔ
23 Ⓐ Ⓑ Ⓒ Ⓓ Ⓔ
24 Ⓐ Ⓑ Ⓒ Ⓓ Ⓔ
25 Ⓐ Ⓑ Ⓒ Ⓓ Ⓔ
26 Ⓐ Ⓑ Ⓒ Ⓓ Ⓔ
27 Ⓐ Ⓑ Ⓒ Ⓓ Ⓔ
28 Ⓐ Ⓑ Ⓒ Ⓓ Ⓔ
29 Ⓐ Ⓑ Ⓒ Ⓓ Ⓔ
30 Ⓐ Ⓑ Ⓒ Ⓓ Ⓔ
31 Ⓐ Ⓑ Ⓒ Ⓓ Ⓔ
32 Ⓐ Ⓑ Ⓒ Ⓓ Ⓔ
33 Ⓐ Ⓑ Ⓒ Ⓓ Ⓔ
34 Ⓐ Ⓑ Ⓒ Ⓓ Ⓔ
35 Ⓐ Ⓑ Ⓒ Ⓓ Ⓔ

Section 4

1 Ⓐ Ⓑ Ⓒ Ⓓ Ⓔ
2 Ⓐ Ⓑ Ⓒ Ⓓ Ⓔ
3 Ⓐ Ⓑ Ⓒ Ⓓ Ⓔ
4 Ⓐ Ⓑ Ⓒ Ⓓ Ⓔ
5 Ⓐ Ⓑ Ⓒ Ⓓ Ⓔ
6 Ⓐ Ⓑ Ⓒ Ⓓ Ⓔ
7 Ⓐ Ⓑ Ⓒ Ⓓ Ⓔ
8 Ⓐ Ⓑ Ⓒ Ⓓ Ⓔ
9 Ⓐ Ⓑ Ⓒ Ⓓ Ⓔ
10 Ⓐ Ⓑ Ⓒ Ⓓ Ⓔ
11 Ⓐ Ⓑ Ⓒ Ⓓ Ⓔ
12 Ⓐ Ⓑ Ⓒ Ⓓ Ⓔ
13 Ⓐ Ⓑ Ⓒ Ⓓ Ⓔ
14 Ⓐ Ⓑ Ⓒ Ⓓ Ⓔ
15 Ⓐ Ⓑ Ⓒ Ⓓ Ⓔ
16 Ⓐ Ⓑ Ⓒ Ⓓ Ⓔ
17 Ⓐ Ⓑ Ⓒ Ⓓ Ⓔ
18 Ⓐ Ⓑ Ⓒ Ⓓ Ⓔ
19 Ⓐ Ⓑ Ⓒ Ⓓ Ⓔ
20 Ⓐ Ⓑ Ⓒ Ⓓ Ⓔ
21 Ⓐ Ⓑ Ⓒ Ⓓ Ⓔ
22 Ⓐ Ⓑ Ⓒ Ⓓ Ⓔ
23 Ⓐ Ⓑ Ⓒ Ⓓ Ⓔ
24 Ⓐ Ⓑ Ⓒ Ⓓ Ⓔ
25 Ⓐ Ⓑ Ⓒ Ⓓ Ⓔ
26 Ⓐ Ⓑ Ⓒ Ⓓ Ⓔ
27 Ⓐ Ⓑ Ⓒ Ⓓ Ⓔ
28 Ⓐ Ⓑ Ⓒ Ⓓ Ⓔ
29 Ⓐ Ⓑ Ⓒ Ⓓ Ⓔ
30 Ⓐ Ⓑ Ⓒ Ⓓ Ⓔ
31 Ⓐ Ⓑ Ⓒ Ⓓ Ⓔ
32 Ⓐ Ⓑ Ⓒ Ⓓ Ⓔ
33 Ⓐ Ⓑ Ⓒ Ⓓ Ⓔ
34 Ⓐ Ⓑ Ⓒ Ⓓ Ⓔ
35 Ⓐ Ⓑ Ⓒ Ⓓ Ⓔ

Section 5

1 Ⓐ Ⓑ Ⓒ Ⓓ Ⓔ
2 Ⓐ Ⓑ Ⓒ Ⓓ Ⓔ
3 Ⓐ Ⓑ Ⓒ Ⓓ Ⓔ
4 Ⓐ Ⓑ Ⓒ Ⓓ Ⓔ
5 Ⓐ Ⓑ Ⓒ Ⓓ Ⓔ
6 Ⓐ Ⓑ Ⓒ Ⓓ Ⓔ
7 Ⓐ Ⓑ Ⓒ Ⓓ Ⓔ
8 Ⓐ Ⓑ Ⓒ Ⓓ Ⓔ

9, 10, 11, 12, 13, 14, 15, 16, 17, 18 (each grid-in box):

	⊘	⊘	
⊙	⊙	⊙	⊙
	⓪	⓪	⓪
①	①	①	①
②	②	②	②
③	③	③	③
④	④	④	④
⑤	⑤	⑤	⑤
⑥	⑥	⑥	⑥
⑦	⑦	⑦	⑦
⑧	⑧	⑧	⑧
⑨	⑨	⑨	⑨

Practice Test 2

Section 6

1 Ⓐ Ⓑ Ⓒ Ⓓ Ⓔ	8 Ⓐ Ⓑ Ⓒ Ⓓ Ⓔ	15 Ⓐ Ⓑ Ⓒ Ⓓ Ⓔ	22 Ⓐ Ⓑ Ⓒ Ⓓ Ⓔ	29 Ⓐ Ⓑ Ⓒ Ⓓ Ⓔ
2 Ⓐ Ⓑ Ⓒ Ⓓ Ⓔ	9 Ⓐ Ⓑ Ⓒ Ⓓ Ⓔ	16 Ⓐ Ⓑ Ⓒ Ⓓ Ⓔ	23 Ⓐ Ⓑ Ⓒ Ⓓ Ⓔ	30 Ⓐ Ⓑ Ⓒ Ⓓ Ⓔ
3 Ⓐ Ⓑ Ⓒ Ⓓ Ⓔ	10 Ⓐ Ⓑ Ⓒ Ⓓ Ⓔ	17 Ⓐ Ⓑ Ⓒ Ⓓ Ⓔ	24 Ⓐ Ⓑ Ⓒ Ⓓ Ⓔ	31 Ⓐ Ⓑ Ⓒ Ⓓ Ⓔ
4 Ⓐ Ⓑ Ⓒ Ⓓ Ⓔ	11 Ⓐ Ⓑ Ⓒ Ⓓ Ⓔ	18 Ⓐ Ⓑ Ⓒ Ⓓ Ⓔ	25 Ⓐ Ⓑ Ⓒ Ⓓ Ⓔ	32 Ⓐ Ⓑ Ⓒ Ⓓ Ⓔ
5 Ⓐ Ⓑ Ⓒ Ⓓ Ⓔ	12 Ⓐ Ⓑ Ⓒ Ⓓ Ⓔ	19 Ⓐ Ⓑ Ⓒ Ⓓ Ⓔ	26 Ⓐ Ⓑ Ⓒ Ⓓ Ⓔ	33 Ⓐ Ⓑ Ⓒ Ⓓ Ⓔ
6 Ⓐ Ⓑ Ⓒ Ⓓ Ⓔ	13 Ⓐ Ⓑ Ⓒ Ⓓ Ⓔ	20 Ⓐ Ⓑ Ⓒ Ⓓ Ⓔ	27 Ⓐ Ⓑ Ⓒ Ⓓ Ⓔ	34 Ⓐ Ⓑ Ⓒ Ⓓ Ⓔ
7 Ⓐ Ⓑ Ⓒ Ⓓ Ⓔ	14 Ⓐ Ⓑ Ⓒ Ⓓ Ⓔ	21 Ⓐ Ⓑ Ⓒ Ⓓ Ⓔ	28 Ⓐ Ⓑ Ⓒ Ⓓ Ⓔ	35 Ⓐ Ⓑ Ⓒ Ⓓ Ⓔ

Section 7

1 Ⓐ Ⓑ Ⓒ Ⓓ Ⓔ	8 Ⓐ Ⓑ Ⓒ Ⓓ Ⓔ	15 Ⓐ Ⓑ Ⓒ Ⓓ Ⓔ	22 Ⓐ Ⓑ Ⓒ Ⓓ Ⓔ	29 Ⓐ Ⓑ Ⓒ Ⓓ Ⓔ
2 Ⓐ Ⓑ Ⓒ Ⓓ Ⓔ	9 Ⓐ Ⓑ Ⓒ Ⓓ Ⓔ	16 Ⓐ Ⓑ Ⓒ Ⓓ Ⓔ	23 Ⓐ Ⓑ Ⓒ Ⓓ Ⓔ	30 Ⓐ Ⓑ Ⓒ Ⓓ Ⓔ
3 Ⓐ Ⓑ Ⓒ Ⓓ Ⓔ	10 Ⓐ Ⓑ Ⓒ Ⓓ Ⓔ	17 Ⓐ Ⓑ Ⓒ Ⓓ Ⓔ	24 Ⓐ Ⓑ Ⓒ Ⓓ Ⓔ	31 Ⓐ Ⓑ Ⓒ Ⓓ Ⓔ
4 Ⓐ Ⓑ Ⓒ Ⓓ Ⓔ	11 Ⓐ Ⓑ Ⓒ Ⓓ Ⓔ	18 Ⓐ Ⓑ Ⓒ Ⓓ Ⓔ	25 Ⓐ Ⓑ Ⓒ Ⓓ Ⓔ	32 Ⓐ Ⓑ Ⓒ Ⓓ Ⓔ
5 Ⓐ Ⓑ Ⓒ Ⓓ Ⓔ	12 Ⓐ Ⓑ Ⓒ Ⓓ Ⓔ	19 Ⓐ Ⓑ Ⓒ Ⓓ Ⓔ	26 Ⓐ Ⓑ Ⓒ Ⓓ Ⓔ	33 Ⓐ Ⓑ Ⓒ Ⓓ Ⓔ
6 Ⓐ Ⓑ Ⓒ Ⓓ Ⓔ	13 Ⓐ Ⓑ Ⓒ Ⓓ Ⓔ	20 Ⓐ Ⓑ Ⓒ Ⓓ Ⓔ	27 Ⓐ Ⓑ Ⓒ Ⓓ Ⓔ	34 Ⓐ Ⓑ Ⓒ Ⓓ Ⓔ
7 Ⓐ Ⓑ Ⓒ Ⓓ Ⓔ	14 Ⓐ Ⓑ Ⓒ Ⓓ Ⓔ	21 Ⓐ Ⓑ Ⓒ Ⓓ Ⓔ	28 Ⓐ Ⓑ Ⓒ Ⓓ Ⓔ	35 Ⓐ Ⓑ Ⓒ Ⓓ Ⓔ

Section 8

1 Ⓐ Ⓑ Ⓒ Ⓓ Ⓔ	5 Ⓐ Ⓑ Ⓒ Ⓓ Ⓔ	9 Ⓐ Ⓑ Ⓒ Ⓓ Ⓔ	13 Ⓐ Ⓑ Ⓒ Ⓓ Ⓔ	17 Ⓐ Ⓑ Ⓒ Ⓓ Ⓔ
2 Ⓐ Ⓑ Ⓒ Ⓓ Ⓔ	6 Ⓐ Ⓑ Ⓒ Ⓓ Ⓔ	10 Ⓐ Ⓑ Ⓒ Ⓓ Ⓔ	14 Ⓐ Ⓑ Ⓒ Ⓓ Ⓔ	18 Ⓐ Ⓑ Ⓒ Ⓓ Ⓔ
3 Ⓐ Ⓑ Ⓒ Ⓓ Ⓔ	7 Ⓐ Ⓑ Ⓒ Ⓓ Ⓔ	11 Ⓐ Ⓑ Ⓒ Ⓓ Ⓔ	15 Ⓐ Ⓑ Ⓒ Ⓓ Ⓔ	19 Ⓐ Ⓑ Ⓒ Ⓓ Ⓔ
4 Ⓐ Ⓑ Ⓒ Ⓓ Ⓔ	8 Ⓐ Ⓑ Ⓒ Ⓓ Ⓔ	12 Ⓐ Ⓑ Ⓒ Ⓓ Ⓔ	16 Ⓐ Ⓑ Ⓒ Ⓓ Ⓔ	20 Ⓐ Ⓑ Ⓒ Ⓓ Ⓔ

Section 9

1 Ⓐ Ⓑ Ⓒ Ⓓ Ⓔ	5 Ⓐ Ⓑ Ⓒ Ⓓ Ⓔ	9 Ⓐ Ⓑ Ⓒ Ⓓ Ⓔ	13 Ⓐ Ⓑ Ⓒ Ⓓ Ⓔ	17 Ⓐ Ⓑ Ⓒ Ⓓ Ⓔ
2 Ⓐ Ⓑ Ⓒ Ⓓ Ⓔ	6 Ⓐ Ⓑ Ⓒ Ⓓ Ⓔ	10 Ⓐ Ⓑ Ⓒ Ⓓ Ⓔ	14 Ⓐ Ⓑ Ⓒ Ⓓ Ⓔ	18 Ⓐ Ⓑ Ⓒ Ⓓ Ⓔ
3 Ⓐ Ⓑ Ⓒ Ⓓ Ⓔ	7 Ⓐ Ⓑ Ⓒ Ⓓ Ⓔ	11 Ⓐ Ⓑ Ⓒ Ⓓ Ⓔ	15 Ⓐ Ⓑ Ⓒ Ⓓ Ⓔ	19 Ⓐ Ⓑ Ⓒ Ⓓ Ⓔ
4 Ⓐ Ⓑ Ⓒ Ⓓ Ⓔ	8 Ⓐ Ⓑ Ⓒ Ⓓ Ⓔ	12 Ⓐ Ⓑ Ⓒ Ⓓ Ⓔ	16 Ⓐ Ⓑ Ⓒ Ⓓ Ⓔ	20 Ⓐ Ⓑ Ⓒ Ⓓ Ⓔ

Section 10

1 Ⓐ Ⓑ Ⓒ Ⓓ Ⓔ	5 Ⓐ Ⓑ Ⓒ Ⓓ Ⓔ	9 Ⓐ Ⓑ Ⓒ Ⓓ Ⓔ	13 Ⓐ Ⓑ Ⓒ Ⓓ Ⓔ	17 Ⓐ Ⓑ Ⓒ Ⓓ Ⓔ
2 Ⓐ Ⓑ Ⓒ Ⓓ Ⓔ	6 Ⓐ Ⓑ Ⓒ Ⓓ Ⓔ	10 Ⓐ Ⓑ Ⓒ Ⓓ Ⓔ	14 Ⓐ Ⓑ Ⓒ Ⓓ Ⓔ	18 Ⓐ Ⓑ Ⓒ Ⓓ Ⓔ
3 Ⓐ Ⓑ Ⓒ Ⓓ Ⓔ	7 Ⓐ Ⓑ Ⓒ Ⓓ Ⓔ	11 Ⓐ Ⓑ Ⓒ Ⓓ Ⓔ	15 Ⓐ Ⓑ Ⓒ Ⓓ Ⓔ	19 Ⓐ Ⓑ Ⓒ Ⓓ Ⓔ
4 Ⓐ Ⓑ Ⓒ Ⓓ Ⓔ	8 Ⓐ Ⓑ Ⓒ Ⓓ Ⓔ	12 Ⓐ Ⓑ Ⓒ Ⓓ Ⓔ	16 Ⓐ Ⓑ Ⓒ Ⓓ Ⓔ	20 Ⓐ Ⓑ Ⓒ Ⓓ Ⓔ

Practice Test 2 1 1 1 1 1 1 1

SECTION 1   Time—25 Minutes   ESSAY

Write your essay on the lines provided on the answer sheet on pages 107–108. Be careful to write legibly. Write on the topic, carefully presenting your point of view. Your essay will be scored on the basis of the ideas it contains and its effectiveness in expressing these ideas. Pay special attention to logic, clarity, and the accurate use of language.

Think about the topic presented in the following excerpt and in the assignment below it.

> *Education has produced a vast population able to read but unable to distinguish what is worth reading.*
>
> —*G.M. Trevelyan, English Social History*

ASSIGNMENT: Is it true that most people today do not know the difference between something that is worthwhile to read and something that is not? Plan and write an essay in which you develop your point of view on this issue. Support your argument with reasoning and examples from your experience, reading, or observations.

2 2 2 2 2 2 2 2 2 2 2

SECTION **2**

Time—25 Minutes
20 Questions

For each problem in this section determine which of the five choices is correct and blacken the corresponding choice on your answer sheet. You may use any blank space on the page for your work.

Notes:

• You may use a calculator whenever you think it will be helpful.

• Only real numbers are used. No question or answer on this test involves a complex or imaginary number.

• Use the diagrams provided to help you solve the problems. Unless you see the words "Note: Figure not drawn to scale" under a diagram, it has been drawn as accurately as possible. Unless it is stated that a figure is three-dimensional, you may assume it lies in a plane.

• For any function, f, the domain, unless specifically restricted, is the set of all real numbers for which $f(x)$ is also a real number.

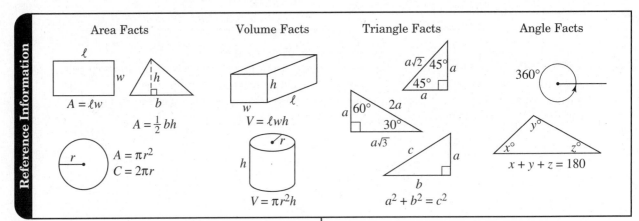

Reference Information

Area Facts

$A = \ell w$

$A = \frac{1}{2} bh$

$A = \pi r^2$
$C = 2\pi r$

Volume Facts

$V = \ell wh$

$V = \pi r^2 h$

Triangle Facts

$a^2 + b^2 = c^2$

Angle Facts

$x + y + z = 180$

1. If $\dfrac{1}{d} + \dfrac{2}{d} + \dfrac{3}{d} + \dfrac{4}{d} = \dfrac{1}{5}$, what is the value of d?

(A) $\dfrac{1}{50}$

(B) $\dfrac{1}{10}$

(C) 2

(D) 10

(E) 50

$(3a + 30)°$

$(4a − 30)°$ $3a°$

Note: Figure not drawn to scale.

2. In the figure above, what is the measure of the smallest angle?

(A) 18°
(B) 24°
(C) 42°
(D) 48°
(E) 54°

GO ON TO THE NEXT PAGE

Practice Test 2

2   2   2   2   2   2   2   2   2   2   2

3. If $x = \dfrac{1}{4}y$ and $y = \dfrac{2}{3}z$, what is z when $x = 7$?

(A) 14
(B) 21
(C) 28
(D) 35
(E) 42

4. How many ordered pairs (m, n) are there such that m and n are both integers and m is the reciprocal of n?

(A) None
(B) 1
(C) 2
(D) 3
(E) More than 3

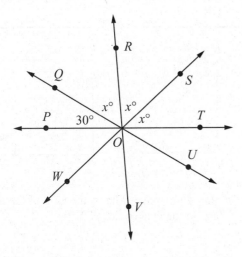

5. In the figure above, four lines intersect at O. What is the measure of $\angle WOU$?

(A) 30°
(B) 60°
(C) 90°
(D) 100°
(E) 150°

6. Consider the infinite sequence

1, 2, 3, 4, 5, 6, 7, 1, 2, 3, 4, 5, 6, 7, . . .

in which the integers from 1 through 7 repeat forever in that order. What is the 188th integer in this sequence?

(A) 6
(B) 5
(C) 4
(D) 3
(E) 2

7. On a certain day in 2011, the exchange rates for the South African ZAR, the Japanese yen, and the Chinese renbini were such that 1 ZAR was equivalent to 11 yen and 66 yen were equivalent to 5 renbini. On that day, how many renbini were equivalent to 18 ZAR?

(A) 10
(B) 12
(C) 15
(D) 16
(E) 20

Questions 8 and 9 refer to the function $A(x)$, defined as follows.

For any positive number x, $A(x)$ is the area of an isosceles right triangle, each of whose legs is x.

8. What is the value of $A\left(\sqrt{2}\right)$?

(A) $2\sqrt{2}$
(B) $4\sqrt{2}$
(C) $\dfrac{1}{2}$
(D) 1
(E) 2

GO ON TO THE NEXT PAGE

Practice Test 2

9. Which of the following is equal to $A(6) + A(8)$?

(A) $A(7)$
(B) $A(10)$
(C) $A(14)$
(D) $A(24)$
(E) $A(48)$

10. The length of rectangle A is 20 percent greater than the length of rectangle B, and the width of rectangle A is 20 percent less than the width of rectangle B. What is the ratio of the area of rectangle A to the area of rectangle B?

(A) 0.80
(B) 0.96
(C) 1.00
(D) 1.04
(E) 1.20

11. If n is a positive integer and the remainder when n is divided by 2 is 1, which of the following could be the remainder when n is divided by 4?

I. 1
II. 2
III. 3

(A) I only
(B) II only
(C) III only
(D) I and III only
(E) I, II, and III

12. If a, b, and c are three consecutive even integers with $a < b < c$, and if $a + b + c = S$, which of the following expressions is equal to c?

(A) $\dfrac{S-6}{3}$
(B) $\dfrac{S-3}{3}$
(C) $\dfrac{S}{3}$
(D) $\dfrac{S+3}{3}$
(E) $\dfrac{S+6}{3}$

13. If 40 percent of a is equal to 8 percent of b, then b is what percent of a?

(A)   5%
(B)   40%
(C)   50%
(D) 400%
(E) 500%

14. If x^2 varies inversely with y, and $x = \dfrac{1}{2}$ when $y = 8$, what is the value of x when $y = 32$?

(A) $\dfrac{1}{4}$
(B) $\dfrac{1}{2}$
(C) 1
(D) 2
(E) 4

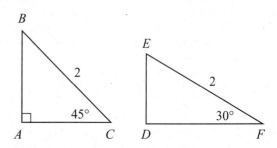

15. In the figure above, what is the ratio of the area of $\triangle ABC$ to the area of $\triangle DEF$?

(A) $\dfrac{2}{\sqrt{2}}$
(B) $\dfrac{\sqrt{2}}{2}$
(C) $\dfrac{2}{\sqrt{3}}$
(D) $\dfrac{\sqrt{3}}{2}$
(E) $\dfrac{\sqrt{2}}{\sqrt{3}}$

GO ON TO THE NEXT PAGE

Practice Test 2

16. A palindrome is a positive integer, such as 77 or 353 or 74247, that reads the same from right to left as it does from left to right. If *A*, *B*, and *C* represent the number of palindromes between 100 and 1,000, between 1,000 and 10,000, and between 10,000 and 100,000, respectively, which of the following statements are true?

    I. $A < B < C$
    II. $B = 10A$
    III. $C = 10B$

    (A) I only
    (B) II only
    (C) III only
    (D) I and III only
    (E) I, II, and III

17. Delphine rode her bike on the bike path from Florence to Amherst at an average rate of 18 miles per hour. She then spent an hour and 20 minutes in Amherst before heading back along the same path. On the ride back to Florence she rode at an average rate of 12 miles per hour. If the total time of her outing, including the time she spent in Amherst, was 3 hours, what is the length, in miles, of the bike path between the two towns?

    (A) 8
    (B) 12
    (C) 16
    (D) 18
    (E) 20

18. Line ℓ, drawn in the *xy*-coordinate plane, has a slope of 2. If line *k* is the reflection of line ℓ across the *y*-axis, which of the following must be true?

    I. The *y*-intercepts of ℓ and *k* are the same
    II. The *x*-intercepts of ℓ and *k* are the same
    III. The slope of line *k* is $-\dfrac{1}{2}$

    (A) I only
    (B) II only
    (C) III only
    (D) I and III only
    (E) II and III only

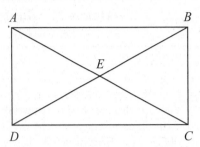

Note: Figure not drawn to scale.

19. In the figure above, the diagonals of rectangle *ABCD* intersect at *E*. $\triangle AED$ is an equilateral triangle whose perimeter is 6 inches. If the perimeter of the rectangle is *P* inches, and the area of the rectangle is *A* square inches, what is the value of $P - A$?

    (A) 2
    (B) 4
    (C) $\sqrt{3}$
    (D) $2\sqrt{3}$
    (E) $4\sqrt{3}$

8	*a*	*b*
c	*d*	7
4	*e*	*f*

20. In the square above, each of the integers from 1 to 9 appears exactly once in the nine small squares, and the sum of the three numbers in each row, each column, and the two diagonals is the same. What is the value of *a*?

    (A) 9
    (B) 6
    (C) 5
    (D) 3
    (E) 1

STOP

4 | 4 4 4 4 4 4 4 4 4 4 | **4**

SECTION **4** | **Time—25 Minutes**
25 Questions | **Choose the best answer to each of the following questions in this section. Then blacken the appropriate space on your answer sheet.**

Each of the following sentences contains one or two blanks, indicating that a word or set of words has been omitted. Beneath each sentence there are five answer choices labeled A to E from which you must select the word or set of words that best fits the meaning of the sentence as a whole.

Example:

Records of colonization can be found as far back as the Phoenicians, but colonization became a major force in world history only when European countries began, in the fifteenth century, to make ---- Asia, the Americas, and Africa.

(A) queries about   (B) incursions into
  (C) tirades against   (D) enemies in
    (E) amends for

1. The Austrian scientist Konrad Lorenz was a pioneer in the study of animal behavior under natural conditions, ---- by human interaction with the subjects.

(A) hampered   (B) untainted
  (C) recapitulated   (D) rejuvenated
    (E) assisted

2. To be ---- about something is to take the position that there is neither enough evidence to believe it nor enough evidence to disbelieve it.

(A) capricious   (B) truthful   (C) cynical
  (D) skeptical   (E) cryptic

3. The mayor prohibited the use of teargas by police against the rioters, saying its use would not help but only ---- the already chaotic situation.

(A) exacerbate   (B) coalesce   (C) remedy
  (D) assuage   (E) instigate

4. Although it is ---- to some people, slang often expresses ideas with great directness, avoiding the circumlocution of more ---- language.

(A) annoying . . pithy
(B) reprehensible . . disgusting
(C) fortuitous . . usual
(D) horrible . . extemporaneous
(E) loathsome . . refined

5. Because of Western preeminence in many fields, such as media, globalization has resulted in the ---- of Western culture increasingly becoming the ---- in many non-western countries.

(A) spread . . news
(B) ascendancy . . rule
(C) creed . . idiosyncrasy
(D) mores . . norm
(E) criticism . . tradition

6. The engineer's view is that the ---- of technology is to construct devices that improve human life.

(A) design   (B) ramification
  (C) raison d'être   (D) prognosis
    (E) proclivity

GO ON TO THE NEXT PAGE

4   4 4 4 4 4 4 4 4 4 4   4

7. ---- is any expression that is substituted for a more common expression on the grounds that it bears more ---- connotations.

   (A) A witticism . . relevant
   (B) A solecism . . benign
   (C) A euphemism . . positive
   (D) A panegyric . . favorable
   (E) A metaphor . . fatuous

8. The book argues that in the 1970s some environmental groups made ---- about population increase and resource scarcity ---- unwarranted assumptions, such as that in the future natural resources would be discovered and utilized at the same rate as they had been in the past.

   (A) estimates . . precluded by
   (B) predictions . . mitigated by
   (C) recommendations . . adumbrated by
   (D) extrapolations . . predicated on
   (E) inquiries . . supported by

GO ON TO THE NEXT PAGE

4   4 4 4 4 4 4 4 4 4 4   **4**

Below are passages followed by questions on them. Questions on a pair of related passages may be about the relationship between the two passages. For each question, select the best answer based on what is stated or implied in the passage (or passages).

Questions 9–12 are based on the following passages.

Passage 1

During the last two decades of the twentieth century, some exponents of Afrocentrism attracted widespread attention with vigorous
Line arguments that Africa and African cultures were
(5) the original sources of world civilization, that peoples of African descent have a unique "humanistic, spiritualistic value system" unmatched by any other racial group, that European cultural and economic systems are
(10) inherently exploitative, and that blacks' high melanin content made them "inherently more creative." Opponents of the more extreme tenets of Afrocentrism charged that its advocates lacked scholarly proof of their claims or based them on
(15) distortions of historical research and that many of the arguments of Afrocentrists were implicitly racist, in particular often viciously anti-Semitic. The debate remained unresolved as the scholarly community continued to appropriate new research
(20) concerning the origins of cultures, societies, and races.

Passage 2

Maybe if I had never set foot here, I could celebrate my own blackness, my "African-ness." Then I might feel a part of this place, and
(25) Africa's pain might be my own. But while I know that "Afrocentrism" has become fashionable for many black Americans searching for identity, I know it cannot work for me. I have been here, I have lived here and seen Africa in all
(30) its horror. I know now that I am a stranger here. I am an American, a black American, and I feel no connection to this strange and violent place. You see? I just wrote "black American." I couldn't even bring myself to write "African-American."
(35) It's a phrase that, for me, doesn't roll naturally off the tongue: "African-American." Is that what we really are? Is there anything really "African" left in the descendants of those original slaves who made that torturous journey across the
(40) Atlantic? Are white Americans whose ancestors sailed west across the same ocean as long ago as the slaves still considered "English Americans" or "Dutch Americans"? And haven't the centuries on America's shores erased all those ancient
(45) connections, so that we descendants of Africa and England and Holland and Ireland and China are now simply "Americans"?

9. Which best describes the relationship between Passage 1 and Passage 2?

   (A) Passage 1 proposes various theories explaining the popularity of the concept of Afrocentrism, whereas Passage 2 is a condemnation of Afrocentrism in all its forms.
   (B) Passage 1 analyzes the reasons that views vary so greatly about a concept, whereas Passage 2 presents views about the concept.
   (C) Passage 1 describes the reasons that have led most scholars to reject a concept, and Passage 2 presents the reasons one particular scholar has rejected the concept.
   (D) Passage 1 is concerned mainly to argue for a moderate view of Afrocentrism, whereas Passage 2 is a personal account of the experiences that led one person to reject Afrocentrism.
   (E) Passage 1 presents an objective description of varying views on a concept, whereas Passage 2 gives a subjective view of that concept based on a person's experience.

10. In line 22, "here" most nearly means

   (A) America
   (B) the land where the writer was born
   (C) anywhere in the world where Africans or their descendents live
   (D) Africa
   (E) a perfect world that exists only in the mind

GO ON TO THE NEXT PAGE

11. It is reasonable to infer that if the author of Passage 2 had never visited Africa he

(A) would have begun to question the tenets of "Afrocentrism" discussed in Passage 1

(B) would not have come to regard "Afrocentrism" as the answer to Black Americans' search for identity

(C) would have come over time to identify more strongly with American culture

(D) would identify more strongly with African culture

(E) would have realized that identity is an over-valued concept

12. Opponents of the more extreme beliefs of Afrocentrism referred to in Passage 1 would be most likely to view the account in Passage 2 as

(A) evidence that race is such a vague concept that it is meaningless

(B) showing that the superior spiritual values of Africans are determined entirely by race

(C) evidence that race and culture are not as closely related as the extreme exponents of Afrocentrism believe

(D) evidence that there will always be a few individuals who will betray their true African identity

(E) proof that Africans can be tricked into believing the lies of European culture about them

Questions 13–25 are based on the following passage.

    The village headman, a man of about fifty, sat cross-legged in the centre of the room, close to the coals burning in a hearth that was hollowed
Line out of the floor; he was inspecting my violin.
(5) Among the possessions brought to this mountain village by the two "city youths"—which was how they saw Luo and me—it was the sole item that exuded an air of foreignness, of civilization, and therefore aroused suspicion.
(10)   One of the peasants came forward with an oil lamp to facilitate identification of the strange object. The headman held the violin upright and peered into the black interior of the body, like an officious customs officer searching for drugs.

(15) I noticed three blood spots in his left eye, one large and two small, all the same shade of bright red.
    Raising the violin to eye level, he shook it, as though convinced something would drop out of
(20) the sound-holes. His investigation was so enthusiastic I was afraid the strings would break.
    Just about everyone in the village had come to the house on stilts way up on the mountain to witness the arrival of the city youths. Men,
(25) women and children swarmed inside the cramped room, clung to the windows, jostled each other by the door. When nothing fell out of my violin, the headman held his nose over the soundholes and sniffed long and hard. Several long, bristly
(30) hairs protruding from his left nostril vibrated gently.
    Still no clues.
    He ran his calloused fingertips over one string, then another . . .
(35)   The strange resonance froze the crowd, as if the sound had won some sort of respect.
    "It's a toy," said the headman solemnly.
    This verdict left us speechless. Luo and I exchanged furtive, anxious glances. Things were
(40) not looking good.
    One peasant took the "toy" from the headman's hands, drummed with his fists on its back, then passed it to the next man. For a while my violin circulated through the crowd and we—
(45) two frail, skinny, exhausted and risible city youths—were ignored. We had been tramping across the mountains all day, and our clothes, faces and hair were streaked with mud. We looked like pathetic little reactionary soldiers
(50) from a propaganda film after their capture by a horde of Communist farm workers.
    "A stupid toy," a woman commented hoarsely.
    "No," the village headman corrected her, "a bourgeois toy."
(55)   I felt chilled to the bone despite the fire blazing in the centre of the room.
    "A toy from the city," the headman continued, "go on, burn it!"

GO ON TO THE NEXT PAGE

His command galvanized the crowd. Everyone
(60) started talking at once, shouting and reaching out
to grab the toy for the privilege of throwing it on
the coals.

"Comrade, it's a musical instrument," Luo said
as casually as he could, "and my friend here's a
(65) fine musician. Truly."

The headman called for the violin and looked
it over once more.

Then he held it out to me.

"Forgive me, comrade," I said, embarrassed,
(70) "but I'm not that good."

I saw Luo giving me a surreptitious wink.
Puzzled, I took my violin and set about tuning it.

"What you are about to hear, comrade, is a
Mozart sonata," Luo announced, as coolly as
(75) before.

I was dumbfounded. Had he gone mad? All
music by Mozart or indeed by any other Western
composer had been banned years ago. In my
sodden shoes my feet turned to ice. I shivered as
(80) the cold tightened its grip on me.

"What's a sonata?" the headman asked warily.

"I don't know," I faltered. "It's Western."

"Is it a song?"

"More or less," I replied evasively.

(85) At that instant the glint of the vigilant
Communist reappeared in the headman's eyes,
and his voice turned hostile.

"What's the name of this song of yours?"

"Well, it's like a song, but actually it's a
(90) sonata."

"I'm asking you what it's called!" he snapped,
fixing me with his gaze.

Again I was alarmed by the three spots of
blood in his left eye.

(95) "*Mozart . . .*" I muttered.

"*Mozart* what?"

"*Mozart Is Thinking of Chairman Mao*," Luo
broke in.

The audacity! But it worked: as if he had
(100) heard something miraculous, the headman's
menacing look softened. He crinkled up his eyes
in a wide, beatific smile.

"Mozart thinks of Mao all the time," he said.

"Indeed, all the time," agreed Luo.

(105) As soon as I had tightened my bow there was
a burst of applause, but I was still nervous.
However, as I ran my swollen fingers over the
strings, Mozart's phrases came flooding back to

me like so many faithful friends. The peasants'
(110) faces, so grim a moment before, softened under
the influence of Mozart's limpid music like
parched earth under a shower, and then, in the
dancing light of the oil lamp, they blurred into
one.

(115) I played for some time, Luo lit a cigarette and
smoked quietly, like a man.

This was our first taste of re-education. Luo
was eighteen years old, I was seventeen.

13. The author's description of the village headman,
"like an officious customs officer searching for
drugs," in lines 13–14 depicts the headman as

(A) prying
(B) curious
(C) official
(D) formal
(E) dispassionate

14. Until the narrator plays the violin the villagers
regard it primarily as

(A) a dangerous weapon
(B) a wondrous, almost magical device
(C) something alien
(D) an object used to transport illicit drugs
(E) a traditional Chinese musical instrument

15. What word most accurately describes how the
narrator views the villagers?

(A) Bourgeois
(B) Materialistic
(C) Reactionary
(D) Uncivilized
(E) Independent-minded

16. In line 39, "furtive" most nearly means

(A) surreptitious
(B) hurried
(C) overt
(D) amused
(E) comical

GO ON TO THE NEXT PAGE

17. The narrator says "Things were not looking good." (lines 39–40) because

(A) the headman doesn't understand how delicate the violin is, and so the narrator and Luo are afraid that he might accidentally break it

(B) the headman has discovered the truth about the violin—that it's a toy—and Luo and the narrator are afraid that he will keep it for himself

(C) Luo and the narrator believe that if the villagers are so ignorant that they don't even know what a violin is, they won't be able to appreciate a Mozart sonata played on it

(D) the headman has just concluded that the violin is a toy, and, therefore, something regarded as bourgeois

(E) Luo and the narrator believe that the headman's verdict about the violin suggests that he has total control of the village

18. In line 74, "coolly" most nearly means

(A) stylishly
(B) calmly
(C) nervously
(D) affectedly
(E) resignedly

19. What is the most likely reason that the villagers in the crowd regard burning the violin as a "privilege" (line 61)?

(A) They regard it as an honor to be the person to destroy something that has caused so much confusion in the village.

(B) They believe that the person who destroys the violin will be richly rewarded by the headman.

(C) They see it as an honor to be the person who destroys a symbol of bourgeois decadence.

(D) They believe that the person who destroys the violin will be likely to become the next headman.

(E) They believe that the person who destroys the violin will be rewarded in the afterlife.

20. What is the most likely reason that Luo gives the narrator "a surreptitious wink" (line 71)?

(A) To reassure the narrator that it is all right if his violin playing is not very good

(B) To indicate to the narrator that he has a plan, and that the narrator should go along with it

(C) To signal that the narrator should be more confidant about his violin playing

(D) To remind the narrator that they should be loyal Communists

(E) To warn the narrator that they are in a very difficult situation

21. The fact that the narrator "took [his] violin and set about tuning it" (line 72) after Luo had winked at him suggests that the narrator

(A) has no idea at all what Luo was trying to communicate to him by winking at him

(B) does not know what to say, so he tunes his violin

(C) wants to distract the attention of the villagers

(D) trusts his friend even though he does not understand his plan

(E) is annoyed with Luo for trying to involve him in a duplicitous plan

22. The most likely reason that the narrator exclaims "The audacity!" (line 99) is that

(A) he believes it is audacious of Luo to interrupt when the headman is waiting for a reply from the narrator

(B) he thinks that making up a song title called *Mozart Is Thinking of Chairman Mao* shows disrespect for one of the great Western classical composers

(C) he thinks that making up a song title shows disrespect to the headman

(D) he regards it as rude to lie to the headman

(E) he thinks it is very bold of Luo to make up a song title called *Mozart Is Thinking of Chairman Mao* because the headman could have reacted angrily and said that the narrator and Luo were trying to trick him

GO ON TO THE NEXT PAGE

23. Which word can *least* accurately be used to describe Luo's actions as they are presented in the passage?

    (A) Risky
    (B) Ingenious
    (C) Bold
    (D) Cowardly
    (E) Enterprising

24. The author makes use of all of the following *except*

    (A) humor
    (B) parody
    (C) description of details
    (D) a building up of tension in the narrative
    (E) simile

25. It can be inferred from the fact that Luo "smoked quietly, like a man" (line 116 that)

    (A) he is worried about what will happen when the narrator stops playing the Mozart sonata
    (B) he is planning another way to fool the gullible headman
    (C) he is justifiably satisfied with himself for orchestrating a daring and successful plan to gain the favor of the villagers
    (D) he realizes that he has been accepted as a full-fledged adult member of the village
    (E) he does not want to say anything more because the headman might become suspicious

STOP

IN ANY REMAINING TIME YOU MAY REVIEW THE ANSWERS YOU CHOSE IN THIS SECTION. DO NOT WORK ON ANY OTHER SECTION OF THE TEST DURING THIS TIME.

5 5 5 5 5 5 5

Practice Test 2

SECTION **5**

Time—25 Minutes
18 Questions

You have 25 minutes to answer the 8 multiple-choice questions and 10 student-produced response questions in this section. For each multiple-choice question, determine which of the five choices is correct and blacken the corresponding choice on your answer sheet. You may use any blank space on the page for your work.

Notes:

- You may use a calculator whenever you think it will be helpful.
- Only real numbers are used. No question or answer on this test involves a complex or imaginary number.
- Use the diagrams provided to help you solve the problems. Unless you see the words "Note: Figure not drawn to scale" under a diagram, it has been drawn as accurately as possible. Unless it is stated that a figure is three-dimensional, you may assume it lies in a plane.
- For any function, f, the domain, unless specifically restricted, is the set of all real numbers for which $f(x)$ is also a real number.

Reference Information

Area Facts

$A = \ell w$

$A = \frac{1}{2}bh$

$A = \pi r^2$
$C = 2\pi r$

Volume Facts

$V = \ell wh$

$V = \pi r^2 h$

Triangle Facts

$a^2 + b^2 = c^2$

Angle Facts

$x + y + z = 180$

1. How many hundredths of an inch are there in one hundred inches?

   (A)   0.01
   (B)   1
   (C)   100
   (D)   1,000
   (E)   10,000

2. Which of the following expressions is equivalent to $\dfrac{a+b}{3+4}$?

   (A) $\dfrac{a}{3}+\dfrac{b}{4}$

   (B) $\dfrac{a}{4}+\dfrac{b}{3}$

   (C) $\dfrac{a}{7}+\dfrac{b}{7}$

   (D) $\dfrac{a+b}{3}+\dfrac{a+b}{4}$

   (E) $\dfrac{a+b}{7}+\dfrac{a+b}{7}$

GO ON TO THE NEXT PAGE ⟹

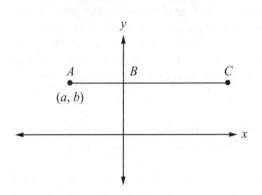

3. In the figure above, line segment $\overline{AC}$ is perpendicular to the *y*-axis, and crosses the *y*-axis at *B*. If $BC = 2AB$, what are the coordinates of point *C*?

(A) $(-2a, b)$
(B) $(-2a, -2b)$
(C) $(2a, b)$
(D) $(a, -2b)$
(E) $(-2a, -b)$

Questions 4–5 refer to the following definition.

For any real numbers *a*, *b*, *c*, and *d*, the symbol [*a*, *b*, *c*, *d*] is defined as [*a*, *b*, *c*, *d*] = *ad* − *bc*.

4. If $\dfrac{r}{s}$ and $\dfrac{t}{u}$ are equivalent fractions, then which of the following is equal to [*r*, *s*, *t*, *u*]?

(A) 0
(B) 1
(C) $\dfrac{rs}{tu}$
(D) *rstu*
(E) It cannot be determined from the information given.

5. If *x* is positive and [*x*, 7, 14, *x*] = 2, what is the value of *x*?

(A)   7
(B)   10
(C)   49
(D)   98
(E)   100

6. Howard and Dee each have the same number of books. Howard packed all his books in 9 cartons, each carton containing the same number of books. Dee packed all of her books in 12 cartons, also with each carton containing the same number of books. If each of Dee's cartons has 5 fewer books than Howard's cartons, how many books does each of them have?

(A)   140
(B)   160
(C)   180
(D)   200
(E)   220

7. What is the value of *x*, if $2^{\sqrt{x}} = 16$?

(A)   4
(B)   9
(C)   16
(D)   144
(E)   256

8. One day Dan rode down a hill at an average speed of 24 miles per hour and then rode up the hill at an average speed of 6 miles per hour. What was his average speed in miles per hour for the round trip?

(A)   4.8
(B)   9.6
(C)   10
(D)   12
(E)   15

GO ON TO THE NEXT PAGE

5 5 5 5 5 5 5

Directions for Student-Produced Response Questions (Grid-ins)

In questions 9–18, first solve the problem, and then enter your answer on the grid provided on the answer sheet. The instructions for entering your answers are as follows:

- First, write your answer in the boxes at the top of the grid.
- Second, grid your answer in the columns below the boxes.
- Use the fraction bar in the first row or the decimal point in the second row to enter fractions and decimal answers.

- Grid only one space in each column.
- Entering the answer in the boxes is recommended as an aid in gridding, but is not required.
- The machine scoring your exam can read only what you grid, so you **must grid in your answers correctly to get credit.**
- If a question has more than one correct answer, grid in only one of these answers.
- The grid does not have a minus sign, so no answer can be negative.
- A mixed number *must* be converted to an improper fraction or a decimal before it is gridded. Enter $1\frac{1}{4}$ as 5/4 or 1.25; the machine will interpret 1 1/4 as $\frac{11}{4}$ and mark it wrong.
- **All decimals must be entered as accurately as possible.** Here are the three acceptable ways of gridding

$$\frac{3}{11} = 0.272727\ldots$$

- Note that rounding to .273 is acceptable, because you are using the full grid, but you would receive **no credit** for .3 or .27, because these answers are less accurate.

Answer: $\frac{8}{15}$ Answer: 1.75

Write your → answer in the boxes.

Grid in → your answer.

Answer: 100

Either position is acceptable

3/11   .272   .273

5 5 5 5 5 5 5

9. Bob set his burglar alarm when he left his house at 8:45 a.m. and turned it off when he returned home later that day at 6:30 p.m. For how many minutes was the alarm set?

10. If $\frac{3}{8}$ the perimeter of a regular pentagon is 15, what is the length of each side of the pentagon?

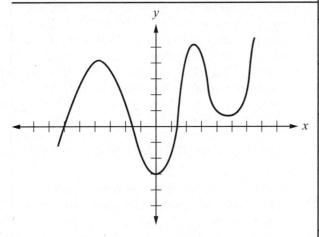

11. The figure above shows the graph of $y = f(x)$ for all values of x between -6 and 7. For how many values of x in that interval is $|f(x)|$ equal to 3?

12. If the product of two positive numbers is 60, and if the larger number is 15 times the smaller number, what is the sum of the two numbers?

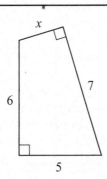

13. The quadrilateral in the figure above has sides of 5, 6, 7, and x. What is the value of x^4?

14. An ordered pair of numbers, (x, y), forms a "triploid" if the sum of their reciprocals is equal to 3. For example, $(1, \frac{1}{2})$, forms a triploid because $\frac{1}{1} + \frac{1}{\frac{1}{2}} = 1 + 2 = 3$. For what value of a does $(\frac{5}{11}, a)$ form a triploid?

15. If $0.6 < \frac{1}{x} < 0.7$, what is one possible value of x?

16. For all real numbers x: $f(x) = x^2 - 2$. If $f(a) = 10$, what is the value of $f(5a)$?

17. Printing press A, working alone at a constant rate, prints n postcards in 12 seconds. Printing press B, working alone at a constant rate prints n postcards in 8 seconds. How many seconds does it take presses A and B, working simultaneously at their respective rates, to print $2n$ postcards?

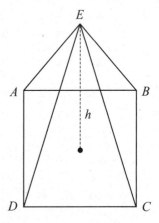

18. In the figure above, square $ABCD$ is the base of pyramid $ABCDE$. If $AC = 4$ inches and the volume of the pyramid is 4 cubic inches, what is the length, in inches, of the height h?

(The formula for the volume of a pyramid is $V = \frac{1}{3}Bh$, where B is the area of the base and h is the height.)

STOP

IN ANY REMAINING TIME YOU MAY REVIEW THE ANSWERS YOU CHOSE IN THIS SECTION. DO NOT WORK ON ANY OTHER SECTION OF THE TEST DURING THIS TIME.

Practice Test 2

6   6 6 6 6 6 6 6 6 6 6   6

SECTION 6	Time—25 Minutes 35 Questions	Choose the best answer to each of the following questions in this section. Then blacken the appropriate space on your answer sheet.

Each sentence below may or may not employ correct or effective expression. If you think that the underlined phrasing makes the most clear and precise sentence, select choice A. If, however, you think that the underlined phrasing makes the meaning of the sentence unclear or awkward, or that it is grammatically incorrect, select another answer from choices B to E.

In choosing your answers, follow the conventions of English as it is used by educated writers. Consider sentence structure, grammar, word choice, and punctuation. Choose the answer that produces the sentence that is the most clear and effective.

Example:

In her comments after the debate the judge said that she had been impressed by the ability of both teams to exploit logical weaknesses and <u>in citing relevant examples</u>.

(A) in citing relevant examples
(B) in that relevant examples had been cited
(C) in the citing of relevant examples
(D) to cite relevant examples
(E) to be able to cite relevant examples

Ⓐ Ⓑ Ⓒ ● Ⓔ

1. In order to capture the reader's attention, Mr. Ward begins his piece <u>by an anecdote, that is,</u> a short account of an interesting or amusing incident.

(A) by an anecdote, that is,
(B) by an anecdote, being
(C) by an anecdote, that is
(D) using an anecdote, it is
(E) with an anecdote, a

2. It is fortuitous that the Earth is well-protected from harmful ultraviolet radiation <u>emitted by the Sun</u>.

(A) emitted by the Sun
(B) emitted in the Sun
(C) emitted with the Sun
(D) that the Sun was emitting
(E) emitted of the Sun

3. Until being told by his teacher that he had no future as a writer, <u>the career Tom was dreaming of was as</u> a screen writer for situation comedies on television.

(A) the career Tom was dreaming of was as
(B) Tom had dreamt of a career as
(C) the career Tom dreamt of was as
(D) the career Tom dreamed of was as
(E) Tom dreamed of a career which was

4. The compositions of Johann Sebastian <u>Bach are at once mathematically precise and</u> deeply emotional, thereby creating an unprecedented fusion of "head and heart."

(A) Bach are at once mathematically precise and
(B) Bach are once and for all mathematically precise and
(C) Bach together are mathematically precise and
(D) Bach are mathematically precise at the same time as being
(E) Bach, mathematically precise and

GO ON TO THE NEXT PAGE

6   6 6 6 6 6 6 6 6 6 6 6   6

5. During the interview Raymond told the <u>investigator that he couldn't hardly remember the events of the night that</u> the accident occurred.

(A) investigator that he couldn't hardly remember the events of the night that

(B) investigator that he could hardly remember the events of the night that

(C) investigator, that when he could hardly remember the events of the night that

(D) investigator, hardly remembering the events of the night that

(E) investigator, when he couldn't remember, the events of the night that

6. The newspaper report says that the government employee was released from his <u>contract as a result stemming from his being involved</u> in extra work outside the area specified in his contract.

(A) contract as a result stemming from his being involved

(B) contract, a result that was stemming from his being involved

(C) contract as a result of him being involved

(D) contract as a result of his being involved

(E) contract, resulting in involvement

7. Rome would have been destroyed if it had not been for Pope Leo I, <u>who, going to the camp of Attila to persuade him</u>, not to attack the city.

(A) who, going to the camp of Attila to persuade him,

(B) who was going to the camp of Attila to persuade him,

(C) who, going to the camp of Attila and persuading him,

(D) who went to the camp of Attila and persuaded him

(E) who had been going to the camp of Attila and he persuaded him

8. The university tends to admit only students with SAT scores of 2250, <u>and it is rare for exceptions to be made on</u> the basis of exceptional talent for students with lower scores.

(A) and it is rare for exceptions to be made on

(B) rarely does it make exceptions on

(C) rarely has it made exceptions on

(D) and it rarely makes exceptions on

(E) and it rarely makes exceptions for

9. All cultures contain certain cultural "universals," such as religion, structure, and economic <u>organization, of which manifestations taken by these universals depend</u> on the peculiarities of each particular culture.

(A) organization, of which manifestations taken by these universals depend

(B) organization, for the manifestations these universals take depend

(C) organization, the universals took manifestations depending

(D) organization; the result is manifestations taken by these universals depending

(E) organization; the manifestations that these universals take depend

10. The newspaper article reported that <u>job prospects for a website designer are now as good as a software engineer</u>.

(A) job prospects for a website designer are now as good as a software engineer

(B) the job prospects of a web designer are now as good as a software engineer

(C) the job prospects for a website designer are now as good as a software engineer's

(D) a website designer's job prospects are now as good as software engineers

(E) a website designer now has job prospects as good as software engineers

11. Carl Jung believed that humanity shares what he called the "collective unconscious," <u>symbols arise out of this that appear</u> in dreams and myths.

(A) symbols arise out of this that appear

(B) these are symbols that arise out of this and appear

(C) it is symbols that arise out of this and appear

(D) out of which symbols, arising and appearing,

(E) out of which arise symbols that appear

GO ON TO THE NEXT PAGE

6 6 6 6 6 6 6 6 6 6 6 6   6

Each of the sentences below contains either one error or no error in grammar or usage. If there is an error, it will be underlined. If the sentence contains an error, indicate this by selecting the letter for the one under-lined part that should be changed to make the sentence correct. Follow the requirements of standard written English in choosing answers. If the sentence is already correct, select choice E.

Example:

The number of stars <u>visible in</u> the sky on any
                         A

<u>given</u> night <u>vary</u>, mainly <u>because of</u> changes in
  B   C   D

atmospheric conditions and in the phases of the

Moon. <u>No Error</u>
          E

12. The two sisters and their cousin from Bangalore,

    <u>who</u> formerly <u>sang</u> in the school's choral group,
    A   B

    now <u>plays</u> the sitar in the school's <u>newly formed</u>
          C   D

    Indian orchestra. <u>No Error</u>
                          E

13. William Shakespeare's <u>fecund</u> imagination <u>covered</u>
                            A   B

    the entire range of human experience, <u>from</u> the
                                            C

    depths of despair <u>to</u> the ecstasy of love. <u>No Error</u>
                        D   E

14. For reasons <u>know only</u> to themselves, neither Alan
                  A

    <u>nor</u> his friends on the soccer team at Richmond
      B

    Preparatory School <u>intend</u> to stay on the team <u>once</u>
                          C   D

    the semester is over. <u>No Error</u>
                              E

15. Perhaps the ultimate bureaucracy <u>is depicted</u> in
                                        A

    George Orwell's novel *1984*, in which Big

    Brother—a <u>supposedly</u> benevolent government—
                  B

watches over citizens and <u>provides for</u> their
                            C

welfare, but <u>stifling</u> individuality. <u>No Error</u>
              D   E

16. <u>For we</u> citizens of a modern democracy such as
    A

    the United States it is difficult to believe that the

    <u>institution of</u> slavery <u>has been</u>, until recently, the
    B   C

    rule <u>rather than</u> the exception throughout history.
          D

    <u>No Error</u>
    E

17. In Chinese philosophy, yin, a passive, negative

    force <u>existing</u> in the universe, is <u>associated with</u>
          A   B

    cold, dark, and earth, <u>whereas</u> yang, an active,
                            C

    positive force, is connected with heat, light,

    heaven, and <u>being creative</u>. <u>No Error</u>
                  D   E

18. If students who <u>have never had</u> the opportunity to
                      A

    visit Korea could spend <u>just</u> a few weeks in Seoul,
                              B

    Daegu, or Jeonju they <u>can</u> develop <u>more of</u> an
                          C   D

    interest in Korean culture. <u>No Error</u>
                                    E

19. The journalist <u>whom</u> we met last night at the
                    A

    gamelan concert, <u>together with</u> his wife and
                        B

    children, <u>are moving</u> back home to Virginia when
                C

    he <u>completes</u> his current assignment in Bali.
          D

    <u>No Error</u>
    E

GO ON TO THE NEXT PAGE ➡

6   6 6 6 6 6 6 6 6 6 6   6

20. After six armed men halted and boarded our
                                    A
    tourist bus outside the town of Phuket, we were
                                                B
    greatly relieved to learn that their aim was to
    protect us from roaming bandits and insurgents
    who continually pose a danger to travelers in
    C   D
    southern Thailand. No Error
                        E

21. Charlene has always drank soy milk, adding it to
                A   B
    her breakfast cereal, her tea and coffee, and any
                                                C
    other food or drink that calls for milk, because she
                              D
    is very allergic to cow's milk. No Error
                                    E

22. On the first day of drama class the demanding
                                        A
    teacher insisted on each student's developing a
                              B
    clear rationale for what and how they were going
                      C   D
    to perform in each exercise. No Error
                                  E

23. The man in the cereal advertisement, who
                                          A
    everyone in our town knows as Mr. Potts, the high
                              B
    school physics teacher, does extra work to
                            C
    supplement his teacher's income. No Error
                        D   E

24. Many people believe that a person with great
                      A
    ambition and who is willing to work hard can
                      B   C
    succeed at anything. No Error
            D   E

25. Rationalization is the process of thinking of
                                    A
    reasons for one's behavior that make you self-
                                    B   C
    satisfied but that are incorrect. No Error
            D   E

26. Nearly every time my brother plays tennis with
                                    A
    Bill Montague, he has lost so miserably that I have
                                B
    had to spend endless hours consoling him.
    C   D
    No Error
    E

27. You may sometimes find it effective to cite the
        A   B
    views of an authority with whom you disagree,
    and you use this as a take-off point to give your
    C   D
    own views. No Error
              E

28. It is unfortunate that my brother is so absorbed in
                      A   B
    his social life and thus he is neglecting his studies.
                    C   D
    No Error
    E

29. The high school teacher, nearing retirement,
                            A
    observed that students became more spontaneous
                            B
    over the years while he had been becoming less
                        C
    spontaneous; or, he wondered, was it just that he
    was becoming older, while they remained the same
        D
    age? No Error
          E

The following early draft of an essay needs to be rewritten to improve sentence structure, choice of words, clarity of expression, organization, and development. After reading the draft, answer each question below it, choosing the answer that best conforms to the requirements of standard written English.

(1) A number of evolutionary theories were proposed in the nineteenth century. (2) The two most notable of these were Lamarckism and Darwinism. (3) Why did Darwinism gain acceptance by scientists to become the foundation of modern biology, whereas Lamarckism became relegated for being a footnote in the history of science?

(4) Perhaps the major reason is that Darwinism proposes a credible mechanism, supported by many scientific studies and observations, for evolution. (5) Darwin's theory of natural selection says that all traits are inherent in the organism (this was before the importance of genetics was known). (6) For example, Darwinism explains the giraffe's long neck by theorizing that as giraffes as we know them today began to evolve, they were born with the trait of necks of various sizes but because giraffes with long necks were more likely to survive and reproduce than giraffes with short necks, resulting in how all giraffes gradually came to have long necks.

(7) Lamarck proposed that organisms can purposefully change their physical structure during their lifetime to adapt to their environment, and then pass this new characteristic on to their progeny. (8) To illustrate his theory of acquired characteristics, Lamarck gave the example of giraffes developing long necks to enable them to eat the foliage of trees more efficiently. (9) Thus, if a giraffe spends its life trying to eat foliage high in trees it will gradually make its neck longer. (10) When the giraffe mates, the trait of a long neck will somehow be passed on to its offspring.

(11) Scientists have not proven that natural selection drives evolution, but numerous studies suggest that it does. (12) Natural selection is, as Darwin believed, the main mechanism by which evolution proceeds.

30. Which of the following is the best version of the underlined portion of sentence 3 (reproduced below)?

    Why did Darwinism gain acceptance by scientists to become the foundation of modern biology, whereas Lamarckism became relegated for being a footnote in the history of science?

    (A) (As it is now)
    (B) while it relegated Lamarckism, becoming a footnote in the history of science?
    (C) whereas it was relegated for Lamarckism to be a footnote in the history of science?
    (D) whereas Lamarckism was relegated to a footnote in the history of science?
    (E) whereas the history of science relegated Lamarckism for being a footnote?

31. Which of the following sentences, if inserted immediately after sentence 5, would most effectively link sentences 5 and 6?

    (A) Darwin was, however, unaware of the role played by genes in the transmission of traits from parents to offspring.
    (B) He believed that traits favorable to specific conditions in the environment become predominant as individuals with these traits survive and reproduce at a higher rate than those without these traits.
    (C) He theorized that traits favorable to reproducing specific environments become predominant as individuals with these traits survive and reproduce at a higher rate than those lacking these traits.
    (D) He believed that favorable conditions in the environment become predominant as individuals with advantageous traits survive and reproduce at higher rates than individuals without such traits.
    (E) Darwin's evolutionary theory is, therefore, superior to Lamarck's.

GO ON TO THE NEXT PAGE

32. Which of the following should be done with sentence 6 (reproduced below)?

    For example, Darwinism explains the giraffe's long neck by theorizing that as giraffes as we know them today began to evolve, they were born with the trait of necks of various sizes but because giraffes with long necks were more likely to survive and reproduce than giraffes with short necks, resulting in how all giraffes gradually came to have long necks.

    (A) (As it is now)
    (B) Change the phrase "as giraffes as we know them today" to "when giraffes evolved."
    (C) Change the phrase "as giraffes as we know them today" to "as giraffes as we knew them."
    (D) Break the sentence into two sentences as follows: "For example, Darwinism explains the giraffe's long neck by theorizing that as giraffes as we know them today began to evolve, they were born with the trait of necks of various sizes. Being that giraffes with long necks were more likely to survive and reproduce than giraffes with short necks, it finally happened that all giraffes developed long necks."
    (E) Delete "resulting in how all giraffes gradually came to have long necks" at the end of the sentence and replace this with "all giraffes gradually came to have long necks."

33. Which of the following sentences, if inserted before sentence 7, would best improve the third paragraph?

    (A) In contrast, the mechanism proposed for evolution by Lamarck has similarities to the one proposed by Darwin.
    (B) Lamarck, however, proposed a mechanism that has received the support of most scientists.
    (C) The mechanism proposed for evolution by Lamarck, on the other hand, has not been supported by empirical evidence.

    (D) Fortunately, Lamarck proposed a mechanism for evolution that was totally different from Darwin's.
    (E) Differently from Darwin, Lamarck's theory of how evolution took place was supported by empirical evidence.

34. Which of the following is the best version of the underlined portion of sentence 8 (reproduced below)?

    To illustrate his theory of acquired characteristics, Lamarck gave the example of giraffes developing long necks to enable them to eat the foliage of trees more efficiently.

    (A) (as it is now)
    (B) of what caused giraffes to develop long necks to enable them to eat
    (C) of why giraffes developed long necks to enable them to eat
    (D) for giraffes developing long necks to enable them to eat
    (E) of the giraffe's development of a long neck resulting in its being able to eat

35. Which of the following, if inserted at the beginning of sentence 12, would make the most logical final sentence for the essay?

    (A) In light of this, some research has recently suggested that some acquired characteristics can be passed on, but most biologists maintain that
    (B) Recently, some research has proven that
    (C) On the other hand, most scientists deny that
    (D) Ultimately, further research is likely to show that Lamarck's theory of
    (E) Recently, some research has suggested that it is possible for some acquired characteristics to be inherited, but most biologists believe that this is relatively rare and that

STOP

IN ANY REMAINING TIME YOU MAY REVIEW THE
ANSWERS YOU CHOSE IN THIS SECTION. DO NOT WORK
ON ANY OTHER SECTION OF THE TEST DURING THIS TIME.

7

SECTION 7	Time—25 Minutes 24 Questions	Choose the best answer to each of the following questions in this section. Then blacken the appropriate space on your answer sheet.

Each of the following sentences contains one or two blanks, indicating that a word or set of words has been omitted. Beneath each sentence there are five answer choices labeled A to E from which you must select the word or set of words that best fits the meaning of the sentence as a whole.

Example:

Records of colonization can be found as far back as the Phoenicians, but colonization became a major force in world history only when European countries began, in the fifteenth century, to make ---- Asia, the Americas, and Africa.

(A) queries about   (B) incursions into
  (C) tirades against   (D) enemies in
    (E) amends for

(A) ● (C) (D) (E)

1. During his first long camping trip, which he enjoyed more than anything else he had done in his life, Sam realized he had ---- outdoor activities.

(A) a disinclination for   (B) a dislike for
  (C) a fear of   (D) a bent for
    (E) misgivings about

2. We were relieved when the guide told our tour group that it was almost certain that the volcano would remain ---- during the two-hour hike into its crater.

(A) hot   (B) stationary
  (C) quiescent   (D) unpredictable
    (E) incipient

3. In his novel *Ulysses*, James Joyce used free association to help portray one day in the life of the ----, Bloom, depicting the ---- of the character's mind as it fixes first on one subject and then on another.

(A) protagonist . . ramblings
(B) accessory . . musings
(C) hero . . altruism
(D) novice . . misgivings
(E) character . . decline

4. Britain's attempts to regulate trade with its American colonies to its advantage by ---- tariffs was one of the major factors causing these colonies to resort to war to achieve independence.

(A) explaining   (B) imposing   (C) validating
  (D) rectifying   (E) obviating

5. In most debates about ---- issues, reasonable evidence can be given to support opposing sides; for example, in the debate on gun control, proponents of strong gun control cite the fact that in countries with strong gun control laws there is generally less violent crime than in countries with weak gun control, but opponents counter with the ---- that crime is lower in these countries to begin with, and that guns are not the central factor in determining crime rates.

(A) disputatious . . tautology
(B) contentious . . dogma
(C) political . . concession
(D) subjective . . rebuttal
(E) controversial . . rejoinder

GO ON TO THE NEXT PAGE ⟩

7

Below are passages followed by questions on them. Questions on a pair of related passages may be about the relationship between the two passages. For each question, select the best answer based on what is stated or implied in the passage (or passages).

Questions 6–7 are based on the following passage.

Textbook economics says that prices rise and fall in order to balance supply and demand. In the oil market, however, supply and demand are
Line extremely slow to respond to price shifts, which
(5) means that prices can undergo big swings before a balance is restored. Oil is a must-have commodity with no exact substitutes; when prices rise, most consumers have little choice in the near term but to pay more rather than buy less. It takes
(10) years to develop new resources, and it is difficult to turn production on or off on short notice. When new supplies (usually years in the making) threaten to flood the market or a sudden drop in demand (for example, due to a recession) leaves
(15) sellers without ready buyers, prices can plunge before producers start shutting the taps. Oil prices naturally tend toward extremes.

6. A drop in demand for oil is likely to be caused by all of the following except

(A) a recession
(B) a warm winter
(C) increased sales taxes for consumers on oil products
(D) a decrease in the stocks of oil available for sale
(E) a decrease in the price of oil

7. Which word or phrase most accurately describes oil prices?

(A) Determined in a manner almost identical to other commodity prices
(B) Volatile
(C) Unlike other commodities, rising in price with declining demand
(D) Uniquely determined almost solely by supply
(E) Unusually fast to respond to market forces

Questions 8–9 are based on the following passage.

Because ground-based optical systems peer through Earth's atmosphere, drawbacks exist. Ground-based optical systems cannot operate
Line during daylight or twilight and are subject to
(5) interference from weather, atmospheric turbulence, scattering from moonlight, and atmospheric attenuation. Significant atmospheric attenuation in the infrared-spectral region prevents these systems from determining accurate
(10) NEO (near-Earth object) sizes. These systems also will have difficulty finding objects in inner-Earth or Earth-like orbits. There will be fewer opportunities to discover these objects from the ground because they are available only at the
(15) beginning and end of the night, when evening and morning twilight brightens the sky. Additionally, ground-based systems can have intangible programmatic issues related to access to the assets,* as well as site and infrastructure
(20) maintenance.

8. Ground-based optical systems will be most useful for

(A) determining the size of NEOs by observing in spectral regions outside the infrared
(B) observing NEOs on cloudless nights with a full moon
(C) observing objects in Earth-like orbits in inner-Earth orbits
(D) looking for NEOs during twilight
(E) observing NEOs in orbits not like Earth's and not in inner-Earth orbits on a moonless night

---

*Assets are possessions and resources available for use.

GO ON TO THE NEXT PAGE

9. All of the following could arise as "issues related to access to the assets" (lines 18–19) *except*

  (A) difficulty in maintaining electric power to the equipment supporting a ground-based optical system because of its remoteness

  (B) a full moon making useful observations with the ground-based optical system difficult

  (C) problems in providing catering for the staff of the ground-based optical system and supporting infrastructure

  (D) a scientist being unable to make a long drive to use a ground-based optical system at a time that is suitable for observing NEOs

  (E) a difficulty in finding technicians and other support staff to work in a remotely located ground-based optical system

Questions 10–15 are based on the following passage.

He was an inch, perhaps two, under six feet, powerfully built, and he advanced straight at you with a slight stoop of the shoulders, head
Line forward, and a fixed from-under stare which
(5) made you think of a charging bull. His voice was deep, loud, and his manner displayed a kind of dogged self-assertion which had nothing aggressive in it. It seemed a necessity, and it was directed apparently as much at himself as at
(10) anybody else. He was spotlessly neat, appareled in immaculate white from shoes to hat, and in the various Eastern ports where he got his living as a ship-chandler's water-clerk he was very popular.

A water-clerk need not pass an examination in
(15) anything under the sun, but he must have Ability in the abstract and demonstrate it practically. His work consists in racing under sail, steam, or oars against other water-clerks for any ship about to anchor, greeting her captain cheerily, forcing
(20) upon him a card—the business card of the ship-chandler—and on his first visit on shore piloting him firmly but without ostentation to a vast, cavern-like shop which is full of things that are eaten and drunk on board ship; where you can get
(25) everything to make her seaworthy and beautiful, from a set of chain-hooks for her cable to a book of gold-leaf for the carvings of her stern; and where her commander is received like a brother by a ship-chandler he has never seen before.
(30) There is a cool parlor, easy-chairs, bottles, cigars, writing implements, a copy of harbor regulations, and a warmth of welcome that melts the salt of a three months' passage out of a seaman's heart. The connection thus begun is kept up, as long as
(35) the ship remains in harbor, by the daily visits of the water-clerk. To the captain he is faithful like a friend and attentive like a son, with the patience of Job, the unselfish devotion of a woman, and the jollity of a boon companion. Later on the bill
(40) is sent in. It is a beautiful and humane occupation. Therefore good water-clerks are scarce. When a water-clerk who possesses Ability in the abstract has also the advantage of having been brought up to the sea, he is worth to his
(45) employer a lot of money and some humoring. Jim had always good wages and as much humoring as would have bought the fidelity of a fiend. Nevertheless, with black ingratitude he would throw up the job suddenly and depart. To
(50) his employers the reasons he gave were obviously inadequate. They said "Confounded fool!" as soon as his back was turned. This was their criticism on his exquisite sensibility.

To the white men in the waterside business
(55) and to the captains of ships he was just Jim—nothing more. He had, of course, another name, but he was anxious that it should not be pronounced. His incognito, which had as many holes as a sieve, was not meant to hide a
(60) personality but a fact. When the fact broke through the incognito he would leave suddenly the seaport where he happened to be at the time and go to another—generally farther east. He kept to seaports because he was a seaman in exile
(65) from the sea, and had Ability in the abstract, which is good for no other work but that of a water-clerk. He retreated in good order towards the rising sun, and the fact followed him casually but inevitably. Thus in the course of years he was
(70) known successively in Bombay, in Calcutta, in Rangoon, in Penang, in Batavia—and in each of these halting-places was just Jim the water-clerk. Afterwards, when his keen perception of the Intolerable drove him away for good from

GO ON TO THE NEXT PAGE ⇨

7

(75) seaports and white men, even into the virgin
forest, the Malays of the jungle village, where
he had elected to conceal his deplorable faculty,
added a word to the monosyllable of his
incognito. They called him Tuan Jim: as one
(80) might say—Lord Jim.

10. The phrase "fidelity of a fiend" (lines 47–48) most
nearly means

(A) loyalty of a devil
(B) faithfulness of a fanatic
(C) respect and love of a good woman
(D) the patience of Job
(E) devotion of a friend

11. Why does Jim regularly give up the job he has in a
particular port and move to another port to take up
a similar position?

(A) He becomes tired of living under a false
name.
(B) A secret about him becomes known in the
area.
(C) He wants to advance his career.
(D) When his real identity becomes known, people
shower him with honors (such as calling him
"Lord"), which he finds so embarrassing that
he has to leave.
(E) He wants to give younger men a chance to
learn the trade he loves.

12. What does the author mean by "His incognito . . .
had as many holes as a sieve" (lines 58–59)?

(A) Jim often let his real identity leak out
deliberately.
(B) Jim's false name was able to hide his real
personality effectively because it was open to
many interpretations.
(C) Jim's false identity was able to keep "the fact"
(line 60) but not his real name secret.
(D) Jim's false identity was generally effective at
keeping people from learning his real identity.
(E) Jim's false identity did a poor job of keeping
people from learning his real identity.

13. The "fact" mentioned in lines 60 and 68 most
likely refers to

(A) something disreputable that Jim did
(B) Jim's real name
(C) the fact that Jim had no formal qualification
for the position of water-clerk
(D) the fact that Jim didn't really know a great
deal about ships
(E) the fact that Jim had been exiled from the sea

14. According to the passage, Jim is

(A) effeminate and extremely neat in appearance
(B) lonely and aggressive
(C) powerfully built and popular
(D) always angry at others but nevertheless liked
by them
(E) academically gifted, especially in abstract
subjects

15. In line 68, "casually" most nearly means

(A) lazily
(B) cautiously
(C) unobtrusively
(D) after various intervals of time
(E) informally

Questions 16–24 are based on the following passage.

Throughout history, artists and writers have
been so candidly contemptuous of commercial
activity between consenting adults, regarding it as
Line an activity that tends to coarsen and trivialize the
(5) human spirit. And since bourgeois society was
above all else a commercial society—the first in
all of recorded history in which the commercial
ethos was sovereign over all others—their
exasperation was bound to be all the more acute.
(10) Later on, the term "philistinism" would emerge to
encapsulate this sentiment.

Though a commercial society may offer artists
and writers all sorts of desirable things—freedom
of expression especially, popularity and affluence

GO ON TO THE NEXT PAGE

(15) occasionally—it did (and does) deprive them of the status that they naturally feel themselves entitled to. Artists and writers and thinkers always have taken themselves to be Very Important People, and they are outraged by a *(20)* society that merely tolerates them, no matter how generously.

A commercial society, a society whose civilization is shaped by market transactions, is always likely to reflect the appetites and *(25)* preferences of common men and women. Each may not have much money, but there are so many of them that their tastes are decisive. Artists and intellectuals see this as an inversion of the natural order of things, since it gives "vulgarity," the *(30)* power to dominate where and when it can. By their very nature "elitists" (as one now says), they believe that a civilization should be shaped by an *aristoi* to which they will be organically attached, no matter how perilously.

(35) In sum, intellectuals and artists will be (as they have been) restive in a bourgeois–capitalist society. The popularity of romanticism in the century after 1750 testifies to this fact, as the artists led an "inner emigration" of the spirit— *(40)* which, however, left the actual world unchanged. But not all such restiveness found refuge in escapism. Rebellion was an alternative route, as the emergence of various socialist philosophies and movements early in the nineteenth century *(45)* demonstrated.

Socialism (of whatever kind) is a romantic passion that operates within a rationalist framework. It aims to construct a human community in which everyone places the *(50)* common good—as defined, necessarily, by an intellectual and moral elite—before his own individual interests and appetites. The intention was not new—there isn't a religion in the world that has failed to preach and expound it. What *(55)* was new was the belief that such self-denial could be realized, not through a voluntary circumscription of individual appetites, but even while the aggregate of human appetites was being increasingly satisfied by ever-growing material *(60)* prosperity. "Scientific" socialism promised to remove the conflict between actual and potentially ideal human nature by creating an economy of such abundance that appetite as a social force would, as it were, wither away.

(65) Behind this promise, of course, was the profound belief that modern science—including the social sciences, and especially including scientific economics—would gradually but ineluctably provide humanity with modes of *(70)* control over nature (and human nature, too) that would permit the modern world radically to transcend all those limitations of the human condition previously taken to be "natural." The trouble with implementing this belief, however, *(75)* was that the majority of men and women were no more capable of comprehending a "science of society" than they were of practicing austere self-denial. A socialist elite, therefore, was indispensable to mobilize the masses for their *(80)* own ultimate self-transformation.

The appeal of any such movement to intellectuals is clear enough. As intellectuals, they are qualified candidates for membership in the elite that leads such movements, and they can *(85)* thus give free expression to their natural impulse for authority and power. They can do so, moreover, within an ideological context, which reassures them that they are disinterestedly serving the "true" interests of the people.

16. The assertion made in the first line that "Throughout history, artists and writers have been so candidly contemptuous of commercial activity between consenting adults, regarding it as an activity that tends to coarsen and trivialize the human spirit" (lines 1–5) could be best strengthened by

(A) evidence supporting the assertion
(B) an explanation of the word "candidly" (line 2)
(C) a fuller definition of "artists and writers" (line 1)
(D) an explanation of the term "commercial activity" (lines 2–3)
(E) evidence showing that artists and writers have felt their spirit "coarsened and trivialized" by commercial activity

GO ON TO THE NEXT PAGE ⟩

7

17. In line 5, "bourgeois" most nearly means

(A) lower class
(B) democratic
(C) middle class
(D) upper class
(E) modern European

18. According to the author, the term "philistinism" (line 10) arose because

(A) there was no euphemism for the word "bourgeoisie"
(B) artists and writers became aware that they would increasingly have to participate in commercial activities
(C) artists and writers became increasingly frustrated and annoyed as society became more commercial and bourgeois
(D) a new word had to be found to refer to the new commercial ethos that was emerging in the eighteenth century
(E) artists and writers needed a word to conveniently describe their changing role in bourgeoisie society

19. The phrase "between consenting adults" (line 3) is used to

(A) exclude commercial activity that is forced upon a person or is necessary for the person's survival from the sort of commercial activity that artists and writers have contempt for
(B) remind the reader that all meaningful activity of any sort is between free adults
(C) suggest that nearly all adults, if given the freedom to do so, resist the urge to engage in commercial activity
(D) suggest that bourgeois society, more than any other, depends on the freely given consent of adults
(E) help the reader understand why artists and writers have been so contemptuous of commercial activity

20. According to the author, as society became more commercial

(A) artists and writers became increasingly constrained in their range of subjects
(B) artists and writers generally tended to follow this trend and increasingly worked only for financial reward
(C) artist and writers became relatively poorer as compared to people who weren't artists or writers
(D) artists and writers came to regard their role in society as increasingly important
(E) the status of artists and writers became lower

21. Which of the following best describes the author's attitude about the tastes of common men and women becoming predominant in commercial society?

(A) Unhappiness that higher art and literature, as well as other intellectual pursuits, have been devalued in commercial society
(B) Resignation to an unfortunate turn of events in history
(C) Celebration that at last the voices of common men and women are being heard
(D) A noncommittal attitude as to whether this is a favorable or an unfavorable development
(E) Surprise that it has taken so long for the superior taste of the masses to be properly recognized

22. According to the author, romanticism

(A) led to the creation of socialist philosophies and movements
(B) culminated in rebellions in the early nineteenth century
(C) had no effect on the real world
(D) was most popular among common men and women after 1750
(E) flourished because it was widely supported by the bourgeoisie

GO ON TO THE NEXT PAGE

23. "Appetite as a social force would, as it were, wither away" (lines 63–64) means that

   (A) the desire of individuals to have and do what they like would gradually cease to have an effect on the nature of society
   (B) common men and women would no longer regard the consumption of goods and services as legitimate
   (C) individual taste would gradually be determined by individuals rather than by society
   (D) the desire on the part of individuals to have more material possessions than others would gradually disappear
   (E) society would gradually come to realize that individual appetites cannot be controlled by intellectual and moral elites

24. In line 88, "disinterestedly" most nearly means

   (A) without genuine interest
   (B) keeping foremost in mind the ultimate goals of the ideological movement they lead
   (C) genuinely
   (D) impartially, and not motivated by self-interest
   (E) with no emotion

STOP

IN ANY REMAINING TIME YOU MAY REVIEW THE ANSWERS YOU CHOSE IN THIS SECTION. DO NOT WORK ON ANY OTHER SECTION OF THE TEST DURING THIS TIME.

8 8 8 8 8 8 8 8 8 8 8

SECTION **8**

Time—20 Minutes
16 Questions

For each problem in this section determine which of the five choices is correct and blacken the corresponding choice on your answer sheet. You may use any blank space on the page for your work.

Notes:

- You may use a calculator whenever you think it will be helpful.
- Only real numbers are used. No question or answer on this test involves a complex or imaginary number.
- Use the diagrams provided to help you solve the problems. Unless you see the words "Note: Figure not drawn to scale" under a diagram, it has been drawn as accurately as possible. Unless it is stated that a figure is three-dimensional, you may assume it lies in a plane.
- For any function f, the domain, unless specifically restricted, is the set of all real numbers for which $f(x)$ is also a real number.

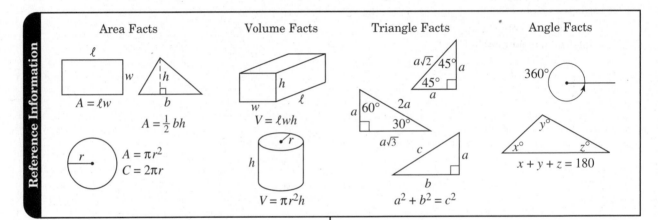

Area Facts   Volume Facts   Triangle Facts   Angle Facts

1. If $5x - 100 = 11$, then what is the value of $5x + 100$?

   (A) 111
   (B) 151
   (C) 201
   (D) 211
   (E) 251

2. In triangle PQR, the measure of angle P is greater than $40°$ and the measure of angle Q is greater than $75°$. Which of the following could be the measure of angle R?

   (A) 64°
   (B) 65°
   (C) 66°
   (D) 70°
   (E) 75°

3. If $cd = 6$, which of the following could not be the value of c?

   (A) −4
   (B) −3
   (C) 0
   (D) 2
   (E) 12

GO ON TO THE NEXT PAGE

8 8 8 8 8 8 8 8 8 8 8

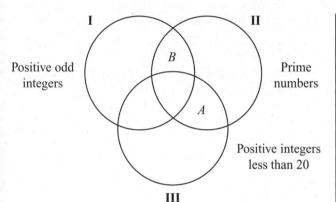

I   II

Positive odd integers

B

Prime numbers

A

Positive integers less than 20

III

4. In the diagram above, circle I represents the set of odd positive integers, circle II represents the set of prime numbers, and circle III represents the set of positive integers less than 20. If *a* is in region *A*, and *b* is the smallest integer in region *B*, what is the value of *a* + *b*?

(A) 21
(B) 22
(C) 23
(D) 24
(E) 25

5. If $0 < a < b < 1$, which of the following statements must be true?

   I. $a^5 < a$
   II. $\sqrt[5]{b} < b$
   III. $ab < a + b$

(A) I only
(B) II only
(C) III only
(D) I and III only
(E) I, II, and III

Questions 6–7 refer to the following graphs.

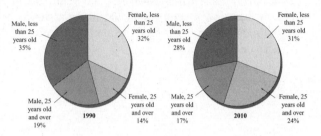

College Enrollment, by Age and Gender

Male, less than 25 years old 35%
Female, less than 25 years old 32%
Male, 25 years old and over 19%
Female, 25 years old and over 14%
1990

Male, less than 25 years old 28%
Female, less than 25 years old 31%
Male, 25 years old and over 17%
Female, 25 years old and over 24%
2010

6. If in 1990 there were 10,000,000 college students, how many more male students were there than female students?

(A) 80,000
(B) 100,000
(C) 200,000
(D) 400,000
(E) 800,000

7. If the total number of students enrolled in college was 40% higher in 2010 than in 1990, what is the ratio of the number of male students in 2010 to the number of male students in 1990?

(A) 6:7
(B) 7:6
(C) 5:6
(D) 6:5
(E) 7:5

8. If *m* markers cost *c* cents, then at this rate how many markers can you buy for *d* dollars?

(A) $\dfrac{dm}{c}$

(B) cdm

(C) $\dfrac{100dm}{c}$

(D) $100cdm$

(E) $\dfrac{100m}{cd}$

GO ON TO THE NEXT PAGE ⟩

Practice Test 2

8 8 8 8 8 8 8 8 8 8 8

9. Central State College has three sections of Math 102. If four students, Bill, Jill, Phil, and Will, decide to transfer from Math 101 into Math 102, in how many ways can the four students be assigned to the three sections if each section must receive at least one new student?

   (A) 12
   (B) 18
   (C) 24
   (D) 27
   (E) 36

10. If the perimeter of a square is P inches, and if the area of that square is A square inches, then which of the following statements could be true?

   I. $P = A$
   II. $P < A$
   III. $P > A$

   (A) None
   (B) II only
   (C) III only
   (D) II and III only
   (E) I, II, and III

11. Let $f(x)$ be the function defined as $f(x) = ax + b$, where a and b are constants. If $f(2) = 10$ and $f(4) = 16$, what is the value of $f(8)$?

   (A) 22
   (B) 24
   (C) 27
   (D) 28
   (E) 36

12. At City Prep, the ratio of boys to girls in the band is 2:3. If $\frac{1}{4}$ of the boys and $\frac{1}{3}$ of the girls in the band are also in the chorus, what fraction of the band members are NOT in the chorus?

   (A) $\frac{3}{10}$
   (B) $\frac{4}{10}$
   (C) $\frac{5}{10}$
   (D) $\frac{6}{10}$
   (E) $\frac{7}{10}$

13. A kindergarten class has c children, s percent of whom have one or more siblings. How many of the children have no brothers or sisters?

   (A) $\frac{sc}{100}$
   (B) $\frac{(1+s)c}{100}$
   (C) $\frac{(100-s)c}{100}$
   (D) $\frac{(1-s)c}{0.01}$
   (E) $\frac{(100-s)c}{0.01}$

14. It is known that in country A, a rare genetic disease affects approximately 0.025 percent of the population. If 800 inhabitants of country A have this disease, which of the following is the best approximation of the population of country A?

   (A) 300,000
   (B) 800,000
   (C) 3,000,000
   (D) 8,000,000
   (E) 30,000,000

GO ON TO THE NEXT PAGE

8 8 8 8 8 8 8 8 8 8 8

15. Let T be the sum of a set of numbers, one of which is x. If x is p percent of the sum of all the other numbers in the set, then x is what fraction of T?

(A) p

(B) $\dfrac{p}{100}$

(C) $\dfrac{p}{100T}$

(D) $\dfrac{p}{100+p}$

(E) $\dfrac{pT}{100+p}$

16. Let $f(n)$ be the function that assigns to each integer greater than 1 the sum of its distinct prime factors. For example, since 2 and 5 are the only prime factors of 20, $f(20) = 7$, and since 5 is the only prime factor of 25, $f(25) = 5$. Which of the following statements *could* be true?

I. $f(2n) = f(n)$
II. $f(2n) = f(n) + 2$
III. $f(2n) = 2f(n)$

(A) I only
(B) II only
(C) I and II only
(D) I and III only
(E) I, II, and III

Practice Test 2

STOP

IN ANY REMAINING TIME YOU MAY REVIEW THE
ANSWERS YOU CHOSE IN THIS SECTION. DO NOT WORK
ON ANY OTHER SECTION OF THE TEST DURING THIS TIME.

9 9 9 9 9 9 9

SECTION 9   Time—20 Minutes
18 Questions

Choose the best answer to each of the following questions in this section. Then blacken the appropriate space on your answer sheet.

Each of the following sentences contains one or two blanks, indicating that a word or set of words has been omitted. Beneath each sentence there are five answer choices labeled A to E from which you must select the word or set of words that best fits the meaning of the sentence as a whole.

Example:

Records of colonization can be found as far back as the Phoenicians, but colonization became a major force in world history only when European countries began, in the fifteenth century, to make ---- Asia, the Americas, and Africa.

(A) queries about   (B) incursions into
  (C) tirades against   (D) enemies in
    (E) amends for

  (A) ● (C) (D) (E)

---

1. The English instructor told his students that they should take ---- approach in their argumentative essays so that the topic would be discussed in a fair and objective way, giving all sides equitable treatment.

   (A) a logical   (B) a balanced
     (C) a limited   (D) a didactic
       (E) an adversarial

2. Some social scientists believe that war is biological—an expression of the ---- human traits of aggression and territoriality.

   (A) extrinsic   (B) capricious   (C) formative
     (D) innate   (E) latent

3. The cyclical view of history posits that societies progress from barbarism to civilization, then become ----, and subsequently decline back to barbarism.

   (A) refined   (B) decadent
     (C) scientific   (D) progressive
       (E) cultured

4. To establish the validity of the ---- that cigarette smoking causes lung cancer, epidemiologists had to show that there were no variables other than smoking or not smoking that were ---- in causing lung cancer.

   (A) generalization . . entities
   (B) induction . . determinants
   (C) inference . . axioms
   (D) conclusion . . inklings
   (E) deduction . . culpable

5. In the view of J.G. Frazer, science developed when people became aware of the degree of regularity and predictability in nature and concluded that it cannot be explained by the exercise of ---- will on the part of a god or gods.

   (A) arbitrary   (B) superfluous
     (C) ambivalent   (D) indefatigable
       (E) robust

6. In a sense, everyone is a prisoner of his or her particular ---- and ---- experience, which inevitably give rise to prejudices.

   (A) biases . . sophomoric
   (B) postulates . . tangential
   (C) assumptions . . didactic
   (D) quandaries . . subjective
   (E) preconceptions . . circumscribed

GO ON TO THE NEXT PAGE

Below are passages followed by questions on them. Questions on a pair of related passages may be about the relationship between the two passages. For each question, select the best answer based on what is stated or implied in the passage (or passages).

Questions 7–18 are based on the following passages.

Passage 1 is an extract from an essay titled "The Clash of Civilizations?" by Professor Samuel P. Huntington. Passage 2 is an extract from the essay "Do Civilizations Hold?" written by Professor Albert L. Weeks in response to Professor Huntington's essay.

Passage 1

Civilization identity will be increasingly important in the future, and the world will be shaped in large measure by the interactions
Line among seven or eight major civilizations. These
(5) include Western, Confucian, Japanese, Islamic, Hindu, Slavic-Orthodox, Latin American and possibly African civilization. The most important conflicts of the future will occur along the cultural fault lines separating these civilizations
(10) from one another. Why will this be the case?

First, differences among civilizations are not only real; they are basic. Civilizations are differentiated from each other by history, language, culture, tradition and, most important,
(15) religion. The people of different civilizations have different views on the relations between God and man, the individual and the group, the citizen and the state, parents and children, husband and wife, as well as differing views
(20) of the relative importance of rights and responsibilities, liberty and authority, equality and hierarchy. These differences are the product of centuries. They will not soon disappear. They are far more fundamental than differences among
(25) political ideologies and political regimes. Differences do not necessarily mean conflict, and conflict does not necessarily mean violence. Over the centuries, however, differences among civilizations have generated the most prolonged
(30) and the most violent conflicts. Second, the world is becoming a smaller place. The interactions between peoples of different civilizations are increasing; these increasing interactions intensify civilization consciousness and awareness of
(35) differences between civilizations and commonalities within civilizations. North African

immigration to France generates hostility among Frenchmen and at the same time increased receptivity to immigration by "good" European
(40) Catholic Poles. Americans react far more negatively to Japanese investment than to larger investments from Canada and European countries.

Similarly, as Donald Horowitz has pointed out,
(45) "An Ibo may be . . . an Owerri Ibo or an Onitsha Ibo in what was the Eastern region of Nigeria. In Lagos, he is simply an Ibo. In London, he is a Nigerian. In New York, he is an African." The interactions among peoples of different
(50) civilizations enhance the civilization-consciousness of people that, in turn, invigorates differences and animosities stretching or thought to stretch back deep into history.

Third, the processes of economic
(55) modernization and social change throughout the world are separating people from longstanding local identities. They also weaken the nation state as a source of identity. In much of the world religion has moved in to fill this gap, often
(60) in the form of movements that are labeled "fundamentalist." Such movements are found in Western Christianity, Judaism, Buddhism, and Hinduism, as well as in Islam. In most countries and most religions the people active in
(65) fundamentalist movements are young, college-educated, middle-class technicians, professionals and business persons. The "unsecularization of the world," George Weigel has remarked, "is one of the dominant social facts of life in the late
(70) twentieth century." The revival of religion, "la revanche de Dieu," as Gilles Kepel labeled it, provides a basis for identity and commitment that transcends national boundaries and unites civilizations.

GO ON TO THE NEXT PAGE ⟩

(75) Fourth, the growth of civilization-consciousness is enhanced by the dual role of the West. On the one hand, the West is at a peak of power. At the same time, however, and perhaps as a result, a return to the roots phenomenon is *(80)* occurring among non-Western civilizations. Increasingly one hears references to trends toward a turning inward and "Asianization" in Japan, the end of the Nehru legacy and the "Hinduization" of India, the failure of Western *(85)* ideas of socialism and nationalism and hence "re-Islamization" of the Middle East, and now a debate over Westernization versus Russianization in Boris Yeltsin's country. A West at the peak of its power confronts non-Wests that increasingly *(90)* have the desire, the will and the resources to shape the world in non-Western ways.

Passage 2

Toynbee distinguished what he called primary, secondary and tertiary civilizations by the time of their appearance in history, contending that their *(95)* attributes continued to influence contemporary events. Wright, likewise applying a historical method, classified civilizations as "bellicose" (including Syrian, Japanese and Mexican), "moderately bellicose" (Germanic, Western, *(100)* Russian, Scandinavian), and "most peaceful" (such as Irish, Indian and Chinese). Like Toynbee and now Huntington, he attributed contemporary significance to these factors. Huntington's classification, while different in several respects *(105)* from those of his illustrious predecessors, also identifies determinants on a grand scale by "civilizations." His endeavor, however, has its own fault lines. The lines are the borders encompassing each distinct nation state and *(110)* mercilessly chopping the alleged civilizations into pieces. With the cultural and religious glue of these "civilizations" thin and cracked, with the nation state's political regime providing the principal bonds, crisscross fracturing and *(115)* cancellation of Huntington's own macro-scale, somewhat anachronistic fault lines are inevitable.

The world remains fractured along political and possibly geopolitical lines; cultural and historical determinants are a great deal less vital *(120)* and virulent. Politics, regimes and ideologies are culturally, historically and "civilizationally" determined to an extent. But it is willful, day-to-

day, crisis-to-crisis, war-to-war political decision-making by nation-state units that remains the *(125)* single most identifiable determinant of events in the international arena. How else can we explain repeated nation-state "defections" from their collective "civilizations"? As Huntington himself points out, in the Persian Gulf War "one Arab *(130)* state invaded another and then fought a coalition of Arab, Western and other states."

Raymond Aron described at length the primacy of a nation state's political integrity and independence, its inviolable territoriality and *(135)* sovereign impermeability. He observed that "men have believed that the fate of cultures was at stake on the battlefields at the same time as the fate of provinces." But, he added, the fact remains that sovereign states "are engaged in a *(140)* competition for power [and] conquests. . . . In our times the major phenomenon [on the international scene] is the heterogeneity of state units [not] supranational aggregations."

7. The term "cultural fault lines" (line 9) suggests that

(A) like geological continental plates, civilizations are distinct from each other, and sometimes collide

(B) like geological continental plates, civilizations are relatively stable, with little meaningful interaction between them

(C) future civilizational conflict will occur in areas difficult to predict

(D) civilizations are subject to the same laws as all natural processes, such as those governing the movement of Earth's tectonic plates

(E) conflicts between civilizations will increasingly come about as a result of differences over the place of the arts in society

8. In line 12, "basic" most nearly means

(A) important
(B) distinct
(C) fundamental
(D) simple
(E) elementary

GO ON TO THE NEXT PAGE →

9 9 9 9 9 9 9

9. The author of Passage 1 would be most likely to agree with the statement that

(A) differences between cultures nearly always lead to conflict between these cultures

(B) most people in the world identify more strongly with the religion they belong to than the political party they belong to

(C) a determined government can, without much difficulty, change the beliefs and values of its citizens

(D) the differing values of people of different civilizations are more superficial than is generally believed

(E) it is not possible to make meaningful generalizations about the values of the world's seven or eight major civilizations

10. What would the author of Passage 1 most likely consider to be the most important implication of the statement "Over the centuries . . . most violent conflicts" (lines 27–30)?

(A) Serious differences among civilizations are generally resolved without conflict.

(B) Differences among civilizations rather than differing political ideologies are likely to cause serious future conflict in the world.

(C) All future conflicts among civilizations will be violent and long-lasting.

(D) Differences among civilizations cause wars of great destruction, but these wars serve, paradoxically, to purify and thus strengthen civilizations.

(E) There will ultimately be a major conflict between all the major civilizations of the world resulting in the destruction of all but one of them.

11. The author of Passage 1 would most likely agree that

(A) the growth of transnational companies is likely to sharply reduce the likelihood of conflict between civilizations

(B) the wide availability of the World Wide Web has lessened, though not eliminated, the likelihood of major civilizational conflict

(C) Hollywood films have played a significant role in creating a "one-world" mentality among the people of the world

(D) the increased frequency of large movements of people between nations belonging to different

civilizations has raised the likelihood of conflict between civilizations

(E) the availability and affordability of modern air transport has, most importantly, fostered understanding between people of different civilizations

12. According to the author of Passage 1, many young well-educated technicians, professionals, and business persons around the world are turning to religion because

(A) social change in many countries has brought more people into contact with the major world religions

(B) economic and technological modernization in poorer countries has given people greater leisure, and thus young people have more opportunity to pursue different spiritual paths

(C) young people in rapidly developing countries believe that identifying with a major world religion will make them more attractive as employees to multi-national companies

(D) they identify less strongly with their local traditions and nation, and so seek identity in religion, especially in fundamentalist religious movements

(E) the nation states of which they are citizens have ceased to provide a national religion for everyone to follow

13. The author of Passage 2 most likely put quotation marks around the word "civilizations" (line 107) to

(A) suggest that it is very possible that what Huntington defines as civilizations are not in actuality civilizations

(B) make it clear that his definition of civilization is not the same as Huntington's

(C) suggest that the term "civilization" has no meaning at all

(D) express his scorn for scholars who use important terms carelessly

(E) distinguish what Huntington defines as civilizations from how civilizations have traditionally been defined

Practice Test 2

GO ON TO THE NEXT PAGE ⟶

9   9   9   9   9   9   9

14. According to the information provided in Passage 2, Toynbee, Wright, and Huntington all believe that

    (A) it is of primary importance to classify civilizations according to how aggressive they are toward other civilizations
    (B) the major civilizations have all developed from a core nation-state
    (C) the term "civilization" is a Western notion that has little meaning when used to describe non-Western cultures and societies
    (D) the nature of a civilization is, above all, determined by the period in history at which it emerged as a full-fledged civilization
    (E) a civilization's past has a significant effect on its future

15. The author of Passage 2

    (A) believes that Raymond Aron is correct in his statement that "men have believed that the fate of cultures was at stake on the battlefields at the same time as the fate of provinces" (lines 135–138)
    (B) believes that the term "civilization" is virtually synonymous with the term "nation-state"
    (C) asserts that ideologies develop independently of civilizations
    (D) suggests that nation-states almost never act to undermine the "civilization" to which they belong
    (E) mentions that although nation-states are still important, the world is moving toward larger cultural and political units that transcend national boundaries

16. Both passages do all of the following EXCEPT

    (A) cite the work of other scholars
    (B) provide examples to support some, although not all, of their contentions
    (C) qualify quite a few of their assertions
    (D) adopt a respectful, scholarly tone
    (E) refer to theories of civilizations that have been formulated in the past

17. The author of Passage 2 says, "Politics, regimes, and ideologies are culturally, historically, and 'civilizationally' determined to an extent" (lines 120–122). In the context of the author's main argument, this sentence is most accurately described as

    (A) a central thesis
    (B) a reasonable inference
    (C) an unnecessary qualification
    (D) a proviso
    (E) a partial concession

18. The author of Passage 1 would be most likely to respond to the example of the Persian Gulf War cited in Passage 2 (lines 128–131) by saying that

    (A) there will continue to be cases in which nation-states act against the interest of the civilization to which they belong, but the more significant trend is for civilizational loyalty to take precedence over loyalty to the nation-state
    (B) most of the Arab states involved in the Persian Gulf War owe their allegiance primarily to the West, not to Islamic civilization
    (C) the Arab states that allied themselves with the West in the Persian Gulf War were forced to do so for larger geopolitical and economic reasons that transcend civilizational concerns
    (D) civilizational loyalty cannot be assessed by the amount of intra-civilizational aggression that occurs
    (E) the fact that a nation-state belonging to a particular civilization invades another nation-state belonging to that same civilization does not mean that the people of these two nation-states identify more strongly with their respective nation-states than with their civilizations

STOP

IN ANY REMAINING TIME YOU MAY REVIEW THE
ANSWERS YOU CHOSE IN THIS SECTION. DO NOT WORK
ON ANY OTHER SECTION OF THE TEST DURING THIS TIME.

Practice Test 2

10   10   10   10   10   10   10

SECTION 10   Time—10 Minutes   14 Questions   Choose the best answer to each of the following questions in this section. Then blacken the appropriate space on your answer sheet.

Each sentence below may or may not employ correct or effective expression. If you think that the underlined phrasing makes the most clear and precise sentence, select choice A. If, however, you think that the underlined phrasing makes the meaning of the sentence unclear or awkward, or that it is grammatically incorrect, select another answer from choices B to E.

In choosing your answers, follow the conventions of English as it is used by educated writers. Consider sentence structure, grammar, word choice, and punctuation. Choose the answer that produces the sentence that is the most clear and effective.

Example:

In her comments after the debate the judge said that she had been impressed by the ability of both teams to exploit logical weaknesses and in citing relevant examples.

(A) in citing relevant examples
(B) in that relevant examples had been cited
(C) in the citing of relevant examples
(D) to cite relevant examples
(E) to be able to cite relevant examples

1. The emperor worried that the enemy had pillaged the churches and other splendid buildings of the city, they carry away all the beautiful and costly sculptures and paintings.

   (A) city, they carry
   (B) city, it carries
   (C) city, and they carry
   (D) city, carrying
   (E) city and carrying

2. Some critics consider the novels of Anthony Trollope to be superior to great writers such as Charles Dickens.

   (A) the novels of Anthony Trollope to be superior to
   (B) the novels of Anthony Trollope are superior to
   (C) the novels of Anthony Trollope to be superior to those of
   (D) that the novels of Anthony Trollope are superior to
   (E) that Anthony Trollope's novels have superiority over those of

3. Critics of the "one person, one vote" principle argue that the framers of the U.S. Constitution were aware that representation would not be equal, and that if they wanted a "one man, one vote" system, they would specify it in the Constitution.

   (A) wanted a "one man, one vote" system, they would specify
   (B) did want a "one man, one vote" system, they would be specifying
   (C) had wanted a "one man, one vote" system, they would have specified
   (D) had wanted a "one man, one vote" system, they would be specifying
   (E) were wanting a "one man, one vote" system, they would specify

4. Déjà vu is the illusory feeling where you have experienced something before.

   (A) where you have
   (B) that you had
   (C) of having
   (D) in which you have
   (E) whereby you have

10   10   10   10   10   10   10

5. The reason new car designs are so rare is that it requires a special combination of originality and conformity.

   (A) The reason new car designs are so rare is that it requires
   (B) The reason new car designs are so rare is because it requires
   (C) New car designs are very rare because it is required to have
   (D) New car designs are so rare because it requires
   (E) The reason new car designs are so rare is that they require

6. Each of these history books are excellent, but I would recommend a more comprehensive book for really advanced students.

   (A) Each of these history books are excellent, but I would
   (B) Each of these history books are excellent, but I will
   (C) Each of these history books being excellent, but I would
   (D) Although each of these history books is excellent, but I would rather
   (E) Each of these history books is excellent, but I would

7. Dissatisfied with the government's weak response to violent crime, citizen groups are being formed by people in the country.

   (A) citizen groups are being formed by people in the country
   (B) citizen groups are forming with people in the country
   (C) people in the country are forming citizen groups
   (D) people in the country were formed into citizen groups
   (E) country people are being formed into citizen groups

8. Many advances in electronics have been pioneered by amateur radio operators, new communications techniques are what they enjoy experimenting with as dilettantes.

   (A) operators, new communications techniques are what they enjoy experimenting with as dilettantes
   (B) operators, dilettantes who enjoy experimenting with new communications techniques
   (C) operators, being that it is new communications techniques that they enjoy experimenting with as dilettantes
   (D) operators, new communications techniques being enjoyed by them as dilettantes
   (E) operators; dilettantes enjoying experimenting with new communications techniques

9. Players at the top levels of international chess must combine an encyclopedic knowledge of openings with being able to analyze extremely complex situations and must be able to predict the consequences of different moves.

   (A) openings with being able to analyze extremely complex situations
   (B) openings, together with an ability to analyze extremely complex situations,
   (C) openings, being able to analyze extremely complex situations,
   (D) openings together with an ability to analyze extremely complex situations
   (E) openings with an ability to analyze extremely complex situations

GO ON TO THE NEXT PAGE

Practice Test 2

10   10   10   10   10   10   10

10. The best known type of map developed to accurately reflect the spherical Earth on a flat surface is the Mercator projection, which depicts directions accurately but which <u>has the drawback where size is increasingly distorted towards the poles</u>.

   (A) has the drawback where size is increasingly distorted towards the poles
   (B) has the drawback, size being increasingly distorted towards the poles
   (C) distorts size increasingly towards the poles, and this is the drawback
   (D) has the drawback of distorting size increasingly towards the poles
   (E) has poles distorted in size increasingly, a drawback

11. Arguing that people have a tendency to judge the <u>past using the prevailing values of their own time rather than to try</u> to assess the past from an objective standpoint, the historian urged schools to require more history courses.

   (A) past using the prevailing values of their own time rather than to try
   (B) past, and they had used the prevailing values of their time rather than to try
   (C) past using the prevailing values of their own time instead of to try
   (D) past using the prevailing values of their own time instead of where trying
   (E) past by which they use the prevailing values of their own time instead of them trying

12. The term "social exclusion" designates <u>the result when people suffer</u> from a combination of related problems such as unemployment, low income, bad health, family breakdown, and poor skills.

   (A) the result when people suffer
   (B) the resulting suffering of people
   (C) what results from the suffering of people
   (D) what can happen when people suffer
   (E) the outcome of when people suffer

13. Although cartography would appear to be a fairly innocuous activity, it is an historical fact that those who <u>drew the maps had considerable political power in that they could</u> dictate how people should perceive the world.

   (A) drew the maps had considerable political power in that they could
   (B) drew the maps are having considerable political power in that they could
   (C) had drawn the maps have had considerable political power in that they can
   (D) draw the maps have considerable political power in that they could
   (E) have drawn the maps had had considerable political power in that they can

14. <u>The pilot of the commercial jetliner's reporting of a UFO sighting was denied by the airline, saying</u> that such claims were the result of "either pilot fatigue or optical illusions."

   (A) The pilot of the commercial jetliner's reporting of a UFO sighting was denied by the airline, saying
   (B) The pilot of the commercial jetliner who reported a UFO sighting was denied by the airline, he said
   (C) The reporting of a UFO sighting by the pilot of the commercial jetliner was denied by the airline, which said
   (D) The reporting of a UFO sighting by the pilot of the commercial jetliner was denied by the airline, it said
   (E) The pilot of the commercial jetliner, reporting the sighting of a UFO, was denied by the airline; they said

STOP

IN ANY REMAINING TIME YOU MAY REVIEW THE ANSWERS YOU CHOSE IN THIS SECTION. DO NOT WORK ON ANY OTHER SECTION OF THE TEST DURING THIS TIME.

Practice Test 2

Answer Key

CRITICAL READING

Section 4

Ans.	Level of Diff.	Ans.	Level of Diff.
1. B	2	13. A	4
2. D	2	14. C	3
3. A	3	15. D	2
4. E	3	16. A	5
5. D	3	17. D	4
6. C	4	18. B	1
7. C	5	19. C	3
8. D	5	20. B	4
9. E	3	21. D	2
10. D	1	22. E	5
11. D	2	23. D	2
12. C	3	24. B	3
		25. C	3

Section 7

Ans.	Level of Diff.	Ans.	Level of Diff.
1. D	1	13. A	4
2. C	2	14. C	2
3. A	3	15. D	4
4. B	3	16. A	2
5. E	4	17. C	3
6. E	3	18. C	5
7. B	4	19. A	5
8. E	5	20. E	4
9. B	2	21. D	3
10. A	3	22. C	1
11. B	2	23. A	3
12. E	3	24. D	3

Section 9

Ans.	Level of Diff.	Ans.	Level of Diff.
1. B	1	11. D	3
2. D	3	12. D	2
3. B	3	13. A	4
4. B	3	14. E	4
5. A	4	15. A	5
6. E	4	16. E	4
7. A	2	17. E	3
8. C	2	18. A	5
9. B	3		
10. B	3		

MATHEMATICS

Section 2

Ans.	Level of Diff.	Ans.	Level of Diff.
1. E	1	11. D	3
2. C	1	12. E	3
3. E	1	13. E	3
4. C	1	14. A	3
5. D	2	15. C	3
6. A	3	16. C	4
7. C	2	17. B	5
8. D	2	18. A	4
9. B	2	19. B	4
10. B	2	20. E	5

Section 5

Ans.	Level of Diff.	Ans.	Level of Diff.
1. E	1	10. 8	2
2. C	1	11. 6	3
3. A	2	12. 32	2
4. A	2	13. 144	3
5. B	3	14. 5/4 or 1.25	4
6. C	3	15. 1.5 or $1.43 < x < 1.66$	3
7. C	4	16. 298	4
8. B	5	17. 9.6	4
9. 585	1	18. 3/2 or 1.5	5

Section 8

Ans.	Level of Diff.	Ans.	Level of Diff.
1. D	1	9. E	3
2. A	1	10. E	3
3. C	1	11. D	4
4. E	2	12. E	3
5. D	2	13. C	4
6. E	3	14. C	4
7. B	3	15. D	5
8. C	3	16. C	4

WRITING

Section 6

Ans.	Level of Diff.	Ans.	Level of Diff.	Ans.	Level of Diff.	Ans.	Level of Diff.
1. E	1	10. C	3	19. C	3	28. C	5
2. A	1	11. E	3	20. E	3	29. B	5
3. B	2	12. C	1	21. A	3	30. D	3
4. A	2	13. E	1	22. D	3	31. B	3
5. B	2	14. E	2	23. A	3	32. E	3
6. D	2	15. D	2	24. B	4	33. C	4
7. D	2	16. A	3	25. C	4	34. A	4
8. D	3	17. D	3	26. A	4	35. E	5
9. E	3	18. C	3	27. C	4		

Section 10

Ans.	Level of Diff.	Ans.	Level of Diff.
1. D	1	9. E	3
2. C	2	10. D	3
3. C	2	11. A	4
4. C	2	12. D	4
5. E	2	13. A	4
6. E	2	14. C	5
7. C	3		
8. B	3		

Practice Test 2

Score Your Own SAT Essay

Use this table as you rate your performance on the essay-writing section of this Practice Test. Circle the phrase that most accurately describes your work. Enter the numbers in the scoring chart below. Add the numbers together and divide by 6 to determine your total score. The higher your total score, the better you are likely to do on the essay section of the SAT.

Note that on the actual SAT two readers will rate your essay; your essay score will be the sum of their two ratings and could range from 12 (highest) to 2 (lowest). Also, they will grade your essay holistically, rating it on the basis of their overall impression of its effectiveness. They will *not* analyze it piece by piece, giving separate grades for grammar, vocabulary level, and so on. Therefore, you cannot expect the score you give yourself on this Practice Test to predict your eventual score on the SAT with any great degree of accuracy. Use this scoring guide instead to help you assess your writing strengths and weaknesses, so that you can decide which areas to focus on as you prepare for the SAT.

Like most people, you may find it difficult to rate your own writing objectively. Ask a teacher or fellow student to score your essay as well. With his or her help you should gain added insights into writing your 25-minute essay.

	6	5	4	3	2	1
POSITION ON THE TOPIC	Clear, convincing, & insightful	Fundamentally clear & coherent	Fairly clear & coherent	Insufficiently clear	Largely unclear	Extremely unclear
ORGANIZATION OF EVIDENCE	Well organized, with strong, relevant examples	Generally well organized, with apt examples	Adequately organized, with some examples	Sketchily developed, with weak examples	Lacking focus and evidence	Unfocused and disorganized
SENTENCE STRUCTURE	Varied, appealing sentences	Reasonably varied sentences	Some variety in sentences	Little variety in sentences	Errors in sentence structure	Severe errors in sentence structure
LEVEL OF VOCABULARY	Mature & apt word choice	Competent word choice	Adequate word choice	Inappropriate or weak vocabulary	Highly limited vocabulary	Rudimentary
GRAMMAR AND USAGE	Almost entirely free of errors	Relatively free of errors	Some technical errors	Minor errors, and some major ones	Numerous major errors	Extensive severe errors
OVERALL EFFECT	Outstanding	Effective	Adequately competent	Inadequate, but shows some potential	Seriously flawed	Fundamentally deficient

Practice Test 2

Self-Scoring Chart

For each of the following categories, rate the essay from 1 (lowest) to 6 (highest)

Position on the Topic   _____

Organization of Evidence   _____

Sentence Structure   _____

Level of Vocabulary   _____

Grammar and Usage   _____

Overall Effect   _____

TOTAL   _____

(To get a score, divide the total by 6)   _____

Scoring Chart (Second Reader)

For each of the following categories, rate the essay from 1 (lowest) to 6 (highest)

Position on the Topic   _____

Organization of Evidence   _____

Sentence Structure   _____

Level of Vocabulary   _____

Grammar and Usage   _____

Overall Effect   _____

TOTAL   _____

(To get a score, divide the total by 6)   _____

Scoring Practice Test 2

Refer to the answer key for Practice Test 2 on page 152. Then use the Scoring Worksheet below to determine your raw scores for Critical Reading, Mathematics, and Writing. For each section, give yourself one point for each answer that is correct. Your total raw score is the total number of correct answer points minus $\frac{1}{4}$ of the total number of incorrect answer points. Round off the total raw score to the nearest whole number to get your Rounded Raw Score. Convert your raw scores to scaled scores using the Conversion Tables on pages 156–157.

SCORING WORKSHEET

Critical Reading

Section 4 $\underset{\text{number correct}}{\underline{\hspace{3cm}}} - \frac{1}{4}\left(\underset{\text{number incorrect}}{\underline{\hspace{3cm}}} \right) = \underline{\hspace{3cm}}$ (A)

Section 7 $\underset{\text{number correct}}{\underline{\hspace{3cm}}} - \frac{1}{4}\left(\underset{\text{number incorrect}}{\underline{\hspace{3cm}}} \right) = \underline{\hspace{3cm}}$ (B)

Section 9 $\underset{\text{number correct}}{\underline{\hspace{3cm}}} - \frac{1}{4}\left(\underset{\text{number incorrect}}{\underline{\hspace{3cm}}} \right) = \underline{\hspace{3cm}}$ (C)

Critical Reading Raw Score = (A) + (B) + (C) = \underline{\hspace{3cm}}

Critical Reading Scaled Score (see Table 1) = \underline{\hspace{3cm}}

Mathematics

Section 2 $\underset{\text{number correct}}{\underline{\hspace{3cm}}} - \frac{1}{4}\left(\underset{\text{number incorrect}}{\underline{\hspace{3cm}}} \right) = \underline{\hspace{3cm}}$ (D)

Section 7
Part I
(1–8) $\underset{\text{number correct}}{\underline{\hspace{3cm}}} - \frac{1}{4}\left(\underset{\text{number incorrect}}{\underline{\hspace{3cm}}} \right) = \underline{\hspace{3cm}}$ (E)

Part II
(9–18) $\underset{\text{number correct}}{\underline{\hspace{3cm}}}$ $= \underline{\hspace{3cm}}$ (F)

Section 8 $\underset{\text{number correct}}{\underline{\hspace{3cm}}} - \frac{1}{4}\left(\underset{\text{number incorrect}}{\underline{\hspace{3cm}}} \right) = \underline{\hspace{3cm}}$ (G)

Mathematics Raw Score = (D) + (E) + (F) + (G) = \underline{\hspace{3cm}}

Mathematics Scaled Score (see Table 2) = \underline{\hspace{3cm}}

Writing

Essay $\dfrac{}{\text{score 1}} + \dfrac{}{\text{score 2}}$ = _____ (H)

Section 6 $\dfrac{}{\text{number correct}} - \dfrac{1}{4}\left(\dfrac{}{\text{number incorrect}} \right)$ = _____ (I)

Section 10 $\dfrac{}{\text{number correct}} - \dfrac{1}{4}\left(\dfrac{}{\text{number incorrect}} \right)$ = _____ (J)

Writing Raw Score = I + J (H is a separate subscore)   = _____

Writing Scaled Score (see Table 3)   = _____

TABLE 1: CRITICAL READING CONVERSION TABLE

Raw Score	Scaled Score	Raw Score	Scaled Score	Raw Score	Scaled Score	Raw Score	Scaled Score
67	800	49	630	31	510	14	400
66	790	48	620	30	510	13	400
65	790	47	610	29	500	12	390
64	780	46	610	28	490	11	380
63	770	45	600	27	490	10	370
62	760	44	590	26	480	9	360
61	750	43	590	25	480	8	350
60	740	42	580	24	470	7	340
59	730	41	570	23	460	6	330
58	720	40	570	22	460	5	320
57	710	39	560	21	450	4	310
56	700	38	550	20	440	3	300
55	690	37	550	19	440	2	280
54	680	36	540	18	430	1	270
53	670	35	540	17	420	0	260
52	660	34	530	16	420	−1	230
51	650	33	520	15	410	−2 and below	210
50	640	32	520				

TABLE 2: MATH CONVERSION TABLE

Math Raw Score	Math Scaled Score	Math Raw Score	Math Scaled Score	Math Raw Score	Math Scaled Score	Math Raw Score	Math Scaled Score
54	800	40	630	26	500	12	390
53	790	39	620	25	500	11	380
52	770	38	610	24	490	10	370
51	750	37	600	23	480	9	360
50	730	36	590	22	470	8	340
49	710	35	580	21	460	7	330
48	700	34	570	20	450	6	320
47	690	33	560	19	450	5	300
46	680	32	560	18	440	4	290
45	670	31	550	17	430	3	270
44	660	30	540	16	420	2	250
43	650	29	530	15	410	1	240
42	640	28	520	14	410	0	230
41	640	27	510	13	400	−1 and below	200

TABLE 3: WRITING CONVERSION TABLE

Writing Raw Score	Essay Score					
	6	5	4	3	2	1
49	800	800	770	740	710	680
48	800	790	750	710	680	650
47	790	760	720	690	660	630
46	770	740	700	670	640	610
45	760	730	690	650	620	590
44	740	710	670	640	610	580
43	730	700	660	620	600	570
42	720	690	650	610	580	550
41	710	670	630	600	570	540
40	690	660	620	590	560	530
39	680	650	610	580	550	520
38	670	640	600	570	540	510
37	670	630	590	560	530	500
36	660	630	590	550	520	490
35	650	620	580	540	510	480
34	640	610	570	530	510	480
33	630	600	560	530	500	470
32	620	590	550	520	490	460
31	620	590	550	510	480	450
30	610	580	540	500	480	450
29	600	570	530	500	470	440
28	590	560	520	490	460	430
27	590	560	520	480	450	430
26	580	550	510	480	450	420
25	570	540	500	470	440	410
24	570	540	500	460	440	410
23	560	530	490	460	430	400
22	560	520	480	450	420	390
21	550	520	480	440	420	390
20	540	510	470	440	410	380
19	540	510	470	430	400	370
18	530	500	460	430	400	370
17	520	490	450	420	390	360
16	520	490	450	410	380	350
15	510	480	440	410	380	350
14	500	470	430	400	370	340
13	500	470	430	390	370	340
12	490	460	420	390	360	330
11	480	450	410	380	350	320
10	480	450	410	370	350	320
9	470	440	400	370	340	310
8	460	430	390	360	330	300
7	460	420	390	350	320	290
6	450	420	380	340	310	280
5	440	410	370	330	310	280
4	430	400	360	320	300	270
3	420	390	350	310	280	250
2	400	360	330	300	270	240
1	390	360	320	290	260	230
0	370	340	300	270	240	210

Practice Test 2

ANSWERS EXPLAINED
Section 2 Mathematics

<u>Note:</u>

1. See page 32 for an explanation of the symbol $\Rightarrow$ that is used in some answer explanations.

2. A calculator icon, 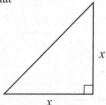, is placed next to the answer explanation of any question for which a calculator *could* be useful. Almost always, the question can be answered easily without using a calculator.

3. If you are unfamiliar with any of the math facts used in the following answer explanations, refer to Barron's *SAT*, which, in addition to having practice tests, has a full review of all the math you need to know.

1. **E** **Solution 1.** $\frac{1}{d} + \frac{2}{d} + \frac{3}{d} + \frac{4}{d} = \frac{1+2+3+4}{d} = \frac{10}{d}$. So, $\frac{10}{d} = \frac{1}{5}$ and by cross-multiplying, we get that $d = 50$.

   Solution 2. Backsolve. Test the choices, starting with 2, choice C.

   Clearly, $\frac{1}{2} + \frac{2}{2} + \frac{3}{2} + \frac{4}{2}$ is much more than 1, and so is greater than $\frac{1}{5}$. To make the fractions smaller, the denominators need to be larger. Eliminate choices A, B, and C, and try choice D or E. Choice E works:

   $\frac{1}{50} + \frac{2}{50} + \frac{3}{50} + \frac{4}{50} = \frac{10}{50} = \frac{1}{5}$.

2. **C** Since the sum of the measures of the three angles in any triangle is 180°,
   $180 = 3a + (3a + 30) + (4a - 30) = 10a$.
   So $a = 18$, and the degree measures of the three angles are
   $3 \times 18 = 54$, $(3 \times 18) + 30 = 84$,   and $(4 \times 18) - 30 = 42$.

3. **E** If $x = 7$, then $7 = \frac{1}{4}y$ and so $y = (4) \times (7) = 28$. Then, $28 = \frac{2}{3}z$ and so, $z = \frac{3}{2} \times (28) = (3) \times (14) = 42$.

4. **C** Since m is the reciprocal of n, we have that $m = \frac{1}{n}$, and so $mn = 1$. There are only two ordered pairs of integers whose product is 1: $(1, 1)$ and $(-1, -1)$.

5. **D** Since $\overrightarrow{PT}$ is a straight line, $30 + x + x + x = 180 \Rightarrow 3x = 150$ and $x = 50$. So, m∠$WOU = 50° + 50° = 100°$. NOTE: Since you aren't told that the diagram is not drawn to scale, it is, which means you can trust it: m∠WOU appears to be slightly more than 90°, so choice (D), 100°, is the only reasonable choice.

6. **A** 188 divided by 7 is 26.857.... So, the quotient is 26 and the remainder is $188 - (7 \times 26) = 188 - 182 = 6$. Therefore, the first 188 terms of the sequence consist of 26 complete sets of the integers from 1 through 7, followed by 6 more terms. Those terms are 1, 2, 3, 4, 5, and 6. So the 188th term is 6.

7. **C** 66 yen $= 6 \times (11$ yen$) = 6 \times (1$ ZAR$) = 6$ ZAR.
   But 66 yen $= 5$ renbini. So 6 ZAR $= 5$ renbini.
   Then, $\frac{6 \text{ ZAR}}{5 \text{ renbini}} = \frac{18 \text{ ZAR}}{x \text{ renbini}}$; so $6x = 5 \times 18 = 90$ and $x = 15$.

8. **D** Using the formula $A = \frac{1}{2}bh$ for the area of a triangle, we see that
   $A(x) = \frac{1}{2}(x)(x) = \frac{1}{2}x^2$. So,
   $A(\sqrt{2}) = \frac{1}{2}(\sqrt{2})^2 = \frac{1}{2}(2) = 1$.

9. **B** $A(6) + A(8) = \frac{1}{2}(6^2) + \frac{1}{2}(8^2) = \frac{1}{2}(36) + \frac{1}{2}(64) = 18 + 32 = 50$.

If $A(x) = 50$, then $\frac{1}{2}x^2 = 50$ and so $x^2 = 100$. Therefore, $x = 10$.

10. **B** The simplest solution is to use easy numbers. Assume rectangle B is a 10 by 10 square. Then the length of rectangle A is 12 (20% more than 10) and the width of rectangle A is 8 (20% less than 10). Then the area of rectangle A is $12 \times 8 = 96$ and the area of rectangle B is $10 \times 10 = 100$. So the desired ratio is $\frac{96}{100} = 0.96$.

11. **D** Since the remainder is 1 when n is divided by 2, n is odd. Since n is odd, the remainder when n is divided by 4 must be 1 (if n is 5 or 9, say) or 3 (if n is 7 or 11, say). Only I and III are true.

12. **E** **Solution 1.** Since a, b, and c are consecutive even integers,

$b = a + 2$ and $c = b + 2 = a + 4$. So, $S = a + b + c = a + (a + 2) + (a + 4) = 3a + 6$. Then, $a = \frac{S-6}{3}$ and

$c = a + 4 = \frac{S-6}{3} + 4 = \frac{S-6}{3} + \frac{12}{3} = \frac{S+6}{3}$.

Solution 2. Pick three consecutive even integers, say $a = 2$, $b = 4$, and $c = 6$. Then $S = 2 + 4 + 6 = 12$. Which

answer choice is equal to 6 when $S = 12$? Choice E: $\frac{12+6}{3} = \frac{18}{3} = 6$.

13. **E** **Solution 1.** $0.40a = 0.08b \Rightarrow b = \frac{0.40}{0.08}a = 5a$. So $b = 500\%$ of a.

Solution 2. Pick an easy-to-use number for a, say $a = 100$, since we are dealing with percents. Then

$40\%(100) = 40 = 8\%(b)$. So $40 = 0.08b \Rightarrow b = \frac{0.40}{0.08} = 500$, and 500 is 500% of 100.

14. **A** If x^2 varies inversely with y, then there is a constant k such that

$x^2 y = k$. Since $x = \frac{1}{2}$ when $y = 8$, we have that $k = \left(\frac{1}{2}\right)^2 (8) = \left(\frac{1}{4}\right)(8) = 2$. So when

$y = 32$, we have $x^2(32) = 2$, and so $x^2 = \frac{2}{32} = \frac{1}{16}$ and $x = \frac{1}{4}$.

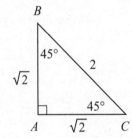

15. **C** Since $\triangle ABC$ is a 45-45-90 isosceles right triangle,

$AC = AB = \frac{AC}{\sqrt{2}} = \frac{2}{\sqrt{2}} = \sqrt{2}$.

Since $\triangle DEF$ is a 30-60-90 right triangle,

$DE = \frac{EF}{2} = \frac{2}{2} = 1$, and $DF = (DE)\sqrt{3} = \sqrt{3}$.

So the area of $\triangle ABC = \frac{1}{2}(\sqrt{2})(\sqrt{2}) = \frac{1}{2}(2) = 1$, and the area of

$\triangle DEF = \frac{1}{2}(\sqrt{3})(1) = \frac{\sqrt{3}}{2}$. So the ratio of the area of $\triangle ABC$ to the

area of $\triangle DEF$ is $1 : \frac{\sqrt{3}}{2} = 2 : \sqrt{3} = \frac{2}{\sqrt{3}}$.

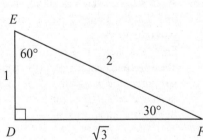

16. **C** The easiest way to answer this is to use the counting principle to evaluate A, B, and C.
- To write a three-digit palindrome, you have nine choices for the first digit (any of the ten digits except 0), ten choices for the second digit, and only one choice for the third digit (since it must be the same as the first digit). So, $A = 9 \times 10 \times 1 = 90$.
- Similarly, to write a four-digit palindrome, you have nine choices for the first digit (any of the ten digits except 0), ten choices for the second digit, only one choice for the third digit (since it must be the same as the second digit), and only one choice for the fourth digit (since it must be the same as the first digit). So, $B = 9 \times 10 \times 1 \times 1 = 90$.
- Finally, to write a five-digit palindrome, you have nine choices for the first digit (any of the ten digits except 0), ten choices for the second digit, ten choices for the third digit, only one choice for the fourth digit (since it must be the same as the second digit), and only one choice for the fifth digit (since it must be the same as the first digit). $C = 9 \times 10 \times 10 \times 1 \times 1 = 900$.

Only Statement III is true.

17. **B** **Solution 1.** Since the entire trip took 3 hours, of which 1 hour and 20 minutes was spent in Amherst, Delphine rode her bike for 1 hour and 40 minutes or $1\frac{2}{3}$ hours or $\frac{5}{3}$ hours. If d represents the distance between the two towns on the bike path, then $\frac{d}{12}$ and $\frac{d}{18}$ are the times, in hours, she spent riding to Amherst and back to Florence, respectively. So, $\frac{d}{12} + \frac{d}{18} = \frac{5}{3}$. Multiply each term by 36, the least common multiple of the denominators.

$$ \overset{3}{\cancel{36}}\left(\frac{d}{\cancel{12}}\right) + \overset{2}{\cancel{36}}\left(\frac{d}{\cancel{18}}\right) = \overset{12}{\cancel{36}}\left(\frac{5}{\cancel{3}}\right) $$

So $3d + 2d = 60 \Rightarrow 5d = 60$, and $d = 12$.

Solution 2. Once you know that Delphine spent $1\frac{2}{3}$ hours riding, you can avoid the algebra by testing the answers. Start with choice (C), 16. If $d = 16$, then in hours, the ride would take $\frac{16}{12} + \frac{16}{18} = \frac{4}{3} + \frac{8}{9} = 2\frac{2}{9}$ hours, which is too much. Since d must be less than 16, eliminate choices (C), (D), and (E). Try choice B: $\frac{12}{12} + \frac{12}{18} = 1 + \frac{2}{3} = 1\frac{2}{3}$. The answer is (B).

18. **A** A simple sketch is all you need to answer this question. We are told that the slope of ℓ is 2, but we may choose any number for its y-intercept, say 2.
From the sketch it is clear that the lines have the same y-intercepts, but different x-intercepts. (I is true; II is false.) Clearly, ℓ and k are *not* perpendicular so the slope of k is *not* the negative reciprocal of the slope of ℓ. (III is false.)
In fact, the slope of k is -2.

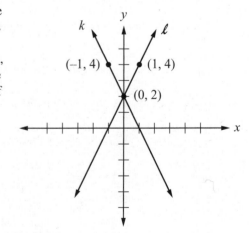

19. **B** Since the perimeter of △AED is 6, each side is 2. Altitude $\overline{EF}$ divides △AED into two 30-60-90 right triangles, whose sides are 1, 2, and $\sqrt{3}$; so $EF = \sqrt{3}$. Since the diagonals of a rectangle bisect each other, $BE = CE = 2$, and since opposite sides of a rectangle are congruent, $BC = 2$. Therefore, △BEC is congruent to △AED, and $FG = 2\sqrt{3}$. So, $AB = DC = 2\sqrt{3}$. Then $P = 4 + 4\sqrt{3}$ and $A = 2(2\sqrt{3}) = 4\sqrt{3}$. Finally, $P - A = 4$.

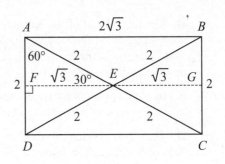

20. **E** The sum of the nine integers from 1 through 9 is 45. Since the sum of the numbers in each of the three rows is the same, each of those sums is $45 \div 3 = 15$, as is the sum of the three numbers in each column, and the sum of the numbers in the two diagonals. So,

- $8 + c + 4 = 15 \Rightarrow c = 3$
- $c + d + 7 = 15 \Rightarrow 3 + d + 7 = 15 \Rightarrow d = 5$
- $4 + d + b = 15 \Rightarrow 4 + 5 + b = 15 \Rightarrow b = 6$
- $8 + a + b = 15 \Rightarrow 8 + a + 6 = 15 \Rightarrow a = 1$

8	$a = 1$	$b = 6$
$c = 3$	$d = 5$	7
4	e	f

Section 4 Critical Reading

1. **B** The phrase "under natural conditions" in the sentence signals that *untainted* (unspoiled) is the best choice.

2. **D** To be *skeptical* is by definition to take the position that there is not enough evidence to believe or to disbelieve something.

3. **A** The mayor "prohibited the use of teargas" because he thought its use would only *exacerbate* (make worse) the chaotic situation. The words "its use would not help but only" signal that the answer should contrast with the word *help*.

4. **E** *Annoying*, *reprehensible* (blameworthy), *horrible*, and *loathsome* (abhorrent) all make sense in the first blank because the word "although" signals that the adjective describing some people's attitude to slang will be negative, in contrast to the positive description of slang given in the next part of the sentence ("great directness" and "avoiding . . . circumlocution"). *Fortuitous* (happening by chance) makes little sense because slang does not happen by chance. *Refined* (cultivated) is the best choice for the second blank, which calls for a type of language that directly contrasts with slang (informal language characterized by the use of vulgar vocabulary and expressions). Refined language also tends to contain circumlocution (an indirect way of saying something), whereas slang uses direct language. *Pithy* (forceful and brief) does not make sense because forceful and brief language would not use circumlocution. Language that is *disgusting* or *extemporaneous* (unrehearsed) cannot be directly compared to slang, and such language does not necessarily contain circumlocution.

5. **D** The sentence says that because the West is preeminent in many fields, the process often called "globalization" has resulted in its *mores* (customs) becoming the *norm* (standard regarded as typical) in many non-Western countries.

6. **C** It is reasonable that an engineer would believe that the *raison d'être* (reason for existing) of technology is to build devices to improve human life.

7. **C** A *euphemism* is by definition an expression that can be substituted for a more common expression on the grounds that it has more *positive* connotations.

8. **D**   The second half of the sentence gives an example of an "unwarranted assumption" made by environmental groups that in the future there would be no change in the rate at which resources are discovered. Some groups made *extrapolations* (estimates based on extending known information) that were *predicated on* (based on) such unwarranted assumptions.

9. **E**   Passage 1 is an objective account of varying views of the concept of Afrocentrism. Passage 2 gives a subjective view of Afrocentrism based on the writer's experience of living in Africa.

10. **D**   The writer is referring to Africa when he uses the word "here" in line 22, as can be seen from lines 28–30: "I have been . . . all its horror."

11. **D**   The author says, "Maybe if I had never set foot here, I could celebrate my own blackness, my 'African-ness.' Then I might feel part of this place . . ." (lines 22–23).

12. **C**   Opponents of the more extreme beliefs of Afrocentrism referred to in Passage 1 are described as saying that "many of the arguments of Afrocentrists [are] implicitly racist" (lines 15–17). Racism entails the belief that certain inherent qualities, not determined by culture, make one race superior to another. It can thus be inferred that the opponents of the more extreme beliefs of Afrocentrism would view the account in Passage 2 as evidence that race and culture are not closely related. This can be inferred because the author of Passage 2 is racially African but does not identify culturally with Africa.

13. **A**   In context "officious" means "prying." The headman is described as "peer[ing] into the black interior of the [violin]."

14. **C**   In lines 7–8 the narrator says, "It [the violin] was the sole item that exuded an air of foreignness. . . ." In lines 11–12, it is described as a "strange object" in the eyes of the villagers. The headman "[holds] his nose over the soundhole and sniffed long and hard" (lines 28–29), but the villagers have no idea what it is until the headman strums a few strings and the violin produces a sound. The only term the villagers have for the violin is "toy." (B) is too positive to describe the villagers' attitude to the violin; they are suspicious of it.

15. **D**   The narrator says that the violin was the only item Luo and he had that "exuded an air of . . . civilization, and therefore aroused suspicion" (lines 8–9). We can infer from this that the narrator regards the villagers as uncivilized.

16. **A**   In context "furtive" means *surreptitious* (marked by stealth). Luo and the narrator's glances are surreptitious because they don't want others to notice them.

17. **D**   After examining the violin thoroughly, the headman concludes that it's a toy. The narrator says, "This verdict left us speechless" (line 38). The narrator says, "Things were not looking good" because he knew that the villagers, as loyal Communists, would regard them as bourgeois.

18. **B**   In context, "coolly" means *calmly*. Earlier the narrator said that Luo spoke to the headman "as casually as he could" (line 64).

19. **C**   We can infer from their comments and behavior that the villagers see themselves as loyal Communists, which means they follow Communist ideology and condemn bourgeois (middle class) values and pastimes, such as playing Western music, as decadent. Thus, the villagers would see it as an honor to be the person who destroys a symbol of bourgeois decadence. The sentence "We looked like . . . Communist farm workers" (lines 48–51) strongly suggests that the villagers are Communists and that the narrator and Luo are "reactionary" (the latter suggests they are bourgeois). Further clues are that the headman condemns the violin as "a bourgeois toy" (lines 53–54) and that the narrator describes the headman as "the vigilant Communist" (lines 85–86).

20. **B**   In the light of what happens after Luo winks at the narrator, we can infer that Luo winked at the narrator to indicate that he had a plan and that the narrator should follow it. Evidently, Luo's plan was to announce that the narrator would play "a Mozart sonata" (lines 73–74) and then say that the sonata was called *Mozart Is Thinking of Chairman Mao*.

21. **D**   The narrator says he was "puzzled" (line 72) by Luo's wink, but he nevertheless takes his violin and tunes it. This suggests he trusts his friend to act intelligently and responsibly even though the narrator does not know what his friend is planning to do.

22.   **E**   We can infer this because we know that the narrator realizes that he and Luo are in a tense, dangerous situation in which they are dependent on the headman.

23.   **D**   There is no suggestion that Luo's actions are cowardly. On the contrary, on the spot he conceives and carries out a clever, daring, and risky plan. Thus, (A), (B), (C), and (E) all can be used to describe Luo's actions.

24.   **B**   Parody is not used in the passage. The passage does not make great use of (A) humor, but some of what happens is mildly amusing, especially when the headman says, "Mozart thinks of Mao all the time" and Luo agrees, "Indeed, all the time" (line 104). There is a lot of description of (C) details; for example, the description of the bloodspots in the headman's eye (lines 15–17). (D) Tension is built up until the climax at the end of the passage. (E) There are several similes; for example, "Mozart's phrases came flooding back to me like so many faithful friends" (lines 108–109).

25.   **C**   The narrator says that Luo was only eighteen years old when the events recounted in the passage occurred. It can be inferred that when Luo lights a cigarette and smokes it while the narrator plays the violin for the villagers he is feeling satisfied with the successful outcome of his daring plan. The fact that the narrator describes Luo as smoking "quietly, like a man" suggests that he has just undergone an experience that made him more mature and that he is aware that he has become more mature.

Section 5 Mathematics
Note:

1.   See page 32 for an explanation of the symbol $\Rightarrow$ that is used in some answer explanations.

2.   A calculator icon, [calculator icon], is placed next to the answer explanation of any question for which a calculator *could* be useful. Almost always, the question can be answered easily without using a calculator.

3.   If you are unfamiliar with any of the math facts used in the following answer explanations, refer to Barron's *SAT*, which, in addition to having practice tests, has a full review of all the math you need to know.

1.   **E**   Divide one hundred by one hundredth:

$$100 \div \frac{1}{100} = 100 \times \frac{100}{1} = 10{,}000$$

2.   **C**   **Solution 1.** $\dfrac{a+b}{3+4} = \dfrac{a+b}{7} = \dfrac{a}{7} + \dfrac{b}{7}$

Solution 2. Solution 1, above, is straightforward, but if you aren't confident that you would do it correctly, plug in numbers and test the choices. For example, if $a = 3$ and $b = 4$, then $\dfrac{a+b}{3+4} = \dfrac{3+4}{3+4} = 1$. Only choice (C) is equal to 1, when $a = 3$ and $b = 4$.

3.   **A**   Since $\overline{AC}$ is perpendicular to the y-axis, it is parallel to the x-axis. Every point on $\overline{AC}$ has the same y-coordinate, namely b, so only choices (A) and (C) are possible. Also, since a is negative, $2a$ is negative, and so cannot be the x-coordinate of C, which clearly is positive. The answer is (A).

4.   **A**   **Solution 1.** Since $\dfrac{r}{s}$ and $\dfrac{t}{u}$ are equivalent, $\dfrac{r}{s} = \dfrac{t}{u}$ and so, by cross-multiplying, we get that $ru = st$. So, $[r, s, t, u] = ru - st = 0$.

Solution 2. Pick simple values for the equivalent fractions $\dfrac{r}{s}$ and $\dfrac{t}{u}$, say $\dfrac{1}{2}$ and $\dfrac{2}{4}$, and evaluate $[1, 2, 2, 4] = 1 \times 4 - 2 \times 2 = 0$.

5.   **B** $[x, 7, 14, x] = x^2 - (7)(14) = x^2 - 98$. Since $[x, 7, 14, x] = 2$, we have that $x^2 - 98 = 2$ and $x^2 = 100$. So $x = 10$.

6. **C** If n represents the number of books in each of Howard's 9 cartons, then $n - 5$ represents the number of books in each of Dee's 12 cartons, and since they have the same number of books, $9n = 12 (n - 5) \Rightarrow 9n = 12n - 60 \Rightarrow 3n = 60 \Rightarrow n = 20$.
So Howard has $9 \times 20 = 180$ books, as does Dee: $12 \times 15 = 180$.
NOTE: This problem is trivial if you realize that 180, choice (C), is the only choice that is a multiple of 9 (or 12).

7. **C** You should know the first few powers of 2 by heart (2, 4, 8, 16, 32, 64) and immediately recognize that $16 = 2^4$. So if $2^{\sqrt{x}} = 16$, then $2^{\sqrt{x}} = 2^4$. Therefore, $\sqrt{x} = 4$ and $x = 16$.

8. **B** Since the answer to this question doesn't depend on the length of the hill, pick an easy-to-use value, say 24 miles. Then since $d = rt$, we have $t = \dfrac{d}{r}$. So,

- The time to go down the hill was $\dfrac{24 \text{ miles}}{24 \text{ miles per hour}} = 1$ hour.
- The time to go up the hill was $\dfrac{24 \text{ miles}}{6 \text{ miles per hour}} = 4$ hours.

Therefore, Dan rode a total of 48 miles in 5 hours, for an average speed of $\dfrac{48}{5} = 9.6$ miles per hour.

9. **585**
- From 8:45 a.m. to 9:00 a.m. is 15 minutes.
- From 9:00 a.m. to 6:00 p.m. is 9 hours or $9 \times 60 = 540$ minutes.
- From 6:00 p.m. to 6:30 p.m. is 30 minutes.
- So the alarm was set for $15 + 540 + 30 = 585$ minutes.

10. **8** To get the perimeter, either note that if $\dfrac{3}{8}$ of the perimeter is 15, then $\dfrac{1}{8}$ of the perimeter is 5, and so the perimeter is $8 \times 5 = 40$, or obtain the same result by letting P represent the perimeter and solving the equation $\dfrac{3}{8}P = 15$. Since the perimeter is 40, each of the 5 sides is $40 \div 5 = 8$.

11. **6** $|f(x)| = 3$ if $f(x) = 3$ or $f(x) = -3$. There is only one value of x for which $f(x) = -3$, namely 0: $(0, 3)$ is the only point on the graph of $y = f(x)$ whose y-coordinate is -3. There are 5 values of x for which $f(x) = 3$, the 5 values where the graph of $y = f(x)$ crosses the horizontal line $y = 3$. So, in total there are $1 + 5 = 6$ values of x between 5 and -5 for which $|f(x)| = 3$.

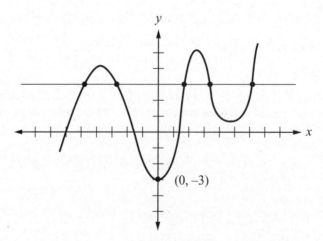

$(0, -3)$

12. **32** Let the numbers be x and y with $x < y$. Then $xy = 60$ and $y = 15x$. Then, $60 = xy = x(15x) = 15x^2$. Therefore, $x^2 = \dfrac{60}{15} = 4$, and $x = 2$. Since $x = 2$, $y = 15(2) = 30$, and $x + y = 32$.

13. **144** Draw in diagonal $\overline{AC}$.
- Applying the Pythagorean theorem to $\triangle ADC$, we get $5^2 + 6^2 = h^2 \Rightarrow h^2 = 25 + 36 = 61$.
- Applying the Pythagorean theorem to $\triangle ABC$, we get $x^2 + 7^2 = h^2 \Rightarrow x^2 + 49 = 61$, so $x^2 = 12$.
- Finally, $x^4 = (x^2)^2 = (12)^2 = 144$.

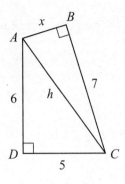

14. $\dfrac{5}{4}$ If $(\dfrac{5}{11}, a)$ forms a triploid, then $3 = \dfrac{1}{\dfrac{5}{11}} + \dfrac{1}{a} = \dfrac{11}{5} + \dfrac{1}{a}$.

Therefore, $\dfrac{1}{a} = 3 - \dfrac{11}{5} = \dfrac{15}{5} - \dfrac{11}{5} = \dfrac{4}{5}$. Since $\dfrac{1}{a} = \dfrac{4}{5}$, $a = \dfrac{5}{4}$.

15. **1.5** or $\dfrac{3}{2}$ (or any number between 1.43 and 1.66).

If $\dfrac{1}{x} = 0.6 = \dfrac{6}{10}$, then $6x = 10$, and $x = \dfrac{10}{6} = 1.666$.

If $\dfrac{1}{x} = 0.7 = \dfrac{7}{10}$, then $7x = 10$, and $x = \dfrac{10}{7} = 1.429$.

Since $0.6 < \dfrac{1}{x} < 0.7$, then $1.429 < x < 1.666$. So grid in 1.5 or $\dfrac{3}{2}$ or any number satisfying $1.43 < x < 1.66$.

16. **298** Since $f(a) = a^2 - 2$, if $f(a) = 10$, then $a^2 - 2 = 10$, and so $a^2 = 12$.
$f(5a) = (5a)^2 - 2 = 25a^2 - 2 = 25(12) - 2 = 300 - 2 = 298$.

17. **9.6** Of course, this problem can be solved algebraically, but on the SAT it is faster and easier to solve it arithmetically.

Solution 1 (non-algebraic). Since 24 is the least common multiple of 8 and 12, it is convenient to use 24 for the number of seconds. And for n, choose 2. Then
- At the rate of 2 postcards every 12 seconds, in 24 seconds, press A can print 4 postcards.
- At the rate of 2 postcards every 8 seconds, in 24 seconds, press B can print 6 postcards.
- So in 24 seconds, presses A and B working together can print 10 postcards.
- So, presses A and B together can print 1 postcard in 2.4 ($\dfrac{1}{10}$ of 24) seconds, and so can print $2n = 4$ cards in $4 \times 2.4 = 9.6$ seconds.

Solution 2 (algebraic). Since press A prints n postcards in 12 seconds, it prints $\dfrac{n}{12}$ postcards per second; similarly, press B prints $\dfrac{n}{8}$ postcards per second. So, together they can print $\dfrac{n}{12} + \dfrac{n}{8} = \dfrac{2n}{24} + \dfrac{3n}{24} = \dfrac{5n}{24}$ postcards per second. Finally, the number of seconds required to print $2n$ postcards is $2n \div \dfrac{5n}{24} = (2n) \times \dfrac{24}{5n} = \dfrac{48}{5} = 9.6$. Generally, this is the kind of algebra you should try to avoid when taking the SAT.

18. $\dfrac{3}{2}$ **or 1.5** To find B, the area of the base of the pyramid, use either of the two

formulas for the area of a square: $A = \dfrac{d^2}{2}$ or $A = s^2$. So $A = \dfrac{4^2}{2} = \dfrac{16}{2} = 8$

or $A = \left(\dfrac{4}{\sqrt{2}}\right)^2 = \dfrac{16}{2} = 8$. Since we are given that the volume is 4, we have

$4 = \dfrac{1}{3}(8)h \Rightarrow h = \dfrac{12}{8} = \dfrac{3}{2}$.

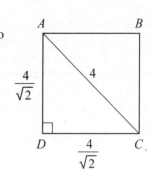

Section 6 Writing

1. **E** The given sentence contains an idiom error. *A short account of an interesting or amusing incident* is an appositive phrase referring to the noun *anecdote*, so there is no need for the words *that is* to introduce it. The correct preposition is *with*, not *by*.

2. **A** The given sentence is clear and grammatical.

3. **B** This corrects the awkwardness and wordiness in the given sentence by making *Tom* the subject of the independent clause beginning after the comma. The participial phrase beginning with the word *until* and ending with the word *writer* refers to *Tom*, so the sentence is best improved by making *Tom* the subject.

4. **A** The given sentence is clear and grammatical.

5. **B** This corrects the error in the given sentence, which contains a double negative, *couldn't hardly*.

6. **D** The given sentence corrects an idiom error. In this context, the phrase *as a result* must be followed by the preposition *of*. Note that the phrase "as a result of" begins an adverb clause (ending in the word *contract*) that modifies the subject complement *released*.

7. **D** *Going to the camp of Attila to persuade him* is a participial phrase, which cannot follow the relative pronoun *who*. Choice (D) creates a correct adjective clause describing *Pope Leo I*.

8. **D** The given sentence has faulty parallelism. This is a compound sentence. The first independent clause is cast in the active voice, with *university* as the subject. There is no need to change the voice to passive in the second independent clause. Choice (D) makes the voice active, with the subject the pronoun *it*, which refers to university.

9. **E** In the given sentence the words after the comma are not grammatical and do not make sense. (E) is the only choice that is grammatical and makes good sense. The semicolon correctly links two independent clauses, with the second clause elaborating on the first clause.

10. **C** This corrects the problem in the given sentence, which contains a faulty comparison between *job prospects* and *software engineer*.

11. **E** This corrects the error in the given sentence, which is a run-on sentence, by changing the part of the sentence after the comma into a dependent clause referring to *collective unconscious*.

12. **C** Subject–verb agreement. The subject of the sentence—*sisters* and *cousin*—is plural, so the singular verb *plays* should be changed to the plural verb *play*.

13. **E** No error.

14. **E** No error. Note that (C) *intend* is correct because it agrees with the second of the compound subjects, *friends*.

15. **D** Tense error. The structure of the sentence requires that the verb *stifles* should follow the coordinating conjunction *but* so that it is consistent with the verbs *watches* and *provides*.

16. **A** Incorrect pronoun. The preposition *for* takes a pronoun in the objective case. Use *us*.

17. **D** Faulty parallelism. *Being creative* should be changed to *creativity* to make it consistent in form with the other items (*heat*, *light*, *heaven*) in the series.

18. **C** Wrong modal verb. Change *can* to *might*.

19. **C** Subject–verb agreement. The singular noun *journalist* requires a singular verb. Change *are moving* to *is moving*.

20. **E** No error.

21. **A** Incorrect verb form. The past participle of drink is *drunk*, not *drank*. Use the past participle of a verb to form the present perfect tense: *has always drunk*.

22. **D** Error in pronoun–antecedent agreement. The antecedent *student* requires the singular subject *he or she*, which in turn requires the singular verb *was*.

23. **A** Wrong pronoun case. Change *who* to *whom* because the relative pronoun is the object of the verb *knows*.

24. **B** Faulty parallelism. The first object of the preposition *with* is a noun, *ambition*, so *who is willing* should be changed to *a willingness* so that it is also a noun that is the object of the preposition *with*.

25. **C** Unnecessary pronoun shift. Change *you* to *one* so that it is consistent with *one's*.

26. **A** Tense error. *Has lost* is the present perfect tense. *Plays* must be changed to *has played* to maintain this tense.

27. **C** The sentence is talking about future possibility (*You may . . .*), so the phrase *you use* is not correct. It can be changed to *you can use* or the less wordy participle *using* so that *using this as a take-off point to give your own views* becomes a participial phrase.

28. **C** Error in idiom. Change *and thus* to *that* to make the correct idiomatic phrase: *so absorbed . . . that he is. . . .*

29. **B** Tense error. *Became* should be changed to the past perfect *had become* because the action it refers to occurred before the teacher *observed* (simple past tense).

30. **D** This clearly and grammatically expresses the meaning. (A) This contains the non-standard phrase *became relegated*. (B) This is awkward and changes the meaning so that Darwinism became a footnote. (C) This makes little sense. The phrase *relegated for* is not grammatical. (E) This would make sense if the word *for* were changed to *to*.

31. **B** This is the best choice because it explains what Darwin believed about traits mentioned in the preceding sentence (sentence 5) and makes a general assertion about these traits that the following sentence (sentence 6) provides an example of. (A) This expresses information very similar to that contained in the parentheses in sentence 5. It is not very relevant to the main point being developed in the paragraph about natural selection. (C) This does not make sense because it is not the environment that is being produced or reproduced. (D) This does not make sense because it is not conditions in the environment that become predominant. (E) This makes little sense because it doesn't help to link sentence 5 to sentence 6 and because it doesn't relate to the main topic of the second paragraph.

32. **E** The coordinating conjunction *but* joins the adverb clause beginning with the subordinating conjunction *because* and ending with *necks* to the first part of the sentence (that is, all the words before *but*). This adverb clause gives the reason *all giraffes gradually came to have long necks*. (A) is incorrect. The phrase *resulting in how* cannot be used because the word *because* conveys the ideas of cause and result. (B) This changes the meaning and is not as clear as the original. (C) This does not make sense because the verb *knew* is the past tense and it is followed by the adverb *today*. (D) This makes sense, but the second sentence is clumsy. *Being that* is non-standard; *finally* is not a suitable word in context.

33. **C** This improves the third paragraph by providing a link between the second paragraph, which discusses the mechanism for evolution proposed by Darwin, and the body of the third paragraph, which discusses the mechanism for evolution proposed by Lamarck. (A) This does not make sense in view of the content of the body of the third paragraph. (B) This does not make sense in view of the content of the body of the third

paragraph. (D) This makes little sense because of the word *fortunately*. (E) This is awkward and makes little sense. Also, it contradicts line 4, in which we are told that natural selection is well-supported by scientific evidence.

34. **A** This is a clear and grammatical sentence. (B) The word *what* changes the meaning of the sentence so that the sentence does not make sense in the passage. (C) The word *why* changes the meaning of the sentence so that the sentence does not make sense in the passage. (D) The word *for* makes this incorrect. (E) This is grammatical and has the same meaning as (A), but it is wordy and not as clear as (A).

35. **E** This creates a suitable concluding sentence because it helps to contrast what scientists now believe about Lamarckism, on the one hand, and Darwinism, on the other hand. Also, it helps to link sentence 11 and sentence 12. (A) This makes little sense because of the phrase *in light of this*. (B) This makes little sense because it contradicts the preceding sentence (sentence 11). (C) This makes no sense because it contradicts what has been said about natural selection in the passage. (D) This makes no sense. Natural selection is not Lamarck's theory.

Section 7 Critical Reading

1. **D** Sam realized that he greatly enjoyed his camping trip, so it makes sense that he has a *bent* (natural inclination) *for* outdoor activities.

2. **C** Members of a tour group into a volcano crater would be relieved to learn that the volcano would remain *quiescent* (inactive) during their visit.

3. **A** The phrase "character's mind" in the sentence signals that a character in a novel is being described and that this character's mind is specifically being discussed. Bloom is the novel's *protagonist* (main character); the *ramblings* (digressions) of his mind are portrayed as they "fix first on one subject and then on another."

4. **B** It makes sense that the American colonies resorted to war to achieve independence as a consequence of Britain's *imposing* (establishing as compulsory) tariffs.

5. **E** The statement "Reasonable evidence can be given to support opposing sides" indicates that (E) *controversial* issues are being discussed. (B) *contentious* (controversial; causing quarrels) and (C) *political* are also acceptable choices for the first blank. For the second blank (D) *rebuttal* (statement that something is not true) and (E) *rejoinder* (answer) are possible. Thus, (E) is the only acceptable answer.

6. **E** The passage says that oil prices "rise and fall in order to balance supply and demand" (lines 1–2). The fact that "supply and demand are extremely slow to respond to price shifts" (lines 3–4) does not mean that oil prices are not determined by supply and demand. Thus, a decrease in the price of oil would result in an increase in demand for oil, not a decrease in the price of oil.

7. **B** According to the passage, "[Oil] prices can undergo big swings before a balance is restored" (lines 5–6) and, "Oil prices naturally tend toward extremes" (lines 16–17). *Volatile* (tending to vary often or widely) thus most accurately describes oil prices.

8. **E** According to the passage, ground-based optical systems "will have difficulty finding objects in inner-Earth or Earth-like orbits" (lines 11–12). The passage also says that such systems "are subject to . . . scattering from moonlight" (lines 4–6). It thus makes sense that such systems will be most useful for observing NEOs in orbits that are not like Earth's and that are not in inner-Earth orbits on a moonless night.

9. **B** A full moon making useful observations difficult is the only choice that is not an example of "[an issue] related to access to the assets."

10. **A** "Fidelity" means *loyalty* and a "fiend" is a *devil*.

11. **B** This can be inferred from information provided in the passage: "Nevertheless . . . he would throw up the job suddenly and depart" (lines 48–49); "His incognito, which . . . go to another . . ." (lines 58–63); "He retreated in . . . casually but inevitably" (lines 67–69). We can infer that the "fact" mentioned in line 60 refers to a secret about Jim.

12. **E** The word "incognito" means *false identity*. The phrase "as many holes as a sieve" means that the false identity did not do a good job of keeping Jim's real identity secret.

13. **A** This can be inferred from the reason that is given for Jim's leaving seaports: "When the fact . . . go to another" (lines 60–63).

14. **C** Jim is described as "powerfully built" (line 2) and "very popular" (line 13).

15. **D** The word "casually" is used to describe the manner in which "the fact" follows Jim. As discussed in the explanation to question 11 and to question 13, a secret about Jim eventually becomes known in the seaport in which he is working. The word "casually" describes how the secret becomes known after various intervals of time.

16. **A** The assertion is about a matter of fact, and thus historical evidence would strengthen the assertion. Examples of this attitude on the part of artists and writers could be given.

17. **C** "Bourgeois" means *middle class*.

18. **C** The phrase "this sentiment" (line 11) refers to the "exasperation" (line 9) of artists and writers with highly commercial society. *Philistinism* (line 10)—*an attitude of smug ignorance and conventionalism toward artistic and cultural values*—neatly describes the attitude that artists and writers found exasperating.

19. **A** We can infer that the writer does not think that artists and writers would have contempt for commercial activity that is forced upon a person or that is necessary for their survival.

20. **E** In lines 5–8 ("And since . . . over all others. . . .") we are told that bourgeois society was the first in which the "commercial ethos" was dominant, so we can infer that the author is discussing a time at which the society was becoming more commercial. In lines 15–17 we are told that "[commercial society] did (and does) deprive [artists and writers] of the status that they naturally feel themselves entitled to."

21. **D** The author is concerned mainly with describing the attitudes of artists and writers and their place in bourgeois society. In lines 22–25 he says, "A commercial society, a society whose civilization is shaped by market transactions, is always likely to reflect the appetites and preferences of common men and women." He does not express a view on whether this was a favorable or unfavorable development. His main concern is to describe its effect on artists and writers.

22. **C** The author says, "The popularity of romanticism in the century after 1750 testifies to this fact, as the artists led an 'inner emigration' of the spirit—which, however, left the actual world unchanged" (lines 37–40).

23. **A** The phrase "social force" refers to anything that affects the nature of society. According to the author, socialists believed that the creation of great material abundance would mean that the demand for goods and services ("appetite," line 63) would no longer affect the nature of society.

24. **D** In context "disinterestedly" means *impartially, not motivated by self-interest*. The author is saying that one of the reasons that "scientific socialism" (line 60) is an appealing ideology to intellectuals is that it supports their belief that they are not exercising control over others because they enjoy power or prestige but because they want to help "mobilize the masses for their own ultimate self-transformation" (lines 79–80).

Section 8 Mathematics

<u>Note:</u>

1. See page 32 for an explanation of the symbol ⇒ that is used in some answer explanations.

2. A calculator icon, 🖩, is placed next to the answer explanation of any question for which a calculator *could* be useful. Almost always, the question can be answered easily without using a calculator.

3. If you are unfamiliar with any of the math facts used in the following answer explanations, refer to Barron's *SAT*, which, in addition to having practice tests, has a full review of all the math you need to know.

1. **D** **Solution 1.** The simplest solution is to recognize that if you start with any number and add 100, the result will be 200 more than if you subtract 100 from that number. So, $5x + 100 = 11 + 200 = 211$.

   Solution 2. Start to solve for x:
   $5x - 100 = 11 \Rightarrow 5x = 111$; so, $5x + 100 = 111 + 100 = 211$

2. **A** Since $m\angle P + m\angle Q + m\angle R = 180°$, and $m\angle P + m\angle Q > (40° + 75°) = 115°$, then $m\angle R$ must be *less than* $180° - 115° = 65°$.

3. **C** Since the product of 0 and any number is 0, if c were 0, then cd would be 0, not 4. All of the other choices are possible. In fact, c could be *any* number other than 0, in which case d would equal $\dfrac{4}{c}$.

4. **E** Region A consists of those positive integers that are prime, less than 20, and not odd. The only number in A is 2, so $a = 2$. Region B consists of odd integers that are prime, but not less than 20. There are infinitely many numbers in B, the smallest of which is 23. So $b = 23$, and $a + b = 2 + 23 = 25$.

5. **D** **Solution 1.**
   * Multiplying both sides of the inequality $a < 1$ by the positive number a, we get $a^2 < a$. So $a^2 < 1$, and again multiplying both sides by a, we see that $a^3 < a$. Similarly, $a^n < a$ for any integer $n > 1$. In particular, $a^5 < a$. I is true.
   * Just as $a^5 < a$ (see above), $b^5 < b$. Taking the fifth root of each side, we see that $b < \sqrt[5]{b}$. So $\sqrt[5]{b}$ is *not* less than b, it's greater than b. II is false.
   * Since $b < 1$ and a is positive, $a(b) < a(1) \Rightarrow ab < a$. But since b is positive, $a < a + b$. So $ab < a < a + b$. III is true.

   Solution 2. You can test some numbers. If $a = 0.5$ and $b = 0.6$, then you can use your calculator to see that $a^5 = 0.03125$, which is much less than a. That doesn't prove that Statement I is true, but it justifies a guess, and, of course, you could test another number. Similarly, since $(0.5) \times (0.6) = 0.30$ and $(0.5) + (0.6) = 1.1$, it appears that Statement III is true. Since $\sqrt[5]{0.6} \approx 0.90$, Statement II is definitely false.

6. **E** From the graph on the left, we see that in 1990, 54% (35% + 19%) of all college students were male, and the other 46% were female. So, of the 10,000,000 students, there were 5,400,000 males and 4,600,000 females—a difference of 800,000.

7. **B** From the two graphs, we see that in 1990, 54% (35% + 19%) of all college students were male, whereas in 1995 the corresponding figure was 45% (28% + 17%). For simplicity, assume that there were 100 college students in 1990, 54 of whom were male. Then in 2010, after a 40% increase in the total number of students, there were 140 students, 63 of whom were male (45% of 140 = 63). So the ratio of the number of male students in 2010 to the number of male students in 1990 is 63:54 = 7:6.

8. **C** **Solution 1.** Replace d dollars by $100d$ cents and set up a proportion:

   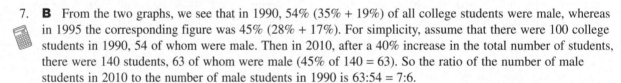

   $$\frac{\text{markers}}{\text{cents}} = \frac{m}{c} = \frac{x}{100d} \Rightarrow x = \frac{100dm}{c}$$

   Solution 2. Plug in easy-to-use numbers, not necessarily ones that are realistic. If 3 markers cost 6 cents, then markers cost 2 cents each and for 2 dollars you can buy 100 of them. Which choice equals 100 when $p = 3$, $c = 6$, and $d = 2$? Only choice (C): $\dfrac{100(2)(3)}{6} = 100$

9. **E** The only way to satisfy the condition that each section receive at least one student is for one student to join each of two of the sections and for two students to join the third section. The best way to answer this type of question is to use the counting principle. Assume that Section 3 receives two students. Then there are 4 ways to assign one of the students to Section 1 and 3 ways to assign one of the three remaining students to Section 2, after which the two remaining students must go to Section 3; so there are $4 \times 3 = 12$ ways to assign the students. Similarly, there are 12 ways to assign the students if Section 2 receives two students, and 12 more ways if Section 1 receives two students. In total there are $3 \times 12 = 36$ ways to assign the students.

10. **E** Let s represent the length of a side of the square. Then $P = 4s$ and $A = s^2$.
- Could $P = A$? Could $4s = s^2$? Yes, if $s = 4$.
- Could $P < A$? Could $4s < s^2$? Yes, if $s > 4$.
- Could $P > A$? Could $4s > s^2$? Yes, if $s < 4$.

NOTE: The question asks, which of the statements *could* be true, not which of the statements *must* be true. *None* of the statements *must* be true.

11. **D** Since $f(x) = ax + b$, $f(2) = 2a + b$, and $f(4) = 4a + b$. So $4a + b = 16$ and $2a + b = 10$. Subtracting the second equation from the first, we get that $2a = 6$, and so $a = 3$. Therefore, $4(3) + b = 16$, and $b = 4$. So, $f(x) = 3x + 4$, and $f(8) = 3(8) + 4 = 24 + 4 = 28$.

12. **E Solution 1.** Let the number of boys in the band be $2x$ and the number of girls in the band be $3x$. Then the number of band members in the chorus is

$$\frac{1}{4}(2x) + \frac{1}{3}(3x) = \frac{x}{2} + x = \frac{3}{2}x$$

Since the total number of band members is $2x + 3x = 5x$, the fraction of band members in the chorus is

$\dfrac{\frac{3}{2}x}{5x} = \dfrac{\frac{3}{2}}{5} = \dfrac{3}{10}$. So the fraction of band members *not* in the chorus is $1 - \dfrac{3}{10} = \dfrac{7}{10}$.

Solution 2. Pick a number for the number of band members. You can pick any number, but since the ratio of boys to girls is 2:3, choose a multiple of 5, say 50. Then there are 20 boys and 30 girls in the band, of whom

$\dfrac{1}{4}(20) = 5$ and $\dfrac{1}{3}(30) = 10$ are in the chorus. So 15 band members are in the chorus and 35 are not: $\dfrac{35}{50} = \dfrac{7}{10}$.

13. **C Solution 1.** If $s\%$ of the c children have a sibling, then

$(100 - s)\%$ of the c children don't have a sibling. Since $x\%$ means $\dfrac{x}{100}$, $(100 - s)\% = \dfrac{100 - s}{100}$.

Finally, $(100 - s)\%$ of c is equal to $\dfrac{(100 - s)}{100}c = \dfrac{(100 - s)c}{100}$.

Solution 2. Pick easy-to-use numbers for c and s. Assume the class has 10 children and 20 percent of them have siblings. Then 2 children have siblings and 8 don't. Which answer choice equals 8 when $c = 10$ and

$s = 20$? Only choice (C): $\dfrac{(100 - 20)(10)}{100} = \dfrac{(80)(10)}{100} = \dfrac{800}{100} = 8$

14. **C** $0.025 = \dfrac{25}{1,000}$ and for any number, x, $x\% = x \div 100$. Therefore, $0.025\% = \dfrac{25}{1,000} \div 100 = \dfrac{25}{100,000} = \dfrac{1}{4,000}$.

So, in country A approximately one person in 4,000 is affected with the disease. Set up a proportion and cross-multiply:

$$\frac{1}{4,000} = \frac{800}{x} \Rightarrow x = 800 \times 4,000 = 3,200,000$$

Of the five choices, choice (C), 3,000,000, is the best approximation.

15. **D Solution 1.** The sum of all the numbers in the set other than x is $T - x$. Then since $x = p\%$ of $(T - x)$,

$x = \dfrac{p}{100}(T - x)$, and so $100x = pT - px \Rightarrow 100x + px = pT$. Then, factoring out an x, we have

$(100 + p)x = pT$, and $x = \dfrac{pT}{100 + p}$. Finally, dividing both sides by T, we get $\dfrac{x}{T} = \dfrac{p}{100 + p}$.

Solution 2. Pick simple numbers. Let the set be $\{1, 2, 3\}$ and let $x = 3$. Then $T = 1 + 2 + 3 = 6$ and x is $\dfrac{1}{2}$ of

T. The sum of the numbers in the set other than 3 is $1 + 2 = 3$, so 3 is 100 percent of the sum of those numbers.

Finally, which of the answer choices is equal to $\dfrac{1}{2}$ when $p = 100$ and $T = 6$? Only choice (D):

$\dfrac{100}{100 + 100} = \dfrac{100}{200} = \dfrac{1}{2}$

16. **C**

- Every prime factor of n is a prime factor of $2n$ and the only additional prime factor $2n$ could have is 2.
  If n is even, then 2 is already one of the prime factors of n, and so $2n$ and n have exactly the same prime factors, and so $f(2n) = f(n)$. I is true.
- If n is odd, the prime factors of $2n$ are the prime factors of n and the number 2. So $f(2n) = f(n) + 2$. II is true.
- If n is even $f(2n) = f(n)$ and so cannot equal $2f(n)$.
  If n is odd $f(2n) = f(n) + 2$, so if $f(2n)$ were equal to $2f(n)$, then $f(n) + 2 = 2f(n)$ and so $f(n)$ would equal 2. But that is impossible if n is odd. III is false.

Section 9 Critical Reading

1. **B** The words "in a fair and objective way, giving all sides equitable treatment" in the sentence signal that the writing instructor would like his students to take (B) *a balanced* approach.

2. **D** If war is "biological" it makes sense that such instincts are (D) *innate* (inborn).

3. **B** The sentence describes a "cyclical view of history," so it is reasonable to conclude that societies become *decadent* (undergoing a process of decline or decay) after becoming civilized.

4. **B** An *induction* is *a general principle arrived at from particular facts*. Epidemiologists (doctors who study the causes and distribution of disease) had to show that the only variable in determining whether or not a person got lung cancer was whether he or she smoked cigarettes. (B) *Determinants* is the best choice for the second blank because it means *something that determines the outcome*.

5. **A** People became aware that "the degree of regularity and predictability in nature" cannot be explained by gods exercising (A) *arbitrary* (determined by whim) will. The key to identifying the correct answer is noticing that "regularity and predictability" would not be produced by an arbitrary will.

6. **E** The word "prisoner" in the sentence signals that something limiting is referred to in both the first blank and the second blank. For the first blank, (A) *biases* (preferences) (C) *assumptions*, and (E) *preconceptions* (prejudices) make sense. For the second blank, (D) *subjective* (personal) and (E) *circumscribed* (narrowly limited) make sense. Thus, (E) is the best choice.

7. **A** "Fault lines" is a term in geology that refers to the place where two tectonic plates meet. The use of the term to refer to civilizations compares civilizations to continental plates, suggesting that like continental plates civilizations are distinct entities that sometimes collide, causing conflict between them.

8. **C** We can infer that the author uses the word *basic* to mean *fundamental* because immediately after the sentence in which he uses the word he describes differences among civilizations that, in his view, determine the essential nature of civilizations: "Civilizations are differentiated . . . equality and hierarchy" (lines 12–22). Also, in line 24 he refers to the differences as "fundamental."

9. **B** The author says, "Civilizations are differentiated from each other by history, language, culture, tradition and, *most important, religion*" (lines 12–15, italics mine) and "[These differences] are far more fundamental than differences among political ideologies . . ." (lines 22–25). We can infer from this that the author believes that most people identify more strongly with their religion than with their political party.

10. **B** The author is arguing that what he considers the most fundamental differences among civilizations (as described in lines 12–22, "Civilizations are differentiated . . . equality and hierarchy") have "over the centuries . . . generated the most prolonged and the most violent conflicts" (lines 27–30). Since the passage is mainly concerned with the cause of future conflict, it makes sense that the author would consider the most important implication of the statement to be that differences among civilizations rather than differing political ideologies will cause serious future conflict in the world.

11. **D** The author says, "The interactions between peoples of different civilizations are increasing; these interactions intensify civilization consciousness and awareness of differences between civilizations and commonalities within civilizations" (lines 31–36). Immediately after this statement he gives examples of such interactions, including North African immigration to France. In lines 48–53 the author says, "The interactions

among peoples of different civilizations enhance the civilization-consciousness of people that, in turn, invigorates differences and animosities stretching or thought to stretch back deep into history." From this information we can infer that the author would be very likely to agree that the increased movements of large numbers of people belonging to different civilizations from one civilization to another has increased the likelihood of conflict between civilizations.

12. **D** The author says, "The processes of economic modernization and social change throughout the world are separating people from longstanding local identities . . . In much of the world religion has moved in to fill this gap. . . . In most countries and most religions the people active in fundamentalist movements are young, college-educated, middle-class technicians, professionals, and business persons" (lines 54–67).

13. **A** After describing Huntington's classification as "[identifying] determinants [of international events] on a grand scale by 'civilizations' " (lines 106–107), the author of Passage 2 describes what he sees as the difficulties with Huntington's classification: "His endeavor, however, has its own fault lines. The lines are borders encompassing each distinct nation and mercilessly chopping the alleged civilizations into pieces" (lines 107–111). From this we can infer that the author of Passage 2 has serious doubts about whether the term "civilization" can be applied to the entities described as such by Huntington.

14. **E** The author of Passage 2 says, "Toynbee . . . contend[ed] that [civilizations'] attributes continue to influence contemporary events" (lines 92–96). and "Like Toynbee and now Huntington, [Wright] attributed contemporary significance to these factors" (lines 101–103).

15. **A** The author of Passage 2 believes Raymond Aron's statement is correct because he agrees with Aron that although culture and civilization are important to people and play a part in determining events in the international arena, nation-states play the decisive role in determining such events.

16. **E** Passage 2 refers to theories of civilizations that have been formulated in the past by Toynbee and Wright. Passage 1 makes no reference to theories of civilizations formulated in the past.

17. **E** The author's main argument is that "It is willful, day-to-day, crisis-to-crisis, war-to-war political decision-making by nation-state units that remains the single most identifiable determinant of events in the international arena" (lines 122–126). In this context the statement in lines 120–123 is most accurately described as a "partial concession" to Huntington's argument that politics, regimes, and ideologies are determined by culture, history, and civilization. The author says Huntington's argument is true "*to an extent*" (line 123; italics mine), a statement that can be described as a partial concession to Huntington's argument.

18. **A** The author of Passage 1 does not argue that *all* conflict is at present caused by conflicts between civilizations or that this will be true in the future. He argues that "the world will be shaped *in large measure* by the interactions among seven or eight major civilizations" (lines 2–4; italics mine) and that "the most important conflicts of the future will occur along the cultural fault lines separating these civilizations from one another" (lines 7–10). Thus, he would be likely to say that the Persian Gulf War is an example of nation-states putting their interests ahead of the interests of the civilization to which they belong, but that this one example does not invalidate his argument that civilizational loyalty is becoming more important than loyalty to the nation-state in causing conflict in the world.

Section 10 Writing

1. **D** This is a run-on sentence. Two independent clauses cannot be joined by a comma. Choice (D) changes the part of the sentence after the comma so that it becomes a participial phrase referring to *enemy*.

2. **C** This corrects the error in the given sentence, which contains a faulty comparison. *Novels* cannot be compared to *writers*.

3. **C** This changes the tense error in the given sentence by changing the tense of the verb *wanted* from the simple past tense to the past perfect tense and the tense of *would specify* from the present tense to the present perfect tense.

4. **C** The given sentence contains an idiom error. The phrase *where you have* is incorrect in this context. Change to *of having*.

5. **E** This corrects the error in pronoun–antecedent agreement in the given sentence. The antecedent of the pronoun *it* is *designs*, a plural noun, so the singular pronoun *it* must be changed to the plural pronoun *they*. Because the pronoun *they* is plural the verb *requires* must in turn be changed to *require* to agree with *they* in number.

6. **E** This corrects the error in subject–verb agreement in the given sentence. The subject of the independent clause beginning with the word *each* is *each*, a singular noun, so the plural verb *are* must be changed to the singular verb *is*.

7. **C** The given sentence contains a dangling participle, *dissatisfied with the government's weak response to violent crime*. Choice (C) corrects this by making *people* the subject of the independent clause that begins after the comma, and placing it at the beginning of the clause, so that the participial phrase clearly refers to *people*.

8. **B** This corrects the error in the given sentence, which is a run-on sentence, by changing the part of the sentence after the comma from an independent clause to an appositive. *Dilettantes* refers to *amateur radio operators*, so it should be placed near it in the sentence.

9. **E** The given sentence has faulty parallelism because the direct objects of the verb *combine* are not in the same form. Choice (E) corrects this by changing *being able* to *an ability to*.

10. **D** The given sentence contains an idiom error. The phrase *where size is increasingly distorted towards the poles* is incorrect in this context. This corrects the error.

11. **A** The given sentence is clear and grammatical.

12. **D** The phrase *the result when people suffer* is not idiomatic. Choice (D) provides the correct idiom.

13. **A** The given sentence is clear and grammatical.

14. **C** The given sentence is awkwardly worded in two ways. The subject of the main clause is *pilot*, but the focus is *reporting*. This requires the use of a possessive structure, which is awkward. Also, it is not clear whether the participial phrase beginning with *saying* refers to the pilot or to the airline. This corrects the awkward wording by changing the subject of the independent clause from the noun *pilot* to the gerund *reporting*. It also changes the incorrect participial phrase beginning with *saying* to a relative clause, which makes clear that the *airline* is being referred to.

Answer Sheet–Practice Test 3

Section 1   ESSAY

Essay (continued)

If a section has fewer questions than answer spaces, leave the extra spaces blank.

Section 2

1 Ⓐ Ⓑ Ⓒ Ⓓ Ⓔ	8 Ⓐ Ⓑ Ⓒ Ⓓ Ⓔ	15 Ⓐ Ⓑ Ⓒ Ⓓ Ⓔ	22 Ⓐ Ⓑ Ⓒ Ⓓ Ⓔ	29 Ⓐ Ⓑ Ⓒ Ⓓ Ⓔ
2 Ⓐ Ⓑ Ⓒ Ⓓ Ⓔ	9 Ⓐ Ⓑ Ⓒ Ⓓ Ⓔ	16 Ⓐ Ⓑ Ⓒ Ⓓ Ⓔ	23 Ⓐ Ⓑ Ⓒ Ⓓ Ⓔ	30 Ⓐ Ⓑ Ⓒ Ⓓ Ⓔ
3 Ⓐ Ⓑ Ⓒ Ⓓ Ⓔ	10 Ⓐ Ⓑ Ⓒ Ⓓ Ⓔ	17 Ⓐ Ⓑ Ⓒ Ⓓ Ⓔ	24 Ⓐ Ⓑ Ⓒ Ⓓ Ⓔ	31 Ⓐ Ⓑ Ⓒ Ⓓ Ⓔ
4 Ⓐ Ⓑ Ⓒ Ⓓ Ⓔ	11 Ⓐ Ⓑ Ⓒ Ⓓ Ⓔ	18 Ⓐ Ⓑ Ⓒ Ⓓ Ⓔ	25 Ⓐ Ⓑ Ⓒ Ⓓ Ⓔ	32 Ⓐ Ⓑ Ⓒ Ⓓ Ⓔ
5 Ⓐ Ⓑ Ⓒ Ⓓ Ⓔ	12 Ⓐ Ⓑ Ⓒ Ⓓ Ⓔ	19 Ⓐ Ⓑ Ⓒ Ⓓ Ⓔ	26 Ⓐ Ⓑ Ⓒ Ⓓ Ⓔ	33 Ⓐ Ⓑ Ⓒ Ⓓ Ⓔ
6 Ⓐ Ⓑ Ⓒ Ⓓ Ⓔ	13 Ⓐ Ⓑ Ⓒ Ⓓ Ⓔ	20 Ⓐ Ⓑ Ⓒ Ⓓ Ⓔ	27 Ⓐ Ⓑ Ⓒ Ⓓ Ⓔ	34 Ⓐ Ⓑ Ⓒ Ⓓ Ⓔ
7 Ⓐ Ⓑ Ⓒ Ⓓ Ⓔ	14 Ⓐ Ⓑ Ⓒ Ⓓ Ⓔ	21 Ⓐ Ⓑ Ⓒ Ⓓ Ⓔ	28 Ⓐ Ⓑ Ⓒ Ⓓ Ⓔ	35 Ⓐ Ⓑ Ⓒ Ⓓ Ⓔ

Section 3

1 Ⓐ Ⓑ Ⓒ Ⓓ Ⓔ	8 Ⓐ Ⓑ Ⓒ Ⓓ Ⓔ	15 Ⓐ Ⓑ Ⓒ Ⓓ Ⓔ	22 Ⓐ Ⓑ Ⓒ Ⓓ Ⓔ	29 Ⓐ Ⓑ Ⓒ Ⓓ Ⓔ
2 Ⓐ Ⓑ Ⓒ Ⓓ Ⓔ	9 Ⓐ Ⓑ Ⓒ Ⓓ Ⓔ	16 Ⓐ Ⓑ Ⓒ Ⓓ Ⓔ	23 Ⓐ Ⓑ Ⓒ Ⓓ Ⓔ	30 Ⓐ Ⓑ Ⓒ Ⓓ Ⓔ
3 Ⓐ Ⓑ Ⓒ Ⓓ Ⓔ	10 Ⓐ Ⓑ Ⓒ Ⓓ Ⓔ	17 Ⓐ Ⓑ Ⓒ Ⓓ Ⓔ	24 Ⓐ Ⓑ Ⓒ Ⓓ Ⓔ	31 Ⓐ Ⓑ Ⓒ Ⓓ Ⓔ
4 Ⓐ Ⓑ Ⓒ Ⓓ Ⓔ	11 Ⓐ Ⓑ Ⓒ Ⓓ Ⓔ	18 Ⓐ Ⓑ Ⓒ Ⓓ Ⓔ	25 Ⓐ Ⓑ Ⓒ Ⓓ Ⓔ	32 Ⓐ Ⓑ Ⓒ Ⓓ Ⓔ
5 Ⓐ Ⓑ Ⓒ Ⓓ Ⓔ	12 Ⓐ Ⓑ Ⓒ Ⓓ Ⓔ	19 Ⓐ Ⓑ Ⓒ Ⓓ Ⓔ	26 Ⓐ Ⓑ Ⓒ Ⓓ Ⓔ	33 Ⓐ Ⓑ Ⓒ Ⓓ Ⓔ
6 Ⓐ Ⓑ Ⓒ Ⓓ Ⓔ	13 Ⓐ Ⓑ Ⓒ Ⓓ Ⓔ	20 Ⓐ Ⓑ Ⓒ Ⓓ Ⓔ	27 Ⓐ Ⓑ Ⓒ Ⓓ Ⓔ	34 Ⓐ Ⓑ Ⓒ Ⓓ Ⓔ
7 Ⓐ Ⓑ Ⓒ Ⓓ Ⓔ	14 Ⓐ Ⓑ Ⓒ Ⓓ Ⓔ	21 Ⓐ Ⓑ Ⓒ Ⓓ Ⓔ	28 Ⓐ Ⓑ Ⓒ Ⓓ Ⓔ	35 Ⓐ Ⓑ Ⓒ Ⓓ Ⓔ

Section 4

1 Ⓐ Ⓑ Ⓒ Ⓓ Ⓔ	8 Ⓐ Ⓑ Ⓒ Ⓓ Ⓔ	15 Ⓐ Ⓑ Ⓒ Ⓓ Ⓔ	22 Ⓐ Ⓑ Ⓒ Ⓓ Ⓔ	29 Ⓐ Ⓑ Ⓒ Ⓓ Ⓔ
2 Ⓐ Ⓑ Ⓒ Ⓓ Ⓔ	9 Ⓐ Ⓑ Ⓒ Ⓓ Ⓔ	16 Ⓐ Ⓑ Ⓒ Ⓓ Ⓔ	23 Ⓐ Ⓑ Ⓒ Ⓓ Ⓔ	30 Ⓐ Ⓑ Ⓒ Ⓓ Ⓔ
3 Ⓐ Ⓑ Ⓒ Ⓓ Ⓔ	10 Ⓐ Ⓑ Ⓒ Ⓓ Ⓔ	17 Ⓐ Ⓑ Ⓒ Ⓓ Ⓔ	24 Ⓐ Ⓑ Ⓒ Ⓓ Ⓔ	31 Ⓐ Ⓑ Ⓒ Ⓓ Ⓔ
4 Ⓐ Ⓑ Ⓒ Ⓓ Ⓔ	11 Ⓐ Ⓑ Ⓒ Ⓓ Ⓔ	18 Ⓐ Ⓑ Ⓒ Ⓓ Ⓔ	25 Ⓐ Ⓑ Ⓒ Ⓓ Ⓔ	32 Ⓐ Ⓑ Ⓒ Ⓓ Ⓔ
5 Ⓐ Ⓑ Ⓒ Ⓓ Ⓔ	12 Ⓐ Ⓑ Ⓒ Ⓓ Ⓔ	19 Ⓐ Ⓑ Ⓒ Ⓓ Ⓔ	26 Ⓐ Ⓑ Ⓒ Ⓓ Ⓔ	33 Ⓐ Ⓑ Ⓒ Ⓓ Ⓔ
6 Ⓐ Ⓑ Ⓒ Ⓓ Ⓔ	13 Ⓐ Ⓑ Ⓒ Ⓓ Ⓔ	20 Ⓐ Ⓑ Ⓒ Ⓓ Ⓔ	27 Ⓐ Ⓑ Ⓒ Ⓓ Ⓔ	34 Ⓐ Ⓑ Ⓒ Ⓓ Ⓔ
7 Ⓐ Ⓑ Ⓒ Ⓓ Ⓔ	14 Ⓐ Ⓑ Ⓒ Ⓓ Ⓔ	21 Ⓐ Ⓑ Ⓒ Ⓓ Ⓔ	28 Ⓐ Ⓑ Ⓒ Ⓓ Ⓔ	35 Ⓐ Ⓑ Ⓒ Ⓓ Ⓔ

Section 5

1 Ⓐ Ⓑ Ⓒ Ⓓ Ⓔ	8 Ⓐ Ⓑ Ⓒ Ⓓ Ⓔ	15 Ⓐ Ⓑ Ⓒ Ⓓ Ⓔ	22 Ⓐ Ⓑ Ⓒ Ⓓ Ⓔ	29 Ⓐ Ⓑ Ⓒ Ⓓ Ⓔ
2 Ⓐ Ⓑ Ⓒ Ⓓ Ⓔ	9 Ⓐ Ⓑ Ⓒ Ⓓ Ⓔ	16 Ⓐ Ⓑ Ⓒ Ⓓ Ⓔ	23 Ⓐ Ⓑ Ⓒ Ⓓ Ⓔ	30 Ⓐ Ⓑ Ⓒ Ⓓ Ⓔ
3 Ⓐ Ⓑ Ⓒ Ⓓ Ⓔ	10 Ⓐ Ⓑ Ⓒ Ⓓ Ⓔ	17 Ⓐ Ⓑ Ⓒ Ⓓ Ⓔ	24 Ⓐ Ⓑ Ⓒ Ⓓ Ⓔ	31 Ⓐ Ⓑ Ⓒ Ⓓ Ⓔ
4 Ⓐ Ⓑ Ⓒ Ⓓ Ⓔ	11 Ⓐ Ⓑ Ⓒ Ⓓ Ⓔ	18 Ⓐ Ⓑ Ⓒ Ⓓ Ⓔ	25 Ⓐ Ⓑ Ⓒ Ⓓ Ⓔ	32 Ⓐ Ⓑ Ⓒ Ⓓ Ⓔ
5 Ⓐ Ⓑ Ⓒ Ⓓ Ⓔ	12 Ⓐ Ⓑ Ⓒ Ⓓ Ⓔ	19 Ⓐ Ⓑ Ⓒ Ⓓ Ⓔ	26 Ⓐ Ⓑ Ⓒ Ⓓ Ⓔ	33 Ⓐ Ⓑ Ⓒ Ⓓ Ⓔ
6 Ⓐ Ⓑ Ⓒ Ⓓ Ⓔ	13 Ⓐ Ⓑ Ⓒ Ⓓ Ⓔ	20 Ⓐ Ⓑ Ⓒ Ⓓ Ⓔ	27 Ⓐ Ⓑ Ⓒ Ⓓ Ⓔ	34 Ⓐ Ⓑ Ⓒ Ⓓ Ⓔ
7 Ⓐ Ⓑ Ⓒ Ⓓ Ⓔ	14 Ⓐ Ⓑ Ⓒ Ⓓ Ⓔ	21 Ⓐ Ⓑ Ⓒ Ⓓ Ⓔ	28 Ⓐ Ⓑ Ⓒ Ⓓ Ⓔ	35 Ⓐ Ⓑ Ⓒ Ⓓ Ⓔ

Section 7

1 Ⓐ Ⓑ Ⓒ Ⓓ Ⓔ 3 Ⓐ Ⓑ Ⓒ Ⓓ Ⓔ 5 Ⓐ Ⓑ Ⓒ Ⓓ Ⓔ 7 Ⓐ Ⓑ Ⓒ Ⓓ Ⓔ
2 Ⓐ Ⓑ Ⓒ Ⓓ Ⓔ 4 Ⓐ Ⓑ Ⓒ Ⓓ Ⓔ 6 Ⓐ Ⓑ Ⓒ Ⓓ Ⓔ 8 Ⓐ Ⓑ Ⓒ Ⓓ Ⓔ

9 **10** **11** **12** **13**

14 **15** **16** **17** **18**

Section 8

1 Ⓐ Ⓑ Ⓒ Ⓓ Ⓔ	5 Ⓐ Ⓑ Ⓒ Ⓓ Ⓔ	9 Ⓐ Ⓑ Ⓒ Ⓓ Ⓔ	13 Ⓐ Ⓑ Ⓒ Ⓓ Ⓔ	17 Ⓐ Ⓑ Ⓒ Ⓓ Ⓔ
2 Ⓐ Ⓑ Ⓒ Ⓓ Ⓔ	6 Ⓐ Ⓑ Ⓒ Ⓓ Ⓔ	10 Ⓐ Ⓑ Ⓒ Ⓓ Ⓔ	14 Ⓐ Ⓑ Ⓒ Ⓓ Ⓔ	18 Ⓐ Ⓑ Ⓒ Ⓓ Ⓔ
3 Ⓐ Ⓑ Ⓒ Ⓓ Ⓔ	7 Ⓐ Ⓑ Ⓒ Ⓓ Ⓔ	11 Ⓐ Ⓑ Ⓒ Ⓓ Ⓔ	15 Ⓐ Ⓑ Ⓒ Ⓓ Ⓔ	19 Ⓐ Ⓑ Ⓒ Ⓓ Ⓔ
4 Ⓐ Ⓑ Ⓒ Ⓓ Ⓔ	8 Ⓐ Ⓑ Ⓒ Ⓓ Ⓔ	12 Ⓐ Ⓑ Ⓒ Ⓓ Ⓔ	16 Ⓐ Ⓑ Ⓒ Ⓓ Ⓔ	20 Ⓐ Ⓑ Ⓒ Ⓓ Ⓔ

Section 9

1 Ⓐ Ⓑ Ⓒ Ⓓ Ⓔ	5 Ⓐ Ⓑ Ⓒ Ⓓ Ⓔ	9 Ⓐ Ⓑ Ⓒ Ⓓ Ⓔ	13 Ⓐ Ⓑ Ⓒ Ⓓ Ⓔ	17 Ⓐ Ⓑ Ⓒ Ⓓ Ⓔ
2 Ⓐ Ⓑ Ⓒ Ⓓ Ⓔ	6 Ⓐ Ⓑ Ⓒ Ⓓ Ⓔ	10 Ⓐ Ⓑ Ⓒ Ⓓ Ⓔ	14 Ⓐ Ⓑ Ⓒ Ⓓ Ⓔ	18 Ⓐ Ⓑ Ⓒ Ⓓ Ⓔ
3 Ⓐ Ⓑ Ⓒ Ⓓ Ⓔ	7 Ⓐ Ⓑ Ⓒ Ⓓ Ⓔ	11 Ⓐ Ⓑ Ⓒ Ⓓ Ⓔ	15 Ⓐ Ⓑ Ⓒ Ⓓ Ⓔ	19 Ⓐ Ⓑ Ⓒ Ⓓ Ⓔ
4 Ⓐ Ⓑ Ⓒ Ⓓ Ⓔ	8 Ⓐ Ⓑ Ⓒ Ⓓ Ⓔ	12 Ⓐ Ⓑ Ⓒ Ⓓ Ⓔ	16 Ⓐ Ⓑ Ⓒ Ⓓ Ⓔ	20 Ⓐ Ⓑ Ⓒ Ⓓ Ⓔ

Section 10

1 Ⓐ Ⓑ Ⓒ Ⓓ Ⓔ	5 Ⓐ Ⓑ Ⓒ Ⓓ Ⓔ	9 Ⓐ Ⓑ Ⓒ Ⓓ Ⓔ	13 Ⓐ Ⓑ Ⓒ Ⓓ Ⓔ	17 Ⓐ Ⓑ Ⓒ Ⓓ Ⓔ
2 Ⓐ Ⓑ Ⓒ Ⓓ Ⓔ	6 Ⓐ Ⓑ Ⓒ Ⓓ Ⓔ	10 Ⓐ Ⓑ Ⓒ Ⓓ Ⓔ	14 Ⓐ Ⓑ Ⓒ Ⓓ Ⓔ	18 Ⓐ Ⓑ Ⓒ Ⓓ Ⓔ
3 Ⓐ Ⓑ Ⓒ Ⓓ Ⓔ	7 Ⓐ Ⓑ Ⓒ Ⓓ Ⓔ	11 Ⓐ Ⓑ Ⓒ Ⓓ Ⓔ	15 Ⓐ Ⓑ Ⓒ Ⓓ Ⓔ	19 Ⓐ Ⓑ Ⓒ Ⓓ Ⓔ
4 Ⓐ Ⓑ Ⓒ Ⓓ Ⓔ	8 Ⓐ Ⓑ Ⓒ Ⓓ Ⓔ	12 Ⓐ Ⓑ Ⓒ Ⓓ Ⓔ	16 Ⓐ Ⓑ Ⓒ Ⓓ Ⓔ	20 Ⓐ Ⓑ Ⓒ Ⓓ Ⓔ

Practice Test 3 $\quad$ 1 $\quad$ 1 $\quad$ 1 $\quad$ 1 $\quad$ 1 $\quad$ 1 $\qquad$ 1

SECTION 1 $\quad$ **Time—25 Minutes** $\qquad$ **ESSAY**

Write your essay on the lines provided on the answer sheet on pages 175–176. Be careful to write legibly. Write on the topic, carefully presenting your point of view. Your essay will be scored on the basis of the ideas it contains and its effectiveness in expressing these ideas. Pay special attention to logic, clarity, and the accurate use of language.

Think about the topic presented in the following excerpt and in the assignment below it.

The government believes that in certain instances it must exercise control over the media, including newspapers and magazines, radio and television, social media such as Facebook, and the World Wide Web in general. Although the government admits that such restrictions are not desirable in themselves because they restrict individual freedom and give government dangerous powers over the people, the government maintains that they are nevertheless essential in some situations, such as those involving national security.

ASSIGNMENT: To what extent, if any, should government restrict the free flow of information in a democracy? Plan and write an essay in which you develop your point of view on this question. Support your position with reasoning and examples taken from your experience, reading, or observations.

2 2 2 2 2 2 2 2 2 2 2

SECTION **2** | Time—25 Minutes 24 Questions | Choose the best answer to each of the following questions in this section. Then blacken the appropriate space on your answer sheet.

Each of the following sentences contains one or two blanks, indicating that a word or set of words has been omitted. Beneath each sentence there are five answer choices labeled A to E from which you must select the word or set of words that best fits the meaning of the sentence as a whole.

Example:

Records of colonization can be found as far back as the Phoenicians, but colonization became a major force in world history only when European countries began, in the fifteenth century, to make ---- Asia, the Americas, and Africa.

(A) queries about   (B) incursions into
    (C) tirades against   (D) enemies in
      (E) amends for

 Ⓐ ● Ⓒ Ⓓ Ⓔ

---

1. Although the general ---- of Americans increased in the 1980s and 1990s, a spate of research has shown that people at the bottom of the economic hierarchy were less likely than ever before to move up the economic ladder.

   (A) skill level   (B) consensus   (C) interest
        (D) affluence   (E) knowledge

2. Knowledge is a double-edged sword that can be used to increase wisdom and do good, or be used for ----.

   (A) technology   (B) malefaction
       (C) research   (D) humanity
        (E) patricide

3. It has been asserted that because a language is ---- part of any culture, for a community to elect or be compelled to speak a language other than the one its members first acquired ---- means that it loses forever a significant part of its culture.

   (A) a peripheral . . unequivocally
   (B) an important . . parenthetically
   (C) an extraneous . . unfortunately
   (D) an intrinsic . . ironically
   (E) an integral . . necessarily

4. Respiration is essentially the ---- the energy producing and storing process of photosynthesis, allowing organisms to break down carbohydrates stored as food to utilize their energy.

   (A) rejoinder to   (B) antithesis of
       (C) parody of   (D) moratorium on
        (E) reciprocation of

5. According to physicists, many elementary particles—such as those created in laboratories—have a ---- existence; such particles are not directly observable but their existence can be deduced from the traces that they leave behind.

   (A) transitory   (B) mundane
       (C) worthwhile   (D) charmed
        (E) nondescript

6. International monitoring of communicable disease by such agencies as the Center for Disease Control in Atlanta, Georgia has helped control the spread of ---- that in the past ---- populations.

   (A) viruses . . inundated
   (B) pandemics . . decimated
   (C) contaminants . . reduced
   (D) illnesses . . ameliorated
   (E) wars . . afflicted

GO ON TO THE NEXT PAGE

7. Some opponents of applying genetic engineering to human beings ---- a "slippery slope" argument, saying that although most people find the idea ---- in principle, they first will be swayed by the prospect of having offspring free of physical imperfection, then by the idea of having highly intelligent children, and so on.

(A) eschew . . repugnant
(B) evoke . . aberrant
(C) invoke . . abhorrent
(D) exhume . . pernicious
(E) overstate . . optional

8. According to the theory of natural selection, our seemingly ---- intellectual abilities, such as the ability to do higher mathematics and write symphonies, evolved as an indirect result of our struggle to survive, and subsequently gave us a monumental advantage over other species in the struggle for survival.

(A) paltry
(B) flamboyant
(C) recurrent
(D) superfluous
(E) palpable

GO ON TO THE NEXT PAGE

2   2 2 2 2 2 2 2 2 2   2

Below are passages followed by questions on them. Questions on a pair of related passages may be about the relationship between the two passages. For each question, select the best answer based on what is stated or implied in the passage (or passages).

Questions 9–12 are based on the following passages.

Passage 1

It may be surprising to some that the use of nuclear energy has direct benefits to the environment, specifically air quality. Although
Line debate continues about the potential for the
(5) disruption of the earth's climate by emissions of carbon dioxide and other greenhouse gases, there is no doubt about the serious health consequences of air pollution from the burning of fossil fuels. Unlike fossil-fuel power plants, nuclear plants do
(10) not produce carbon dioxide, sulfur or nitrogen oxides. Nuclear power production in the U.S. annually avoids the emission of more than 175 million tons of carbon that would have been released into the environment if the same amount
(15) of electricity had instead been generated by burning coal.

Passage 2

Nuclear energy is claimed to be the answer to our climate problems since it is clean-burning. However, a life-cycle analysis, which takes into
(20) account the energy-intensive processes of mining and enriching the uranium ore, constructing and dismantling the nuclear plant, and disposing the hazardous waste, shows that nuclear is definitely not carbon-free. In fact, emissions from a nuclear
(25) plant in the U.S. can range from 16–55 grams of CO_2 per kilowatt-hour over the lifetime of the plant. Compared to wind (11–37 gCO_2/kWh) and biomass (29–62 gCO_2/kWh), nuclear is no cleaner than renewables. Furthermore, nuclear power will
(30) only become more polluting in the future since increased nuclear production will decrease the supply of high-grade uranium and much more

energy is required to enrich uranium at lower grades. At the same time, the International
(35) Atomic Energy Agency has already acknowledged that current uranium resources are not sufficient to meet increased demand in the future. A report from The Oxford Research Group predicts that in 45 to 70 years, nuclear energy
(40) will emit more carbon dioxide than gas-fired electricity.

9. Passage 1 and Passage 2 both

(A) offer information that supports the argument for the increased use of nuclear energy to produce power

(B) compare the amount of pollution generated by nuclear power plants with the amount of pollution generated by coal and gas-burning power plants

(C) compare the amount of pollution produced by nuclear power plants with the amount of pollution produced by renewable energy sources

(D) consider the pollution generated from mining uranium and related activities necessary to generate power as well as the pollution generated solely by the production of electricity

(E) agree that direct emissions of pollutants from nuclear plants is relatively low

GO ON TO THE NEXT PAGE ⇒

2 2 2 2 2 2 2 2 2 2

10. How would the author of Passage 2 most likely respond to the statement in Passage 1 that "Nuclear power production in the U.S. annually avoids the emission of more than 175 million tons of carbon that would have been released into the environment if the same amount of electricity had instead been generated by burning coal" (lines 11–16)?

    (A) Wind and biomass power generation annually avoid the emission of more than 175 million tons of carbon.

    (B) This is a completely fallacious and deliberately misleading statement made to support the nuclear power industry.

    (C) This is a misleading figure because it does not take into account the great amount of carbon released by the related activities necessary for the generation of nuclear power.

    (D) This figure does not take into consideration the fact that much more energy is required to enrich low-grade uranium than high-grade uranium.

    (E) This is laudable in that it is the one major area in which the use of nuclear power helps solve the climate problem.

11. Which of the following future developments would offer support for the argument made in Passage 1?

    (A) A study showing that supplies of high-grade uranium are running out faster than previously believed

    (B) New technological developments that greatly reduce emissions from coal-burning power plants

    (C) A study showing conclusively that Earth's climate has been significantly changed by the emissions of carbon dioxide and other greenhouse gases

    (D) New technological developments that greatly reduce the pollution produced in the process of mining uranium ore

    (E) A definitive study showing that the effects of air pollution—already known to be serious— on human health are far worse than previously thought

12. The author of Passage 1 would be most likely to say that the information presented in Passage 2 would be made more valuable in deciding how much electric power should be generated by nuclear energy over the next 30 years by

    (A) the inclusion of a life-cycle analysis of the amount of emissions from coal and gas electric power generation

    (B) the inclusion of a life-cycle analysis of the amount of emissions from other renewable energy sources in addition to wind and biomass

    (C) the inclusion of a life-cycle analysis comparing the amount of emissions produced by wind and biomass

    (D) information providing support for the assertion that "Nuclear energy is . . . clean-burning" (lines 17–18).

    (E) Details of the Oxford Research Group's prediction that "in 45–70 years, nuclear energy will emit more carbon dioxide than gas fired electricity" (lines 39–41).

Questions 13–24 are based on the following passage.

    The following is an excerpt from The Great Boer War *by Arthur Conan Doyle.*

    Take a community of Dutchmen of the type of those who defended themselves for fifty years against all the power of Spain at a time when
Line Spain was the greatest power in the world.
 (5) Intermix with them a strain of those inflexible French Huguenots who gave up home and fortune and left their country for ever at the time of the revocation of the Edict of Nantes. The product must obviously be one of the most rugged, virile,
(10) unconquerable races ever seen upon earth. Take this formidable people and train them for seven generations in constant warfare against savage men and ferocious beasts, in circumstances under which no weakling could survive, place them so
(15) that they acquire exceptional skill with weapons and in horsemanship, give them a country which is eminently suited to the tactics of the huntsman,

GO ON TO THE NEXT PAGE ➡

the marksman, and the rider. Then, finally, put a finer temper upon their military qualities by a

(20) dour fatalistic Old Testament religion and an ardent and consuming patriotism. Combine all these qualities and all these impulses in one individual, and you have the modern Boer—the most formidable antagonist who ever crossed the

(25) path of Imperial Britain. Our military history has largely consisted in our conflicts with France, but Napoleon and all his veterans have never treated us so roughly as these hard-bitten farmers with their ancient theology and their inconveniently

(30) modern rifles.

Look at the map of South Africa, and there, in the very center of the British possessions, like the stone in a peach, lies the great stretch of the two republics, a mighty domain for so small a people.

(35) How came they there? Who are these Teutonic folk who have burrowed so deeply into Africa? It is a twice-told tale, and yet it must be told once again if this story is to have even the most superficial of introductions. No one can know or

(40) appreciate the Boer who does not know his past, for he is what his past has made him.

It was about the time when Oliver Cromwell was at his zenith—in 1652, to be pedantically accurate—that the Dutch made their first

(45) lodgment at the Cape of Good Hope. The Portuguese had been there before them, but, repelled by the evil weather, and lured forwards by rumors of gold, they had passed the true seat of empire and had voyaged further to settle along

(50) the eastern coast. Some gold there was, but not much, and the Portuguese settlements have never been sources of wealth to the mother country, and never will be until the day when Great Britain signs her huge check for Delagoa Bay. The coast

(55) upon which they settled reeked with malaria. A hundred miles of poisonous marsh separated it from the healthy inland plateau. For centuries these pioneers of South African colonization strove to obtain some further footing, but save

(60) along the courses of the rivers they made little progress. Fierce natives and an enervating climate barred their way.

But it was different with the Dutch. That very rudeness of climate which had so impressed the

(65) Portuguese adventurer was the source of their success. Cold and poverty and storm are the nurses of the qualities which make for empire. It

is the men from the bleak and barren lands who master the children of the light and the heat. And

(70) so the Dutchmen at the Cape prospered and grew stronger in that robust climate. They did not penetrate far inland, for they were few in number and all they wanted was to be found close at hand. But they built themselves houses, and they

(75) supplied the Dutch East India Company with food and water, gradually budding off little townlets, Wynberg, Stellenbosch, and pushing their settlements up the long slopes which lead to that great central plateau which extends for

(80) fifteen hundred miles from the edge of the Karoo to the Valley of the Zambesi.

Then came the additional Huguenot emigrants—the best blood of France, three hundred of them, a handful of the choicest seed

(85) thrown in to give a touch of grace and soul to the solid Teutonic strain. Again and again in the course of history, with the Normans, the Huguenots, the Émigrés, one can see the great hand dipping into that storehouse and sprinkling

(90) the nations with the same splendid seed. France has not founded other countries, like her great rival, but she has made every other country the richer by the mixture with her choicest and best. The Rouxs, Du Toits, Jouberts, Du Plessis,

(95) Villiers, and a score of other French names are among the most familiar in South Africa.

For a hundred more years the history of the colony was a record of the gradual spreading of the Afrikaners over the huge expanse of veld

(100) which lay to the north of them. Cattle raising became an industry, but in a country where six acres can hardly support a sheep, large farms are necessary for even small herds. Six thousand acres was the usual size, and five pounds a year

(105) the rent payable to Government. The diseases which follow the white man had in Africa, as in America and Australia, been fatal to the natives, and an epidemic of smallpox cleared the country for the newcomers. Further and further north they

(110) pushed, founding little towns here and there, such as Graaf-Reinet and Swellendam, where a Dutch

GO ON TO THE NEXT PAGE

2   2 2 2 2 2 2 2 2 2   2

Reformed Church and a store for the sale of the bare necessaries of life formed a nucleus for a few scattered dwellings. Already the settlers were
(115) showing that independence of control and that detachment from Europe which has been their most prominent characteristic. Even the sway of the Dutch Company (an older but weaker brother of John Company in India) had caused them to
(120) revolt. The local rising, however, was hardly noticed in the universal cataclysm which followed the French Revolution. After twenty years, during which the world was shaken by the Titanic struggle between England and France, in
(125) the final counting up of the game and paying of the stakes, the Cape Colony was added in 1814 to the British Empire.

13. Which of the following, according to the author, did *not* go into the making of "the modern Boer" (line 23)?

    (A) Dutch ancestry
    (B) Seven generations of constant warfare
    (C) A country well-suited to the tactics the Boer were good at
    (D) A religion that valued pleasure above all else
    (E) Patriotism

14. What does the author mean by "treated us so roughly" (lines 27–28)?

    (A) Was such a difficult foe to defeat on the battlefield
    (B) Denied us vital exports of farm products
    (C) Insulted our national honor
    (D) Slaughtered so many of our helpless women and children
    (E) Judged us unfairly

15. What does the writer mean when he describes the Boers' rifles as "inconveniently modern" (lines 29–30)?

    (A) The Boers' rifles were up-to-date but poorly designed.
    (B) The Boers' rifles were very effective.
    (C) The Boers' rifles were effective but inconveniently stored so that there was difficulty in getting them to the troops before battle.
    (D) The Boers' rifles were old-fashioned.
    (E) The Boers' rifles were rather modern, but they were not as advanced as those used by British forces.

16. In line 61, "enervating" most nearly means

    (A) draining energy
    (B) energizing
    (C) saving energy
    (D) wasting energy
    (E) favoring the enemy

17. What, according to the author, was the main reason that the Dutch, rather than the Portuguese, succeeded in establishing a successful colony in Africa?

    (A) The Dutch had more financial support from their mother country.
    (B) The Dutch were more ruthless than the Portuguese.
    (C) The Dutch were stronger than the Portuguese because they were from a harsher climate.
    (D) The religion of the Dutch placed more emphasis on colonization of other lands than did that of the Portuguese.
    (E) The Dutch were better carpenters than the Portuguese.

GO ON TO THE NEXT PAGE

Practice Test 3

2 2 2 2 2 2 2 2 2 2

18. What is "the choicest seed" (line 84)?

(A) The best seeds from Holland used to grow hardy crops
(B) Germans
(C) People from France who migrated to Africa to join the Dutch colony there
(D) Blood donated by the smartest and most courageous people of France
(E) Three hundred of the greatest works of French literature

19. The phrase "her great rival" (lines 91–92) refers to

(A) Portugal
(B) Germany
(C) Australia
(D) England
(E) the United States

20. Which of the following words best describes the attitude of the writer toward the Boers?

(A) Skeptical
(B) Admiring
(C) Hostile
(D) Angry
(E) Neutral

21. In line 19, "temper" most nearly means

(A) composure
(B) irritability
(C) hardness
(D) a characteristic general quality
(E) disposition

22. In line 21, "consuming" most nearly means

(A) reckless
(B) self-destructive
(C) deeply felt
(D) aggressive
(E) wasteful

23. Which of the following would the author be *least* likely to say is a characteristic of the modern Boer?

(A) Readiness to compromise
(B) Independent spirit
(C) Determination
(D) Patriotism
(E) A willingness to work hard

24. The author does which one of the following?

(A) Quotes representative people among the community he describes
(B) Questions the premises of some of his central assertions
(C) Recounts historical events
(D) Cites authorities to support some of his assertions
(E) Contrasts his view of the Boer with that of other writers

IN ANY REMAINING TIME YOU MAY REVIEW THE ANSWERS YOU CHOSE IN THIS SECTION. DO NOT WORK ON ANY OTHER SECTION OF THE TEST DURING THIS TIME.

3   3 3 3 3 3 3 3 3 3 3   3

SECTION **3**

Time—25 Minutes
20 Questions

For each problem in this section determine which of the five choices is correct and blacken the corresponding choice on your answer sheet. You may use any blank space on the page for your work.

Notes:

- You may use a calculator whenever you think it will be helpful.
- Only real numbers are used. No question or answer on this test involves a complex or imaginary number.
- Use the diagrams provided to help you solve the problems. Unless you see the words "Note: Figure not drawn to scale" under a diagram, it has been drawn as accurately as possible. Unless it is stated that a figure is three-dimensional, you may assume it lies in a plane.
- For any function, f, the domain, unless specifically restricted, is the set of all real numbers for which $f(x)$ is also a real number.

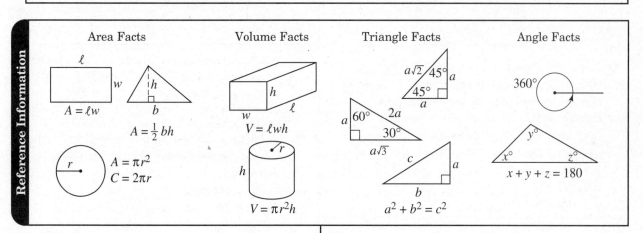

Reference Information

Area Facts

$A = \ell w$

$A = \frac{1}{2} bh$

$A = \pi r^2$
$C = 2\pi r$

Volume Facts

$V = \ell wh$

$V = \pi r^2 h$

Triangle Facts

$a^2 + b^2 = c^2$

Angle Facts

$360°$

$x + y + z = 180$

1. At Frank's Fancy Fruits, Frank makes up gift baskets containing 1 pineapple, 3 kiwis, and 5 passion fruits. What is the maximum number of complete gift baskets he can assemble on a day that he has 50 pineapples, 100 kiwis, and 200 passion fruits on hand?

   (A) 50
   (B) 40
   (C) 33
   (D) 30
   (E) 25

2. In a class of 36 children there are 3 times as many boys as girls. How many boys are in the class?

   (A) 6
   (B) 9
   (C) 12
   (D) 18
   (E) 27

3. If the ratio of the circumference of circle 1 to the circumference of circle 2 is 2:1, what is the ratio of the radius of circle 1 to the radius of circle 2?

   (A) 2:1
   (B) 1:2
   (C) π:1
   (D) π:2
   (E) 2π:1

GO ON TO THE NEXT PAGE

Practice Test 3

3 3 3 3 3 3 3 3 3 3 3 **3**

4. If the product of six integers is odd, what is the smallest number of them that could be odd?

(A) 0
(B) 1
(C) 3
(D) 5
(E) 6

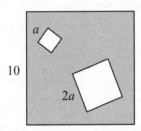

5. In the figure above, two white squares are drawn inside a larger square. Which of the following expressions represents the area of the shaded region?

(A) $10 - 3a$
(B) $40 - 12a$
(C) $100 - 3a^2$
(D) $100 - 5a^2$
(E) $100 - 9a^2$

6. Sally had three times as much money as Heidi did. After giving Heidi $200, Sally had twice as much money as Heidi did. How much money did Sally originally have?

(A) 600
(B) 900
(C) 1,200
(D) 1,500
(E) 1,800

7. If u and t are the units digits and the tens digits of the product $123,456,789 \times 987,654,321$, what is the value of $u - t$?

(A) −3
(B) −1
(C) 0
(D) 3
(E) 5

8. If the average (arithmetic mean) of $a, a, a, a, \frac{1}{6}$, and $\frac{1}{3}$ is $\frac{1}{4}$, then what is the value of a?

(A) $\frac{1}{6}$

(B) $\frac{1}{4}$

(C) $\frac{1}{3}$

(D) $\frac{1}{2}$

(E) $\frac{3}{4}$

9. A delivery service has two fees: $5 for a package weighing less than 10 pounds and $8 for a package weighing at least 10 pounds but not more than 20 pounds. Packages weighing more than 20 pounds are not accepted. Which of the following inequalities can be used to determine if a package weighing p pounds should be charged $8 to be delivered?

(A) $|p - 20| \le 10$
(B) $|p - 10| \le 20$
(C) $|p - 15| \le 5$
(D) $|p + 15| \le 5$
(E) $|p + 15| \ge 5$

10. What is the slope of the line whose equation is $4y - 5x = 6$?

(A) −5

(B) $-\frac{5}{4}$

(C) $-\frac{4}{5}$

(D) $\frac{3}{2}$

(E) $\frac{5}{4}$

GO ON TO THE NEXT PAGE

Practice Test 3

3   3 3 3 3 3 3 3 3 3 3   3

$$8a + 5b = 100$$
$$5a + 8b = 98$$

11. If a and b satisfy the two equations above, what is the value of $a - b$?

  (A) $\dfrac{2}{3}$

  (B) $\dfrac{3}{2}$

  (C) 1

  (D) 2

  (E) 6

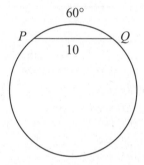

60°

P   Q

10

12. In the circle above, the degree measure of arc PQ is 60° and the length of chord $\overline{PQ}$ is 10. What is the circumference of the circle?

  (A) 10π

  (B) 20π

  (C) 30π

  (D) 40π

  (E) 60π

13. If $\dfrac{3a - 2b}{3a + 2b} = \dfrac{2}{3}$, what is the value of $\dfrac{a}{b}$?

  (A) $-\dfrac{10}{3}$

  (B) $-\dfrac{3}{10}$

  (C) $\dfrac{3}{10}$

  (D) $\dfrac{10}{3}$

  (E) $\dfrac{13}{3}$

14. A jar contains fewer than 100 marbles. If one marble is removed from the jar at random, the probability that it will be red is $\dfrac{1}{3}$, the probability that it will be white is $\dfrac{1}{5}$, and the probability that it will be blue is $\dfrac{1}{4}$. How many of the marbles in the jar are not red, white, or blue?

  (A) 13

  (B) 23

  (C) 40

  (D) 47

  (E) It cannot be determined from the information given.

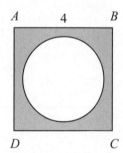

A   4   B

D   C

15. In the figure above, if the length of each side of square $ABCD$ is 4 and the area of the shaded region is 6, what is the circumference of the white circle?

  (A) $\dfrac{10}{\pi}$

  (B) $\dfrac{10}{\sqrt{\pi}}$

  (C) $20\sqrt{\pi}$

  (D) $\sqrt{10\pi}$

  (E) $2\sqrt{10\pi}$

GO ON TO THE NEXT PAGE

16. Each member of the Eastside Women's Club has at most two children, and no one has two children of the same sex. If 25 of the women have exactly one child and in total the women have 32 boys and 37 girls, how many of the women have both a boy and a girl?

(A) 5
(B) 7
(C) 19
(D) 22
(E) 44

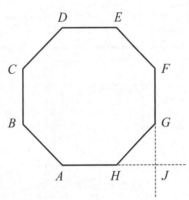

17. In the figure above, *ABCDEFGH* is a regular octagon whose sides are 2. If $\overline{AH}$ and $\overline{FG}$ are extended and intersect at *J* as shown, what is the area of $\triangle GHJ$?

(A) 0.5
(B) 1.0
(C) 2.0
(D) $\sqrt{2}$
(E) $\dfrac{1}{\sqrt{2}}$

18. If *m* and *n* are positive integers, which of the following could be true?

I. $\dfrac{m}{n} = \dfrac{m+1}{n+1}$

II. $\dfrac{m}{n} < \dfrac{m+1}{n+1}$

III. $\dfrac{m}{n} > \dfrac{m+1}{n+1}$

(A) I only
(B) II only
(C) III only
(D) I and III only
(E) I, II, and III

19. If the sum of all the positive integers from 1 to 1,000, inclusive, is *S*, what is the sum of all the positive integers from 1 to 2,000?

(A) $1,000 + S$
(B) $1,000 + 2S$
(C) $2,000 + S$
(D) $1,000,000 + S$
(E) $1,000,000 + 2S$

20. If the function f is defined for all real numbers, x, by $f(x) = ax^2 + bx + c$, where a, b, and c are all negative and $a < b$, which of the following could be the graph of $y = f(x)$?

(A)

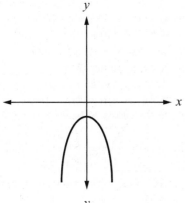

(B)

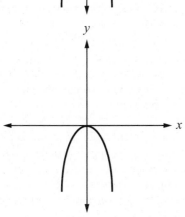

(C)

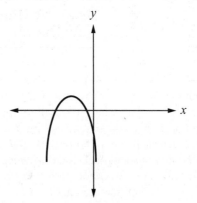

(D)

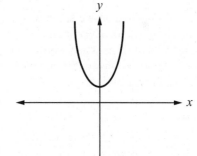

(E)

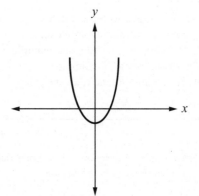

IN ANY REMAINING TIME YOU MAY REVIEW THE
ANSWERS YOU CHOSE IN THIS SECTION. DO NOT WORK
ON ANY OTHER SECTION OF THE TEST DURING THIS TIME.

4 **4** **4** **4** **4** **4** **4** **4** **4** **4** **4**

SECTION **4** | Time—25 Minutes 35 Questions | Choose the best answer to each of the following questions in this section. Then blacken the appropriate space on your answer sheet.

Each sentence below may or may not employ correct or effective expression. If you think that the underlined phrasing makes the most clear and precise sentence, select choice A. If, however, you think that the underlined phrasing makes the meaning of the sentence unclear or awkward, or that it is grammatically incorrect, select another answer from choices B to E.

In choosing your answers, follow the conventions of English as it is used by educated writers. Consider sentence structure, grammar, word choice, and punctuation. Choose the answer that produces the sentence that is the most clear and effective.

Example:

In her comments after the debate the judge said that she had been impressed by the ability of both teams to exploit logical weaknesses and in citing relevant examples.

(A) in citing relevant examples
(B) in that relevant examples had been cited
(C) in the citing of relevant examples
(D) to cite relevant examples
(E) to be able to cite relevant examples

1. Kim Stanley Robinson is a science fiction writer that is able to make a living at it.
   (A) Kim Stanley Robinson is a science fiction writer that is able to make a living at it.
   (B) Able to make a living from it, Kim Stanley Robinson is a science fiction writer.
   (C) Through writing science fiction Kim Stanley Robinson is able to make a living as a writer.
   (D) Kim Stanley Robinson is able to make a living as a science fiction writer.
   (E) A science fiction writer, Kim Stanley Robinson is able to make a living from it.

2. For Geoff, becoming a vegetarian meant eating tofu rather than beef, eggplant rather than chicken, and to eating beans rather than pork.
   (A) to eating beans rather than
   (B) to beans rather than
   (C) beans rather than
   (D) to beans rather than eating
   (E) to the eating of beans instead of

3. Chess and bridge are an example of games that require great skill to play well.
   (A) are an example of games that require great skill
   (B) is an example of games that require great skill
   (C) exemplify games where great skill is required
   (D) are examples of games that require great skill
   (E) are examples from some games that require great skill

4. The largest migration in recorded history had occurred in the approximately one hundred years between the early nineteenth century and the early twentieth century, when there was an exodus of thirty-five million people from Europe to the United States.
   (A) had occurred in the approximately
   (B) had occurred in the approximate
   (C) occurs in the approximately
   (D) occurred in the approximately
   (E) was occurring in the approximate

GO ON TO THE NEXT PAGE

5. Louise was happy to find her lost cell phone walking along the street near her friend's house.

   (A) Louise was happy to find her lost cell phone walking along the street near her friend's house
   (B) Walking along the street near her friend's house, Louise was happy to find her lost cell phone
   (C) It caused Louise to be happy finding her lost cell phone while she was walking along the street near her friend's house
   (D) It made Louise happy to find her lost cell phone walking along the street near her friend's house
   (E) Louise, happy to find her lost cell phone, while walking along the street near her friend's house

6. One of the great achievements in aviation history was Charles Lindbergh, who flew solo across the Atlantic Ocean.

   (A) Charles Lindbergh, who flew solo across the Atlantic Ocean
   (B) Charles Lindbergh's crossing the Atlantic Ocean by flying solo
   (C) Charles Lindbergh's solo flight across the Atlantic Ocean
   (D) the time Charles Lindbergh flew solo across the Atlantic Ocean
   (E) Charles Lindbergh, in his flying solo across the Atlantic Ocean

7. Because of continually complaining about low pay and poor working conditions, the workers went on strike to protest against the company's policies.

   (A) Because of continually complaining about low pay and poor working conditions,
   (B) While they continually complain about low pay and poor working conditions,
   (C) Continually complaining about low pay and poor working conditions, eventually
   (D) They have continually complained about low pay and poor working conditions, later
   (E) After continually complaining about low pay and poor working conditions

8. Anthony Trollope, an English Victorian novelist, believed that the most important duty of a novelist is to entertain readers, the second duty he believed was to inform the reader.

   (A) readers, the second duty he believed was to inform the reader
   (B) readers; he believed the second duty was to inform the reader
   (C) readers; to inform the reader he believed was the second duty
   (D) readers; informing the reader was what he believed the second duty was to be
   (E) readers; and another thing he believed was the novelist's duty to inform the reader

9. The school provides a wide range of extra-curricular activities for students, in addition it will arrange extra lessons for the weaker students.

   (A) students, in addition it will arrange
   (B) students and also arranges
   (C) students, in addition arranging
   (D) students, it arranges
   (E) students; it is also arranging

10. Hoping to finally have his novel published by a major publisher, Norman sent to them each a package, which had in it a copy of his novel.

    (A) Norman sent to them each a package, which had in it a copy of his novel
    (B) a copy of his novel was sent by Norman in a package to them each
    (C) a package containing a copy of his novel was sent by Norman to them each
    (D) Norman sent each of them a package containing a copy of his novel
    (E) Norman sent each of them a package, containing a copy of his novel

11. New research shows that there might be twice as many habitable planets in our galaxy than previously thought.

    (A) than previously thought
    (B) when compared to what was previously thought
    (C) as was believed to be the case previously
    (D) than was believed previously to be the case
    (E) than was thought to be true in earlier times

GO ON TO THE NEXT PAGE ▷

4 4 4 4 4 4 4 4 4 4 4 **4**

Each of the sentences below contains either one error or no error in grammar or usage. If there is an error, it will be underlined. If the sentence contains an error, indicate this by selecting the letter for the one underlined part that should be changed to make the sentence correct. Follow the requirements of standard written English in choosing answers. If the sentence is already correct, select choice E.

Example:

The number of stars <u>visible in</u> the sky on any
            A

<u>given</u> night <u>vary</u>, mainly <u>because of</u> changes in
 B   C   D

atmospheric conditions and in the phases of the

Moon. <u>No Error</u>
     E

Ⓐ Ⓑ ● Ⓓ Ⓔ

12. <u>Paradoxically</u>, law <u>can be</u> used either to tyrannize
   A   B

the populace, <u>denying</u> them liberty, or to protect
         C

their rights, <u>enables</u> them to live as free citizens
        D

expressing their views and doing as they wish.

<u>No Error</u>
  E

13. Because of the <u>unprecedented</u> number of
         A

immigrants who had to be assimilated <u>into</u>
                     B

American culture, the United States used

institutions such as schools to socialize new

arrivals, so that they <u>will</u> gradually lose the norms
               C

of their home cultures and <u>become</u> part of the
                 D

"melting pot"—the new American culture.

<u>No Error</u>
  E

14. A trinket has <u>only</u> an ephemeral appeal <u>but</u> can
        A   B

<u>have existed</u> a long time in a landfill because <u>it's</u>
    C   D

made of plastic, which is durable. <u>No Error</u>
                        E

15. <u>The Stoics</u> taught that virtue is <u>based on</u> knowledge
   A   B

and that the wise <u>is</u> indifferent to suffering and <u>the</u>
           C   D

changing fortunes of life. <u>No Error</u>
               E

16. A competent sociologist can determine the social

class of a person <u>quite</u> accurately from such
          A

<u>seemingly</u> trivial facts <u>as</u> the hobbies <u>they</u> pursue.
  B   C   D

<u>No Error</u>
  E

17. The terms *aphorism* and *maxim* <u>share</u> the same
                        A

general meaning: A <u>pithy</u> and familiar statement
             B

<u>expressing</u> an observation or principle commonly
  C

accepted <u>as</u> true. <u>No Error</u>
       D   E

18. Terry's <u>incredible</u> bad performance in the jazz
        A

concert last Friday night was <u>due to</u> his <u>weakened</u>
                   B   C

condition from the flu that <u>was going</u> around.
                   D

<u>No Error</u>
  E

19. The writer of a <u>very</u> popular novel that I am
          A

reading <u>creates</u> irony by <u>him</u> having the narrator
    B   C

continually <u>undercut</u> his own assertions. <u>No Error</u>
       D   E

GO ON TO THE NEXT PAGE ▷

Practice Test 3

4   4   4   4   4   4   4   4   4   4   4

20. Perhaps an accurate depiction of the American
                        A

   society is a mosaic, in which each group retains its
                    B

   identity but also is blending into the whole.
           C   D

   No Error
     E

21. If a jury indicts a person, the trial takes place
                           A

   before another jury or a judge following the
                      B

   procedures of an adversarial system in which the
               C

   government prosecutor and the accused person's

   defense lawyer each does his best to present
             D

   evidence in a light that discredits his opponent's

   argument. No Error
         E

22. The belief that music is the paradigm by the other
                 A   B

   arts and best exemplifies the power of art to
          C

   express subtle feelings was aptly expressed by the

   critic Walter Pater: "All art constantly aspires
                          D

   towards the condition of music." No Error
                     E

23. According to this book on the Supreme Court,

   Chief Justice Earl Warren frequently lobbied other

   justices on the court, seeking to build a consensus
           A   B

   for the liberal, socially activist positions he
     C   D

   favored. No Error
         E

24. Although that country has a few natural resources,
                       A

   through the hard work of its people it has become
      B   C   D

   one of the richest countries in the world. No Error
                           E

25. Teachers who do not enforce rules govern the time
           A   B

   allowed for the completion of assignments
     C

   are encouraging procrastination on the part of
         D

   students. No Error
            E

26. Scientists have built up a compelling picture of a
               A

   universe that is in the words of one physicist, "Not
                          B

   only strange, and stranger than we can imagine."
             C   D

   No Error
     E

27. The romantic movement in music reached its
                          A

   zenith in the music of composers such as Hector

   Berlioz, Franz Liszt, and Frederic Chopin, all of
                          B

   their work has become an important part of the
              C

   repertoire of many contemporary performers.
     D

   No Error
     E

28. We heard the wife and children of the recently
       A

   deceased man in praising the doctors and nurses
            B

   for the care they gave him during his extended
              C   D

   hospital stay. No Error
            E

29. In the case of many dynamic new art forms,
     A

   Cubism had its inception as a revolt against the
          B   C

   predominant style of art of the day, which was
                 D

   highly expressive and emotional. No Error
                       E

GO ON TO THE NEXT PAGE

$$\boxed{4} \quad \boxed{4 \quad 4 \quad 4 \quad 4 \quad 4 \quad 4 \quad 4 \quad 4 \quad 4 \quad 4 \qquad 4}$$

The following early draft of an essay needs to be rewritten to improve sentence structure, choice of words, clarity of expression, organization, and development. After reading the draft, answer each question below it, choosing the answer that best conforms to the requirements of standard written English.

(1) Students often have difficulty knowing what type of writing is considered acceptable. (2) Generally, in the rather formal sort of writing that you do in school, you should follow as much as possible what is often called "standard usage." (3) It's just the sort being accepted by educated users of English in America at the present time. (4) Although there is continuing discussion about exactly what constitutes standard usage, there is broad agreement. (5) Generally speaking, most educated users agree on matters of grammar. (6) Everyone agrees, for example, that verbs must agree with their subjects. (7) Most users agree that run-on sentences should be avoided.

(8) How can you determine whether a particular word or phrase that you want to use is "standard"? (9) Perhaps the best way is to consult a good dictionary, such as *Merriam-Webster's Collegiate Dictionary* or *The American Heritage College Dictionary*. (10) *The American Heritage College Dictionary*, fourth edition, lists many meanings first under the noun form and then under the verb form of the word. (11) With a stick to the verb form of "stick," we learn that there are more than twelve distinct formal meanings and half a dozen or so informal or colloquial meanings. (12) According to the experts at American Heritage, the use of "stick to" in the previous sentence is acceptable, but the phrases "stick around" and "stick (one's) neck out" are not because they are informal.

(13) If you really want to stick to your guns and use an expression that your dictionary labels informal because it's colorful and expresses your meaning clearly, you have two choices: one, consult another reputable dictionary and hope that it says the expression is standard; two, hope that your teacher doesn't notice it—or, better, notices it, praises your creativity and boldness in using non-standard English, and sticks up for your right to use informal language.

30. In context, which of the following is the best way to phrase the underlined portion of sentence 3 (reproduced below)?

    It's just the sort being accepted by educated users of English in America at the present time.

    (A) (As it is now)
    (B) It is a language being accepted by
    (C) It's the sort of language having been accepted by
    (D) This is language that is accepted by
    (E) Language being accepted by

31. Which of the following sentences, if inserted immediately after sentence 7, would most effectively link sentences 7 and 8?

    (A) These are sentences that are not properly structured.
    (B) These are errors in sentences that many students ignore.
    (C) Such sentences consist of words and phrases.
    (D) Grammar is not the only area of writing on which most educated users of English agree.
    (E) The greatest difficulties tend to appear at the level of words and phrases.

32. Which of the following sentences would be best to insert before sentence 10?

    (A) Both are very good dictionaries; but I prefer the layout and definitions in the latter.
    (B) Let's take the word "stick" as an example.
    (C) These are both excellent dictionaries.
    (D) These dictionaries define both the noun form and the verb form of many words.
    (E) We can take a word as an example.

GO ON TO THE NEXT PAGE

4 4 4 4 4 4 4 4 4 4 4 | 4

33. Which of the following is the best version of the underlined portion of sentence 11 (reproduced below)?

With a stick to the verb form of "stick," we learn that there are more than twelve distinct formal meanings and half a dozen or so informal or colloquial meanings.

(A) (As it is now)
(B) Sticking to the verb form of "stick,"
(C) On sticking to the verb form of "stick,"
(D) Stuck to the verb form of "stick,"
(E) What sticks to the verb form of "stick,"

34. Of the following, which is the best version of the underlined portion of sentence 13 (reproduced below)?

If you really want to stick to your guns and use an expression that your dictionary labels informal because it's colorful and expresses your meaning clearly, *you have two choices: one, consult another (reputable) dictionary and hope that it says the expression is standard; two, hope that your teacher doesn't notice it—or, better, notices it, praises your creativity and boldness in using non-standard English, and sticks up for your right to use informal language.*

(A) (as it is now)
(B) that you think is colorful and expresses your meaning clearly because your dictionary labels it informal,
(C) because you think it's colorful, expresses your meaning clearly, and your dictionary labels it informal,
(D) that is colorful and expresses your meaning clearly, and is labeled to be informal by your dictionary,
(E) because you think it's colorful and expresses your meaning clearly, but your dictionary labels it informal,

35. The primary effect of the final paragraph (sentence 13) is to

(A) leave the reader with the impression that language is inflexible
(B) call into question what was said earlier in the passage
(C) create humor
(D) make fun of people who worry about correct English usage
(E) discourage students from being creative in their writing

STOP

IN ANY REMAINING TIME YOU MAY REVIEW THE ANSWERS YOU CHOSE IN THIS SECTION. DO NOT WORK ON ANY OTHER SECTION OF THE TEST DURING THIS TIME.

Practice Test 3

5 5 5 5 5 5 5

| SECTION 5 | Time—25 Minutes 24 Questions | Choose the best answer to each of the following questions in this section. Then blacken the appropriate space on your answer sheet. |

Each of the following sentences contains one or two blanks, indicating that a word or set of words has been omitted. Beneath each sentence there are five answer choices labeled A to E from which you must select the word or set of words that best fits the meaning of the sentence as a whole.

Example:

Records of colonization can be found as far back as the Phoenicians, but colonization became a major force in world history only when European countries began, in the fifteenth century, to make ---- Asia, the Americas, and Africa.

(A) queries about   (B) incursions into
  (C) tirades against   (D) enemies in
    (E) amends for

Ⓐ ● Ⓒ Ⓓ Ⓔ

1. Samuel Huntington's main thesis in his book *The Clash of Civilizations and the Remaking of World Order* is that future international ---- will be more the result of differing cultural values than of varying political and economic interests.

   (A) friendship   (B) relations   (C) treaties
     (D) colloquy   (E) animosity

2. Students who pursue a professional qualification often do so on the ---- that they are trading off hard work in the present for rewards in the future.

   (A) theme   (B) foundation   (C) quandary
     (D) premise   (E) accretion

3. ---- city planners allow for the movement of people from the city center to the suburbs as they move up the socio-economic ----.

   A. Jaded . . ladder
   B. Prudent . . hierarchy
   C. Sagacious . . quagmire
   D. Circumspect . . indicator
   E. Judicious . . bureaucracy

4. Careful observation of popular culture as presented in the mass media reveals that many songs, movies, and television programs are ----, teaching the values of society through entertainment.

   (A) expedient   (B) bombastic   (C) didactic
     (D) acerbic   (E) prosaic

5. The writer introduced ---- evidence that sounded ---- upon first hearing, but which upon deeper reflection was seen to be flawed.

   (A) elusive . . plausible
   (B) multi-faceted . . preconceived
   (C) convincing . . facile
   (D) spurious . . credible
   (E) beguiling . . circuitous

GO ON TO THE NEXT PAGE

5   5   5   5   5   5   5

Below are passages followed by questions on them. Questions on a pair of related passages may be about the relationship between the two passages. For each question, select the best answer based on what is stated or implied in the passage (or passages).

Questions 6–7 are based on the following passage.

Style is character expressive of definite conceptions, as of grandeur, gaiety, or solemnity. An historic style is the particular phase, the
Line characteristic manner of design, which prevails at
(5) a given time and place. It is not the result of caprice, but of intellectual, moral, social, religious, and even political conditions. Gothic architecture could never have been invented by the Greeks, nor could the Egyptian styles have
(10) grown up in Italy. Each style is based upon some fundamental principle springing from its surrounding civilization, which undergoes successive developments until it either reaches perfection or its possibilities are exhausted, after
(15) which a period of decline usually sets in. This is followed either by a reaction and the introduction of some radically new principle leading to the evolution of a new style, or by the final decay and extinction of the civilization and its
(20) replacement by some younger and more virile element.

6. In line 6, "caprice" most nearly means

(A) intangible elements
(B) utilitarian concerns
(C) aesthetic judgment
(D) a sudden and unaccountable change of views
(E) chance

7. Based on what is said in the passage, the author would most likely agree that

(A) once a style of art exhausts its possibilities, it inevitably and immediately declines
(B) when an architectural style achieves perfection, it does so independently of the nature of the civilization in which it developed
(C) terms such as "Gothic architecture" are useful but ultimately are too general to have any real meaning
(D) the study of architectural styles is closely related to the study of the history of civilizations
(E) it is impossible to assign an absolute aesthetic value to any style of architecture because each style is rooted in a particular civilization, and the nature of civilizations varies greatly

Questions 8–9 are based on the following passage.

Art in all its phases was not only an adornment but a necessity of Christian civilization. The Church taught people by
Line sculpture, mosaic, miniature, and fresco. It was
(5) an object-teaching, a grasping of ideas by forms seen in the mind, not a presenting of abstract ideas as in literature. Printing was not known. There were few manuscripts, and the majority of people could not read. Ideas came to them for
(10) centuries through form and color, until at last the Italian mind took on a plastic and pictorial character. It saw things in symbolic figures, and when the Renaissance came and art took the lead as one of its strongest expressions, painting was
(15) but the color-thought and form-language of the people. And these people, by reason of their peculiar education, were an exacting people, knowing what was good and demanding it from

GO ON TO THE NEXT PAGE ⟩

5　　5　　5　　5　　5　　5　　5

the artists. Every Italian was, in a way, an art
(20) critic, because every church in Italy was an art
school. The artists may have led the people, but
the people spurred on the artists, and so the
Italian mind went on developing and unfolding
until at last it produced the great art of the
Renaissance.

8. Which of the following is one of the reasons the
author says that art was "a necessity of Christian
civilization" (lines 2–3)?

   (A) The Christian religion believes that only art
   can reflect God's glory and power.
   (B) Printing was not known for much of the time
   that Christian civilization existed.
   (C) Only art can present abstract ideas in a
   manner similar to literature.
   (D) Reading books was so popular that the Church
   had to use art to capture people's attention.
   (E) Christian civilization was for many centuries
   centered in Italy, whose government required
   that religious ideas be communicated
   primarily through art.

9. Which of the following factors helped produce the
great art of the Renaissance?

   (A) Artists had a receptive and appreciative
   audience.
   (B) By the time of the Renaissance, nearly every
   church in Italy had been converted from a
   church into an art school.
   (C) During the Renaissance, people became more
   able to appreciate literature.
   (D) Books had become widely available by the
   time of the Renaissance, enabling artists to
   pass on their knowledge to the next generation
   of artists.
   (E) Most of the best artists of the Renaissance
   were not Christians.

Questions 10–14 are based on the following passage.

The periodical cicadas, most notably
Magicicada septendecim, have the longest life
cycle of any insect. Their unique life cycle begins
Line underground, where the nymphs patiently suck
(5) the juice from the roots of trees. Then, after 17
years of waiting, the adult cicadas emerge from
the ground, swarm in vast numbers, and
temporarily swamp the landscape. Within a few
weeks they mate, lay their eggs, and die.
(10)　　The question that puzzled biologists was, *Why
is the cicada's life cycle so long*? And is there
any significance to the life cycle being a prime
number of years? Another species, *Magicicada
tredecim*, swarms every 13 years, implying that
(15) life cycles lasting a prime number of years offer
some evolutionary advantage.
　　One theory suggests that the cicada has a
parasite that also goes through a lengthy life
cycle and that the cicada is trying to avoid. If the
(20) parasite has a life cycle of, say, 2 years then the
cicada wants to avoid a life cycle that is divisible
by 2, otherwise the parasite and the cicada will
regularly coincide. Similarly, if the parasite has a
life cycle of 3 years then the cicada wants to
(25) avoid a life cycle that is divisible by 3, otherwise
the parasite and the cicada will once again
regularly coincide. Ultimately, to avoid meeting
its parasite, the cicadas' best strategy is to have a
long life cycle lasting a prime number of years.
(30) Because nothing will divide into 17, *Magicicada
septendecim* will rarely meet its parasite. If the
parasite has a 2-year life cycle they will meet
only every 34 years, and if it has a longer life
cycle, say 16 years, then they will meet only
(35) every 272 (16 × 17) years.
　　In order to fight back, the parasite has only
two life cycles that will increase the frequency of
coincidences—the annual cycle and the same 17-
year cycle as the cicada. However, the parasite is
(40) unlikely to survive reappearing 17 years in a row,
because for the first 16 appearances there will be

GO ON TO THE NEXT PAGE

5 5 5 5 5 5 5

no cicadas for it to parasitize. On the other hand, in order to reach the 17-year life cycle, the generations of parasites would first have to
(45) evolve through the 16-year life cycle. This would mean at some stage of evolution the parasite and cicada would not coincide for 272 years! In either case the cicada's long prime life cycle protects it.

This might explain why the alleged parasite
(50) has never been found! In the race to keep up with the cicada, the parasite probably kept extending its life cycle until it hit the 16-year hurdle. Then it failed to coincide for 272 years, by which time the lack of coinciding with cicadas had driven it
(55) to extinction. The result is a cicada with a 17-year life cycle, which it no longer needs because its parasite no longer exists.

10. Scientists theorize that cicadas have a 17-year life cycle because

(A) 17 years is the optimum length of time for cicadas to most efficiently use available food and other resources in order to reproduce

(B) no parasite species can survive 17 years without reproducing

(C) it evolved as the most advantageous way for cicadas to co-exist with a parasite that has now become extinct

(D) it evolved as a successful defense against a parasite that no longer exists

(E) all insects have a life cycle lasting a number of years that is some randomly selected prime number

11. *Magicicada tredecim* probably has a 13-year life cycle rather than a 17-year one because

(A) it is a less advanced species than *Magicicada septendecim*

(B) two species of cicada having the same life cycle would create unnecessary competition for both species, so one evolved a different long prime number life cycle

(C) its parasite is still extant, so it cannot evolve a life cycle lasting so long

(D) its parasite became extinct so it had no need to evolve a life cycle lasting a longer prime number of years

(E) it has a parasite with a 16-year life cycle, which means that it will meet its parasite only once every 208 (16 × 13) years

12. According to the theory described in the passage, which of the following statements is NOT true?

(A) The cicada wants to decrease the frequency with which its life cycle coincides with its parasite.

(B) The cicada's parasite wants to increase the frequency with which its life cycle coincides with that of the cicadas.

(C) For the cicada's parasite, the longer the life cycle of the cicadas the better.

(D) To avoid meeting its parasite it is advantageous for the cicada to have a long life cycle.

(E) To avoid meeting its parasite it is advantageous for cicadas to have a life cycle lasting a prime number of years.

13. Which of the following most accurately describes the explanation given in the passage for the fact that *Magicicada septendecim* has a 17-year life cycle?

(A) It is based on a scientific theory that has excellent theoretical and empirical support.

(B) It is based entirely on conjecture.

(C) It is based on a scientific theory that has good theoretical support but no real empirical support.

(D) It is a mathematician's tongue-in-cheek attempt to offer a mathematical explanation for a biological phenomenon that cannot be mathematically explained.

(E) It is based on a theory with excellent empirical support but almost no theoretical support.

GO ON TO THE NEXT PAGE

14. If an organism is discovered that parasitizes *Magicicada septendecim* it would

    (A) totally invalidate the theory that *Magicicada septendecim* evolved a long life cycle lasting a prime number of years to protect itself from a parasite

    (B) demonstrate conclusively that Magicicada Septendecim evolved a long life cycle lasting a prime number of years in order to protect itself from a parasite

    (C) suggest that the theory that *Magicicada septendecim* evolved a long life cycle lasting a prime number of years to protect itself from a parasite is probably not true

    (D) show conclusively that certain parasites can survive 272 years without a host to parasitize

    (E) suggest that parasites have evolved at a faster rate than cicadas

Questions 15–24 are based on the following passages.

Passage 1

    Sustainability of renewable resources can be defined in different ways. Maintaining the economic output of an ecosystem (e.g., in a
Line commercially exploited forest) is one option and
(5) maintaining the integrity of the whole ecosystem (e.g., in an old-growth forest) is another possibility. In addition to the immediate value associated with its economic outputs, the ecosystem that supports the resource flows may
(10) have option values for possible future uses, and existence values simply because people value its continued existence. Ecosystems have information value as working models of complex interacting life-sustaining systems, about which
(15) we still have much to learn. Option and existence values are less tangible and more difficult to measure than the immediate economic output, but may be of comparable importance, especially in a long-term perspective.
(20)   Renewable resources are subject to a variety of stresses, often more powerful than those acting on non-renewables. They are inexhaustible in the sense that they can be continually recycled, but this does not mean they are infinite in amount
(25) and does not prevent their degradation.

Renewable resources, including air, water and land, are subject to pressures for different uses, which may be incompatible. Air and water are particularly susceptible to pollutants because of
(30) the ease with which they can be used as open-access resources for receiving and disseminating waste. Habitat for plant and animal species may be very sensitive to environmental impacts, and easily destroyed. Thus renewable resources
(35) should be seen as finite and vulnerable to pressures.

    For example, a river system can be dedicated to a variety of purposes: power generation, drinking water, irrigation, industrial use, sport
(40) and commercial fishing, recreation in various forms such as rafting and canoeing, swimming, sailing or motor-boating on lakes and reservoirs, scenery for hikers and campers, sites for resorts or cottages, or pure wilderness. Once dedicated, it
(45) cannot be used again without disturbing the constituencies that use its features and whose property values depend on them. Some of these uses may degrade the quality of the water, or spoil it for other uses. In some cases, so much
(50) water is withdrawn for various uses that not much reaches the sea or ocean—the Nile and the Colorado are in this condition at times. This in turn can have an impact on coastal currents and water quality, salinity of water in the delta, etc.
(55) Policy for renewable resources, including pricing policy, should reflect their scarcity value, multiple uses, and susceptibility to degradation or irreversible loss.

Passage 2

    Many instances of unsustainable resource use
(60) can be attributed not only to a lack of a well-functioning market, but to perverse institutional or legal incentives, such as a lack of property rights to resources, or (especially in underdeveloped nations) a lack of ready resource
(65) alternatives. Groundwater resources in the U.S., for instance, are often overused because of subsidies, a lack of tradable rights to water ("use

GO ON TO THE NEXT PAGE

5　5　5　5　·　5　5　5

it or lose it"), and a lack of clear property rights to water tables. Overfishing in the oceans
(70) provides a better example. It is easy to imagine that cattle might be scarce, just as buffalo became scarce, if they were owned in common and were taken from one vast domain, rather than being privately owned on separate ranches. While the
(75) exact analogue to barbed wire for fishing grounds in the ocean may be hard to conceive, assigning ownership rights to the ocean should not be much more difficult than assigning ownership rights to the radio frequency spectrum, as is currently
(80) being done throughout the world.

　　The United States should encourage developing nations to follow this general strategy. Much of the destruction of forest resources that is of present concern is due to unsound government
(85) policies that private owners would not likely have undertaken to the same extent, if at all. Vice President Al Gore notes in Earth in the Balance: "the most serious examples of environmental degradation in the world today are tragedies that
(90) were created or actively encouraged by governments—usually in pursuit of some notion that a dramatic reordering of the material world would enhance the greater good."

　　There is much enthusiasm for "getting the
(95) incentives right." This produces nods of agreement on the general level, and furious disagreement about its specific application. "Getting the incentives right" should mean chiefly assigning property rights to environmental
(100) goods, rather than using government power to set the "correct price" for the use of a commonly held environmental good. Any so-called "market-based incentive" policy that involves government setting the "correct price" to establish a "level
(105) playing field" is inherently flawed, because it misunderstands the nature of markets and prices. The government will always lack the necessary knowledge to set the "right" price, and such policies will usually introduce new distortions
(110) into the marketplace that will likely be counterproductive and wasteful of resources.

15. The term "option values" as it is used in line 10 refers to
(A) optional financial transactions
(B) uses other than the present ones to which an ecosystem could be put
(C) commercial worth
(D) marketable commodities
(E) values that can be converted to cash under certain circumstances

16. According to the author of Passage 1, a renewable resource such as land is "inexhaustible" (line 22) but not "infinite in amount" (line 24). This means that a particular resource, such as a 10-acre tract of land,
(A) can be used for activities without worrying about the effects of these activities on it for the foreseeable future
(B) can be put to an infinite number of uses but eventually it will have no value for anything
(C) can be used for first one purpose, then another, and another, and so on indefinitely, but the total amount of land cannot be increased
(D) is so large that it is effectively infinite
(E) is inexhaustible in that the supply of land is infinite, but there are so many types of uses to which it can be put that it ultimately will not be worthwhile maintaining

17. According to the author of Passage 1, once a river system is reserved for certain uses
(A) it can never be used for any other purpose
(B) it can be used for other purposes, but this will affect those already using it
(C) it is always harmful to the river's ecosystem to change those uses
(D) it is a mistake to change those uses because property values are likely to drop in the area
(E) it is inevitable that water quality in the system will be degraded

GO ON TO THE NEXT PAGE

5   5   5   5   5   5   5

18. In line 61, "perverse" most nearly means

    (A) convoluted
    (B) corrupt
    (C) caused by selfishness
    (D) arising from obstinate persistence in an error
    (E) controlled by government

19. According to the author of Passage 2, a lack of tradable rights to water encourages people with rights to water to

    (A) buy water they don't need
    (B) speculate on price rises for water
    (C) use other unsustainable resources in place of water
    (D) conserve the water they have
    (E) use the water they have rights to

20. We can infer that the author of Passage 2 believes that cattle might become scarce if they "were owned in common and were taken from one vast domain" (lines 72–73) because

    (A) people would have little incentive to conserve cattle
    (B) cattle would be much easier to kill
    (C) people would have little incentive to care for the cattle by providing food and so forth
    (D) fatal diseases would spread easily through the cattle population
    (E) private ownership is always better than common or public ownership

21. According to the information provided in the passage, we can infer that the author of Passage 2 believes that

    (A) government shouldn't be at all involved in the conservation of unsustainable resources
    (B) one of the most important roles of government in the conservation of unsustainable resources is to assign property rights to environmental goods
    (C) if property rights are assigned to environmental goods, there will be no more instances of unsustainable resource use
    (D) the private market has no role in the conservation of unsustainable resources
    (E) only government has the expertise, access to information, and manpower to set the price of a commonly held economic good

22. Passage 1 and Passage 2 differ in that

    (A) Passage 1 provides four definitions of sustainability of renewable resources; Passage 2 discusses several examples of unsustainable resource use
    (B) Passage 1 describes the difficulties involved in promoting the sustainable use of resources, Passage 2 discusses some important concepts related to the sustainable use of resources and argues for more government involvement in the conservation of resources
    (C) Passage 1 outlines a policy for encouraging the sustainable use of resources; Passage 2 discusses the role of government in preserving the environment through promoting the sustainable use of resources
    (D) Passage 1 analyzes problems with sustainable resource use in general; Passage 2 argues for a particular approach to solving the problem of unsustainable resource use that can be applied in all cases
    (E) Passage 1 discusses various issues related to the sustainability of renewable resources and makes some general recommendations about the issue; Passage 2 analyzes certain examples of unsustainable resource use and makes firm recommendations about how some such problems in this area can be corrected

 **GO ON TO THE NEXT PAGE**

Practice Test 3

5 **5** **5** **5** **5** **5** **5**

23. What comment would the author of Passage 1 be most likely to make about the suggestion in Passage 2 that ownership rights should be assigned to the ocean?

   (A) It might have some merit, but the results would have to be closely monitored because habitats could be destroyed and what is done by one owner could have a great effect on the areas of the ocean owned by others.
   (B) It has some merit, but ownership rights to the ocean should be given only for fishing.
   (C) It would be an excellent idea both for fostering economic activity and for environmental conservation.
   (D) It is a good idea as long as owners are prohibited from oil exploration and promise to provide scientists with information on the effects of their commercial activities on the ecosystem.
   (E) It would be good environmental policy, but governments are unlikely to agree.

24. Based on the information provided in Passage 1 and Passage 2, which of the following would most accurately reflect the probable views of the author of Passage 1 about the main argument made in Passage 2?

   (A) He would unreservedly agree with it.
   (B) He would say that a market-based approach should be encouraged in some instances, but that there are many problems related to the sustainability of renewable resources that cannot be solved by this approach alone.
   (C) He would agree with it with certain relatively minor reservations.
   (D) He would say that it is entirely misguided because the free-market has no place in the conservation of resources.
   (E) He would say that it is unrealistic because most governments will not grant property rights to resources.

STOP

IN ANY REMAINING TIME YOU MAY REVIEW THE ANSWERS YOU CHOSE IN THIS SECTION. DO NOT WORK ON ANY OTHER SECTION OF THE TEST DURING THIS TIME.

7

SECTION 7

Time—25 Minutes
18 Questions

You have 25 minutes to answer the 8 multiple-choice questions and 10 student-produced response questions in this section. For each multiple-choice question, determine which of the five choices is correct and blacken the corresponding choice on your answer sheet. You may use any blank space on the page for your work.

Notes:
- You may use a calculator whenever you think it will be helpful.
- Only real numbers are used. No question or answer on this test involves a complex or imaginary number.
- Use the diagrams provided to help you solve the problems. Unless you see the words "Note: Figure not drawn to scale" under a diagram, it has been drawn as accurately as possible. Unless it is stated that a figure is three-dimensional, you may assume it lies in a plane.
- For any function f, the domain, unless specifically restricted, is the set of all real numbers for which $f(x)$ is also a real number.

Reference Information

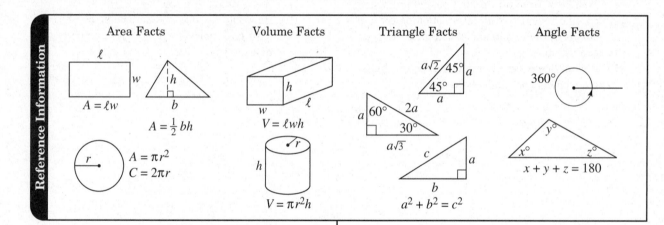

Area Facts

$A = \ell w$

$A = \frac{1}{2}bh$

$A = \pi r^2$
$C = 2\pi r$

Volume Facts

$V = \ell wh$

$V = \pi r^2 h$

Triangle Facts

$a^2 + b^2 = c^2$

Angle Facts

$x + y + z = 180$

1. If $7x - 3 = 13$, what is the value of $7x + 3$?

   (A) 6
   (B) 7
   (C) 10
   (D) 16
   (E) 19

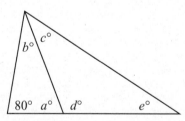

2. In the figure above, what is the value of $a + b + c + d + e$?

   (A) 240
   (B) 270
   (C) 280
   (D) 360
   (E) 440

GO ON TO THE NEXT PAGE

7

3. At Sam's Superette, the regular price for apples is 3 for $1.99. When they are on sale, the price is 3 for $1.59. How many apples would you have to buy at the sale price to save $2.00?

(A) 12
(B) 15
(C) 18
(D) 24
(E) 30

4. If the average (arithmetic mean) of a, b, and c is 19 and the average of b, c, and d is 17, what is the value of $a - d$?

(A) 2
(B) 4
(C) 6
(D) 18
(E) 54

5. On Tuesday, Cheryl had $12 more in her bank account than on Monday, and on Wednesday she had $15 more than on Tuesday. If on Wednesday she had 4 times as much money in her account as on Monday, how much money was in her account on Tuesday?

(A) $ 9
(B) $15
(C) $21
(D) $24
(E) $27

6. What is the area of a circle if one-fourth of its circumference is $\dfrac{4}{\pi}$?

(A) $\dfrac{\pi}{16}$

(B) $\dfrac{\pi}{4}$

(C) $\dfrac{16}{\pi^2}$

(D) $\dfrac{1}{4\pi^3}$

(E) $\dfrac{64}{\pi^3}$

7. Karl and Kathy each drove the same distance from point A to point B. It took Kathy exactly 2 hours to make the trip. If Karl drove 10 miles per hour faster than Kathy, how many minutes less did it take him to make the trip?

(A) 12
(B) 20
(C) 30
(D) 60
(E) It cannot be determined from the information given.

8. Given that for any positive integer n, the sum, $S(n)$, of the first n positive integers can be evaluated using the formula $S(n) = \dfrac{n(n+1)}{2}$, what is the sum of all integers, n, such that $50 < n < 100$?

(A) 3,625
(B) 3,675
(C) 3,725
(D) 3,775
(E) 3,825

GO ON TO THE NEXT PAGE

7

Directions for Student-Produced Response Questions (Grid-ins)

In questions 9–18, first solve the problem, and then enter your answer on the grid provided on the answer sheet. The instructions for entering your answers are as follows:

- First, write your answer in the boxes at the top of the grid.
- Second, grid your answer in the columns below the boxes.
- Use the fraction bar in the first row or the decimal point in the second row to enter fractions and decimal answers.

Answer: $\dfrac{8}{15}$ Answer: 1.75

Write your → answer in the boxes.

Grid in → your answer.

Answer: 100

Either position is acceptable

- Grid only one space in each column.
- Entering the answer in the boxes is recommended as an aid in gridding, but is not required.
- The machine scoring your exam can read only what you grid, so you **must grid in your answers correctly to get credit.**
- If a question has more than one correct answer, grid in only one of these answers.
- The grid does not have a minus sign, so no answer can be negative.
- A mixed number *must* be converted to an improper fraction or a decimal before it is gridded. Enter $1\frac{1}{4}$ as 5/4 or 1.25; the machine will interpret 1 1/4 as $\dfrac{11}{4}$ and mark it wrong.
- **All decimals must be entered as accurately as possible.** Here are the three acceptable ways of gridding

$$\frac{3}{11} = 0.272727\ldots$$

3/11   .272   .273

- Note that rounding to .273 is acceptable, because you are using the full grid, but you would receive **no credit** for .3 or .27, because these answers are less accurate.

GO ON TO THE NEXT PAGE

7

9. If $5 - a = b - 5$, what is the value of $5a + 5b$?

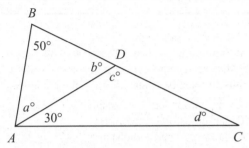

Note: Figure not drawn to scale.

10. In the figure above, $\overline{BD}$ divides $\triangle ABC$ into two smaller triangles. What is the value of $a + b + c + d$?

11. For all numbers a, b, c such that $abc \neq 0$, define ▲ to be $\dfrac{a+b}{c} \cdot \dfrac{b+c}{a} \cdot \dfrac{a+c}{b}$. What is the value of ▲?

12. At South Central High School, the name of each tenth-, eleventh-, and twelfth-grader who bought a raffle ticket was placed in a bag. One name was drawn from the bag to determine the winner. If the bag contained the names of 85 tenth-graders and 95 eleventh-graders, and if the probability of the winner being a twelfth-grader was $\dfrac{1}{5}$, how many students bought raffle tickets?

13. In a group of 2 girls and 8 boys, the average (arithmetic mean) weight of the 10 children is 90 pounds. If the average weight of the girls is 80 pounds, what is the average weight of the boys?

14. In a major league baseball season, each team plays 162 games, none of which ends in a tie. If team A won 62 more games than it lost, how many games did it lose?

15. Geraldine and Jerome each drive exactly 5 miles from point A to point B. If Geraldine's average speed is 50 miles per hour, and Jerome's average speed is 60 miles per hour, how much longer, in seconds, will it take Geraldine than Jerome to drive the 5 miles?

16. The function f is defined for all real numbers x, as $f(x) = ax + b$, where a and b are constants. If $f(10) = 65$ and $f(15) = 100$, what is the value of $a + b$?

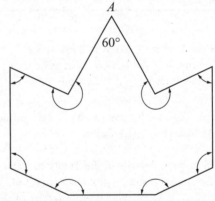

17. In the figure above, if the m$\angle A = 60°$, what is the average (arithmetic mean) measure, in degrees, of the eight other marked angles?

18. How many positive integers less than 1,000 contain the digit 7?

STOP

Practice Test 3

8 8 8 8 8 8 8 8 8 8 8

SECTION 8   Time—20 Minutes   19 Questions   Choose the best answer to each of the following questions in this section. Then blacken the appropriate space on your answer sheet.

Each of the following sentences contains one or two blanks, indicating that a word or set of words has been omitted. Beneath each sentence there are five answer choices labeled A to E from which you must select the word or set of words that best fits the meaning of the sentence as a whole.

Example:

Records of colonization can be found as far back as the Phoenicians, but colonization became a major force in world history only when European countries began, in the fifteenth century, to make ---- Asia, the Americas, and Africa.

(A) queries about   (B) incursions into
(C) tirades against   (D) enemies in
(E) amends for

---

1. As a result of the Cold War, early space exploration was politicized, each system of government trying to demonstrate the ---- of its ideology in the "space race."

   (A) origins   (B) superiority   (C) influence
   (D) history   (E) failure

2. ---- in varying degrees to the Treaty of Versailles, the Great Depression, nationalism, and militarism, the causes of World War II are a matter of debate.

   (A) Apportioned   (B) Allocated
   (C) Assigned   (D) Attributed
   (E) Disclosed

3. An opinion is ---- belief based on available evidence; as more evidence becomes available an opinion must be changed to ---- the evidence.

   (A) an unfounded . . substantiate
   (B) an unjustified . . confirm
   (C) a stereotyped . . bolster
   (D) a provisional . . accommodate
   (E) a religious . . establish

4. Good writers often use ---- devices intuitively, knowing that effective communication depends on a range of techniques that must be adapted to each situation.

   (A) electronic   (B) rhetorical   (C) modern
   (D) antiquated   (E) literal

5. Nineteenth century ---- capitalism provided a rationalization for the exploitation of the poor by the rich by drawing ---- between the free market of capitalism and the struggle for existence in nature described by Charles Darwin, in which the fit survive.

   (A) champions of . . a graph
   (B) polemicists for . . a bridge
   (C) apologists for . . an analogy
   (D) demagogues of . . a connection
   (E) satirists of . . a picture

6. For centuries literary critics have debated whether drama ---- unhealthy passions such as pity and fear, as Plato contended, or ---- them by allowing them to be released, as Aristotle believed.

   (A) embellishes . . engenders
   (B) decreases . . diffuses
   (C) incites . . enhances
   (D) sanctions . . expurgates
   (E) arouses . . purges

GO ON TO THE NEXT PAGE

8   8 8 8 8 8 8 8 8 8   8

Below are passages followed by questions on them. Questions on a pair of related passages may be about the relationship between the two passages. For each question, select the best answer based on what is stated or implied in the passage (or passages).

Questions 7–19 are based on the following passage.

In *Finishing The Hat*, Stephen Sondheim
zeroes in on the essential difference between the
art of the lyricist and that of the poet: "Poetry
Line doesn't need music," he writes, "lyrics do."
(5) Poetry is the art of "concision," written to stand
on its own; lyrics, the art of "expansion," written
to accommodate music.

And yet, the line between song and poem is
not as firm as Sondheim suggests. William Blake
(10) called his greatest books of poetry *Songs of
Innocence* and *Songs of Experience*. Walt
Whitman called the opening poem of *Leaves of
Grass* "Song of Myself." In both cases, their
work straddles the line between the genres.
(15) Blake's

> Piping down the valleys wild,
> Piping songs of pleasant glee,
> On a cloud I saw a child,
> And he laughing said to me

(20) practically begs to be set to music, and has been
by more than one composer. Whitman's great
elegy, beginning

> In the dooryard fronting an old farm-house
> near the white-wash'd palings,
(25) Stands the lilac-bush tall-growing . . .

is one of the loveliest "songs" in the Kurt Weill /
Langston Hughes musical, *Street Scene*.

Perhaps the most significant divergence
between these sister arts today is the way in
(30) which poets and songwriters imagine their
audiences. Whereas poetry is aimed almost
exclusively at a limited number of fellow poets,
hundreds of millions of men and women listen to
songs on iPods and smart phones and millions
(35) more sing them in showers, kitchens, and karaoke
bars.

Poets who want to achieve wider readership
might consider the qualities that attract millions
of intelligent men and women to their sister art.
(40) First in importance, the primary mission of the
poem should be the same as the primary mission

of the song: *to make the listener want to hear the
song again and again*!

If I'm satisfied with listening to a song once,
(45) the song is a failure! Yet, how many times have I
heard poets introduce their poems with words
like these:

> "I think I may have read this poem here
> before. If so, I hope you'll bear with me.
(50) Hopefully there are others here who haven't
> heard it."

Imagine Paul Simon saying, "If there's anyone
here who has already heard 'Bridge Over
Troubled Water' I apologize for boring you with
(55) it again." If Frost came back from the grave
would audiences shout, "We only want to hear
new work, Robert. Don't you dare read 'Birches'
or 'The Road Not Taken'!" Frost acknowledged
poetry's ambition to be heard again and again
(60) when he explained that his goal was "to lodge a
few poems where they will be hard to get rid of."

Too many poets programmatically eschew the
memory cues songwriters unabashedly use to
accomplish this mission. After talking to writing
(65) students, conditioned by their professors to
tolerate no rhyme or meter in poetry, James
Fenton suggests (in *The American Scholar*) that
they would "be happier if they accepted that the
person who was studying creative writing, with
(70) the aim of producing poetry, was the same person
who had a car full of country and western tapes,
or whatever the music was that delighted them."

The aversion to rhyme and meter, Fenton
implies, is an artificially-acquired, counter-
(75) intuitive, schizophrenic taste. The popularity of
rap, rock, and country music, as well as the
power of advertising, remind us that our desire
for repetition is based on pulse and heartbeat and

GO ON TO THE NEXT PAGE

8   8 8 8 8 8 8 8 8 8   8

the nature of the human brain. It's suicidal for
(80) poets to reject their own biology!

Still, I hear critics admonishing me for
ignoring the singing elephant in the room. It's not
the lyric, they protest, but the music that makes
us want to hear a song again and again. And
(85) music is something poets do not have in their
arsenal.

Or do they? To be sure, poets cannot rely on
actual musical tones; still the poems I love
(formal or open) have a quasi-melodic structure
(90) that has an effect not unlike melody proper.

Melody seizes us, picks us up, and holds us
with the progression of its tones, never putting us
back on the ground until the final note stops
vibrating. Great poems use purely verbal
(95) elements—syllables, words, accent—to build a
rhetorical arc that provides a similar experience.
Here's an example of a poetic "melody" by Walt
Whitman:

I think I could turn and live with animals, they
(100) are so placid and self-contained,
I stand and look at them long and long.
They do not sweat and whine about their
condition,
They do not lie awake in the dark and weep
(105) for their sins,
They do not make me sick discussing their
duty to God,
Not one is dissatisfied, not one is demented
with the mania of owning things,
(110) Not one kneels to another, nor to his kind that
lived thousands of years ago,
Not one is respectable or unhappy over the
whole earth.

Walt reminds us that poetic music can be
(115) achieved without fixed form as long as it
embraces repetition: I think, I turn, I live; I stand,
look, long; they do not sweat, whine, lie awake,
weep, make me sick; not one is dissatisfied,
demented; not one kneels, not one is respectable,
(120) unhappy. Whitman's verse may be "free," but it
is loaded with alliteration, assonance, and
anaphora. His "melody" seizes us by the
imagination, turns us towards his beloved
animals, and keeps us wholly focused on them
(125) until the final reverberating syllable returns us to
"earth."

There can be relief and contrast in poetic
melody akin to what we find in a musical bridge;
but no prefacing, meandering, digression,
(130) parentheses. Once a successful poem begins the
reader surrenders to the exhilarating ride its
verbal "tune" provides. The possibilities are
infinite:

We real cool. We
(135) Left school. We
Lurk late. We
Strike straight. We
Sing sin. We
Thin gin. We
(140) Jazz June. We
Die soon.

In contrast to Whitman's affectionate,
languorous, comforting melody, Gwendolyn
Brooks' tune is jazzy, aggressive, staccato,
(145) disturbing. Whitman plays the cello; Brooks the
trumpet; both instruments are perfectly suited to
the subjects and quasi-musical effects the poets
produce. Like Whitman, Brooks does not fear
repetition. Not only does she pepper her poem
(150) with rhyme and eight clusters of three strong
beats; she uses the word "We" seven times at the
end of each line where its effect is like a trumpet
blast. Both poets have crafted verbal melodies
that have brought me back to these poems again
(155) and again.

At a time when too many poets have so
purged their "poetry" of repetition and melody
that it reads and sounds like outright prose,
songwriters continue to satisfy a human craving
(160) that cannot and should not be denied. Whether or
not poets can again become relevant to non-
practitioners of their art may depend on how well
they listen to their big sister.

GO ON TO THE NEXT PAGE

8   8 8 8 8 8   8 8 8 8   8

7. Which of the following statements about Stephen Sondheim's description of the difference between the art of the lyricist and that of the poet would the author of this passage be most likely to agree with?

(A) It is untrue.
(B) It is simplistic, but contains an element of truth.
(C) It expresses a truth about only one relatively minor aspect of the difference between the two arts.
(D) It is fundamentally true, yet at times the difference between them is not so clear.
(E) It is impossible to generalize meaningfully either about lyrics or poetry.

8. The author quotes lines from Blake's' *Songs of Innocence* in order to

(A) illustrate how very different a poem is from a lyric
(B) provide an example of a poem that is very much like a lyric
(C) demonstrate that the fact that an author calls a poem a song doesn't make it a song
(D) show that only a simple poem can successfully be set to music
(E) show that there is no difference between melody in music and repetition in poetry

9. According to the author, one of the main reasons that poems are not as popular as songs is that

(A) poets tend to write for a limited audience, whereas songwriters tend to write for a mass audience
(B) poets are not sufficiently trained in music theory and composition
(C) poems have become too complex for most people to understand
(D) poems have become too much like songs, thus losing the distinctiveness that gives them their appeal
(E) unlike most poems, songs deal with the concerns of everyday life

10. In line 62, "programmatically eschew" most nearly means

(A) automatically embrace as part of a program
(B) unconsciously reject
(C) slavishly copy
(D) avoid something because one thinks it is conformist
(E) avoid something because it isn't part of one's customary system

11. The quotation by James Fenton, "[They would] be happier . . . that delighted them" (lines 68–72) suggests that

(A) more music lovers should enroll in writing courses aimed at producing poets
(B) writing students aiming to produce poetry should not use techniques from songwriting when they write poems
(C) writing students should listen to more music
(D) writing students wanting to become poets tend not to draw on their knowledge and appreciation of music in their attempts to produce poetry
(E) writing students are not happy because their professors do not allow them to draw on their knowledge and appreciation of music in their writing of poetry

12. In line 75, "schizophrenic" most nearly means

(A) characterized by delusional thought patterns
(B) characterized by the coexistence of antagonistic qualities
(C) paranoid about not being respected
(D) outside the bounds of what is normally accepted
(E) mentally unstable

13. The phrase "singing elephant in the room," as it is used in line 82, can be described accurately by all of the following words EXCEPT

(A) idiomatic
(B) metaphorical
(C) jocular
(D) colorful
(E) elegiac

GO ON TO THE NEXT PAGE

14. In line 90, "melody proper" most nearly means

    (A) musical melody
    (B) properly used melody
    (C) poetic "melody"
    (D) melody like that in old-time songs
    (E) poetic techniques

15. The author probably refers to Walt Whitman as "Walt" in line 114 in order to

    (A) help maintain the deceptively simple terse style of the lines he has just cited from Whitman's poetry
    (B) suggest that Walt Whitman and his poetry is held in high and affectionate regard by poetry lovers
    (C) help create a rhythmic pattern in the sentence that the word is in that is akin to melody
    (D) suggest that the author and Walt Whitman are friends
    (E) illustrate how a writer can bend the rules of language to achieve an effect

16. According to the author, which of the following characteristics does the verse by Walt Whitman quoted in lines 93–113 and the verse by Gwendolyn Brooks quoted in lines 134–141 share?

    (A) Frequent use of rhyme
    (B) Prose-like sentences
    (C) Use of repetition
    (D) Rigid adherence to a traditional form
    (E) A staccato rhythm

17. What is the author probably suggesting when he says, "But no prefacing, meandering, digression, parentheses" (lines 129–130)?

    (A) Poets who want to create a "poetic melody" in a poem must not use poetic techniques, only musical ones.
    (B) Poets who want to be widely popular must not insert parenthetical, self-referring comments into their poems.

(C) Poets who want to be popular among non-poets must not use too many poetic techniques.
(D) Poets who want to create a "poetic melody" in a poem must not insert material that interrupts this "melody."
(E) Poets must never change the rhythm of a poem.

18. In the last line of the passage the author says, "Whether or not poets can again become relevant to non-practitioners of their art may depend on how well they listen to their big sister" (lines 160–163). The author is most likely suggesting that

    (A) to increase significantly the popularity of their work among people who are not poets themselves, poets should strongly consider learning some of the techniques that songwriters use and employing them when they write poetry
    (B) to become popular outside poetry circles poets should write poems just like song lyrics
    (C) how popular a poet becomes depends on how sophisticated his or her musical tastes are
    (D) young poets must heed the advice of senior poets, including listening to popular music to develop their sense of rhythm and melody
    (E) young poets, especially male poets, should pay special attention to the advice of senior poets in writing their poems

19. Based on the information in the passage, the author would be most likely to agree with the statement that

    (A) a poem can be both excellent and popular
    (B) popular poetry is almost by definition bad poetry
    (C) the more like a song a poem becomes, the better it is
    (D) most songwriters are better poets than most poets
    (E) a poem without a lot of "musical" qualities cannot be a good poem

IN ANY REMAINING TIME YOU MAY REVIEW THE
ANSWERS YOU CHOSE IN THIS SECTION. DO NOT WORK
ON ANY OTHER SECTION OF THE TEST DURING THIS TIME.

9   9   9   9   9   9   9

SECTION 9

Time—20 Minutes
16 Questions

For each problem in this section determine which of the five choices is correct and blacken the corresponding choice on your answer sheet. You may use any blank space on the page for your work.

Notes:

- You may use a calculator whenever you think it will be helpful.
- Only real numbers are used. No question or answer on this test involves a complex or imaginary number.
- Use the diagrams provided to help you solve the problems. Unless you see the words "Note: Figure not drawn to scale" under a diagram, it has been drawn as accurately as possible. Unless it is stated that a figure is three-dimensional, you may assume it lies in a plane.
- For any function, f, the domain, unless specifically restricted, is the set of all real numbers for which $f(x)$ is also a real number.

Reference Information

Area Facts

$A = \ell w$

$A = \frac{1}{2} bh$

$A = \pi r^2$
$C = 2\pi r$

Volume Facts

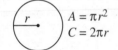

$V = \ell wh$

$V = \pi r^2 h$

Triangle Facts

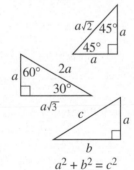

$a^2 + b^2 = c^2$

Angle Facts

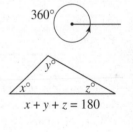

$360°$

$x + y + z = 180$

1. If $\dfrac{1}{2} \times \dfrac{2}{3} \times \dfrac{3}{4} \times \dfrac{4}{5} \times \dfrac{5}{6} = \dfrac{a}{b}$ and $\dfrac{a}{b}$ is written in lowest terms, what is the value of $a + b$?

   (A) 6
   (B) 7
   (C) 8
   (D) 9
   (E) 10

2. If $2x + 3y < 3x + 2y$, which of the following could be the values of x and y?

   (A) $x = 1$ and $y = 1$
   (B) $x = -1$ and $y = -1$
   (C) $x = -1$ and $y = 2$
   (D) $x = -1$ and $y = -2$
   (E) $x = 2$ and $y = 2$

3. What is the value of x if $3^{x-3} = 81$?

   (A) 4
   (B) 5
   (C) 6
   (D) 7
   (E) 8

GO ON TO THE NEXT PAGE

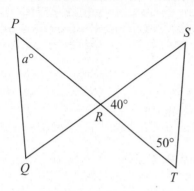

Note: Figure not drawn to scale.

4. If in the figure above, $PR = QR$, what is the value of a?

(A)   40
(B)   50
(C)   70
(D)   90
(E)   140

5. If $-1 < a < b < 0$, which of the following statements must be true?

  I. $\dfrac{1}{a} < \dfrac{1}{b}$
  II. $ab < a + b$
  III. $\sqrt{ab} = \sqrt{a} \times \sqrt{b}$

(A) None
(B) I only
(C) II only
(D) III only
(E) I, II, and III

6. A jar contains 100 marbles, each of which is red, white, or blue. If 60 of the marbles are white and the ratio of the number of red marbles to blue marbles is 3 to 5, how many of the marbles are blue?

(A)   10
(B)   15
(C)   20
(D)   25
(E)   30

Questions 7–8 refer to the following definition: **for any numbers a and b, $a \odot b = (a + b) - ab$**

7. What is the value of $-\dfrac{1}{3} \odot 4$?

(A) $\dfrac{5}{3}$

(B) $\dfrac{7}{3}$

(C) $\dfrac{11}{3}$

(D)   5
(E)   7

8. If $a \odot a = -a$ and $a \neq 0$, what is the value of a?

(A)   −2
(B)   −1
(C)   0
(D)   2
(E)   3

GO ON TO THE NEXT PAGE

9　9　9　9　9　9　9

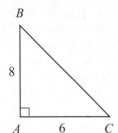

9. In the figure above, △ABC is a right triangle whose legs are 6 and 8. △DEF is an equilateral triangle whose sides are 8. Which of the following statements about △ABC and △DEF are true?

   I. The perimeter of △ABC is equal to the perimeter of △DEF.

  II. The average (arithmetic mean) of the measures of the three angles in △ABC is equal to the average of the measures of the three angles in △DEF.

 III. The area of △ABC is equal to the area of △DEF.

(A) I only
(B) II only
(C) I and II only
(D) I and III only
(E) I, II, and III

10. The average (arithmetic mean) of a set of 25 positive integers is 25, and the median of those 25 integers is 25. What is the greatest possible sum of the 10 largest numbers in the set?

(A) 250
(B) 386
(C) 498
(D) 538
(E) 586

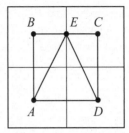

11. In the figure above, a large square, whose area is 16, is divided into four small squares. If A, B, C, and D are the centers of the four squares and E is the midpoint of $\overline{BC}$, what is the perimeter of △AED?

(A) $3\sqrt{3}$
(B) $3\sqrt{5}$
(C) $4+\sqrt{3}$
(D) $2+2\sqrt{3}$
(E) $2+2\sqrt{5}$

12. For all positive numbers x, let the function A be defined as $A(x)$ = the area of a square whose sides are x. Which of the following are equal to $A(5) - A(4)$?

   I. $A(5 - 4)$

  II. $A(3)$

 III. $A\left(\sqrt{35}\right) - A\left(\sqrt{26}\right)$

(A) I only
(B) II only
(C) III only
(D) II and III only
(E) I, II, and III

13. If $a^2 + b^2 = 5\pi$ and $ab = 2\pi$, which of the following is equal to $(a - b)^2$?

(A) 1
(B) 9
(C) π
(D) 4π
(E) 9π

GO ON TO THE NEXT PAGE

9   9   9   9   9   9   9

14. Let d_1 and d_2 and P_1 and P_2 be the diagonals and perimeters of squares 1 and 2, respectively. If $d_2 = d_1 + 1$, what is $P_2 - P_1$?

(A) 2

(B) 4

(C) $\sqrt{2}$

(D) $2\sqrt{2}$

(E) $4\sqrt{2}$

15. If $f(x) = 2^x$ and $g(x) = f(x - 2)$ and if $g(a) = b$, which of the following is equal to $f(a)$?

(A) b

(B) $4b$

(C) $f(b)$

(D) $\dfrac{1}{4} f(b)$

(E) $4f(b)$

16. Caleb's car averages 24 miles per gallon on the highway and 18 miles per gallon in the city. On his summer vacation last year, Caleb drove 4,500 miles. If 80 percent of his driving was on highways and the rest in cities, what was his car's average number of miles per gallon during the entire vacation?

(A) 20.5

(B) 21.4

(C) 22.8

(D) 22.5

(E) 23.0

STOP

IN ANY REMAINING TIME YOU MAY REVIEW THE ANSWERS YOU CHOSE IN THIS SECTION. DO NOT WORK ON ANY OTHER SECTION OF THE TEST DURING THIS TIME.

Practice Test 3

10   10   10   10   10   10   10

Each sentence below may or may not employ correct or effective expression. If you think that the underlined phrasing makes the most clear and precise sentence, select choice A. If, however, you think that the underlined phrasing makes the meaning of the sentence unclear or awkward, or that it is grammatically incorrect, select another answer from choices B to E.

In choosing your answers, follow the conventions of English as it is used by educated writers. Consider sentence structure, grammar, word choice, and punctuation. Choose the answer that produces the sentence that is the most clear and effective.

Example:

In her comments after the debate the judge said that she had been impressed by the ability of both teams to exploit logical weaknesses and in citing relevant examples.

(A) in citing relevant examples
(B) in that relevant examples had been cited
(C) in the citing of relevant examples
(D) to cite relevant examples
(E) to be able to cite relevant examples

Ⓐ Ⓑ Ⓒ ● Ⓔ

1. This week's Independence Day fireworks being much more exciting than last year's.

(A) being
(B) had been
(C) that was
(D) was
(E) were

2. Many governments use a civil service system for employing workers, one of the reasons is to eliminate or at least reduce nepotism.

(A) Many governments use a civil service system for employing workers, one of the reasons is
(B) Many governments use a civil service system for employing workers, and one of the reasons is
(C) Many governments use a civil service system for employing workers, they do it, for one reason,
(D) One of the reasons many governments use a civil service system for employing workers is
(E) One of the reasons many governments use a civil service system employing workers is

3. If your conjecture is correct, Simon had become the new principal of the high school in 1998.

(A) is correct, Simon had become
(B) is correct, Simon has become
(C) is correct, Simon became
(D) was correct, Simon was becoming
(E) was correct, Simon is becoming

4. The Greek root *pan*, and this is found in the English words *pantheism*, *panorama*, and *Pan-American*, means "all" or "every."

(A) *pan*, and this is found in the English words
(B) *pan*, and this is being found in the English words
(C) *pan*, founded in the English words
(D) *pan*, found in the English words
(E) *pan* that is founded in the English words

GO ON TO THE NEXT PAGE

10   10   10   10   10   10   10

5. The country's finance minister described foreign investors as <u>vultures, feeding on a market in a country</u> for a few months, then taking off for another country.

   (A) vultures, feeding on a market in a country
   (B) vultures who feed on a market in a country
   (C) vultures, first they feed on a market
   (D) vultures in a country feeding on a market
   (E) vultures, they feed on a market in a country

6. Reading widely in books and magazines, studying vocabulary regularly, and <u>frequent practice on reading comprehension exercises</u> helped Tim to do well on the English examination.

   (A) frequent practice on reading comprehension exercises
   (B) practicing frequently on reading comprehension exercises
   (C) practicing frequent on reading comprehension exercises, these
   (D) by frequent practice on reading comprehension exercises
   (E) through practicing on reading comprehension exercises frequently, this

7. <u>The literary critic is writing her own novel, which is more satisfying to her than evaluating the novels of others.</u>

   (A) The literary critic is writing her own novel, which is more satisfying than evaluating the novels of others.
   (B) Writing her own novel is found by the literary critic to be more satisfying than evaluating the novels of others.
   (C) The literary critic, who evaluates the novels of others, is writing her own novel, which she finds more satisfying.
   (D) The literary critic finds writing her own novel more satisfying than evaluating the novels of others.
   (E) The literary critic is finding writing her own novel is more satisfying than evaluating the novels of others.

8. In the chess match against world champion Gary Kasparov, the IBM computer Deep Blue took advantage of an error by Kasparov to win an important game and take the <u>lead; unfortunately, Kasparov was</u> unable to even the score in the remaining games.

   (A) lead; unfortunately, Kasparov was
   (B) lead; unfortunately, Kasparov is
   (C) lead, unfortunately Kasparov was
   (D) lead; too bad, but Kasparov was
   (E) lead; unfortunately, but Kasparov was

9. <u>Extrapolating from present trends, the prediction of experts is</u> that the population of the world will be ten billion in the year 2020.

   (A) Extrapolating from present trends, the prediction of experts is
   (B) When experts extrapolate from present trends, it is predicted
   (C) In extrapolating from present trends, the prediction by experts is
   (D) Extrapolating from present trends, it is a prediction of experts
   (E) Extrapolating from present trends, experts predict

10. In the belief that watching French language movies would improve his grades in French, <u>Matt will spend endless hours watching them every weekend.</u>

   (A) Matt will spend endless hours watching them every weekend
   (B) Matt spent endless hours watching them every weekend
   (C) endless hours every weekend are spent watching them by Matt
   (D) Matt spends endless hours watching them every weekend
   (E) every weekend Matt will be found spending endless hours watching them

GO ON TO THE NEXT PAGE

11. It is often difficult for policy makers to balance competing interests when deciding what use renewable <u>resources should be put to, such as lakes</u>.

    (A) resources should be put to, such as lakes
    (B) resources, such as lakes, should be put to
    (C) resources should be put to such as lakes
    (D) resources should lakes be put to
    (E) resources, such as lakes, are being put to

12. When choosing a college to attend, it is a good idea to consider how much a particular college costs, how effective the teachers are, and <u>its reputation</u>.

    (A) its reputation
    (B) how good its reputation is
    (C) is it a college with a good reputation
    (D) what kind of reputation it has
    (E) whether or not the college has a good reputation

13. <u>The writer produced works that are now highly praised despite poverty and misfortune.</u>

    (A) The writer produced works that are now highly praised despite poverty and misfortune.
    (B) The writer produced works that, despite poverty and misfortune, are now highly praised.
    (C) Despite being poor and facing misfortune, the writer produced works that are now highly praised.
    (D) Despite the fact of her facing poverty and misfortune, the writer produced works that are now highly praised.
    (E) Despite poverty and misfortune, the writer produced works that are now highly praised.

14. The <u>lawyers representing the doctor contended as to the defensibility of his practices as legal and ethical.</u>

    (A) lawyers representing the doctor contended as to the defensibility of his practices as legal and ethical
    (B) lawyers, who contended that the practices of the doctor are both legal and ethical, represent the doctor
    (C) lawyers representing the doctor contended that his practices are legally and ethically defensible
    (D) lawyers represented the doctor, who contended that his practices are legal and ethical
    (E) lawyers representing the doctor contended, in regard to the matter of the defensibility of the doctor's practices, that they are legally and ethically defensible

STOP

IN ANY REMAINING TIME YOU MAY REVIEW THE ANSWERS YOU CHOSE IN THIS SECTION. DO NOT WORK ON ANY OTHER SECTION OF THE TEST DURING THIS TIME.

Practice Test 3

Answer Key

CRITICAL READING

	Section 2				Section 5				Section 8		
Ans.	Level of Diff.	Ans.	Level of Diff.	Ans.	Level of Diff.	Ans.	Level of Diff.	Ans.	Level of Diff.	Ans.	Level of Diff.
1. D	1	13. D	2	1. E	2	13. C	4	1. B	1	11. D	5
2. B	3	14. A	2	2. D	3	14. C	5	2. D	2	12. B	4
3. E	3	15. B	1	3. B	3	15. B	3	3. D	3	13. E	5
4. B	3	16. A	1	4. C	4	16. C	5	4. B	3	14. A	1
5. A	3	17. C	2	5. D	5	17. B	3	5. C	4	15. B	4
6. B	4	18. C	3	6. D	4	18. D	4	6. E	5	16. C	2
7. C	4	19. D	4	7. D	3	19. E	4	7. D	4	17. D	3
8. D	5	20. B	2	8. B	2	20. A	1	8. B	3	18. A	4
9. E	2	21. D	5	9. A	4	21. B	2	9. A	2	19. A	5
10. C	3	22. C	3	10. D	1	22. E	4	10. E	4		
11. E	4	23. A	2	11. D	5	23. A	4				
12. A	5	24. C	2	12. C	3	24. B	3				

MATH

	Section 3				Section 7				Section 9		
Ans.	Level of Diff.	Ans.	Level of Diff.	Ans.	Level of Diff.	Ans.	Level of Diff.	Ans.	Level of Diff.	Ans.	Level of Diff.
1. C	1	11. A	3	1. E	1	10. 280	2	1. B	1	9. C	3
2. E	1	12. B	3	2. C	1	11. 45/4	3	2. D	2	10. D	3
3. A	2	13. D	3	3. B	2	12. 225	3	3. D	2	11. E	3
4. E	1	14. A	3	4. C	2	13. 92.5	3	4. C	2	12. D	4
5. D	2	15. E	4	5. C	3	14. 50	3	5. A	3	13. C	3
6. E	3	16. D	3	6. E	3	15. 60	4	6. D	3	14. D	5
7. D	2	17. B	4	7. E	4	16. 2	4	7. D	3	15. B	4
8. B	2	18. E	4	8. B	4	17. 150	4	8. E	3	16. D	5
9. C	3	19. E	5	9. 50	1	18. 271	5				
10. E	3	20. A	5								

WRITING

	Section 4								Section 10		
Ans.	Level of Diff.	Ans.	Level of Diff.	Ans.	Level of Diff.	Ans.	Level of Diff.	Ans.	Level of Diff.	Ans.	Level of Diff.
1. D	1	10. D	4	19. C	3	28. B	4	1. E	1	9. E	3
2. C	1	11. C	5	20. D	3	29. A	5	2. D	1	10. B	3
3. D	1	12. D	1	21. E	3	30. D	2	3. C	1	11. B	3
4. D	2	13. C	2	22. B	3	31. E	2	4. D	2	12. B	4
5. B	2	14. C	2	23. E	3	32. B	1	5. A	2	13. E	4
6. C	2	15. C	3	24. A	4	33. B	3	6. B	3	14. C	5
7. E	3	16. D	3	25. B	4	34. A	5	7. D	3		
8. B	3	17. E	3	26. C	4	35. C	4	8. A	3		
9. B	3	18. A	3	27. B	4						

Score Your Own SAT Essay

Use this table as you rate your performance on the essay-writing section of this Practice Test. Circle the phrase that most accurately describes your work. Enter the numbers in the scoring chart below. Add the numbers together and divide by 6 to determine your total score. The higher your total score, the better you are likely to do on the essay section of the SAT.

Note that on the actual SAT two readers will rate your essay; your essay score will be the sum of their two ratings and could range from 12 (highest) to 2 (lowest). Also, they will grade your essay holistically, rating it on the basis of their overall impression of its effectiveness. They will *not* analyze it piece by piece, giving separate grades for grammar, vocabulary level, and so on. Therefore, you cannot expect the score you give yourself on this Practice Test to predict your eventual score on the SAT with any great degree of accuracy. Use this scoring guide instead to help you assess your writing strengths and weaknesses, so that you can decide which areas to focus on as you prepare for the SAT.

Like most people, you may find it difficult to rate your own writing objectively. Ask a teacher or fellow student to score your essay as well. With his or her help you should gain added insights into writing your 25-minute essay.

	6	5	4	3	2	1
POSITION ON THE TOPIC	Clear, convincing, & insightful	Fundamentally clear & coherent	Fairly clear & coherent	Insufficiently clear	Largely unclear	Extremely unclear
ORGANIZATION OF EVIDENCE	Well organized, with strong, relevant examples	Generally well organized, with apt examples	Adequately organized, with some examples	Sketchily developed, with weak examples	Lacking focus and evidence	Unfocused and disorganized
SENTENCE STRUCTURE	Varied, appealing sentences	Reasonably varied sentences	Some variety in sentences	Little variety in sentences	Errors in sentence structure	Severe errors in sentence structure
LEVEL OF VOCABULARY	Mature & apt word choice	Competent word choice	Adequate word choice	Inappropriate or weak vocabulary	Highly limited vocabulary	Rudimentary
GRAMMAR AND USAGE	Almost entirely free of errors	Relatively free of errors	Some technical errors	Minor errors, and some major ones	Numerous major errors	Extensive severe errors
OVERALL EFFECT	Outstanding	Effective	Adequately competent	Inadequate, but shows some potential	Seriously flawed	Fundamentally deficient

Self-Scoring Chart

For each of the following categories, rate the essay from 1 (lowest) to 6 (highest)

Position on the Topic   _____

Organization of Evidence   _____

Sentence Structure   _____

Level of Vocabulary   _____

Grammar and Usage   _____

Overall Effect   _____

TOTAL   _____

(To get a score, divide the total by 6)   _____

Scoring Chart (Second Reader)

For each of the following categories, rate the essay from 1 (lowest) to 6 (highest)

Position on the Topic   _____

Organization of Evidence   _____

Sentence Structure   _____

Level of Vocabulary   _____

Grammar and Usage   _____

Overall Effect   _____

TOTAL   _____

(To get a score, divide the total by 6)   _____

Scoring Practice Test 3

Refer to the answer key for Practice Test 3 on page 222. Then use the Scoring Worksheet below to determine your raw scores for Critical Reading, Mathematics, and Writing. For each section, give yourself one point for each answer that is correct. Your total raw score is the total number of correct answer points minus $\frac{1}{4}$ of the total number of incorrect answer points. Round off the total raw score to the nearest whole number to get your Rounded Raw Score. Convert your raw scores to scaled scores using the Conversion Tables on pages 226–227.

SCORING WORKSHEET

Critical Reading

Section 2 $\underline{\hspace{2cm}}_{\text{number correct}} - \frac{1}{4}\left(\underline{\hspace{2cm}}_{\text{number incorrect}} \right) = \underline{\hspace{2cm}}$ (A)

Section 5 $\underline{\hspace{2cm}}_{\text{number correct}} - \frac{1}{4}\left(\underline{\hspace{2cm}}_{\text{number incorrect}} \right) = \underline{\hspace{2cm}}$ (B)

Section 8 $\underline{\hspace{2cm}}_{\text{number correct}} - \frac{1}{4}\left(\underline{\hspace{2cm}}_{\text{number incorrect}} \right) = \underline{\hspace{2cm}}$ (C)

Critical Reading Raw Score = (A) + (B) + (C) = $\underline{\hspace{2cm}}$

Critical Reading Scaled Score (see Table 1) = $\underline{\hspace{2cm}}$

Mathematics

Section 3 $\underline{\hspace{2cm}}_{\text{number correct}} - \frac{1}{4}\left(\underline{\hspace{2cm}}_{\text{number incorrect}} \right) = \underline{\hspace{2cm}}$ (D)

Section 7
Part I
(1–8) $\underline{\hspace{2cm}}_{\text{number correct}} - \frac{1}{4}\left(\underline{\hspace{2cm}}_{\text{number incorrect}} \right) = \underline{\hspace{2cm}}$ (E)

Part II
(9–18) $\underline{\hspace{2cm}}_{\text{number correct}}$ $= \underline{\hspace{2cm}}$ (F)

Section 9 $\underline{\hspace{2cm}}_{\text{number correct}} - \frac{1}{4}\left(\underline{\hspace{2cm}}_{\text{number incorrect}} \right) = \underline{\hspace{2cm}}$ (G)

Mathematics Raw Score = (D) + (E) + (F) + (G) = $\underline{\hspace{2cm}}$

Mathematics Scaled Score (see Table 2) = $\underline{\hspace{2cm}}$

Writing

Essay $$\frac{}{\text{score 1}} + \frac{}{\text{score 2}} = \underline{} \text{ (H)}$$

Section 4 $$\frac{}{\text{number correct}} - \frac{1}{4}\left(\frac{}{\text{number incorrect}}\right) = \underline{} \text{ (I)}$$

Section 10 $$\frac{}{\text{number correct}} - \frac{1}{4}\left(\frac{}{\text{number incorrect}}\right) = \underline{} \text{ (J)}$$

Writing Raw Score = I + J (H is a separate subscore) = _____

Writing Scaled Score (see Table 3) = _____

TABLE 1: CRITICAL READING CONVERSION TABLE

Raw Score	Scaled Score	Raw Score	Scaled Score	Raw Score	Scaled Score	Raw Score	Scaled Score
67	800	49	630	31	510	14	400
66	790	48	620	30	510	13	400
65	790	47	610	29	500	12	390
64	780	46	610	28	490	11	380
63	770	45	600	27	490	10	370
62	760	44	590	26	480	9	360
61	750	43	590	25	480	8	350
60	740	42	580	24	470	7	340
59	730	41	570	23	460	6	330
58	720	40	570	22	460	5	320
57	710	39	560	21	450	4	310
56	700	38	550	20	440	3	300
55	690	37	550	19	440	2	280
54	680	36	540	18	430	1	270
53	670	35	540	17	420	0	260
52	660	34	530	16	420	−1	230
51	650	33	520	15	410	−2 and below	210
50	640	32	520				

Table 2: Math Conversion Table

Math Raw Score	Math Scaled Score	Math Raw Score	Math Scaled Score	Math Raw Score	Math Scaled Score	Math Raw Score	Math Scaled Score
54	800	40	630	26	500	12	390
53	790	39	620	25	500	11	380
52	770	38	610	24	490	10	370
51	750	37	600	23	480	9	360
50	730	36	590	22	470	8	340
49	710	35	580	21	460	7	330
48	700	34	570	20	450	6	320
47	690	33	560	19	450	5	300
46	680	32	560	18	440	4	290
45	670	31	550	17	430	3	270
44	660	30	540	16	420	2	250
43	650	29	530	15	410	1	240
42	640	28	520	14	410	0	230
41	640	27	510	13	400	−1 and below	200

Practice Test 3

TABLE 3: WRITING CONVERSION TABLE

Writing Raw Score	Essay Score					
	6	5	4	3	2	1
49	800	800	770	740	710	680
48	800	790	750	710	680	650
47	790	760	720	690	660	630
46	770	740	700	670	640	610
45	760	730	690	650	620	590
44	740	710	670	640	610	580
43	730	700	660	620	600	570
42	720	690	650	610	580	550
41	710	670	630	600	570	540
40	690	660	620	590	560	530
39	680	650	610	580	550	520
38	670	640	600	570	540	510
37	670	630	590	560	530	500
36	660	630	590	550	520	490
35	650	620	580	540	510	480
34	640	610	570	530	510	480
33	630	600	560	530	500	470
32	620	590	550	520	490	460
31	620	590	550	510	480	450
30	610	580	540	500	480	450
29	600	570	530	500	470	440
28	590	560	520	490	460	430
27	590	560	520	480	450	430
26	580	550	510	480	450	420
25	570	540	500	470	440	410
24	570	540	500	460	440	410
23	560	530	490	460	430	400
22	560	520	480	450	420	390
21	550	520	480	440	420	390
20	540	510	470	440	410	380
19	540	510	470	430	400	370
18	530	500	460	430	400	370
17	520	490	450	420	390	360
16	520	490	450	410	380	350
15	510	480	440	410	380	350
14	500	470	430	400	370	340
13	500	470	430	390	370	340
12	490	460	420	390	360	330
11	480	450	410	380	350	320
10	480	450	410	370	350	320
9	470	440	400	370	340	310
8	460	430	390	360	330	300
7	460	420	390	350	320	290
6	450	420	380	340	310	280
5	440	410	370	330	310	280
4	430	400	360	320	300	270
3	420	390	350	310	280	250
2	400	360	330	300	270	240
1	390	360	320	290	260	230
0	370	340	300	270	240	210

ANSWERS EXPLAINED
Section 2 Critical Reading

1. **D** *Although* signals a contrast with "were less likely than ever before to move up the economic ladder." *Affluence* means "wealth."

2. **B** A contrast is signaled by "or." *Malefaction* (evil-doing) contrasts with "increase wisdom and do good."

3. **E** "Means that it loses forever a significant part of its culture" signals that language is an *integral* (necessary for completeness) part of culture. If a community speaks a language other than the one it first acquired it will *necessarily* lose part of its culture.

4. **B** Respiration allows organisms to utilize stored energy, so it is the *antithesis* (direct opposite of) photosynthesis.

5. **A** It makes sense that particles that are not directly observable are *transitory* (existing only for a short time).

6. **B** International monitoring of communicable disease has helped control the spread of *pandemics* (epidemics over a wide geographic area) that in the past *decimated* (killed a large part of) the population.

7. **C** Some opponents of applying genetic engineering to human beings *invoke* (apply) a "slippery slope" argument, saying that most people find the idea *abhorrent* (loathsome) but will gradually come to support it as they come to know its benefits.

8. **D** The sentence says our intellectual abilities "gave us a monumental advantage," so we know the adjective describing these abilities must be a word with a positive meaning. *Seemingly* is the clue that these great abilities might appear to be *superfluous* (beyond what is required).

9. **E** Passage 1 says, "Nuclear plants do not produce carbon dioxide, sulfur or nitrogen oxides" (lines 9–11) and that "Nuclear power production . . . avoids the emission of more than 175 million tons of carbon . . ." (lines 11–13). In line 18, Passage 2 strongly suggests that it agrees with the claim that nuclear energy is "clean-burning," (which means that relatively little pollution is produced in the actual process of generating power).

10. **C** Passage 2 says, "However, a life-cycle . . . of the plant" (lines 19–27).

11. **E** The argument in Passage 1 is that burning fossil fuels to generate electricity has serious health consequences, and that switching to nuclear power would greatly reduce the amount of pollution. Thus, a study showing that air pollution is even worse than previously believed would strengthen the argument made in Passage 1.

12. **A** The author's main point in Passage 1 is that nuclear power plants produce less air pollution than fossil-fuel power plants. Passage 2 cites a life-cycle analysis comparing nuclear power with power generated by renewables. The author of Passage 1 would probably say that a life-cycle analysis of power from coal and gas would be helpful because its results could be compared to the results of the life-cycle analysis of nuclear power, thus providing a picture of the total amount of carbon produced by each.

13. **D** The author says that Boers had "a dour fatalistic Old Testament religion" (lines 19–20). The word *dour* means stern and gloomy.

14. **A** In lines 25–30 the author is comparing Napoleon's troops with Boer soldiers, so in context this phrase refers to the fact that the Boer soldiers were harder for the British to defeat than Napoleon's troops.

15. **B** As discussed in Question 14 above, the author says the Boers were very difficult foes on the battlefield, so it makes sense that they would have very effective rifles. The word "modern" is used humorously, referring to the word "ancient" in the phrase "ancient theology" (line 29).

16. **A** Enervating means "draining energy," which makes good sense in context because the climate "barred their way" (line 62).

17. **C** In lines 63–71 ("But it was . . . that robust climate"), the author explains why the Dutch succeeded where the Portuguese had not.

18.   **C**   "The choicest seed" refers to "the additional Huguenot emigrants" (lines 82–83) from France.

19.   **D**   There is no evidence that any of the choices besides England was a great rival of France during the time period being discussed. There are several clues that England is being referred to. For example, lines 25–26: "Our military history has largely consisted in our conflicts with France." Also, the lines 122–127 ("After twenty years . . . The British Empire") tell us that England and France were great rivals.

20.   **B**   Throughout the passage the writer has an admiring attitude toward the Boers. This is well illustrated in the first paragraph, in which the author describes the origin and qualities of the Boers.

21.   **D**   *Temper* in context means a characteristic general quality.

22.   **C**   *Consuming* in context means "deeply felt."

23.   **A**   There is no suggestion that the modern Boers are willing to compromise. All of the other choices are either mentioned or implied.

24.   **C**   The author mainly recounts events in the course of describing the history of the Boers.

Section 3 Mathematics
<u>Note</u>:

1.   See page 32 for an explanation of the symbol $\Rightarrow$ that is used in some answer explanations.

2.   A calculator icon, 🖩, is placed next to the answer explanation of any question for which a calculator *could* be useful. Almost always, the question can be answered easily without using a calculator.

3.   If you are unfamiliar with any of the math facts used in the following answer explanations, refer to Barron's *SAT*, which, in addition to having practice tests, has a full review of all the math you need to know.

1.   **C**   Frank has enough pineapples for $50 \div 1 = 50$ baskets. Since $100 \div 3 = 33\frac{1}{3}$, Frank has enough kiwis for 33 baskets, and he would have 1 kiwi left over. He has enough passion fruits for $200 \div 5 = 40$ baskets. So he has enough fruit on hand to make 33 gift baskets.

2.   **E**   **Solution 1.** If x represents the number of girls in the class, then $3x$ represents the number of boys. So, $36 = 3x + x = 4x$, and $x = 9$. Therefore, the number of boys is $3x = 27$.

   Solution 2. Since there are more boys than girls, the number of boys is more than $\frac{1}{2}(36) = 18$. Only choice (E), 27, is greater than 18.

3.   **A**   **Solution 1.** The ratios of any corresponding linear measurements in two circles is the same. Here $\frac{r_1}{r_2} = \frac{d_1}{d_2} = \frac{C_1}{C_2} = \frac{2}{1}$.

   Solution 2. Choose an easy-to-use number for the radius of circle 2, say 1. So, $C_2 = 2\pi r_2 = 2\pi(1) = 2\pi$. Then, $C_1 = 2(2\pi) = 4\pi$. But $C_1 = 2\pi r_1$, so $r_1 = 2$ and $\frac{r_1}{r_2} = \frac{2}{1}$.

4.   **E**   If even one of the six integers were even, then their product would be even, so all six of the integers *must* be odd.

5.   **D**   **Solution 1.** The areas of the two white squares are a^2 and $(2a)^2 = 4a^2$, respectively, and the area of the large square is $10^2 = 100$. To find the area of the shaded region, subtract the area of the white regions from the total area: $100 - (a^2 + 4a^2) = 100 - 5a^2$.

   Solution 2. Plug in a number for a, say $a = 1$. Then the areas of the two white squares are $1^2 = 1$ and $2^2 = 4$. So the shaded area is $100 - 5 = 95$. Only choice (D) is equal to 95 when $a = 1$.

6. **E** **Solution 1.** (The straightforward algebraic solution.)

Let x and $3x$ represent the amount of money, in dollars, that Heidi and Sally had originally. After Sally gave Heidi $200, Sally had $3x - 200$ and Heidi had $x + 200$. So $3x - 200 = 2(x + 200) = 2x + 400 \Rightarrow x = 600$. Originally, Heidi had $600 and Sally had $1,800.

Solution 2. (Backsolving.)

Test the answers starting with choice (C). If Sally originally had $1,200, Heidi would have had $400. After giving Heidi $200, Sally would have had $1,000 and Heidi, $600. Since $1,000 is less than twice $600, choice (C) is wrong. Clearly, we need a larger amount. Test choice (D) or choice (E). Choice (D) doesn't work. Choice (E) does.

7. **D** The only digits of the two factors that can affect u and t are the units digits and tens digits. So u and t are equal to the units digits and tens digits, respectively, of $89 \times 21 = 1869$. So $u = 9$, $t = 6$, and $u - t = 3$.

8. **B** Since the average of the 6 numbers $a, a, a, a, \dfrac{1}{6}$, and $\dfrac{1}{3}$ is $\dfrac{1}{4}$, their sum is $6 \times \dfrac{1}{4} = \dfrac{6}{4} = \dfrac{3}{2}$.

So, $\dfrac{3}{2} = a + a + a + a + \dfrac{1}{6} + \dfrac{1}{3} = 4a + \dfrac{1}{2}$. Hence, $4a = 1$ and $a = \dfrac{1}{4}$.

9. **C** A package costing $8 for delivery must weigh between 10 and 20 pounds, inclusive. Therefore, it must weigh within 5 pounds of 15: no more than 5 pounds less than 15 pounds and no more than 5 pounds more than 15 pounds. The inequality that expresses that fact is $|p - 15| \le 5$.

10. **E** Solve the given equation for y. Then the slope will be the coefficient of x. Since, $4y - 5x = 6$, $4y = 5x + 6$

and $y = \dfrac{5x}{4} + \dfrac{6}{4} = \dfrac{5}{4}x + \dfrac{3}{2}$. So the slope is $\dfrac{5}{4}$.

11. **A** Subtracting the second equation from the first equation, we get that $3a - 3b = 2$. Dividing both sides by 3, we get $a - b = \dfrac{2}{3}$.

12. **B** Draw in O, the center of the circle, and radii $\overline{OP}$ and $\overline{OQ}$.

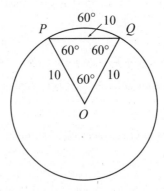

Since arc PQ measures 60°, so does central angle O, and since m$\angle P$ = m$\angle Q$, they are also both 60°. So $\triangle POQ$ is equilateral, and therefore, radius $OQ = 10$. So the diameter is 20, and the circumference is $\pi d = 20\pi$.

13. **D** Cross-multiply the given proportion:

$$\frac{3a - 2b}{3a + 2b} = \frac{2}{3} \Rightarrow 3(3a - 2b) = 2(3a + 2b).$$

So $9a - 6b = 6a + 4b$. Then $3a = 10b$ and $\dfrac{a}{b} = \dfrac{10}{3}$.

14. **A** Since the probability of drawing a red marble is $\frac{1}{3}$, the number of marbles in the jar must be a multiple of 3. Similarly, the number of marbles must be a multiple of 4 and of 5. The only number less than 100 that is a multiple of 3, 4, and 5 is 60. So the numbers of red, white, and blue marbles are $\frac{1}{3}(60) = 20$, $\frac{1}{5}(60) = 12$, and $\frac{1}{4}(60) = 15$, respectively. So $20 + 12 + 15 = 47$ marbles are red, white, or blue, and the other $60 - 47 = 13$ marbles are not red, white, or blue.

15. **E** **Solution 1.** Since the area of the square is $4^2 = 16$ and the area of the shaded region is 6, the area of the white circle is $16 - 6 = 10$. If r is the radius of the circle, then $\pi r^2 = 10$. So $r^2 = \frac{10}{\pi}$ and $r = \sqrt{\frac{10}{\pi}}$. Finally, the circumference of the circle is

$$2\pi r = 2\pi\sqrt{\frac{10}{\pi}} = \frac{2\pi\sqrt{10}}{\sqrt{\pi}} = 2\sqrt{\pi}\sqrt{10} = 2\sqrt{10\pi}.$$

NOTE: If you get that the circumference is equal to $2\pi\sqrt{\frac{10}{\pi}}$ but can't simplify that expression, just use your calculator.

$2\pi\sqrt{\frac{10}{\pi}} \approx 11.2$. Now check the answer choices. Only choice (E) is equal to 11.2.

Solution 2. Trust the diagram. Since the side of the square is 4, the diameter of the circle is about 3.5. So the circumference is about $3.5\pi \approx 3.5 \times 3.14 = 10.99$. Now evaluate the answer choices. Only choice E is even close.

16. **D** Draw a Venn diagram, letting x = the number of women who have both a boy and a girl.

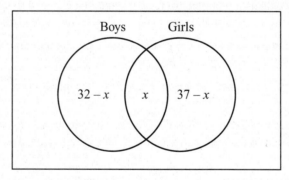

Then, $(32 - x) + (37 - x) = 25$. So, $69 - 2x = 25$.
Therefore, $2x = 44$ and $x = 22$.

17. **B** The sum of the measures of the interior angles of a polygon with n sides is $(n - 2) \times 180°$. So the sum of the 8 interior angles of octagon *ABCDEFGH* is $6 \times 180° = 1{,}080°$. Since the octagon is regular, each of the 8 *interior* angles measures $1{,}080° \div 8 = 135°$. Therefore, the measure of each *exterior* angle is $180° - 135° = 45°$.

So, $\triangle GHJ$ is a 45-45-90 right triangle whose hypotenuse is 2 and each of whose legs is $\frac{2}{\sqrt{2}} = \sqrt{2}$.

So the area of the triangle is $\frac{1}{2}(\sqrt{2})(\sqrt{2}) = \frac{1}{2}(2) = 1$.

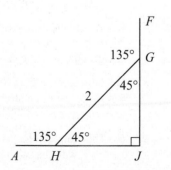

18. **E** The best way to compare two fractions is to cross-multiply. $\dfrac{m}{n}$ is less than, equal to, or greater than $\dfrac{m+1}{n+1}$ if and only if $m(n + 1)$ is less than, equal to, or greater than $n(m + 1)$, respectively. Since

$$m(n + 1) = mn + m \qquad \text{and} \qquad n(m + 1) = nm + n,$$

we can subtract mn from both expressions and just compare m and n.
- I is true whenever $m = n$.
- II is true whenever $m < n$.
- III is true whenever $m > n$.

Since we are asked which of the statements *could* be true, the answer is I, II, and III.

19. **E** The sum of the integers from 1,001 to 2,000 is

   $1,001 + 1,002 + \ldots + 1,999 + 2,000 = (1 + 1000) + (2 + 1000) + \ldots + (999 + 1000) + (1,000 + 1,000) =$
   $(1 + 2 + \ldots + 1,000) + (1,000 + 1,000 + \ldots + 1,000) = S + 1,000 \times 1,000 = S + 1,000,000.$

   So the sum of the positive integers from 1 to 2,000 is $S + (S + 1,000,000) = 2S + 1,000,000.$

20. **A**
- $f(0) = c$, which is negative, so the y-intercept of the graph must be negative. Eliminate choices (B) and (D).
- $f(1) = a + b + c$, which is negative, and since a and b are negative, $a + b + c < c$. So $f(1) < f(0)$. Eliminate choice (E).
- $f(-1) = a + (-b) + c$. Since $a < b$, $a - b$ is negative, and $a - b + c < c$. Therefore, $f(-1) < f(0)$. Eliminate choice (C).
- Only choice (A) is possible.
- NOTE: if you know that whenever a is negative the graph of $y = ax^2 + bx + c$ is a parabola that opens downward, you could have immediately eliminated choices D and E.

Section 4 Writing

1. **D** The given sentence contains a pronoun error. *That* should be changed to *who* because a person, Kim Stanley Robinson, is being referred to. Choice (D) also makes the meaning more clear.

2. **C** This corrects the faulty parallelism in the given sentence by maintaining the structure *eating tofu rather than beef, eggplant rather than chicken, and beans rather than pork.*

3. **D** This corrects the error in the given sentence. *Examples*, the subject complement of the verb *are*, must agree with it in number.

4. **D** This corrects the error in tense in the given sentence. The simple past tense is correct because the migration is regarded as a single event in the past, and no other events are mentioned, so there is no need for a perfect tense.

5. **B** The given sentence contains a dangling participle. Choice (B) corrects this so that it is clear that it was Louise who was walking along the street near her friend's house, not her cell phone.

6. **C** This corrects the error in the given sentence: *Charles Lindbergh* cannot be an *achievement*. (C) corrects this by making Lindberg's *flight* the achievement.

7. **E** The given sentence makes little sense because workers would not go on strike *because* they were complaining about low pay and poor working conditions. Choice (E) improves the sentence by the use of the adverb after to indicate the relationship between the two events (*complaining* and *went on strike*).

8. **B** This corrects the error in the given sentence, which is a run-on sentence. It also maintains parallelism by following the basic structure of the first part of the sentence, which is the subject (*Trollope*) followed by a main verb (*believed*).

9. **B** This corrects the given sentence, which is a run-on sentence (comma splice), by creating a compound sentence with the two independent clauses linked by the conjunction *and*.

10. **D** The given sentence is grammatically correct, but the part of the sentence after the comma is awkward. Choice (D) expresses the meaning clearly and concisely.

11. **C** The given sentence is clear and grammatically correct.

12. **D** Faulty parallelism. The phrase referring to *protect their rights* should have the same grammatical form as the phrase referring to *tyrannize the populace*. Therefore, the word *enables* should be changed to *enabling* so that it is a participle, like *denying*.

13. **C** Wrong tense. Events in the past are referred to, so the future tense (*will*) is incorrect. Change *will* to the past tense, *would*.

14. **C** Tense error. The present perfect *have existed* must be changed to the simple present tense *exist* because the present tense is used to state general facts or laws.

15. **C** Subject–verb agreement. The phrase *the wise* means people who are *wise*. Because the word *people* is plural, *is* must be changed to *are*.

16. **D** Pronoun–antecedent agreement. The pronoun *they* refers to *person*, which is singular. Change *they* to *he or she*.

17. **E** No error.

18. **A** Wrong part of speech. An adverb is needed to modify the adjective *bad*. Change *incredible* to *incredibly*.

19. **C** The phrase *having the narrator continually undercut his own assertions* is the object of the preposition *by*, so there is no need for a possessive pronoun.

20. **D** Faulty parallelism. The phrase *is blending* should be changed to *blends* so that it is in the same grammatical form as *retains*.

21. **E** No error.

22. **B** Idiom error. In context, the standard usage is *paradigm for*.

23. **E** No error.

24. **A** In context *a few natural resources* doesn't make sense. Change *a few* to *few*.

25. **B** The structure of the sentence requires that the word *govern*, which refers to *rules,* must be a participle, *governing*, so that *governing the time allowed for the completion of assignments* becomes a participial phrase referring to the noun *rules*.

26. **C** Idiom error. The quotation begins with the words *Not only*. In standard usage this is linked to the second part of the sentence by the coordinating conjunction *but*.

27. **B** Run-on sentence (comma splice). Either the independent clause after the word *Chopin* must be linked to the first independent clause with a semicolon, or two sentences must be made by putting a period after *Chopin*.

28. **B** *Praising* is a verb expressing the action of the subject *wife and children*, so the prepositional phrase *in praising* is incorrect.

29. **A** Idiom error. The given sentence is not grammatical. Change *In the case of* to *As is the case with*.

30. **D** This is the best choice because the word *This* makes it clear that *standard usage* in the preceding sentence (sentence 2) is being referred to and because it is standard usage. (A) This is a bit unclear because *the sort being accepted* is not standard usage in context. (B) The phrase *a language* is incorrect because *standard usage* is not a language. (C) *Having been accepted* is not grammatical in context. Also *standard usage* is not a language. (E) This does not form a complete sentence because *being* is a participle.

31. **E** This is the best choice because it links the three sentences preceding sentence 8 (sentences 5, 6, and 7), which deal with grammar, with the four sentences after sentence 8 (sentences 9, 10, 11, and 12), which deal with words and phrases. (A) This elaborates on sentence 7. It is not as good a choice as (E) because sentence 7 provides an example and does not require further elaboration, whereas (E) links the sentences as described in (E) above. (B) The same explanation as (A) above applies. (C) This sentence makes some link between the discussion of grammar and the discussion of words and phrases, but it does not do so nearly as well as (E). (D) This does not link the two topics, grammar and words/phrases.

32. **B** This effectively links sentences 9 and 10. Sentence 9 suggests consulting a dictionary to see if a word is "standard." Choice (B) suggests a word to check in the dictionary. Sentence 10 describes what is found in the dictionary. (A) This elaborates on the dictionaries mentioned in sentence 9 but does not relate to sentence 10. (C) Like choice (A), this elaborates on the dictionaries mentioned in sentence 9 but does not relate to sentence 10. (D) Like choices (A) and (B), this elaborates on the dictionaries mentioned in sentence 9 but does not relate to sentence 10. (E) This provides a link between sentences 9 and 10, but it is not as good a choice as (B) because it does not specify the word to be used as an example.

33. **B** The sentence preceding sentence 11, sentence 10, states that there are meanings under the noun form and under the verb form. Thus, this is the best choice because it links sentence 11 to sentence 10 by referring to one of the two forms mentioned in sentence 10. (A) This does not make sense because it is not idiomatic in the context. (C) This is not as good a choice as (B) because the phrase *on sticking to* is not standard usage in this context. (D) This does not make sense. (E) This does not form a complete sentence and makes little sense.

34. **A** This is grammatical, clear, and makes good sense. (B) The clause beginning with *because* makes poor sense in that position in the sentence. (C) This makes sense, but is awkward because it does not maintain parallel structure. (D) This is awkward. Also, the phrase *labeled to be* is not standard usage. (E) This is awkward and not as clear as choice (A).

35. **C** The final paragraph's main effect is to create humor through the offering of somewhat tongue-in-cheek advice and idiomatic use of the verb *stick*. (A) Language is used flexibly in the paragraph, so it does not discourage the flexible use of language. (B) The paragraph does not call into question anything that was said earlier in the paragraph. (D) The paragraph does not make fun of people who worry about correct English usage. (E) It could be argued that one of the main effects of the final paragraph is to encourage students to be creative. Certainly, its effect is not to discourage creativity.

Section 5 Critical Reading

1. **E** It makes sense that future *animosity* (active hatred) will be based on differing cultural values.

2. **D** *Premise* (a proposition from which a conclusion is drawn) makes good sense because such students pursue a professional qualification based on the idea that hard work in the present will be rewarded in the future.

3. **B** It makes good sense that as people move up the socioeconomic *hierarchy* (categorization of a group of people according to status) many of them move from the city center to the suburbs, which *prudent* (careful) city planners allow for.

4. **C** "Teaching the values of society" signals that many songs, etc., are *didactic* (instructional).

5. **D** "Was seen to be flawed" signals that the evidence was *spurious* (false) although it sounded *credible* (believable) "on first hearing."

6. **D** The word "caprice" is used to describe how an historic style does not develop. This is signaled by the fact that it is contrasted with "conditions" (line 7). The author is saying an historic style is not caused by people's changing their views for no apparent reason but by the nature of society.

7. **D** The author says, "An historic style is the particular phase, the characteristic manner of design, which prevails at a given time and place" (lines 3–5) and, "Each style is based upon some fundamental principle springing from the surrounding civilization" (lines 10–12). From this it can be inferred that the author would agree that the study of architectural style and the study of the history of civilizations are closely related.

8. **B** Line 7 says, "Printing was not known." One of the reasons that the Church taught through art was that there were no books.

9. **A** The author says, "When the Renaissance came . . . painting was but the color-thought and form-language of the people. And these people . . . were an exacting people, knowing what was good and demanding it from artists" (lines 13–19) and, "The people spurred on the artists" (line 22).

10. **D** The theory is outlined in lines 17–57.

11. **D** We can infer this from the theory described in lines 17–57. As described in the theory, the parasite must keep extending its life cycle to keep up with the cicada's increasing life cycle. The parasite thus must have become extinct after *Magicicada tredecim's* life cycle became 13 years.

12. **C** This is not true because, according to the theory described in the passage, the longer the cicada's life cycle is, the more difficult it will be for its parasite to survive.

13. **C** The theory explains the phenomenon very well, but the fact that the parasite has not been found (lines 49–50) does not provide good empirical support.

14. **C** As mentioned in 13 above, the fact that the parasite hasn't been found provides good support for the theory. The discovery of the parasite would be strong evidence against the theory, but it wouldn't invalidate it because it's possible that the parasite survived even though it had to make it through the difficult 272-year period mentioned in line 53, in which there were no cicadas to parasitize.

15. **B** The phrase "for possible future uses" (line 10) signals that values (which means "uses") in the future are being referred to.

16. **C** "They can be continually recycled" (line 23) signals that land can be used successively for an infinite number of purposes. "Does not mean they are infinite in amount" (line 24) indicates that the amount of land cannot be increased.

17. **B** "Once dedicated, [a river system] cannot be used again without disturbing the constituencies that use its features" (lines 44–46).

18. **D** In context "perverse" means *arising from obstinate persistence in an error*. The author is saying that often unsustainable resource use is encouraged by policies that continue despite evidence that they do not work.

19. **E** The author uses groundwater resources in the U.S. as an example of a situation in which there exists a "perverse institutional or legal incentives" (lines 61–62). The phrase "use it or lose it" lines 67–68 in parentheses immediately after "a lack of tradable rights to water" (line 67) signals that the author is saying that because people cannot trade water rights they have an incentive to use the water they have before others gain access to it and use it through digging wells.

20. **A** The author cites the example of cattle to illustrate the principle that private ownership often results in more effective conservation of resources than public ownership. We can infer that the author believes that cattle might become scarce if they were owned in common because individuals would have little incentive to care for cattle and limit the number of cattle they consume. (In fact, the author might argue that people would have an incentive to kill as many cattle as they can before others do.)

21. **B** The author argues throughout the passage that in many cases assigning ownership rights is the most effective way to conserve unsustainable resources. In line 98 he says, "Getting the incentives right" should mean chiefly assigning property rights to environmental goods.

22. **E** This is the most accurate characterization of each passage.

23. **A** The author of Passage 1 says, "Air and water are particularly susceptible to pollutants because of the ease with which they can be used as open-access resources for receiving and disseminating waste" (lines 28–32). Thus, he would probably argue for close monitoring of the result of assigning ownership rights. In his discussion of the example of a river system, the author stresses that the various uses it is put to can have a great effect on other uses it has, on the system itself, and on things outside the system related to it. Therefore, it is likely he would be concerned about the effects of the activity of one owner on the parts of the ocean owned by others.

24. **B** The author of Passage 1 does not discuss the value of a market-based approach, but there is no reason to think that he would rule out some use of a market-based approach if the results achieved by it were carefully monitored and the approach helped to effectively sustain renewable resources. However, he would also be likely to say that granting ownership rights cannot be the sole solution in the case of resources that have many, often competing, uses, such as a river system. He says (in lines 55–58), "Policy for renewable . . . or irreversible loss."

Section 7 Mathematics

<u>Note:</u>

1. See page 32 for an explanation of the symbol ⇒ that is used in some answer explanations.

2. A calculator icon, 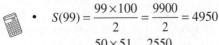, is placed next to the answer explanation of any question for which a calculator *could* be useful. Almost always, the question can be answered easily without using a calculator.

3. If you are unfamiliar with any of the math facts used in the following answer explanations, refer to Barron's *SAT*, which, in addition to having practice tests, has a full review of all the math you need to know.

1. **E** **Solution 1.** If $7x - 3 = 13$, then $7x = 16$. Stop. *Do not solve for x.*

   If $7x = 16$, then $7x + 3 = 16 + 3 = 19$.

   Solution 2. If you immediately notice that $7x + 3$ is 6 more than $7x - 3$, then simply add 6: $13 + 6 = 19$.

2. **C** The sum of the six angles in the two triangles is $2 \times 180° = 360°$. Since one of the angles measures 80°, the sum of the other five angles is $360° - 80° = 280°$.

3. **B** Each time you buy 3 apples, you save $\$1.99 - \$1.59 = \$0.40$. To save $\$2.00$, you would have to do that $2.00 \div 0.40 = 5$ times, so you would have to buy $5 \times 3 = 15$ apples.

4. **C** Since $\dfrac{a+b+c}{3} = 19$ and $\dfrac{b+c+d}{3} = 17$, then $a + b + c = 3 \times 19 = 57$ and $b + c + d = 3 \times 17 = 51$.
   Subtracting the second equation from the first, we get $a - d = 57 - 51 = 6$.

5. **C** Let M, T, and W represent the amounts, in dollars, that Cheryl had in her bank account on Monday, Tuesday, and Wednesday, respectively.
   Then $T = M + 12$, $W = T + 15$, and $W = 4M$.
   Since $W = T + 15 = (M + 12) + 15 = M + 27$ and $W = 4M$, then
   $4M = M + 27 \Rightarrow 3M = 27 \Rightarrow M = 9$. So $T = 9 + 12 = 21$.

6. **E** If $\dfrac{1}{4}C = \dfrac{4}{\pi}$, then $C = \dfrac{16}{\pi}$. Since $C = 2\pi r$, we have $\dfrac{16}{\pi} = 2\pi r$.

   So, $16 = 2\pi^2 r$ and $r = \dfrac{16}{2\pi^2} = \dfrac{8}{\pi^2}$. Finally, $A = \pi r^2 = \pi \left(\dfrac{8}{\pi^2}\right)^2 = \pi \left(\dfrac{64}{\pi^4}\right) = \dfrac{64}{\pi^3}$.

7. **E** Use the formula $d = rt$ (distance = rate × time). Let r represent Kathy's rate, in miles per hour, and $r + 10$, Karl's rate. Kathy's trip took 2 hours, and let t represent the time for Karl's trip. Then for Kathy, $d = 2r$, and for Karl, $d = (r + 10)t$. Since the distances are equal, $2r = (r + 10)t$ and $t = \dfrac{2r}{r+10}$, which clearly depends on r. For example, if Kathy's rate, r, were 10, then Karl's time, t, would be $\dfrac{20}{20} = 1$ hour; whereas if $r = 50$, then Karl's time would be $\dfrac{100}{60} = 1\dfrac{2}{3}$ hours.

8. **B** To evaluate $51 + 52 + 53 + \ldots + 98 + 99$, first evaluate $S(99)$, the sum of all the integers from 1 through 99, and then subtract from that $S(50)$, the sum of the integers from 1 through 50.

   - $S(99) = \dfrac{99 \times 100}{2} = \dfrac{9900}{2} = 4950$

   - $S(50) = \dfrac{50 \times 51}{2} = \dfrac{2550}{2} = 1275$

   - $S(99) - S(50) = 4,950 - 1,275 = 3,675$

9. **50** **Solution 1.** $5 - a = b - 5 \Rightarrow a + b = 10$. Then, $5a + 5b = 5(a + b) = 50$.

   Solution 2. Pick a number for a, say $a = 1$. Then $5 - 1 = b - 5$; so, $4 = b - 5$ and $b = 9$. Then, $5a + 5b = 5(1) + 5(9) = 5 + 45 = 50$.

10. **280** The sum of the measures of the three angles in $\triangle ABC$ is

    $180°$. So, $50 + (a + 30) + d = 180$, and so $a + d = 100$. Since $\angle ADC$ is a straight angle, $b + c = 180$. So, $a + b + c + d = 100 + 180 = 280$.

    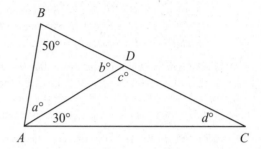

11. $\dfrac{\mathbf{45}}{\mathbf{4}}$ $\triangle$ $= \dfrac{2+4}{8} \cdot \dfrac{4+8}{2} \cdot \dfrac{2+8}{4} = \dfrac{\overset{3}{\cancel{6}} \times \overset{}{\cancel{12}} \times \overset{5}{\cancel{10}}}{\underset{1}{\cancel{8}} \times \cancel{2} \times \cancel{4}_1} = \dfrac{45}{4}$.

    Note that $\dfrac{45}{4} = 11.25$, but grids only have four columns and 11.25 would require five columns. Also, you would get no credit if you rounded off to 11.2 or 11.3. When it is possible to grid in the exact answer, you must do so.

12. **225** Since the probability that a twelfth-grader's name would be chosen was $\dfrac{1}{5}$, the probability was $\dfrac{4}{5}$ that one of the $85 + 95 = 180$ tenth- and eleventh-graders would be chosen. So if S represents the number of students who bought raffle tickets, $\dfrac{4}{5}S = 180$ and $S = \dfrac{5}{4}(180) = 225$.

13. **92.5**
    - Since the average weight of the 10 children is 90 pounds, their total weight is $10 \times 90 = 900$ pounds.
    - The 2 girls weigh a total of $2 \times 80 = 160$ pounds.
    - So the 8 boys weigh a total of $900 - 160 = 740$ pounds.
    - Finally, the average weight of the 8 boys is $740 \div 8 = 92.5$.

14. **50** **Solution 1.** Let L represent the number of games that team A lost. Then $62 + L$ is the number of games team A won. So,

    $$162 = L + (62 + L) \Rightarrow 2L = 100 \Rightarrow L = 50$$

    Solution 2. Test numbers for wins and losses that add up to 162, refining your guesses until you have the correct answer.
    - Try 100 wins and 62 losses. 100 is 38 more than 62. We need more wins.
    - Try 110 wins and 52 losses. 110 is 58 more than 52. Still too few wins, but we're very close.
    - 111 and 51? No.
    - 112 and 50? Yes.

15. **60** Use the formula $d = rt$ in the form $t = \dfrac{d}{r}$. Then

    Geraldine: $t = \dfrac{5 \text{ miles}}{50 \text{ miles per hour}} = \dfrac{1}{10} \text{ hour} = 6 \text{ minutes}$

    Jerome: $t = \dfrac{5 \text{ miles}}{60 \text{ miles per hour}} = \dfrac{1}{12} \text{ hour} = 5 \text{ minutes}$

    The difference in times is exactly 1 minute, or 60 seconds.

16. **2**
   - $f(15) = 100 \Rightarrow 15a + b = 100$
   - $f(10) = 65 \Rightarrow 10a + b = 65$
   - Subtracting the two equations, we get $5a = 35$, and so $a = 7$.
   - Replacing a by 7 in the second equation, we get
     $10(7) + b = 65 \Rightarrow 70 + b = 65$ and so $b = -5$.
   - Finally, $a + b = 7 + (-5) = 2$.

17. **150**   The polygon in the figure has 9 sides. In general, if a polygon has n sides, the sum of the measures of its interior angles is $(n - 2) \times 180°$. So the sum of the measures of all 9 interior angles in the given figure is $(9 - 2) \times 180° = 7 \times 180° = 1260°$. Since $m\angle A = 60°$, the sum of the measures of the 8 other angles is $1260° - 60° = 1200°$. Finally, the average degree measure of those 8 angles is $1200 \div 8 = 150$.

18. **271**   **Solution 1.** Think of every non-negative integer less than 1,000 as a three-digit number from 000 to 999: $001, \ldots, 009, 010, 011, \ldots, 099, 100, \ldots, 999$. Then, using the counting principle, the number of ways to write a three-digit number that has *no* 7s is $9 \times 9 \times 9$, since there are 9 choices for each digit: $9 \times 9 \times 9 = 729$. So, 729 integers from 0 to 999 don't contain the digit 7, and $1,000 - 729 = 271$ integers do.

Solution 2.
   - Of course, all 100 integers from 700 to 799 contain the digit 7.
   - From 1 through 99 there are 10 integers whose ten's digit is 7: $70, 71, \ldots, 79$, and 10 integers whose unit's digit is 7: $7, 17, \ldots, 97$. Of these 20 numbers, one of them (77) was counted twice; so 19 integers less than 100 contain the digit 7.
   - From 100 to 199 there are also 19 integers that contain the digit 7: the 19 integers found by writing a 1 in front of each number less than 100 containing a 7: $107, 117, \ldots, 197; 170, 171, \ldots, 179$.
   - Similarly there are 19 numbers in the 200s, 300s, 400s, 500s, 600s, 800s, and 900s.
   - In total, there are $9 \times 19 + 100 = 171 + 100 = 271$ integers less than 1,000 that include the digit 7.

Section 8 Critical Reading

1. **B**   It makes sense that two systems of government in a "space race" were trying to demonstrate the superiority of their ideology (set of beliefs that are the basis of a political system).

2. **D**   The causes of World War II are *attributed* (related as a cause) to various things.

3. **D**   "Based on available evidence" signals that a belief is *provisional* (temporary). "More evidence" signals that an opinion must be changed to *accommodate* (allow for) new evidence.

4. **B**   "Writers" and "effective communication" signal that *rhetorical* (concerned with speaking or writing effectively) devices are being discussed.

5. **C**   "Provided a rationalization for the exploitation of the poor" signals that it was *apologists* (persons who justify something) for capitalism who gave capitalism an excuse for exploiting the poor by drawing an *analogy* (comparison based on a similarity) between the free market and the struggle for existence.

6. **E**   The words "debated" and "or" signal that two effects of drama are being contrasted. (E) is the only choice that creates a sentence with a clear contrast. Plato believed that drama *arouses* unhealthy passions, whereas Aristotle believed that drama *purges* (purifies) them.

7. **D**   The author says Stephen Sondheim "Zeroes in on the *essential* differences between the art of the lyricist and that of the poet" (lines 2–3; italics mine), but he also says, "And yet, the line between song and poem is not as firm as Sondheim suggests" (lines 8–9).

8. **B**   The author says, "[Blake's *Songs of Innocence* and *Songs of Experience* and Whitman's 'Song of Myself' straddle] the line between genres" (lines 9–14). He then quotes from *Songs of Innocence,* and says the lines "Practically [beg] to be set to music" (line 20).

9. **A**   The author says, "Whereas poetry is aimed almost exclusively at a limited number of fellow poets, hundreds of millions of men and women listen to songs . . ." (lines 31–34).

10. **E**   As it is used in line 62, "eschew" means *avoid*, and "pragmatically" means *following a set program or system*.

11. **D**   Robert Fenton is suggesting that writing students tend to be one "person"—that is, think in a certain way—when listening to music and another "person" when writing poems, and thus do not apply what they know about music to their writing of poetry.

12. **B**   In context "schizophrenic" refers to taste that is divided by two antagonistic qualities. We can infer that one of these qualities is a liking for rhyme, meter, and other "musical" qualities in poetry, and the other is a dislike for these qualities. A clue to the meaning is Robert Fenton's reference to "the person" in line 69 and "the same person" in line 70, suggesting a division in taste in one person.

13. **E**   The expression "elephant in the room" is a colorful metaphorical idiom meaning *"an obvious truth that is being ignored."* The author's adjective "singing" is a "jocular" (joking) reference to the idea that it is the music, not the lyric, that makes a person want to hear a song again. *Elegiac* (related to an elegy or mourning) can be eliminated because the expression has nothing to do with an elegy or mourning.

14. **A**   The author says, "Poets cannot rely on musical tones; still the poems I love . . . have a quasi-melodic structure that has an effect not unlike melody proper" (lines 87–90). The author is saying that some poems have an effect that is very similar to musical melody.

15. **B**   The fact that an author writing about poetry refers to a poet by only his first name suggests that he and other poetry lovers regard him with some affection. It also implies that they hold his poetry in high regard because such "short-hand" references generally are only to highly respected poets. We can infer that the author regards Walt Whitman as a great poet by the fact that he uses Whitman's verse as an example of "great poems [that] use purely verbal elements" (lines 94–95).

16. **C**   The verses by Walt Whitman and Gwendolyn Brooks that are quoted are different in many ways, but both writers use repetition. The author says, "Walt reminds us that poetic music can be achieved . . . as long as it embraces *repetition*" (lines 114–116; italics mine) and, "Brooks does not fear repetition . . . she uses the word 'we' seven times" (lines 148–151).

17. **D**   The word "but" in line 129 signals a contrast with "There can be relief and contrast in poetic melody" (lines 127–128). All the words in the parentheses in line 130 refer to things that would interrupt the "ride" (line 131).

18. **A**   In the sentence preceding the last line ("At a time . . . not be denied," lines 156–160) the author says that poets are no longer using repetition and melody, but that songwriters continue to use these techniques, which help make their songs popular. It makes sense, therefore, that in the last sentence the author is suggesting that to become more widely popular poets should use some of the techniques of their "big sister" (line 163)—that is, songwriting.

19. **A**   One of the author's main points is that poets can use some of the techniques of songwriters to make their poems more popular. There is nothing in the passage to suggest that the author believes that a poem cannot be both excellent and popular.

Section 9 Mathematics

<u>Note</u>:

1.   See page 32 for an explanation of the symbol ⇒ that is used in some answer explanations.

2.   A calculator icon, 🖩, is placed next to the answer explanation of any question for which a calculator *could* be useful. Almost always, the question can be answered easily without using a calculator.

3.   If you are unfamiliar with any of the math facts used in the following answer explanations, refer to Barron's *SAT*, which, in addition to having practice tests, has a full review of all the math you need to know.

1. **B** $\dfrac{1}{\cancel{2}} \times \dfrac{\cancel{2}}{\cancel{3}} \times \dfrac{\cancel{3}}{\cancel{4}} \times \dfrac{\cancel{4}}{\cancel{5}} \times \dfrac{\cancel{5}}{6} = \dfrac{1}{6}$, so $\dfrac{a}{b} = \dfrac{1}{6}$, and $a + b = 1 + 6 = 7$.

2. **D** $2x + 3y < 3x + 2y \Rightarrow y < x$. Only in choice D, $x = -1$ and $y = -2$, is $y < x$.

3. **D** **Solution 1.** Since $81 = 3^4$, $3^{x-3} = 81 = 3^4$. So, $x - 3 = 4$ and $x = 7$.

    Solution 2. Backsolve: Test the answers starting with 6, choice (C).
   $3^{6-3} = 3^3 = 27$. So, 6 is too small; eliminate choices (A), (B), and (C)
   and try choice (D) or (E). Choice (D) works.

4. **C** Since $PR = QR$, triangle PQR is isosceles and $m\angle P = m\angle Q = a°$.
   Since $\angle PRQ$ and $\angle PRT$ are vertical angles, their measures are equal.
   So $m\angle PRQ = 40°$. Since the sum of the measures of the three angles in
   $\triangle PRQ$ is 180°, we have
   $a + a + 40 = 180 \Rightarrow 2a + 40 = 180 \Rightarrow 2a = 140 \Rightarrow a = 70$.
   Note that we made no use of the fact that $m\angle T = 50°$, and, in fact,
   it was irrelevant. If $m\angle T$ were 60° or 90° or 110°, a would still be equal
   to 70.

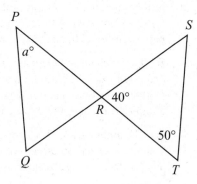

5. **A**

   - Test some numbers. If $a = -\dfrac{1}{2}$ and $b = -\dfrac{1}{3}$, then $\dfrac{1}{a} = -2$ and $\dfrac{1}{b} = -3$. So it is not true that $\dfrac{1}{a} < \dfrac{1}{b}$. I is false.
   - Since a and b are both negative, ab is positive and $a + b$ is negative. So $ab > a + b$. Therefore, II is false.
   - Since ab is positive, we can take its square root, but since a and b are negative numbers, their square roots don't exist. So III is false. Note that on the SAT, all numbers are real, but even if you used imaginary numbers to get the square roots of a and b, statement III would be false.

6. **D** Since 60 of the marbles are white, the other $100 - 60 = 40$ marbles are red or blue. Since the ratio red:blue = 3:5, the number of red and blue marbles can be represented by $3x$ and $5x$, respectively. Then $3x + 5x = 40$. So $8x = 40$, and $x = 5$. The number of blue marbles, therefore, is $5 \times 5 = 25$.

7. **D** $-\dfrac{1}{3} ☺ 4 = \left(-\dfrac{1}{3} + 4\right) - \left(-\dfrac{1}{3}\right)(4) = \dfrac{11}{3} + \dfrac{4}{3} = \dfrac{15}{3} = 5$.

8. **E** $a ☺ a = -a \Rightarrow (a + a) - (a)(a) = -a$
   So, $2a - a^2 = -a$. Then, $a^2 = 3a$, and since $a \neq 0$, $a = 3$.

9. **C**
   - $\triangle ABC$ is a 6-8-10 right triangle.
   - Since the perimeter of each triangle is 24, I is true.
   - The average of three numbers is their sum divided by 3, and since the sum of the measures of the three angles in *any* triangle is 180°, the average of the measures of the three angles in *any* triangle is $\dfrac{180°}{3} = 60°$.

     II is true.
   - The area of $\triangle ABC$ is $\dfrac{1}{2}(6)(8) = 24$. The area of an equilateral triangle whose sides are s

     is $\dfrac{s^2 \sqrt{3}}{4}$. So the area of $\triangle DEF$ is $\dfrac{64\sqrt{3}}{4} = 16\sqrt{3}$, which is not equal to 24. III is false.
   - If you don't know the formula for the area of an equilateral triangle,

     draw in an altitude and use the standard formula: $A = \dfrac{1}{2}bh$.

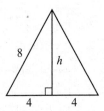

   STOP. You don't have to calculate the area, you just need to know if it is equal to 24. $\dfrac{1}{2}(8)h = 24$,

   only if $h = 6$. But it isn't. If h were 6, then we would have that $4^2 + 6^2 = 8^2$. But $16 + 36 \neq 64$.

10. **D** Since the average of the 25 integers is 25, their sum is $25 \times 25 = 625$. For the sum of the 10 largest numbers to be as big as possible, the other 15 numbers must be as small as possible. The least value of the sum of the 12 smallest integers is 12 (if each of them were 1); the 13th integer is 25, since it is the median. The least possible values of the 14th and 15th numbers are each 25, since they must be greater than or equal to the median. So the sum of the 15 smallest integers is at least $12 + 25 + 25 + 25 = 87$ and the greatest possible sum of the other 10 numbers is $625 - 87 = 538$.

11. **E** Since the area of the large square is 16, each side is 4, each side of square $ABCD$ is 2, and $BE = EC = 1$. To find AE (and ED), use the Pythagorean theorem.

$$2^2 + 1^2 = (AE)^2 \Rightarrow (AE)^2 = 5 \Rightarrow AE = \sqrt{5}$$

So the perimeter of $\triangle AED = AD + AE + ED = 2 + \sqrt{5} + \sqrt{5} = 2 + 2\sqrt{5}$.

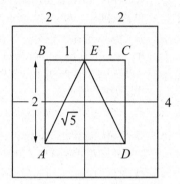

12. **D** Since the area of a square whose side is s is s^2, $A(x) = x^2$.
Then $A(5) - A(4) = 5^2 - 4^2 = 25 - 16 = 9$.
- $A(5 - 4) = A(1) = 1^2 = 1 \neq 9$. I is false.
- $A(3) = 3^2 = 9$. II is true.
- $A\left(\sqrt{35}\right) - A\left(\sqrt{26}\right) = \left(\sqrt{35}\right)^2 - \left(\sqrt{26}\right)^2 = 35 - 26 = 9$. III is true.

So II and III only are true.

13. **C** $(a - b)^2 = a^2 - 2ab + b^2 = (a^2 + b^2) - 2ab = 5\pi - 2(2\pi) = 5\pi - 4\pi = \pi$

14. **D** Let s_1 and s_2 be the sides of squares 1 and 2, respectively.

Then, $d_1 = s_1\sqrt{2}$. So $s_1 = \dfrac{d_1}{\sqrt{2}}$ and $P_1 = \dfrac{4d_1}{\sqrt{2}}$. Also, $s_2 = \dfrac{d_2}{\sqrt{2}}$.

So, $P_2 = 4s_2 = \dfrac{4d_2}{\sqrt{2}} = \dfrac{4(d_1 + 1)}{\sqrt{2}} = \dfrac{4d_1 + 4}{\sqrt{2}} = \dfrac{4d_1}{\sqrt{2}} + \dfrac{4}{\sqrt{2}} = P_1 + \dfrac{4}{\sqrt{2}}$.

So, $P_2 - P_1 = \dfrac{4}{\sqrt{2}} = \dfrac{4}{\sqrt{2}} \times \dfrac{\sqrt{2}}{\sqrt{2}} = \dfrac{4\sqrt{2}}{2} = 2\sqrt{2}$.

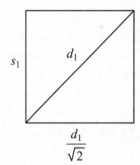

15. **B** $b = g(a) = f(a - 2) = 2^{a-2} = \dfrac{2^a}{2^2} = \dfrac{2^a}{4} = \dfrac{1}{4}(2^a) = \dfrac{1}{4}f(a)$

So, $b = \dfrac{1}{4}f(a)$ and $f(a) = 4b$.

16. **D** Since $80\%(4{,}500) = 3{,}600$ and $20\%(4{,}500) = 900$, Caleb drove 3,600 miles on highways and 900 miles in cities.

3,600 miles ÷ 24 miles per gallon = 150 gallons.
900 miles ÷ 18 miles per gallon = 50 gallons.
So Caleb used 200 gallons of gas to drive 4,500 miles:

$$\dfrac{4{,}500 \text{ miles}}{200 \text{ gallons}} = 22.5 \text{ miles per gallon}.$$

Section 10 Writing

1. **E** This corrects the incorrect verb form in the given sentence by using the simple past tense. *Was* agrees with *fireworks*, which is plural.

2. **D** This corrects the run-on sentence (comma splice).

3. **C** This corrects the tense error in the given sentence. The simple past tense is correct because only one event in the past is referred to in the main clause.

4. **D** The words "the Greek root *pan*" do not form an independent clause, so they cannot be joined to the rest of the sentence by a coordinating conjunction, which the word *and* is. Coordinating conjunctions can only join words or groups of words of equal status. Choice (D) corrects the error by the use of a parenthetical phrase set off by commas.

5. **A** The given sentence is clear and grammatical.

6. **B** This corrects the faulty parallelism in the given sentence. *Reading* and *studying* are gerunds, so using *practicing* instead of *practice* improves the sentence.

7. **D** This is the best choice because it is concise and makes clear that *writing her own novel* is being compared to *evaluating the novels of others*.

8. **A** The given sentence is correct. The independent clause is linked to the main clause by a semicolon and adds information relevant to that given in the main clause.

9. **E** The given sentence contains a dangling participle, *extrapolating from present trends*. This participial phrase refers to the subject of the sentence, *experts*, so the word *experts* should be placed at the beginning of the independent clause.

10. **B** This corrects the tense error in the given sentence. The fact that the verb *enhance* in the first part of the sentence is in the past tense (*enhanced*) signals that *spend* should also be in the past tense (*spent*).

11. **B** This makes the sentence more clear by placing the phrase *such as lakes* closer to the word *resources*, which it gives an example of.

12. **B** The given sentence contains faulty parallelism. *Its reputation* is not the same form as *how much a particular college costs* and *how effective the teachers are*. This maintains correct parallelism: *how much, how effective, how good*.

13. **E** This corrects the given sentence so that it is clear *that despite poverty and misfortune* refers to *the writer*, not *works*.

14. **C** This corrects the error in the given sentence. Normal usage requires that the verb *contended* have an object. In choice (C) the clause beginning with the word *that* becomes its object.

Answer Sheet—Practice Test 4

Section 1   **ESSAY**

Practice Test 4

Essay (continued)

If a section has fewer questions than answer spaces, leave the extra spaces blank.

Section 2

1 Ⓐ Ⓑ Ⓒ Ⓓ Ⓔ	8 Ⓐ Ⓑ Ⓒ Ⓓ Ⓔ	15 Ⓐ Ⓑ Ⓒ Ⓓ Ⓔ	22 Ⓐ Ⓑ Ⓒ Ⓓ Ⓔ	29 Ⓐ Ⓑ Ⓒ Ⓓ Ⓔ
2 Ⓐ Ⓑ Ⓒ Ⓓ Ⓔ	9 Ⓐ Ⓑ Ⓒ Ⓓ Ⓔ	16 Ⓐ Ⓑ Ⓒ Ⓓ Ⓔ	23 Ⓐ Ⓑ Ⓒ Ⓓ Ⓔ	30 Ⓐ Ⓑ Ⓒ Ⓓ Ⓔ
3 Ⓐ Ⓑ Ⓒ Ⓓ Ⓔ	10 Ⓐ Ⓑ Ⓒ Ⓓ Ⓔ	17 Ⓐ Ⓑ Ⓒ Ⓓ Ⓔ	24 Ⓐ Ⓑ Ⓒ Ⓓ Ⓔ	31 Ⓐ Ⓑ Ⓒ Ⓓ Ⓔ
4 Ⓐ Ⓑ Ⓒ Ⓓ Ⓔ	11 Ⓐ Ⓑ Ⓒ Ⓓ Ⓔ	18 Ⓐ Ⓑ Ⓒ Ⓓ Ⓔ	25 Ⓐ Ⓑ Ⓒ Ⓓ Ⓔ	32 Ⓐ Ⓑ Ⓒ Ⓓ Ⓔ
5 Ⓐ Ⓑ Ⓒ Ⓓ Ⓔ	12 Ⓐ Ⓑ Ⓒ Ⓓ Ⓔ	19 Ⓐ Ⓑ Ⓒ Ⓓ Ⓔ	26 Ⓐ Ⓑ Ⓒ Ⓓ Ⓔ	33 Ⓐ Ⓑ Ⓒ Ⓓ Ⓔ
6 Ⓐ Ⓑ Ⓒ Ⓓ Ⓔ	13 Ⓐ Ⓑ Ⓒ Ⓓ Ⓔ	20 Ⓐ Ⓑ Ⓒ Ⓓ Ⓔ	27 Ⓐ Ⓑ Ⓒ Ⓓ Ⓔ	34 Ⓐ Ⓑ Ⓒ Ⓓ Ⓔ
7 Ⓐ Ⓑ Ⓒ Ⓓ Ⓔ	14 Ⓐ Ⓑ Ⓒ Ⓓ Ⓔ	21 Ⓐ Ⓑ Ⓒ Ⓓ Ⓔ	28 Ⓐ Ⓑ Ⓒ Ⓓ Ⓔ	35 Ⓐ Ⓑ Ⓒ Ⓓ Ⓔ

Section 3

1 Ⓐ Ⓑ Ⓒ Ⓓ Ⓔ	8 Ⓐ Ⓑ Ⓒ Ⓓ Ⓔ	15 Ⓐ Ⓑ Ⓒ Ⓓ Ⓔ	22 Ⓐ Ⓑ Ⓒ Ⓓ Ⓔ	29 Ⓐ Ⓑ Ⓒ Ⓓ Ⓔ
2 Ⓐ Ⓑ Ⓒ Ⓓ Ⓔ	9 Ⓐ Ⓑ Ⓒ Ⓓ Ⓔ	16 Ⓐ Ⓑ Ⓒ Ⓓ Ⓔ	23 Ⓐ Ⓑ Ⓒ Ⓓ Ⓔ	30 Ⓐ Ⓑ Ⓒ Ⓓ Ⓔ
3 Ⓐ Ⓑ Ⓒ Ⓓ Ⓔ	10 Ⓐ Ⓑ Ⓒ Ⓓ Ⓔ	17 Ⓐ Ⓑ Ⓒ Ⓓ Ⓔ	24 Ⓐ Ⓑ Ⓒ Ⓓ Ⓔ	31 Ⓐ Ⓑ Ⓒ Ⓓ Ⓔ
4 Ⓐ Ⓑ Ⓒ Ⓓ Ⓔ	11 Ⓐ Ⓑ Ⓒ Ⓓ Ⓔ	18 Ⓐ Ⓑ Ⓒ Ⓓ Ⓔ	25 Ⓐ Ⓑ Ⓒ Ⓓ Ⓔ	32 Ⓐ Ⓑ Ⓒ Ⓓ Ⓔ
5 Ⓐ Ⓑ Ⓒ Ⓓ Ⓔ	12 Ⓐ Ⓑ Ⓒ Ⓓ Ⓔ	19 Ⓐ Ⓑ Ⓒ Ⓓ Ⓔ	26 Ⓐ Ⓑ Ⓒ Ⓓ Ⓔ	33 Ⓐ Ⓑ Ⓒ Ⓓ Ⓔ
6 Ⓐ Ⓑ Ⓒ Ⓓ Ⓔ	13 Ⓐ Ⓑ Ⓒ Ⓓ Ⓔ	20 Ⓐ Ⓑ Ⓒ Ⓓ Ⓔ	27 Ⓐ Ⓑ Ⓒ Ⓓ Ⓔ	34 Ⓐ Ⓑ Ⓒ Ⓓ Ⓔ
7 Ⓐ Ⓑ Ⓒ Ⓓ Ⓔ	14 Ⓐ Ⓑ Ⓒ Ⓓ Ⓔ	21 Ⓐ Ⓑ Ⓒ Ⓓ Ⓔ	28 Ⓐ Ⓑ Ⓒ Ⓓ Ⓔ	35 Ⓐ Ⓑ Ⓒ Ⓓ Ⓔ

Section 5

1 Ⓐ Ⓑ Ⓒ Ⓓ Ⓔ	8 Ⓐ Ⓑ Ⓒ Ⓓ Ⓔ	15 Ⓐ Ⓑ Ⓒ Ⓓ Ⓔ	22 Ⓐ Ⓑ Ⓒ Ⓓ Ⓔ	29 Ⓐ Ⓑ Ⓒ Ⓓ Ⓔ
2 Ⓐ Ⓑ Ⓒ Ⓓ Ⓔ	9 Ⓐ Ⓑ Ⓒ Ⓓ Ⓔ	16 Ⓐ Ⓑ Ⓒ Ⓓ Ⓔ	23 Ⓐ Ⓑ Ⓒ Ⓓ Ⓔ	30 Ⓐ Ⓑ Ⓒ Ⓓ Ⓔ
3 Ⓐ Ⓑ Ⓒ Ⓓ Ⓔ	10 Ⓐ Ⓑ Ⓒ Ⓓ Ⓔ	17 Ⓐ Ⓑ Ⓒ Ⓓ Ⓔ	24 Ⓐ Ⓑ Ⓒ Ⓓ Ⓔ	31 Ⓐ Ⓑ Ⓒ Ⓓ Ⓔ
4 Ⓐ Ⓑ Ⓒ Ⓓ Ⓔ	11 Ⓐ Ⓑ Ⓒ Ⓓ Ⓔ	18 Ⓐ Ⓑ Ⓒ Ⓓ Ⓔ	25 Ⓐ Ⓑ Ⓒ Ⓓ Ⓔ	32 Ⓐ Ⓑ Ⓒ Ⓓ Ⓔ
5 Ⓐ Ⓑ Ⓒ Ⓓ Ⓔ	12 Ⓐ Ⓑ Ⓒ Ⓓ Ⓔ	19 Ⓐ Ⓑ Ⓒ Ⓓ Ⓔ	26 Ⓐ Ⓑ Ⓒ Ⓓ Ⓔ	33 Ⓐ Ⓑ Ⓒ Ⓓ Ⓔ
6 Ⓐ Ⓑ Ⓒ Ⓓ Ⓔ	13 Ⓐ Ⓑ Ⓒ Ⓓ Ⓔ	20 Ⓐ Ⓑ Ⓒ Ⓓ Ⓔ	27 Ⓐ Ⓑ Ⓒ Ⓓ Ⓔ	34 Ⓐ Ⓑ Ⓒ Ⓓ Ⓔ
7 Ⓐ Ⓑ Ⓒ Ⓓ Ⓔ	14 Ⓐ Ⓑ Ⓒ Ⓓ Ⓔ	21 Ⓐ Ⓑ Ⓒ Ⓓ Ⓔ	28 Ⓐ Ⓑ Ⓒ Ⓓ Ⓔ	35 Ⓐ Ⓑ Ⓒ Ⓓ Ⓔ

Section 6

1 Ⓐ Ⓑ Ⓒ Ⓓ Ⓔ	3 Ⓐ Ⓑ Ⓒ Ⓓ Ⓔ	5 Ⓐ Ⓑ Ⓒ Ⓓ Ⓔ	7 Ⓐ Ⓑ Ⓒ Ⓓ Ⓔ	
2 Ⓐ Ⓑ Ⓒ Ⓓ Ⓔ	4 Ⓐ Ⓑ Ⓒ Ⓓ Ⓔ	6 Ⓐ Ⓑ Ⓒ Ⓓ Ⓔ	8 Ⓐ Ⓑ Ⓒ Ⓓ Ⓔ	

9   10   11   12   13

(grid-in answer boxes numbered 0–9 for each of questions 9 through 13)

Practice Test 4

14 · · · · (grid) **15** · · · · (grid) **16** · · · · (grid) **17** · · · · (grid) **18** · · · · (grid)

Section 7

1 Ⓐ Ⓑ Ⓒ Ⓓ Ⓔ 8 Ⓐ Ⓑ Ⓒ Ⓓ Ⓔ 15 Ⓐ Ⓑ Ⓒ Ⓓ Ⓔ 22 Ⓐ Ⓑ Ⓒ Ⓓ Ⓔ 29 Ⓐ Ⓑ Ⓒ Ⓓ Ⓔ
2 Ⓐ Ⓑ Ⓒ Ⓓ Ⓔ 9 Ⓐ Ⓑ Ⓒ Ⓓ Ⓔ 16 Ⓐ Ⓑ Ⓒ Ⓓ Ⓔ 23 Ⓐ Ⓑ Ⓒ Ⓓ Ⓔ 30 Ⓐ Ⓑ Ⓒ Ⓓ Ⓔ
3 Ⓐ Ⓑ Ⓒ Ⓓ Ⓔ 10 Ⓐ Ⓑ Ⓒ Ⓓ Ⓔ 17 Ⓐ Ⓑ Ⓒ Ⓓ Ⓔ 24 Ⓐ Ⓑ Ⓒ Ⓓ Ⓔ 31 Ⓐ Ⓑ Ⓒ Ⓓ Ⓔ
4 Ⓐ Ⓑ Ⓒ Ⓓ Ⓔ 11 Ⓐ Ⓑ Ⓒ Ⓓ Ⓔ 18 Ⓐ Ⓑ Ⓒ Ⓓ Ⓔ 25 Ⓐ Ⓑ Ⓒ Ⓓ Ⓔ 32 Ⓐ Ⓑ Ⓒ Ⓓ Ⓔ
5 Ⓐ Ⓑ Ⓒ Ⓓ Ⓔ 12 Ⓐ Ⓑ Ⓒ Ⓓ Ⓔ 19 Ⓐ Ⓑ Ⓒ Ⓓ Ⓔ 26 Ⓐ Ⓑ Ⓒ Ⓓ Ⓔ 33 Ⓐ Ⓑ Ⓒ Ⓓ Ⓔ
6 Ⓐ Ⓑ Ⓒ Ⓓ Ⓔ 13 Ⓐ Ⓑ Ⓒ Ⓓ Ⓔ 20 Ⓐ Ⓑ Ⓒ Ⓓ Ⓔ 27 Ⓐ Ⓑ Ⓒ Ⓓ Ⓔ 34 Ⓐ Ⓑ Ⓒ Ⓓ Ⓔ
7 Ⓐ Ⓑ Ⓒ Ⓓ Ⓔ 14 Ⓐ Ⓑ Ⓒ Ⓓ Ⓔ 21 Ⓐ Ⓑ Ⓒ Ⓓ Ⓔ 28 Ⓐ Ⓑ Ⓒ Ⓓ Ⓔ 35 Ⓐ Ⓑ Ⓒ Ⓓ Ⓔ

Section 8

1 Ⓐ Ⓑ Ⓒ Ⓓ Ⓔ 5 Ⓐ Ⓑ Ⓒ Ⓓ Ⓔ 9 Ⓐ Ⓑ Ⓒ Ⓓ Ⓔ 13 Ⓐ Ⓑ Ⓒ Ⓓ Ⓔ 17 Ⓐ Ⓑ Ⓒ Ⓓ Ⓔ
2 Ⓐ Ⓑ Ⓒ Ⓓ Ⓔ 6 Ⓐ Ⓑ Ⓒ Ⓓ Ⓔ 10 Ⓐ Ⓑ Ⓒ Ⓓ Ⓔ 14 Ⓐ Ⓑ Ⓒ Ⓓ Ⓔ 18 Ⓐ Ⓑ Ⓒ Ⓓ Ⓔ
3 Ⓐ Ⓑ Ⓒ Ⓓ Ⓔ 7 Ⓐ Ⓑ Ⓒ Ⓓ Ⓔ 11 Ⓐ Ⓑ Ⓒ Ⓓ Ⓔ 15 Ⓐ Ⓑ Ⓒ Ⓓ Ⓔ 19 Ⓐ Ⓑ Ⓒ Ⓓ Ⓔ
4 Ⓐ Ⓑ Ⓒ Ⓓ Ⓔ 8 Ⓐ Ⓑ Ⓒ Ⓓ Ⓔ 12 Ⓐ Ⓑ Ⓒ Ⓓ Ⓔ 16 Ⓐ Ⓑ Ⓒ Ⓓ Ⓔ 20 Ⓐ Ⓑ Ⓒ Ⓓ Ⓔ

Section 9

1 Ⓐ Ⓑ Ⓒ Ⓓ Ⓔ 5 Ⓐ Ⓑ Ⓒ Ⓓ Ⓔ 9 Ⓐ Ⓑ Ⓒ Ⓓ Ⓔ 13 Ⓐ Ⓑ Ⓒ Ⓓ Ⓔ 17 Ⓐ Ⓑ Ⓒ Ⓓ Ⓔ
2 Ⓐ Ⓑ Ⓒ Ⓓ Ⓔ 6 Ⓐ Ⓑ Ⓒ Ⓓ Ⓔ 10 Ⓐ Ⓑ Ⓒ Ⓓ Ⓔ 14 Ⓐ Ⓑ Ⓒ Ⓓ Ⓔ 18 Ⓐ Ⓑ Ⓒ Ⓓ Ⓔ
3 Ⓐ Ⓑ Ⓒ Ⓓ Ⓔ 7 Ⓐ Ⓑ Ⓒ Ⓓ Ⓔ 11 Ⓐ Ⓑ Ⓒ Ⓓ Ⓔ 15 Ⓐ Ⓑ Ⓒ Ⓓ Ⓔ 19 Ⓐ Ⓑ Ⓒ Ⓓ Ⓔ
4 Ⓐ Ⓑ Ⓒ Ⓓ Ⓔ 8 Ⓐ Ⓑ Ⓒ Ⓓ Ⓔ 12 Ⓐ Ⓑ Ⓒ Ⓓ Ⓔ 16 Ⓐ Ⓑ Ⓒ Ⓓ Ⓔ 20 Ⓐ Ⓑ Ⓒ Ⓓ Ⓔ

Section 10

1 Ⓐ Ⓑ Ⓒ Ⓓ Ⓔ 5 Ⓐ Ⓑ Ⓒ Ⓓ Ⓔ 9 Ⓐ Ⓑ Ⓒ Ⓓ Ⓔ 13 Ⓐ Ⓑ Ⓒ Ⓓ Ⓔ 17 Ⓐ Ⓑ Ⓒ Ⓓ Ⓔ
2 Ⓐ Ⓑ Ⓒ Ⓓ Ⓔ 6 Ⓐ Ⓑ Ⓒ Ⓓ Ⓔ 10 Ⓐ Ⓑ Ⓒ Ⓓ Ⓔ 14 Ⓐ Ⓑ Ⓒ Ⓓ Ⓔ 18 Ⓐ Ⓑ Ⓒ Ⓓ Ⓔ
3 Ⓐ Ⓑ Ⓒ Ⓓ Ⓔ 7 Ⓐ Ⓑ Ⓒ Ⓓ Ⓔ 11 Ⓐ Ⓑ Ⓒ Ⓓ Ⓔ 15 Ⓐ Ⓑ Ⓒ Ⓓ Ⓔ 19 Ⓐ Ⓑ Ⓒ Ⓓ Ⓔ
4 Ⓐ Ⓑ Ⓒ Ⓓ Ⓔ 8 Ⓐ Ⓑ Ⓒ Ⓓ Ⓔ 12 Ⓐ Ⓑ Ⓒ Ⓓ Ⓔ 16 Ⓐ Ⓑ Ⓒ Ⓓ Ⓔ 20 Ⓐ Ⓑ Ⓒ Ⓓ Ⓔ

Practice Test 4   1 1 1 1 1 1   1

SECTION 1   **Time—25 Minutes**   **ESSAY**

Write your essay on the lines provided on the answer sheet on pages 243–244. Be careful to write legibly. Write on the topic, carefully presenting your point of view. Your essay will be scored on the basis of the ideas it contains and its effectiveness in expressing these ideas. Pay special attention to logic, clarity, and the accurate use of language.

Think about the topic presented in the following excerpt and in the assignment below it.

Modern science has brought humanity a vast amount of knowledge, and in many cases this knowledge has been put to good use. However, in other cases the knowledge gained has created serious problems.

ASSIGNMENT: Have the achievements of modern science been more beneficial or more detrimental to the well-being of humanity? Plan and write an essay in which you develop your point of view on this question. Support your position with reasoning and examples taken from your experience, reading, or observations.

2 2 2 2 2 2 2 2 2 2 2

SECTION 2   Time—25 Minutes
24 Questions

Choose the best answer to each of the following questions in this section. Then blacken the appropriate space on your answer sheet.

Each of the following sentences contains one or two blanks, indicating that a word or set of words has been omitted. Beneath each sentence there are five answer choices labeled A to E from which you must select the word or set of words that best fits the meaning of the sentence as a whole.

Example:

Records of colonization can be found as far back as the Phoenicians, but colonization became a major force in world history only when European countries began, in the fifteenth century, to make ---- Asia, the Americas, and Africa.

(A) queries about   (B) incursions into
  (C) tirades against   (D) enemies in
      (E) amends for

Ⓐ ● Ⓒ Ⓓ Ⓔ

1. Tom's grandfather says that the surest way to spoil a child is to ---- his or her every whim.

  (A) indulge   (B) raise   (C) punish
   (D) criticize   (E) control

2. Darwin's theory of evolution is the foundation upon which the ---- of modern biology is built.

  (A) buttress   (B) tableau   (C) question
   (D) edifice   (E) dream

3. Scholars ---- the theory, saying it is based more on wishful thinking than on solid evidence.

  (A) admire   (B) corroborate   (C) endorse
   (D) aver   (E) dismiss

4. Recent evidence suggests that evolution might be largely ---- process in which there are relatively short periods of radical change followed by periods of ---- .

  (A) a reactionary . . quiescence
  (B) a muted . . senescence
  (C) a sporadic . . perturbation
  (D) an intermittent . . prescience
  (E) a fitful . . stasis

5. The belief in the perfectibility of man contributed to the rise of the idea of progress, the idea that humanity could, by steady effort, ---- social problems and ultimately achieve a nearly perfect society.

  (A) annul   (B) ameliorate
    (C) exacerbate   (D) assimilate
        (E) repeal

6. One of the virtues of the scientific method as it is practiced in science today is that scientific findings are subject to rigorous and objective international testing and review by ---- peers, and thus it is difficult for any one person or institution to ---- what those findings are.

  (A) innocent . . question
  (B) distinguished . . admit
  (C) intelligent . . remember
  (D) anonymous . . dictate
  (E) altruistic . . exemplify

7. This biography cannot be considered reliable because it does not distinguish ---- material from well-substantiated material.

  (A) old   (B) theoretical
    (C) written   (D) apocryphal
        (E) verified

8. Marxists believe in a type of ---- in that they theorize that when communism predominates, the state will ---- wither away and people will live harmoniously.

  (A) government . . gradually
  (B) policy . . ineluctably
  (C) anarchism . . inevitably
  (D) democracy . . occasionally
  (E) socialism . . never

GO ON TO THE NEXT PAGE

2   2 2 2 2 2 2 2 2 2   2

Below are passages followed by questions on them. Questions on a pair of related passages may be about the relationship between the two passages. For each question, select the best answer based on what is stated or implied in the passage (or passages).

Questions 9–10 are based on the following passage.

The Egyptians regarded man as composed of various different entities, each having its separate life and functions. First, there was the body;
Line then the *Ka* or double, which was a less solid
(5) duplicate of the corporeal form—a colored but ethereal projection of the individual, reproducing him feature for feature. The double of a child was as a child; the double of a woman was as a woman; the double of a man was as a man.
(10) After the double (*Ka*) came the Soul (*Bi* or *Ba*), which was popularly represented as a human-headed bird; after the Soul came the "*Khû*," or "the Luminous," a spark from the divine fire. None of these elements were in their own nature
(15) imperishable. Left to themselves, they would hasten to dissolution, and the man would thus die a second time; that is to say, he would be annihilated. The piety of the survivors found means, however, to avert this catastrophe. By
(20) the process of embalmment, they could for ages suspend the decomposition of the body; while by means of prayer and offerings, they saved the Double, the Soul, and the "Luminous" from the second death, and secured to them all that was
(25) necessary for the prolongation of their existence.

9. According to the author, the Egyptians believed that the four entities that man is composed of

(A) can exist forever if they interact with one another in a certain way
(B) are illusions projected by the human mind
(C) are intrinsically destructible
(D) are each a spark of the divine fire
(E) can exist forever if the body is properly embalmed

10. The Egyptians believed that

(A) the soul and body are inseparable
(B) the soul is part of the divine fire
(C) the soul is potentially immortal
(D) the soul is immortal
(E) the existence of the soul can be prolonged by the pious acts of living people

Questions 11–12 are based on the following passage.

The ancient belief system of the Jains rests on a concrete understanding of the working of karma, its effects on the living soul (jiva), and the
Line conditions for extinguishing action and the soul's
(5) release. According to the Jain view, the soul is a living substance that combines with various kinds of nonliving matter and through action accumulates particles of matter that adhere to it and determine its fate. Most of the matter
(10) perceptible to human senses, including all animals and plants, is attached in various degrees to living souls and is in this sense alive. Any action has consequences that necessarily follow the embodied soul, but the worst accumulations
(15) of matter come from violence against other living beings. The ultimate Jain discipline, therefore, rests on complete inactivity and absolute nonviolence (ahimsa) against any living beings. Extreme renunciation, including the refusal of all
(20) food, lies at the heart of a discipline that purges the mind and body of all desires and actions and, in the process, burns off the consequences of actions performed in the past.

GO ON TO THE NEXT PAGE

11. In line 16, "discipline" most nearly means

(A) religious orthodoxy

(B) nonviolence against living things

(C) religious worship

(D) ways to ensure the adherence of believers to traditional doctrines

(E) techniques aimed at helping an individual to achieve a specific purpose

12. It can be inferred from the information in the passage that karma, referred to in line 3, is

(A) fate

(B) human desires

(C) human actions

(D) the interconnectedness of all living things

(E) the total effect of one's actions, regarded as determining one's destiny

Questions 13–24 are based on the following passages.

Passage 1

The principal welcomed "parents and friends" and asked the Baptist minister to lead us in prayer. His invocation was brief and punchy,
Line and for a second I thought we were getting on
(5) the high road to right action. When the principal came back to the dais, however, his voice had changed. Sounds always affected me profoundly and the principal's voice was one of my favorites. During assembly it melted and lowed weakly into
(10) the audience. It had not been in my plan to listen to him, but my curiosity was piqued and I straightened up to give him my attention.

He was talking about Booker T. Washington, our "late great leader," who said we can be as
(15) close as the fingers on the hand, etc. . . . Then he said a few vague things about friendship and the friendship of kindly people to those less fortunate than themselves. With that his voice nearly faded, thin, away. Like a river diminishing to a stream
(20) and then to a trickle. But he cleared his throat and said, "Our speaker tonight, who is also our friend, came from Texarkana to deliver the commencement address, but due to the irregularity of the train schedule, he's going to,
(25) as they say, 'speak and run.'" He said that we understood and wanted the man to know that we were most grateful for the time he was able to give us and then something about how we were

willing always to adjust to another's program,
(30) and without more ado—"I give you Mr. Edward Donleavy."

Not one but two white men came through the door off-stage. The shorter one walked to the speaker's platform, and the tall one moved to the
(35) center seat and sat down. But that was our principal's seat, and already occupied. The dislodged gentleman bounced around for a long breath or two before the Baptist minister gave him his chair, then with more dignity than the
(40) situation deserved, the minister walked off the stage.

Donleavy looked at the audience once (on reflection, I'm sure that he wanted only to reassure himself that we were really there),
(45) adjusted his glasses and began to read from a sheaf of papers.

He was glad "to be here and to see the work going on just as it was in the other schools."

At the first "Amen" from the audience I willed
(50) the offender to immediate death by choking on the word. But Amens and Yes, sir's began to fall around the room like rain through a ragged umbrella.

He told us of the wonderful changes we
(55) children in Stamps had in store. The Central School (naturally, the white school was Central) had already been granted improvements that would be in use in the fall. A well-known artist was coming from Little Rock to teach art to
(60) them. They were going to have the newest microscopes and chemistry equipment for their laboratory. Mr. Donleavy didn't leave us long in the dark over who made these improvements available to Central High. Nor were we to be
(65) ignored in the general betterment scheme he had in mind.

He said that he had pointed out to people at a very high level that one of the first-line football tacklers at Arkansas Agricultural and Mechanical
(70) College had graduated from good old Lafayette County Training School. Here fewer Amen's were heard. Those few that did break through lay dully in the air with the heaviness of habit.

GO ON TO THE NEXT PAGE →

He went on to praise us. He went on to say
(75) how he had bragged that "one of the best
basketball players at Fisk sank his first ball right
here at Lafayette County Training School."

The white kids were going to have a chance to
become Galileos and Madame Curies and
(80) Edisons and Gaugins, and our boys (the girls
weren't even in on it) would try to be Jesse
Owenses and Joe Louises.

Owens and the Brown Bomber were great
heroes in our world, but what school official in
(85) the white-goddom of Little Rock had the right to
decide that those two men must be our only
heroes? Who decided that for Henry Reed to
become a scientist he had to work like George
Washington Carver, as a bootblack, to buy a
(90) lousy microscope? Bailey was obviously always
going to be too small to be an athlete, so which
concrete angel glued to what country seat had
decided that if my brother wanted to become a
lawyer he had to first pay penance for his skin by
(95) picking cotton and hoeing corn and studying
correspondence books at night for twenty years?

The man's dead words fell like bricks around
the auditorium and too many settle in my belly.
Constrained by hard-learned manners I couldn't
(100) look behind me, but to my left and right the
proud graduating class of 1940 had dropped their
heads. Every girl in my row had found something
new to do with her handkerchief. Some folded
the tiny squares into love knots, some into
(105) triangles, but most were wadding them, then
pressing them flat on their yellow laps.

On the dais, the ancient tragedy was being
replayed. Professor Parsons sat, a sculptor's
reject, rigid. His large, heavy body seemed
(110) devoid of will or willingness, and his eyes said
he was no longer with us. The other teachers
examined the flag (which was draped stage right)
or their notes, or the window which opened on
our now-famous playing diamond.
(115) Graduation, the hush-hush magic time of frills
and gifts and congratulations and diplomas, was
finished for me before my name was called. The
accomplishment was nothing. The meticulous
maps, drawn in three colors of ink, learning and
(120) spelling decasyllabic words, memorizing the
whole of *The Rape of Lucrece*—it was for
nothing. Donleavy had exposed us.

We were maids and farmers, handymen and
washerwomen, and anything higher that we
(125) aspired to was farcical and presumptuous.

Passage 2

Being a problem is a strange experience—
peculiar even for one who has never been
anything else, save perhaps in babyhood and in
Europe. It is in the early days of rollicking
(130) boyhood that the revelation first bursts upon one,
all in a day, as it were. I remember well when the
shadow swept across me. I was a little thing,
away up in the hills of New England, where the
dark Housatonic winds between Hoosac and
(135) Taghkanic to the sea. In a wee wooden
schoolhouse, something put it into the boys' and
girls' heads to buy gorgeous visiting-cards—ten
cents a package—and exchange. The exchange
was merry, till one girl, a tall newcomer, refused
(140) my card—refused it peremptorily, with a glance.
Then it dawned upon me with a certain
suddenness that I was different from the others;
or like, mayhap, in heart and life and longing, but
shut out from their world by a vast veil. I had
(145) thereafter no desire to tear down that veil, to
creep through; I held all beyond it in common
contempt, and lived above it in a region of blue
sky and great wandering shadows. That sky was
bluest when I could beat my mates at
(150) examination-time, or beat them at a foot-race, or
even beat their stringy heads. Alas, with the years
all this fine contempt began to fade; for the
words I longed for, and all their dazzling
opportunities, were theirs, not mine. But they
(155) should not keep these prizes, I said; some, all, I
would wrest from them. Just how I would do it I
could never decide: by reading law, by healing
the sick, by telling the wonderful tales that swam
in my head—some way. With other black boys
(160) the strife was not so fiercely sunny: their youth
shrunk into tasteless sycophancy, or into silent
hatred of the pale world about them and mocking
distrust of everything white; or wasted itself in a
bitter cry, Why did God make me an outcast and
(165) a stranger in mine own house? The shades of the

GO ON TO THE NEXT PAGE ⟶

prison-house closed round about us all: walls strait and stubborn to the whitest, but relentlessly narrow, tall, and unscalable to sons of night who must plod darkly on in resignation, or beat

(170) unavailing palms against the stone, or steadily, half hopelessly, watch the streak of blue above.

13. What would most likely be the attitude of the author of Passage 1 about the principal's comment that the speaker "is also our friend" (lines 21–22)?

   (A) She would have respect for the principal's sincere belief in the value of friendship and trust that Donleavy is truly a friend.
   (B) She would be puzzled that the principal would be bringing up the topic of friendship in his introduction of a great speech.
   (C) She would be amazed that the principal would dare to claim a person of such high status as a friend.
   (D) She would be confused because she can't understand how the principal and Donleavy could be old friends.
   (E) She would believe that the principal is naive because he apparently thinks that men like Donleavy are truly kindly toward blacks.

14. "At the first 'Amen' from the audience I willed the offender to immediate death by choking on the word" (lines 49–51). What is the reader most likely meant to infer from this statement in Passage 1?

   (A) The author was repelled by such a blatant display of religious feeling.
   (B) The author was disgusted that her fellow students, their parents, and other guests would believe anything said by a white person.
   (C) The author believes that the audience was docile and fawning to Mr. Donleavy.
   (D) The author is upset that a classmate would be so rude to the commencement speaker.
   (E) The author is embarrassed that a fellow student would be so ignorant as to use religious language at a secular event.

15. We can infer that the reason that one of the two white men in Passage 1 sat down in the center seat was most likely that

   (A) he was not familiar with protocol at Lafayette County Training School
   (B) he was nervous and wanted to find the nearest vacant seat
   (C) he believed that no one was occupying it
   (D) he thought that it had been reserved for him
   (E) he felt superior to the assembled people and felt he should sit wherever he wanted to

16. The phrase "the ancient tragedy," mentioned in line 107, refers to

   (A) similar commencements at black schools in the South in the past
   (B) the loss of self-respect on the part of young blacks in the South in the present
   (C) the wasted talent of young blacks who become laborers instead of doctors or teachers
   (D) the loss of interest in teaching on the part of senior black teachers at Lafayette County Training School
   (E) age old racial prejudice and its consequences

17. The author of Passage 1 most likely intends the final sentence—"We were maids and farmers, handymen and washerwomen, and anything higher that we aspired to was farcical and presumptuous" (lines 123–125)—to be taken as

   (A) reflecting the author's view at the time of the commencement assembly described in the passage
   (B) reflecting only the view of young black people at the time
   (C) reflecting the view of most white people and many black people at the time
   (D) an exaggeration
   (E) reflecting only the view of white people at the time

GO ON TO THE NEXT PAGE ▷

18. The author of Passage 1 makes use of all of the following EXCEPT

   (A) parenthetical remark
   (B) simile
   (C) anecdote
   (D) paradox
   (E) rhetorical question

19. According to the author of Passage 2, the other black boys at his school

   (A) were largely unaware of the attitude of white people toward blacks
   (B) often reacted violently to their bad treatment by white people
   (C) came to either cow-tow to white people, hate the world of white people, or become bitter
   (D) learned to accept that they were different and would never have the opportunities that white people did
   (E) either resigned themselves to living in the world of white people or ended up in prison later in their lives

20. The word "revelation" in line 130 refers to

   (A) the author's realization that despite their different skin color whites and blacks were fundamentally the same
   (B) the author's realization that blacks were not part of the white people's world
   (C) the author's faith that God would look after him
   (D) the author's learning that not everyone was kind
   (E) the author's realization that he could beat his white classmates at examinations or in a foot-race

21. The word "stubborn," as it is used in line 167, suggests that the author believed that

   (A) there were more obstacles for white people than there were for black people
   (B) prisons housing white people had thicker walls than prisons housing black people
   (C) black people were, in general, more stubborn than white people in following the accepted way of thinking of the time
   (D) white people were confined by prevailing attitudes and limited opportunities, but could overcome these with sufficient effort
   (E) white people were generally more stubborn than black people in following the accepted way of thinking of the time

22. The author of Passage 2 would be most likely to describe the behavior of the principal of Lafayette County Training School at the commencement assembly portrayed in Passage 1 as

   (A) opportunistic
   (B) mature
   (C) impeccable
   (D) baffling
   (E) obsequious

23. Compared to Passage 2, the tone of Passage 1 is more

   (A) restrained
   (B) nostalgic
   (C) sarcastic
   (D) respectful
   (E) serious

24. Unlike Passage 1, Passage 2 makes considerable use of

   (A) irony
   (B) hyperbole
   (C) description
   (D) symbolism
   (E) humor

STOP

IN ANY REMAINING TIME YOU MAY REVIEW THE
ANSWERS YOU CHOSE IN THIS SECTION. DO NOT WORK
ON ANY OTHER SECTION OF THE TEST DURING THIS TIME.

Practice Test 4

3   3 3 3 3 3 3 3 3 3 3   **3**

Reference Information

Area Facts

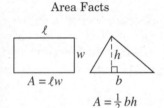

$A = \ell w$

$A = \frac{1}{2} bh$

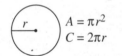

$A = \pi r^2$
$C = 2\pi r$

Volume Facts

$V = \ell w h$

$V = \pi r^2 h$

Triangle Facts

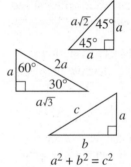

$a^2 + b^2 = c^2$

Angle Facts

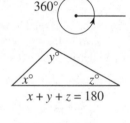

$x + y + z = 180$

1. If $a + 2a + 3a + 4a = 5a + 30$, what is the value of a?

   (A) 3
   (B) 6
   (C) 9
   (D) 12
   (E) 15

2. If 1 bap equals 6 daps, and 8 daps equal 1 hap, how many baps are equal to 3 haps?

   (A) 2
   (B) 3
   (C) 4
   (D) 6
   (E) 8

3. If $a(b - c) = 0$ and if a is negative, which of the following must be true?

   (A) $b = c$
   (B) $b = -c$
   (C) $ab = 0$
   (D) $ac = 0$
   (E) $bc = 0$

GO ON TO THE NEXT PAGE ⟩

3   3 3 3 3 3 3 3 3 3 3   3

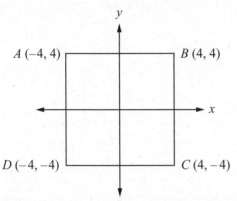

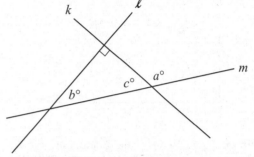

Note: Figure not drawn to scale.

4. In the figure above, how many points in the interior of square *ABCD* have *x*- and *y*-coordinates that are both integers?

(A) 36
(B) 42
(C) 48
(D) 49
(E) 64

5. The average (arithmetic mean) of a set of *n* numbers is what percent of the sum of those numbers?

(A) *n*

(B) $\dfrac{1}{n}$

(C) $\dfrac{n}{100}$

(D) $\dfrac{100}{n}$

(E) 100*n*

6. *x* and *y* are integers, neither of which is a multiple of 8. If R_x and R_y represent the remainders when *x* and *y* are divided by 8, respectively, what is the maximum possible value of $R_x - R_y$?

(A) 8
(B) 7
(C) 6
(D) 4
(E) 1

7. In the diagram above, lines *l* and *k* are perpendicular and line *m* intersects both of them as shown. If $a = 5b$, what is the value of *c*?

(A)   18
(B)   22.5
(C)   67.5
(D)   72
(E)   112.5

8. If a machine produces *b* bolts in *h* hours, how many hours will it take to produce *c* bolts?

(A) $\dfrac{bc}{h}$

(B) $\dfrac{ch}{b}$

(C) $\dfrac{bh}{c}$

(D) $\dfrac{c}{bh}$

(E) $\dfrac{c}{h}$

9. Maria purchased a vase that was on sale for 25% less than the original price. If Maria paid $180 for the vase, what was the vase's original price?

(A) $135
(B) $155
(C) $205
(D) $225
(E) $240

GO ON TO THE NEXT PAGE

Practice Test 4

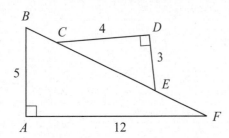

10. In the figure above, *C* and *E* are points on $\overline{BF}$. What is the perimeter of hexagon *ABCDEF*?

   (A) 29
   (B) 32
   (C) 35
   (D) 37
   (E) 42

11. On a certain college application, students are instructed to describe themselves in a paragraph of at least 60 and no more than 100 words. If a student writes a paragraph of *w* words, which of the following inequalities can be used to determine if the paragraph is acceptable?

   (A) $|w - 60| \le 40$
   (B) $|w - 100| \le 40$
   (C) $|w - 80| \le 20$
   (D) $|w + 60| \le 40$
   (E) $|w + 80| \le 20$

12. If 12 years from now Fran will be 4 times as old as she was 15 years ago, how old is she now?

   (A) 9
   (B) 12
   (C) 15
   (D) 21
   (E) 24

13. If $A = \{1, 3, 5\}$, $B = \{2, 4, 6\}$, and *C* is the set consisting of all numbers which are the sum of a number in *A* and a number in *B*, how many numbers are in set *C*?

   (A) 3
   (B) 5
   (C) 6
   (D) 7
   (E) 9

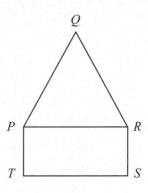

14. In pentagon *PQRST* above, *PQR* is an equilateral triangle and *PRST* is a rectangle whose length, *PR*, is twice as long as its width, *PT*. Which of the following statements is true?

   (A) The perimeter of $\triangle PQR$ is less than the perimeter of rectangle *PRST*.
   (B) The perimeter of $\triangle PQR$ is greater than the perimeter of rectangle *PRST*.
   (C) The perimeter of $\triangle PQR$ is equal to the perimeter of rectangle *PRST*, and the area of $\triangle PQR$ is equal to the area of rectangle *PRST*.
   (D) The perimeter of $\triangle PQR$ is equal to the perimeter of rectangle *PRST*, and the area of $\triangle PQR$ is less than the area of rectangle *PRST*.
   (E) The perimeter of $\triangle PQR$ is equal to the perimeter of rectangle *PRST*, and the area of $\triangle PQR$ is greater than the area of rectangle *PRST*.

15. Let *f* be the function defined for all numbers, *x*, as $f(x) = x^2 + x$. For what value of *a* is $f(a) = f(a + 2)$?

   (A) $-\dfrac{3}{2}$
   (B) -1
   (C) 0
   (D) 1
   (E) $\dfrac{3}{2}$

GO ON TO THE NEXT PAGE

16. How many integers, n, satisfy the inequality $|3n - 17| < n$?

    (A) None
    (B) 2
    (C) 4
    (D) 6
    (E) Infinitely many

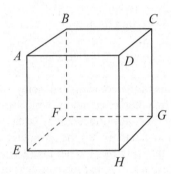

17. The volume of the cube in the figure above is 64. If M and N (not shown) are the midpoints of $\overline{EH}$ and $\overline{CG}$, respectively, what is the length of line segment $\overline{MN}$?

    (A) 4
    (B) 8
    (C) 24
    (D) $\sqrt{24}$
    (E) $\sqrt{96}$

18. For all positive integers m and n, let $m \star n$ be the sum of n consecutive integers, beginning with m. For example, $6 \star 3$ is the sum of three consecutive integers, beginning with 6: $6 \star 3 = 6 + 7 + 8 = 21$. What is the value of $25 \star 26 - 26 \star 25$?

    (A) 0
    (B) 1
    (C) 25
    (D) 26
    (E) 51

19. If $a^7 = 11$ and $a^5 = 5b$, what is the value of b in terms of a?

    (A) $\dfrac{11}{5a^2}$

    (B) $\dfrac{5}{11a^2}$

    (C) $\dfrac{55}{a^2}$

    (D) $\dfrac{11a^2}{5}$

    (E) $\dfrac{5a^2}{11}$

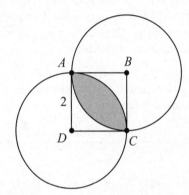

20. In the figure above, vertices B and D of square $ABCD$ are the centers of the two congruent circles and A and C are the points of intersection of those circles. If $AD = 2$, what is the area of the shaded region?

    (A) $\dfrac{1}{2}\pi - 1$
    (B) $\pi - 2$
    (C) $2\pi - 2$
    (D) $2\pi - 4$
    (E) $4\pi - 8$

STOP

IN ANY REMAINING TIME YOU MAY REVIEW THE
ANSWERS YOU CHOSE IN THIS SECTION. DO NOT WORK
ON ANY OTHER SECTION OF THE TEST DURING THIS TIME.

5 5 5 5 5 5 5

SECTION **5** Time—25 Minutes 25 Questions Choose the best answer to each of the following questions in this section. Then blacken the appropriate space on your answer sheet.

Each of the following sentences contains one or two blanks, indicating that a word or set of words has been omitted. Beneath each sentence there are five answer choices labeled A to E from which you must select the word or set of words that best fits the meaning of the sentence as a whole.

Example:

Records of colonization can be found as far back as the Phoenicians, but colonization became a major force in world history only when European countries began, in the fifteenth century, to make ---- Asia, the Americas, and Africa.

(A) queries about (B) incursions into
  (C) tirades against (D) enemies in
    (E) amends for

Ⓐ ● Ⓒ Ⓓ Ⓔ

1. ---- criteria must be met for the results of an experiment to be accepted by the scientific community.

(A) Stringent (B) Recent (C) Interesting
  (D) General (E) Active

2. The editor checked the manuscript for ---- language so that the author's meaning would be clear.

(A) original (B) serious (C) ambiguous
  (D) immature (E) descriptive

3. The study shows that ---- dealings often do irreparable harm to a person's standing in the business community.

(A) scrupulous (B) duplicitous
  (C) prudent (D) honest
    (E) inconsequential

4. In their search for truth, philosophers build on the work of their ----, striving to create a more ---- view of reality.

(A) benefactors . . compliant
(B) legacy . . redundant
(C) pedants . . optimistic
(D) advocates . . soporific
(E) predecessors . . comprehensive

5. Champions of the command economy ---- that, unlike a free market economy, which responds mostly to short-term fluctuations in the market, a command economy has the advantage of being able to effectively incorporate long-term strategies, such as resource ---- and management of the impact of economic activity on the environment.

(A) fear . . utilization
(B) argue . . scarcity
(C) hope . . wastage
(D) contend . . husbanding
(E) deny . . preservation

6. A language, it is said, is ---- philosophy of the world, and to speak a particular language is to ---- the philosophy it embodies.

(A) a comprehensive . . question
(B) a metaphysical . . underscore
(C) an implicit . . subscribe to
(D) an ancient . . reify
(E) a linguistic . . deny

GO ON TO THE NEXT PAGE ⇒

5 **5** **5** **5** **5** **5** 5

Below are passages followed by questions on them. Questions on a pair of related passages may be about the relationship between the two passages. For each question, select the best answer based on what is stated or implied in the passage (or passages).

Questions 7–10 are based on the following passages.

Passage 1

In subject Raphael was religious and mythological, but he was imbued with neither of these so far as the initial spirit was concerned. He
Line looked at all subjects in a calm, intellectual,
(5) artistic way. Even the celebrated Sistine Madonna is more intellectual than pietistic, a Christian Minerva ruling rather than helping to save the world. The same spirit ruled him in classic and theological themes. He did not feel them keenly
(10) or execute them passionately—at least there is no indication of it in his work. The doing so would have destroyed unity, symmetry, repose. The theme was ever held in check by a regard for proportion and rhythm. To keep all artistic
(15) elements in perfect equilibrium, allowing no one to predominate, seemed the mainspring of this action, and in doing this he created that harmony which his admirers sometimes refer to as pure beauty.

Passage 2

(20) When Lomazzo assigned emblems to the chief painters of the Renaissance, he gave to Michael Angelo the dragon of contemplation, and to Mantegna the serpent of sagacity. For Raphael, by a happier instinct, he reserved man, the
(25) microcosm, the symbol of powerful grace, incarnate intellect. This quaint fancy of the Milanese critic touches the truth. What distinguishes the whole work of Raphael, is its humanity in the double sense of the humane and
(30) human. Phoebus, as imagined by the Greeks, was not more radiant, more victorious by the marvel of his smile, more intolerant of things obscene or ugly. Like Apollo chasing the Eumenides from his Delphian shrine, Raphael will not suffer his
(35) eyes to fall on what is loathsome or horrific. Even sadness and sorrow, tragedy and death, take loveliness from him. His men and women are either glorious with youth or dignified in hale old age. Touched by his innocent and earnest genius,
(40) mankind is once more gifted with the harmony of intellect and flesh and feeling, that belonged to Hellas.* Instead of asceticism, Hellenic temperance is the virtue prized by Raphael.

7. In line 24, "happier" most nearly means

(A) more virtuous
(B) more optimistic
(C) more in keeping with human instinct
(D) more in keeping with the truth
(E) showing more awareness of artistic beauty

8. The most likely reason that the author of Passage 2 wrote the phrase "harmony of intellect and flesh and feeling" (lines 40–41) rather than "harmony of intellect, flesh, and feeling" is that

(A) he wanted to convey the idea that intellect, flesh, and feeling are of equal importance
(B) he wanted to suggest that intellect and flesh were more important to Raphael than feeling
(C) he wanted to imitate the structure of Greek grammar to reinforce the idea that Raphael was Hellenic in temperament
(D) he wanted to reinforce his point that Raphael, like the Greeks, combined diverse elements harmoniously
(E) he wanted to suggest that Raphael regarded intellect, flesh, and feeling as one entity

---

* Hellas is the Greek word for Greece.

GO ON TO THE NEXT PAGE

5   5   5   5   5   5   5

9. The authors of both passages would be most likely to agree that

(A) one of the factors that allowed Raphael to create great art was his unparalleled ability to express his feelings through his art

(B) one of the chief virtues of Raphael's art is its harmony

(C) the greatest virtues of Raphael's art derive from Raphael's love of all things Hellenic

(D) religious feeling is, in the final analysis, what makes Raphael's art great

(E) Raphael was more successful in portraying religious themes than mythological themes

10. Which of the following is the most accurate description of the difference between Passage 1 and Passage 2?

(A) Passage 1 stresses Raphael's intellectual approach in his art that helped him create harmony, and thus beauty, whereas Passage 2 emphasizes the profound humanity that allowed Raphael to create art that harmonized the diverse elements that make up man.

(B) Passage 1 describes how Raphael successfully combined themes from classical mythology and Christian belief in his art, whereas Passage 2 stresses the Hellenic virtues that helped Raphael create art that has at once innocent, pure beauty, and deep humanity.

(C) Passage 1 emphasizes the beauty created by Raphael in his art, whereas Passage 2 stresses Raphael's ability to depict ordinary everyday reality in his art.

(D) Passage 1 describes how Raphael achieved harmony in his art, whereas Passage 2 describes how Raphael uses themes from Greek mythology to create powerful works of art.

(E) Passage 1 describes the technique Raphael used in his art to achieve works of great beauty, whereas Passage 2 compares Raphael's art to that of Michelangelo and Montegna, stressing the former's use of classical themes and techniques.

Questions 11–16 are based on the following passage.

First, the real Japanese-Japanese were rounded up. These real Japanese-Japanese were Japanese nationals who had the misfortune to be diplomats *Line* and businessmen and visiting professors. They
(5) were put on a boat and sent back to Japan.

Then the alien Japanese, the ones who had been in America for two, three, or even four decades, were screened, and those found to be too actively Japanese were transported to the
(10) hinterlands and put in a camp.

The security screen was sifted once more and, this time, the lesser lights were similarly plucked and deposited. An old man, too old, too feeble, and too scared, was caught in the net. In his
(15) pocket was a little, black book. He had been a collector for the Japan-Help-the-Poor-and-Starving—and Flooded-Out-and-Homeless-and-Crippled-and-What-Have-You Fund. "Yamada-san, 50 American cents; Okada-san, two
(20) American dollars; Watanabe-san, 24 American cents; Takizaki-san, skip this month because boy broke leg"; and so on down the page. Yamada-san, Okada-san, Watanabe-san, Takizaki-san, and so on down the page were whisked away from
(25) their homes while weeping families wept until the tears must surely have been wept dry, and then wept some more.

By now, the snowball was big enough to wipe out the rising sun. The big rising sun would take
(30) a little more time, but the little rising sun which was the Japanese in countless Japanese communities in the coastal states of Washington, Oregon, and California presented no problem. The whisking and transporting of Japanese and
(35) the construction of camps with bared wire and ominous towers supporting fully armed soldiers in places like Idaho and Wyoming and Arizona, places which even Hollywood scorned for background, had become skills which demanded
(40) the utmost of America's great organizing ability.

And so, a few months after the seventh day of December of the year nineteen forty-one, the only Japanese left on the west coast of the United

GO ON TO THE NEXT PAGE ⟹

5   5   5   5   5   5   5

States was Matsusaburo Inabukuro who, while it
(45) has been forgotten whether he was Japanese-
American or American-Japanese, picked up an
"I am Chinese"—not American or American-
Chinese or Chinese-American but "I am
Chinese"—button and got a job in a California
(50) shipyard.

Two years later a good Japanese-American
who had volunteered for the army sat smoking in
the belly of a B-24 on his way back to Guam
from a reconnaissance flight to Japan. His job
(55) was to listen through his earphones, which were
attached to a high-frequency set, and jot down
air-ground messages spoken by Japanese-
Japanese in Japanese planes and in Japanese radio
shacks.

(60) The lieutenant who operated the radar-
detection equipment was a blond giant from
Nebraska.

The lieutenant from Nebraska said: Where you
from?"

(65) The Japanese-American who was an American
soldier answered: "No place in particular."

"You got folks?"

"Yeah, I got folks."

"Where at?"

(70) "Wyoming, out in the desert."

"Farmers, huh?"

"Not quite."

"What's that mean?"

"Well, it's this way . . . ." And then the
(75) Japanese-American whose folks were still
Japanese-Japanese, or else they would not be in
a camp with barbed wire and watchtowers with
soldiers holding rifles, told the blond giant from
Nebraska about the removal of the Japanese from
(80) the Coast, which was called the evacuation, and
about the concentration camps, which were called
relocation centers.

The lieutenant listened and he didn't believe
it. He said: "That's funny. Now, tell me again."
(85) The Japanese-American soldier of the
American army told it again and didn't change
a word.

The lieutenant believed him this time. "Hell's
bells," he exclaimed, "if they'd done that to me, I
(90) wouldn't be sitting in the belly of a broken-down
B-24 going back to Guam from a reconnaissance
mission to Japan."

"I got reasons," said the Japanese-American
soldier soberly.

11. The word "hinterlands" as it is used in line 10
most nearly means

(A) lands outside the continental United States
(B) a special area outside the border of the United
States
(C) barren lands in the western United States
(D) camps within the United States for housing
people displaced by order of the United States
government
(E) a region remote from urban areas

12. The "snowball" mentioned in line 28 most likely
refers to

(A) America's steadily growing fear of Japanese
people living in America
(B) the accumulating tears of Japanese family
members who have seen their relatives moved
to relocation camps
(C) the steadily increasing, accumulating efforts of
Americans to defeat the Japanese
(D) the steadily growing efforts of Americans to
relocate Japanese aliens living in America
(E) the steadily accumulating efforts of Japanese
aliens living in America to return to Japan to
fight for their country

GO ON TO THE NEXT PAGE

5　5　5　5　5　5　5

13. Which of the following words best describes the author's tone in lines 34–40: "The whisking and transporting of Japanese and the construction of camps with barbed wire and ominous towers supporting fully armed soldiers in places like Idaho and Wyoming and Arizona, places which even Hollywood scorned for background, had become skills which demanded the utmost of America's great organizing ability"?

    (A) Neutral
    (B) Jocular
    (C) Sarcastic
    (D) Apologetic
    (E) Solemn

14. We can infer that the button saying "I am Chinese" that Matsusaburo Inabukuro wore helped him get a job because

    (A) people believed that he wasn't Japanese
    (B) people thought he was a Japanese person trying to make people believe he was a Chinese person
    (C) people believed that Chinese people are hardworking
    (D) people believed that a Chinese person in America was likely to be an American citizen
    (E) people thought that he was a Chinese alien

15. The author would be most likely to describe the term "relocation center" (line 82) as

    (A) a malapropism
    (B) hyperbole
    (C) an understatement
    (D) a euphemism
    (E) a cliché

16. In line 84, "funny" most nearly means

    (A) remarkable
    (B) strange
    (C) exaggerated
    (D) humorous
    (E) not true

Questions 17–25 are based on the following passage.

There are some striking examples in the laws of nuclear physics of numerical accidents that seem to conspire to make the universe habitable.
Line The strength of the attractive nuclear force is just
(5) sufficient to overcome the electrical repulsion between the positive charges in the nuclei or ordinary atoms such as oxygen or iron. But the nuclear forces are not quite strong enough to bind together two protons (hydrogen nuclei) into a
(10) bound system which would be called a diproton if it existed. If the nuclear forces had been slightly stronger than they are, the diproton would exist and almost all the hydrogen in the universe would have been combined into
(15) diprotons and heavier nuclei. Hydrogen would be a rare element, and stars like the sun, which live for a long time by the slow burning of hydrogen in their cores, could not exist. On the other hand, if the nuclear forces had been substantially
(20) weaker than they are, hydrogen could not burn at all and there would be no heavy elements. If, as seems likely, the evolution of life requires a star like the sun, supplying energy at a constant rate for billions of years, then the strength of nuclear
(25) forces had to lie within a rather narrow range to make life possible.

A similar but independent numerical accident appears in connection with the weak interaction by which hydrogen actually burns in the sun. The
(30) weak interaction is millions of times weaker than the nuclear force. It is just weak enough so that the hydrogen in the sun burns at a slow and steady rate. If the weak interaction were much stronger or much weaker, any forms of life
(35) dependent on sunlike stars would again have difficulties.

The facts of astronomy include some other numerical accidents that work to our advantage. For example, the universe is built on such a scale
(40) that the average distance between stars in an average galaxy like ours is about twenty trillion miles—an extravagantly large distance by human

GO ON TO THE NEXT PAGE

5   5   5   5   5   5   5

standards. If a scientist asserts that the stars at these immense distances have a decisive effect on
(45) the possibility of human existence, he will be suspected of being a believer in astrology. But it happens to be true that we could not have survived if the average distance between stars were only two trillion miles instead of twenty. If
(50) the distances had been smaller by a factor of ten, there would have been a high probability that another star, at some time during the four billion years that the earth has existed, would have passed by the sun close enough to disrupt with its
(55) gravitational field the orbits of the planets. To destroy life on earth, it would not be necessary to pull the earth out of the solar system. It would be sufficient to pull the earth into a moderately eccentric elliptical orbit.

(60)   All the rich diversity of organic chemistry depends on a delicate balance between electrical and quantum-mechanical forces. The balance exists only because the laws of physics include an "exclusion principle" which forbids two
(65) electrons to occupy the same state. If the laws were changed so that electrons no longer excluded each other, none of our essential chemistry would survive. There are many other lucky accidents in atomic physics. Without such
(70) accidents, water could not exist as a liquid, chains of carbon atoms could not form complex organic molecules, and hydrogen atoms could not form breakable bridges between molecules.

    I conclude from the existence of these
(75) accidents of physics and astronomy that the universe is an unexpectedly hospitable place for living creatures to make their home. Being a scientist, trained in the habits of thought and language of the twentieth century rather than the
(80) eighteenth, I do not claim that the architecture of the universe proves the existence of God. I claim only that the architecture of the universe is consistent with the hypothesis that mind plays an essential role in its functioning.

17. According to the author, if the nuclear forces in atoms had been slightly stronger than they are

(A) there would be many more stars like the Sun than there are
(B) the universe would be made up of over 99 percent hydrogen
(C) most of the hydrogen in the universe would have burned up
(D) stars like the Sun would not exist
(E) it would make very little difference to the composition of the universe

18. In line 42, "extravagantly" most nearly means

(A) erroneously
(B) extraneously
(C) imprudently
(D) incomprehensibly
(E) in a way that exceeds a reasonable amount

19. The author most likely refers to astrology in line 46 to

(A) show that he is familiar with ways of thinking outside of conventional science
(B) support his assertion that stars greatly affect human beings
(C) emphasize how remarkable it is that far away stars affect life on earth
(D) support his contention that far away stars can come near the Sun and disrupt the Earth's orbit around it
(E) show how ridiculous belief in astrology is

20. In line 44, "decisive" most nearly means

(A) resolute
(B) beyond hope
(C) important
(D) extreme
(E) conclusive

GO ON TO THE NEXT PAGE ⟹

5　　5　　5　　5　　5　　5　　5

21. According to the author, which of the following does not contribute to making the universe "an unexpectedly hospitable place for living creatures to make their home" (lines 76–77)?

(A) The weak interaction by which hydrogen burns in the Sun lies within a narrow range.

(B) The "exclusion principle" forbids two electrons to occupy the same state.

(C) The strength of the attractive nuclear force lies within a narrow range.

(D) Hydrogen atoms cannot form breakable bridges between molecules.

(E) The average distance between stars in galaxies like the Milky Way is about twenty trillion miles rather than only two trillion miles.

22. In line 78, "habits of thought" most nearly means

(A) recurrent patterns of thinking

(B) scientific thinking

(C) unconscious thinking

(D) thinking trained by the discipline of science and mathematics

(E) philosophical thinking

23. Which of the following specialists would be *least* likely to find the argument made by the author in this passage interesting?

(A) A paleontologist searching for the place in which the human species originated

(B) A theologian developing an argument for the existence of God

(C) A college physics professor giving an introductory lecture called "Physics and the Big Picture"

(D) A philosopher writing a paper entitled "The Place of Life in the Universe"

(E) An astronomer specializing in the search for life outside our solar system

24. Which of the following, if it occurred, would support the conclusion reached by the author?

(A) The discovery of a diproton

(B) Proof that no organic compounds exist on planets in several nearby solar systems

(C) The discovery of life on a planet in orbit around another star in our galaxy

(D) The discovery that stars like the Sun are burning hydrogen at a rapidly increasing rate

(E) Good evidence that Earth's orbit around the Sun was significantly changed by another star passing by the Sun

25. The author would be most likely to agree that the argument he makes in this passage

(A) shows conclusively that the universe was designed by some superhuman agency

(B) offers good but far from decisive support for philosophers who argue that the highly ordered structure of the universe proves the existence of God

(C) demonstrates the futility of speculating about how and why the universe was created

(D) shows that scientists should believe in God

(E) strongly suggests that life exists on some planets in solar systems near to Earth

STOP

IN ANY REMAINING TIME YOU MAY REVIEW THE ANSWERS YOU CHOSE IN THIS SECTION. DO NOT WORK ON ANY OTHER SECTION OF THE TEST DURING THIS TIME.

6 6 6 6 6 6 6 6 6 6 6 6

SECTION **6**

Time—25 Minutes
18 Questions

You have 25 minutes to answer the 8 multiple-choice questions
and 10 student-produced response questions in this section.
For each multiple-choice question, determine which of the five
choices is correct and blacken the corresponding choice on your
answer sheet. You may use any blank space on the page for your
work.

Notes:

- You may use a calculator whenever you think it will be helpful.
- Only real numbers are used. No question or answer on this test involves a complex or imaginary number.
- Use the diagrams provided to help you solve the problems. Unless you see the words "Note: Figure not drawn to scale" under a diagram, it has been drawn as accurately as possible. Unless it is stated that a figure is three-dimensional, you may assume it lies in a plane.
- For any function f, the domain, unless specifically restricted, is the set of all real numbers for which $f(x)$ is also a real number.

Reference Information

Area Facts

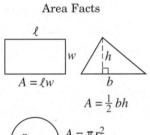

$A = \ell w$

$A = \frac{1}{2} bh$

$A = \pi r^2$
$C = 2\pi r$

Volume Facts

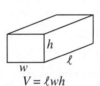

$V = \ell wh$

$V = \pi r^2 h$

Triangle Facts

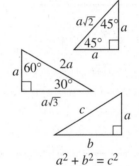

$a^2 + b^2 = c^2$

Angle Facts

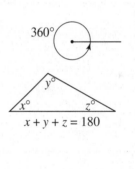

$x + y + z = 180$

1. If $\frac{1}{n}+\frac{1}{n}+\frac{1}{n}+\frac{1}{n}=\frac{b}{4}$, which of the following is an expression for n in terms of b?

(A) b

(B) $\frac{b}{4}$

(C) $\frac{b}{16}$

(D) $\frac{4}{b}$

(E) $\frac{16}{b}$

2. A kilometer is approximately $\frac{5}{8}$ of a mile. If Daniel drove 100 miles from town A to town B, which of the following is closest to the number of kilometers he drove?

(A) 63
(B) 85
(C) 145
(D) 160
(E) 183

GO ON TO THE NEXT PAGE

Practice Test 4

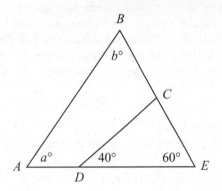

3. In the figure above, what is the value of $a + b$?

(A) 120
(B) 140
(C) 180
(D) 220
(E) 240

4. Which of the following is equal to 3 times 300% of 3?

(A) 301% of 3
(B) 303% of 3
(C) 900% of 3
(D) 903% of 3
(E) 2,700% of 3

5. A, B, and C are three cities in New York State. The distance between A and B is m miles and the distance between B and C is n miles. If, on a map of New York, A and B are c centimeters apart, on that map how many centimeters apart are B and C?

(A) $\dfrac{cn}{m}$

(B) $\dfrac{cm}{n}$

(C) $\dfrac{mn}{c}$

(D) $\dfrac{c}{mn}$

(E) $\dfrac{n}{cm}$

6. If $3 \times 8^{100} + 4 \times 8^{98} = k \times 8^{99}$, what is the value of k?

(A) 12
(B) 24.5
(C) 88
(D) 88.5
(E) 89

7. In the sequence a_1, a_2, a_3, a_4, a_5, . . . the first term, a_1, is 1 and the fourth term, a_4, is 10. From the third term on, each term is equal to 5 more than the sum of the two previous terms. What is the second term, a_2, of this sequence?

(A) $-\dfrac{1}{2}$

(B) $\dfrac{1}{2}$

(C) $\dfrac{3}{2}$

(D) $\dfrac{5}{2}$

(E) $5\dfrac{1}{2}$

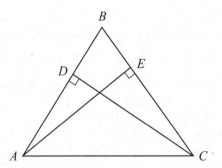

8. In $\triangle ABC$ in the figure above, $AE \perp BC$ and $CD \perp AB$. If $CD = 11$, $AE = 10$, and $AB = 12$, what is the value of BC?

(A) 10.8
(B) 12.0
(C) 12.6
(D) 13.0
(E) 13.2

GO ON TO THE NEXT PAGE

6 6 6 6 6 6 6 6 6 6 6 6 6

Directions for Student-Produced Response Questions (Grid-ins)

In questions 9–18, first solve the problem, and then enter your answer on the grid provided on the answer sheet. The instructions for entering your answers are as follows:

- First, write your answer in the boxes at the top of the grid.
- Second, grid your answer in the columns below the boxes.
- Use the fraction bar in the first row or the decimal point in the second row to enter fractions and decimal answers.

- Grid only one space in each column.
- Entering the answer in the boxes is recommended as an aid in gridding, but is not required.
- The machine scoring your exam can read only what you grid, so you **must grid in your answers correctly to get credit.**
- If a question has more than one correct answer, grid in only one of these answers.
- The grid does not have a minus sign, so no answer can be negative.
- A mixed number *must* be converted to an improper fraction or a decimal before it is gridded. Enter $1\frac{1}{4}$ as 5/4 or 1.25; the machine will interpret 1 1/4 as $\frac{11}{4}$ and mark it wrong.
- **All decimals must be entered as accurately as possible.** Here are the three acceptable ways of gridding

$$\frac{3}{11} = 0.272727\ldots$$

- Note that rounding to .273 is acceptable, because you are using the full grid, but you would receive **no credit** for .3 or .27, because these answers are less accurate.

Answer: $\frac{8}{15}$ Answer: 1.75

Write your answer in the boxes.

Grid in your answer.

Answer: 100

Either position is acceptable

GO ON TO THE NEXT PAGE →

6   **6 6 6 6 6 6 6 6 6 6**   **6**

9. Ali can stuff 330 envelopes per hour. At this rate, how many minutes will it take Ali to stuff 88 envelopes?

10. For what value of x is the sum of 3, 4, and x equal to the product of 3, 4, and x?

11. If $b > 0$ and $(5b + 2)(5b - 2) = 96$, what is the value of b?

12. When a is increased by 10 percent, the result is c, and when b is increased by 20 percent, the result is d. If $d:c = 2$, what is $a:b$?

13. A school planning committee consists of five students, 12 teachers, and three administrators. A three-person subcommittee needs to be formed that consists of one student, one teacher, and one administrator. If one of the students and two of the teachers are not eligible to serve because of other commitments, in how many different ways can the subcommittee be formed?

14. If the circumference of circle 1 is 1 foot greater than the circumference of circle 2, then to the nearest inch how much greater is the radius of circle 1 than the radius of circle 2?

15. If $x = 1{,}000{,}000$ and $y = 999{,}999$ then what is the sum of the digits of $x^2 - y^2$?

16. If $h(x) = 7x - 2$ and $h(11) = b$, what is the value of $h(b - 11)$?

17. Of the 326 children at North Central preschool, 211 have a dog and 174 have a cat. If 83 of the children have neither a cat nor a dog, how many have both?

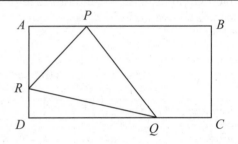

18. In rectangle $ABCD$ above, P, Q, and R are such that $AP = \dfrac{1}{3}AB$, $CQ = \dfrac{1}{3}CD$, and $DR = \dfrac{1}{3}DA$. The area of $\triangle PQR$ is what fraction of the area of rectangle $ABCD$?

IN ANY REMAINING TIME YOU MAY REVIEW THE ANSWERS YOU CHOSE IN THIS SECTION. DO NOT WORK ON ANY OTHER SECTION OF THE TEST DURING THIS TIME.

SECTION **7**   Time—25 Minutes
35 Questions

Choose the best answer to each of the following questions in this section. Then blacken the appropriate space on your answer sheet.

Each sentence below may or may not employ correct or effective expression. If you think that the underlined phrasing makes the most clear and precise sentence, select choice A. If, however, you think that the underlined phrasing makes the meaning of the sentence unclear or awkward, or that it is grammatically incorrect, select another answer from choices B to E.

In choosing your answers, follow the conventions of English as it is used by educated writers. Consider sentence structure, grammar, word choice, and punctuation. Choose the answer that produces the sentence that is the most clear and effective.

Example:

In her comments after the debate the judge said that she had been impressed by the ability of both teams to exploit logical weaknesses and in citing relevant examples.

(A) in citing relevant examples
(B) in that relevant examples had been cited
(C) in the citing of relevant examples
(D) to cite relevant examples
(E) to be able to cite relevant examples

Ⓐ Ⓑ Ⓒ ● Ⓔ

---

1. Applying the concept of "high-tech" retrospectively to past technological developments, which had a great influence on society, we can conclude, for example, that paper was probably considered high-tech in ancient China.

   (A) developments, which had a great influence on society, we
   (B) developments which had a great influence on society we
   (C) developments that had a great influence on society, we
   (D) developments, that had a great influence on society, we
   (E) developments, that had a great influence on society we

2. A common misconception of racists is that culture and race is congruent.

   (A) and race is congruent
   (B) is something that is congruent with race
   (C) and race are congruent
   (D) and race be congruent
   (E) is congruent for race

3. As suggested by what it is called, linguistic determinism postulates that language is the primary factor in determining how we think.

   (A) As suggested by what it is called, linguistic determinism
   (B) Linguistic determinism, as its name suggests,
   (C) What linguistic determinism is called, as its name suggests,
   (D) As what it is called, suggested by its name linguistic determinism
   (E) By its name, linguistic determinism

4. The human heart can be seen as analogous of the fuel pump in a gasoline engine.

   (A) as analogous of
   (B) as analogous for
   (C) as analogous as
   (D) as analogous to
   (E) as analogous in regard to

5. The development of effective, inexpensive, and contraceptives that are relatively safe has been the catalyst for sweeping social changes.

   (A) effective, inexpensive, and contraceptives that are relatively safe
   (B) effective and inexpensive contraceptives, and they are relatively safe
   (C) effective, inexpensive contraceptives, being relatively safe,
   (D) effective, inexpensive contraceptives, and these being relatively safe
   (E) effective, inexpensive, and relatively safe contraceptives

GO ON TO THE NEXT PAGE

7

6. One may be surprised to learn that precursors to the inoculation of modern Western medicine existed in some ancient <u>civilizations, these included</u> India, China, and Persia.

   (A) civilizations, these included
   (B) civilizations, including
   (C) civilizations, inclusive of
   (D) civilizations, which were including
   (E) civilization, and these were inclusive of

7. In a pluralistic society the mass media are generally far from <u>monolithic; they</u> respect and reflect a wide range of views and perspectives.

   (A) monolithic; they
   (B) monolithic, they
   (C) monolithic, where it
   (D) monolithic that it
   (E) monolithic, but they

8. <u>A rarely found trait, according to psychological research, in young children is altruism.</u>

   (A) A rarely found trait, according to psychological research, in young children is altruism.
   (B) According to psychological research, altruism, a rarely found trait, is found in young children.
   (C) According to psychological research, altruism is a rarely found trait in young children.
   (D) According to psychological research, a rarely found trait in young children, is altruism.
   (E) Altruism, according to psychological research, a rarely found trait, is found in young children.

9. <u>The professor's e-mail address was given by her to her class</u> so that they could send her any queries they might have about their term papers during the vacation.

   (A) The professor's e-mail address was given by her to her class
   (B) Given by her to her class, the professor's e-mail address was
   (C) Given by the professor to her class, her e-mail address was
   (D) Her e-mail address was given by the professor to her class
   (E) The professor gave her e-mail address to her class

10. The sociologist Max Weber believed that with the rise of Calvinism people wanted to demonstrate to themselves and others that they were among the elect by becoming affluent, <u>and thus worked hard to achieve wealth, in a self-fulfilling prophecy.</u>

    (A) affluent, and thus worked hard to achieve wealth, in a self-fulfilling prophecy
    (B) affluent. In a self-fulfilling prophecy it was hard work to achieve wealth
    (C) affluent; and thus worked hard to achieve wealth in a self-fulfilling prophecy
    (D) affluent, it was hard work to achieve wealth in a self-fulfilling prophecy
    (E) affluent, they were working hard to achieve wealth in a self-fulfilling prophecy

11. Warren Burger succeeded Earl Warren as chief justice, presiding over the Supreme Court from 1969 until 1986; favoring a policy of judicial <u>restraint, a major role was played by Burger in making the court more conservative in its rulings.</u>

    (A) restraint, a major role was played by Burger in making the court more conservative in its rulings
    (B) restraint was a major role played by Burger in making the court more conservative in its rulings
    (C) restraint, in its rulings the court was made more conservative because of the major role played by Burger
    (D) restraint, Burger played a major role in making the court more conservative in its rulings
    (E) restraint, it was Burger who played a major role in making the court more conservative in its dealings

GO ON TO THE NEXT PAGE ▷

7

Each of the sentences below contains either one error or no error in grammar or usage. If there is an error, it will be underlined. If the sentence contains an error, indicate this by selecting the letter for the one under-lined part that should be changed to make the sen-tence correct. Follow the requirements of standard written English in choosing answers. If the sentence is already correct, select choice E.

Example:

The number of stars <u>visible in</u> the sky on any
                           A

<u>given</u> night <u>vary</u>, mainly <u>because of</u> changes in
   B   C   D

atmospheric conditions and in the phases of the

Moon. <u>No Error</u>
          E

Ⓐ Ⓑ ● Ⓓ Ⓔ

12. The music of the French composer Claude

Debussy can be characterized <u>as</u> Impressionistic in
                                  A

<u>it's</u> stress on atmosphere and on <u>creating</u> nuances
  B   C

of mood, <u>as opposed to</u> the expression of emotion.
              D

<u>No Error</u>
    E

13. Although humanity probably has <u>sufficiently</u>
                                       A

advanced technology for a manned mission to

Mars, <u>there is</u> difficult political and financial
         B

obstacles that <u>must be overcome</u> before <u>it can</u>
                     C   D

become a reality. <u>No Error</u>
                      E

14. Many of the scientists <u>which</u> <u>were presenting</u>
                              A   B

papers at the annual conference <u>had never spoken</u>
                                       C

to such a large gathering <u>before</u>. <u>No Error</u>
                              D   E

15. Religion has had such a profound <u>effect on</u>
                                         A

<u>nearly every</u> area of life and thought <u>which</u> many
     B   C

subjects <u>can only</u> be understood by a person with
             D

some knowledge of religious thinking. <u>No Error</u>
                                          E

16. Some philosophers believe that differences

<u>between</u> one thing and another are illusory; <u>that is</u>,
   A   B

such ostensible differences <u>need</u> exist in the mind
                                C

rather <u>than</u> in reality. <u>No Error</u>
          D   E

17. The recent <u>interest in</u> ecumenism is seen by some
                   A

observers <u>as</u> an indication of a growing recognition
             B

of a need for <u>whole</u> humanity to recognize
                  C

common themes in religions that are often

<u>obscured by</u> cosmetic differences. <u>No Error</u>
    D   E

18. Artists <u>working in</u> the film industry today <u>bear</u> a
                A   B

solemn responsibility to society <u>that</u> the
                                     C

unprecedented power <u>of their medium</u> to influence
                          D

people. <u>No Error</u>
            E

19. Investigators of psychic phenomena <u>have set up</u>
       A   B

audio and video recorders around the house that

<u>is believed</u> to be haunted, hoping <u>that it will</u>
    C   D

record the nocturnal activities of ghosts. <u>No Error</u>
                                              E

GO ON TO THE NEXT PAGE ⟩

7

20. There is <u>little that</u> international legal bodies such
      A
    as the World Court and the International Court of
    Justice <u>can do</u> to enforce their decisions
            B
    <u>in the case of</u> countries that refuse to <u>accede by</u>
          C   D
    their decisions. <u>No Error</u>
                          E

21. <u>In the case of</u> many dynamic new art forms,
          A
    Cubism <u>had</u> its inception <u>as</u> a revolt against the
            B   C
    predominant style of the art of the day, which was
    <u>highly</u> expressive and emotional. <u>No Error</u>
      D   E

22. Student leaders at the college called a meeting to
    discuss their next <u>course of action</u> after the
                          A
    college administration <u>rejected</u> their <u>proposal of</u>
                              B   C
    a delay in <u>implementing</u> an increase in tuition fees.
                    D
    <u>No Error</u>
      E

23. Pro-democracy activists <u>maintain that</u> the country's
                                  A
    new government <u>have not</u> implemented new laws
                        B
    <u>granting</u> voting rights <u>to</u> minorities. <u>No Error</u>
      C   D   E

24. Although the members of the <u>newly formed</u> rock
                                      A
    climbing class were <u>initially</u> very concerned
                            B
    <u>to be injured</u> in the activity, they became less
        C
    worried when the instructor assured them <u>that</u>
                                                  D
    stringent safety measures had been taken. <u>No Error</u>
                                                    E

25. It is important <u>knowing</u> that with the rise of
                      A
    science belief in God was challenged in the minds
    of many people, and a view called agnosticism
    <u>arose</u> that said that God <u>may exist</u>, but that this
      B   C
    cannot be <u>rationally</u> proved. <u>No Error</u>
                  D   E

26. Concerned citizens, <u>hoping to prevent</u> or <u>at least</u>
                            A   B
    delay the construction of the dam, have met with
    officials from both local and state governments to
    outline <u>their argument</u> that the dam <u>will do</u> more
                C   D
    harm than good. <u>No Error</u>
                        E

27. The <u>idea of</u> a golden age <u>in which</u> humanity
            A   B
    inhabited a paradisiacal world <u>unsullied on</u>
                                        C
    problems <u>is found</u> in many cultures. <u>No Error</u>
                  D   E

28. Most economists believe that <u>raising</u> taxes on
                                      A
    business <u>to very high</u> levels discourages
                B
    investment, <u>causing</u> the number of workers <u>to be</u>
                    C   D
    employed to drop. <u>No Error</u>
                          E

29. It seems a reasonable contention <u>that</u> the social
                                          A
    sciences <u>have had</u> a major impact on jurisprudence,
                B
    <u>inclining</u> contemporary legislators, jurists, and
      C
    others involved in law toward placing a greater
    stress on social and economic determinants in
    crime than <u>did</u> their predecessors. <u>No Error</u>
                  D   E

GO ON TO THE NEXT PAGE

7

The following early draft of an essay needs to be rewritten to improve sentence structure, choice of words, clarity of expression, organization, and development. After reading the draft, answer each question below it, choosing the answer that best conforms to the requirements of standard written English.

(1) On October 4, 1957, the Soviet Union launched Sputnik 1, Earth's first artificial satellite. (2) This shocked many Americans, who thought of themselves as living in the most scientifically and technologically advanced country in the world. (3) American leaders responded by increasing research on rockets and space flight in general. (4) On January 31, 1958, America orbited its own satellite, Explorer 1, toward restoring America's confidence. (5) However, there was another Soviet surprise in store: On April 12, 1961, the Soviets launched a human being into space.

(6) Yuri Gagarin circled Earth in the Vostok 1 spacecraft. (7) The reaction to Gagarin's flight in America was similar to the reaction to Sputnik 1, perhaps greater. (8) On May 25, 1961, President Kennedy surprised the world with a bold declaration "To land a man on the Moon and return him safely to Earth, before the end of the decade." (9) It meant that America's scientists and engineers would have to develop new and powerful rockets, space craft, guidance systems, and solve a host of problems in just a few years. (10) Yet, the problems were overcome and, as almost everyone knows, on July 21, 1969, Neil Armstrong became the first man to walk on the Moon.

(11) After the first Moon landing was achieved by the mission called Apollo 11, another six missions to the Moon were carried out, giving scientists more valuable information, especially about the geology of the Moon. (12) The final mission, Apollo 17, which landed on the Moon on December 11, 1972, and returned to Earth eight days later, brought to a close one of the most spectacular periods of exploration in history. (13) The success of Apollo, actually maybe because of it, some people wonder why the United States did not continue to explore the Moon, possibly even building a base there. (14) Perhaps the combined cost of the manned space program and the war in Vietnam made it politically unpopular to continue the missions. (15) Some experts think that there might be a third surprise in store for Americans before very long—a Chinese citizen walking on the Moon!

30. Which of the following is the best version of the underlined portion of sentence 4 (reproduced below)?

On January 31, 1958, America orbited its own satellite, Explorer 1, toward restoring America's confidence.

(A) (As it is now)
(B) going toward restoring America's confidence
(C) an orbiting that went a way toward restoring America's confidence
(D) which went a way to restoring America's confidence
(E) going in some way for restoring America's confidence

31. In context, which is the best way to deal with sentence 6?

(A) Leave it as it is.
(B) Delete it.
(C) Place it at the end of the first paragraph, after sentence 5.
(D) Combine it with sentence 5 in the following way: However, there was another Soviet surprise in store: On April 12, 1961, the Soviets launched Yuri Gagarin into space in the Vostok 1 spacecraft, becoming the first human being to orbit Earth.
(E) Combine it with sentence 5 in the following way: However, there was another Soviet surprise in store: On April 12, 1961, the Soviets launched the Vostok 1 spacecraft into space with Yuri Gagarin, he became the first human being to orbit Earth.

GO ON TO THE NEXT PAGE

7

32. In context, which of the following would be most appropriately inserted at the beginning of sentence 9?

(A) A number of experts commented that it was an ambitious but realistic promise because

(B) Some experts believed that it would be easy to keep this pledge because

(C) Many experts thought that such pledges were just political stunts because

(D) However, the project was never completed because

(E) Many experts thought it was a foolish promise because

33. In context, which of the following would be the best sentence to insert between sentence 9 and sentence 10?

(A) The task seemed easy, with little risk of failure that would damage national prestige.

(B) The problems were considerable, but posed no great difficulty; consequently, failure would not damage national prestige.

(C) It seemed impossible; furthermore, failure would deal an embarrassing blow to national prestige.

(D) It seemed impossible, and failure dealt an embarrassing blow to national prestige.

(E) American's leading scientists and engineers got to work so that failure would not deal an embarrassing blow to national prestige.

34. Which of the following is the best version of the underlined portion of sentence 13 (reproduced below)?

The success of Apollo, actually maybe because of it, some people wonder why the United States did not continue to explore the Moon, possibly even building a base there.

(A) (As it is now)

(B) Furthermore, forgetting the success of Apollo,

(C) However, because of—*despite* the success of Apollo—

(D) However, despite the success of Apollo—or perhaps *because* of it—

(E) On the contrary, perhaps *because* of the success of Apollo,

35. Which of the following sentences would be most logical to insert before sentence 15?

(A) Because of this it seems unlikely that anyone will walk on the Moon again for many years.

(B) Despite this, America is bound to resume manned space flights outside of Earth's orbit.

(C) On the other hand, it is unlikely that any country other than the United States and Russia has the technology to mount a manned mission to the Moon.

(D) Many Americans would like to see an American base on the Moon rather than a Chinese one.

(E) At any rate, the world is waiting for the next person to land on the Moon.

STOP

IN ANY REMAINING TIME YOU MAY REVIEW THE
ANSWERS YOU CHOSE IN THIS SECTION. DO NOT WORK
ON ANY OTHER SECTION OF THE TEST DURING THIS TIME.

SECTION 8	Time—20 Minutes 18 Questions	Choose the best answer to each of the following questions in this section. Then blacken the appropriate space on your answer sheet.

Each of the following sentences contains one or two blanks, indicating that a word or set of words has been omitted. Beneath each sentence there are five answer choices labeled A to E from which you must select the word or set of words that best fits the meaning of the sentence as a whole.

Example:

Records of colonization can be found as far back as the Phoenicians, but colonization became a major force in world history only when European countries began, in the fifteenth century, to make ---- Asia, the Americas, and Africa.

  (A) queries about   (B) incursions into
    (C) tirades against   (D) enemies in
      (E) amends for

                Ⓐ ● Ⓒ Ⓓ Ⓔ

1. Controversial irrigation projects often engender ---- among various competing vested interests.

  (A) agreement   (B) debate   (C) harmony
    (D) consensus   (E) apathy

2. Many people are forced to ---- the salary from their primary job by taking a part-time job.

  (A) augment   (B) reduce
    (C) temper   (D) redistribute
      (E) eschew

3. The congressman's ---- generally support even his most sweeping declamations condemning the ---- portrayal of violence and sex on television and in movies.

  (A) supporters . . profound
  (B) colleagues . . abstruse
  (C) critics . . gratuitous
  (D) constituents . . lurid
  (E) opponents . . graphic

4. In Anthony Trollope's novel *Barchester Towers*, Dr. Proudie is the ---- henpecked husband, a commonly ---- figure in literature.

  (A) serious . . ridiculed
  (B) apocryphal . . mocked
  (C) unfriendly . . travestied
  (D) intrepid . . depicted
  (E) archetypal . . caricatured

5. The term "taste" is often used loosely and neutrally to refer to any kind of preference based on pleasure, or which is in any way the result of ---- judgment.

  (A) nominal   (B) aesthetic   (C) intuitive
    (D) rational   (E) impartial

6. ---- reasoning involves making generalizations on the basis of a number of specific examples, whereas ---- reasoning involves the opposite— drawing conclusions about a specific example on the basis of a generalization.

  (A) Inferential . . sophistical
  (B) Inductive . . deductive
  (C) Logical . . syllogistic
  (D) Mathematical . . valid
  (E) Scientific . . analytical

GO ON TO THE NEXT PAGE ▷

8   8   8   8   8   8   8   8   8   8   8

Below are passages followed by questions on them. Questions on a pair of related passages may be about the relationship between the two passages. For each question, select the best answer based on what is stated or implied in the passage (or passages).

Questions 7–18 are based on the following passage.

It is customary to place the date for the beginnings of modern medicine somewhere in the mid-1930s, with the entry of sulfonamides and
Line penicillin into the pharmacopoeia, and it is usual
(5) to ascribe to these events the force of a revolution in medical practice. This is what things seemed like at the time. Medicine was upheaved, revolutionized indeed. Therapy had been discovered for great numbers of patients whose
(10) illnesses had previously been untreatable. Cures were now available. As we saw it then, it seemed a totally new world. Doctors could now cure disease, and this was astonishing, most of all to the doctors themselves.
(15)   It was, no doubt about it, a major occurrence in medicine, and a triumph for biological science applied to medicine but perhaps not a revolution after all, looking back from this distance. For the real revolution in medicine, which set the stage
(20) for antibiotics and whatever else we have in the way of effective therapy today, had already occurred one hundred years before penicillin. It did not begin with the introduction of science into medicine. That came years later. Like a good
(25) many revolutions this one began with the destruction of dogma. It was discovered, sometime in the 1830s, that the greater part of medicine was nonsense.
    The history of medicine has never been a
(30) particularly attractive subject in medical education, and one reason for this is that it is so unrelievedly deplorable a story. For century after century, all the way into the remote millennia of its origins, medicine got along by sheer
(35) guesswork and the crudest sort of empiricism. It is hard to conceive of a less scientific enterprise among human endeavors. Virtually anything that could be thought up for treatment of disease was tried out at one time or another, and once tried,
(40) lasted decades or even centuries before being given up. It was, in retrospect, the most frivolous and irresponsible kind of human experimentation, based on nothing but trial and error, and usually

resulting in precisely that sequence. Bleeding,
(45) purging, cupping, the administration of infusions of every known plant, solutions of every known metal, every conceivable diet including total fasting, most of these based on the weirdest imaginings about the cause of disease, concocted
(50) out of nothing but thin air—this was the heritage of medicine until a little over a century ago. It is astounding that the profession survived so long, and got away with so much with so little outcry. Almost everyone seems to have been taken in.
(55) Evidently one had to be born a skeptic, like Montaigne, to see through the old nonsense; but even Montaigne, who wrote scathingly about the illnesses caused by doctoring centuries before Ivan Illich, had little effect. Most people were
(60) convinced of the magical powers of medicine and put up with it.
    Then, sometime in the early nineteenth century, it was realized by a few of the leading figures in medicine that almost all of the
(65) complicated treatments then available for disease did not really work, and the suggestion was made by several courageous physicians, here and abroad, that most of them actually did more harm than good. Simultaneously, the surprising
(70) discovery was made that certain diseases were self-limited, got better by themselves, possessed so to speak, a "natural history." It is hard for us now to imagine the magnitude of this discovery and its effect on the practice of medicine. That
(75) long habit, extending back into the distant past, had been to treat everything with something, and it was taken for granted that every disease demanded treatment and might in fact end fatally if not treated. In a sober essay written on this
(80) topic in 1876, Professor Edward H. Clarke of Harvard reviewed what he regarded as the major scientific accomplishment of medicine in the

GO ON TO THE NEXT PAGE ▶

8   8   8   8   8   8   8   8   8   8   8

preceding fifty years, which consisted of studies
proving that patients with typhoid and typhus

(85) fever could recover all by themselves, without
medical intervention, and often did better for
being untreated than when they received the
bizarre herbs, heavy metal and fomentations that
were popular at that time. Delirium tremens, a

(90) disorder long believed to be fatal in all cases
unless subjected to constant and aggressive
medical intervention, was observed to subside by
itself more readily in patients left untreated, with
a substantially improved rate of survival.

(95)   Gradually, over succeeding decades, the
traditional therapeutic ritual of medicine was
given up, and what came to be called the "art of
medicine" emerged to take its place. In
retrospect, this art was really the beginning of the

(100) science of medicine. It was based on meticulous,
objective, even cool observations of sick people.
From this endeavor we learned the details of the
natural history of illness, so that, for example, it
came to be understood that typhoid and typhus

(105) were really two entirely separate, unrelated
disorders, with quite different causes. Accurate
diagnosis became the central purpose and
justification for medicine, and as the methods for
diagnosis improved, accurate prognosis also

(110) became possible, so that patients and their
families could be told not only the name of the
illness but also, with some reliability, how it was
likely to turn out. By the time this century had
begun, these were becoming generally accepted

(115) as the principal responsibilities of the physician.
In addition, a new kind of much less ambitious
and flamboyant therapy began to emerge, termed
"supportive treatment" and consisting in large
part of plain common sense: good nursing care,

(120) appropriate bed rest, sensible diet, avoidance of
traditional nostrums and patent medicine, and a
measured degree of trust that nature, in taking its
course, would very often bring things to a
satisfactory conclusion.

(125)   The doctor became a considerably more useful
and respected professional. For all his limitations,
and despite his inability to do much in the way of
preventing or terminating illness, he could be
depended on to explain things, to relieve

(130) anxieties, and to be on hand. He was trusted as
an adviser and guide in difficult times, including
the time of dying.

7. In line 4, "pharmacopoeia" most nearly means

(A) a collection of drugs approved by the
    government for medical use
(B) accepted medical practice
(C) pharmacy
(D) a stock of medical drugs
(E) doctors' knowledge

8. Why, according to the author, were doctors
   astonished around the mid-1930s?

(A) They were amazed that drugs were able to
    cure diseases.
(B) Cures were becoming available for some
    illnesses, whereas before this doctors had little
    capacity to cure illnesses.
(C) The practice of medicine was being
    revolutionized by a bold young breed of
    doctors.
(D) They were surprised that people still had so
    much respect for doctors and medicine.
(E) They were shocked to learn that some
    illnesses were still untreatable, even with new
    drugs like sulfonamides and penicillin.

9. Which of the following is part of the "dogma"
   referred to in line 26?

(A) Every illness must be treated.
(B) Every illness ends in the patient's death if it is
    not treated.
(C) Some diseases get better if left untreated.
(D) Accurate diagnosis, not treatment, is the most
    important purpose of medicine.
(E) Plenty of bed rest and a nutritious diet are
    often as important as medicine in the
    treatment of illness.

GO ON TO THE NEXT PAGE ▷

8   8   8 8   8 8   8   8 8   8   8

10. In line 35, "the crudest sort of empiricism" most nearly means

(A) acquisition of scientific knowledge by careful experimentation

(B) extremely impolite experimentation on patients

(C) very unsophisticated use of observation and experimentation to gain knowledge

(D) the use of powerful drugs without a scientific understanding of their compositions

(E) the most ridiculous treatments of disease imaginable

11. What is the most likely reason that the author says, "It is astounding that the profession survived so long" (lines 51–52)?

(A) He believes that being a doctor in the time before the development of modern medicine was extremely demanding and he's amazed that so few doctors left the medical profession.

(B) He believes it is very surprising that the medical profession was not assimilated into the larger field of biological science as the latter field made huge advances in the early years of the twentieth century.

(C) He believes it is remarkable that a profession that was so poor at doing its job was so popular.

(D) He believes it is amazing that the medical profession was not more appreciated by the public before the mid-1930s.

(E) He believes that it is remarkable that most doctors did not become so ill from the demands of the medical profession that they could no longer continue to practice medicine.

12. In line 55, "skeptic" most nearly means

(A) a person of very high intelligence

(B) a cynical person

(C) a person who analyzes things objectively

(D) a naive person

(E) a person who questions generally accepted ideas

13. It can be inferred that the author describes "several physicians" as "courageous" (line 67) because

(A) he believes that it took courage for physicians to risk injuring their own health by administering new drugs to patients

(B) he believes that it took courage for physicians to suggest that the methods used in their profession were almost completely wrong because doing so would make them unpopular with other members of the profession

(C) he believes that it took courage for American physicians to question the accepted medical practice of European doctors with a far longer tradition of medicine

(D) he believes that it took courage for physicians to suggest that the profession should try new methods of treating patients

(E) he believes that it took courage for such physicians to admit to their fellow professionals that they had been wrong in their criticism of accepted medical practice

14. Why does the author describe the "discovery" mentioned in lines 69–70 as "surprising"?

(A) Because it comes as a surprise even to doctors today that some diseases get better without medical treatment

(B) Because doctors at the time believed that medical intervention in illness was generally unhelpful

(C) Because doctors at the time believed that there were some diseases that could not be cured

(D) Because most people, including doctors, believed that all illnesses had to be treated

(E) Because medicine has advanced so much since the early nineteenth century that it is surprising that such a discovery was made then

GO ON TO THE NEXT PAGE

15. The word that would best describe "the major scientific accomplishment of medicine in the preceding fifty years" (lines 81–83) is

    (A) ironic
    (B) unsubstantiated
    (C) humorous
    (D) ridiculous
    (E) unethical

16. In line 91, "aggressive" most nearly means

    (A) dangerous
    (B) destructive
    (C) irresponsible
    (D) very intensive
    (E) hostile

17. In line 117, "flamboyant" most nearly means

    (A) invasive
    (B) ornate
    (C) scientific
    (D) showy and elaborate
    (E) not based on scientifically established facts

18. According to the author, all of the following are important components of modern medical practice EXCEPT

    (A) supportive treatment
    (B) providing advice to patients
    (C) aggressive medical intervention in nearly all illnesses
    (D) diagnosis of illness
    (E) prognosis of illness

STOP

IN ANY REMAINING TIME YOU MAY REVIEW THE
ANSWERS YOU CHOSE IN THIS SECTION. DO NOT WORK
ON ANY OTHER SECTION OF THE TEST DURING THIS TIME.

Practice Test 4

SECTION 9

Time—20 Minutes
16 Questions

For each problem in this section determine which of the five choices is correct and blacken the corresponding choice on your answer sheet. You may use any blank space on the page for your work.

Notes:
- You may use a calculator whenever you think it will be helpful.
- Only real numbers are used. No question or answer on this test involves a complex or imaginary number.
- Use the diagrams provided to help you solve the problems. Unless you see the words "Note: Figure not drawn to scale" under a diagram, it has been drawn as accurately as possible. Unless it is stated that a figure is three-dimensional, you may assume it lies in a plane.
- For any function f, the domain, unless specifically restricted, is the set of all real numbers for which $f(x)$ is also a real number.

Reference Information

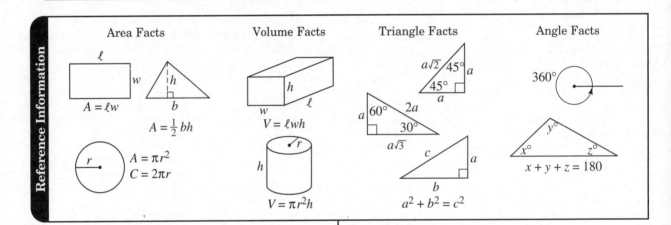

Area Facts

$A = \ell w$

$A = \frac{1}{2} bh$

$A = \pi r^2$
$C = 2\pi r$

Volume Facts

$V = \ell wh$

$V = \pi r^2 h$

Triangle Facts

$x + y + z = 180$

$a^2 + b^2 = c^2$

Angle Facts

$360°$

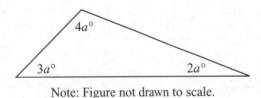

Note: Figure not drawn to scale.

1. In the figure above, what is the measure of the largest angle?

(A) 60°
(B) 80°
(C) 90°
(D) 100°
(E) 120°

2. 20 books were packed in two boxes. If the number of books in the smaller box was $\frac{1}{4}$ the number of books in the larger box, how many books were in the larger box?

(A) 4
(B) 5
(C) 12
(D) 15
(E) 16

GO ON TO THE NEXT PAGE

9　　9　　9　　9　　9　　9　　9

3. If p, q, and r are consecutive positive integers and $p < q < r$, which of the following must be an odd integer?

(A) pqr
(B) $p + q + r$
(C) $p + qr$
(D) $p(q + r)$
(E) $(p + q)(q + r)$

4. If $|a + 5| = 10$ and $|b - 5| = 10$, which of the following could be true?

  I. $a = b$
 II. $a - b = 10$
III. $a + b = 10$

(A) I only
(B) II only
(C) III only
(D) I and II only
(E) I, II, and III

5. If the average (arithmetic mean) of 11 numbers, each of which is equal to n is 13, what is the average of 13 numbers, each of which is equal to n?

(A) $\dfrac{13}{11}$
(B) 11
(C) 13
(D) 24
(E) 143

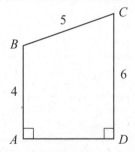

Note: Figure not drawn to scale.

6. In the diagram above, what is the length of side $\overline{AD}$ of quadrilateral $ABCD$?

(A) 4
(B) 4.5
(C) 5
(D) $\sqrt{21}$
(E) $\sqrt{29}$

7. If a is directly proportional to b and inversely proportional to c, and if $a = 2$ when $b = 4$ and $c = 3$, what is the value of $b + c$ when $a = 12$?

(A) $8\dfrac{1}{3}$
(B) 12
(C) 15
(D) $18\dfrac{2}{3}$
(E) $24\dfrac{1}{2}$

8. If n is a positive integer, what is the remainder when $n + 2n + 3n + 4n + 5$ is divided by 10?

(A) 0
(B) 1
(C) 2
(D) 3
(E) 5

9. If $f(x) = 3x + 5$ and $g(x) = 5x + 3$, how many integers, n, satisfy both of the following inequalities: $|n| < 5$ and $f(n) > g(n)$?

(A) None
(B) 1
(C) 3
(D) 5
(E) More than 5

10. If the length of one side of a triangle is 2, which of the following could be the perimeter of the triangle?

  I. 4
 II. 24
III. 44

(A) None
(B) I only
(C) I and II only
(D) II and III only
(E) I, II, and III

GO ON TO THE NEXT PAGE

11. If the average (arithmetic mean) of a, $2a + 8$, and $6a - 11$ is 11, what is the median of the three numbers?

    (A)   6
    (B) 11
    (C) 13
    (D) 16
    (E) 26

12. For any positive integer n, define $\textcircled{n}$ as the greatest prime factor of n. If a and b are positive integers, which of the following statements must be true?

    I. $\textcircled{a + b} = \textcircled{a} + \textcircled{b}$
    II. $\textcircled{ab} = \textcircled{a} \times \textcircled{b}$
    III. $\textcircled{a}^2 = \textcircled{a}$

    (A) None
    (B) I only
    (C) II only
    (D) III only
    (E) II and III only

13. The 28 members of a high school club include 4 seniors, 8 juniors, 10 sophomores, and 6 freshmen. In how many ways can a 5-person committee be formed from the members of the club that consists of 2 seniors, 1 junior, 1 sophomore, and 1 freshman?

    (A)   30
    (B)   480
    (C)   960
    (D) 2,880
    (E) 3,840

14. If m and n are positive integers, how many integers are greater than $m(n - 2)$ and less than $m(n + 2)$?

    (A) 4
    (B) $2m$
    (C) $4m$
    (D) $2m - 1$
    (E) $4m - 1$

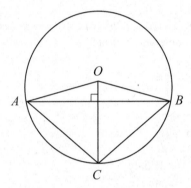

Note: Figure not drawn to scale.

15. In circle O, in the figure above, radius $\overline{OC}$ is perpendicular to chord $\overline{AB}$. If $OC = 8$ and $AB = 8$, what is the area of quadrilateral $AOBC$?

    (A) 16
    (B) 32
    (C) 64
    (D) $16\sqrt{3}$
    (E) $32\sqrt{3}$

16. How many integers, n, satisfy the inequality $|2n + 5| < n$?

    (A) None
    (B) 1
    (C) 2
    (D) 3
    (E) More than 3

STOP

IN ANY REMAINING TIME YOU MAY REVIEW THE
ANSWERS YOU CHOSE IN THIS SECTION. DO NOT WORK
ON ANY OTHER SECTION OF THE TEST DURING THIS TIME.

10   10   10   10   10   10   10

Each sentence below may or may not employ correct or effective expression. If you think that the underlined phrasing makes the most clear and precise sentence, select choice A. If, however, you think that the underlined phrasing makes the meaning of the sentence unclear or awkward, or that it is grammatically incorrect, select another answer from choices B to E.

In choosing your answers, follow the conventions of English as it is used by educated writers. Consider sentence structure, grammar, word choice, and punctuation. Choose the answer that produces the sentence that is the most clear and effective.

Example:

In her comments after the debate the judge said that she had been impressed by the ability of both teams to exploit logical weaknesses and <u>in citing relevant examples</u>.

(A) in citing relevant examples
(B) in that relevant examples had been cited
(C) in the citing of relevant examples
(D) to cite relevant examples
(E) to be able to cite relevant examples

Ⓐ Ⓑ Ⓒ ● Ⓔ

1. John Glenn, the first American to orbit Earth, <u>and later became a U.S. Senator from Ohio, in which he served for twenty-five years</u>.

(A) and later became a U.S. Senator from Ohio, in which he served for twenty-five years
(B) later became a U.S. Senator from Ohio, serving for twenty-five years
(C) later becoming a U.S. Senator from Ohio, serving for twenty-five years
(D) he later became a U.S. Senator from Ohio, serving for twenty-five years
(E) later served for twenty-five years, becoming a U.S. Senator from Ohio

2. The Hollywood star worked at several jobs before becoming a full-time <u>actor, first he was a bank teller, then a carpenter, and his last job before acting was in sales</u>.

(A) actor, first he was a bank teller, then a carpenter, and his last job before acting was in sales
(B) actor, first being a bank teller, second working as a carpenter, and later as a salesperson
(C) actor; he was first a bank teller, second he worked as a carpenter, and he did sales in his last job
(D) actor; first he was a bank teller, next he was a carpenter, and then he was a salesperson
(E) actor; first a bank teller, then carpentry, then a sales job

3. <u>An elaborate concept of the afterlife was not had by the Jews of antiquity</u>, but the early Christians developed an elaborate cosmology of heaven and hell.

(A) An elaborate concept of the afterlife was not had by the Jews of antiquity
(B) An elaborate concept of the afterlife was not a view had by the Jews of antiquity
(C) An elaborate concept of the afterlife had not been had by the Jews of antiquity
(D) The Jews of antiquity did not have an elaborate concept of the afterlife
(E) The Jews of antiquity did not have an elaborate concept when it came to the thought about the afterlife

10   10   10   10   10   10   10

4. Writing, that is full of clichéd ideas and expressions, is generally insipid.

   (A) Writing, that is full of clichéd ideas and expressions, is generally insipid.
   (B) Writing, full of clichéd ideas and expressions, is generally insipid.
   (C) Writing, in cases where it is full of clichéd ideas and expressions, is generally insipid.
   (D) Writing that is full of clichéd ideas and expressions is generally insipid.
   (E) Full of clichéd ideas and expressions, writing is generally insipid.

5. Many forms of electromagnetic radiation, of which X-rays can be considered one form, bombard our bodies constantly, interacting with organic molecules.

   (A) of which X-rays can be considered one form
   (B) which X-rays are included in
   (C) including X-rays
   (D) and X-rays are considered one of them
   (E) X-rays are included in these

6. By raising peripheral issues was how the lawyer tried to obfuscate the main issue.

   (A) By raising peripheral issues was how the lawyer tried to obfuscate the main issue.
   (B) The raising of peripheral issues was how the lawyer tried to obfuscate the main issue.
   (C) Raising peripheral issues, the lawyer trying to obfuscate the main issue.
   (D) The lawyer, trying to obfuscate the main issue, he raised peripheral issues.
   (E) The lawyer tried to obfuscate the main issue by raising peripheral issues.

7. In the "clockwork universe" of eighteenth century philosophy, God is relegated to the role of a "clockmaker" who creates the cosmos and then withdraws to allow human beings autonomous action.

   (A) God is relegated to the role of a "clockmaker"
   (B) it had been God relegated to the role of a "clockmaker"
   (C) God is relegated into the role of a "clockmaker"
   (D) the role of a "clockmaker" relegates to God
   (E) God relegates the role of a "clockmaker"

8. Humanism, one of the major belief systems in the West today, is most commonly held by agnostics and atheists, and there are even some Jewish and Christian humanists as well.

   (A) atheists, and there are even some Jewish and Christian humanists as well
   (B) atheists; and there are even some Jewish and Christian humanists as well
   (C) atheists, but there are some Jewish and Christian humanists as well
   (D) atheists; on the other hand there are even some Jewish and Christian humanists
   (E) atheists, being some Jewish and Christian humanists also

9. The hobby of amateur radio is made up of many people around the world who, although of diverse backgrounds and speakers of many different languages, share a passion for the many forms of radio communication.

   (A) who, although of diverse backgrounds and speakers of many different languages,
   (B) who, although they have diverse backgrounds and speak many different languages,
   (C) who have diverse backgrounds and speak many different languages,
   (D) who, having diverse backgrounds and speaking many different languages,
   (E) whose diverse backgrounds and speaking of many different languages

GO ON TO THE NEXT PAGE →

10   10   10   10   10   10   10

10. Classical historians generally take a subjective
    view of historical events, although modern
    historians strive to gain an objective view of events
    through comprehensive research and careful
    analysis.

    (A) Classical historians generally take a subjective
        view of historical events, although modern
        historians
    (B) Classical historians generally take a subjective
        view of historical events, but modern
        historians, they
    (C) Classical historians generally took a subjective
        view of historical events, but modern
        historians
    (D) Classical historians generally have taken a
        subjective view of historical events, although
        modern historians
    (E) Classical historians generally had taken a
        subjective view of historical events, but
        modern historians

11. Access to coal allowing the development of
    processes requiring great heat, the proximity of
    coal to the surface has been a major determinant in
    industrialization.

    (A) Access to coal allowing
    (B) Access to coal allowing,
    (C) Allowing access to coal,
    (D) Although access to coal allows
    (E) Because access to coal allows

12. Some contemporary writers have expressed
    concern about the intense scrutiny that their work
    is subjected to, dissecting every sentence and
    analyzing every nuance.

    (A) to, dissecting every sentence and analyzing
        every nuance
    (B) to; every sentence is dissected and every
        nuance is analyzed
    (C) to, being the dissection of every sentence and
        the analysis of every nuance
    (D) to, the every sentence being dissected and
        every nuance analyzed
    (E) to, them dissecting every sentence and
        analyzing every nuance

13. The leading English-language newspaper in
    Singapore, *The Straits Times*, publishes more
    international news than most towns in the United
    States.

    (A) than most towns in the United States
    (B) than do most of the leading newspapers found
        in towns in the United States
    (C) compared to what is published in leading
        newspapers in most towns in the United States
    (D) than do leading newspapers in most towns in
        the United States
    (E) than most of the United States' town
        newspapers

14. The philosopher Bertrand Russell commented that
    people want not knowledge but certainty, by which
    he meant that most people are not interested in
    discovering the truth about philosophical questions
    but rather in believing in something that makes
    them feel secure.

    (A) by which he meant that most people are not
        interested in discovering the truth about
        philosophical questions but rather in believing
        in something
    (B) and he meant by this that most people are not
        interested in discovering the truth about
        philosophical questions but rather in believing
        in something
    (C) by which he meant that most people are
        interested not in discovering the truth about
        philosophical questions out rather believe in
        something
    (D) what he meant by that was most people are
        not interested in discovering the truth about
        philosophical questions but rather in
        certainty—having something to believe in
    (E) his meaning was that most people are not
        interested in discovering the truth about
        philosophical questions but rather in believing
        in something

IN ANY REMAINING TIME YOU MAY REVIEW THE
ANSWERS YOU CHOSE IN THIS SECTION. DO NOT WORK
ON ANY OTHER SECTION OF THE TEST DURING THIS TIME.

Answer Key

CRITICAL READING

Section 2

Ans.	Level of Diff.	Ans.	Level of Diff.
1. A	1	13. E	5
2. D	1	14. C	3
3. E	2	15. E	3
4. E	3	16. E	3
5. B	3	17. C	5
6. D	3	18. D	4
7. D	4	19. C	2
8. C	5	20. B	1
9. C	4	21. D	3
10. E	3	22. E	4
11. E	4	23. C	3
12. E	3	24. D	3

Section 5

Ans.	Level of Diff.	Ans.	Level of Diff.
1. A	1	13. C	4
2. C	2	14. A	3
3. B	3	15. D	5
4. E	4	16. B	2
5. D	5	17. D	3
6. C	5	18. E	4
7. D	4	19. C	3
8. D	5	20. E	3
9. B	3	21. D	3
10. A	4	22. A	5
11. E	3	23. A	3
12. C	4	24. C	4
		25. B	4

Section 8

Ans.	Level of Diff.	Ans.	Level of Diff.
1. B	1	11. C	3
2. A	2	12. E	3
3. D	3	13. B	3
4. E	4	14. D	3
5. B	4	15. A	4
6. B	5	16. D	3
7. D	4	17. D	5
8. B	3	18. C	3
9. A	2		
10. C	3		

MATH

Section 3

Ans.	Level of Diff.	Ans.	Level of Diff.
1. B	1	11. C	3
2. C	1	12. E	3
3. A	1	13. B	3
4. D	2	14. D	3
5. D	2	15. A	4
6. C	3	16. C	3
7. C	2	17. D	4
8. B	3	18. C	4
9. E	3	19. A	5
10. B	3	20. D	5

Section 6

Ans.	Level of Diff.	Ans.	Level of Diff.
1. E	1	11. 2	2
2. D	1	12. 6/11 or	3
3. A	2	.545	
4. C	2	13. 120	3
5. A	3	14. 2	3
6. B	3	15. 55	4
7. A	4	16. 446	4
8. E	4	17. 142	4
9. 16	1	18. 5/18 or	5
10. 7/11 or	1	.277	
.636		or .278	
or .637			

Section 9

Ans.	Level of Diff.	Ans.	Level of Diff.
1. B	1	9. D	4
2. E	1	10. D	3
3. E	2	11. C	3
4. B	2	12. A	4
5. C	2	13. D	4
6. D	3	14. E	4
7. E	3	15. B	5
8. E	3	16. A	5

WRITING

Section 7

Ans.	Level of Diff.	Ans.	Level of Diff.	Ans.	Level of Diff.
1. B	1	10. A	4	19. D	2
2. C	1	11. D	4	20. D	3
3. B	2	12. B	1	21. A	3
4. D	2	13. B	1	22. E	3
5. E	2	14. A	1	23. B	3
6. C	3	15. C	2	24. C	3
7. A	3	16. C	2	25. A	3
8. C	3	17. C	2	26. E	3
9. E	3	18. C	2	27. C	4

Section 10

Ans.	Level of Diff.	Ans.	Level of Diff.	Ans.	Level of Diff.
28. D	4	1. B	1	9. B	3
29. E	5	2. D	1	10. C	3
30. D	5	3. D	2	11. E	4
31. C	3	4. D	2	12. B	4
32. E	3	5. C	2	13. D	4
33. C	4	6. E	2	14. A	5
34. D	4	7. A	3		
35. E	4	8. C	3		

Score Your Own SAT Essay

Use this table as you rate your performance on the essay-writing section of this Practice Test. Circle the phrase that most accurately describes your work. Enter the numbers in the scoring chart below. Add the numbers together and divide by 6 to determine your total score. The higher your total score, the better you are likely to do on the essay section of the SAT.

Note that on the actual SAT two readers will rate your essay; your essay score will be the sum of their two ratings and could range from 12 (highest) to 2 (lowest). Also, they will grade your essay holistically, rating it on the basis of their overall impression of its effectiveness. They will *not* analyze it piece by piece, giving separate grades for grammar, vocabulary level, and so on. Therefore, you cannot expect the score you give yourself on this Practice Test to predict your eventual score on the SAT with any great degree of accuracy. Use this scoring guide instead to help you assess your writing strengths and weaknesses, so that you can decide which areas to focus on as you prepare for the SAT.

Like most people, you may find it difficult to rate your own writing objectively. Ask a teacher or fellow student to score your essay as well. With his or her help you should gain added insights into writing your 25-minute essay.

	6	5	4	3	2	1
POSITION ON THE TOPIC	Clear, convincing, & insightful	Fundamentally clear & coherent	Fairly clear & coherent	Insufficiently clear	Largely unclear	Extremely unclear
ORGANIZATION OF EVIDENCE	Well organized, with strong, relevant examples	Generally well organized, with apt examples	Adequately organized, with some examples	Sketchily developed, with weak examples	Lacking focus and evidence	Unfocused and disorganized
SENTENCE STRUCTURE	Varied, appealing sentences	Reasonably varied sentences	Some variety in sentences	Little variety in sentences	Errors in sentence structure	Severe errors in sentence structure
LEVEL OF VOCABULARY	Mature & apt word choice	Competent word choice	Adequate word choice	Inappropriate or weak vocabulary	Highly limited vocabulary	Rudimentary
GRAMMAR AND USAGE	Almost entirely free of errors	Relatively free of errors	Some technical errors	Minor errors, and some major ones	Numerous major errors	Extensive severe errors
OVERALL EFFECT	Outstanding	Effective	Adequately competent	Inadequate, but shows some potential	Seriously flawed	Fundamentally deficient

Self-Scoring Chart

For each of the following categories, rate the essay from 1 (lowest) to 6 (highest)

Position on the Topic _____

Organization of Evidence _____

Sentence Structure _____

Level of Vocabulary _____

Grammar and Usage _____

Overall Effect _____

TOTAL _____

(To get a score, divide the total by 6) _____

Scoring Chart (Second Reader)

For each of the following categories, rate the essay from 1 (lowest) to 6 (highest)

Position on the Topic _____

Organization of Evidence _____

Sentence Structure _____

Level of Vocabulary _____

Grammar and Usage _____

Overall Effect _____

TOTAL _____

(To get a score, divide the total by 6) _____

Scoring Practice Test 4

Refer to the answer key for Practice Test 2 on page 286. Then use the Scoring Worksheet below to determine your raw scores for Critical Reading, Mathematics, and Writing. For each section, give yourself one point for each answer that is correct. Your total raw score is the total number of correct answer points minus $\frac{1}{4}$ of the total number of incorrect answer points. Round off the total raw score to the nearest whole number to get your Rounded Raw Score. Convert your raw scores to scaled scores using the Conversion Tables on pages 290–291.

SCORING WORKSHEET

Critical Reading

Section 2 $\underset{\text{number correct}}{\rule{3cm}{0.4pt}} - \frac{1}{4}\left(\underset{\text{number incorrect}}{\rule{3cm}{0.4pt}} \right) = \underset{}{\rule{3cm}{0.4pt}}$ (A)

Section 5 $\underset{\text{number correct}}{\rule{3cm}{0.4pt}} - \frac{1}{4}\left(\underset{\text{number incorrect}}{\rule{3cm}{0.4pt}} \right) = \underset{}{\rule{3cm}{0.4pt}}$ (B)

Section 8 $\underset{\text{number correct}}{\rule{3cm}{0.4pt}} - \frac{1}{4}\left(\underset{\text{number incorrect}}{\rule{3cm}{0.4pt}} \right) = \underset{}{\rule{3cm}{0.4pt}}$ (C)

Critical Reading Raw Score = (A) + (B) + (C) = _____

Critical Reading Scaled Score (See Table 1) = _____

Mathematics

Section 3 $\underset{\text{number correct}}{\rule{3cm}{0.4pt}} - \frac{1}{4}\left(\underset{\text{number incorrect}}{\rule{3cm}{0.4pt}} \right) = \underset{}{\rule{3cm}{0.4pt}}$ (D)

Section 6
Part I
(1–8) $\underset{\text{number correct}}{\rule{3cm}{0.4pt}} - \frac{1}{4}\left(\underset{\text{number incorrect}}{\rule{3cm}{0.4pt}} \right) = \underset{}{\rule{3cm}{0.4pt}}$ (E)

Part II
(9–18) $\underset{\text{number correct}}{\rule{3cm}{0.4pt}}$ $= \underset{}{\rule{3cm}{0.4pt}}$ (F)

Section 9 $\underset{\text{number correct}}{\rule{3cm}{0.4pt}} - \frac{1}{4}\left(\underset{\text{number incorrect}}{\rule{3cm}{0.4pt}} \right) = \underset{}{\rule{3cm}{0.4pt}}$ (G)

Mathematics Raw Score = (D) + (E) + (F) + (G) = _____

Mathematics Scaled Score (See Table 2) = _____

Writing

Essay $\dfrac{}{\text{score 1}} + \dfrac{}{\text{score 2}}$ = _____ (H)

Section 7 $\dfrac{}{\text{number correct}} - \dfrac{1}{4}\left(\dfrac{}{\text{number incorrect}} \right)$ = _____ (I)

Section 10 $\dfrac{}{\text{number correct}} - \dfrac{1}{4}\left(\dfrac{}{\text{number incorrect}} \right)$ = _____ (J)

Writing Raw Score = I + J (H is a separate subscore) = _____

Writing Scaled Score (See Table 3) = _____

TABLE 1: CRITICAL READING CONVERSION TABLE

Raw Score	Scaled Score	Raw Score	Scaled Score	Raw Score	Scaled Score	Raw Score	Scaled Score
67	800	49	630	31	510	14	400
66	790	48	620	30	510	13	400
65	790	47	610	29	500	12	390
64	780	46	610	28	490	11	380
63	770	45	600	27	490	10	370
62	760	44	590	26	480	9	360
61	750	43	590	25	480	8	350
60	740	42	580	24	470	7	340
59	730	41	570	23	460	6	330
58	720	40	570	22	460	5	320
57	710	39	560	21	450	4	310
56	700	38	550	20	440	3	300
55	690	37	550	19	440	2	280
54	680	36	540	18	430	1	270
53	670	35	540	17	420	0	260
52	660	34	530	16	420	−1	230
51	650	33	520	15	410	−2 and below	210
50	640	32	520				

TABLE 2: MATH CONVERSION TABLE

Math Raw Score	Math Scaled Score	Math Raw Score	Math Scaled Score	Math Raw Score	Math Scaled Score	Math Raw Score	Math Scaled Score
54	800	40	630	26	500	12	390
53	790	39	620	25	500	11	380
52	770	38	610	24	490	10	370
51	750	37	600	23	480	9	360
50	730	36	590	22	470	8	340
49	710	35	580	21	460	7	330
48	700	34	570	20	450	6	320
47	690	33	560	19	450	5	300
46	680	32	560	18	440	4	290
45	670	31	550	17	430	3	270
44	660	30	540	16	420	2	250
43	650	29	530	15	410	1	240
42	640	28	520	14	410	0	230
41	640	27	510	13	400	−1 and below	200

TABLE 3: WRITING CONVERSION TABLE

Writing Raw Score	Essay Score					
	6	5	4	3	2	1
49	800	800	770	740	710	680
48	800	790	750	710	680	650
47	790	760	720	690	660	630
46	770	740	700	670	640	610
45	760	730	690	650	620	590
44	740	710	670	640	610	580
43	730	700	660	620	600	570
42	720	690	650	610	580	550
41	710	670	630	600	570	540
40	690	660	620	590	560	530
39	680	650	610	580	550	520
38	670	640	600	570	540	510
37	670	630	590	560	530	500
36	660	630	590	550	520	490
35	650	620	580	540	510	480
34	640	610	570	530	510	480
33	630	600	560	530	500	470
32	620	590	550	520	490	460
31	620	590	550	510	480	450
30	610	580	540	500	480	450
29	600	570	530	500	470	440
28	590	560	520	490	460	430
27	590	560	520	480	450	430
26	580	550	510	480	450	420
25	570	540	500	470	440	410
24	570	540	500	460	440	410
23	560	530	490	460	430	400
22	560	520	480	450	420	390
21	550	520	480	440	420	390
20	540	510	470	440	410	380
19	540	510	470	430	400	370
18	530	500	460	430	400	370
17	520	490	450	420	390	360
16	520	490	450	410	380	350
15	510	480	440	410	380	350
14	500	470	430	400	370	340
13	500	470	430	390	370	340
12	490	460	420	390	360	330
11	480	450	410	380	350	320
10	480	450	410	370	350	320
9	470	440	400	370	340	310
8	460	430	390	360	330	300
7	460	420	390	350	320	290
6	450	420	380	340	310	280
5	440	410	370	330	310	280
4	430	400	360	320	300	270
3	420	390	350	310	280	250
2	400	360	330	300	270	240
1	390	360	320	290	260	230
0	370	340	300	270	240	210

ANSWERS EXPLAINED
Section 2 Critical Reading

1. **A** The phrase "surest way to spoil" signals that the best choice is to *indulge* (pander to) a child's every whim.

2. **D** *Edifice* (elaborate conceptual structure) is the best choice because it makes sense that the theory of evolution is built on an elaborate conceptual structure.

3. **E** The words "based more on wishful thinking than on solid evidence" signal that scholars *dismiss* (reject) the theory.

4. **E** Evolution might be largely a process in which there are short periods of change, so *fitful* intermittent) makes sense. These periods are followed by other periods, which presumably are different in nature, so *stasis* (motionless state) makes sense.

5. **B** The adjective *nearly* in the sentence signals that social problems cannot be totally solved but they can be *ameliorated* (improved).

6. **D** It makes sense that having *anonymous* (unknown) peers review scientific findings makes it difficult for any one person or institution to *dictate* (control) what those findings are.

7. **D** The words "from well-substantiated material" signal that the answer requires a contrasting word. *Apocryphal* (made up), therefore, is the best choice.

8. **C** *Anarchism* is the theory that all government is unnecessary and should be abolished. Marxists believe that with Communism government will *inevitably* (in a way that is impossible to avoid) cease to exist.

9. **C** In lines 14–16 the author says, "None of these elements were in their own natures imperishable. Left to themselves, they would hasten to dissolution" (termination by disintegration).

10. **E** The author says, "The piety of . . . of their existence" (lines 18–25). The words "suspend" (line 21) and "prolongation" (line 25) signal that this process cannot continue forever.

11. **E** The Jains believe that the *discipline* (technique aimed at helping an individual to achieve a specific purpose) of inactivity and nonviolence "purges the mind and body of all desires and actions" (lines 20–21), achieving the goal of "burn[ing] off the consequences of actions performed in the past" (lines 22–23).

12. **E** The author explains the Jain view that the soul "through action accumulates particles of matter that . . . determine its fate" (lines 7–9).

13. **E** From how she describes Mr. Donleavy's speech we can infer that the author thinks he is part of a system that favors whites over blacks. Thus, she most likely believed that the principal was naive because he seemed to think men like Mr. Donleavy were kindly toward blacks.

14. **C** From the writer's attitude to Mr. Donleavy throughout the passage it can be seen that she believes the audience accepted whatever he said without question. Thus, we can infer that she believes that the "Amens" and "Yes, sirs" showed that the audience was docile and fawning.

15. **E** It is unlikely that the white man did not know that the empty seat belonged to the principal, who was at the speaker's platform. Thus, it is reasonable to infer that he felt superior to the assembled people.

16. **E** Choice E makes the best sense because the word "ancient" suggests the many forms of racial prejudice on the part of whites against blacks over the years rather than a specific form or example of it.

17. **C** The author emphasizes that the school authorities regarded blacks as not being suitable for jobs requiring a high level of education, so it is reasonable to infer that the author intended these remarks as reflecting the view of most white people at the time. Also, the author portrays most of the black students as largely accepting— however reluctantly—their inferior position in society, so it is reasonable to infer that the author intends these remarks to reflect the view of many black people.

18. **D** There is no use of *paradox* (apparent contradiction) in Passage 1. All of the others are used.

19. **C** The author of Passage 2 says, "With other black . . . mine own house?" (lines 159–165).

20. **B** In lines 129–144 ("It is in . . . a vast veil."), the author of Passage 2 describes how as a child he came to realize that black people are treated differently than white people and are not accepted by them.

21. **D** In lines 165–171 ("The shades of . . . of blue above."), the author of Passage 2 describes how "the prison-house closed round us all." It can be inferred that the prison house symbolizes the prevailing attitudes and limited opportunities available to both whites and blacks. The author says that the prison's walls were "stubborn"—that is difficult, but not impossible to scale—to the white people but "unscalable" to blacks.

22. **E** The author of Passage 2 describes how as a child he reacted to being excluded from the white people's world, first holding it in "contempt" (line 147) and beating white children at various things, and then desiring to "wrest [prizes] from them" (line 156). Also, he describes some black boys as reacting by "[shrinking] into tasteless sycophancy" (line 161); *sycophancy* means *servile flattery*. It is thus reasonable to infer that the author would describe the principal's behavior as *obsequious* (full of servile compliance).

23. **C** The tone of Passage 2 is predominantly matter-of-fact and rather dignified. It is certainly not sarcastic. In contrast, sarcasm is used regularly in Passage 1. There are a number of examples, a striking one of which is the parenthetical remark, "naturally, the white school was Central" (line 56).

24. **D** Passage 1 does not use symbolism, whereas it is important in Passage 2, notably the "shadow" (line 132), the "vast veil" (line 144), the "blue sky" (lines 147–148), and the "prison-house" (line 166).

Section 3 Mathematics

<u>Note:</u>

1. See page 32 for an explanation of the symbol $\Rightarrow$ that is used in some answer explanations.

2. A calculator icon, is placed next to the answer explanation of any question for which a calculator *could* be useful. Almost always, the question can be answered easily without using a calculator.

3. If you are unfamiliar with any of the math facts used in the following answer explanations, refer to Barron's *SAT*, which, in addition to having practice tests, has a full review of all the math you need to know.

1. **B** $5a + 30 = a + 2a + 3a + 4a = 10a$. So $10a = 5a + 30$. Subtracting $5a$ from each side, we get that $5a = 30$, and so $a = 6$.

2. **C** Since 1 hap = 8 daps, then 3 haps = $3 \times (8 \text{ daps}) = 24$ daps. Now set up a proportion. $\dfrac{x \text{ baps}}{3 \text{ haps}} = \dfrac{x \text{ baps}}{24 \text{ daps}} = \dfrac{1 \text{ bap}}{6 \text{ daps}}$. So $6x = 24$, and $x = 4$.

3. **A** If a product is equal to 0, then one of the factors must be 0. So if $a(b - c) = 0$, then either $a = 0$ or $b - c = 0$. Since it is given that a is negative, $a \neq 0$, and, therefore, $b - c = 0$. So $b = c$.

4. **D** If (x, y) is in the interior of square $ABCD$ and x and y are both integers, then there are seven possible values for x: $-3, -2, -1, 0, 1, 2,$ and 3, and the same seven values for y.
   So there are $7 \times 7 = 49$ points inside the square with integer coordinates:
   $$(-3, 3), (-3, 2), (-3, 1), (-3, 0), (-3, -1), (-3, -2), (-3, -3)$$
   $$(-2, 3), (-2, 2)\dots\dots\dots\dots\dots\dots\dots\dots\dots\dots\dots (-2, -3)$$
   $$\dots\dots\dots\dots\dots\dots\dots\dots\dots\dots\dots\dots\dots\dots\dots\dots\dots\dots$$
   $$(3, 3), (3, 2)\dots\dots\dots\dots\dots\dots\dots\dots\dots\dots\dots (3, -3)$$

5. **D** **Solution 1.** Let A and S represent the average and sum of the set of n numbers. Then by the definition of average, $S = nA$. So,
   $$A = x\%(S) = \frac{x}{100} S = \frac{x}{100}(nA)$$
   Dividing by A, we get $1 = \dfrac{x}{100} n$ and $x = \dfrac{100}{n}$.

Solution 2. Pick an easy example. The average of the three numbers, 4, 5, and 6, is 5, and their sum is 15. 5 is $\frac{1}{3}$ or $33\frac{1}{3}\%$ of 15. Which answer choice is equal to $33\frac{1}{3}$ when $n = 3$? Only choice (D): $\frac{100}{3} = 33\frac{1}{3}$

6. **C** To maximize $R_x - R_y$, choose the largest possible value for R_x and subtract the smallest possible value for R_y. When an integer is divided by 8, the possible remainders are 0, 1, 2, 3, 4, 5, 6, and 7. So, the largest possible value of R_x is 7. R_y cannot equal 0, because only multiples of 8 have a remainder of 0 when divided by 8, so the smallest possible value of R_y is 1. Finally, $7 - 1 = 6$.

7. **C** **Solution 1.** Since the measure of an exterior angle of a triangle is equal to the sum of the measures of the two opposite interior angles, $a = b + 90$. Since $a = 5b$, we have $b + 90 = 5b$, so $4b = 90$ and $b = 22.5$. Then, $c + 90 + 22.5 = 180 \Rightarrow c + 112.5 = 180 \Rightarrow c = 67.5$.

Solution 2. Since $a + c = 180$, $c = 180 - a$. Then, since $b + c + 90 = 180$, we have $b + (180 - a) + 90 = 180$ and so $b - a + 90 = 0$. But $a = 5b$, so $b - 5b + 90 = 0 \Rightarrow 4b = 90$. So, $b = 22.5$ and, as above, $c = 67.5$.

8. **B** **Solution 1.** Set up a proportion: $\dfrac{b \text{ bolts}}{h \text{ hours}} = \dfrac{c \text{ bolts}}{x \text{ hours}}$.

Cross-multiply $bx = ch$, so $x = \dfrac{ch}{b}$.

Solution 2. Plug in some easy-to-use numbers, say $b = 4$ and $h = 2$. Then, since the machine produces four bolts in 2 hours, it is producing bolts at the rate of two per hour. So it will take 3 hours to produce six bolts.

Which answer choices are equal to 3 when $b = 4$, $h = 2$, and $c = 6$? Only choice (B): $\dfrac{(6)(2)}{4} = 3$

E **Solution 1.** If P represents the vase's original price, then the sale price was $P - 25\%P = 75\%P$. So, $0.75P = 180$ and $P = 180 \div 0.75 = 240$.

Solution 2. Equivalently, you could use fractions. Since $75\% = \dfrac{3}{4}$, we have

$$\frac{3}{4}P = 180 \Rightarrow P = 180 \div \frac{3}{4} = \overset{60}{\cancel{180}} \times \frac{4}{\cancel{3}_1} = 240.$$

Solution 3. If you get stuck, this is the type of question that can easily be answered by backsolving. Test choice (C), $205: 25\%$ of $205 = 51.25$ and $205 - 51.25 = 153.75$, which is too small. Eliminate choices (A), (B), and (C) and test choice (D) or (E). (D) is also too small; (E) works: 25% of $240 = 60$, and $240 - 60 = 180$.

10. **B** The lengths of four of the six sides of hexagon *ABCDEF* are given in the diagram. It is impossible to determine the lengths of the other two—$\overline{BC}$ and $\overline{EF}$—but all we need is the sum of their lengths, which we can calculate as follows: Since triangle *ABC* is a 5-12-13 right triangle, $BF = 13$; and since triangle *CDE* is a 3-4-5 right triangle, $CE = 5$. So $BC + EF = 13 - 5 = 8$. Finally, $5 + 12 + 3 + 4 + 8 = 32$.

11. **C** The midpoint of the range from 60 to 100 is 80, and a paragraph of *w* words will be acceptable if *w* differs from 80 by no more than 20 (i.e., *w* could be as much as 20 less than 80 or 20 more than 80). The inequality that expresses this is $|x - 80| \le 20$.

12. **E** **Solution 1.** If *x* represents Fran's age now, then 12 years from now she will be $x + 12$, and 15 years ago she was $x - 15$. Therefore, $x + 12 = 4(x - 15) = 4x - 60$. Hence, $3x = 72$ and $x = 24$.

Solution 2. Even if you don't like word problems such as these, you must answer them. Eliminate all the absurd answer choices and then test the others or guess. Clearly, choices (A), (B), and (C) are wrong because if Fran were 9 or 12 or 15 now, 15 years ago her age would have been 0 or negative. So the answer must be (D) or (E). If Fran is now 21, 15 years ago she was 6, and 12 years from now she will be 33, which is *not* 4 times 6. The answer must be (E), which, of course, you can verify is correct.

13. **B Solution 1.** If a is in A, and b is in B, then a is odd, b is even, and so $a + b$ is odd. The smallest value of $a + b$ is $1 + 2 = 3$ and the largest value of $a + b$ is $5 + 6 = 11$. So the only possibilities for $a + b$ are the five odd integers 3, 5, 7, 9, and 11, and it is easy to verify that each of them is possible.

Solution 2. Simply list all the sums and eliminate duplicates.

+	2	4	6
1	③	⑤	⑦
3	~~5~~	~~7~~	⑨
5	~~7~~	~~9~~	⑪

14. **D** Let $PT = x$. Then, $PR = 2x$ and the perimeter of $\triangle PQR$ is equal to $2x + 2x + 2x = 6x$. The perimeter of rectangle $PRST = x + 2x + x + 2x = 6x$. So the perimeters are equal: eliminate choices (A) and (B). The area of rectangle $PRST = lw = (2x)x = 2x^2$.

The area of $\triangle PQR = \dfrac{1}{2}bh = \dfrac{1}{2}(2x)(x\sqrt{3}) = \sqrt{3}x^2$

Since $\sqrt{3} < 2$, the area of $\triangle PQR <$ the area of rectangle $PRST$.

15. **A Solution 1.** $f(a + 2) = (a + 2)^2 + (a + 2) = (a^2 + 4a + 4) + (a + 2) = a^2 + 5a + 6$. Then, since $f(a) = f(a + 2)$,

we have $\cancel{a^2} + a = \cancel{a^2} + 5a + 6 \Rightarrow a = 5a + 6 \Rightarrow -4a = 6$. So $a = -\dfrac{6}{4} = -\dfrac{3}{2}$.

Solution 2. You can backsolve, starting with the integers. You can easily verify that $f(-1) \neq f(1)$, $f(0) \neq f(2)$, and $f(1) \neq f(3)$. Now try the fractions:

$f\left(-\dfrac{3}{2}\right) = \left(-\dfrac{3}{2}\right)^2 + \left(-\dfrac{3}{2}\right) = \dfrac{9}{4} - \dfrac{3}{2} = \dfrac{9}{4} - \dfrac{6}{4} = \dfrac{3}{4}$ and $f\left(\dfrac{1}{2}\right) = \left(\dfrac{1}{2}\right)^2 + \left(\dfrac{1}{2}\right) = \dfrac{1}{4} + \dfrac{1}{2} = \dfrac{1}{4} + \dfrac{2}{4} = \dfrac{3}{4}$. So, choice (A) works.

16. **C** If $|3n - 17| < n$, then n must be positive and $-n < (3n - 17) < n$. Therefore, $-4n < -17 < -2n$. Multiplying the inequality above by -1, and remembering to reverse the signs because we are multiplying by a negative

number, we get $4n > 17 > 2n$. So $4n > 17$, which means that $n > \dfrac{17}{4} = 4.25$

and $17 > 2n$, which means that $n < \dfrac{17}{2} = 8.5$. There are four integers that

satisfy the inequality $4.25 < n < 8.5$, namely, 5, 6, 7, and 8.

17. **D** Since the volume of the cube is 64, we have $64 = e^3$, and so each edge of the cube is 4. $\overline{MG}$ is the hypotenuse of right triangle MHG, so by the Pythagorean theorem, $(MG)^2 = 2^2 + 4^2 = 4 + 16 = 20$. Also, $\overline{MN}$ is the hypotenuse of right triangle MGN, so by the Pythagorean theorem, $(MN)^2 = (MG)^2 + 2^2 = 20 + 4 = 24$, and $MN = \sqrt{24}$.

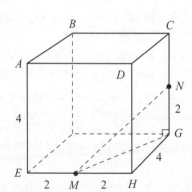

18. **C**
   - $26 \star 25 = 26 + 27 + \ldots + 50$.
   - $25 \star 26 = 25 + 26 + 27 + \ldots + 50$.
   - So $(25 \star 26) - (26 \star 25) = (25 + \cancel{26} + \cancel{27} + \ldots + \cancel{50}) - (\cancel{26} + \cancel{27} + \ldots + \cancel{50}) = 25$.

19. **A** **Solution 1.** $a^7 = a^5 a^2 = (5b)a^2$. But, $a^7 = 11$. So, $5ba^2 = 11 \Rightarrow b = \dfrac{11}{5a^2}$.

    Solution 2. Since $a^5 = 5b$, then $b = \dfrac{a^5}{5}$. But $\dfrac{a^5}{5}$ isn't an answer choice, so you have to find an equivalent

    expression. Since $a^5 = \dfrac{a^7}{a^2} = \dfrac{11}{a^2}$, $\dfrac{a^5}{5} = \dfrac{\frac{11}{a^2}}{5} = \dfrac{11}{5a^2}$.

     Solution 3. Use your calculator: $a \approx 1.4$, the seventh root of 11; $a^2 \approx 2$; and $a^5 \approx 5.5$.
    Since $a^5 = 5b$, we have that $b \approx 1.1$. Only answer choice A is even close.

20. **D** **Solution 1.** Since the radius of each circle is 2, the area of each circle
    is $\pi(2)^2 = 4\pi$. Then the area of quarter-circle DAC is π. So the striped area
    in the diagram at the right is $4 - \pi$, the area of the square minus the area of
    the quarter-circle. Finally, since the area of quarter circle BAC is π, the
    shaded area is $\pi - (4 - \pi) = 2\pi - 4$.

    Solution 2. Estimate. The shaded region appears to take up about half of the
    square, whose area is 4. Approximating π by 3, quickly evaluate the answer

    choices. They are: $\dfrac{1}{2}$, 1, 4, 2, and 4. Clearly the answer is (D).

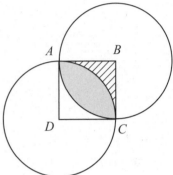

Section 5 Critical Reading

1. **A** It makes sense that *stringent* (imposing rigorous standards) criteria must be met for the results of an experiment to be accepted.

2. **C** The words *so that the author's meaning would be clear* signal that the editor checked for language that was *ambiguous* (unclear in meaning).

3. **B** The words "do irreparable harm" signal that a negative word is needed to describe the dealings; therefore, the best choice is *duplicitous* (deliberately deceptive).

4. **E** The words "build on the work of" signal that *predecessors* (ones who precede others in time) is the best choice for the first blank. *Comprehensive* (thorough) makes the best sense for the second blank because it is reasonable that philosophers build on past work to create a more complete view of reality.

5. **D** Choices (B) *argue*, and (D) *contend* both make sense for the first blank. (A) *utilization*, (D) *husbanding* (conserving) and, to a lesser extent, (E) *preservation* all make sense for the second blank. Therefore, choice (D) is correct.

6. **C** Choices (A) *a comprehensive* (thorough) and (C) *an implicit* (understood but not stated) both make sense for the first blank. (C) *subscribe to* (express approval of) makes good sense with *implicit*, whereas (A) *question* does not make sense with *comprehensive*.

7. **D** The author is saying that Lomazzo's choice of man as Raphael's emblem was more in keeping with Raphael's art than were Lomazzo's choices of emblems for the other artists.

8. **D** The author is stressing that Raphael's art was harmonious, so it makes sense that he would reinforce his point with a balanced, harmonious phrase expressing this idea.

9. **B** Both authors emphasize that harmony is one of the main virtues of Raphael's art. The author of Passage 1 stresses harmony, saying, "To keep all artistic elements in perfect equilibrium . . . seemed the mainspring of this action" (lines 14–17). The author of Passage 2 does not stress harmony as much as the author of Passage 1 does, but he says the following, suggesting harmony is an important virtue of Raphael's art: "Mankind is once more gifted with the harmony of intellect and flesh and feeling" (lines 40–41).

10. **A** Choice (A) accurately summarizes the main argument made in each passage.

11. **E** *Hinterlands* means *remote country regions* and makes good sense in context.

12. **C** Presumably, the image of the snowball was used by the author in an earlier part of the book from which this passage was taken. However, it can be inferred that the "snowball" mentioned in line 28 refers to the

accumulating efforts of Americans to destroy the Japanese because the author is describing the steps taken by Americans to prevent Japanese nationals, Japanese aliens, and Japanese-Americans in America from aiding Japan in the war against America. He says, "The snowball was big enough to wipe out the rising sun" (lines 28–29), suggesting that these efforts had stopped the Japanese threat on American soil.

13. **C** *Sarcastic* (characterized by words that mean the opposite of what they seem to mean and are intended to mock) is the best choice. It is likely that the author is being sarcastic because it would not require "the utmost of America's great organizing ability" (line 40) to construct camps and put people in them as described in the passage.

14. **A** Because America was at war with Japan, it makes sense that some people would hire a person that they believed was Chinese but not a person they believed to be Japanese.

15. **D** A *euphemism* (a word or phrase used in place of a term that might be considered too direct, unpleasant, or offensive) is the best choice because "relocation center" can be seen as a pleasant way of saying "concentration camp" (line 81).

16. **B** *Strange* is the best choice because the lieutenant says, "That's funny," after he is told about the removal of the Japanese from the coast and the construction of relocation centers for them. The narrator says, "He didn't believe it" (lines 83–84), suggesting that the lieutenant thought it was strange that this was being done.

17. **D** The author says, "If the nuclear forces had been slightly stronger then they are . . . hydrogen would be a rare element, and stars like the sun . . . could not exist" (lines 11–18).

18. **E** The author uses the word *extravagantly* to emphasize that the stars in an average galaxy are separated by a distance that is far greater than appears to be necessary.

19. **C** After referring to astrology, the author says, "But it happens to be true that we could not have survived if the average distance between stars were only two trillion miles instead of twenty" (lines 46–49). It makes sense that the author refers to astrology to stress how remarkable it is that far away stars affect life on Earth because astrology also says that far away stars affect life on Earth.

20. **E** The main argument in the passage is that the universe seems designed for life, so it is reasonable that the word "decisive" in line 44 means *conclusive*. The author is saying that without the great distances between stars life would be impossible.

21. **D** The author says, "Without such accidents . . . hydrogen atoms could not form breakable bridges between molecules" (lines 69–73).

22. **A** The author says he is "a scientist, trained in the habits of thought and language of the twentieth century rather than the eighteenth" (lines 77–80). He is contrasting the way a twentieth-century scientist is trained to think with the way people were trained to think in the eighteenth century. Such training produces "habits of thought"—that is, recurrent patterns of thinking.

23. **A** This is the best choice because the passage is mainly about the place of life, in general, in the universe, not about how the human species originated.

24. **C** The author says, "I conclude from the existence of these accidents of physics and astronomy that the universe is an unexpectedly hospitable place for living creatures to make their home" (lines 74–77). The discovery of life on a planet of another star in our galaxy would provide evidence that life is not unique to Earth.

25. **B** The author says, "I do not claim that the architecture of the universe proves the existence of God. I claim only that the architecture of the universe is consistent with the hypothesis that mind plays an essential role in its functioning" (lines 80–84) The author would probably agree that what he calls the "accidents" of physics and astronomy suggest fairly strongly that the universe was designed, presumably by some powerful agency, such as God.

Section 6 Mathematics

Note:

1. See page 32 for an explanation of the symbol ⇒ that is used in some answer explanations.

2. A calculator icon, 🖩, is placed next to the answer explanation of any question for which a calculator *could* be useful. Almost always, the question can be answered easily without using a calculator.

3. If you are unfamiliar with any of the math facts used in the following answer explanations, refer to Barron's *SAT*, which, in addition to having practice tests, has a full review of all the math you need to know.

1. **E** **Solution 1.**

$\frac{1}{n}+\frac{1}{n}+\frac{1}{n}+\frac{1}{n}=\frac{4}{n}$. So, $\frac{4}{n}=\frac{b}{4}$. Therefore, $nb = 16$, and $n=\frac{16}{b}$.

Solution 2. Plug in a number for n, say $n = 2$. Then $\frac{1}{2}+\frac{1}{2}+\frac{1}{2}+\frac{1}{2}=\frac{b}{4}$.

So, $2=\frac{b}{4}$ and $b = 8$. Which of the choices is equal to 2 when $b = 8$? Only choice (E): $\frac{16}{8}=2$

2. **D** Let x represent the number of kilometers Daniel drove, and set up a proportion:

$$\frac{\text{kilometers}}{\text{miles}}: \quad \frac{1 \text{ kilometer}}{\frac{5}{8}\text{ miles}}=\frac{x \text{ kilometers}}{100 \text{ miles}}$$

Then, cross-multiplying, we get $100=\frac{5}{8}x \Rightarrow x=\frac{8}{\overset{1}{\cancel{5}}}(\overset{20}{\cancel{100}})=160$.

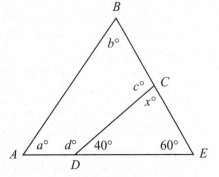

3. **A** **Solution 1.** The easiest solution is to realize that line segment $\overline{CD}$ is irrelevant. In triangle ABE, $a + b + 60 = 180$, and so $a + b = 120$.

Solution 2. If you didn't see that, then consider the diagram at the right. Since $40 + 60 + x = 180$, we have $x = 80$. Then since $x + c = 180$ and $40 + d = 180$, we have $c = 100$ and $d = 140$.
Finally, since the sum of the measures of the four angles in quadrilateral $ABCD$ is 360°, we have $a + b + 100 + 140 = 360$, and so $a + b = 120$.

4. **C** 300% of 3 is equal to $\frac{300}{100}\times 3=3\times 3=9$. So $3 \times 300\%$ of 3 is equal to $3 \times 9 = 27$. Only choice (C), 900% of 3, is equal to 27. (900% of 3: $\frac{900}{100}\times 3=9\times 3=27$)

5. **A** To answer any question about maps or scale drawings, set up a proportion and cross-multiply:

$$\frac{\text{miles}}{\text{centimeters}}: \quad \frac{m}{c}=\frac{n}{x} \Rightarrow mx=cn$$

So, $x=\frac{cn}{m}$.

6. **B**
   - $3 \times 8^{100} = 3 \times (8 \times 8^{99}) = 24 \times 8^{99}$.
   - $4\times 8^{98}=4\times \frac{8^{99}}{8}=\frac{4}{8}\times 8^{99}=\frac{1}{2}\times 8^{99}$.
   - So $3\times 8^{100}+4\times 8^{98}=24\times 8^{99}+\frac{1}{2}\times 8^{99}=24\frac{1}{2}\times 8^{99}=24.5\times 8^{99}$.

7. **A** Since $a_4 = a_2 + a_3 + 5$, and since $a_4, = 10$, we have $a_2 + a_3 = 5$. Similarly, since $a_3 = a_1 + a_2 + 5$, and since $a_1 = 1$, we have $a_3 = 1 + a_2 + 5 = a_2 + 6$. Then, $5 = a_2 + a_3 = a_2 + (a_2 + 6) = 2a_2 + 6$. So, $2a_2 = -1$, and $a_2 = -\dfrac{1}{2}$.

8. **E** Using the formula $A = \dfrac{1}{2}bh$, we can calculate the area of $\triangle ABC$ in two ways: $A = \dfrac{1}{2}(AB)(CD)$ and

$A = \dfrac{1}{2}(BC)(AE)$.

- $\dfrac{1}{2}(AB)(CD) = \dfrac{1}{2}(12)(11) = 66$

- $\dfrac{1}{2}(BC)(AE) = \dfrac{1}{2}(BC)(10) = 5(BC)$

- So, $5(BC) = 66$ and $BC = \dfrac{66}{5} = 13\dfrac{1}{5} = 13.2$

9. **16** **Solution 1.** Set up a proportion:

$$\frac{330 \text{ envelopes}}{1 \text{ hour}} = \frac{330 \text{ envelopes}}{60 \text{ minutes}} = \frac{88 \text{ envelopes}}{m \text{ minutes}}$$

Then $330m = (60) \times (88) = 5{,}280$, and $m = 5{,}280 \div 330 = 16$.

Solution 2. Since Ali stuffs 330 envelopes in 60 minutes, it takes her $\dfrac{60}{330} = \dfrac{6}{33}$ minutes to stuff 1 envelope

and so it takes $^8\cancel{88} \times \dfrac{\cancel{6}^2}{\cancel{33}_{\cancel{3}_1}} = 8 \times 2 = 16$ minutes.

10. $\dfrac{\mathbf{7}}{\mathbf{11}}$ or **.636** or **.637**

If $3 + 4 + x = (3)(4)x$, then $7 + x = 12x$. So, $7 = 11x$ and $x = \dfrac{7}{11}$.

11. **2** $96 = (5b + 2)(5b - 2) = 25b^2 - 4$. So, $25b^2 = 100 \Rightarrow b^2 = 4 \Rightarrow b = 2$.

12. $\dfrac{\mathbf{6}}{\mathbf{11}}$ or **.545** Since $c = 1.1a$ and $d = 1.2b$, and since $\dfrac{d}{c} = 2$, we have $\dfrac{1.2b}{1.1a} = 2$. So, $1.2b = 2.2a$ and

$\dfrac{a}{b} = \dfrac{1.2}{2.2} = \dfrac{12}{22} = \dfrac{6}{11}$.

13. **120** The only reasonable way to answer this question is to use the counting principle. There are 4 ways to choose the student, 10 ways to choose the teacher, and 3 ways to choose the administrator. So there are $4 \times 10 \times 3 = 120$ different ways to form the subcommittee.

14. **2** Let r_1, r_2, C_1, and C_2 represent the radii and the circumferences of circles 1 and 2, respectively. Then $C_1 - C_2 = 1$ foot. So $1 = 2\pi r_1 - 2\pi r_2 = 2\pi(r_1 - r_2)$. Then $r_1 - r_2 = \dfrac{1}{2\pi} \approx \dfrac{1}{6.28} \approx \dfrac{1}{6}$. Finally, $\dfrac{1}{6}$ of a foot is 2 inches. A more precise answer would be, $\dfrac{1}{2\pi}(12)$, which is approximately 1.9, but you were asked for the difference to the nearest inch.

15. **55** $x^2 - y^2 = (x + y)(x - y) = (1{,}000{,}000 + 999{,}999)(1{,}000{,}000 - 999{,}999) = (1{,}999{,}999)(1) = 1{,}999{,}999$. The sum of the digits of $1{,}999{,}999$ is $1 + 9 + 9 + 9 + 9 + 9 + 9 = 55$.

16. **446** Since $h(x) = 7x - 2$, then $h(11) = 7(11) - 2 = 77 - 2 = 75$. So $b = 75$ and $b - 11 = 64$. Finally, $h(b - 11) = h(64) = 7(64) - 2 = 448 - 2 = 446$.

17. **142** Let x = the number of children who have both a cat and a dog. Then $211 - x$ children have a dog but no cat, and $174 - x$ children have a cat but no dog. This is illustrated in the Venn diagram below.

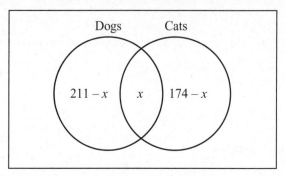

Since 83 children have neither a dog nor a cat, $326 - 83 = 243$ children have a dog, a cat, or both. So,
$(211 - x) + x + (174 - x) = 243 \Rightarrow 385 - x = 243 \Rightarrow x = 385 - 243 = 142.$

18. $\dfrac{5}{18}$ or **.277** or **.278** From the wording of the question it is clear that the answer does not depend on the

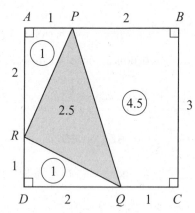

dimensions of rectangle $ABCD$. So, simplify the problem by assuming

that $ABCD$ is a square whose sides are 3. Then the areas of triangles PAR and QDR are each

$\dfrac{1}{2}(1)(2) = 1$, and the area of trapezoid $PBCQ$ is

$\dfrac{1}{2}(3)(1+2) = \dfrac{1}{2}3(3) = \dfrac{9}{2} = 4.5$. So the area of the

white region is $1 + 1 + 4.5 = 6.5$.
If you don't know the formula for the area of a
trapezoid, draw in the dotted line to divide the

trapezoid into a triangle of area $\dfrac{1}{2}(1)(3) = 1\dfrac{1}{2} = 1.5$ and

a rectangle of area $1 \times 3 = 3$. So, again, the total
area of the white region is $1 + 1 + 1.5 + 3 = 6.5$.
Then, the area of the shaded triangle is
9 (the area of the square) $-$ 6.5 (the white area) = 2.5.

Finally, $\dfrac{2.5}{9} = \dfrac{5}{18}$.

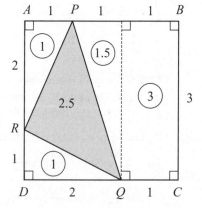

Section 7 Writing

1. **B** This improves the given sentence by making it less wordy.

2. **C** Subject–verb agreement. This changes the given sentence so that the verb *is* agrees with the subjects *culture* and *race*.

3. **B** The given sentence is grammatical, but awkward and wordy. Choice (B) improves the sentence by putting the subject, *linguistic determinism*, at the beginning of the sentence.

4. **D** Idiom error. The correct expression is *analogous to*.

5. **E** Faulty parallelism. This changes the sentence so that the three adjectives in series describe the noun *contraceptives*.

6. **C** This corrects the given sentence so that it makes better sense by changing the nonrestrictive clause *which had a great influence on society* to the restrictive clause *that had a great influence on society*, which specifies the type of past technological developments the concept of "high-tech" is being applied to.

7. **A** The given sentence is clear and grammatical. Note that the noun *media* is plural.

8. **C** Wrong word order. Choice (C) corrects this by changing the word order in the sentence.

9. **E** The given sentence is wordy and awkward because the passive voice, *given by her*, is used. Choice (E) changes this to the active voice.

10. **A** The given sentence is clear and grammatical.

11. **D** This improves the given sentence by placing *Burger*, the noun that the participial phrase *favoring a policy of judicial restraint* refers to near to it and changing the voice from passive to active so that *Burger* is the subject.

12. **B** The contraction *it's* does not make sense here. Change *it's* to the possessive pronoun *its*, referring to *music*.

13. **B** Subject–verb agreement. Change the verb *is* to *are* so that it agrees with the subject *obstacles*.

14. **A** Pronoun error. The pronoun *which* refers to scientists, who are people. Use the relative pronoun *who* in the restrictive relative clause *who were presenting papers at the annual conference*.

15. **C** The phrase *has had such a* requires the relative pronoun *that*.

16. **C** Incorrect verb. Delete the word *need*.

17. **C** Idiom error. Change *whole* to *the whole of*.

18. **C** Delete *that* and substitute *in view of*, *because of*, or *considering*.

19. **D** Wordy and vague pronoun reference. In the participial phrase beginning with the word *hoping*, it is not clear whether the pronoun *it* refers to the setting up of recorders or to the recorders themselves. Change *that it will* to *to*. This is not only clearer and less wordy, it makes better sense because the subject of the sentence is *investigators*.

20. **D** Wrong preposition. The phrase *accede by* is incorrect. The correct preposition to use with the verb *accede* is *to*.

21. **A** Incorrect idiom. The sentence requires the phrase *as is the case with*.

22. **E** No error. If the past perfect action occurred at a specific time, the simple past tense can be used instead of the past perfect tense when "before" or "after" are used in the sentence. The adverb "after" tells what happens first, so the past perfect is optional.

23. **B** Subject–verb agreement error. Change *have* to *has* so that it agrees with government.

24. **C** The predicate adjective *concerned* cannot be followed by the infinitive phrase *to be injured*. Change *to be injured* to the prepositional phrase *about being injured*, which functions as an adverb modifying *concerned*.

25. **A** The predicate adjective *important* cannot be modified by the gerund *knowing*. Change *knowing* to the infinitive phrase *to know*.

26. **E** No error.

27. **C** Wrong preposition. If a preposition is used after the verb *unsullied*, it must be *by*. Use *unsullied by*.

28. **D** The phrase *of workers to be employed* is a prepositional phrase referring to *number*. In context the phrase *to be* does not make good sense. Change *to be* to *who are* so that *who are employed* is a restrictive relative clause modifying *workers*.

29. **E** No error.

30. **D** This corrects choice (A), which is not grammatical, with a nonrestrictive relative clause, which makes the sentence clear and grammatical. (A) This is not grammatical because it does not form a complete sentence. (B) This is not grammatical because a nonrestrictive relative clause cannot begin with the relative pronoun "that." (C) This is grammatical but somewhat awkward and wordy. (E) This is not grammatical because the preposition "for" is not correct here.

31. **C** This is the best choice because sentence 6 elaborates on sentence 5. (A) Sentence 6 is not a good sentence to begin the second paragraph with because the paragraph is about America's reaction to Gagarin's flight. (B) Sentence 6 should not be deleted because it elaborates on sentence 5, providing important information. (D) This is not grammatical because *becoming the first human being to orbit Earth* is a dangling participle. (E) This is not grammatical because a run-on sentence is created.

32. **E** This is the best choice because it helps to link sentence 8 to sentence 9. (A) This makes little sense because sentence 9 describes how difficult it would be to put a man on the Moon. (B) This makes little sense for the same reason that choice (A) does not make sense. (C) Whether the pledge was a political stunt or not is not relevant to what is stated in sentence 9. (D) This makes sense in the sentence. However, it is incorrect because sentence 10 says, "The problems were overcome and . . . Neil Armstrong became the first man to walk on the Moon."

33. **C** This is the best choice because it elaborates on the preceding sentence, sentence 9, and sentence 10 follows logically from it. Note that the word "yet" in sentence 10 signals a contrast with "It seemed impossible." Also, it serves to link the Apollo mission to the idea of American confidence that was emphasized in the first paragraph. (A) This does not make sense because sentence 9 describes the difficulty of the task. (B) This does not make good sense because failure would be likely to damage American prestige. Also, sentence 9 stresses the difficulty of the task. (D) This does not make sense because there was no failure. (E) This sentence follows logically from sentence 9. However, sentence 10 does not follow logically from it because sentence 10 is about overcoming the problems and the successful landing of a man on the Moon.

34. **D** This is the best choice because it is reasonable that some people would wonder why the United States did not continue to explore the Moon as a result of the success of Apollo. Note that this structure is grammatical, whereas choice (A) is not. Note also that dashes should not be used often, but if used effectively can add variety to writing. Similarly, italics for emphasis should be used sparingly. In this case, italicizing *because* helps contrast *because* with *despite*. (A) This does not form a complete sentence. (B) This does not make good sense because if people forgot the success of Apollo they would be unlikely to wonder why the United States did not continue to explore the Moon. (C) The words "Despite the success of Apollo" make no sense here because they follow the words "because of." (E) The phrase *on the contrary* makes little sense because a contrary point was made in the previous sentence (sentence 12).

35. **E** This is the best choice because it helps to link sentence 14 to sentence 15. Sentence 14 gives possible reasons the United States did not continue the Apollo missions, and sentence 15 suggests that the Chinese might land a person on the Moon. The phrase *at any rate* helps provide a transition between sentence 14 and choice (E). (A) This follows logically from sentence 14. However, it does not make sense because sentence 15 says that a Chinese citizen might soon walk on the Moon. (B) This makes little sense because sentence 15 is about the possibility of a Chinese citizen walking on the Moon. (C) This makes no sense because sentence 15 is about the possibility of a Chinese citizen walking on the Moon. (D) This makes no sense because sentence 15 is about the possibility of a Chinese citizen walking on the Moon.

Section 8 Critical Reading

1. **B** The words "debate between various competing vested interests" signal that modern irrigation projects *engender* (cause) debate.

2. **A** It makes sense that the salary from a part-time job would *augment* (make greater) the salary from a primary job.

3. **D** It is possible that a congressman's *constituents* (residents of the district that elects a member of Congress) would support his declarations. It makes sense that he would condemn the *lurid* (sensational) portrayal of violence and sex.

4. **E** The word "commonly" signals that the henpecked husband is a figure that appears often in literature, so *archetypal* (referring to an ideal example) is a good choice for the first blank. It makes sense that a henpecked husband would be *caricatured* (portrayed in an exaggerated way).

5. **B** The term "taste" can refer to *aesthetic* (related to art or beauty) judgment.

6. **B** By definition *inductive* reasoning involves making generalizations on the basis of specific examples, whereas *deductive* reasoning involves drawing conclusions about a specific example on the basis of a generalization.

7. **D** The words "the entry of sulfonamides and penicillin" signal that *pharmacopoeia* refers to a stock of medical drugs.

8. **B** The author says, "Therapy [new and effective drugs] had been discovered for great numbers of patients whose illnesses had previously been untreatable" (lines 8–10) and "Doctors could now cure disease, and this was astonishing, most of all to the doctors themselves" (lines 12–14).

9. **A** The author says, "That long habit . . . had been to treat everything with something" (lines 74–76).

10. **C** "Crudest" means *very unsophisticated* and "empiricism" means *the use of observation and experimentation to gain knowledge.*

11. **C** Before commenting, "It is astounding that the profession survived so long" (lines 51–52), the author describes how medicine was practiced throughout most of history. He describes this practice as "irresponsible" (line 42), as having no scientific basis, and as often harming patients more than helping them.

12. **E** A *skeptic* is a person who questions generally accepted ideas. The author says that Montaigne (a sixteenth-century French essayist) saw through "the old nonsense" (established medical practice, that is) because he was a skeptic.

13. **B** It makes sense that the author believes it took courage for physicians to suggest that their profession was using faulty methods because members of a profession who criticize their profession would be likely to be regarded as disloyal by other members of the profession.

14. **D** The author says, "It is hard for us now to imagine the magnitude of this discovery and its effect on the practice of medicine. That long habit . . . had been to treat everything with something, and it was taken for granted that every disease demanded treatment" (lines 72–78). The discovery that certain diseases are self-limited was surprising because it contradicted what nearly everyone thought.

15. **A** *Ironic* (involving an incongruity between what might be expected and what actually occurs) is the best word to describe the accomplishment because it is ironic that the major scientific accomplishment of medicine, which exists to cure people of disease, is the discovery that patients often are better off without medical treatment.

16. **D** In context *aggressive* refers to *very intensive* medical treatment.

17. **D** In context *flamboyant* refers to *showy* treatment. This can be inferred from the fact that the author is contrasting the new therapy with the established therapy as described previously in the passage. A good example of this is, "Virtually anything that . . . but thin air" (lines 37–50).

18. **C** All of the other answers are mentioned in the author's description of the science of medicine in lines 100–132: "It was based . . . time of dying." Choice (C) is not mentioned, and it is suggested that aggressive intervention is not a major component of modern medicine: The author says, "Accurate diagnosis became the central justification of medicine," "a new kind of much less ambitious . . . therapy began to emerge," and "despite his inability to do much in the way of . . . terminating illness."

Section 9 Mathematics

<u>Note:</u>

1. See page 32 for an explanation of the symbol $\Rightarrow$ that is used in some answer explanations.

2. A calculator icon, 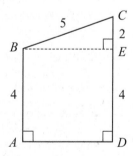, is placed next to the answer explanation of any question for which a calculator *could* be useful. Almost always, the question can be answered easily without using a calculator.

3. If you are unfamiliar with any of the math facts used in the following answer explanations, refer to Barron's *SAT*, which, in addition to having practice tests, has a full review of all the math you need to know.

1. **B** Since the sum of the measures of the three angles in any triangle is $180°$, $180 = 2a + 3a + 4a = 9a$, and so $a = 20$. Therefore, the measures of the angles are $40°$, $60°$, and $80°$.

2. **E** Since the smaller box had $\dfrac{1}{4}$ the number of books as the larger box, the larger box had 4 times as many books as the smaller box. Let x and $4x$ represent the number of books in the smaller and larger boxes, respectively. Then $20 = x + 4x = 5x$, and so $x = 4$ and $4x = 16$.

3. **E** There are two possibilities. Either (i) p and r are even and q is odd, or (ii) p and r are odd and q is even.
   - Since at least one of p, q, and r is even, pqr must be even.
   - $p + q + r$ *could be odd* (if p were even), but if p were odd, then $p + q + r$ would be even.
   - Similarly, $p + qr$ and $p(q + r)$ *could be odd* (if p were odd), but both of them would be even if p were even. Since $p + q$ and $q + r$ are each the sum of an even integer and an odd integer, both of them must be odd, and so their product $(p + q)(q + r)$ *must be odd*.

4. **B**
   - $|a + 5| = 10 \Rightarrow a + 5 = 10$ or $a + 5 = -10 \Rightarrow a = 5$ or $a = -15$
   - $|b - 5| = 10 \Rightarrow b - 5 = 10$ or $b - 5 = -10 \Rightarrow b = 15$ or $b = -5$
   - Neither value for a equals either value for b. I is false.
   - If $a = 5$ and $b = -5$, then $a - b = 10$. II is true.
   - The only possible values for $a + b$ are 0, 20, and -20. III is false.

5. **C** The average of any number of n's is n. If the average of 11 n's is 13, then $n = 13$, and the average of 13 n's is also 13.

6. **D** Draw in line segment $\overline{BE}$ perpendicular to $\overline{CD}$, dividing quadrilateral $ABCD$ into right triangle BEC and rectangle $ABED$. Since opposite sides of a rectangle are congruent, $ED = 4$ and so $CE = 2$. Then, by the Pythagorean theorem,
   $(BE)^2 + 2^2 = 5^2 \Rightarrow (BE)^2 = 25 - 4 = 21$, and so $BE = \sqrt{21}$.
   Finally, since $AD = BE$, $AD = \sqrt{21}$.

7. **E**
   - Since a is directly proportional to b, there is a constant k such that $\dfrac{a}{b} = k$. So, $k = \dfrac{2}{4} = \dfrac{1}{2}$. Then, when $a = 12$, $b = 24$.
   - Since a is inversely proportional to c, there is a constant m such that $ac = m$. So, $m = 2 \times 3 = 6$. Then, when $a = 12$, $c = \dfrac{1}{2}$.
   - Finally, $b + c = 24\dfrac{1}{2}$.

8. **E** **Solution 1.** $n + 2n + 3n + 4n + 5 = 10n + 5$, which is 5 more than a multiple of 10, and so the remainder when it is divided by 10 is 5.

    Solution 2. Plug in an easy-to-use number for n. If $n = 1$, then the numbers are 1, 2, 3, 4, and 5. Their sum is 15, and when 15 is divided by 10, the quotient is 1 and the remainder is 5.

9. **D** If $f(n) > g(n)$, then $3n + 5 > 5n + 3$, and so $2 > 2n$. Therefore, $1 > n$, or equivalently, $n < 1$. Nine integers satisfy the inequality $|n| < 5$: $-4, -3, -2, -1, 0, 1, 2, 3$, and 4. Of these, the first five are less than 1.

10. **D** Let x and y be the lengths of the other two sides of the triangle. Then, by the triangle inequality, $x + y > 2$. So the perimeter of the triangle, $x + y + 2$, is greater than $2 + 2 = 4$. (I is false.) Isosceles triangles with sides of 2, 11, 11 and 2, 21, 21 have perimeters of 24 and 44, respectively. (II and III are true.) In fact, a triangle with one side equal to 2 can have any perimeter greater 4.

11. **C** $11 = \dfrac{a + (2a + 8) + (6a - 11)}{3} = \dfrac{9a - 3}{3} = 3a - 1$.
    So, $3a - 1 = 11 \Rightarrow 3a = 12 \Rightarrow a = 4$.
    So the three numbers are: 4, $2(4) + 8 = 16$, and $6(4) - 11 = 13$.
    The median of 4, 16, and 13 is the middle one, 13.

12. **A** All of the statements *could* be true, but plugging in almost any values for a and b shows that none of the three statements *must* be true. For example:

    - $\widehat{4 + 8} = \widehat{12} = 3$, whereas $\widehat{4} + \widehat{8} = 2 + 2 = 4$.
    - $\widehat{4 \times 8} = \widehat{32} = 2$, whereas $\widehat{4} \times \widehat{8} = 2 \times 2 = 4$.
    - $(\widehat{4})^2 = 2^2 = 4$, whereas $\widehat{4} = 2$.

    If you happen to pick numbers that work for a particular statement, then you know that the statement *could* be true, not that it *must* be true. So you would have to try other numbers. However, if you pick numbers that don't work for a statement, then you know that the statement does not have to be true, and you are through.

13. **D** Label the four seniors A, B, C, and D. Then the number of ways to choose two of them is 6: AB, AC, AD, BC, BD, and CD. Clearly the number of ways to choose one junior is 8, one sophomore is 10, and one freshman is 6. So by the counting principle, the total number of ways to form the committee is:
    $6 \times 8 \times 10 \times 6 = 2{,}880$.

14. **E** **Solution 1.** In this problem, it is much easier to plug in some small positive integers for m and n, say $m = 2$ and $n = 3$, than to reason it out with the letters. Then $m(n - 2) = 2(3 - 2) = 2$ and $m(n + 2) = 2(3 + 2) = 10$. There are seven integers greater than 2 and less than 10 (3, 4, 5, 6, 7, 8, and 9). Only answer choice (E), $4m - 1$, equals 7 when $m = 2$.

    Solution 2. If x is a positive integer, the set of positive integers less than x consists of the $x - 1$ integers: 1, $2, \ldots, x - 1$. So the set of positive integers less than $m(n + 2)$ has $m(n + 2) - 1$ members, namely the integers $1, 2, \ldots, m(n + 2) - 1$. Since we want the number of integers that are not only less than $m(n + 2)$, but also greater than $m(n - 2)$, we now have to eliminate the $m(n - 2)$ integers from 1 to $m(n - 2)$, inclusive. Then, the number of integers left is $[m(n + 2) - 1] - (mn - 2m) = mn + 2m - 1 - mn + 2m = 4m - 1$. Clearly, Solution 1 is preferable.

15. **B** **Solution 1.** The areas of $\triangle OBC$ and $\triangle OAC$ are each
    $\dfrac{1}{2}(8)(4) = 16$. So the sum of their two areas is $16 + 16 = 32$.

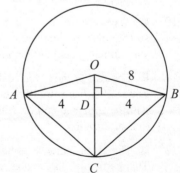

Solution 2. Since *BD* is one-half of *BO*, right triangle *ODB* is a 30-60-90 triangle, and so $OD = 4\sqrt{3}$. So the area of $\triangle AOB$ is $\frac{1}{2}(8)(4\sqrt{3}) = 16\sqrt{3}$.

$CD = OC - OD = 8 - 4\sqrt{3}$. So the area of $\triangle ACB$ is $\frac{1}{2}(8)(8 - 4\sqrt{3}) = 4(8 - 4\sqrt{3}) = 32 - 16\sqrt{3}$. Finally, the area of quadrilateral *AOBC* is $16\sqrt{3} - (32 - 16\sqrt{3}) = 32$.

16. **A** For any number, x, $|x| \geq 0$, so $|2n + 5| \geq 0$ and since $n > |2n + 5|$, n must be positive. If n is positive, then $2n + 5$ is also positive, and so $|2n + 5| = 2n + 5$. But when n is positive, $2n + 5$ is clearly greater than n. So, there are no values for n that satisfy the given inequality.

Section 10 Writing

1. **B** This corrects the grammar error in the given sentence. *The first American to orbit Earth* is an appositive phrase, so the conjunction *and* must be deleted. This choice also corrects the unclear reference in the clause "in which he served for twenty-five years" (John Glenn didn't serve in *Ohio*; he served in the Senate as a *senator*) by replacing it with the participial phrase *serving for twenty-five years*.

2. **D** This corrects the run-on sentence. A comma cannot join two independent clauses. Choice (D) joins the two independent clauses with a semicolon, which is a good choice because the second independent clause adds detail to what is said in the first independent clause.

3. **D** This changes the voice of the verb in the independent clause beginning with *An* from passive to active. This change in voice corrects the awkwardness of the clause and makes it consistent with the second part of the sentence beginning with *but*. Note that the subject of the first clause is now *Jews*, making it clear that the beliefs of Jews are being compared to the beliefs of *Christians*, the subject of the second clause.

4. **D** The clause in the given sentence is set off by commas, making it a nonrestrictive clause. However, modern usage requires the use of *which* rather than *that* in nonrestrictive clauses. Deleting the commas changes the clause to a restrictive clause telling what type of writing is considered insipid.

5. **C** This improves the given sentence by changing the wordy clause *of which X-rays can be considered one form* to a short participial phrase, *including X-rays*.

6. **E** A prepositional phrase (*by raising peripheral issues*) cannot be the subject of a verb (*was*). Choice (E) corrects the sentence by making *lawyer* the subject of the sentence and placing the adverb prepositional phrase *by raising peripheral issues* at the end of the sentence.

7. **A** The given sentence is clear and grammatical.

8. **C** This makes the given sentence clearer because replacing the conjunction *and* with the conjunction *but* signals the contrast between, on the one hand, the number of agnostic and atheist humanists and, on the other hand, the number of Jewish and Christian humanists.

9. **B** This corrects the faulty parallelism in the part of the clause beginning with *who* that is set off by commas by making the pronoun *they* the subject of the verbs *have* and *speak*.

10. **C** There are two errors in the given sentence. First, there is a tense error. *Classical historians* wrote in the past, so *take* must be changed to *took*. Second, the two independent clauses are incorrectly joined by the subordinating conjunction *although*. Choice (C) changes *although* to the coordinating conjunction *but*.

11. **E** The part of the given sentence before the comma is a long participial phrase that makes the meaning of the sentence difficult to understand. Choice (E) makes the meaning clear by the use of an adverb clause (beginning with *because* and ending with *heat*) giving the reason that proximity to coal has been a major determinant in industrialization.

12. **B** The given sentence contains a dangling participle, *dissecting every sentence and analyzing every nuance*. This participial phrase does not refer clearly to a noun. Choice (B) corrects this by changing the participial phrase to an independent clause.

13. **D** There is a faulty comparison in the given sentence. *News* should not be compared to *towns*. Choice (D) corrects the faulty comparison in the given sentence by changing the sentence so that the amount of international *news* published by the newspaper in Singapore is compared to the amount of international *news* published by newspapers in the United States.

14. **A** The given sentence is clear and grammatical.

Answer Sheet—Practice Test 5

Section 1　　　　　　　　　　　**ESSAY**

Essay (continued)

Practice Test 5

If a section has fewer questions than answer spaces, leave the extra spaces blank.

Section 2

1 Ⓐ Ⓑ Ⓒ Ⓓ Ⓔ   8 Ⓐ Ⓑ Ⓒ Ⓓ Ⓔ   15 Ⓐ Ⓑ Ⓒ Ⓓ Ⓔ   22 Ⓐ Ⓑ Ⓒ Ⓓ Ⓔ   29 Ⓐ Ⓑ Ⓒ Ⓓ Ⓔ
2 Ⓐ Ⓑ Ⓒ Ⓓ Ⓔ   9 Ⓐ Ⓑ Ⓒ Ⓓ Ⓔ   16 Ⓐ Ⓑ Ⓒ Ⓓ Ⓔ   23 Ⓐ Ⓑ Ⓒ Ⓓ Ⓔ   30 Ⓐ Ⓑ Ⓒ Ⓓ Ⓔ
3 Ⓐ Ⓑ Ⓒ Ⓓ Ⓔ   10 Ⓐ Ⓑ Ⓒ Ⓓ Ⓔ   17 Ⓐ Ⓑ Ⓒ Ⓓ Ⓔ   24 Ⓐ Ⓑ Ⓒ Ⓓ Ⓔ   31 Ⓐ Ⓑ Ⓒ Ⓓ Ⓔ
4 Ⓐ Ⓑ Ⓒ Ⓓ Ⓔ   11 Ⓐ Ⓑ Ⓒ Ⓓ Ⓔ   18 Ⓐ Ⓑ Ⓒ Ⓓ Ⓔ   25 Ⓐ Ⓑ Ⓒ Ⓓ Ⓔ   32 Ⓐ Ⓑ Ⓒ Ⓓ Ⓔ
5 Ⓐ Ⓑ Ⓒ Ⓓ Ⓔ   12 Ⓐ Ⓑ Ⓒ Ⓓ Ⓔ   19 Ⓐ Ⓑ Ⓒ Ⓓ Ⓔ   26 Ⓐ Ⓑ Ⓒ Ⓓ Ⓔ   33 Ⓐ Ⓑ Ⓒ Ⓓ Ⓔ
6 Ⓐ Ⓑ Ⓒ Ⓓ Ⓔ   13 Ⓐ Ⓑ Ⓒ Ⓓ Ⓔ   20 Ⓐ Ⓑ Ⓒ Ⓓ Ⓔ   27 Ⓐ Ⓑ Ⓒ Ⓓ Ⓔ   34 Ⓐ Ⓑ Ⓒ Ⓓ Ⓔ
7 Ⓐ Ⓑ Ⓒ Ⓓ Ⓔ   14 Ⓐ Ⓑ Ⓒ Ⓓ Ⓔ   21 Ⓐ Ⓑ Ⓒ Ⓓ Ⓔ   28 Ⓐ Ⓑ Ⓒ Ⓓ Ⓔ   35 Ⓐ Ⓑ Ⓒ Ⓓ Ⓔ

Section 3

1 Ⓐ Ⓑ Ⓒ Ⓓ Ⓔ   8 Ⓐ Ⓑ Ⓒ Ⓓ Ⓔ   15 Ⓐ Ⓑ Ⓒ Ⓓ Ⓔ   22 Ⓐ Ⓑ Ⓒ Ⓓ Ⓔ   29 Ⓐ Ⓑ Ⓒ Ⓓ Ⓔ
2 Ⓐ Ⓑ Ⓒ Ⓓ Ⓔ   9 Ⓐ Ⓑ Ⓒ Ⓓ Ⓔ   16 Ⓐ Ⓑ Ⓒ Ⓓ Ⓔ   23 Ⓐ Ⓑ Ⓒ Ⓓ Ⓔ   30 Ⓐ Ⓑ Ⓒ Ⓓ Ⓔ
3 Ⓐ Ⓑ Ⓒ Ⓓ Ⓔ   10 Ⓐ Ⓑ Ⓒ Ⓓ Ⓔ   17 Ⓐ Ⓑ Ⓒ Ⓓ Ⓔ   24 Ⓐ Ⓑ Ⓒ Ⓓ Ⓔ   31 Ⓐ Ⓑ Ⓒ Ⓓ Ⓔ
4 Ⓐ Ⓑ Ⓒ Ⓓ Ⓔ   11 Ⓐ Ⓑ Ⓒ Ⓓ Ⓔ   18 Ⓐ Ⓑ Ⓒ Ⓓ Ⓔ   25 Ⓐ Ⓑ Ⓒ Ⓓ Ⓔ   32 Ⓐ Ⓑ Ⓒ Ⓓ Ⓔ
5 Ⓐ Ⓑ Ⓒ Ⓓ Ⓔ   12 Ⓐ Ⓑ Ⓒ Ⓓ Ⓔ   19 Ⓐ Ⓑ Ⓒ Ⓓ Ⓔ   26 Ⓐ Ⓑ Ⓒ Ⓓ Ⓔ   33 Ⓐ Ⓑ Ⓒ Ⓓ Ⓔ
6 Ⓐ Ⓑ Ⓒ Ⓓ Ⓔ   13 Ⓐ Ⓑ Ⓒ Ⓓ Ⓔ   20 Ⓐ Ⓑ Ⓒ Ⓓ Ⓔ   27 Ⓐ Ⓑ Ⓒ Ⓓ Ⓔ   34 Ⓐ Ⓑ Ⓒ Ⓓ Ⓔ
7 Ⓐ Ⓑ Ⓒ Ⓓ Ⓔ   14 Ⓐ Ⓑ Ⓒ Ⓓ Ⓔ   21 Ⓐ Ⓑ Ⓒ Ⓓ Ⓔ   28 Ⓐ Ⓑ Ⓒ Ⓓ Ⓔ   35 Ⓐ Ⓑ Ⓒ Ⓓ Ⓔ

Section 5

1 Ⓐ Ⓑ Ⓒ Ⓓ Ⓔ   8 Ⓐ Ⓑ Ⓒ Ⓓ Ⓔ   15 Ⓐ Ⓑ Ⓒ Ⓓ Ⓔ   22 Ⓐ Ⓑ Ⓒ Ⓓ Ⓔ   29 Ⓐ Ⓑ Ⓒ Ⓓ Ⓔ
2 Ⓐ Ⓑ Ⓒ Ⓓ Ⓔ   9 Ⓐ Ⓑ Ⓒ Ⓓ Ⓔ   16 Ⓐ Ⓑ Ⓒ Ⓓ Ⓔ   23 Ⓐ Ⓑ Ⓒ Ⓓ Ⓔ   30 Ⓐ Ⓑ Ⓒ Ⓓ Ⓔ
3 Ⓐ Ⓑ Ⓒ Ⓓ Ⓔ   10 Ⓐ Ⓑ Ⓒ Ⓓ Ⓔ   17 Ⓐ Ⓑ Ⓒ Ⓓ Ⓔ   24 Ⓐ Ⓑ Ⓒ Ⓓ Ⓔ   31 Ⓐ Ⓑ Ⓒ Ⓓ Ⓔ
4 Ⓐ Ⓑ Ⓒ Ⓓ Ⓔ   11 Ⓐ Ⓑ Ⓒ Ⓓ Ⓔ   18 Ⓐ Ⓑ Ⓒ Ⓓ Ⓔ   25 Ⓐ Ⓑ Ⓒ Ⓓ Ⓔ   32 Ⓐ Ⓑ Ⓒ Ⓓ Ⓔ
5 Ⓐ Ⓑ Ⓒ Ⓓ Ⓔ   12 Ⓐ Ⓑ Ⓒ Ⓓ Ⓔ   19 Ⓐ Ⓑ Ⓒ Ⓓ Ⓔ   26 Ⓐ Ⓑ Ⓒ Ⓓ Ⓔ   33 Ⓐ Ⓑ Ⓒ Ⓓ Ⓔ
6 Ⓐ Ⓑ Ⓒ Ⓓ Ⓔ   13 Ⓐ Ⓑ Ⓒ Ⓓ Ⓔ   20 Ⓐ Ⓑ Ⓒ Ⓓ Ⓔ   27 Ⓐ Ⓑ Ⓒ Ⓓ Ⓔ   34 Ⓐ Ⓑ Ⓒ Ⓓ Ⓔ
7 Ⓐ Ⓑ Ⓒ Ⓓ Ⓔ   14 Ⓐ Ⓑ Ⓒ Ⓓ Ⓔ   21 Ⓐ Ⓑ Ⓒ Ⓓ Ⓔ   28 Ⓐ Ⓑ Ⓒ Ⓓ Ⓔ   35 Ⓐ Ⓑ Ⓒ Ⓓ Ⓔ

Section 6

1 Ⓐ Ⓑ Ⓒ Ⓓ Ⓔ   3 Ⓐ Ⓑ Ⓒ Ⓓ Ⓔ   5 Ⓐ Ⓑ Ⓒ Ⓓ Ⓔ   7 Ⓐ Ⓑ Ⓒ Ⓓ Ⓔ
2 Ⓐ Ⓑ Ⓒ Ⓓ Ⓔ   4 Ⓐ Ⓑ Ⓒ Ⓓ Ⓔ   6 Ⓐ Ⓑ Ⓒ Ⓓ Ⓔ   8 Ⓐ Ⓑ Ⓒ Ⓓ Ⓔ

9   10   11   12   13

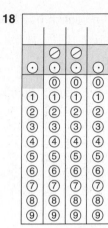

Section 7

1 Ⓐ Ⓑ Ⓒ Ⓓ Ⓔ   8 Ⓐ Ⓑ Ⓒ Ⓓ Ⓔ   15 Ⓐ Ⓑ Ⓒ Ⓓ Ⓔ   22 Ⓐ Ⓑ Ⓒ Ⓓ Ⓔ   29 Ⓐ Ⓑ Ⓒ Ⓓ Ⓔ
2 Ⓐ Ⓑ Ⓒ Ⓓ Ⓔ   9 Ⓐ Ⓑ Ⓒ Ⓓ Ⓔ   16 Ⓐ Ⓑ Ⓒ Ⓓ Ⓔ   23 Ⓐ Ⓑ Ⓒ Ⓓ Ⓔ   30 Ⓐ Ⓑ Ⓒ Ⓓ Ⓔ
3 Ⓐ Ⓑ Ⓒ Ⓓ Ⓔ   10 Ⓐ Ⓑ Ⓒ Ⓓ Ⓔ   17 Ⓐ Ⓑ Ⓒ Ⓓ Ⓔ   24 Ⓐ Ⓑ Ⓒ Ⓓ Ⓔ   31 Ⓐ Ⓑ Ⓒ Ⓓ Ⓔ
4 Ⓐ Ⓑ Ⓒ Ⓓ Ⓔ   11 Ⓐ Ⓑ Ⓒ Ⓓ Ⓔ   18 Ⓐ Ⓑ Ⓒ Ⓓ Ⓔ   25 Ⓐ Ⓑ Ⓒ Ⓓ Ⓔ   32 Ⓐ Ⓑ Ⓒ Ⓓ Ⓔ
5 Ⓐ Ⓑ Ⓒ Ⓓ Ⓔ   12 Ⓐ Ⓑ Ⓒ Ⓓ Ⓔ   19 Ⓐ Ⓑ Ⓒ Ⓓ Ⓔ   26 Ⓐ Ⓑ Ⓒ Ⓓ Ⓔ   33 Ⓐ Ⓑ Ⓒ Ⓓ Ⓔ
6 Ⓐ Ⓑ Ⓒ Ⓓ Ⓔ   13 Ⓐ Ⓑ Ⓒ Ⓓ Ⓔ   20 Ⓐ Ⓑ Ⓒ Ⓓ Ⓔ   27 Ⓐ Ⓑ Ⓒ Ⓓ Ⓔ   34 Ⓐ Ⓑ Ⓒ Ⓓ Ⓔ
7 Ⓐ Ⓑ Ⓒ Ⓓ Ⓔ   14 Ⓐ Ⓑ Ⓒ Ⓓ Ⓔ   21 Ⓐ Ⓑ Ⓒ Ⓓ Ⓔ   28 Ⓐ Ⓑ Ⓒ Ⓓ Ⓔ   35 Ⓐ Ⓑ Ⓒ Ⓓ Ⓔ

Section 8

1 Ⓐ Ⓑ Ⓒ Ⓓ Ⓔ   5 Ⓐ Ⓑ Ⓒ Ⓓ Ⓔ   9 Ⓐ Ⓑ Ⓒ Ⓓ Ⓔ   13 Ⓐ Ⓑ Ⓒ Ⓓ Ⓔ   17 Ⓐ Ⓑ Ⓒ Ⓓ Ⓔ
2 Ⓐ Ⓑ Ⓒ Ⓓ Ⓔ   6 Ⓐ Ⓑ Ⓒ Ⓓ Ⓔ   10 Ⓐ Ⓑ Ⓒ Ⓓ Ⓔ   14 Ⓐ Ⓑ Ⓒ Ⓓ Ⓔ   18 Ⓐ Ⓑ Ⓒ Ⓓ Ⓔ
3 Ⓐ Ⓑ Ⓒ Ⓓ Ⓔ   7 Ⓐ Ⓑ Ⓒ Ⓓ Ⓔ   11 Ⓐ Ⓑ Ⓒ Ⓓ Ⓔ   15 Ⓐ Ⓑ Ⓒ Ⓓ Ⓔ   19 Ⓐ Ⓑ Ⓒ Ⓓ Ⓔ
4 Ⓐ Ⓑ Ⓒ Ⓓ Ⓔ   8 Ⓐ Ⓑ Ⓒ Ⓓ Ⓔ   12 Ⓐ Ⓑ Ⓒ Ⓓ Ⓔ   16 Ⓐ Ⓑ Ⓒ Ⓓ Ⓔ   20 Ⓐ Ⓑ Ⓒ Ⓓ Ⓔ

Section 9

1 Ⓐ Ⓑ Ⓒ Ⓓ Ⓔ   5 Ⓐ Ⓑ Ⓒ Ⓓ Ⓔ   9 Ⓐ Ⓑ Ⓒ Ⓓ Ⓔ   13 Ⓐ Ⓑ Ⓒ Ⓓ Ⓔ   17 Ⓐ Ⓑ Ⓒ Ⓓ Ⓔ
2 Ⓐ Ⓑ Ⓒ Ⓓ Ⓔ   6 Ⓐ Ⓑ Ⓒ Ⓓ Ⓔ   10 Ⓐ Ⓑ Ⓒ Ⓓ Ⓔ   14 Ⓐ Ⓑ Ⓒ Ⓓ Ⓔ   18 Ⓐ Ⓑ Ⓒ Ⓓ Ⓔ
3 Ⓐ Ⓑ Ⓒ Ⓓ Ⓔ   7 Ⓐ Ⓑ Ⓒ Ⓓ Ⓔ   11 Ⓐ Ⓑ Ⓒ Ⓓ Ⓔ   15 Ⓐ Ⓑ Ⓒ Ⓓ Ⓔ   19 Ⓐ Ⓑ Ⓒ Ⓓ Ⓔ
4 Ⓐ Ⓑ Ⓒ Ⓓ Ⓔ   8 Ⓐ Ⓑ Ⓒ Ⓓ Ⓔ   12 Ⓐ Ⓑ Ⓒ Ⓓ Ⓔ   16 Ⓐ Ⓑ Ⓒ Ⓓ Ⓔ   20 Ⓐ Ⓑ Ⓒ Ⓓ Ⓔ

Section 10

1 Ⓐ Ⓑ Ⓒ Ⓓ Ⓔ   5 Ⓐ Ⓑ Ⓒ Ⓓ Ⓔ   9 Ⓐ Ⓑ Ⓒ Ⓓ Ⓔ   13 Ⓐ Ⓑ Ⓒ Ⓓ Ⓔ   17 Ⓐ Ⓑ Ⓒ Ⓓ Ⓔ
2 Ⓐ Ⓑ Ⓒ Ⓓ Ⓔ   6 Ⓐ Ⓑ Ⓒ Ⓓ Ⓔ   10 Ⓐ Ⓑ Ⓒ Ⓓ Ⓔ   14 Ⓐ Ⓑ Ⓒ Ⓓ Ⓔ   18 Ⓐ Ⓑ Ⓒ Ⓓ Ⓔ
3 Ⓐ Ⓑ Ⓒ Ⓓ Ⓔ   7 Ⓐ Ⓑ Ⓒ Ⓓ Ⓔ   11 Ⓐ Ⓑ Ⓒ Ⓓ Ⓔ   15 Ⓐ Ⓑ Ⓒ Ⓓ Ⓔ   19 Ⓐ Ⓑ Ⓒ Ⓓ Ⓔ
4 Ⓐ Ⓑ Ⓒ Ⓓ Ⓔ   8 Ⓐ Ⓑ Ⓒ Ⓓ Ⓔ   12 Ⓐ Ⓑ Ⓒ Ⓓ Ⓔ   16 Ⓐ Ⓑ Ⓒ Ⓓ Ⓔ   20 Ⓐ Ⓑ Ⓒ Ⓓ Ⓔ

Practice Test 5 $\quad$ 1 $\quad$ 1 $\quad$ 1 $\quad$ 1 $\quad$ 1 $\quad$ 1 $\quad$ 1

SECTION 1 $\qquad$ **Time—25 Minutes** $\qquad$ **ESSAY**

Write your essay on the lines provided on the answer sheet on pages 309–310. Be careful to write legibly. Write on the topic, carefully presenting your point of view on it. Your essay will be scored on the basis of the ideas it contains and its effectiveness in expressing these ideas. Pay special attention to logic, clarity, and the accurate use of language.

Think about the topic presented in the following excerpt and in the assignment below it.

> *Some people say that society is becoming so intolerant of dissent that most people are afraid to express their views for fear they will be criticized by one group or another. Certainly public debate on public issues should be civil, but by the same token it should encourage the expression of a diverse range of views, even if some people feel offended.*

ASSIGNMENT: Has the free expression of opinion been stifled, endangering the open discussion of issues that democracy thrives on? Plan and write an essay in which you develop your point of view on this question. Support your position with reasoning and examples taken from your experience, reading, or observations.

2 2 2 2 2 2 2 2 2 2 2

SECTION **2**

Time—25 Minutes
20 Questions

For each problem in this section determine which of the five choices is correct and blacken the corresponding choice on your answer sheet. You may use any blank space on the page for your work.

Notes:

- You may use a calculator whenever you think it will be helpful.
- Only real numbers are used. No question or answer on this test involves a complex or imaginary number.
- Use the diagrams provided to help you solve the problems. Unless you see the words "Note: Figure not drawn to scale" under a diagram, it has been drawn as accurately as possible. Unless it is stated that a figure is three-dimensional, you may assume it lies in a plane.
- For any function f, the domain, unless specifically restricted, is the set of all real numbers for which $f(x)$ is also a real number.

Area Facts

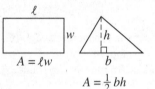

$A = \ell w$

$A = \frac{1}{2}bh$

$A = \pi r^2$
$C = 2\pi r$

Volume Facts

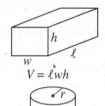

$V = \ell wh$

$V = \pi r^2 h$

Triangle Facts

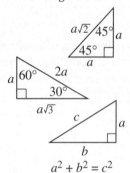

$a^2 + b^2 = c^2$

Angle Facts

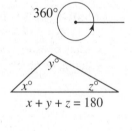

$360°$

$x + y + z = 180$

1. If $a = \frac{1}{3}b$ and $b = \frac{3}{4}c$, what is a when $c = 60$?

   (A) 12
   (B) 15
   (C) 20
   (D) 24
   (E) 30

2. Mrs. Smith purchased $13.00 worth of groceries at the supermarket. She gave the cashier a coupon that entitled her to a discount of 10 percent off her entire purchase. If she paid for her groceries with a $20 bill, how much change should she have received?

   (A) $ 5.70
   (B) $ 8.30
   (C) $ 8.70
   (D) $ 9.30
   (E) $11.70

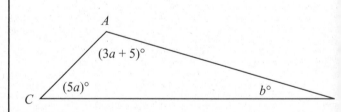

3. In triangle ABC above, if m$\angle A = 50°$, what is the value of b?

   (A) 15
   (B) 55
   (C) 60
   (D) 75
   (E) 120

GO ON TO THE NEXT PAGE

2   2 2 2 2 2 2 2 2   2

4. The perimeter of a rectangle is 10 inches. Which of the following could be the length of one of the sides of the rectangle?

   I. 1 inch
  II. 4.5 inches
 III. 5 inches

(A) I only
(B) II only
(C) I and II only
(D) I and III only
(E) I, II, and III

5. A $150 prize was shared by Liz and Dani. If Liz received $30 more than Dani, what percent of the prize did Liz get?

(A) 50%
(B) 60%
(C) 70%
(D) 75%
(E) 90%

6. What fraction of 8 kilometers is 8 centimeters?
(1 kilometer = 1,000 meters and 1 meter = 100 centimeters)

(A) $\dfrac{8}{1,000}$

(B) $\dfrac{1}{8,000}$

(C) $\dfrac{1}{64,000}$

(D) $\dfrac{1}{100,000}$

(E) $\dfrac{8}{100,000}$

7. Some coins are in a jar, and each coin is a nickel, a dime, or a quarter. If $\dfrac{1}{4}$ of the coins are nickels, and $\dfrac{1}{3}$ of the coins that are not nickels are quarters, what is the ratio of the number of nickels to the number of dimes in the jar?

(A) 1:1
(B) 1:2
(C) 1:3
(D) 2:3
(E) 3:4

8. Which of the following numbers is NOT a factor of 10^{100}?

(A) 125
(B) 375
(C) 625
(D) 10^{25}
(E) 10^{35}

9. Marianne will be traveling from Chicago to Marseille, passing through New York and Paris. From Chicago to New York, Marianne can go by train, bus, or plane; from New York to Paris, she can go by plane or boat; and from Paris to Marseille she can take a regular train, the high-speed train, a bus, or a plane. In how many different ways can Marianne arrange her trip?

(A) 9
(B) 12
(C) 16
(D) 24
(E) 36

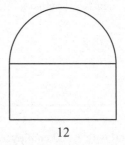

12

Note: Figure not drawn to scale.

10. In the figure above, a rectangle is surmounted by a semicircle, and the area of the semicircle is one-half the area of the rectangle. If the length of the rectangle is 12, what is the width of the rectangle?

(A) π
(B) 2π
(C) 3π
(D) 4π
(E) 6π

GO ON TO THE NEXT PAGE

2   **2**   **2**   **2**   **2**   **2**   **2**   **2**   **2**   **2**   **2**

11. For how many integers, n, between 25 and 75, inclusive, is the remainder 2 when $14n$ is divided by 10?

   (A)   2
   (B)   5
   (C)   8
   (D) 10
   (E) 15

12. If $f(x) = x^2 + 1$ and if a is a positive number such that $f(a) = f(-3)$, what is the value of $f(3a)$?

   (A)   10
   (B)   18
   (C)   64
   (D)   82
   (E) 100

13. Chris and Claire each chose a number. When each of them subtracted 3 from her number and squared the result, they both wound up with 100. If Chris and Claire started with different numbers, what is the sum of their two original numbers?

   (A) −14
   (B)   0
   (C)   6
   (D) 10
   (E) 26

14. At a hospital with 1,200 employees, consisting of doctors, nurses, and other staff, 80 percent of the employees attended this year's holiday party. 20 percent of those attending were nurses, and 180 were doctors. If exactly half of the hospital's employees are staff other than doctors and nurses, what percent of those staff members did *not* attend the party?

   (A)   2%
   (B) 10%
   (C) 12%
   (D) 20%
   (E) 25%

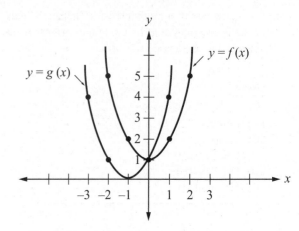

15. The figure above shows the graphs of $y = f(x)$ and $y = g(x)$. Which of the following expresses the relationship between $f(x)$ and $g(x)$?

   (A) $g(x) = f(x) - 1$
   (B) $g(x) = f(x - 1)$
   (C) $g(x) = f(x) + 1$
   (D) $g(x) = f(x + 1)$
   (E) $g(x) = f(x + 1) - 1$

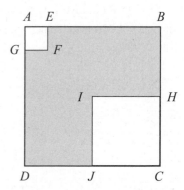

16. In the figure above, the area of square *ABCD* is 50, the area of square *AEFG* is 2, and the area of square *HIJC* is 18. What is the perimeter of the shaded region?

   (A) 20
   (B) 25
   (C) 30
   (D) $16\sqrt{2}$
   (E) $20\sqrt{2}$

GO ON TO THE NEXT PAGE

2 2 2 2 2 2 2 2 2 2 2

17. If h, t, and u represent the hundreds' digit, tens' digit, and units' digit, respectively, of the positive integer n, which of the following is equal to $\dfrac{n}{20}$?

    (A) $\dfrac{h+t+u}{20}$

    (B) $\dfrac{htu}{20}$

    (C) $5h + \dfrac{t+u}{20}$

    (D) $5h + \dfrac{10t+u}{20}$

    (E) $\dfrac{10h+5t+u}{2}$

18. Each of two boys, Al and Bob, and two girls, Carol and Dee, were given cards with a different integer from 1 to 4, inclusive, written on them. What is the probability that the sum of the numbers on the cards given to the two boys is even?

    (A) $\dfrac{1}{6}$

    (B) $\dfrac{1}{4}$

    (C) $\dfrac{1}{3}$

    (D) $\dfrac{1}{2}$

    (E) $\dfrac{2}{3}$

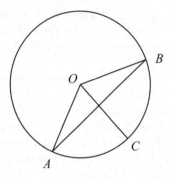

19. In the figure above, chord $\overline{AB}$ is the perpendicular bisector of radius $\overline{OC}$. If $OA = 10$, what is the area of triangle AOB?

    (A) 25
    (B) $25\sqrt{3}$
    (C) $50\sqrt{3}$
    (D) $20 + 10\sqrt{3}$
    (E) $20 + 20\sqrt{3}$

20. At Central High School n students work on the school newspaper and y students work on the yearbook. If b students work on both the newspaper and the yearbook, which of the following is the number who work on either the newspaper or the yearbook, but not both?

    (A) $n + y + b$
    (B) $n + y + 2b$
    (C) $n + y - b$
    (D) $n + y - 2b$
    (E) $b - (n + y)$

STOP

IN ANY REMAINING TIME YOU MAY REVIEW THE
ANSWERS YOU CHOSE IN THIS SECTION. DO NOT WORK
ON ANY OTHER SECTION OF THE TEST DURING THIS TIME.

Practice Test 5

3   3 3 3 3 3 3 3 3 3 3   3

SECTION 3   **Time—25 Minutes**
24 Questions

Choose the best answer to each of the following questions in this section. Then blacken the appropriate space on your answer sheet.

Each of the following sentences contains one or two blanks, indicating that a word or set of words has been omitted. Beneath each sentence there are five answer choices labeled A to E from which you must select the word or set of words that best fits the meaning of the sentence as a whole.

Example:

Records of colonization can be found as far back as the Phoenicians, but colonization became a major force in world history only when European countries began, in the fifteenth century, to make ---- Asia, the Americas, and Africa.

(A) queries about
(B) incursions into
(C) tirades against
(D) enemies in
(E) amends for

1. It is easy to ---- efforts to create a just society as idealistic and unrealistic; it is far more difficult to actually do something to help bring about such a society.

(A) initiate   (B) extol   (C) imitate
    (D) deride   (E) expedite

2. The critic has a reputation for ---- the efforts of new writers rather than encouraging them by offering constructive criticism.

(A) evaluating   (B) analyzing   (C) describing
    (D) imitating   (E) belittling

3. Assumptions are often ----; that is, they underlie a statement or argument without being stated.

(A) unfounded   (B) illogical   (C) implicit
    (D) extrinsic   (E) subjective

4. The ---- of an empirical approach to ---- the truth is to rely on intuition.

(A) goal . . substantiating
(B) apotheosis . . analyzing
(C) antithesis . . discerning
(D) veracity . . venerating
(E) fallacy . . sanctioning

5. One of the difficulties scientists sometimes face is ---- data to determine whether it is ----.

(A) precluding . . valid
(B) assessing . . spurious
(C) quantifying . . qualified
(D) embellishing . . true
(E) substantiating . . interesting

GO ON TO THE NEXT PAGE

3   3 3 3 3 3 3 3 3 3 3   3

Below are passages followed by questions on them. Questions on a pair of related passages may be about the relationship between the two passages. For each question, select the best answer based on what is stated or implied in the passage (or passages).

Questions 6–7 are based on the following passage.

Passage 1

Early Islamic polity was intensely expansionist, fueled both by fervor for the faith and by economic and social factors. After gaining
Line control of Arabia and the Persian Gulf region,
(5) conquering armies swept out of the peninsula, spreading Islam.

Members of the Bani Abd al Qais tribe that controlled the eastern coast of Arabia when the tribe converted to Islam were traders having close
(10) contacts with Christian communities in Mesopotamia. Such contacts may have introduced the tribe to the ideal of one God and so prepared it to accept the Prophet's message. The Arabs of Oman also figure prominently among the early
(15) converts to Islam. According to tradition, the Prophet sent one of his military leaders to Oman to convert not only the Arab inhabitants, some of whom were Christian, but also the Persian garrison, which was Zoroastrian. The Arabs
(20) accepted Islam, but the Persians did not. It was partly the zeal of the newly converted Arabs that inspired them to expel the Persians from Oman.

6. According to the author, a factor that helped Islam to gain control of Oman was

(A) the faith that Persians in Oman had in Zoroastrianism
(B) the military weakness of the Christians in Oman
(C) the religious enthusiasm of some of the Arabs in Oman
(D) the reluctance of the Persian military force in Oman to do battle with Arab soldiers
(E) a conflict in the Omani leadership between loyalty to their fellow Arabs and loyalty to Persia

7. Based on the information in the passage, which of the following statements is most likely to be true?

(A) Followers of Islam had almost no success in converting people who had been influenced by Christian belief.
(B) Islam is a monotheistic religion.
(C) Early in its history Islam spread almost exclusively as a result of the rapidly growing prestige of Arabic culture.
(D) During the early period of Islam, its adherents sought to convert only Arabs.
(E) Islamic belief was more influenced by Zoroastrianism than by Christianity.

Questions 8–9 are based on the following passage.

Passage 2

Considerable cultural exchange occurred between Japan and the continent of Asia late in the Kofun period. Buddhism was introduced from
Line Korea, probably in A.D. 538, exposing Japan to a
(5) new body of religious doctrine. The Soga, a Japanese court family that rose to prominence with the accession of the Emperor Kimmei about A.D. 531, favored the adoption of Buddhism and of governmental and cultural models based on
(10) Chinese Confucianism. But some at the court—such as the Nakatomi family, which was responsible for performing Shinto rituals at court, and the Mononobe, a military clan—were set on maintaining their prerogatives and resisted the
(15) alien religious influence of Buddhism. Acrimony continued between the Soga and the Nakatomi and Mononobe clans for more than a century, during which the Soga temporarily emerged ascendant.

GO ON TO THE NEXT PAGE

8. It can be inferred that the author believes that the Nakatomi family and the Mononobe clan were not sympathetic to Buddhist doctrine primarily because

   (A) the Soga family favored its adoption
   (B) it was at odds with Chinese Confucianism
   (C) they feared that Buddhist influence would lead to increased Korean interference in Japanese affairs
   (D) they believed that Buddhist teaching would lead to Chinese dominance of Japan
   (E) they feared that changes in religious belief would lead to major changes in Japanese society and politics, threatening their position in society

9. It can be inferred from the information provided in the passage that it is probable that

   (A) Korea had a greater influence on Japanese culture than did China
   (B) Buddhism found almost no adherents in Japan
   (C) Chinese Confucianism significantly influenced Japanese life
   (D) historically, the Japanese Emperor has little part in deciding which religion is practiced by the people
   (E) Shinto is a belief system introduced into Japan from Korea

Questions 10–18 are based on the following passage.

"Professedly prudent" is the phrase that I have chosen to apply to Benjamin Franklin. For the one thing that is clear, as we turn to look at him
Line and the other men who stood with Washington, is
(5) that, whatever their philosophical professions may have been, they were not controlled by prudence. They were really imprudent, and at heart willing to take all risks of poverty and death in a struggle whose cause was just though its
(10) issue was dubious. If it be rashness to commit honor and life and property to a great adventure for the general good, then these men were rash to the verge of recklessness. They refused no peril, they withheld no sacrifice, in the following of
(15) their ideal.

I hear John Dickinson saying: "It is not our duty to leave wealth to our children, but it is our duty to leave liberty to them. We have counted the cost of this contest, and we find nothing so
(20) dreadful as voluntary slavery." I see Samuel Adams, impoverished, living upon a pittance, hardly able to provide a decent coat for his back, rejecting with scorn the offer of a profitable office, wealth, a title even, to win him from his
(25) allegiance to the cause of America. I see Robert Morris, the wealthy merchant, opening his purse and pledging his credit to support the Revolution, and later devoting all his fortune and his energy to restore and establish the financial honor of the
(30) Republic, with the memorable words, "The United States may command all that I have, except my integrity." I hear the proud John Adams saying to his wife, "I have accepted a seat in the House of Representatives, and thereby
(35) have consented to my own ruin, to your ruin, and the ruin of our children;" and I hear her reply, with the tears running down her face, "Well, I am willing in this cause to run all risks with you, and be ruined with you, if you are ruined." I see
(40) Benjamin Franklin, in the Congress of 1776, already past his seventieth year, prosperous, famous, by far the most celebrated man in America, accepting without demur the difficult and dangerous mission to France, and whispering
(45) to his friend, Dr. Rush, "I am old and good for nothing, but as the store-keepers say of their remnants of cloth, 'I am but a fag-end, and you may have me for what you please.'"

Here is a man who will illustrate and prove,
(50) perhaps better than any other of those who stood with Washington, the point at which I am aiming. There was none of the glamour of romance about old Ben Franklin. He was shrewd, canny, humorous. The chivalric Southerners disliked his
(55) philosophy, and the solemn New-Englanders mistrusted his jokes. He made no extravagant claims for his own motives, and some of his ways were not distinctly ideal. He was full of prudential proverbs, and claimed to be a follower
(60) of the theory of enlightened self-interest. But there was not a faculty of his wise old head which he did not put at the service of his country, nor was there a pulse of his slow and steady heart

GO ON TO THE NEXT PAGE

which did not beat loyal to the cause of
(65) freedom.

He forfeited profitable office and sure
preferment under the crown, for hard work,
uncertain pay, and certain peril in behalf of the
colonies. He followed the inexorable logic, step
(70) by step, which led him from the natural rights of
his countrymen to their liberty, from their liberty
to their independence. He endured with a grim
humor the revilings of those whom he called
"malevolent critics and bug-writers." He broke
(75) with his old and dear associates in England,
writing to one of them, "You and I were long
friends; you are now my enemy and I am Yours,
B. Franklin."

10. In applying the term "professedly prudent" (line 1)
to Benjamin Franklin, the author is most likely
suggesting that

(A) Benjamin Franklin claimed to be prudent but
in many ways was not
(B) Benjamin Franklin did not claim to be prudent
(C) many of Benjamin Franklin's contemporaries
believed that he was prudent
(D) historians are unsure whether Benjamin
Franklin was prudent or not
(E) Benjamin Franklin was prudent in professional
matters

11. In line 5, "professions" most nearly means

(A) fields of study
(B) areas of expertise
(C) misgivings
(D) occupations
(E) avowals of belief

12. In line 10, "issue" most nearly means

(A) offspring
(B) basis
(C) moral principle
(D) outcome
(E) controversial topic

13. The author most likely quotes Robert Morris's
words, "The United States may command all that I
have, except my integrity" (lines 30–32) to suggest
that Robert Morris

(A) had no integrity
(B) was not loyal to the United States
(C) was a person of both great integrity and great
patriotism
(D) was not completely reliable
(E) could not be trusted with money

14. In line 42, "celebrated" most nearly means

(A) iconoclastic
(B) highly decorated for military service
(C) intrepid
(D) known and praised widely
(E) feted

15. Based on the information in the passage, which of
the following is *not* true of Benjamin Franklin?

(A) He generally put the welfare of his country
before his own welfare.
(B) He was wise.
(C) He believed deeply in natural rights and
liberty.
(D) He never went to Europe.
(E) He was widely admired in his country.

16. According to the information given in the passage,
Benjamin Franklin claimed to be a man who

(A) acted from enlightened self-interest
(B) was motivated by the highest ideals
(C) was chivalrous
(D) was the true father of his country
(E) was the most useful person that his country
could send on a mission to France

GO ON TO THE NEXT PAGE

3 **3** **3** **3** **3** **3** **3** **3** **3** **3** **3** **3**

17. The most appropriate title of this passage would be

(A) Ben Franklin: A Study in Prudence
(B) Benjamin Franklin: An American Hero
(C) John Dickinson, Robert Morris, John Adams, and Benjamin Franklin: Flawed Heroes of the American Revolution
(D) Benjamin Franklin's Theory of Enlightened Self-Interest
(E) Benjamin Franklin: Myth and Fact

18. The quotation from Benjamin Franklin's letter in lines 76–78 ("You and I were long friends; you are now my enemy and I am Yours.") shows

(A) how upset Benjamin Franklin was after his decision to support American independence
(B) that Benjamin Franklin was not a loyal friend
(C) that Benjamin Franklin was a less than perfect man
(D) that some of Benjamin Franklin's friends in England did not have a good character
(E) that Benjamin Franklin was so patriotic that he sacrificed friendships for his love of country

Questions 19–24 are based on the following passage.

Some years ago, being with a camping party in the mountains, I returned from a solitary ramble to find everyone engaged in a ferocious
Line metaphysical dispute. The corpus of the dispute
(5) was a squirrel—a live squirrel supposed to be clinging to one side of a tree-trunk; while over against the tree's opposite side a human being was imagined to stand. This human witness tries to get sight of the squirrel by moving rapidly
(10) round the tree, but no matter how fast he goes, the squirrel moves as fast in the opposite direction, and always keeps the tree between himself and the man, so that never a glimpse of him is caught. The resultant metaphysical
(15) problem now is this: Does the man go round the squirrel or not? He goes round the tree, sure enough, and the squirrel is on the tree; but does he go round the squirrel? In the unlimited leisure of the wilderness, discussion had been worn
(20) threadbare. Everyone had taken sides, and was obstinate; and the numbers on both sides were even. Each side, when I appeared, therefore appealed to me to make it a majority. Mindful of

the scholastic adage that whenever you meet a
(25) contradiction you must make a distinction, I immediately sought and found one, as follows: "Which party is right," I said, "depends on what you practically mean by 'going round' the squirrel. If you mean passing from the north of
(30) him to the east, then to the south, then to the west, and then to the north of him again, obviously the man does go round him, for he occupies these successive positions. But if on the contrary you mean being first in front of him,
(35) then on the right of him, then behind him, then on his left, and finally in front again, it is quite as obvious that the man fails to go round him, for by the compensating movements the squirrel makes, he keeps his belly turned towards the man
(40) all the time, and his back turned away. Make the distinction, and there is no occasion for any farther dispute. You are both right and both wrong according as you conceive the verb 'to go round' in one practical fashion or the other."
(45) Although one or two of the hotter disputants called my speech a shuffling evasion, saying they wanted no quibbling or scholastic hair-splitting, but meant just plain honest English "round," the majority seemed to think that the distinction had
(50) assuaged the dispute.
I tell this trivial anecdote because it is a peculiarly simple example of what I wish now to speak of as the pragmatic method. The pragmatic method is primarily a method of settling
(55) metaphysical disputes that otherwise might be interminable. Is the world one or many?—fated or free?—material or spiritual?—here are notions either of which may or may not hold good of the world; and disputes over such notions are
(60) unending. The pragmatic method in such cases is to try to interpret each notion by tracing its respective practical consequences. What difference would it practically make to anyone if this notion rather than that notion were true? If
(65) no practical difference whatever can be traced, then the alternatives mean practically the same thing, and all dispute is idle. Whenever a dispute

GO ON TO THE NEXT PAGE ➤

is serious, we ought to be able to show some practical difference that must follow from one (70) side or the other's being right.

19. The phrase "hair-splitting" as it is used in line 47 most nearly means

(A) asking a rhetorical question
(B) introducing a red herring into the discussion
(C) making unreasonably fine distinctions
(D) begging the question
(E) "splitting" the difference between the two sides and "agreeing to disagree"

20. A "shuffling evasion" (line 46) is

(A) a popular dance
(B) the dance created when a man chases a squirrel around a tree
(C) a meaningless metaphysical dispute
(D) the inexplicable interaction of spiritual and physical forces in the universe
(E) equivocation

21. The author uses the dispute about whether the man goes around the squirrel in the tree

(A) to show that metaphysical disputes can never be solved
(B) to illustrate his point that there is no point in defining clearly the words used in a metaphysical dispute since words can mean anything one wants them to
(C) to give a clear example of how the pragmatic approach can solve metaphysical disputes
(D) to demonstrate the stupidity of most people
(E) to give a simple example of a shuffling evasion

22. Based on the information given in the passage, which of the following statements would the author be most likely to agree with?

(A) Metaphysical questions can't be solved by the "Pragmatic Method."
(B) It is important to define carefully the terms in a philosophical discussion.
(C) The world is primarily spiritual in nature.
(D) Defining terms in a philosophical discussion is mere quibbling.
(E) Philosophical truth is best determined by majority vote.

23. In line 67, "idle" most nearly means

(A) lacking value
(B) employing circular reasoning
(C) something done by lazy people
(D) endless
(E) lacking energy

24. The passage makes use of all of the following EXCEPT

(A) anecdote
(B) rhetorical question
(C) parody
(D) definition
(E) adage

STOP

IN ANY REMAINING TIME YOU MAY REVIEW THE ANSWERS YOU CHOSE IN THIS SECTION. DO NOT WORK ON ANY OTHER SECTION OF THE TEST DURING THIS TIME.

5 5 5 5 5 5 5

SECTION **5** **Time—25 Minutes** **35 Questions** Choose the best answer to each of the following questions in this section. Then blacken the appropriate space on your answer sheet.

Each sentence below may or may not employ correct or effective expression. If you think that the underlined phrasing makes the most clear and precise sentence, select choice A. If, however, you think that the underlined phrasing makes the meaning of the sentence unclear or awkward, or that it is grammatically incorrect, select another answer from choices B to E.

In choosing your answers, follow the conventions of English as it is used by educated writers. Consider sentence structure, grammar, word choice, and punctuation. Choose the answer that produces the sentence that is the most clear and effective.

Example:

In her comments after the debate the judge said that she had been impressed by the ability of both teams to exploit logical weaknesses and in citing relevant examples.

(A) in citing relevant examples
(B) in that relevant examples had been cited
(C) in the citing of relevant examples
(D) to cite relevant examples
(E) to be able to cite relevant examples

1. Although the Scottish writer David Lindsay's novel *A Voyage to Arcturus* is not as well known as C.S. Lewis's *Perelandra*, there are some critics and writers, such as Colin Wilson, who consider it the greatest novel of the two.

(A) the greatest novel
(B) the greater novel
(C) the great novel
(D) the novel that is greater
(E) a great novel

2. Lacking a solid foundation in basic mathematics, the calculus course was something that was difficult for Terry.

(A) the calculus course was something that was difficult for Terry
(B) there were difficulties for Terry in the calculus course
(C) Terry, in the calculus course, had difficulties
(D) something difficult for Terry was the calculus course
(E) Terry found the calculus course difficult

3. The witness testified as to the whereabouts of the accused on the day that the crime was committed.

(A) as to
(B) as for
(C) over
(D) describing
(E) what was

4. Because bullets, traveling faster than sound, there is a saying among soldiers that you do not hear the sound of the gun firing the bullet that kills you.

(A) Because bullets, traveling faster than sound, there is a saying among soldiers that
(B) Because there is a saying among soldiers that bullets travel faster than sound
(C) There is a saying among soldiers that because bullets travel faster than sound
(D) Among soldiers because bullets travel faster than sound there is a saying
(E) A saying among soldiers there is that because bullets travel faster than sound

5 5 5 5 5 5 5

5. Singapore's population of about four million is composed of people who, although they share English as a common language, <u>a number of mother tongue languages such as Tamil, Cantonese, and Malay are spoken</u>.

(A) a number of mother tongue languages such as Tamil, Cantonese, and Malay are spoken
(B) they are speaking a number of mother tongue languages such as Tamil, Cantonese, and Malay
(C) mother tongue languages, such as Tamil, Cantonese, and Malay, are spoken
(D) speak a number of mother tongue languages such as Tamil, Cantonese, and Malay
(E) spoken are a number of mother tongue languages such as Tamil, Cantonese, and Malay

6. Major Smith and his family moved many times during his military career, <u>moving from California, first they went to Texas, then later they went from the United States to Germany</u>.

(A) moving from California, first they went to Texas, then later they went from the United States to Germany
(B) first to Texas from California and later from the United States to Germany
(C) first from California to Texas and later from the United States to Germany
(D) first from California they moved to Texas, later they went to Germany from the United States
(E) the first move the family made was from California to Texas, and then they went from the United States to Germany

7. During the time when the bridge into the city was being repaired, the flow of traffic was slowed, <u>and this as a result caused delays that made people late for work</u>.

(A) and this as a result caused delays that made people late for work
(B) causing delays that made people late for work
(C) causing delays, which made people late for work
(D) by which delays were caused making people late for work
(E) as a result of which people were late for work because of delays

8. <u>In view of his great personal charm and firm grasp of public policy, Troy is</u> a politician who one day might become a U.S. Senator.

(A) In view of his great personal charm and firm grasp of public policy, Troy is
(B) Having great personal charm, combined with having a firm grasp of public policy, Troy is
(C) Great personal charm and a grasp of public policy that is firm make Troy
(D) Considering his great personal charm, combined with a firm grasp of public policy, Troy is
(E) By virtue of his having great personal charm, as well as his firm grasp of public policy, Troy is

9. Benjamin Franklin is revered not only as a courageous patriot but also <u>he discovered and invented many things</u>.

(A) he discovered and invented many things
(B) for discovering and inventing many things
(C) for his many discoveries and inventions
(D) as someone who made many discoveries and invented many things
(E) as having made many discoveries and invented many things

Practice Test 5

GO ON TO THE NEXT PAGE ➡

10. After Jerry Garcia died in 1995, he was eulogized by Bob Dylan, among many musicians, who said, "There's no way to measure his greatness as a person or as a player.... He is the very spirit personified of whatever is muddy river country at its core and screams up into the spheres. He really had no equal."

(A) by Bob Dylan, among many musicians, who said,

(B) by Bob Dylan, among many musicians who said,

(C) by many musicians, Bob Dylan saying,

(D) by many musicians, including Bob Dylan, who said,

(E) among many musicians, including Bob Dylan, who said,

11. The most common excuses given by students for not handing in assignments are that they are busy with other school work and not understanding the requirements fully.

(A) are that they are busy with other school work and not understanding the requirements fully

(B) are being busy with school work and they do not understand the requirements fully

(C) are being busy with other assignments and, in addition, not having a full understanding of what is required

(D) is being busy with other assignments and not fully understanding the requirements

(E) are that they are busy with other school work and that they do not understand the requirements fully

GO ON TO THE NEXT PAGE ➡

5 **5** **5** **5** **5** **5** **5**

Each of the sentences below contains either one error or no error in grammar or usage. If there is an error, it will be underlined. If the sentence contains an error, indicate this by selecting the letter for the one under-lined part that should be changed to make the sentence correct. Follow the requirements of standard written English in choosing answers. If the sentence is already correct, select choice E.

Example:

The number of stars <u>visible in</u> the sky on any
               A
<u>given</u> night <u>vary</u>, mainly <u>because of</u> changes in
 B   C   D
atmospheric conditions and in the phases of the

Moon. <u>No Error</u>
      E

12. A very good maxim to remember is, "What goes online stays online," <u>which means</u> that information
                 A
a person puts on the World Wide Web <u>stays</u> there;
                        B
so, if you put a picture of yourself on a social
network site, for example, <u>its</u> sensible to keep in
                     C
mind that others might <u>be looking</u> at it in ten
                 D
years' time. <u>No Error</u>
        E

13. <u>Interesting</u>, one of the main drivers <u>behind</u> the
   A   B
ever-increasing power of personal computers is the
<u>need of</u> game players for machines that can
 C
process information at <u>greater speed</u>. <u>No Error</u>
               D   E

14. The <u>prominent</u> civil rights movement leader Martin
     A
Luther King, Jr. was <u>influenced by</u> the precepts of
                B
Mohandas Gandhi, the Indian political and spiritual
leader who <u>seeked</u> justice <u>through</u> nonviolence.
         C   D
<u>No Error</u>
 E

15. In the 1980s there were numerous predictions of a "paperless office" that <u>had come about</u> because
               A
computers <u>would make</u> paper unnecessary for
         B
many purposes; however, a quick look
<u>around almost</u> any office would tell us that paper
  C
is still <u>greatly</u> used. <u>No Error</u>
    D   E

16. The Romans <u>believed</u> that each person <u>has</u> a
        A   B
"genius," a spirit that guides <u>the person</u> from birth
               C
to death, <u>much like</u> the "guardian angel" of
       D
Christianity. <u>No Error</u>
      E

17. The film *The Right Stuff*, <u>based on</u> the book <u>in</u> the
               A   B
same title by Tom Wolfe, tells the <u>story of</u> the
                  C
courageous test pilots and astronauts who
<u>paved the way</u> for American space exploration in
 D
the 1950s and 1960s. <u>No Error</u>
           E

Practice Test 5

GO ON TO THE NEXT PAGE

5 5 5 5 5 5 5

18. According to the article in the latest <u>issue of</u> the
                                            A
psychology journal, <u>increasing numbers</u> of young
                        B
people in Japan <u>are becoming</u> alienated <u>from</u>
                    C   D
society. <u>No Error</u>
          E

19. One of the <u>best-known</u> amateur radio operators
                    A
<u>was</u> Senator Barry Goldwater, a U.S. Senator from
  B
Arizona <u>who</u> ran for President in 1964 <u>by</u> the
            C   D
Republican ticket. <u>No Error</u>
                      E

20. Australia has a land area <u>approximately</u> four-fifths
                                    A
<u>the size of</u> the continental United States, but has a
  B
population of about twenty million, <u>compared to</u>
                                        C
the United States, <u>with having</u> a population of over
                        D
three hundred million. <u>No Error</u>
                          E

21. <u>The rabbit</u>, introduced <u>into</u> Australia by English
      A   B
settlers, <u>bred prolific</u> and quickly became a pest,
            C
<u>eating</u> farmers' grain and animal feed. <u>No Error</u>
  D   E

22. The "Queenslander" is <u>one of</u> the most
                            A
<u>recognizable</u> architectural styles of Australia: a
    B
spacious house with a <u>sweeping</u> veranda
                          C
<u>mounted by</u> poles. <u>No Error</u>
  D   E

23. Apostrophes were <u>originally</u> used in English
                        A
<u>to indicate</u> missing letters in words (*lyin'*, for
  B
example); <u>only</u> later <u>did they come</u> to be used to
            C   D
indicate possession (*Phil's book*, for example).

<u>No Error</u>
  E

24. The tennis coach <u>allowed</u> the members of the team
                        A
to decide whether <u>he or she</u> would play
                      B
<u>singles or doubles</u> in the <u>team's</u> final match of the
  C   D
year. <u>No Error</u>
        E

25. According to psychologists, peer groups <u>normally</u>
                                                A
have a leader, a deputy leader, and various
members, among <u>whom</u> there <u>are</u> sometimes a
                    B   C
"joker" and an "isolate" (a person who doesn't
form a bond <u>with</u> the other members). <u>No Error</u>
              D   E

26. <u>When</u> Mr. Johnson, a forklift operator <u>by trade</u>,
      A   B
was unemployed during the severe recession of
2001, he <u>had</u> difficulty simply <u>to put</u> food on the
            C   D
table for his family. <u>No Error</u>
                        E

GO ON TO THE NEXT PAGE

5 **5** **5** **5** **5** **5** **5**

27. According to the research of psychologists,
                                 A
    romantic love lasts an average of thirty months,
                         B
    after which a relationship becomes more
         C
    oriented in companionship. No Error
         D   E

28. The primary mission of Médicins Sans Frontières,
            A
    a renowned aid organization founded by a group
        B   C
    of French doctors, is to provide people in

    disaster striked areas of the world with medicine
         D
    and health care experts. No Error
                              E

29. Experts in space flight say that in the early years
        A
    of the "space race" between the Soviet Union and

    the United States, engineers in the former had a
                                    B
    significant advantage in they had rockets available
                          C
    that could carry much larger payloads than those
                                             D
    available to American engineers could. No Error
                                            E

GO ON TO THE NEXT PAGE ⟶

5 5 5 5 5 5 5

The following early draft of an essay needs to be rewritten to improve sentence structure, choice of words, clarity of expression, organization, and development. After reading the draft, answer each question below it, choosing the answer that best conforms to the requirements of standard written English.

(1) The Pilbara is a rugged area in Western Australia. **(2)** It is a part of Earth that has stayed at the surface for about 3.5 billion years, which is approximately three-quarters of the age of Earth. **(3)** Studying rocks in the Pilbara helps geologists to gain a better understanding of what was happening on the planet in the early period of its development. **(4)** Microbes existed on Earth as early as 3.5 billion years ago. **(5)** Geologists reached this conclusion because they found stromatolites, which are shapes created by microbes, in the rocks.

(6) What is more, it raises a tantalizing question: If life could have arisen so early on Earth, could it also have arisen billions of years ago elsewhere in the solar system? **(7)** Astonishingly, evidence of just that has been found! **(8)** Recently, scientists from the Search for Extraterrestrial Intelligence Institute discovered that certain rocks on Mars might contain fossilized remains of ancient life. **(9)** The rocks are in an area of Mars called Nili Fossae and the scientists say that their composition is very similar to that of the rocks in the Pilbara. **(10)** They both contain carbonate, which can be formed from the bones and shells of organisms that have died. **(11)** Some researchers believe it is very likely that the rocks contain stromatolites like those in the Pilbara. **(12)** If stromatolites are found it would demonstrate conclusively that life originated on Mars under less than ideal conditions, suggesting in turn that it is very likely that life has arisen elsewhere in the solar system.

30. In context, which of the following would be the best phrase to link sentences 1 and 2?

(A) that geologists are finding to be fascinating because
(B) that fascinates geologists because
(C) that is one of the areas in the world that most interests geologists because
(D) that is ancient because
(E) that puzzles geologists because

31. What would be the best way to deal with sentence 4?

(A) Leave it as it is.
(B) Delete it.
(C) Add "For instance" to the beginning of the sentence.
(D) Insert "One of the scientists' most important discoveries was that" at the beginning of the sentence.
(E) Insert "being one of the most important scientific discoveries" at the end of the sentence.

32. Which of the following sentences would be best inserted before sentence 6 to introduce paragraph 2?

(A) However, scientists cannot determine from stromatolites what type of microbes they were.
(B) The importance of the Pilbara for geology thus cannot be underestimated.
(C) It is interesting to learn that life existed on Earth at such an early stage of its development.
(D) It is, therefore, possible that life could have arisen on other planets, too.
(E) However, not all scientists agree with this conclusion, and so more research is needed.

GO ON TO THE NEXT PAGE

5   5   5   5   5   5   5

33. Which would be the best way to revise the underlined portion of sentence 7 (reproduced below)?

    Astonishingly, evidence <u>of just that</u> has been found!

(A) of even more advanced forms of life in the Pilbara

(B) that is irrefutable proof that life exists outside Earth

(C) that life could have arisen elsewhere in the solar system

(D) that shows that life could not have existed on other planets in the solar system

(E) that life exists throughout the solar system

34. Which of the following words or phrases would best improve sentence 10 if added to the beginning of the sentence?

(A) On the other hand,

(B) Mysteriously,

(C) In point of fact,

(D) Most notably,

(E) Unfortunately,

35. Which would be the best way to revise the underlined portion of Sentence 12 (reproduced below)?

    If stromatolites are found it would demonstrate conclusively that life originated on Mars under less than ideal <u>conditions, suggesting in turn that</u> it is very likely that life has arisen elsewhere in the solar system.

(A) conditions; suggesting in turn that

(B) conditions, something that would then suggest that

(C) conditions, this would then suggest that

(D) conditions, which in turn would suggest that

(E) conditions, which, as a consequence of this, would suggest that

STOP

IN ANY REMAINING TIME YOU MAY REVIEW THE ANSWERS YOU CHOSE IN THIS SECTION. DO NOT WORK ON ANY OTHER SECTION OF THE TEST DURING THIS TIME.

SECTION 6

Time—25 Minutes
18 Questions

You have 25 minutes to answer the 8 multiple-choice questions and 10 student-produced response questions in this section. For each multiple-choice question, determine which of the five choices is correct and blacken the corresponding choice on your answer sheet. You may use any blank space on the page for your work.

Notes:

- You may use a calculator whenever you think it will be helpful.
- Only real numbers are used. No question or answer on this test involves a complex or imaginary number.
- Use the diagrams provided to help you solve the problems. Unless you see the words "Note: Figure not drawn to scale" under a diagram, it has been drawn as accurately as possible. Unless it is stated that a figure is three-dimensional, you may assume it lies in a plane.
- For any function, *f*, the domain, unless specifically restricted, is the set of all real numbers for which *f*(*x*) is also a real number.

Reference Information

Area Facts

$A = \ell w$

$A = \frac{1}{2} bh$

$A = \pi r^2$
$C = 2\pi r$

Volume Facts

$V = \ell wh$

$V = \pi r^2 h$

Triangle Facts

$a^2 + b^2 = c^2$

Angle Facts

$x + y + z = 180$

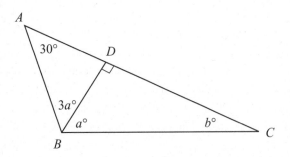

1. In the figure above, what is the value of *b*?

(A) 20
(B) 30
(C) 45
(D) 60
(E) 70

2. If $6a - 3 < 3a + 6$, which of the following CANNOT be the value of *a*?

(A) −3
(B) −1
(C) 0
(D) 1
(E) 3

GO ON TO THE NEXT PAGE

6   6 6 6 6 6 6 6 6 6 6   6

3. If $|a - b| = 5$ and $|b - c| = 5$, which of the following could be the value of $|a - c|$?

   I.   0
  II.   5
 III. 10

(A) I only
(B) II only
(C) III only
(D) I and III only
(E) I, II, and III

4. For how many values of x does $(x - 2)(x - 3) = x^2 - 5x - 6$?

(A) None
(B) 1
(C) 2
(D) 3
(E) Infinitely many

5. x and y are integers, such that $2 < x < 9$ and $5 < y < 9$. If G is the greatest possible value of $x - y$ and L is the least possible value of $x - y$, what is the value of $G - L$?

(A) −3
(B) −2
(C) 3
(D) 7
(E) 12

6. If $x^2 = 12$, what is the value of $(x + 4)^2 + (x - 4)^2$?

(A) 24
(B) 32
(C) 36
(D) 48
(E) 56

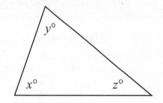

Note: Figure not drawn to scale.

7. In the figure above, the average (arithmetic mean) of x and y is z. If x is four times y, what is the average of x and z?

(A) 42
(B) 60
(C) 72
(D) 78
(E) 96

8. Elaine had d dollars. She used 60 percent of her money to buy pencils that cost p cents each. She spent the rest of her money to buy markers that cost m cents each. Which of the following expressions represents the number of markers she bought?

(A) $\dfrac{2d}{5m}$

(B) $\dfrac{5d}{2m}$

(C) $\dfrac{40d}{m}$

(D) $\dfrac{40d}{mp}$

(E) $\dfrac{2dp}{5m}$

GO ON TO THE NEXT PAGE

Practice Test 5

6   6 6 6 6 6 6 6 6 6 6   6

Directions for Student-Produced Response Questions (Grid-ins)

In questions 9–18, first solve the problem, and then enter your answer on the grid provided on the answer sheet. The instructions for entering your answers are as follows:
- First, write your answer in the boxes at the top of the grid.
- Second, grid your answer in the columns below the boxes.
- Use the fraction bar in the first row or the decimal point in the second row to enter fractions and decimal answers.

- Grid only one space in each column.
- Entering the answer in the boxes is recommended as an aid in gridding, but is not required.
- The machine scoring your exam can read only what you grid, so you **must grid in your answers correctly to get credit**.
- If a question has more than one correct answer, grid in only one of these answers.
- The grid does not have a minus sign, so no answer can be negative.
- A mixed number *must* be converted to an improper fraction or a decimal before it is gridded. Enter $1\frac{1}{4}$ as 5/4 or 1.25; the machine will interpret 1 1/4 as $\frac{11}{4}$ and mark it wrong.
- **All decimals must be entered as accurately as possible.** Here are the three acceptable ways of gridding

$$\frac{3}{11} = 0.272727\ldots$$

Answer: $\frac{8}{15}$ Answer: 1.75

Write your →
answer in
the boxes.

Grid in →
your
answer.

Answer: 100

Either position is acceptable

3/11   .272   .273

• Note that rounding to .273 is acceptable, because you are using the full grid, but you would receive **no credit** for .3 or .27, because these answers are less accurate.

GO ON TO THE NEXT PAGE →

6   6 6 6 6 6 6 6 6 6 6 6   6

9. If $a^2 + b^2 = 15$, what is the value of $(3a)^2 + (3b)^2$?

10. What is $\dfrac{1}{2}$ of 10% of 40?

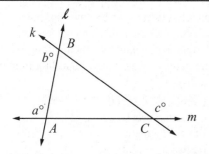

11. In the figure above, lines k, ℓ, and m intersect to form triangle ABC. If m∠$BAC = 83°$, what is the value of $a + b + c$?

12. John's father gave him a box of coins in which the ratio of the number of American coins to the number of foreign coins was 3:1. Later John received a gift of 80 foreign coins. The ratio of the number of American coins to the number of foreign coins he then had was 1:3. How many American coins did John have originally?

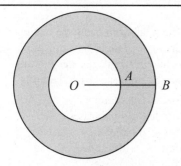

Note: Figure not drawn to scale.

13. In the figure above, O is the center of both circles. Point A is a point on the small circle and lies on $\overline{OB}$, which is a radius of the large circle. If $OA = 9$ and the area of the shaded region is 144π, what is the length of segment $\overline{AB}$?

14. How many different integers, x, satisfy the inequality $7 < 7x + 77 < 777$?

15. Olivier has an envelope with 100 bills in it. Each bill is either a $5 bill or a $10 bill. If the total value of the bills in the envelope is $865, how many of the bills are $10 bills?

16. For all real numbers x: $f(x) = x^2 - 2$. For what value of a is it true that $f(a) = f(a - 1)$?

17. In a survey of 500 families, each family has at least one child. If 345 of the families have at least one boy and 245 of the families have at least one girl, how many families have only boys?

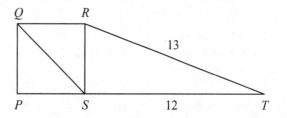

18. In the figure above, side $\overline{PS}$ of square $PQRS$ is extended to T, $ST = 12$, and $RT = 13$. If the perimeter of quadrilateral $QRTS$ is expressed as $a + b\sqrt{2}$, where a and b are integers, what is the value of $a + b$?

IN ANY REMAINING TIME YOU MAY REVIEW THE ANSWERS YOU CHOSE IN THIS SECTION. DO NOT WORK ON ANY OTHER SECTION OF THE TEST DURING THIS TIME.

Practice Test 5

7

SECTION 7	Time—25 Minutes 24 Questions	Choose the best answer to each of the following questions in this section. Then blacken the appropriate space on your answer sheet.

Each of the following sentences contains one or two blanks, indicating that a word or set of words has been omitted. Beneath each sentence there are five answer choices labeled A to E from which you must select the word or set of words that best fits the meaning of the sentence as a whole.

Example:

Records of colonization can be found as far back as the Phoenicians, but colonization became a major force in world history only when European countries began, in the fifteenth century, to make ---- Asia, the Americas, and Africa.

(A) queries about   (B) incursions into
   (C) tirades against   (D) enemies in
    (E) amends for

1. Censorship presents a major problem for democratic societies: democracy depends on free expression and censorship ---- that expression.

   (A) enhances   (B) nurtures   (C) inhibits
     (D) spurs   (E) supplements

2. Within a scientist's professional frame of reference, spiritual beliefs have little relevance; however, outside this framework it is ---- for a scientist to have such beliefs.

   (A) facile   (B) dangerous
     (C) bombastic   (D) legitimate
      (E) difficult

3. Language reflects ----: By investigating the organization and use of language systems we can gain some understanding of something basic in human nature, in particular regarding human ---- ability.

   (A) the world . . social
   (B) culture . . artistic
   (C) life . . linguistic
   (D) reality . . verbal
   (E) mind . . cognitive

4. People considering acting on the ---- "The ends justify the means" would do well to keep in mind the ---- advice of Augustus William Hare: "He who does evil that good may come, pays a toll to the devil to let him into heaven."

   (A) quotation . . encouraging
   (B) doctrine . . modest
   (C) belief . . facile
   (D) idea . . absurd
   (E) principle . . wise

5. If it is true that all humans are equipped with identical ---- for language acquisition, then it follows that all languages, despite their superficial ----, share a number of basic features.

   (A) classes . . variations
   (B) aptitudes . . similarities
   (C) skills . . parallels
   (D) faculties . . differences
   (E) brains . . likenesses

GO ON TO THE NEXT PAGE

7

6. In his book *The Golden Bough*, ---- study, J. G. Frazer proposed that human societies progress by virtue of different ways of thinking about the world.

   (A) an anthropomorphic
   (B) an anthropological
   (C) an aesthetic
   (D) a linguistic
   (E) a philanthropic

7. Upon reading Charles Darwin's *On the Origin of Species*, which systematically and ---- outlined the theory of natural selection as the impetus for evolution, the eminent scientist T. H. Huxley ---- not having thought of such a simple idea: "How extremely stupid not to have thought of that," he said.

   (A) painstakingly . . lamented
   (B) meticulously . . ignored
   (C) languidly . . belabored
   (D) loquaciously . . decried
   (E) methodically . . berated

GO ON TO THE NEXT PAGE >

7

Below are passages followed by questions on them. Questions on a pair of related passages may be about the relationship between the two passages. For each question, select the best answer based on what is stated or implied in the passage (or passages).

Questions 8–11 are based on the following passages.

Passage 1

The health-care system today is dominated by fee-for-service payment; the health-care system of the future needs to be dominated by fee-for-
Line value payment. The difference is crucial: one
(5) payment system drives up quantity; the other, quality. The health bill takes some steps, albeit modest ones, toward creating a system based on paying for quality. For example, it creates penalties for hospitals with high rates of hospital-
(10) acquired infections and other avoidable conditions by reducing Medicare payments for hospitals in the top 25 percent of the distribution for such problems. It includes a variety of pilot programs involving bundled payments, which
(15) provide incentives to coordinate care for patients with chronic illnesses by paying a fixed sum for treating a specific condition rather than paying for each individual treatment.

Passage 2

Medicare currently makes separate payments
(20) to providers for the services they furnish to beneficiaries for a single illness or course of treatment, leading to fragmented care with minimal coordination across providers and health care settings. Payment is based on how much a
(25) provider does, not how well the provider does in treating the patient. Under the Bundled Payment Initiative, Centers for Medicare Services would link payments for multiple services patients receive during an episode of care. For example,
(30) instead of a surgical procedure generating multiple claims from multiple providers, the entire team is compensated with a "bundled" payment that provides incentives to deliver health care services more efficiently while maintaining
(35) or improving quality of care. Providers will have flexibility to determine which episodes of care and which services would be bundled together. Research has shown that bundled payments can align incentives for providers—hospitals, post

(40) acute care providers, doctors, and other practitioners—to partner closely across all specialties and settings that a patient may encounter to improve the patient's experience of care during a hospital stay in an acute care
(45) hospital, and during post-discharge recovery.

8. According to the author of Passage 1, health care systems based on fee-for-service payment
   (A) tend to encourage health care providers to be efficient
   (B) encourage health care providers to give high-quality service
   (C) are the fairest way of providing health care
   (D) have not been studied enough to reach a sensible conclusion about its merit
   (E) tend to encourage health care providers to give a greater amount of service

9. The phrase "albeit modest" in lines 6–7 most nearly means
   (A) although not large
   (B) poorly planned
   (C) although respectful and non-confrontational
   (D) although not controversial
   (E) notably large

10. Which of the following topics, mentioned in Passage 1, is focused on in Passage 2?
    (A) Reduced Medicare payments to hospitals with high rates of hospital-acquired infections
    (B) Weaknesses of the fee-for-service approach to payment for medical care
    (C) Bundled payments
    (D) The advantage of the fee-for-value approach to payment for medical care
    (E) Incentives to encourage health care providers to coordinate treatment of patients with chronic conditions

GO ON TO THE NEXT PAGE

11. Which of the following most accurately describes the relationship of Passage 1 to Passage 2?

(A) Passage 1 describes measures taken to improve the health care system; Passage 2 describes how one of the measures mentioned in Passage 1 would be implemented.

(B) Passage 1 compares fee-for-service-based payment for health care with fee-for-value-based payment for health care; Passage 2 describes how a bundled payment system would work.

(C) Passage 1 analyzes some of the measures taken to improve the quality of medical care; Passage 2 discusses how three of these measures would work in practice.

(D) Passage 1 discusses inefficiencies in the health care system caused by the dominance of the fee-for-service payment for health care model; Passage 2 discusses some of the difficulties that may arise in switching from the fee-for-service payment for health care model to the fee-for-quality/value payment for health care model.

(E) Passage 1 describes incentives and disincentives that the health bill includes to make health care more efficient; Passage 2 describes how Medicare now causes inefficiencies in the health care system.

Questions 12–24 are based on the following passages.

Passage 1

Do not all cultures have to cope with the natural turbulence of adolescence, even though it may not be given institutional expression? Dr.
Line Mead has studied this question in Samoa. There
(5) the girl's life passes through well-marked periods. Her first years out of baby-hood are passed in small neighborhood gangs of age mates from which the little boys are strictly excluded. The corner of the village to which she belongs is all-
(10) important, and the little boys are traditional enemies. She has one duty, that of baby-tending, but she takes the baby with her rather than stay home to mind it, and her play is not seriously hampered. A couple of years before puberty,
(15) when she grows strong enough to have more difficult tasks required of her and old enough to

learn more skilled techniques, the little girls' play group in which she grew up ceases to exist. She assumes woman's dress and must contribute to
(20) the work of the household. It is an uninteresting period of life to her and quite without turmoil. Puberty brings no change at all.

A few years after she has come of age, she will begin the pleasant years of casual and
(25) irresponsible love affairs that she will prolong as far as possible into the period when marriage is already considered fitting. Puberty itself is marked by no social recognition, no change of attitude or of expectancy. Her preadolescent
(30) shyness is supposed to remain unchanged for a couple of years. The girl's life in Samoa is blocked out by other considerations than those of physiological sex maturity, and puberty falls in a particularly unstressed and peaceful period during
(35) which no adolescent conflicts manifest themselves. Adolescence, therefore, may not only be culturally passed over without ceremonial; it may also be without importance in the emotional life of the child and in the attitude of the village
(40) toward her.

Passage 2

If we assume that a transitional period of the life cycle, akin to adolescence, organized around puberty and of variable length, exists almost universally, the next question is what forms it
(45) takes and whether its features, too, are universal. Ethnographic research in Samoa conducted by anthropologist Margaret Mead brought the issue of cultural difference in the experience of adolescence to the fore. Her book, *Coming of Age*
(50) *in Samoa,* famously challenged Hall's "storm and stress" model and argued that Samoan culture influenced psychological development of girls in such a way that the transition from childhood to adulthood was smooth and lacked the "natural"
(55) turbulence with which it had been characterized by the evolutionary view. Unlike American culture, Samoan culture, she argued, did not place judgments and pressures on adolescents and was

GO ON TO THE NEXT PAGE

more relaxed, for example, in its views about
(60) sexuality.

All of these factors were thought to make Samoan adolescence relatively tranquil and enjoyable and led to Mead's assertion of the primacy of nurture over nature. While Derek
(65) Freeman later critiqued Mead's culturally deterministic approach for a number of methodological reasons her ethnographic approach has been important for subsequent cross-cultural approaches to adolescence. Since
(70) then, a sizeable literature in psychology and anthropology has developed which has addressed cross-cultural differences in adolescence.

Schlegel and Barry's cross-cultural study of adolescents in tribal and traditional societies
(75) using data collected from over 175 societies around the world demonstrated that adolescence as a distinctive, socially marked stage of life is ubiquitous. These researchers put forward a biosocial theory, arguing that the social stage of
(80) adolescence is a response to the development of the reproductive capacity. Most notably, however, these cross-cultural studies challenge the notion that features of "storm and stress" and a period of psychological crisis are universal inevitabilities in
(85) adolescence. For example, while mild forms of antisocial behavior were present in some societies, it was certainly not generalizable as a feature. Similarly, aggressive and violent behavior occurred in a minority of cultures and when
(90) present was heavily gendered with aggression in girls being particularly low. Cross-cultural researchers stress that the *meanings* of developmental tasks associated with adolescence such as the establishment of independence or
(95) autonomy may differ according to culture, and may be subject to change over time. For example, developing independence in some cultures may mean taking on duties to care for siblings or elders, and not necessarily separating from adults
(100) and orienting towards peers. Based on a study comparing five cultures that could be contrasted as "traditional" and "modern" or "collectivistic" and "individualistic," Trommsdorff suggested that "turbulent" features such as intergenerational
(105) conflict stem from the focus on attaining independence from parents during this period and are linked to cultural values of individualism in Western societies. Certainly, in many cultures, particularly in pre-industrial societies,

(110) adolescence is not marked by such a characterization or psychological turmoil, and thus, both the characterization and length of this life stage vary according to culture. Puberty, too, which is clearly grounded in biology across
(115) cultures, interacts with the local environment. Menarche, which marks the beginning of puberty in girls, is occurring increasingly early in industrialized countries such as Japan or the United States. This finding may be connected to
(120) changes in dietary intake. Even if puberty could be the biological marker of the start of adolescence in every culture, the end point is less clear.

In summary, adolescence conceptualized as a
(125) prolonged period of identity development linked to increased autonomy, intergenerational conflict, peer-relatedness and social psychological anxieties, is not the norm across cultures.

Indeed, these features seem to depend on
(130) degrees of individualism, social/economic role expectations, gender and class. A historical appreciation of adolescence as a category of science as well as cross-cultural investigations of the experience of adolescence demonstrates that
(135) characteristics associated with this developmental stage may not only have biological bases but also social and cultural origins.

12. Which of the following is most likely to have been one of the main reasons that Dr. Mead chose to study the question of "whether all cultures have to cope with the natural turbulence of adolescence" (lines 1–2) in Samoa?

(A) Samoan culture attaches greater importance to young people than does American culture.
(B) The lives of Samoans go through clearly marked periods, whereas the lives of Americans do not.
(C) Samoan culture places less stress on the individual than does American culture.
(D) Samoans belong to a different racial group than most Americans.
(E) Samoan culture is very different from American culture.

GO ON TO THE NEXT PAGE

13. In line 3, "given institutional expression" most nearly means

   (A) officially recognized by the government
   (B) made part of the religious practices of the society
   (C) explicitly recognized by society and made a part of the culture
   (D) acknowledged as important by anthropologists
   (E) made a part of the school curriculum

14. The author says, "The corner of the village to which she belongs is all-important" (lines 8–10). It is most likely that the author means by this that

   (A) the area of the village in which pre-adolescent girls play is the most important area in the village
   (B) the area of the village in which a young girl's father, mother, and siblings live is the most important area in a young girl's life
   (C) activities in the area of the village in which a group of pre-adolescent girls play are by far the most important activities in a young girl's life
   (D) the area where a pre-adolescent girl and her age mates are to play must be carefully selected by village elders
   (E) the man that a girl eventually marries is determined by which part of the village she plays in as a child

15. The author of Passage 1 writes, "A few years after she has come of age, she will begin the pleasant years of casual and irresponsible love affairs that she will prolong as far as possible into the period when marriage is already considered fitting" (lines 23–27). The author's tone in this sentence can most accurately be described as

   (A) laudatory
   (B) patronizing
   (C) outraged
   (D) puzzled
   (E) matter-of-fact

16. In line 65, "critiqued" most nearly means

   (A) admired
   (B) criticized
   (C) extolled
   (D) evaluated objectively
   (E) imitated

17. According to the author of Passage 2, from her observation that adolescence in Samoa is different from adolescence in America, Margaret Mead argued that

   (A) Samoan culture is different from American culture
   (B) culture has a larger part in shaping human behavior than does genetics
   (C) girls are treated better in Samoa than they are in America
   (D) adolescence in any society varies greatly from adolescence in any other society
   (E) people go through the same basic life experiences in all societies but do so at different times in their lives

18. According to the author of Passage 2, Schlegel and Barry's cross-cultural study of adolescents in tribal and traditional societies showed that

   (A) the phenomenon of adolescence is found everywhere
   (B) adolescence is a time of great conflict in every society
   (C) anti-social behavior always increases during adolescence
   (D) adolescent boys become aggressive in every society
   (E) in every society adolescents focus on developing independence from adults

19. In line 84, "inevitabilities" most nearly means

   (A) stages of life
   (B) assumptions
   (C) occasional events
   (D) unavoidable occurrences
   (E) rare happenings

20. In line 90, "gendered" most nearly means

   (A) free of bias toward either males or females
   (B) biased toward females
   (C) based on genetics
   (D) characteristic of one gender
   (E) seen from a male perspective

GO ON TO THE NEXT PAGE ⟩

7

21. Trommsdorff, whose study is cited in Passage 2, would most likely agree that

   (A) modern cultures are "collectivistic"
   (B) individualistic cultures are "traditional" cultures
   (C) adolescents in "collectivist" cultures do not argue with their parents as much as adolescents in "individualistic" cultures do
   (D) adolescents in "individualistic" cultures never argue with their parents
   (E) adolescents in "collectivist" societies never become fully adult because they never achieve independence from their parents

22. What would be Margaret Mead's most likely response to the following statement in Passage 2: "In summary, adolescence conceptualized as a prolonged period of identity development linked to increased autonomy, intergenerational conflict, peer-relatedness and social psychological anxieties, is not the norm across cultures" (lines 124–128)?

   (A) She would completely disagree with it.
   (B) She would say that there is not enough evidence to justify such a generalization.
   (C) She would say that it reflects the view of most psychologists, but not the view of most anthropologists.
   (D) She would say that cross-cultural studies of any social phenomenon are meaningless because the meaning of any particular social behavior varies so greatly between cultures that comparisons are meaningless.
   (E) She would agree with it.

23. Based on what is said in Passage 2, it can be inferred that its author most likely believes that

   (A) one of the main features of adolescence everywhere is rebellion by young people against parental authority
   (B) adolescence as a distinct period of life is unique to industrialized societies

   (C) adolescence is entirely a social phenomenon with no relation to biology
   (D) adolescence occurs in every culture (or at least nearly every culture), but the form that it takes varies from culture to culture
   (E) adolescence as a distinct period of life occurs only in "individualistic" societies

24. Which of the following most accurately describes the relationship of Passage 1 to Passage 2?

   (A) Passage 1 describes a study that reached a conclusion about a question; Passage 2 addresses the question raised in Passage 1, making use of the study described in Passage 1, as well as other studies, to help reach a conclusion about the question.
   (B) Passage 1 examines the strengths and weaknesses of a particular study, but reaches no conclusion about it; Passage 2 addresses the question raised in Passage 1, presents several answers to it that have been suggested, but reaches no conclusion about the answer to the question.
   (C) Passage 1 examines two competing theories and concludes that there is more evidence for one of them than the other; Passage 2 examines several studies and concludes that they all point to one basic answer to a fundamental question.
   (D) Passage 1 describes a study that the author believes is interesting but which has little relevance today; Passage 2 discusses the relationship between the study described in Passage 1 and subsequent research in the same area.
   (E) Passage 1 describes a study conducted by its author that reached a conclusion about a question; Passage 2 describes later studies that support the conclusion reached by the author of Passage 1.

STOP

8   8 8 8 8 8 8 8 8 8   8

SECTION 8

Time—20 Minutes
16 Questions

For each problem in this section determine which of the five choices is correct and blacken the corresponding choice on your answer sheet. You may use any blank space on the page for your work.

Notes:

- You may use a calculator whenever you think it will be helpful.
- Only real numbers are used. No question or answer on this test involves a complex or imaginary number.
- Use the diagrams provided to help you solve the problems. Unless you see the words "Note: Figure not drawn to scale" under a diagram, it has been drawn as accurately as possible. Unless it is stated that a figure is three-dimensional, you may assume it lies in a plane.
- For any function, f, the domain, unless specifically restricted, is the set of all real numbers for which $f(x)$ is also a real number.

Reference Information

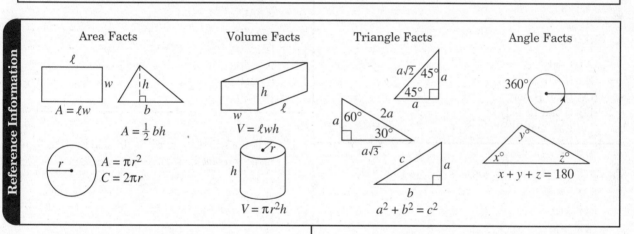

Area Facts

$A = \ell w$

$A = \frac{1}{2} bh$

$A = \pi r^2$
$C = 2\pi r$

Volume Facts

$V = \ell wh$

$V = \pi r^2 h$

Triangle Facts

$a^2 + b^2 = c^2$

Angle Facts

$360°$

$x + y + z = 180$

1. If 85 percent of the stamps in Jon's stamp collection are from countries in Europe, and if 600 of his stamps are from non-European countries, how many stamps are in his collection?

(A) 1,800
(B) 2,400
(C) 3,400
(D) 3,600
(E) 4,000

2. Points P, Q, R, S, and T lie on a line in that order. Q is the midpoint of $\overline{PR}$, R is the midpoint of $\overline{QS}$, and S is the midpoint of $\overline{RT}$. If $QS = 8$, what is the value of PT?

(A) 12
(B) 16
(C) 18
(D) 20
(E) 24

3. If n is an even integer, what is the smallest odd integer greater than $n - 7$?

(A) $n - 6$
(B) $n - 5$
(C) $n - 7$
(D) $n - 8$
(E) $n - 9$

4. If a is equal to $\frac{1}{5}$ of 0.001%, what is the value of a?

(A) .02
(B) .002
(C) .0002
(D) .00002
(E) .000002

GO ON TO THE NEXT PAGE

8   8   8 8 8 8 8 8 8 8   8

5. Let a and b be the two solutions of the equation $|x - 2.5| = 1.5$ and let c and d be the two solutions of the equation $|x - 1.5| = 2.5$. What is the value of $a + b + c + d$?

(A) 4
(B) 5
(C) 6
(D) 8
(E) 10

6. If n is a non-zero integer, which of the following could be the result of dividing n by its reciprocal?

   I. 8
   II. 9
   III. 10

(A) I only
(B) II only
(C) I and II only
(D) II and III only
(E) I, II, and III

7. If $f(x) = x^3 - 2x + 1$, what is the value of $f(2) - f(-2)$?

(A) −10
(B) −8
(C) 0
(D) 8
(E) 10

8. What is the perimeter of an equilateral triangle whose area is $\sqrt{3}$?

(A) $\sqrt{3}$
(B) $3\sqrt{3}$
(C) $6\sqrt{3}$
(D) 2
(E) 6

9. Last year, Tom's car averaged 25 miles per gallon of gas. If Tom drove 10,000 miles and if each time he purchased gas he paid between $3.00 and $3.25 per gallon, which of the following could be the amount of money he paid for gas last year?

(A) $ 879
(B) $1,047
(C) $1,111
(D) $1,234
(E) $1,326

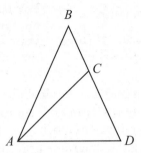

Note: Figure not drawn to scale.

10. In the figure above, $AC = AD$ and $BA = BD$. If $m\angle ADB = 80°$, what is the measure, in degrees, of $\angle BAC$?

(A) 20
(B) 40
(C) 50
(D) 60
(E) 80

11. If the remainder when n is divided by 11 is 7, what is the remainder when $7n$ is divided by 11?

(A) 1
(B) 3
(C) 5
(D) 7
(E) 9

12. For all real numbers, x: $f(x) = x^2 - 18$ and $g(x) = x^2 + 18$. If $k = f(5)$, what is $g(k)$?

(A)   5
(B)   31
(C)   67
(D) 1,831
(E) 1,867

GO ON TO THE NEXT PAGE

8   8   8   8   8   8   8   8   8   8   8

13. If the circumference of a right circular cylinder is 12π inches and the volume of the cylinder is 12π cubic inches, what is the length, in inches, of the height of the cylinder?

(A) π

(B) $\frac{1}{3}\pi$

(C) $\frac{1}{3}$

(D) 1

(E) 3

14. When the positive integer n is divided by 15, the remainder is 11. Which of the following must be a multiple of 15?

  I. $n - 11$
 II. $3n - 3$
III. $4n + 1$

(A) I only
(B) I and II only
(C) I and III only
(D) II and III only
(E) I, II, and III

15. Consider the sequence that begins 1, 1, 2, 3, 5,…, in which the first two terms are each 1 and every term after the second is the sum of the two previous terms (for example: $2 = 1 + 1$, $3 = 1 + 2$, and $5 = 2 + 3$). How many of the first 500 terms of this sequence are odd?

(A) 166
(B) 167
(C) 333
(D) 334
(E) 500

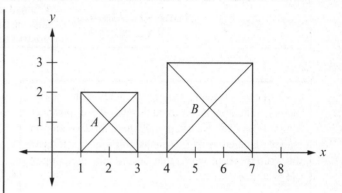

16. The diagram above shows two squares, each with one side on the x-axis. Points A and B are the points of intersection of the diagonals of the two squares, respectively. What is the slope of the line (not shown) that passes through A and B?

(A) $\frac{1}{7}$

(B) $\frac{1}{6}$

(C) $\frac{1}{5}$

(D) $\frac{1}{4}$

(E) $\frac{1}{3}$

Practice Test 5

STOP

IN ANY REMAINING TIME YOU MAY REVIEW THE
ANSWERS YOU CHOSE IN THIS SECTION. DO NOT WORK
ON ANY OTHER SECTION OF THE TEST DURING THIS TIME.

9   9   9   9   9   9   9

SECTION **9**   **Time –20 Minutes**   Choose the best answer to each of the following questions in
           19 Questions   this section. Then blacken the appropriate space on your
answer sheet.

Each of the following sentences contains one or two blanks, indicating that a word or set of words has been omitted. Beneath each sentence there are five answer choices labeled A to E from which you must select the word or set of words that best fits the meaning of the sentence as a whole.

Example:

Records of colonization can be found as far back as the Phoenicians, but colonization became a major force in world history only when European countries began, in the fifteenth century, to make ---- Asia, the Americas, and Africa.

(A) queries about   (B) incursions into
   (C) tirades against   (D) enemies in
     (E) amends for

---

1. A summary is a short statement of the ---- points of a piece of discourse.

   (A) only   (B) trivial   (C) secondary
      (D) main   (E) emotional

2. It was understandable that the two rivals for Pamela's affection felt some ---- one another.

   (A) equanimity about
   (B) amusement about
   (C) affability toward
   (D) sympathy for
   (E) antagonism toward

3. The hospital's board of governors is looking for ---- so that the children's ward can be expanded.

   (A) a benefactor   (B) a mercenary
      (C) a misanthrope   (D) a hedonist
        (E) an opportunist.

4. A hypothesis is ---- the status of a theory when sufficient evidence for it accumulates so that no competing hypothesis is ---- .

   (A) elevated to . . credible
   (B) reduced to . . plausible
   (C) advanced to . . convoluted
   (D) precluded by . . legitimate
   (E) countenanced by . . nuanced

5. Asked how he had produced so many books, the ---- author said, "Every day I get up and write steadily until dinner time."

   (A) sedentary   (B) seminal   (C) prolific
      (D) novice   (E) pious

6. The theme of Franz Kafka's *The Castle* is the ---- of modern man, which Kafka depicts by creating an impersonal, bureaucratic, and ---- world.

   (A) animation . . foreboding
   (B) lassitude . . natural
   (C) legacy . . optimistic
   (D) anodyne . . forlorn
   (E) alienation . . sinister

GO ON TO THE NEXT PAGE ⟩

9　　　9　　　9　　　9　　　9　　　9　　　9

Below are passages followed by questions on them. Questions on a pair of related passages may be about the relationship between the two passages. For each question, select the best answer based on what is stated or implied in the passage (or passages).

Questions 7—19 are based on the following passage.

Apart from elementary schoolmasters, instructors of scribes and the like, the first professional higher educators in the Western
Line world were the group of brilliant talkers and keen
(5) thinkers who appeared in Greece during the fifth century B.C. They were called "sophists."

They were exclusively lecturers. All that we hear of them shows them as phenomenally graceful and subtle talkers, usually to fairly large
(10) audiences. In that they are the direct ancestors of the modern "authority" who tours the large cities giving a carefully prepared speech in which his own personal power or charm is combined with well-spaced jokes and memorable epigrams, the
(15) whole varying very little from one repetition to another. Like him, they were highly paid and widely advertised and welcomed by a reception committee and entertained by ambitious hosts. But unlike him, some of them professed to be
(20) authorities on everything. They said they could lecture on any subject under the sun. Often they were challenged to speak on odd and difficult topics, and accepted the dare. However, they did not usually pretend to know more facts than
(25) others, but rather to be able to think and talk better. In that, perhaps, they are the ancestors of the modern journalists who have the knack of turning out a bright and interesting article on any new subject, without using special or expert
(30) information. The sophists dazzled everyone without convincing anyone of anything positive. They argued unsystematically and unfairly, but painted over the gaps in their reasoning with glossy rhetoric. They had few constructive ideas,
(35) and won most applause by taking traditional notions and showing they were based on convention rather than logic. They demonstrated that almost anything could be proved by a fast talker—sometimes, as a stunt, they made a
(40) powerful speech on one side of a question in the morning, and an equally powerful speech on the opposite side in the afternoon. And they never allowed anyone else to get a word in edgewise.

To some of his contemporaries Socrates
(45) looked like a sophist. But he distrusted and

opposed the sophists wherever possible. They toured the whole Greek world. Socrates stayed in Athens, talking to his fellow-citizens. They made carefully prepared continuous speeches; he only
(50) asked questions. They took rich fees for their teaching; he refused regular payment, living and dying poor. They were elegantly dressed, turned out like film-stars on a personal-appearance tour, with secretaries and personal servants and
(55) elaborate advertising. Socrates wore the workingman's clothes, bare feet and a smock; in fact, he had been a stonemason and carver by trade, and came from a working-class family. They spoke in specially prepared lecture-halls; he
(60) talked to people at street-corners and in the gymnasium (like public baths and bathing-beaches nowadays), where every afternoon the young men exercised, and old men talked, while they all sunbathed. He fitted in so well there that
(65) he sometimes compared himself to the athletic coach, who does not run or wrestle, but teaches others how to run and wrestle better: Socrates said he trained people to think. Lastly, the sophists said they knew everything and were
(70) ready to explain it. Socrates said he knew nothing and was trying to find out.

The sophists were the first lecturers. Socrates was the first tutor. His invention was more radical than theirs. Speeches such as they delivered could
(75) be heard elsewhere—in the new democratic law-courts, where clever orators tried to sway large juries by dozens of newly developed oratorical tricks, and in the theaters, where tragic kings, queens, gods, and heroes accused and defied one
(80) another in mortal tirades, and in the assemblies of the people, where any citizen could speak on the destinies of Athens. And travelling virtuosi like the sophists were fairly common in other fields—touring musicians, painters, and sculptors,
(85) eminent poets like Simonides, were all welcome

GO ON TO THE NEXT PAGE ▷

9   9   9   9   9   9   9

in Greek cities and at the rich courts of the
"tyrants." It was not too hard, then, for the
sophists to work out a performance of their own,
as brilliant and sometimes as impermanent as a
(90) harpist's recital. The innovations Socrates made
were to use ordinary conversation as a method of
teaching, and to act on one society only, his own
city of Athens, instead of detaching himself and
traveling. He was not even a "brilliant
(95) conversationalist," in the style of Oscar Wilde.
He does not seem to have made memorable
epigrams or thrown off eloquent paragraphs of
improvisation like Coleridge. His talk was not
"full of flowers and stars." He made the other
(100) fellow do most of the talking. He merely asked
questions.
    But anyone who has watched a cross-
examination in court knows that this is more
difficult than making a prepared speech. Socrates
(105) questioned all sorts and conditions, from
schoolboys to elderly capitalists, from orthodox
middle-of-the-road citizens to extremists, friends
and enemies, critics and admirers, the famous and
the obscure, prostitutes and politicians, artists and
(110) soldiers, average Athenians and famous visitors.
It was incredibly difficult for him to adapt
himself to so many different characters and
outlooks, and yet we know that he did. Socrates
looked ugly. He had good manners, but no
(115) aristocratic polish. Yet he was able to talk to the
cleverest and the toughest minds of this age and
to convince them that they knew no more than he
did. His methods were, first, the modest
declaration of his own ignorance—which
(120) imperceptibly flattered the other man and made
him eager to explain to such an intelligent but
naive inquirer; second, his adaptability—which
showed him the side on which each man could be
best approached; and, third, his unfailing good
(125) humor—which allowed him always to keep the
conversation going and at crises, when the other
lost his temper, to dominate it. Some of the most
delightful dramatic scenes in literature are those
dialogues in which we see him confronted by a
(130) brilliant fanatic and drenched with a shower of
words that would have silenced most others, and
then emerging, with a humorous pretense of
timidity, to shake off the rhetoric and pursue the
truth, until at last, under his gently persistent
(135) questions, his opponent is—not forced, but led, to
admit that he was wrong, and to fall into helpless
silence.

7. In line 16, "him" most nearly means
   (A) the typical sophist
   (B) a well-known lecturer
   (C) the modern authority
   (D) Socrates
   (E) professional higher education

8. In line 13, "personal power or charm" most nearly
   means
   (A) opulence
   (B) volubility
   (C) affability
   (D) decorum
   (E) charisma

9. The author would be most likely to say that
   modern journalists often produce articles that are
   (A) not authoritative
   (B) poorly written
   (C) insipid
   (D) poorly researched
   (E) not understandable by readers who are not
       experts in the subject of the article

10. In line 34, "glossy rhetoric" most nearly means
    (A) colorful language
    (B) elaborate language with little meaning
    (C) complex logic
    (D) specious conclusions
    (E) fascinating but distracting details

11. According to the author, all of the following were
    true about the sophists *except*
    (A) they made speeches that had been prepared in
        advance
    (B) they were well paid
    (C) some of them said that they were experts on
        everything
    (D) they were very articulate
    (E) they were always scrupulously fair in
        argument

GO ON TO THE NEXT PAGE

9   9   9   9   9   9   9

12. According to the author, Socrates

(A) traveled extensively in the Greek world,
talking to all sorts of people
(B) was well paid for his teaching
(C) taught using methods developed and refined
by the sophists
(D) preferred lecturing to conversing
(E) was from a working class family

13. It can be inferred that the author believes that
Socrates "opposed the sophists wherever possible"
(line 46) because he believes that Socrates

(A) was seeking the truth, whereas the sophists
had little concern for the truth
(B) resented the popularity of the sophists
(C) believed that emphasizing his rivalry with the
sophists would help make him popular
(D) tended to attack anyone with views and
methods different from his own
(E) believed that the sophists were undermining
conventional thinking

14. According to the author, all of the following
contributed to the acceptance and success of the
sophists EXCEPT

(A) they were articulate
(B) people were accustomed to attending
performance by virtuoso artists and poets
(C) speeches of high quality by others besides
sophists were common in Athens
(D) they and similar traveling virtuosos were
welcomed by the wealthy rulers
(E) they offered people clear and profound new
answers to their philosophical perplexities

15. The most appropriate title for this passage would
be

(A) Sophists and Socrates
(B) The Greek World at the Time of Socrates
(C) The Influence of Ancient Greece on Western
Education
(D) The Influence of the Sophists on Socrates
(E) Socrates: A Man in Search of Truth

16. Based on the information in the passage, which of
the following statements would Socrates have been
LEAST likely to agree with?

(A) It is more important to seek the truth than to
impress other people.
(B) The truth is often hidden by language.
(C) Many people do not carefully examine their
beliefs and assumptions.
(D) A rich person is more likely to be correct in
his or her views than a poor person.
(E) Most truths have already been discovered.

17. In line 122, "naive" most nearly means

(A) innocent
(B) guileless
(C) uninformed
(D) stupid
(E) credulous

18. It can be inferred that people with whom Socrates
was discussing ideas sometimes lost their temper
because

(A) they became frustrated at their inability to
refute Socrates' arguments
(B) they regarded Socrates' debating tactics as
unfair
(C) they became upset because Socrates could not
understand their argument
(D) they felt that they were wasting their time
(E) Socrates continually insulted them

19. Based on the author's description of Socrates, it
can be inferred that Socrates possessed which of
the following qualities not mentioned in the
passage?

(A) A superb grasp of the day-to-day workings of
politics in Athens
(B) The ability to write entertaining dramatic
literature
(C) An excellent understanding of human nature
(D) An ability to charm women
(E) Great legal acumen

IN ANY REMAINING TIME YOU MAY REVIEW THE
ANSWERS YOU CHOSE IN THIS SECTION. DO NOT WORK
ON ANY OTHER SECTION OF THE TEST DURING THIS TIME.

10   10   10   10   10   10   10

SECTION 10 | Time—10 Minutes 14 Questions | Choose the best answer to each of the following questions in this section. Then blacken the appropriate space on your answer sheet.

Each sentence below may or may not employ correct or effective expression. If you think that the underlined phrasing makes the most clear and precise sentence, select choice A. If, however, you think that the underlined phrasing makes the meaning of the sentence unclear or awkward, or that it is grammatically incorrect, select another answer from choices B to E.

In choosing your answers, follow the conventions of English as it is used by educated writers. Consider sentence structure, grammar, word choice, and punctuation. Choose the answer that produces the sentence that is the most clear and effective.

Example:

In her comments after the debate the judge said that she had been impressed by the ability of both teams to exploit logical weaknesses and in citing relevant examples.

(A) in citing relevant examples
(B) in that relevant examples had been cited
(C) in the citing of relevant examples
(D) to cite relevant examples
(E) to be able to cite relevant examples

1. It is sensible for teachers to keep in mind that it is easy to become so engrossed in one's subject, so that one forgets that most students mainly want to learn what they need to know to get a good grade.

(A) subject, so that one forgets
(B) subject that one forgets
(C) subject, which one forgets
(D) subject, and one forgets
(E) subject, so forgetting

2. The cross-country coach uses a variety of approaches to improving the endurance of his runners; including one in which they have to run up a steep hill twenty times.

(A) runners; including one in which they have to run up a steep hill twenty times
(B) runners, included in these are one in which they have to run up a steep hill twenty times
(C) runners and including one in which they have to run up a steep hill twenty times
(D) runners, including one in which they have to run up a steep hill twenty times
(E) runners, and running up a steep hill twenty times is one that runners must do

3. By reading widely in the subject and doing well-designed practice exercises, a good score can be attained by a student on the examination.

(A) a good score can be attained by a student
(B) attaining a good score can be done by a student
(C) a student can attain a good score
(D) a student's good score can be attained
(E) your good score can be attained

4. Teachers should strive to give students a balanced view of controversial issues, at the same time they should stimulate student interest in such issues.

(A) at the same time they should stimulate student interest in such issues
(B) aiming at the same time they do this to stimulate student interest in such issues
(C) and while doing this they also should stimulate student interest in such issues
(D) while at the same time stimulating student interest in such issues
(E) stimulating their students, at the same time, to have interest in such issues

10 10 10 10 10 10 10

5. Quite a few drivers in the suburbs are forming <u>carpools, the reason being to reduce</u> the cost of driving to work.

(A) carpools, the reason being to reduce
(B) carpools to reduce
(C) carpools for the reason of reducing
(D) carpools, by which they want to reduce
(E) carpools; they are doing this to reduce

6. Before signing the contract, <u>its details must be carefully studied by both parties.</u>

(A) its details must be carefully studied by both parties
(B) careful study must be given to the details of it by both parties
(C) the details of it must be carefully studied by both parties
(D) both parties must carefully study its details
(E) by both parties careful attention to its details must be given

7. Because of the World Wide Web, students today have convenient access to far more information <u>than</u> the 1960s.

(A) than
(B) comparing
(C) than was available until
(D) than did
(E) than did students in

8. Growing up in a small town, <u>it was only when Jessica moved to Chicago that she realized how many interesting things there are to do in a city.</u>

(A) it was only when Jessica moved to Chicago that she realized how many interesting things there are to do in a city
(B) Jessica did not realize how many interesting things there are to do in a city until she moved to Chicago
(C) moving to Chicago made Jessica realize how many interesting things there are to do in a city
(D) when Jessica moved to Chicago, only then did she realize how many interesting things there are to do in a city
(E) when Jessica moved to Chicago she then realized that there are many interesting things to do in a city

9. In 1907 the Rabbit Proof Fence was built in Western Australia in an attempt to control rabbits, <u>and they are not</u> indigenous to Australia.

(A) and they are not
(B) they are not
(C) not that they are
(D) which are not
(E) being not

10. <u>The goal of the scientists having been reached,</u> the exhausted scientists celebrated by having a small party.

(A) The goal of the scientists having been reached,
(B) The goal of the scientists being reached,
(C) After they reached their goal,
(D) After having the goal of their research as scientists finally reached,
(E) Finally reaching the scientists' goal,

11. The <u>author is a noted scientist, taking the reader on a journey through time,</u> skillfully interweaving factual accounts of several great discoveries with fictional portrayals of the lives of the scientists who made them.

(A) author is a noted scientist, taking the reader on a journey through time,
(B) author, who is a noted scientist taking the reader on a journey through time,
(C) reader is taken by the author, a noted scientist, on a journey through time,
(D) author, a noted scientist, takes the reader on a journey through time,
(E) reader, taken by the author, a noted scientist on a journey through time, which is

GO ON TO THE NEXT PAGE

Practice Test 5

10   10   10   10   10   10   10

12. The philosophers of ancient Greece were proud of their ability to discourse on any subject imaginable as well as their debating skills, and these they sometimes demonstrated by taking first one side of an issue and then the other.

(A) skills, and these they sometimes demonstrated by taking first one side of an issue and then the other

(B) skills: Sometimes they demonstrated these by taking first one side of an issue and then the other side

(C) skills; sometimes these skills were demonstrated by them taking first one side of an issue and then the other

(D) skills, which, by taking first one side of an issue and then the other, they sometimes demonstrated

(E) skills, which they sometimes demonstrated by taking first one side of an issue and then the other

13. Some people believe that humans should not only explore Mars but that colonization of the planet should also be done.

(A) humans should not only explore Mars but that colonization of the planet should also be done

(B) humans should not only explore Mars but that they should also colonize it

(C) not only should humans explore Mars but that there should also be colonization of the planet

(D) not only should humans explore Mars but that colonization should also be done of the planet

(E) Mars should not only be explored by humans but that humans should also colonize it

14. Because high-frequency radio waves can be reflected back to Earth by the ionosphere and because the ionosphere is fairly uniform around Earth, this makes it possible to transmit radio signals large distances.

(A) Earth, this makes it

(B) Earth, it is

(C) Earth, making it

(D) Earth, thus making it

(E) Earth; it is therefore

STOP

IN ANY REMAINING TIME YOU MAY REVIEW THE
ANSWERS YOU CHOSE IN THIS SECTION. DO NOT WORK
ON ANY OTHER SECTION OF THE TEST DURING THIS TIME.

Practice Test 5

Answer Key

CRITICAL READING

Section 3

Ans.	Level of Diff.	Ans.	Level of Diff.
1. D	2	15. D	3
2. E	2	16. A	1
3. C	3	17. B	3
4. C	4	18. E	3
5. B	4	19. C	4
6. C	3	20. E	4
7. B	4	21. C	3
8. E	3	22. B	4
9. C	4	23. A	4
10. A	2	24. C	5
11. E	5		
12. D	5		
13. C	3		
14. D	3		

Section 7

Ans.	Level of Diff.	Ans.	Level of Diff.
1. C	1	15. E	3
2. D	2	16. B	3
3. E	3	17. B	2
4. E	3	18. A	3
5. D	3	19. D	2
6. B	4	20. D	4
7. A	4	21. C	4
8. E	1	22. E	3
9. A	3	23. D	4
10. C	2	24. A	5
11. A	3		
12. E	3		
13. C	3		
14. C	3		

Section 9

Ans.	Level of Diff.	Ans.	Level of Diff.
1. D	1	12. E	2
2. E	2	13. A	3
3. A	3	14. E	3
4. A	3	15. A	4
5. C	4	16. E	4
6. E	5	17. C	3
7. C	1	18. A	5
8. E	3	19. C	3
9. A	3		
10. B	4		
11. E	3		

MATH

Section 2

Ans.	Level of Diff.	Ans.	Level of Diff.
1. B	1	11. D	3
2. B	1	12. D	3
3. B	1	13. C	3
4. C	2	14. A	3
5. B	1	15. E	4
6. D	2	16. E	3
7. B	2	17. D	4
8. B	3	18. C	4
9. D	3	19. B	5
10. C	3	20. D	5

Section 6

Ans.	Level of Diff.	Ans.	Level of Diff.
1. E	1	11. 360	2
2. E	1	12. 30	3
3. D	2	13. 6	3
4. A	2	14. 109	3
5. D	3	15. 73	4
6. E	3	16. 1/2 or .5	4
7. D	4	17. 255	5
8. C	5	18. 35	5
9. 135	1		
10. 1/50 or .02	1		

Section 8

Ans.	Level of Diff.	Ans.	Level of Diff.
1. E	1	9. D	3
2. B	1	10. D	3
3. B	2	11. C	3
4. E	2	12. C	3
5. D	2	13. C	4
6. B	3	14. E	4
7. D	3	15. D	5
8. E	3	16. A	5

WRITING

Section 5

Ans.	Level of Diff.	Ans.	Level of Diff.	Ans.	Level of Diff.	Ans.	Level of Diff.
1. B	1	10. D	5	19. D	3	28. D	4
2. E	2	11. E	5	20. D	3	29. C	5
3. A	2	12. C	1	21. C	3	30. B	4
4. C	2	13. A	1	22. D	4	31. D	3
5. D	3	14. C	1	23. E	4	32. C	3
6. C	3	15. A	2	24. B	4	33. C	3
7. B	4	16. E	2	25. E	4	34. D	4
8. A	4	17. B	3	26. D	4	35. D	5
9. C	5	18. E	3	27. D	4		

Section 10

Ans.	Level of Diff.	Ans.	Level of Diff.
1. B	2	9. D	3
2. D	2	10. C	3
3. C	2	11. D	3
4. D	2	12. E	3
5. B	2	13. B	3
6. D	2	14. B	5
7. E	2		
8. B	2		

Score Your Own SAT Essay

Use this table as you rate your performance on the essay-writing section of this Practice Test. Circle the phrase that most accurately describes your work. Enter the numbers in the scoring chart below. Add the numbers together and divide by 6 to determine your total score. The higher your total score, the better you are likely to do on the essay section of the SAT.

Note that on the actual SAT two readers will rate your essay; your essay score will be the sum of their two ratings and could range from 12 (highest) to 2 (lowest). Also, they will grade your essay holistically, rating it on the basis of their overall impression of its effectiveness. They will *not* analyze it piece by piece, giving separate grades for grammar, vocabulary level, and so on. Therefore, you cannot expect the score you give yourself on this Practice Test to predict your eventual score on the SAT with any great degree of accuracy. Use this scoring guide instead to help you assess your writing strengths and weaknesses, so that you can decide which areas to focus on as you prepare for the SAT.

Like most people, you may find it difficult to rate your own writing objectively. Ask a teacher or fellow student to score your essay as well. With his or her help you should gain added insights into writing your 25-minute essay.

	6	5	4	3	2	1
POSITION ON THE TOPIC	Clear, convincing, & insightful	Fundamentally clear & coherent	Fairly clear & coherent	Insufficiently clear	Largely unclear	Extremely unclear
ORGANIZATION OF EVIDENCE	Well organized, with strong, relevant examples	Generally well organized, with apt examples	Adequately organized, with some examples	Sketchily developed, with weak examples	Lacking focus and evidence	Unfocused and disorganized
SENTENCE STRUCTURE	Varied, appealing sentences	Reasonably varied sentences	Some variety in sentences	Little variety in sentences	Errors in sentence structure	Severe errors in sentence structure
LEVEL OF VOCABULARY	Mature & apt word choice	Competent word choice	Adequate word choice	Inappropriate or weak vocabulary	Highly limited vocabulary	Rudimentary
GRAMMAR AND USAGE	Almost entirely free of errors	Relatively free of errors	Some technical errors	Minor errors, and some major ones	Numerous major errors	Extensive severe errors
OVERALL EFFECT	Outstanding	Effective	Adequately competent	Inadequate, but shows some potential	Seriously flawed	Fundamentally deficient

Self-Scoring Chart

For each of the following categories, rate the essay from 1 (lowest) to 6 (highest)

Position on the Topic _____

Organization of Evidence _____

Sentence Structure _____

Level of Vocabulary _____

Grammar and Usage _____

Overall Effect _____

TOTAL _____

(To get a score, divide the total by 6) _____

Scoring Chart (Second Reader)

For each of the following categories, rate the essay from 1 (lowest) to 6 (highest)

Position on the Topic _____

Organization of Evidence _____

Sentence Structure _____

Level of Vocabulary _____

Grammar and Usage _____

Overall Effect _____

TOTAL _____

(To get a score, divide the total by 6) _____

Practice Test 5

Scoring Practice Test 5

Refer to the answer key for Practice Test 5 on page 353. Then use the Scoring Worksheet below to determine your raw scores for Critical Reading, Mathematics, and Writing. For each section, give yourself one point for each answer that is correct. Your total raw score is the total number of correct answer points minus $\frac{1}{4}$ of the total number of incorrect answer points. Round off the total raw score to the nearest note number to get your Rounded Raw Score. Convert your raw scores to scaled scores using the Conversion Tables on pages 357–358.

SCORING WORKSHEET

Critical Reading

Section 3 $\underline{\hspace{2cm}}_{\text{number correct}} - \frac{1}{4}\left(\underline{\hspace{2cm}}_{\text{number incorrect}} \right) = \underline{\hspace{2cm}}$ (A)

Section 7 $\underline{\hspace{2cm}}_{\text{number correct}} - \frac{1}{4}\left(\underline{\hspace{2cm}}_{\text{number incorrect}} \right) = \underline{\hspace{2cm}}$ (B)

Section 9 $\underline{\hspace{2cm}}_{\text{number correct}} - \frac{1}{4}\left(\underline{\hspace{2cm}}_{\text{number incorrect}} \right) = \underline{\hspace{2cm}}$ (C)

Critical Reading Raw Score = (A) + (B) + (C) = $\underline{\hspace{2cm}}$

Critical Reading Scaled Score (see Table 1) = $\underline{\hspace{2cm}}$

Mathematics

Section 2 $\underline{\hspace{2cm}}_{\text{number correct}} - \frac{1}{4}\left(\underline{\hspace{2cm}}_{\text{number incorrect}} \right) = \underline{\hspace{2cm}}$ (D)

Section 6
Part I
(1–8) $\underline{\hspace{2cm}}_{\text{number correct}} - \frac{1}{4}\left(\underline{\hspace{2cm}}_{\text{number incorrect}} \right) = \underline{\hspace{2cm}}$ (E)

Part II
(9–18) $\underline{\hspace{2cm}}_{\text{number correct}}$ $= \underline{\hspace{2cm}}$ (F)

Section 8 $\underline{\hspace{2cm}}_{\text{number correct}} - \frac{1}{4}\left(\underline{\hspace{2cm}}_{\text{number incorrect}} \right) = \underline{\hspace{2cm}}$ (G)

Mathematics Raw Score = (D) + (E) + (F) + (G) = $\underline{\hspace{2cm}}$

Mathematics Scaled Score (see Table 2) = $\underline{\hspace{2cm}}$

Writing

Essay $\dfrac{}{\text{score 1}} + \dfrac{}{\text{score 2}}$ = _____ (H)

Section 5 $\dfrac{}{\text{number correct}} - \dfrac{1}{4}\left(\dfrac{}{\text{number incorrect}}\right)$ = _____ (I)

Section 10 $\dfrac{}{\text{number correct}} - \dfrac{1}{4}\left(\dfrac{}{\text{number incorrect}}\right)$ = _____ (J)

Writing Raw Score = I + J (H is a separate subscore) = _____

Writing Scaled Score (see Table 3) = _____

TABLE 1: CRITICAL READING CONVERSION TABLE

Raw Score	Scaled Score	Raw Score	Scaled Score	Raw Score	Scaled Score	Raw Score	Scaled Score
67	800	49	630	31	510	14	400
66	790	48	620	30	510	13	400
65	790	47	610	29	500	12	390
64	780	46	610	28	490	11	380
63	770	45	600	27	490	10	370
62	760	44	590	26	480	9	360
61	750	43	590	25	480	8	350
60	740	42	580	24	470	7	340
59	730	41	570	23	460	6	330
58	720	40	570	22	460	5	320
57	710	39	560	21	450	4	310
56	700	38	550	20	440	3	300
55	690	37	550	19	440	2	280
54	680	36	540	18	430	1	270
53	670	35	540	17	420	0	260
52	660	34	530	16	420	−1	230
51	650	33	520	15	410	−2 and below	210
50	640	32	520				

TABLE 2: MATH CONVERSION TABLE

Math Raw Score	Math Scaled Score	Math Raw Score	Math Scaled Score	Math Raw Score	Math Scaled Score	Math Raw Score	Math Scaled Score
54	800	40	630	26	500	12	390
53	790	39	620	25	500	11	380
52	770	38	610	24	490	10	370
51	750	37	600	23	480	9	360
50	730	36	590	22	470	8	340
49	710	35	580	21	460	7	330
48	700	34	570	20	450	6	320
47	690	33	560	19	450	5	300
46	680	32	560	18	440	4	290
45	670	31	550	17	430	3	270
44	660	30	540	16	420	2	250
43	650	29	530	15	410	1	240
42	640	28	520	14	410	0	230
41	640	27	510	13	400	−1 and below	200

TABLE 3: WRITING CONVERSION TABLE

Writing Raw Score	Essay Score					
	6	5	4	3	2	1
49	800	800	770	740	710	680
48	800	790	750	710	680	650
47	790	760	720	690	660	630
46	770	740	700	670	640	610
45	760	730	690	650	620	590
44	740	710	670	640	610	580
43	730	700	660	620	600	570
42	720	690	650	610	580	550
41	710	670	630	600	570	540
40	690	660	620	590	560	530
39	680	650	610	580	550	520
38	670	640	600	570	540	510
37	670	630	590	560	530	500
36	660	630	590	550	520	490
35	650	620	580	540	510	480
34	640	610	570	530	510	480
33	630	600	560	530	500	470
32	620	590	550	520	490	460
31	620	590	550	510	480	450
30	610	580	540	500	480	450
29	600	570	530	500	470	440
28	590	560	520	490	460	430
27	590	560	520	480	450	430
26	580	550	510	480	450	420
25	570	540	500	470	440	410
24	570	540	500	460	440	410
23	560	530	490	460	430	400
22	560	520	480	450	420	390
21	550	520	480	440	420	390
20	540	510	470	440	410	380
19	540	510	470	430	400	370
18	530	500	460	430	400	370
17	520	490	450	420	390	360
16	520	490	450	410	380	350
15	510	480	440	410	380	350
14	500	470	430	400	370	340
13	500	470	430	390	370	340
12	490	460	420	390	360	330
11	480	450	410	380	350	320
10	480	450	410	370	350	320
9	470	440	400	370	340	310
8	460	430	390	360	330	300
7	460	420	390	350	320	290
6	450	420	380	340	310	280
5	440	410	370	330	310	280
4	430	400	360	320	300	270
3	420	390	350	310	280	250
2	400	360	330	300	270	240
1	390	360	320	290	260	230
0	370	340	300	270	240	210

ANSWERS EXPLAINED
Section 2 Mathematics
<u>Note:</u>

1. See page 32 for an explanation of the symbol $\Rightarrow$ that is used in some answer explanations.

2. A calculator icon, is placed next to the answer explanation of any question for which a calculator *could* be useful. Almost always, the question can be answered easily without using a calculator.

3. If you are unfamiliar with any of the math facts used in the following answer explanations, refer to Barron's *SAT*, which, in addition to having practice tests, has a full review of all the math you need to know.

1. **B** $b = \dfrac{3}{4}(60) = 45$. So $a = \dfrac{1}{3}(45) = 15$.

2. **B** Since 10% of $13.00 is $1.30, Mrs. Smith owed $13.00 − $1.30 = $11.70 for her groceries. The amount of change she should have received is $20.00 − $11.70 = $8.30.

3. **B** $3a + 5 = 50 \Rightarrow 3a = 45 \Rightarrow a = 15$. So, $m\angle C = (5 \times 15)° = 75°$.

   Then $m\angle A + m\angle B + m\angle C = 180 \Rightarrow 50 + b + 75 = 180 \Rightarrow b = 180 - 125 = 55$.

4. **C** Since the lengths of the opposite sides of a rectangle are equal, no side could be greater than or equal to 5 inches, because if two sides were 5 inches long (or more), then the sum of those two sides alone would be greater than or equal to 10. Roman numeral III is false. The four sides could be 1, 4, 1, and 4, and could be 0.5, 4.5, 0.5, and 4.5. Only I and II are true.

5. **B** **Solution 1.** Let x be the amount that Dani received. Then $x + 30$ is the amount that Liz received. So, $x + (x + 30) = 150 \Rightarrow 2x = 120$ and $x = 60$. Therefore, Dani received $60 and Liz received $90. So, Liz got $\dfrac{90}{150} = 0.6 = 60\%$ of the prize.

   Solution 2. Think of the division of the prize this way: first Liz got $30 and the remaining $150 − $30 = $120 was divided equally. So, Liz received $30 + \dfrac{1}{2}($120$) = $30 + $60 = 90, which is 60% of $150.

6. **D** 1 kilometer = 1,000 meters = 1,000 × (100 centimeters) = 100,000 centimeters. So,

   $$\frac{8 \text{ centimeters}}{8 \text{ kilometers}} = \frac{8 \text{ centimeters}}{800,000 \text{ centimeters}} = \frac{1}{100,000}$$

7. **B** **Solution 1.** Let n represent the number of coins in the jar. Then the number of nickels is $\dfrac{1}{4}n$ and the number of dimes and quarters together is $\dfrac{3}{4}n$. So $\dfrac{1}{3}\left(\dfrac{3}{4}n\right) = \dfrac{1}{4}n$ is the number of quarters. Since $\dfrac{1}{4}n + \dfrac{1}{4}n = \dfrac{1}{2}n$, half the coins are nickels or quarters and the other half are dimes. So the ratio of nickels to dimes is $\dfrac{1}{4} : \dfrac{1}{2} = 1 : 2$.

   Solution 2. Pick any multiple of 4 for n, say $n = 8$. Then $\dfrac{1}{4}(8) = 2$; so 2 coins are nickels, and 6 are not nickels. Since $\dfrac{1}{3}(6) = 2$, there are 2 quarters and the other 4 coins are dimes. Finally, the ratio of the number of nickels to the number of dimes is 2:4, which equals 1:2.

8. **B** Since $10 = 2 \times 5$, $10^{100} = (2 \times 5)^{100} = 2^{100} \times 5^{100}$. So the only prime factors of 10^{100} are 2 and 5. Since $375 = 3 \times 5 \times 5 \times 5$ is divisible by 3, it cannot be a factor of 10^{100}. The other four choices *are* factors of 10^{100}:

    - $10^{100} = 10^3 \times 10^{97} = 1{,}000 \times 10^{97} = (125 \times 8) \times 10^{97}$
    - $10^{100} = 10^4 \times 10^{96} = 10{,}000 \times 10^{96} = (625 \times 16) \times 10^{96}$
    - $10^{100} = 10^{25} \times 10^{75}$
    - $10^{100} = 10^{35} \times 10^{65}$

9. **D** The best way to solve this problem is to use the counting principle. Since there are 3 ways to go from Chicago to New York, 2 ways to go from New York to Paris, and 4 ways to go from Paris to Marseille, there are $3 \times 2 \times 4 = 24$ ways to arrange the trip.

10. **C** Since *ABCD* is a rectangle, $BC = AD = 12$. So the diameter of the semicircle is 12 and, hence, its radius is 6. Therefore, the area of the semicircle is
    $\frac{1}{2}\pi r^2 = \frac{1}{2}\pi(6)^2 = 18\pi$. Then the area of the rectangle is $2 \times 18\pi = 36\pi$. So $36\pi = lw = 12w$, and *w*, the width of the rectangle, is 3π.

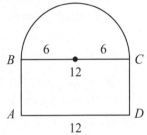

11. **D** When an integer, *n*, is divided by 10, the remainder is the units digits of *n*. (For example, when 27 is divided by 10, the quotient is 2 and the remainder is 7: $27 = 2 \times 10 + 7$.) So when $14n$ is divided by 10, the remainder will be 2 only if the units digit of $14n$ is 2, which can happen only if the units digit of *n* is 3 or 8. (4 is the units digit of 14, and since $4 \times 3 = 12$ and $4 \times 8 = 32$, the product of 14 and a number whose units' digit is 3 or 8 is a number whose units' digit is 2.) Between 25 and 75 there are 10 such integers: 28, 33, 38, 43, 48, 53, 58, 63, 68, and 73. (For example, $14 \times 28 = 392 = 39 \times 10 + 2$.)

12. **D** Since $f(-3) = (-3)^2 + 1 = 9 + 1 = 10$, $f(a) = 10$.

    Then $f(a) = a^2 + 1 = 10$, so $a^2 = 9$ and $a = 3$.

    Finally, $3a = 9$ and $f(3a) = f(9) = 9^2 + 1 = 81 + 1 = 82$.

13. **C** Chris's number and Claire's number each satisfied the equation $(x - 3)^2 = 100$. So one of their numbers satisfied the equation $x - 3 = 10$ and the other number satisfied the equation $x - 3 = -10$. So the two numbers were 13 and −7, whose sum is 6.

14. **A** The number of employees attending the party was 960 (80% of $1200 = 0.80 \times 1200 = 960$). Of these 960 people, 192 were nurses (20% of $960 = 0.2 \times 960 = 192$) and 180 were doctors. Therefore, $960 - (192 + 180) = 960 - (372) = 588$ of those attending were other staff members. Since there are 600 staff members (half of 1200), all but 12 attended the party. Finally, $\frac{12}{600} = \frac{2}{100} = 0.02 = 2\%$.

15. **E** The graph of $y = g(x)$ is obtained by shifting the graph of $y = f(x)$ down 1 unit and 1 unit to the left. In the diagram on the left, $y = h(x) = f(x + 1)$ is the result of shifting $y = f(x)$ 1 unit to the left, and then $g(x)$ is obtained by shifting $h(x)$ down 1 unit: $g(x) = h(x) - 1 = f(x + 1) - 1$. Alternatively, as shown in the diagram on the right, $y = k(x) = f(x) - 1$ is the result of shifting $y = f(x)$ 1 unit down, and $g(x)$ is obtained by shifting $y = k(x)$ 1 unit to the left: $g(x) = k(x + 1) = f(x + 1) - 1$.

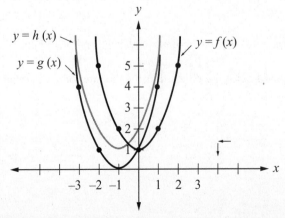

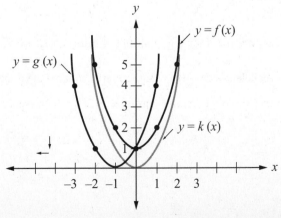

16. **E** **Solution 1.** Since the area of square *ABCD* is 50, each side is $\sqrt{50} = 5\sqrt{2}$, and the perimeter of the square is $4 \times 5\sqrt{2} = 20\sqrt{2}$. Now, notice that the perimeter of the shaded region is exactly the same as the perimeter of the square. (For example, *AB* = *GF* + *EB* and *BC* = *BH* + *IJ*).

Solution 2. The length of each side of square *ABCD* is $\sqrt{50} = 5\sqrt{2}$. The sides of the two white squares are $\sqrt{2}$ and $\sqrt{18} = 3\sqrt{2}$ (see diagram at right). So the shaded perimeter is $\sqrt{2} + 4\sqrt{2} + 2\sqrt{2} + 3\sqrt{2} + 3\sqrt{2} + 2\sqrt{2} + 4\sqrt{2} + \sqrt{2} = 20\sqrt{2}$.

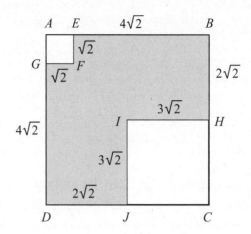

17. **D** **Solution 1.** $n = 100h + 10t + u$, so,

$$\frac{n}{20} = \frac{100h + 10t + u}{20} = 5h + \frac{t}{2} + \frac{u}{20} = 5h + \frac{10t + u}{20}$$

Solution 2. Pick a 3-digit value for *n*, say *n* = 130. Then $\frac{n}{20} = \frac{130}{20} = \frac{13}{2} = 6.5$. Which of the choices is equal to 6.5 when *h* = 1, *t* = 3, and *u* = 0? Only choice D,

$$5(1) + \frac{10(3) + 0}{20} = 5 + \frac{30}{20} = 5 + 1.5 = 6.5$$

18. **C** **Solution 1.** No matter what number is assigned to Al, only 1 of the 3 remaining numbers can be assigned to Bob to make the sum of their numbers even. So the desired probability is $\frac{1}{3}$. For example, if Al has the 1 then Bob needs the 3, and if Al has the 2, then Bob needs the 4.

Solution 2. If Al's and Bob's numbers have an even sum, then either both of their numbers are even or both are odd.

* The probability that an even number is assigned to Al is $\frac{2}{4} = \frac{1}{2}$.

* The probability that the other even number is assigned to Bob is $\frac{1}{3}$.

* So the probability they both have even numbers is $\frac{1}{2} \times \frac{1}{3} = \frac{1}{6}$.

* Similarly, the probability they both have odd numbers is $\frac{1}{6}$.

* Finally, the probability they both have even numbers or both have odd numbers is $\frac{1}{6} + \frac{1}{6} = \frac{1}{3}$.

19. **B** *OA* = *OB* = *OC* = 10, and since $\overline{AB}$ bisects $\overline{OC}$, *OD* = 5. Then use the Pythagorean theorem (or recognize that $\triangle AOD$ is a 30-60-90 right triangle) to evaluate *AD*:
$(AD)^2 + 5^2 = 10^2 \Rightarrow (AD)^2 + 25 = 100 \Rightarrow (AD)^2 = 75 \Rightarrow AD = \sqrt{75} = 5\sqrt{3}$.
Since *AD* = *BD*, base $\overline{AB}$ of $\triangle AOB$ is $10\sqrt{3}$. Finally, the area of $\triangle AOB$ is

$$\frac{1}{2}bh = \frac{1}{2}\left(10\sqrt{3}\right)(5) = \left(5\sqrt{3}\right)(5) = 25\sqrt{3}.$$

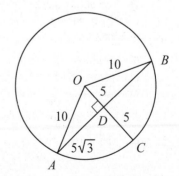

20. **D** **Solution 1.**
* Of the *n* students who work on the newspaper, *b* also work on the yearbook, and so *n* − *b* work only on the newspaper.

- Of the *y* students who work on the yearbook, *b* also work on the newspaper, and so *y* − *b* work only on the yearbook.
- So the number of students who work only on the newspaper or only on the yearbook is
$(n - b) + (y - b) = n + y - 2b$.

Solution 2. Suppose that the students who work on the newspaper are Al, Bob, and Carol, and that the students who work on the yearbook are Carol, Diane, Ed, and Frank. Then $n = 3$, $y = 4$, and $b = 1$. So 5 students—Al, Bob, Diane, Ed, and Frank—work on only one of the two publications. Of the five answer choices, only choice D, $n + y - 2b$, equals 5 when $n = 3$, $y = 4$, and $b = 1$.

Section 3 Critical Reading

1. **D** The phrase it *is far more difficult* signals that the second part of the sentence contrasts with the first part of the sentence. It is easy to *deride* (ridicule) efforts to create a just society as unrealistic and idealistic.

2. **E** The phrase *rather than encouraging them* signals a contrast with the first part of the sentence. The critic has a reputation for *belittling* (mocking) the efforts of new writers.

3. **C** The second part of the sentence describes the defining feature of *implicit* (unstated) assumptions.

4. **C** The *antithesis* (exact opposite) of an empirical (based on observation and experiment) approach to *discerning* (detecting) the truth is to rely on intuition.

5. **B** Scientists face the difficulty of *assessing* (evaluating) data to determine whether it is *spurious* (false).

6. **C** The author says, "It was partly the zeal of the newly converted Arabs that inspired them to expel the Persians from Oman" (lines 20–22). Note that "zeal" means *fervor*.

7. **B** The author says, "Such contacts may have introduced the tribe to the ideal of one God and so prepared it to accept the Prophet's message" (lines 11–13). A monotheistic religion is a religion whose followers believe in one God.

8. **E** The author says, "The Nakatomi family…and the Mononobe…clan were set on maintaining their prerogative and resisted the alien religious influence of Buddhism" (lines 11–15).

9. **C** The author says, "The Soga, a Japanese court family that rose to prominence with the accession of the Emperor Kimmei about A.D. 531, favored the adoption of…governmental and cultural models based on Chinese Confucianism" (lines 5–10). Also, in lines 16–17 we are told that the Soga were ascendant "for more than a century." It is thus reasonable to infer that Chinese Confucianism significantly affected Japanese life.

10. **A** The author says, "Whatever [Franklin's and the other men's who stood with Washington] philosophical professions may have been, they were not controlled by prudence" (lines 5–7). The word "professions" in this context means *avowals of belief*. The phrase "professedly prudent" means that Franklin professed—that is *avowed*—to be *prudent* (cautious and sensible).

11. **E** As stated in the previous explanation, *professions* in this context means *avowals of belief*.

12. **D** The author says, "They were…willing to take all risks…in a struggle whose course was just though its issue was dubious" (lines 7–10). It makes sense that the word "issue" means *outcome* here because a struggle results in an outcome.

13. **C** It can be inferred that the author quotes these words to show that Robert Morris had great integrity and patriotism because Morris said he will do anything asked of him by his country unless it would mean a loss of his integrity.

14. **D** In context the word "celebrated" means *known and praised widely*.

15. **D** The author says, "I see Benjamin Franklin…accepting without demur the difficult and dangerous mission to France" (lines 39–44).

16. **A** The author says that Benjamin Franklin "claimed to be a follower of the theory of enlightened self-interest" (lines 59–60).

17. **B** This is the best title because the passage concentrates on the important role Benjamin Franklin had in American history and the sacrifices he made for America.

18. **E** The quotation referred to is in the last sentence of a paragraph describing the great sacrifices that Benjamin Franklin made for his country.

19. **C** In context "hair-splitting" means *making unreasonably fine distinctions*. The words "wanted no quibbling" (line 47) and "They wanted…just plain honest English" (lines 46–48) are clues to the meaning.

20. **E** The author says that "one or two of the hotter disputants" (line 45) said his speech was "a shuffling evasion" (line 46). Since an "evasion" means *avoiding the problem*, it can be inferred that they believed that his solution to the dispute was *equivocation* (evading an issue by avoiding the making of a clear statement).

21. **C** The author refers to the argument about the squirrel as a "metaphysical dispute" (line 4). He tells the disputants "You are both right and wrong according to how you conceive the verb 'to go round' in one practical fashion or the other" (lines 42–44). Also, the author says, "The pragmatic method is primarily a method of settling metaphysical disputes" (lines 53–55).

22. **B** The author tells the disputants, "Which party is right…depends on what you practically mean by 'going round' the squirrel" (lines 27–29). He then defines the phrase in two ways, showing that the conclusion reached to the dispute depends on carefully defining the important terms in it.

23. **A** In context the word "idle" means *lacking value*. The author says, "If no practical difference whatever can be traced, then the alternatives mean practically the same thing, and all dispute is idle" (lines 64–67). The author is saying that there is no value in arguing about which of two ideas is true if we see that it makes no difference in reality which is true.

24. **C** The passage makes use of all of these except *parody* (copying another work in a comic or satirical way).

Section 5 Writing

1. **B** "The greatest novel" is incorrect because two novels are being compared. This corrects the incorrect superlative adjective *greatest* by changing it to the comparative adjective *greater*. The comparative is used when two items are being compared.

2. **E** Dangling participle. The participial phrase *lacking a solid foundation in basic mathematics* refers to *Terry*, not *the calculus course*. Choice (E) makes *Terry* the subject of the independent clause so that it is clear that the participial phrase refers to Terry. This choice is also more concise.

3. **A** The given sentence is clear and grammatical. *As to* is the correct idiom.

4. **C** The given sentence is not correct because the adverb clause beginning with the word *because* is not grammatical. Choice (C) changes the sentence so that the subject, *saying*, comes before a relative clause (beginning with the word *that*) that contains the adverb clause (beginning with *because*). Putting the subject first makes the sentence clearer.

5. **D** The given sentence is incorrect because the relative clause beginning with the word *who* is not grammatical. Choice (D) corrects the sentence so that the relative pronoun *who* is the first word in a relative clause (*who speak a number of languages such as Tamil, Cantonese, and Malay*), referring to *people*. This is a difficult question because the relative clause is interrupted by the adverb clause *although they share English as a common language*.

6. **C** Run-on sentence. The words after the first comma (beginning with *moving*) are independent clauses. They cannot be joined to the first independent clause by a comma. Choice (C) creates an adverb clause modifying the verb *moved*, thus making a complete sentence.

7. **B** The given sentence is grammatical, but the phrase *and this as a result* makes it wordy. This improves the sentence by changing the independent clause (which consists of the words after the comma) to a participial phrase, which expresses the idea more concisely.

8. **A** The given sentence is clear and grammatical.

9. **C** Faulty parallelism. This improves the given sentence by changing the independent clause *he discovered and invented many new things* to an adverb clause modifying the verb *revered*. This makes it parallel in structure to the adverb clause *not only as a courageous patriot*.

10. **D** The underlined part of the sentence is awkward and unclear. This improves the sentence by making it clear that Jerry Garcia was eulogized by many musicians, one of whom was Bob Dylan.

11. **E** Faulty parallelism. The subject complements of the linking verb are not parallel in form. This changes them so they are both relative clauses.

12. **C** *Its* is incorrect because it is a possessive pronoun. The context requires the contraction *it's*.

13. **A** Wrong part of speech. Change the adjective *interesting*, which is incorrect here, to the correct word, the adverb *interestingly*.

14. **C** Tense error. Change *seeked*, which is not a word, to *sought*, which is the past tense of *seek*.

15. **A** Tense error. Change *had come about* from the incorrect past perfect tense to the correct modal form *would come about* to indicate what the people in the past thought would happen in the future.

16. **E** No error.

17. **B** Wrong preposition. *In* is the wrong preposition. Change it to *of*.

18. **E** No error.

19. **D** Incorrect idiom. *By* is incorrect. The correct idiom is *ran…on*.

20. **D** *With having a population of over three hundred million* refers to *the United States*, so the words *with having* should be changed to *which has*. This creates a nonrestrictive relative clause referring to *the United States*.

21. **C** Incorrect part of speech. *Prolific* modifies the verb *bred*, it should be changed to the adverb form, *prolifically*.

22. **D** Wrong preposition. Change *mounted by* to *mounted on*.

23. **E** There are no errors in grammar or usage.

24. **B** Pronoun–antecedent error. The antecedent of the pronouns *he or she* is *members*, which is plural. Change *he or she* to the plural pronoun *they*.

25. **E** No error.

26. **D** In the given sentence, the infinitive phrase beginning with *to put* incorrectly modifies the noun *difficulty*. Change *to put* to the present participle *putting* so that the phrase beginning with *putting* is a participial phrase modifying *difficulty*.

27. **D** Wrong preposition. The correct preposition to follow the verb *oriented* in this context is *toward*.

28. **D** The correct compound adjective is *disaster-stricken*.

29. **C** Incorrect idiom. Change *in they had* to *in that they had* or *in having*.

30. **B** This is the best choice because it provides a clear and logical link between sentences 1 and 2. It connects the description of the Pilbara given in sentence 1 with the information about its age given in sentence 2. Also, mentioning geologists in the first sentence makes sense because they are referred to later in the passage. (A) This is acceptable but wordy. (C) This is acceptable but wordy. (D) This does not make sense. (E) This makes sense as a link between sentences 1 and 2. However, it does not make sense when the rest of the passage is considered; the passage emphasizes the information being found in the Pilbara, not that it is puzzling.

31. **D** This is the best choice because it helps to link sentence 4, which describes a discovery made by geologists studying rocks in the Pilbara, to sentence 3, which says that studying rocks in the Pilbara helps geologists to gain a better understanding of what was happening on the planet in the early period of its development. (A) This is a poor choice because there is no information provided about the significance of the fact mentioned in sentence 4. (B) This makes no sense because sentence 5 follows from sentence 4. (C) This makes no sense. (E) This makes little sense. (D) is a better choice.

32. **C** This sentence serves to link paragraph 1, which describes how scientists discovered that life existed on Earth billions of years ago, to paragraph 2, which immediately raises the question of whether life also could have arisen billions of years ago elsewhere in the solar system. Also, the word *it* in sentence 6, the first sentence in paragraph 2, refers to the fact that life existed on Earth at an early stage of its development, providing a link between the new sentence and sentence 6. (A) This does not help to introduce paragraph 2. (B) This does not help to introduce paragraph 2. (D) This introduces the main topic of paragraph 2, but it does not make sense to do this before sentence 6, which does the same thing. (E) This does not help to introduce paragraph 2.

33. **C** This improves the sentence by making it clear what evidence has been found. (A) This does not make sense. (B) This is not mentioned in the sentences after sentence 7. (D) This is not mentioned in the sentences after sentence 7. (E) This is not mentioned in the sentences after sentence 7.

34. **D** This is the best choice because it provides a link to the previous sentence (sentence 9) and signals to the reader that the rest of the sentence is about a notable similarity between the rocks in the Nili Fossae area of Mars and rocks in the Pilbara. (A) This makes no sense. (B) This makes little sense because finding such evidence of life would not be mysterious. (C) This makes little sense. (E) This makes no sense.

35. **D** This makes clear what would be suggested if it is demonstrated that life originated on Mars under less than ideal conditions. Also, the sentence is a conditional (signaled by the word *if*), so it makes sense to maintain the same grammatical structure used in the main clause (*it would demonstrate*). (A) This would not create a complete sentence. (B) This is similar to the given sentence and is wordy. (C) This would not create a complete sentence. (E) This is acceptable but unnecessarily wordy.

Section 6 Mathematics

<u>Note:</u>

1. See page 32 for an explanation of the symbol $\Rightarrow$ that is used in some answer explanations.

2. A calculator icon, 🖩, is placed next to the answer explanation of any question for which a calculator *could* be useful. Almost always, the question can be answered easily without using a calculator.

3. If you are unfamiliar with any of the math facts used in the following answer explanations, refer to Barron's *SAT*, which, in addition to having practice tests, has a full review of all the math you need to know.

1. **E** **Solution 1.** In $\triangle ABD$, $30 + 90 + 3a = 180 \Rightarrow 3a + 120 = 180$. So $3a = 60$ and $a = 20$. Then in $\triangle BDC$, $20 + 90 + b = 180 \Rightarrow b = 70$.

   Solution 2. After getting that $a = 20$, from the first step in Solution 1, we see that m$\angle ABC = 80$, and so in $\triangle ABC$, $30 + 80 + b = 180 \Rightarrow b = 70$.

2. **E** $6a - 3 < 3a + 6 \Rightarrow 3a < 9 \Rightarrow a < 3$. Only choice (E), 3, is not less than 3.

3. **D** **Solution 1.**
   * $|a - b| = 5 \Rightarrow a - b = 5$ or $a - b = -5$; so, $b = a - 5$ or $b = a + 5$
   * Similarly, $|b - c| = 5 \Rightarrow c = b - 5$ or $c = b + 5$
   * If $c = b - 5$, then $c = (a - 5) - 5 = a - 10$ or $c = (a + 5) - 5 = a$.
   * If $c = b + 5$, then $c = (a - 5) + 5 = a$ or $c = (a + 5) + 5 = a + 10$.
   * So the only possible values of c are a, $a - 10$, and $a + 10$.
   * If $c = a$, then $|a - c| = 0$.
   * If $c = a - 10$ or $c = a + 10$, then $|a - c| = 10$.
   * Only statements I and III are true.

   Solution 2. Essentially, do exactly the same thing as above, except choose a number for a, say $a = 10$.
   * Then b is either 5 or 15.
   * If $b = 5$, then $c = 0$ or 10.
   * If $b = 15$, then $c = 10$ or 20.
   * So, $c = 0, 10, 20$.
   * Then $c = a$ (in which case, $|a - c| = 0$) or c is 10 less than or 10 more than a (in which case, $|a - c| = 10$).

4. **A** $(x - 2)(x - 3) = x^2 - 5x + 6$. So, if $(x - 2)(x - 3) = x^2 - 5x - 6$, then $x^2 - 5x - 6 = x^2 - 5x + 6$. Subtracting $x^2 - 5x$ from each side of this equation, we get $-6 = 6$, which clearly is false. So there is no value of x that satisfies the given equation.

5. **D**
   - For the difference $x - y$ to be as large as possible, take the greatest possible value for x, 8, and subtract from it the least possible value for y, 6. So, $G = 8 - 6 = 2$.
   - For the difference $x - y$ to be as small as possible, take the least possible value for x, 3, and subtract from it the greatest possible value for y, 8. So, $L = 3 - 8 = -5$.
   - So, $G - L = 2 - (-5) = 2 + 5 = 7$.

6. **E Solution 1.**
   $(x + 4)^2 + (x - 4)^2 = (x^2 + 8x + 16) + (x^2 - 8x + 16) = 2x^2 + 32 = 2(12) + 32 = 24 + 32 = 56$

   Solution 2. On your calculator, simply evaluate $\left(\sqrt{12} + 4\right)^2 + \left(\sqrt{12} - 4\right)^2$. If you enter this all in one step, the value will be 56. If you do it in steps, and round off to the nearest thousandth, you will get:

   - $\left(\sqrt{12} + 4\right)^2 = (3.464 + 4)^2 = (7.464)^2 = 55.711$
   - $\left(\sqrt{12} - 4\right)^2 = (3.464 - 4)^2 = (-0.536)^2 = 0.287$
   - $55.711 + 0.287 = 55.998$. So clearly the answer is choice (E): 56.

7. **D** Since $\dfrac{x + y}{2} = z$, we have $x + y = 2z$. Then, since $x + y + z = 180$, we see that $2z + z = 180$.

   So, $3z = 180$ and $z = 60$. So, $x + y = 120$. But, $x = 4y$, so $4y + y = 120 \Rightarrow 5y = 120 \Rightarrow y = 24$. Finally,

   $x = 4(24) = 96$, and the average of x and z is $\dfrac{96 + 60}{2} = \dfrac{156}{2} = 78$.

8. **C** Note that it is irrelevant how much each pencil cost, so the correct answer cannot contain p.

   Solution 1. Elaine used $\dfrac{60}{100} d$ dollars to buy pencils and $\dfrac{40}{100} d$ dollars to buy markers. To find out how many

   markers she bought, divide the number of dollars she spent on markers, $\dfrac{40}{100} d = \dfrac{40d}{100}$, by the cost, in dollars of

   each marker. Each marker cost m *cents* or $\dfrac{m}{100}$ dollars. Then $\dfrac{40d}{100} \div \dfrac{m}{100} = \dfrac{40d}{100} \times \dfrac{100}{m} = \dfrac{40d}{m}$.

   Solution 2. Plug in numbers. Assume Elaine had \$100 and spent \$60 on pens and the other \$40 on markers, which cost \$2 or 200 cents each. Then she bought 20 markers. Which answer choice is equal to 20 when

   $d = 100$ and $m = 200$? Only choice (C): $\dfrac{40d}{m} = \dfrac{40 \times 100}{200} = 20$.

9. **135** $(3a)^2 + (3b)^2 = 9a^2 + 9b^2 = 9(a^2 + b^2) = 9(15) = 135$

10. $\dfrac{1}{50}$ **or .02** $\dfrac{1}{2}\%$ of 10% of 40 = 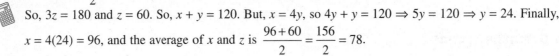 $\dfrac{1}{2}\left(\dfrac{1}{100}\right) \times \left(\dfrac{\overset{1}{\cancel{10}}}{\underset{10_1}{\cancel{100}}}\right) \times \overset{\overset{2}{\cancel{40}}}{\cancel{40}}^{\overset{2}{20}} = \dfrac{2}{100} = \dfrac{1}{50} = .02$

11. **360 Solution 1.** The easiest solution is to recall that the sum of the measures of the three exterior angles, one at each vertex, in any triangle is 360°.

    Solution 2. The measures of the three interior angles of $\triangle ABC$ are 83°, $(180 - b)°$, and $(180 - c)°$, so, $83 + 180 - b + 180 - c = 180 \Rightarrow 263 = b + c$. Finally, since $a = 180 - 83 = 97$, we have $a + b + c = 97 + 263 = 360$.

12. **30** Assume that John originally had $3x$ American coins and x foreign coins. After receiving 80 foreign coins,

    he had $80 + x$ foreign coins. The $3x$ American coins he had were now $\dfrac{1}{3}$ of the $80 + x$ foreign coins. So,

    $3x = \dfrac{1}{3}(80 + x) \Rightarrow 9x = 80 + x$. Therefore, $8x = 80$, $x = 10$, and $3x = 30$.

13. **6** Since $OA = 9$, the area of the white circle is $\pi(9)^2 = 81\pi$. Therefore, the area of the large circle is $81\pi + 144\pi = 225\pi$. If r is the radius of the large circle, then $\pi r^2 = 225\pi \Rightarrow r^2 = 225$, and so $r = 15$. So $OB = 15$ and $AB = OB - OA = 15 - 9 = 6$.

14. **109**
    - $7 < 7x + 77 < 777$
    - Subtract 77: $-70 < 7x < 700$
    - Divide by 7: $-10 < x < 100$

    This last inequality is satisfied by 9 negative integers: $-9, -8, \ldots, -1$ and 99 positive integers: $1, 2, \ldots, 99$, as well as the 1 integer that is neither positive nor negative, 0. So, there are $9 + 99 + 1 = 109$ integers that satisfy the original inequality.

15. **73** **Solution 1.** Let f and t be the number of \$5 bills and \$10 bills, respectively. Then, $5f + 10t = 865$ and $f + t = 100$. Multiply the second equation by 5: $5f + 5t = 500$. Now subtract this equation from the first one:

$$
\begin{array}{r}
5f + 10t = 865 \\
-\ 5f +\ 5t = 500 \\
\hline
5t = 365, \text{ and so } t = 73.
\end{array}
$$

 Solution 2. Test values, starting with $f = t = 50$, and refine your guesses as necessary.

- $(50 \times 5) + (50 \times 10) = 750$, which is too small, so we need more \$10 bills and fewer \$5 bills.
- Here is a table showing one way of zooming in on the right answer—as t goes from 50 to 60 to 70 to 73.

f	t	Value
50	50	750
40	60	800
30	70	850
27	73	865

 Solution 3. Zoom in even faster. Again, start with $f = t = 50$, which has a value of \$750. Now realize that each time you reduce f by 1 (taking away a five-dollar bill) and increase t by 1 (adding a ten-dollar bill) the total value goes up by \$5. Since $865 - 750 = 115$, we need $115 \div 5 = 23$ more \$10 bills: $50 + 23 = 73$.

16. $\dfrac{1}{2}$ or **.5** $\quad f(a) = a^2 - 2$ and $f(a - 1) = (a - 1)^2 - 2 = (a^2 - 2a + 1) - 2 = a^2 - 2a - 1$. So, if $f(a) = f(a - 1)$, then $\cancel{a^2} - 2 = \cancel{a^2} - 2a - 1$, and so $-2 = -2a - 1$. Multiplying both sides of this equation by -1, we get $2 = 2a + 1$. So, $2a = 1$ and $a = \dfrac{1}{2}$.

17. **255** Let x represent the number of families that had at least one boy and at least one girl, and draw a Venn diagram to illustrate the situation.

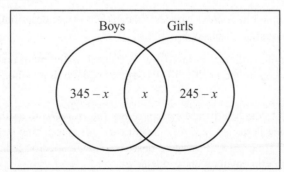

 So, $345 - x$ families have only boys and $245 - x$ families have only girls. Therefore, $(345 - x) + x + (245 - x) = 500 \Rightarrow 590 - x = 500 \Rightarrow x = 90$. So, $345 - 90 = 255$ families had only boys.

18. **35** $\triangle SRT$ is a 5–12–13 right triangle. If you don't recognize that immediately, let $x = RS$ and use the Pythagorean theorem:

$$x^2 + 12^2 = 13^2 \Rightarrow x^2 + 144 = 169 \Rightarrow x^2 = 25 \Rightarrow x = 5$$

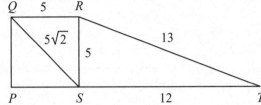

Then, since $QR = RS$, $QR = 5$ and since QS is the hypotenuse of an isosceles right triangle, $QS = 5\sqrt{2}$. So the perimeter of $QRTS$ is $5 + 13 + 12 + 5\sqrt{2} = 30 + 5\sqrt{2}$. Therefore, $a = 30$, $b = 5$, and $a + b = 35$.

Section 7 Critical Reading

1. **C** The words "Censorship presents a major problem" signal that censorship *inhibits* (hampers) the free expression that democracy depends on.

2. **D** The word "however" signals a contrast in the second part of the sentence with the first part of the sentence. It is *legitimate* (justifiable) for a scientist to have spiritual beliefs outside his professional frame of reference.

3. **E** This is a difficult question. All ten words make sense by themselves. However, the only choice that has two words that make good sense together is (E). Language reflects *mind;* therefore, by studying language we can learn something about human *cognitive* (relating to thought processes) ability.

4. **E** This is the best choice because the statement "The ends justify the means" is a *principle* (a standard of ethical decision-making). The phrase "do well to keep in mind" signals that the advice is *wise*.

5. **D** For the first blank, choices (B) *aptitudes* (abilities), (C) *skills*, and (D) *faculties* (capacities possessed by the human mind) are all good choices. (E) *Brains* is not a good choice because brains are not identical. For the second blank, only choice (D) *differences* makes sense with the word in the first blank.

6. **B** *Anthropological* (relating to the study of humankind, especially the study of cultures) is the best choice because the book is about human societies.

7. **A** (A) *Painstakingly* (carefully), (B) *meticulously* (carefully), and (E) *methodically* (systematically) are all good choices for the first blank. However, only (A) *lamented* (expressed regret) makes sense for the second blank because T.H. Huxley said, "How extremely stupid not to have thought of that."

8. **E** The author says that "one payment system drives up quantity" (lines 4–5). We can infer that the author is referring to healthcare systems based on fee-for-service payment here because this type of system is mentioned first in both the first and second sentence.

9. **A** "Albeit" means *although* and in context "modest" means *not large*, describing "steps…toward creating a system based on paying for quality" (lines 6–8).

10. **C** (C) Bundled payments are mentioned in line 14 of Passage 1 as the main feature of various pilot programs that are some of the steps taken by the health bill. Passage 2 explains how a bundled payments program would work in one case.

11. **A** (A) Passage 1 asserts that "the health care system of the future needs to be dominated by fee-for-value payment" (lines 2–4) and then describes how "the health care bill takes some steps…toward creating a system based on paying for quality" (lines 6–8). Passage 2 describes how a specific measure mentioned in Passage 1, bundled payments, would be implemented under Medicare.

12. **E** It makes sense that the reason Dr. Mead chose to study the question in Samoa was that Samoa has a culture that is very different from American culture. This is because to answer a question about "all cultures" it makes sense to study a culture that is very different from the one with which you are familiar.

13. **C** In context the word "institutional" means *related to a practice or custom in a society*. If something is expressed as an institution it becomes something that is recognized and practiced as part of the society's culture.

14. **C** The author is describing the childhood of a typical Samoan female. In the preceding sentence she described how a young girl spends her time "in small neighborhood gangs of age mates" (lines 6–7). Thus it makes sense that the "corner of the village" refers to the activities of young girls who belong to a particular gang of girls. It can be inferred that the area is "all-important" to the girl because she is growing up to a large extent in the group.

15. **E** In the passage the author is describing Dr. Mead's findings in an objective, matter-of-fact way, not inserting her own views, so it makes sense that her tone here is also matter-of-fact.

16. **B** The author says, "*While* Derek Freeman later critiqued Mead's culturally determined approach" (lines 64–66; italics mine), so we can infer that by "critique" the author means "criticized."

17. **B** The author says, "All of these were thought to make Samoan adolescence relatively tranquil and enjoyable and led to Mead's assertion of the primacy of nurture over nature" (lines 61–64). "Nurture" refers to cultural influences and "nature" refers to the influence of a person's genetic make-up.

18. **A** The author says, "Schlegal and Barry's cross-cultural study of adolescents…demonstrated that adolescence…is ubiquitous" (lines 73–78). In context, "ubiquitous" means *existing everywhere*.

19. **D** In context the word "inevitabilities" (line 84) means *unavoidable occurrences*.

20. **D** In context the word "gendered" (line 90) means *characteristic of one gender*. The phrase "with aggression in girls being particularly low" (lines 90–91) provides a clue to the meaning.

21. **C** According to the author, based on a study "Trommsdorff suggested that 'turbulent'" features such as inter-generational conflict stem from the focus on attaining independence from parents during this period and are linked to cultural values of individualism in Western societies" (lines 103–108). From this it can be inferred that Trommsdorff would probably agree that adolescents in individualistic cultures would be more likely to argue with their parents than adolescents in collective cultures.

22. **E** Based both on the account of Margaret Mead's research and conclusions in Passage 1 and on the first two paragraphs of Passage 2, we can infer that Margaret Mead would agree with this statement. She believed that adolescence is greatly influenced by culture, and that because cultures vary adolescence varies.

23. **D** The author says, "If we assume that a transitional period of the life cycle, akin to adolescence, organized around puberty and of variable length, exists almost universally…" (lines 41–44). The author also says, "Adolescence conceptualized as a prolonged period of identity development linked to increased autonomy, intergenerational conflict, peer-relatedness and social psychological anxieties, is not the norm across cultures" (lines 124–128).

24. **A** Passage 1 describes Margaret Mead's study of adolescence in Samoa, from which she concluded that adolescence there is not marked by conflict and stress; Passage 2 reviews Margaret Mead's study of adolescence and her conclusions, and makes use of two other studies to help reach a conclusion.

SECTION 8 MATHEMATICS

<u>Note:</u>

1. See page 32 for an explanation of the symbol ⇒ that is used in some answer explanations.

2. A calculator icon, ⌨, is placed next to the answer explanation of any question for which a calculator *could* be useful. Almost always, the question can be answered easily without using a calculator.

3. If you are unfamiliar with any of the math facts used in the following answer explanations, refer to Barron's *SAT*, which, in addition to having practice tests, has a full review of all the math you need to know.

1. **E** Since 85% of Jon's stamps are from European countries, the other 15% are from non-European countries. So if T represents the total number of stamps in his collection, $15\%T = 600$. Then, $0.15T = 600 \Rightarrow T = 600 \div 0.15 = 4,000$.

2. **B** Draw a line, label the points, and let $PQ = x$.

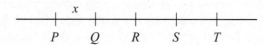

Since Q is the midpoint of $\overline{PR}$, then $QR = x$.

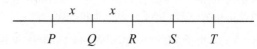

But R is the midpoint of $\overline{QS}$, so $RS = QR = x$.

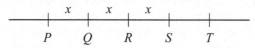

Finally, since S is the midpoint of $\overline{RT}$, $ST = RS = x$.

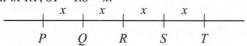

Then $QS = 2x$ and it was given that $QS = 8$. So $x = 4$ and $PT = 4x = 16$.

3. **B** **Solution 1.** Pick a value for n, say $n = 10$. Then $n - 7 = 3$, and the smallest odd integer greater than 3 is 5. Which answer choice is equal to 5 when $n = 10$? Choice (B): $n - 5$

   Solution 2. If n is even, then, since 7 is odd, $n - 7$ is odd. To get the smallest odd integer greater than a given odd integer, add 2: $(n - 7) + 2 = n - 5$.

4. **E** For any number x, $x\% = \dfrac{x}{100}$. So $0.001\% = \dfrac{0.001}{100} = 0.00001$, and $\dfrac{1}{5}(0.00001) = 0.000002$.

5. **D**
   - If $|x - 2.5| = 1.5$, then either

     $$x - 2.5 = 1.5 \quad \text{or} \quad x - 2.5 = -1.5$$
     $$x = 4 \quad \text{or} \quad x = 1$$

   - If $|x - 1.5| = 2.5$, then either

     $$x - 1.5 = 2.5 \quad \text{or} \quad x - 1.5 = -2.5$$
     $$x = 4 \quad \text{or} \quad x = -1$$

   So, a and b are 4 and 1, and c and d are 4 and -1.

   Finally, $a + b + c + d = 4 + 1 + 4 + (-1) = 8$.

6. **B** For any non-zero number n, its reciprocal is $\dfrac{1}{n}$ and $n \div \dfrac{1}{n} = n \times n = n^2$. Of 8, 9, and 10, only 9 is the square of an integer.

7. **D**
   - $f(2) = (2)^3 - 2(2) + 1 = 8 - 4 + 1 = 5$.
   - $f(-2) = (-2)^3 - 2(-2) + 1 = -8 + 4 + 1 = -3$.
   - So $f(2) - f(-2) = 5 - (-3) = 5 + 3 = 8$.

8. **E** **Solution 1.** The quickest solution is to use the formula for the area of an equilateral triangle whose sides are s: $A = \dfrac{s^2\sqrt{3}}{4}$.

Then, $\dfrac{s^2\sqrt{3}}{4} = \sqrt{3} \Rightarrow s^2\sqrt{3} = 4\sqrt{3} \Rightarrow s^2 = 4 \Rightarrow s = 2$.

Since each side of the triangle is 2, its perimeter is 6.

Solution 2. If you don't know the special formula for the area of an equilateral triangle, simply use $A = \dfrac{1}{2}bh$.

Since altitude $\overline{BD}$ divides equilateral triangle ABC into two 30-60-90 triangles, $BD = \dfrac{1}{2}s\sqrt{3}$.

So, $A = \dfrac{1}{2}(s)\left(\dfrac{1}{2}s\sqrt{3}\right) = \dfrac{1}{4}s^2\sqrt{3}$, and, as above, $s = 2$ and $p = 6$.

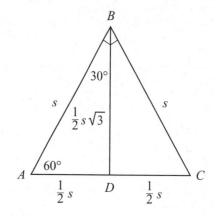

9. **D**

- 10,000 miles ÷ 25 miles per gallon = 400 gallons.
- 400 gallons × $3.00 per gallon = $1,200.
- 400 gallons × $3.25 per gallon = $1,300.

So, last year Tom spent between $1,200 and $1,300 for gas. Only choice (D), $1,234, is in that range.

10. **D**
- Since $AC = AD$, $\triangle ACD$ is isosceles and $b = 80$.
- Then $80 + 80 + a = 180$, and so $a = 20$.
- Since $BA = BD$, $\triangle ABD$ is isosceles and $(a + c) = 80$.
- Finally, since $a + c = 80$ and $a = 20$, then $c = 60$.

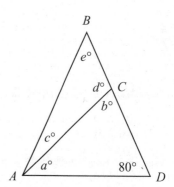

11. **C** **Solution 1.** Pick a number n that has a remainder of 7 when divided by 11, say $n = 18$. Then

$7n = 7 \times 18 = 126$, and when 126 is divided by 11, the quotient is 11 and the remainder is 5 ($126 = 11 \times 11 + 5$).

Solution 2. If the remainder when n is divided by 11 is 7, then n is 7 more than a multiple of 11. So $n = 11q + 7$, where q is an integer. Then $7n = 7(11q + 7) = 77q + 49 = 77q + 44 + 5 = 11(7q + 4) + 5$, which is 5 more than a multiple of 11.

12. **C** $f(5) = 5^2 - 18 = 25 - 18 = 7$. So $k = 7$. Then $g(k) = g(7) = 7^2 + 18 = 49 + 18 = 67$.

13. **C** Let r, h, C, and V be the radius, height, circumference, and volume of the cylinder.

Since $C = 2\pi r$, we have $12\pi = 2\pi r$, and so $r = 6$. Then, since $V = \pi r^2 h$, we get $12\pi = \pi(6)^2 h$. So, $12\pi = 36\pi h \Rightarrow h = \dfrac{1}{3}$.

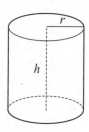

14. **E** Since n is 11 more than a multiple of 15, $n = 15m + 11$, for some integer m.

- $n - 11 = (15m + 11) - 11 = 15m$, which *is* a multiple of 15.
- $3n - 3 = 3(15m + 11) - 3 = (45m + 33) - 3 = 45m + 30 = 15(3m + 2)$, which *is* a multiple of 15.
- $4n + 1 = 4(15m + 11) + 1 = (60m + 44) + 1 = 60m + 45 = 15(4m + 1)$, which *is* a multiple of 15.

I, II, and III are all true.

15. **D** If you list several terms of this sequence—

$$1, 1, 2, 3, 5, 8, 13, 21, 34, \ldots$$

you should see the following pattern of odd and even numbers: (odd, odd, even), (odd, odd, even), (odd, odd, even), which continues indefinitely. So, it appears that in every three consecutive terms of the sequence, two are odd and one is even. Since $500 ÷ 3 = 166.66$, since $166 \times 3 = 498$, and since $500 = 498 + 2$, we have that the first 500 terms consists of 166 complete groups of three numbers followed by two more numbers. The 166 groups consist of 166 even numbers and $2 \times 166 = 332$ odd numbers. The next two numbers are the first two numbers of the next group of three, both of which are odd. Therefore, in the first 500 terms there are 334 odd numbers and 166 even numbers.

16. **A** From the diagram below, we see that the coordinates of *A* and *B* are (2, 1) and (5.5, 1.5), respectively. So the slope of the line that passes through *A* and *B* is $\dfrac{1.5-1}{5.5-2} = \dfrac{0.5}{3.5} = \dfrac{5}{35} = \dfrac{1}{7}$.

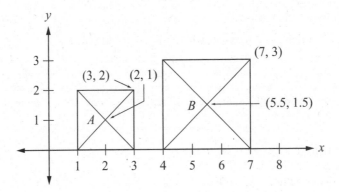

Section 9 Critical Reading

1. **D** A summary is a short statement of the *main* points in a piece of discourse (a lengthy written discussion of a topic).

2. **E** It makes sense that two rivals for a woman's affection would feel some *antagonism* (hostility) toward one another.

3. **A** This is the best choice because a *benefactor* (financial supporter) could donate money to the hospital's board of governors to help it expand the children's ward.

4. **A** A common definition of a theory is that it is a hypothesis that has been *elevated* (raised) to the status of a theory because enough evidence has accumulated for it so that no competing hypothesis is *credible* (convincing).

5. **C** The words "produced so many books" signal that the author is *prolific* (highly productive).

6. **E** The meanings of the other adjectives describing the world of *The Castle*, "impersonal" and "bureaucratic," are quite closely related to (E) *alienation* (a feeling that you do not belong to a particular group). (E) *Sinister* (menacing) makes good sense because we can imagine such a world also being sinister.

7. **C** In lines 10–20 ("In that they…authorities on everything") the author compares the sophists to the modern "authority." The pronoun *him* here refers to the modern "authority."

8. **E** In context "personal power or charm" refers to *charisma* (personal magnetism).

9. **A** The author says modern journalists can produce articles "without using…expert information" (lines 29–30). It can be inferred that he would say that modern journalists often produce articles that are not authoritative because such articles require expert information that journalists normally do not have.

10. **B** "Rhetoric" in context means *language that is elaborate but has little meaning*. The author says the sophists used rhetoric to hide the gaps in their logic. The adjective "glossy" means *slick, smooth,* suggesting that the sophist used rhetoric to, metaphorically, paint over the gaps in their reasoning with slick language.

11. **E** The author says the sophists "argued unsystematically and unfairly" (line 32).

12. **E** The author says that Socrates "came from a working-class family" (line 58).

13. **A** The author believes that Socrates "opposed the sophists wherever possible" because he believes that Socrates, unlike the sophists, was seeking the truth. This can be inferred from what the author says about the sophists and about Socrates. First, the sophists: "The sophists dazzled everyone without convincing anyone of anything positive.... They argued unsystematically and unfairly.... They had few constructive ideas.... They demonstrated that almost anything could be proved by a fast talker" (lines 30–39). Second, Socrates: "He distrusted...the sophists" (lines 45–46). "He only asked questions" (lines 49–50). "Socrates said he knew nothing and was trying to find out" (lines 70–71). Finally, "[Socrates] shakes[s] off the rhetoric and pursues[s] the truth" (lines 133–134). It is thus reasonable that the author believes that Socrates opposed the sophists because he believed that they not only were not seeking the truth, they were detrimental to the search for the truth.

14. **E** The other choices are mentioned in lines 72–87. It is unlikely that the sophists had new philosophical answers that helped them become successful because the author says that the sophists "dazzled without convincing anyone of anything positive" (lines 30–31) and "had few constructive ideas" (line 34), and generally were not concerned with finding the truth.

15. **A** This is the best choice because the passage is mainly concerned with the sophists and Socrates.

16. **E** According to the author, "Socrates said he knew nothing and was trying to find out" (lines 70–71). He spent his life questioning all sorts of people "and convinc[ing] them that they knew no more than he did" (lines 116–118). Thus, it is very unlikely that Socrates would believe that most truths have been discovered.

17. **C** In context the word "naive" means *uninformed*. This can be inferred because the author says that Socrates convinced people they "knew no more than he did" (lines 117–118) by first telling them that he knew nothing. This made the person eager to explain to Socrates because they believed he was "intelligent" (line 121) but uninformed.

18. **A** The author describes how in some of the dialogues Socrates listens to a "fanatic" (line 130) patiently. He then "shake[s] off the rhetoric" (line 133) by relentlessly questioning the person, leading the person to admit that "he was wrong." We can infer from this description that some people lost their temper because they became frustrated at their inability to refute Socrates' arguments.

19. **C** The author says that Socrates questioned "all sorts and conditions" (line 105) of people and that he adapted to them. He also says that Socrates' "adaptability...showed him the side on which each man could be best approached" (lines 122–124). We can infer from this information about Socrates that he had an excellent understanding of human nature because it would have been difficult for him to adapt to so many people without it.

Section 10 Writing

1. **B** This corrects the error in the given sentence. The words "become so engrossed in one's subject" must be followed by the word *that*.

2. **D** In the given sentence, the participial phrase beginning with the word *including* is incorrectly linked to the independent clause by a semicolon. This corrects the error in the sentence by changing the semicolon to a comma.

3. **C** This corrects the error in the given sentence. The part of the sentence before the comma is a prepositional phrase referring to *student*, so the word *student* should become the subject of the independent clause, which consists of the words after the comma.

4. **D** Run-on sentence. This makes the sentence grammatical by creating an adverb clause modifying the verb *strive* in the independent clause.

5. **B** Run-on sentence. This makes a complete sentence by creating an adverb infinitive phrase beginning with *to reduce*, modifying the verb *are forming*.

6. **D** Dangling participle. This improves the sentence by changing the words after the comma so that *parties* is the subject of the independent clause. The participial phrase *before signing the contract* now clearly refers to the subject, *parties*.

7. **E** Faulty comparison. The given sentence compares how much convenient access to information students today have to the 1960s. This corrects the error by comparing how much convenient access to information students today have to how much convenient access to information students had in the 1960s.

8. **B** Dangling participle. *Growing up in a small town* is a participial phrase referring to "Jessica." Choice (B) changes the independent clause (which consists of the words after the comma) so that "Jessica" is its subject. This makes it clear that the participial phrase refers to Jessica.

9. **D** The given sentence is awkward because the second independent clause (beginning with *they*) is a main clause in a compound sentence, but its content is of secondary importance. Choice (D) improves the sentence by making the words after the comma a nonrestrictive relative clause referring to *rabbits*.

10. **C** Faulty parallelism. The participial phrase beginning with the word *the* is cast in the passive voice, whereas the independent clause is cast in the active voice. This improves the sentence by changing the part of the sentence before the comma from a participial phrase to an adverb clause, cast in the active voice, telling when *the exhausted scientists celebrated*. Note that choice (C) also avoids the awkward repetition of the word *scientists*.

11. **D** The given sentence is awkward. This improves the sentence by changing it so that the most central idea—the scientist takes the reader on a journey through time—is expressed in an independent clause. The phrase "a noted scientist" becomes an appositive phrase referring to *author*.

12. **E** The given sentence is somewhat wordy. This improves the sentence by changing it so that the part of the sentence after the comma becomes a relative clause referring to *skills*.

13. **B** Faulty parallelism. The verb in the first relative clause is cast in the active voice, whereas the verb in the second relative clause is cast in the passive voice. Choice (B) improves the sentence by making the form of the second clause the same as the form of the first clause.

14. **B** The words *this makes it* are incorrect because two adverb clauses each give a reason, so the pronoun *this* is not needed. *It is* creates a correct sentence.

Answer Sheet–Practice Test 6

Section 1 ESSAY

Essay (continued)

If a section has fewer questions than answer spaces, leave the extra spaces blank.

Section 2

1 Ⓐ Ⓑ Ⓒ Ⓓ Ⓔ   8 Ⓐ Ⓑ Ⓒ Ⓓ Ⓔ   15 Ⓐ Ⓑ Ⓒ Ⓓ Ⓔ   22 Ⓐ Ⓑ Ⓒ Ⓓ Ⓔ   29 Ⓐ Ⓑ Ⓒ Ⓓ Ⓔ
2 Ⓐ Ⓑ Ⓒ Ⓓ Ⓔ   9 Ⓐ Ⓑ Ⓒ Ⓓ Ⓔ   16 Ⓐ Ⓑ Ⓒ Ⓓ Ⓔ   23 Ⓐ Ⓑ Ⓒ Ⓓ Ⓔ   30 Ⓐ Ⓑ Ⓒ Ⓓ Ⓔ
3 Ⓐ Ⓑ Ⓒ Ⓓ Ⓔ   10 Ⓐ Ⓑ Ⓒ Ⓓ Ⓔ   17 Ⓐ Ⓑ Ⓒ Ⓓ Ⓔ   24 Ⓐ Ⓑ Ⓒ Ⓓ Ⓔ   31 Ⓐ Ⓑ Ⓒ Ⓓ Ⓔ
4 Ⓐ Ⓑ Ⓒ Ⓓ Ⓔ   11 Ⓐ Ⓑ Ⓒ Ⓓ Ⓔ   18 Ⓐ Ⓑ Ⓒ Ⓓ Ⓔ   25 Ⓐ Ⓑ Ⓒ Ⓓ Ⓔ   32 Ⓐ Ⓑ Ⓒ Ⓓ Ⓔ
5 Ⓐ Ⓑ Ⓒ Ⓓ Ⓔ   12 Ⓐ Ⓑ Ⓒ Ⓓ Ⓔ   19 Ⓐ Ⓑ Ⓒ Ⓓ Ⓔ   26 Ⓐ Ⓑ Ⓒ Ⓓ Ⓔ   33 Ⓐ Ⓑ Ⓒ Ⓓ Ⓔ
6 Ⓐ Ⓑ Ⓒ Ⓓ Ⓔ   13 Ⓐ Ⓑ Ⓒ Ⓓ Ⓔ   20 Ⓐ Ⓑ Ⓒ Ⓓ Ⓔ   27 Ⓐ Ⓑ Ⓒ Ⓓ Ⓔ   34 Ⓐ Ⓑ Ⓒ Ⓓ Ⓔ
7 Ⓐ Ⓑ Ⓒ Ⓓ Ⓔ   14 Ⓐ Ⓑ Ⓒ Ⓓ Ⓔ   21 Ⓐ Ⓑ Ⓒ Ⓓ Ⓔ   28 Ⓐ Ⓑ Ⓒ Ⓓ Ⓔ   35 Ⓐ Ⓑ Ⓒ Ⓓ Ⓔ

Section 3

1 Ⓐ Ⓑ Ⓒ Ⓓ Ⓔ   8 Ⓐ Ⓑ Ⓒ Ⓓ Ⓔ   15 Ⓐ Ⓑ Ⓒ Ⓓ Ⓔ   22 Ⓐ Ⓑ Ⓒ Ⓓ Ⓔ   29 Ⓐ Ⓑ Ⓒ Ⓓ Ⓔ
2 Ⓐ Ⓑ Ⓒ Ⓓ Ⓔ   9 Ⓐ Ⓑ Ⓒ Ⓓ Ⓔ   16 Ⓐ Ⓑ Ⓒ Ⓓ Ⓔ   23 Ⓐ Ⓑ Ⓒ Ⓓ Ⓔ   30 Ⓐ Ⓑ Ⓒ Ⓓ Ⓔ
3 Ⓐ Ⓑ Ⓒ Ⓓ Ⓔ   10 Ⓐ Ⓑ Ⓒ Ⓓ Ⓔ   17 Ⓐ Ⓑ Ⓒ Ⓓ Ⓔ   24 Ⓐ Ⓑ Ⓒ Ⓓ Ⓔ   31 Ⓐ Ⓑ Ⓒ Ⓓ Ⓔ
4 Ⓐ Ⓑ Ⓒ Ⓓ Ⓔ   11 Ⓐ Ⓑ Ⓒ Ⓓ Ⓔ   18 Ⓐ Ⓑ Ⓒ Ⓓ Ⓔ   25 Ⓐ Ⓑ Ⓒ Ⓓ Ⓔ   32 Ⓐ Ⓑ Ⓒ Ⓓ Ⓔ
5 Ⓐ Ⓑ Ⓒ Ⓓ Ⓔ   12 Ⓐ Ⓑ Ⓒ Ⓓ Ⓔ   19 Ⓐ Ⓑ Ⓒ Ⓓ Ⓔ   26 Ⓐ Ⓑ Ⓒ Ⓓ Ⓔ   33 Ⓐ Ⓑ Ⓒ Ⓓ Ⓔ
6 Ⓐ Ⓑ Ⓒ Ⓓ Ⓔ   13 Ⓐ Ⓑ Ⓒ Ⓓ Ⓔ   20 Ⓐ Ⓑ Ⓒ Ⓓ Ⓔ   27 Ⓐ Ⓑ Ⓒ Ⓓ Ⓔ   34 Ⓐ Ⓑ Ⓒ Ⓓ Ⓔ
7 Ⓐ Ⓑ Ⓒ Ⓓ Ⓔ   14 Ⓐ Ⓑ Ⓒ Ⓓ Ⓔ   21 Ⓐ Ⓑ Ⓒ Ⓓ Ⓔ   28 Ⓐ Ⓑ Ⓒ Ⓓ Ⓔ   35 Ⓐ Ⓑ Ⓒ Ⓓ Ⓔ

Section 5

1 Ⓐ Ⓑ Ⓒ Ⓓ Ⓔ   3 Ⓐ Ⓑ Ⓒ Ⓓ Ⓔ   5 Ⓐ Ⓑ Ⓒ Ⓓ Ⓔ   7 Ⓐ Ⓑ Ⓒ Ⓓ Ⓔ
2 Ⓐ Ⓑ Ⓒ Ⓓ Ⓔ   4 Ⓐ Ⓑ Ⓒ Ⓓ Ⓔ   6 Ⓐ Ⓑ Ⓒ Ⓓ Ⓔ   8 Ⓐ Ⓑ Ⓒ Ⓓ Ⓔ

9 ⬚ 10 ⬚ 11 ⬚ 12 ⬚ 13 ⬚

14 ⬚ 15 ⬚ 16 ⬚ 17 ⬚ 18 ⬚

Section 6

1 Ⓐ Ⓑ Ⓒ Ⓓ Ⓔ	8 Ⓐ Ⓑ Ⓒ Ⓓ Ⓔ	15 Ⓐ Ⓑ Ⓒ Ⓓ Ⓔ	22 Ⓐ Ⓑ Ⓒ Ⓓ Ⓔ	29 Ⓐ Ⓑ Ⓒ Ⓓ Ⓔ
2 Ⓐ Ⓑ Ⓒ Ⓓ Ⓔ	9 Ⓐ Ⓑ Ⓒ Ⓓ Ⓔ	16 Ⓐ Ⓑ Ⓒ Ⓓ Ⓔ	23 Ⓐ Ⓑ Ⓒ Ⓓ Ⓔ	30 Ⓐ Ⓑ Ⓒ Ⓓ Ⓔ
3 Ⓐ Ⓑ Ⓒ Ⓓ Ⓔ	10 Ⓐ Ⓑ Ⓒ Ⓓ Ⓔ	17 Ⓐ Ⓑ Ⓒ Ⓓ Ⓔ	24 Ⓐ Ⓑ Ⓒ Ⓓ Ⓔ	31 Ⓐ Ⓑ Ⓒ Ⓓ Ⓔ
4 Ⓐ Ⓑ Ⓒ Ⓓ Ⓔ	11 Ⓐ Ⓑ Ⓒ Ⓓ Ⓔ	18 Ⓐ Ⓑ Ⓒ Ⓓ Ⓔ	25 Ⓐ Ⓑ Ⓒ Ⓓ Ⓔ	32 Ⓐ Ⓑ Ⓒ Ⓓ Ⓔ
5 Ⓐ Ⓑ Ⓒ Ⓓ Ⓔ	12 Ⓐ Ⓑ Ⓒ Ⓓ Ⓔ	19 Ⓐ Ⓑ Ⓒ Ⓓ Ⓔ	26 Ⓐ Ⓑ Ⓒ Ⓓ Ⓔ	33 Ⓐ Ⓑ Ⓒ Ⓓ Ⓔ
6 Ⓐ Ⓑ Ⓒ Ⓓ Ⓔ	13 Ⓐ Ⓑ Ⓒ Ⓓ Ⓔ	20 Ⓐ Ⓑ Ⓒ Ⓓ Ⓔ	27 Ⓐ Ⓑ Ⓒ Ⓓ Ⓔ	34 Ⓐ Ⓑ Ⓒ Ⓓ Ⓔ
7 Ⓐ Ⓑ Ⓒ Ⓓ Ⓔ	14 Ⓐ Ⓑ Ⓒ Ⓓ Ⓔ	21 Ⓐ Ⓑ Ⓒ Ⓓ Ⓔ	28 Ⓐ Ⓑ Ⓒ Ⓓ Ⓔ	35 Ⓐ Ⓑ Ⓒ Ⓓ Ⓔ

Section 7

1 Ⓐ Ⓑ Ⓒ Ⓓ Ⓔ	8 Ⓐ Ⓑ Ⓒ Ⓓ Ⓔ	15 Ⓐ Ⓑ Ⓒ Ⓓ Ⓔ	22 Ⓐ Ⓑ Ⓒ Ⓓ Ⓔ	29 Ⓐ Ⓑ Ⓒ Ⓓ Ⓔ
2 Ⓐ Ⓑ Ⓒ Ⓓ Ⓔ	9 Ⓐ Ⓑ Ⓒ Ⓓ Ⓔ	16 Ⓐ Ⓑ Ⓒ Ⓓ Ⓔ	23 Ⓐ Ⓑ Ⓒ Ⓓ Ⓔ	30 Ⓐ Ⓑ Ⓒ Ⓓ Ⓔ
3 Ⓐ Ⓑ Ⓒ Ⓓ Ⓔ	10 Ⓐ Ⓑ Ⓒ Ⓓ Ⓔ	17 Ⓐ Ⓑ Ⓒ Ⓓ Ⓔ	24 Ⓐ Ⓑ Ⓒ Ⓓ Ⓔ	31 Ⓐ Ⓑ Ⓒ Ⓓ Ⓔ
4 Ⓐ Ⓑ Ⓒ Ⓓ Ⓔ	11 Ⓐ Ⓑ Ⓒ Ⓓ Ⓔ	18 Ⓐ Ⓑ Ⓒ Ⓓ Ⓔ	25 Ⓐ Ⓑ Ⓒ Ⓓ Ⓔ	32 Ⓐ Ⓑ Ⓒ Ⓓ Ⓔ
5 Ⓐ Ⓑ Ⓒ Ⓓ Ⓔ	12 Ⓐ Ⓑ Ⓒ Ⓓ Ⓔ	19 Ⓐ Ⓑ Ⓒ Ⓓ Ⓔ	26 Ⓐ Ⓑ Ⓒ Ⓓ Ⓔ	33 Ⓐ Ⓑ Ⓒ Ⓓ Ⓔ
6 Ⓐ Ⓑ Ⓒ Ⓓ Ⓔ	13 Ⓐ Ⓑ Ⓒ Ⓓ Ⓔ	20 Ⓐ Ⓑ Ⓒ Ⓓ Ⓔ	27 Ⓐ Ⓑ Ⓒ Ⓓ Ⓔ	34 Ⓐ Ⓑ Ⓒ Ⓓ Ⓔ
7 Ⓐ Ⓑ Ⓒ Ⓓ Ⓔ	14 Ⓐ Ⓑ Ⓒ Ⓓ Ⓔ	21 Ⓐ Ⓑ Ⓒ Ⓓ Ⓔ	28 Ⓐ Ⓑ Ⓒ Ⓓ Ⓔ	35 Ⓐ Ⓑ Ⓒ Ⓓ Ⓔ

Section 8

1 Ⓐ Ⓑ Ⓒ Ⓓ Ⓔ	5 Ⓐ Ⓑ Ⓒ Ⓓ Ⓔ	9 Ⓐ Ⓑ Ⓒ Ⓓ Ⓔ	13 Ⓐ Ⓑ Ⓒ Ⓓ Ⓔ	17 Ⓐ Ⓑ Ⓒ Ⓓ Ⓔ
2 Ⓐ Ⓑ Ⓒ Ⓓ Ⓔ	6 Ⓐ Ⓑ Ⓒ Ⓓ Ⓔ	10 Ⓐ Ⓑ Ⓒ Ⓓ Ⓔ	14 Ⓐ Ⓑ Ⓒ Ⓓ Ⓔ	18 Ⓐ Ⓑ Ⓒ Ⓓ Ⓔ
3 Ⓐ Ⓑ Ⓒ Ⓓ Ⓔ	7 Ⓐ Ⓑ Ⓒ Ⓓ Ⓔ	11 Ⓐ Ⓑ Ⓒ Ⓓ Ⓔ	15 Ⓐ Ⓑ Ⓒ Ⓓ Ⓔ	19 Ⓐ Ⓑ Ⓒ Ⓓ Ⓔ
4 Ⓐ Ⓑ Ⓒ Ⓓ Ⓔ	8 Ⓐ Ⓑ Ⓒ Ⓓ Ⓔ	12 Ⓐ Ⓑ Ⓒ Ⓓ Ⓔ	16 Ⓐ Ⓑ Ⓒ Ⓓ Ⓔ	20 Ⓐ Ⓑ Ⓒ Ⓓ Ⓔ

Section 9

1 Ⓐ Ⓑ Ⓒ Ⓓ Ⓔ	5 Ⓐ Ⓑ Ⓒ Ⓓ Ⓔ	9 Ⓐ Ⓑ Ⓒ Ⓓ Ⓔ	13 Ⓐ Ⓑ Ⓒ Ⓓ Ⓔ	17 Ⓐ Ⓑ Ⓒ Ⓓ Ⓔ
2 Ⓐ Ⓑ Ⓒ Ⓓ Ⓔ	6 Ⓐ Ⓑ Ⓒ Ⓓ Ⓔ	10 Ⓐ Ⓑ Ⓒ Ⓓ Ⓔ	14 Ⓐ Ⓑ Ⓒ Ⓓ Ⓔ	18 Ⓐ Ⓑ Ⓒ Ⓓ Ⓔ
3 Ⓐ Ⓑ Ⓒ Ⓓ Ⓔ	7 Ⓐ Ⓑ Ⓒ Ⓓ Ⓔ	11 Ⓐ Ⓑ Ⓒ Ⓓ Ⓔ	15 Ⓐ Ⓑ Ⓒ Ⓓ Ⓔ	19 Ⓐ Ⓑ Ⓒ Ⓓ Ⓔ
4 Ⓐ Ⓑ Ⓒ Ⓓ Ⓔ	8 Ⓐ Ⓑ Ⓒ Ⓓ Ⓔ	12 Ⓐ Ⓑ Ⓒ Ⓓ Ⓔ	16 Ⓐ Ⓑ Ⓒ Ⓓ Ⓔ	20 Ⓐ Ⓑ Ⓒ Ⓓ Ⓔ

Section 10

1 Ⓐ Ⓑ Ⓒ Ⓓ Ⓔ	5 Ⓐ Ⓑ Ⓒ Ⓓ Ⓔ	9 Ⓐ Ⓑ Ⓒ Ⓓ Ⓔ	13 Ⓐ Ⓑ Ⓒ Ⓓ Ⓔ	17 Ⓐ Ⓑ Ⓒ Ⓓ Ⓔ
2 Ⓐ Ⓑ Ⓒ Ⓓ Ⓔ	6 Ⓐ Ⓑ Ⓒ Ⓓ Ⓔ	10 Ⓐ Ⓑ Ⓒ Ⓓ Ⓔ	14 Ⓐ Ⓑ Ⓒ Ⓓ Ⓔ	18 Ⓐ Ⓑ Ⓒ Ⓓ Ⓔ
3 Ⓐ Ⓑ Ⓒ Ⓓ Ⓔ	7 Ⓐ Ⓑ Ⓒ Ⓓ Ⓔ	11 Ⓐ Ⓑ Ⓒ Ⓓ Ⓔ	15 Ⓐ Ⓑ Ⓒ Ⓓ Ⓔ	19 Ⓐ Ⓑ Ⓒ Ⓓ Ⓔ
4 Ⓐ Ⓑ Ⓒ Ⓓ Ⓔ	8 Ⓐ Ⓑ Ⓒ Ⓓ Ⓔ	12 Ⓐ Ⓑ Ⓒ Ⓓ Ⓔ	16 Ⓐ Ⓑ Ⓒ Ⓓ Ⓔ	20 Ⓐ Ⓑ Ⓒ Ⓓ Ⓔ

Practice Test 6 1 1 1 1 1 1 1

Write your essay on the lines provided on the answer sheet on pages 375–376. Be careful to write legibly. Write on the topic, carefully presenting your point of view on it. Your essay will be scored on the basis of the ideas it contains and its effectiveness in expressing these ideas. Pay special attention to logic, clarity, and the accurate use of language.

Think about the topic presented in the following excerpt and in the assignment below it.

> *The singer and songwriter Bob Dylan said, "What's money? A man is a success if he gets up in the morning and goes to bed at night and in between does what he wants to do."*
>
> *There are many ways to define success. To some people it means a good paying job and a respected position in society. To other people it means having the opportunity to do interesting work in science, the arts, or other areas. And to still other people it means contributing to society and helping others to achieve their goals.*

ASSIGNMENT: What does success mean to you? Plan and write an essay in which you develop your point of view on this question. Support your position with reasoning and examples taken from your experience, reading, or observations.

2   2 2 2 2 2 2 2 2 2   2

SECTION **2**

Time—25 Minutes
20 Questions

For each problem in this section determine which of the five choices is correct and blacken the corresponding choice on your answer sheet. You may use any blank space on the page for your work.

Notes:

- You may use a calculator whenever you think it will be helpful.
- Only real numbers are used. No question or answer on this test involves a complex or imaginary number.
- Use the diagrams provided to help you solve the problems. Unless you see the words "Note: Figure not drawn to scale" under a diagram, it has been drawn as accurately as possible. Unless it is stated that a figure is three-dimensional, you may assume it lies in a plane.
- For any function, f, the domain, unless specifically restricted, is the set of all real numbers for which $f(x)$ is also a real number.

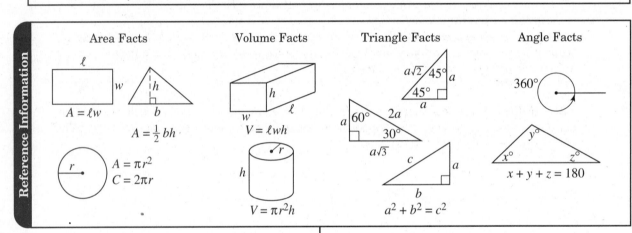

1. How many integers, n, satisfy the inequality
$$\frac{2}{5} < \frac{9}{n} < \frac{3}{4}\,?$$
   (A) None
   (B) 9
   (C) 10
   (D) 11
   (E) Infinitely many

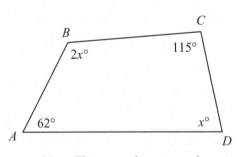

Note: Figure not drawn to scale.

2. For what value of a is $\dfrac{x^2 - a}{x^2 + 2} = 1$?

   (A) -2
   (B) 0
   (C) 1
   (D) 2
   (E) No value of a satisfies the given equation.

3. In quadrilateral *ABCD* above, what is the value of x?

   (A) 1
   (B) 31
   (C) 61
   (D) 91
   (E) 122

GO ON TO THE NEXT PAGE

4. Chloe has 12 nickels and 8 dimes. What is the ratio of the value of her nickels to the value of her dimes?

(A) 1:2
(B) 2:3
(C) 3:4
(D) 3:2
(E) 4:3

5. If the average (arithmetic mean) of a, b, c, and d is 2 less than the average of b, c, d, and e, then e is how much greater than a?

(A) 2
(B) 4
(C) 6
(D) 8
(E) 10

6. How many integers from 1 to 100, inclusive, have a remainder of 2 when divided by 7?

(A) 7
(B) 10
(C) 14
(D) 15
(E) 21

7. What is the length of each diagonal of a rectangle whose width is 15 and whose perimeter is 70?

(A) 18
(B) 20
(C) 24
(D) 25
(E) 30

8. If x, y are integers such that $|xy| = 6$, what is the greatest possible value of $x - y$?

(A) 5
(B) 6
(C) 7
(D) 8
(E) 9

9. Heather wants to buy a ring, a necklace, and a bracelet. Together, the ring and necklace would cost $123, the ring and bracelet would cost $113, and the necklace and bracelet would cost $86. If Heather has $140, how much more money, in dollars, does she need to buy all three items?

(A) 20
(B) 21
(C) 22
(D) 23
(E) 24

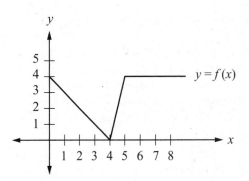

10. The figure above, consisting of three line segments, is the graph of the function of $y = f(x)$. If $f(6) = a$, what is $f(a)$?

(A) 0
(B) 2
(C) 4
(D) 6
(E) 8

GO ON TO THE NEXT PAGE

$$2 \quad 2 \; 2 \; 2 \; 2 \; 2 \; 2 \; 2 \; 2 \; 2 \quad 2$$

11. Julie hired a handyman to come to her house to hang some paintings. The handyman charged d dollars to come to the house, $\frac{3d}{10}$ dollars per painting for the first five paintings, and $\frac{d}{10}$ dollars per painting for each additional painting. If the total cost to hang ten paintings was $75, what is the value of d?

(A) 5
(B) 15
(C) 25
(D) 35
(E) 45

12. The radius of circle 2 is 1 foot longer than the radius of circle 1. If the radius of circle 1 is 1 mile, then the difference between the circumferences of the two circles is in which of the following intervals? (1 mile = 5,280 feet)

(F)   0 to 5 feet
(G)   5 to 10 feet
(H)   10 to 50 feet
(I)   50 to 100 feet
(J)   100 to 500 feet

13. For any numbers, x and y, $x \blacksquare y$ is defined as $x \blacksquare y = x^2 - y$.

If $a \blacksquare b = (a + 2) \blacksquare (b + 2)$, which of the following must be true?

(A) $a = 0$

(B) $a = -\frac{1}{2}$

(C) $a = -1$
(D) $b = 0$
(E) $b = -1$

14. If p and q are prime numbers, which of the following could not be the value of $p - q$?

(A) 3
(B) 4
(C) 5
(D) 6
(E) 7

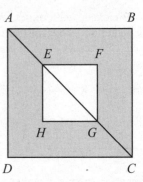

15. In the figure above, vertices E and G of square $EFGH$ lie on diagonal $\overline{AC}$ of square $ABCD$. If $EG = 6$, and the area of the shaded region is 82, what is the length of $\overline{AB}$?

(A) $3\sqrt{2}$
(B) $6\sqrt{2}$
(C) $10\sqrt{2}$
(D)   8
(E)   10

16. For all real numbers, x, let f be the function defined by $f(x) = x^2 + 7$. For what value of a is $4f\left(\frac{1}{2}\sqrt{a}\right) = 30$?

(A) $\frac{1}{2}$

(B) 1

(C) 2

(D) $\sqrt{\frac{1}{2}}$

(E) $\sqrt{2}$

17. If $x^3 < x^2 < x^4$, which of the following CANNOT be true?

   I. $x^2 < 1$
  II. $x^3 > 1$
 III. $x^3 < x^5$

(A) I only
(B) II only
(C) III only
(D) I and II only
(E) I, II, and III

GO ON TO THE NEXT PAGE

2   2 2 2 2 2 2 2 2 2   2

18. *A* and *B* are sets of numbers and *C* is the intersection of *A* and *B*. If the number of elements in *A*, *B*, and *C* are *a*, *b*, and *c*, respectively, how many numbers are in exactly one of the two sets *A* and *B*?

(A) $a + b$
(B) $a + b + c$
(C) $a + b - c$
(D) $2(a + b - c)$
(E) $a + b - 2c$

20. Eileen and Bob each drove the same distance from point *X* to point *Y*. It took Eileen exactly 2 hours to make the trip. If Bob drove 20 percent faster than Eileen, how many minutes less did it take him to make the trip?

(A) 12
(B) 20
(C) 30
(D) 60
(E) It cannot be determined from the information given.

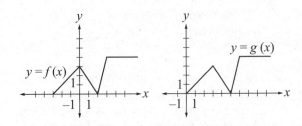

19. In the figure above, the graph of $y = f(x)$ is on the left and the graph of $y = g(x)$ is on the right. Which of the following equations expresses the relationship between $f(x)$ and $g(x)$?

(A) $g(x) = f(x + 3)$
(B) $g(x) = f(x - 3)$
(C) $g(x) = f(x) + 3$
(D) $g(x) = f(x) - 3$
(E) $g(x) = f(x - 3) + 3$

STOP

IN ANY REMAINING TIME YOU MAY REVIEW THE
ANSWERS YOU CHOSE IN THIS SECTION. DO NOT WORK
ON ANY OTHER SECTION OF THE TEST DURING THIS TIME.

Practice Test 6

3 3 3 3 3 3 3 3 3 3 3 **3**

SECTION **3**   Time—25 Minutes
24 Questions

Choose the best answer to each of the following questions in this section. Then blacken the appropriate space on your answer sheet.

Each of the following sentences contains one or two blanks, indicating that a word or set of words has been omitted. Beneath each sentence there are five answer choices labeled A to E from which you must select the word or set of words that best fits the meaning of the sentence as a whole.

Example:

Records of colonization can be found as far back as the Phoenicians, but colonization became a major force in world history only when European countries began, in the fifteenth century, to make ---- Asia, the Americas, and Africa.

(A) queries about   (B) incursions into
  (C) tirades against   (D) enemies in
    (E) amends for

Ⓐ ● Ⓒ Ⓓ Ⓔ

---

1. Generally, the main purpose of planning an essay is to select and organize ---- material.

   (A) left over   (B) personal   (C) obsolete
     (D) humorous   (E) relevant

2. There is strong evidence that any human being, given the exposure at the age during which language is first ----, can learn to speak any language.

   (A) memorized   (B) refined   (C) acquired
     (D) allowed   (E) hypothesized

3. Some scholars believe that the impetus for the building of the great pyramids at Giza was for reasons other than the purely functional one of providing ---- and secure burial chambers for pharaohs; these experts see ---- meaning behind their design.

   (A) large . . a pragmatic
   (B) insipid . . a recondite
   (C) apocryphal . . a nefarious
   (D) imposing . . an arcane
   (E) mercurial . . a sportive

4. The ---- of people from Europe between the early nineteenth century and early twentieth century resulted in European settlements in the Western Hemisphere, Australia, and New Zealand, which gradually overwhelmed their ---- cultures.

   (A) flood . . foreign
   (B) antipathy . . native
   (C) emigration . . heterogeneous
   (D) exodus . . indigenous
   (E) adversity . . parochial

5. In contrast to the Judeo-Christian tradition, the Hindu, Jain, and Buddhist traditions ---- a continuum of beings, each with spiritual value, so that any one cannot be ---- regarded as superior.

   (A) postulate . . initially
   (B) reject . . objectively
   (C) posit . . arbitrarily
   (D) circumscribe . . provisionally
   (E) presage . . dogmatically

GO ON TO THE NEXT PAGE ⟶

3   3 3 3 3 3 3 3 3 3 3   3

Below are passages followed by questions on them. Questions on a pair of related passages may be about the relationship between the two passages. For each question, select the best answer based on what is stated or implied in the passage (or passages).

Questions 6–9 are based on the following passages.

Passage 1

Passage 1 is from a letter written in 1859 by the nineteenth-century civil rights leader Susan B. Anthony to the organization Friends of Human Progress. Passage 2 is from an editorial in The Hartford Post in Hartford, Connecticut, on October 29, 1869.

I would exhort all women to be discontented with their present condition and to assert their individuality of thought, word and action by the
Line energetic doing of noble deeds. Idle wishes, vain
(5) repinings, loud-sounding declamations never can bring freedom to any human soul. What woman most needs is a true appreciation of her womanhood, a self-respect which shall scorn to eat the bread of dependence. Whoever consents
(10) to live by "the sweat of the brow" of another human being inevitably humiliates and degrades herself. . . . No genuine equality, no real freedom, no true manhood or womanhood can exist on any foundation save that of pecuniary independence.
(15) As a right over a man's subsistence is a power over his moral being, so a right over a woman's subsistence enslaves her will, degrades her pride and vitiates her whole moral nature.

Passage 2

Of late years, the country has been occupied in
(20) discussing the claim of man to hold property in his fellow-man, and has decided the question in the negative. Still another form of slavery remains to be disposed of; the old idea yet prevails that woman is owned and possessed by
(25) man, to be clothed and fed and cared for by his generosity. All the wrongs, arrogances and antagonisms of modern society grow out of this false condition of the relations between man and woman. The present agitation rises from a
(30) demand of the soul of woman for the right to own and possess herself. It is said that as a rule man does sufficiently provide for woman, and that she ought to remain content. The great facts of the world are at war with this assumption.

6. It can be inferred that the phrase "noble deeds" mentioned in line 4 refers to

(A) voluntary organizing of programs to aid indigent women
(B) heroic endeavors to advance human rights and end slavery
(C) sacrifices made by a woman for her husband and children
(D) altruistic actions to help all of humanity
(E) selfless efforts to advance the cause of women's freedom and equality

7. Which of the following would both the author of Passage 1 and the author of Passage 2 be most likely to agree with?

(A) Women should not marry.
(B) Women should not have children.
(C) Women should take salaried jobs outside their home.
(D) Women should spend more of their time making speeches to advance the cause of the equality of women.
(E) Women should neither marry nor have children.

8. One of the ways in which Passage 2 differs from Passage 1 is that

(A) Passage 2 cites an authority to support its argument
(B) Passage 2 considers a counter argument to the main argument that it is advancing
(C) Passage 2 does not consider the financial position of women in relation to the financial position of men
(D) Passage 2 stresses the importance of men's rights as well as women's rights
(E) Passage 2 takes a considerably less extreme position on the issue of women's rights

GO ON TO THE NEXT PAGE

Practice Test 6

3   **3 3 3 3 3 3 3 3 3 3**   **3**

9. Which of the following most accurately characterizes the relationship between the two passages?

(A) Passage 1 is mainly a call to women to action; Passage 2 is firm expression of support for women's rights and equality.

(B) Passage 1 is mainly a plea to women to take salaried employment; Passage 2 is concerned mainly with the broad issue of slavery.

(C) Passage 1 is largely a call for married women to divorce their husbands; Passage 2 is a sober analysis of the pros and cons of women gaining equality with men.

(D) Passage 1 is a caution to women that the struggle for equality will entail self-sacrifice; Passage 2 is an analysis of the pernicious effects of male domination of women on society.

(E) Passage 1 is a declaration that a woman's rights are more important than a man's rights; Passage 2 argues for granting women certain limited rights.

Questions 10–15 are based on the following passage.

With Union troops in the South and an increasing number of federal officials, most of whom were loyal Republicans, the latter sought
Line to build up a strong Southern wing of their party.
(5) Many Freedmen's Bureau officials were interested not only in the welfare of the freedman but in the growth of the Republican party as well. Moreover, missionary groups and teachers from the North, who saw in the Republican party an
(10) instrument by which the South could be saved from barbarism, supported it enthusiastically. It would be incorrect, however, to conclude that these groups were primarily political in their motives or activities. But the special agency that
(15) recruited Republicans, primarily among blacks, was the Union League.

The Union League of America was organized in the North during the war. It did an effective job in rallying support for the war wherever there
(20) was much opposition. Later it branched out into the South to protect the fruits of Northern victory. As a protective and benevolent society, it welcomed black members and catechized them on political activity. As the Freedmen's Bureau
(25) and other Northern agencies grew in the South,

the Union League became powerful, attracting a large number of blacks. With the establishment of Radical Reconstruction, the league became the spearhead for Southern Republicanism. Since
(30) black males were the most numerous enfranchised group in many areas, the league depended on them for the bulk of Republican strength. Black women also played a role in "getting out the vote" and in shaping political
(35) decisions in their communities. In October 1867 a reporter for the *New York Times* noted the presence of black women in the audience at local Republican and state constitutional conventions. He and other observers were impressed that, in
(40) contrast to white women who were quiet spectators at political meetings, black women shouted from the balconies, forcing their voices into the debates. As Elsa Barkley Brown has pointed out: "African-American women in
(45) Virginia, Mississippi, South Carolina and elsewhere understood themselves to have a vital stake in African-American men's franchise." The fact that only men could exercise the franchise did not at all mean that women were not
(50) involved.

By the fall of 1867 chapters of the league were all over the South. South Carolina alone had eighty-eight, and it was said that almost every black in the state was enrolled. Ritual, secrecy,
(55) night meetings, and an avowed devotion to freedom and equal rights made the league especially attractive to blacks. At elections they looked to their chapters for guidance on voting. If they had any doubt about the straight Republican
(60) ticket, the league had only to remind them that this was the party of Abraham Lincoln and of deliverance. A vote for Democrats, they said, was a vote for the return of slavery. During most of Reconstruction, the Union League and such
(65) smaller organizations as the Lincoln Brotherhood and the Red Strings delivered the black vote to the Republican party in national as well as state and local elections.

GO ON TO THE NEXT PAGE

3   **3**   **3**   **3**   **3**   **3**   **3**   **3**   **3**   **3**   **3**   **3**

10. In line 23, "catechized them" most nearly means

    (A) advised
    (B) pledged to secrecy
    (C) administered an oath of loyalty
    (D) warned
    (E) instructed in important basic principles

11. In line 48, "exercise the franchise" most nearly means

    (A) run for government office
    (B) be members of the Republican Party
    (C) vote to elect government officials
    (D) participate in political activities
    (E) take an oath to become full-fledged American citizens

12. It can be inferred that black women were more vocal than white women at political meetings primarily because

    (A) they were more confident than white women because they played a larger role in their community than white women did in theirs
    (B) they were better educated than white women
    (C) they realized that black men could not attain equality for blacks through the exercise of the franchise because politics were still dominated by whites, whereas white women believed that they didn't have to participate because white men already dominated politics in the South
    (D) there was a long tradition in the South of black women participating in political activities, whereas there was no such tradition for white women
    (E) they believed that increased political power for blacks in the South could improve the position of blacks and they wanted to support and be a part of the political process despite not being allowed to vote, whereas white women did not feel this need because whites were dominant

13. The Union League of America depended on black males to strengthen the Republican Party in the South during the Radical Reconstruction period because

    (A) in many areas they were the only people who could read and write
    (B) in many areas they were the largest group of people who could vote
    (C) the leaders of the Union League of America were male chauvinists
    (D) they had a history of supporting the Republican Party
    (E) black women generally did not support Republican candidates for office

14. The passage states that all of the following wanted to build up the Republican Party in the South EXCEPT

    (A) missionary groups and teachers from the North
    (B) many officials of the Freedman's Bureau
    (C) the Union League of America
    (D) many Union troops in the South
    (E) many Federal officials in the South

15. According to the information in the passage, all of the following are true about the Union League of America EXCEPT

    (A) it did not exist before the war
    (B) it was organized in the North
    (C) it worked to increase support for the war
    (D) it attracted many blacks as members
    (E) it was the only organization organizing black support for the Republican Party during Reconstruction

GO ON TO THE NEXT PAGE

3 3 3 3 3 3 3 3 3 3 3 **3**

Questions 16–24 are based on the following passage.

I have said that in one respect my mind has changed during the last twenty or thirty years. Up to the age of thirty, or beyond it, poetry of many
Line kinds, such as the works of Milton, Gray, Byron,
(5) Wordsworth, Coleridge, and Shelley, gave me great pleasure, and even as a schoolboy I took intense delight in Shakespeare, especially in the historical plays. I have also said that formerly pictures gave me considerable, and music very
(10) great delight. But now for many years I cannot endure to read a line of poetry: I have tried lately to read Shakespeare, and found it so intolerably dull that it nauseated me. I have also almost lost my taste for pictures or music. Music generally
(15) sets me thinking too energetically on what I have been at work on, instead of giving me pleasure. I retain some taste for fine scenery, but it does not cause me the exquisite delight which it formerly did. On the other hand, novels which are works
(20) of the imagination, though not of a very high order, have been for years a wonderful relief and pleasure to me, and I often bless all novelists. A surprising number have been read aloud to me, and I like all if moderately good, and if they do
(25) not end unhappily—against which a law ought to be passed. A novel, according to my taste, does not come into the first class unless it contains some person whom one can thoroughly love, and if a pretty woman all the better.
(30)   This curious and lamentable loss of the higher aesthetic tastes is all the odder, as books on history, biographies, and travels (independently of any scientific facts which they may contain), and essays on all sorts of subjects interest me as
(35) much as ever they did. My mind seems to have become a kind of machine for grinding general laws out of large collections of facts, but why this should have caused the atrophy of that part of the brain alone, on which the higher tastes
(40) depend, I cannot conceive. A man with a mind more highly organized or better constituted than mine, would not, I suppose, have thus suffered; and if I had to live my life again, I would have made a rule to read some poetry and listen to
(45) some music at least once every week; for perhaps the parts of my brain now atrophied would thus have been kept active through use. The loss of these tastes is a loss of happiness, and may

possibly be injurious to the intellect, and more
(50) probably to the moral character, by enfeebling the emotional part of our nature.
    I have no great quickness of apprehension or wit which is so remarkable in some clever men, for instance, Huxley. I am therefore a poor critic:
(55) a paper or book, when first read, generally excites my admiration, and it is only after considerable reflection that I perceive the weak points. My power to follow a long and purely abstract train of thought is very limited; and
(60) therefore I could never have succeeded with metaphysics or mathematics. My memory is extensive, yet hazy: it suffices to make me cautious by vaguely telling me that I have observed or read something opposed to the
(65) conclusion which I am drawing, or on the other hand in favor of it; and after a time I can generally recollect where to search for my authority. So poor in one sense is my memory, that I have never been able to remember for more
(70) than a few days a single date or a line of poetry.
    Some of my critics have said, "Oh, he is a good observer, but he has no power of reasoning!" I do not think that this can be true, for *The Origin of Species* is one long argument
(75) from the beginning to the end, and it has convinced not a few able men. No one could have written it without having some power of reasoning. I have a fair share of invention, and of common sense or judgment, such as every fairly
(80) successful lawyer or doctor must have, but not, I believe, in any higher degree.
    On the favorable side of the balance, I think that I am superior to the common run of men in noticing things which easily escape attention, and
(85) in observing them carefully. My industry has been nearly as great as it could have been in the observation and collection of facts. What is far more important, my love of natural science has been steady and ardent.
(90)   This pure love has, however, been much aided by the ambition to be esteemed by my fellow naturalists. From my early youth I have had the

GO ON TO THE NEXT PAGE ➡

strongest desire to understand or explain whatever I observed,—that is, to group all facts (95) under some general laws. These causes combined have given me the patience to reflect or ponder for any number of years over any unexplained problem. As far as I can judge, I am not apt to follow blindly the lead of other men. I have (100) steadily endeavored to keep my mind free so as to give up any hypothesis, however much beloved (and I cannot resist forming one on every subject), as soon as facts are shown to be opposed to it. Indeed, I have had no choice but to (105) act in this manner, for with the exception of the Coral Reefs, I cannot remember a single first-formed hypothesis which had not after a time to be given up or greatly modified. This has naturally led me to distrust greatly deductive (110) reasoning in the mixed sciences. On the other hand, I am not very skeptical,—a frame of mind which I believe to be injurious to the progress of science. A good deal of skepticism in a scientific man is advisable to avoid much loss of time, but (115) I have met with not a few men, who, I feel sure, have often thus been deterred from experiment or observations, which would have proved directly or indirectly serviceable.

16. When the author writes "against which a law ought to be passed" (lines 25–26) he is most likely being

(A) satirical
(B) serious
(C) ironic
(D) jocular
(E) sarcastic

17. In lines 30–31, "the higher aesthetic tastes" refers to

(A) the ability to read and understand the poetic works of great poets like Milton and Wordsworth
(B) the ability to appreciate the beauties of nature
(C) the ability to appreciate beauty created by first-rate art
(D) the ability to relate scientific facts to art
(E) the ability to enjoy a novel

18. Which of the following would the author have probably most enjoyed doing when he was the age at which he wrote this passage?

(A) Reading a poem by William Wordsworth
(B) Reading a play by William Shakespeare
(C) Listening to a symphony
(D) Reading an essay on English history
(E) Studying advanced mathematics

19. The author believes that he has considerable ability in all of the following areas EXCEPT

(A) thinking independently
(B) evaluating the worth of hypotheses he has formed
(C) reasoning clearly
(D) quickly evaluating the worth of a book or paper written by someone else
(E) observing carefully

20. Which of the following best characterizes the main process the author says he employs in his study of nature?

(A) Skepticism
(B) Deduction
(C) Induction
(D) Impartiality
(E) Invention

21. The author believes that

(A) the more skeptical a scientist is the better the scientist he or she will be
(B) a scientist must be somewhat skeptical but not excessively so
(C) skepticism has no place in science
(D) skepticism is irrelevant to the pursuit of scientific research
(E) he should have been more skeptical in his scientific career

GO ON TO THE NEXT PAGE

22. In line 52, "apprehension" most nearly means

    (A) trepidation
    (B) prodigality
    (C) diligence
    (D) understanding
    (E) anticipation

23. The author says "independently of any scientific facts which they may contain" (lines 32–33). This is most likely intended to make clear that

    (A) he is interested in reading books on history, biographies, and travels for their intrinsic merit and not only for the scientific facts they may contain
    (B) he is interested in reading books on history, biographies, and travels only for the scientific facts they contained
    (C) he is interested in reading books on history, biographies, and travels only for reasons other than the scientific facts they contained
    (D) books on history, biographies, and travels do not contain any scientific facts
    (E) facts found in books on history, biographies, and travels cannot be related to the facts found by science

24. In line 78, "invention" most nearly means

    (A) discovery
    (B) mechanical aptitude
    (C) logical ability
    (D) insight
    (E) creativity

STOP

IN ANY REMAINING TIME YOU MAY REVIEW THE
ANSWERS YOU CHOSE IN THIS SECTION. DO NOT WORK
ON ANY OTHER SECTION OF THE TEST DURING THIS TIME.

5 **5** **5** **5** **5** **5** 5

SECTION 5

Time—25 Minutes
18 Questions

You have 25 minutes to answer the 8 multiple-choice questions and 10 student-produced response questions in this section. For each multiple-choice question, determine which of the five choices is correct and blacken the corresponding choice on your answer sheet. You may use any blank space on the page for your work.

Notes:

- You may use a calculator whenever you think it will be helpful.
- Only real numbers are used. No question or answer on this test involves a complex or imaginary number.
- Use the diagrams provided to help you solve the problems. Unless you see the words "Note: Figure not drawn to scale" under a diagram, it has been drawn as accurately as possible. Unless it is stated that a figure is three-dimensional, you may assume it lies in a plane.
- For any function, f, the domain, unless specifically restricted, is the set of all real numbers for which $f(x)$ is also a real number.

Reference Information

Area Facts

$A = \ell w$

$A = \frac{1}{2} bh$

$A = \pi r^2$
$C = 2\pi r$

Volume Facts

$V = \ell wh$

$V = \pi r^2 h$

Triangle Facts

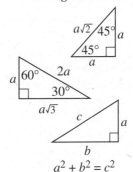

$a^2 + b^2 = c^2$

Angle Facts

$360°$

$x + y + z = 180$

1. $\frac{2}{3}$ of 60 is what fraction of 100?

 (A) $\frac{1}{3}$

 (B) $\frac{2}{5}$

 (C) $\frac{1}{2}$

 (D) $\frac{3}{5}$

 (E) $\frac{3}{4}$

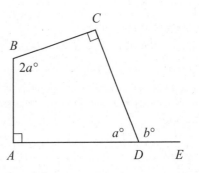

2. In the diagram above, side $\overline{AD}$ of quadrilateral $ABCD$ is extended to E. What is the value of b?

 (A) 60
 (B) 75
 (C) 120
 (D) 135
 (E) 150

GO ON TO THE NEXT PAGE

5 5 5 5 5 5 5

3. If $c^2 + d^2 = 20$ and $cd = 10$, what is the value of $(c + d)^2$?

(A) 20
(B) 30
(C) 40
(D) 50
(E) 60

4. Chris and Claire each collect antique dolls. Claire has 40 percent fewer dolls in her collection than Chris does. If Claire has 90 dolls, how many dolls does Chris have?

(A) 50
(B) 54
(C) 130
(D) 144
(E) 150

5. In a set of 50 different integers, 40 of them are greater than 19 and 30 of them are less than 50. How many of the integers have a ten's digit that is equal to 2, 3, or 4?

(A) 10
(B) 20
(C) 25
(D) 30
(E) 40

6. Jar 1 contains 10 red and 5 blue marbles.

Jar 2 contains 12 blue and 6 green marbles.

Jar 3 contains 7 red and 7 green marbles.

If one marble is drawn at random from each jar, what is the probability that the three marbles are all different colors?

(A) $\dfrac{3}{18}$

(B) $\dfrac{4}{18}$

(C) $\dfrac{5}{18}$

(D) $\dfrac{6}{18}$

(E) $\dfrac{7}{18}$

7. If three lines are drawn in a plane, which of the following could be the number of nonoverlapping regions into which the plane is divided?

 I. 4
 II. 6
III. 7

(A) I only
(B) II only
(C) III only
(D) I and II only
(E) I, II, and III

8. Palindromes are integers such as 444 and 1551 that read the same from right to left as they do from left to right. If a and b are both palindromes between 300 and 3,000, with $a > b$, what is the least possible value of $a - b$?

(A) 2
(B) 9
(C) 10
(D) 11
(E) 110

GO ON TO THE NEXT PAGE ⟹

5   5   5   5   5   5   5

Directions for Student-Produced Response Questions (Grid-ins)

In questions 9–18, first solve the problem, and then enter your answer on the grid provided on the answer sheet. The instructions for entering your answers are as follows:

- First, write your answer in the boxes at the top of the grid.
- Second, grid your answer in the columns below the boxes.
- Use the fraction bar in the first row or the decimal point in the second row to enter fractions and decimal answers.

- Grid only one space in each column.
- Entering the answer in the boxes is recommended as an aid in gridding, but is not required.
- The machine scoring your exam can read only what you grid, so you **must grid in your answers correctly to get credit.**
- If a question has more than one correct answer, grid in only one of these answers.
- The grid does not have a minus sign, so no answer can be negative.
- A mixed number *must* be converted to an improper fraction or a decimal before it is gridded. Enter $1\frac{1}{4}$ as 5/4 or 1.25; the machine will interpret 1 1/4 as $\frac{11}{4}$ and mark it wrong.
- **All decimals must be entered as accurately as possible.** Here are the three acceptable ways of gridding

$$\frac{3}{11} = 0.272727\ldots$$

Answer: $\frac{8}{15}$ Answer: 1.75

Write your → answer in the boxes.

Grid in → your answer.

Answer: 100

Either position is acceptable

3/11   .272   .273

- Note that rounding to .273 is acceptable, because you are using the full grid, but you would receive **no credit** for .3 or .27, because these answers are less accurate.

GO ON TO THE NEXT PAGE →

5   5   5   5   5   5   5

9. Ten minutes is what fraction of the time between 6:00 A.M. and 3:00 P.M. of the same day?

10. If the point $(-5, b)$ lies on the line whose equation is $2x + 3y + 4 = 0$, what is the value of b?

11. If $a^{10} = 2$, what is the value of a^{100}?

12. Michael, Chris, and Lauren were each assigned a code number. Michael's code is 5 more than 3 times Lauren's code, and Chris's code is 7 times Lauren's code. If Michael's code is 44, what is the sum of Lauren's code and Chris's code?

13. If $f(x) = x^2 - 1$ and $f(7) = a$, what is the value of $f(a)$?

14. If 5 years from now Ezra will be twice as old as he was 5 years ago, in how many years will he be 5 times as old as he is now?

15. A box contains some big disks and some small disks. The total weight of all the disks in the box is 6 pounds. If each big disk weighs 7 ounces and each small disk weighs 5 ounces, what is the largest possible number of small disks that could be in the box? (16 ounces = 1 pound)

16. The first nine terms of a sequence are 7, a, b, c, 25, d, e, f, and g. If the difference between any two consecutive terms in the sequence is the same, what is the value of g?

17. The sum of two numbers is equal to one-half their product. If one of the numbers is 10, what is the other number?

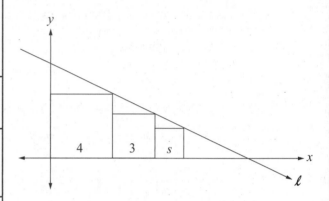

18. In the figure above, one side of the largest square lies on the y-axis, one side of each of the three squares lies on the x-axis, and one vertex of each square is on line l. If the lengths of the sides of the three squares are 4, 3, and s, respectively, what is the value of s?

STOP

IN ANY REMAINING TIME YOU MAY REVIEW THE ANSWERS YOU CHOSE IN THIS SECTION. DO NOT WORK ON ANY OTHER SECTION OF THE TEST DURING THIS TIME.

6 6 6 6 6 6 6 6 6 6 6 6

SECTION **6**   Time—25 Minutes   Choose the best answer to each of the following questions in
35 Questions   this section. Then blacken the appropriate space on your
answer sheet.

Each sentence below may or may not employ correct or effective expression. If you think that the underlined phrasing makes the most clear and precise sentence, select choice A. If, however, you think that the underlined phrasing makes the meaning of the sentence unclear or awkward, or that it is grammatically incorrect, select another answer from choices B to E.

In choosing your answers, follow the conventions of English as it is used by educated writers. Consider sentence structure, grammar, word choice, and punctuation. Choose the answer that produces the sentence that is the most clear and effective.

Example:

In her comments after the debate the judge said that she had been impressed by the ability of both teams to exploit logical weaknesses and <u>in citing relevant examples</u>.

(A) in citing relevant examples
(B) in that relevant examples had been cited
(C) in the citing of relevant examples
(D) to cite relevant examples
(E) to be able to cite relevant examples

Ⓐ Ⓑ Ⓒ ● Ⓔ

1. <u>Double-entry bookkeeping revolutionized business, was</u> devised in Venice in 1494 by Luca Pacioli, a brilliant mathematician who taught mathematics to Leonardo da Vinci.

(A) Double-entry bookkeeping revolutionized business, was
(B) Double-entry bookkeeping, it revolutionized business, was
(C) Double-entry bookkeeping, which revolutionized business, was
(D) It was double-entry bookkeeping that revolutionized business, being
(E) The double entry-bookkeeping, and it revolutionized business, was

2. The great baseball player Babe Ruth, who, according to legend, once pointed his bat to the spot in the grandstand where he hit a home run on his next swing, <u>and</u> famous for his exploits both on and off the baseball diamond.

(A) and
(B) and who became
(C) is
(D) and has been
(E) had who was

3. Paul Fussell, one of America's leading literary critics and <u>essayists, he taught for many years</u> at Rutgers University and at the University of Pennsylvania.

(A) essayists, he taught for many years
(B) essayists, taught for many years
(C) essayists, and taught for many years
(D) essayists, when he had been teaching for many years
(E) essayists, he was a teacher for many years

4. The new restaurant <u>priced items on its menu</u> cheaply in order to gain a clientele, which grew steadily by word of mouth.

(A) priced items on its menu
(B) is pricing items on its menu
(C) prices items on its menu
(D) has menu items priced
(E) has items on its menu priced

GO ON TO THE NEXT PAGE

Practice Test 6

5. The stock <u>market recovered later in the week and had been quite low earlier in the week</u>.

(A) market recovered later in the week and had been quite low earlier in the week
(B) market recovered later in the week, earlier in the week it had been quite low
(C) market, which had been quite low earlier in the week, recovered later in the week
(D) market's recovery came later in the week and had been quite low earlier in the week
(E) market, recovering later in the week, from being quite low earlier in the week

6. <u>The sorting of genetic material in new combinations, which is done by mutation and sexual reproduction, is how the genetic variation required for the process of natural selection is produced.</u>

(A) The sorting of genetic material in new combinations, which is done by mutation and sexual reproduction, is how the genetic variation required for the process of natural selection is produced.
(B) Sorting genetic material in new combinations, which is done by mutation and sexual reproduction, is the way the genetic variation required for the process of natural selection is produced.
(C) By sorting of genetic material in new combinations, which is done by mutation and sexual reproduction, the genetic variation required for the process of natural selection is produced.
(D) By sorting genetic material in new combinations, mutation and sexual reproduction produce the genetic variation required for natural selection.
(E) Mutation and sexual reproduction sort the genetic material in new combinations, and that is how the genetic variation required for the process of natural selection is produced.

7. Though now regarded as one of the great composers, <u>Igor Stravinsky had been reviled, for many years, by concert-goers</u>.

(A) Igor Stravinsky had been reviled, for many years, by concert-goers
(B) Igor Stravinsky was for many years reviled by concert-goers
(C) concert-goers for many years reviled Igor Stravinsky
(D) concert-goers, for many years, reviled Igor Stravinsky
(E) concert-goers were reviling Igor Stravinsky for many years

8. According to scientists the human body needs a certain amount of natural radiation in order to stay healthy, <u>but doses that are large and especially those received in a short amount of time</u> can be very harmful and even fatal.

(A) but doses that are large and especially those received in a short amount of time
(B) but large doses, those especially received in a short amount of time,
(C) but large doses received and in an especially short amount of time
(D) but large doses, especially if received in a short amount of time,
(E) but large doses received, if it is especially in a short amount of time,

GO ON TO THE NEXT PAGE →

9. Declining in numbers, relocation programs are being implemented to increase the population of the northwestern fairy wren.

(A) Declining in numbers, relocation programs are being implemented to increase the population of the northwestern fairy wren.

(B) Declining in numbers, relocation programs are being implemented and they increase the population of the northwestern fairy wren.

(C) Declining in numbers, relocation programs that are being implemented increase the population of the northwestern fairy wren.

(D) The population of the northwestern fairy wren is declining in numbers while being increased by the implementation of relocation programs.

(E) Relocation programs are being implemented to increase the population of the northwestern fairy wren, which is declining in numbers.

10. It was not until after World War II that college football and basketball became big business, previously they were popular but not the huge money-earners they are today.

(A) business, previously

(B) business, in comparison with previous times when

(C) business compared to previously when

(D) business; previously

(E) business, in earlier times

11. Ursula K. Le Guin's novel *The Left Hand of Darkness* not only is a novel that is a superbly entertaining story of political intrigue, but it also is a fascinating exploration of the relationship between male and female on an alien world.

(A) not only is a novel that is a superbly entertaining story of political intrigue, but it also is

(B) is not only a story of political intrigue that is a superbly entertaining novel, but it is also

(C) is not only a superbly entertaining story of political intrigue; but it is also

(D) is a superbly entertaining story of political intrigue but also

(E) not only is a superbly entertaining story of political intrigue; it is also

GO ON TO THE NEXT PAGE

6   6 6 6 6 6 6 6 6 6 6 6   6

Each of the sentences below contains either one error or no error in grammar or usage. If there is an error, it will be underlined. If the sentence contains an error, indicate this by selecting the letter for the one underlined part that should be changed to make the sentence correct. Follow the requirements of standard written English in choosing answers. If the sentence is already correct, select choice E.

Example:

The number of stars <u>visible in</u> the sky on any
                         A

<u>given</u> night <u>vary</u>, mainly <u>because of</u> changes in
  B   C   D

atmospheric conditions and in the phases of the

Moon. <u>No Error</u>
          E

Ⓐ Ⓑ ● Ⓓ Ⓔ

12. <u>Far less known</u> outside Australia <u>than</u> the
         A   B
    kangaroo, the echidna <u>it is</u> another fascinating
                              C
    animal <u>native to</u> Australia. <u>No Error</u>
                D   E

13. <u>Unlike</u> many retired couples, neither Ruth <u>or</u> her
        A   B
    husband Samuel <u>has</u> an interest <u>in traveling</u> around
                      C   D
    the world. <u>No Error</u>
                   E

14. <u>Some</u> ecosystems are fragile, <u>they are</u> susceptible
        A   B
    <u>to</u> small changes in conditions, <u>whereas</u> others are
    C   D
    robust. <u>No Error</u>
                E

15. Babies <u>born to</u> Aboriginal mothers in Australia
               A
    <u>die at</u> twice the rate of other Australian babies, and
        B
    <u>experienced</u> higher rates of <u>preventable illness</u>
         C   D
    such as heart disease, kidney disease, and diabetes.

    <u>No Error</u>
        E

16. The <u>university's</u> physics department, <u>under</u>
            A   B
    pressure to have more female professors, <u>are taking</u>
                                                 C
    measures to encourage female undergraduates

    <u>to pursue</u> careers in physics. <u>No Error</u>
        D   E

17. If—like many people—you have trouble

    <u>to remember</u> the difference between *it's* and *its*, it
         A
    <u>might be</u> helpful to keep in mind that *it's* is a
        B
    <u>contraction of</u> *it is*, <u>whereas</u> *its* is a possessive
         C   D
    pronoun, which do not have an apostrophe.

    <u>No Error</u>
        E

18. One of the important missions <u>of</u> amateur radio is
                                     A
    <u>to provide</u> communications in emergencies, <u>when</u>
         B   C
    normal means of communication such as cell

    phones and e-mail <u>disrupted</u>. <u>No Error</u>
                          D   E

GO ON TO THE NEXT PAGE ⟹

6   6 6 6 6 6 6 6 6 6 6   6

19. One of the problems faced with intelligence-
                        A
gathering bodies such as the Central Intelligence

Agency is identifying important information so that
             B
it can be thoroughly analyzed and evaluated.
C   D
No Error
      E

20. A number of the rockets used in the American
       A
space program in the 1950s and 1960s were

modified Intercontinental Ballistic Missiles

(ICBMs), which had been developed to
                  B
be launched from the U.S. and travel thousands of
C
miles to targets in the Soviet Union and elsewhere.
                                              D
No Error
      E

21. Knowledge of basic English grammar, including
       A
common used terms, is helpful to people who are
   B
developing their writing skills because it helps
                                        C
them to understand the grammatical structure of
      D
the sentences they write. No Error
                             E

22. During the long sleepless night before the battle
       A
the two soldiers, who were friends since high
                    B
school, talked about what they were going to do
                    C   D
after the war. No Error
               E

23. The French Impressionist artist Camille Pissarro

once gave this prediction about his contemporary,
                         A   B
Vincent Van Gogh: "This man is either going to go
                              C
mad, or he'd leave us all far behind." No Error
        D   E

24. During the Cold War between the United States
    A
and the Soviet Union, the former relied on a three-

prong approach to deterring Soviet aggression
                 B
through the threat of a nuclear counter attack:

Land-based intercontinental ballistic missiles,

submarines armed with missiles that could strike
           C
targets thousands of miles away, and bombers

carrying bombs on constant alert. No Error
D   E

25. The historic Traders Hotel on Chesterton Road was

built around the turn of the century from the
      A   B
dismantling materials of old buildings, including
   C   D
the eighteenth century post office in Waterville.

No Error
   E

26. Performance activities lay at the heart of our jazz
    A   B
course and each semester we organize an exciting
       C
program of events that complements students'
                          D
academic studies. No Error
                   E

GO ON TO THE NEXT PAGE

Practice Test 6

6   6   6   6   6   6   6   6   6   6   6   **6**

27. Journalist and UCLA professor Tom Plate <u>once</u>
                                                    A

    gave some good advice to young people who want

    to acquire the <u>wide</u> general knowledge a good
                       B

    journalist needs; he said whenever you

    <u>would browse</u> in the magazine section of a store,
            C

    buy one or two magazines <u>in</u> areas you have very
                                         D

    little knowledge of. <u>No Error</u>
                          E

28. The life of Jean-Baptiste Lamarck <u>is</u> the old story
                                        A

    of a man of genius who lived <u>far</u> in advance <u>of</u> his
                              B   C

    age, and who died <u>in comparative</u> unappreciated
                              D

    and neglected. <u>No Error</u>
                      E

29. <u>Like</u> many other technologies, the Internet <u>has had</u>
     A   B

    both good and bad effects on society; and, <u>as is</u> the
                                             C

    case with other technologies, whether the Internet

    will ultimately help humanity more than it will

    harm it depends on those who <u>had used</u> it.
                                            D

    <u>No Error</u>
      E

GO ON TO THE NEXT PAGE ➡

6 6 6 6 6 6 6 6 6 6 6 6 6

The following early draft of an essay needs to be rewritten to improve sentence structure, choice of words, clarity of expression, organization, and development. After reading the draft, answer each question below it, choosing the answer that best conforms to the requirements of standard written English.

(1) Most people would agree that obedience to authority is necessary. **(2)** Without obedience it would be difficult, if not impossible, for society to function.

(3) A famous experiment conducted by Stanley Millgram at Yale University in the Unites States in the 1960s went toward answering this question. **(4)** The experiment is too complex to describe here in detail, but it showed that most people will obey authority even if it goes against what they think is morally right. **(5)** Subjects were deceived by the experimenter into thinking that they were inflicting pain on others by electric shocks. **(6)** The experimenters told the subjects that what they were doing was important for science and that they must continue to administer the shocks. **(7)** The finding was that about 65 percent of subjects in the experiment regularly administered what they believed to be very painful shocks.

(8) Some people have suggested that the phenomenon could to some extent explain the horrific acts of men such as Adolf Eichmann and the other Nazi officials responsible for Hitler's Holocaust. **(9)** At their trial after World War II Eichmann and the others consistently maintained that they did not act out of hatred or cruelty but because they had been ordered to do so by their superiors.

(10) Stanley Millgram himself observed, "It is psychologically easy to ignore responsibility when one is only an intermediate link in a chain of evil action. **(11)** Thus there is a fragmentation of the total human act; no one man decides to carry out the evil act and is confronted with its consequences."

30. In context, which of the following is the best word or phrase to insert at the beginning of sentence 2?

(A) Consequently,
(B) On the other hand,
(C) After all,
(D) However,
(E) Oddly enough though,

31. Which of the following is the best sentence to insert at the end of the first paragraph?

(A) How could it be otherwise?
(B) Would society break down into total anarchy?
(C) For example, without obedience how could a country have an army?
(D) However, can too much obedience be bad?
(E) However, some political scientists dispute this claim.

32. Of the following, which is the best version of the underlined portion of sentence 3 (reproduced below)?

A famous experiment conducted by Stanley Millgram at Yale University in the 1960s went toward answering this question.

(A) (As it is now)
(B) was something helpful in
(C) helped to be
(D) went somewhere in the direction of
(E) went some way toward

33. Where in the essay could the following sentence best be inserted to improve the essay?

The experiment has been repeated in a number of countries around the world with similar results, suggesting that the phenomenon is not unique to the United States.

(A) After sentence 3
(B) After sentence 5
(C) After sentence 6
(D) After sentence 7
(E) After sentence 8

GO ON TO THE NEXT PAGE

6   6 6 6 6 6 6 6 6 6 6   6

34. Which of the following best describes the function of the final paragraph?

   (A) To cast doubt on the suggestion made in sentence 8
   (B) To provide evidence to support the suggestion made in sentence 8
   (C) To provide a statement of the possible significance of the experiment described in paragraph 2, especially as it relates to what is discussed in the second paragraph
   (D) To give an example to illustrate the point made in sentence 2
   (E) To suggest areas for further experimentation

35. All of the following strategies or techniques are used by the author EXCEPT

   (A) direct quotation
   (B) indirect quotation
   (C) irony
   (D) citing of evidence
   (E) explanation of a procedure

STOP

IN ANY REMAINING TIME YOU MAY REVIEW THE ANSWERS YOU CHOSE IN THIS SECTION. DO NOT WORK ON ANY OTHER SECTION OF THE TEST DURING THIS TIME.

7

SECTION 7   **Time—25 Minutes**   **Choose the best answer to each of the following questions in**
                 24 Questions   **this section. Then blacken the appropriate space on your**
                                                    answer sheet.

Each of the following sentences contains one or two blanks, indicating that a word or set of words has been omitted. Beneath each sentence there are five answer choices labeled A to E from which you must select the word or set of words that best fits the meaning of the sentence as a whole.

Example:

Records of colonization can be found as far back as the Phoenicians, but colonization became a major force in world history only when European countries began, in the fifteenth century, to make ---- Asia, the Americas, and Africa.

(A) queries about   (B) incursions into
   (C) tirades against   (D) enemies in
     (E) amends for

---

1. Frequently, immigrants are not easily ---- into a society.

(A) yoked   (B) usurped   (C) waived
   (D) tempered   (E) assimilated

2. It has been proposed that there exist "----universals"—features common to all human languages irrespective of period or place.

(A) cultural   (B) objective   (C) immutable
   (D) linguistic   (E) ostensible

3. A common campaign promise in American politics is to "Get government off the backs of the people" by reducing government ----; however, this is difficult to achieve because citizens expect government to perform a ---- of tasks, from regulating industry to protecting the environment.

(A) expenditures . . minimum
(B) bureaucracy . . myriad
(C) leadership . . multitude
(D) interference . . selection
(E) control . . modicum

4. The use of a physical journey to symbolize a personal voyage of discovery and transformation reached its ---- in *The Odyssey*, a long poem about the wanderings of Odysseus, which remains one of the greatest stories ever told.

(A) juncture   (B) nadir   (C) apogee
   (D) beginning   (E) apotheosis

5. ---- refers to meanings suggested by or associated with a word.

(A) Definition   (B) Connotation
   (C) Symbolism   (D) Allegory
     (E) Rhetoric

6. Advocates of strict pollution control measures argue that they are necessary to ---- an environmental disaster.

(A) forestall   (B) presage   (C) prescribe
   (D) engender   (E) proscribe

7. ---- is a statement accepted as true for the purpose of argument or ---- investigation.

(A) A cliché . . further
(B) A maxim . . iconoclastic
(C) An incantation . . forensic
(D) A postulate . . empirical
(E) A dictum . . cursory

8. The nucleus of an atom occupies only a ---- fraction of an atom's volume, but contains almost all of its mass.

(A) divergent   (B) profligate   (C) blithe
   (D) negligible   (E) protean

GO ON TO THE NEXT PAGE ⟩

7

Below are passages followed by questions on them. Questions on a pair of related passages may be about the relationship between the two passages. For each question, select the best answer based on what is stated or implied in the passage (or passages).

Questions 9–10 are based on the following passage.

The Romans had become masters of the world, only that the sea from one end of their dominions to the other should be patrolled by
Line organized rovers. For many years, as Roman
(5) commerce extended, the Mediterranean had become a profitable field of enterprise for this group of people. From every country which they had overrun or occupied the conquests of the Roman Empire had let loose swarms of restless
(10) patriots who, if they could not save the liberties of their own countries, could prey upon the oppressor. Illyrians from the Adriatic, Greeks from the islands and the Asiatic ports, Syrians, Egyptians, Africans, Spaniards, Gauls, and
(15) disaffected Italians, many of them trained to the sea from their childhood, took to the water in their light galleys with all the world before them. Under most circumstances society is protected against thieves by their inability to combine. But
(20) the pirates of the Mediterranean had learnt from the Romans the advantage of union, and had drifted into a vast confederation.

9. According to the author, piracy was common in the Mediterranean at the height of the Roman Empire because of all of the following EXCEPT

(A) the growth of Roman trade in the region
(B) the fact that there were many competent sailors in the area
(C) several countries recruited and trained pirates to harass Roman shipping
(D) it was lucrative to plunder ships involved in commerce with Rome
(E) there were many people who were looking for an opportunity to retaliate against the Romans for conquering their countries

10. In line 15, "disaffected" most nearly means

(A) disingenuous
(B) not pretentious
(C) no longer loyal to their group
(D) not effective
(E) no longer citizens of a country

Questions 11–12 are based on the following passage.

The medical and scientific advancement of Japan in the seventeenth and eighteenth centuries was not co-ordinate with her progress in the arts.
Line They were hampered by the old Chinese notions
(5) about a male principle and a female principle which were conceived to prevail in nature, and with the five elements to which the human organs were supposed to correspond. Fortunately nature has ways of healing diseases in spite of theories
(10) and drugs. To this benign principle must be assigned the fact that the human race has survived the surgery and medicines of medieval Europe as well as medieval China and Japan.

11. In line 10, "benign" most nearly means

(A) universal
(B) innocuous
(C) utilitarian
(D) mundane
(E) beneficial

12. Based on the information in the passage the author would be most likely to agree that

(A) medieval Japanese medicine was more advanced than medieval European medicine
(B) more research should be done on the idea that a male and a female principle prevail in nature to see how they can be used in modern medicine
(C) drugs used in medieval Japanese medicine, although not as effective as those used in modern Western medicine, often benefited patients
(D) traditional beliefs can slow medical progress
(E) theories of medicine usually have little effect on medical practice

GO ON TO THE NEXT PAGE

Questions 13–24 are based on the following passages.

Passage 1

The vast majority of earthquakes and volcanic eruptions occur near tectonic plate boundaries, but there are some exceptions. For example, the
Line Hawaiian Islands, which are entirely of volcanic
(5) origin, have formed in the middle of the Pacific Ocean more than 3,200 km from the nearest plate boundary. How do the Hawaiian Islands and other volcanoes that form in the interior of plates fit into the plate-tectonics picture?

(10) In 1963, J. Tuzo Wilson, the Canadian geophysicist who discovered transform faults, came up with an ingenious idea that became known as the "hotspot" theory. Wilson noted that in certain locations around the world, such as
(15) Hawaii, volcanism has been active for very long periods of time. This could only happen, he reasoned, if relatively small, long-lasting, and exceptionally hot regions—called hotspots— existed below the plates that would provide
(20) localized sources of high heat energy (thermal plumes) to sustain volcanism. Specifically, Wilson hypothesized that the distinctive linear shape of the Hawaiian Island-Emperor Seamounts chain resulted from the Pacific Plate moving over
(25) a deep, stationary hotspot in the mantle, located beneath the present-day position of the Island of Hawaii. Heat from this hotspot produced a persistent source of magma by partly melting the overriding Pacific Plate. The magma, which is
(30) lighter than the surrounding solid rock, then rises through the mantle and crust to erupt onto the seafloor, forming an active seamount. Over time, countless eruptions cause the seamount to grow until it finally emerges above sea level to form an
(35) island volcano. Wilson suggested that continuing plate movement eventually carries the island beyond the hotspot, cutting it off from the magma source, and volcanism ceases. As one island volcano becomes extinct, another develops over
(40) the hotspot, and the cycle is repeated. This process of volcano growth and death, over many millions of years, has left a long trail of volcanic islands and seamounts across the Pacific Ocean floor.

(45) According to Wilson's hotspot theory, the volcanoes of the Hawaiian chain should get progressively older and become more eroded the farther they travel beyond the hotspot. The oldest volcanic rocks on Kauai, the northwesternmost
(50) inhabited Hawaiian island, are about 5.5 million years old and are deeply eroded. By comparison, on the "Big Island" of Hawaii—southeasternmost in the chain—the oldest exposed rocks are less than 0.7 million years old and new volcanic rock
(55) is continually being formed.

Passage 2

The Hawaiian Islands are one of the outstanding volcanic features on Earth, but their origins have been shrouded in mystery. Still in debate has been a theory proposed 40 years ago,
(60) which states that mid-tectonic plate hotspots such as Hawaii are generated by upwelling plumes of lava from the base of Earth's lower mantle.

A multi-institutional team of scientists put the theory to the test. They deployed a large network
(65) of sea-floor seismometers in Hawaii, through a National Science Foundation funded expedition called the Plume-Lithosphere Undersea Melt Experiment (PLUME), opening up a window into the Earth. PLUME allowed scientists to obtain
(70) the best picture yet of a mantle plume originating from the lower mantle, and revealed Hawaii's deep roots.

"The hypothesis that hot spots like Hawaii originate from mantle plumes is one of the
(75) longest-standing and most controversial topics in geology," says Robert Detrick, director of National Science Foundation's Division of Earth Sciences. "This pioneering experiment combining large numbers of broadband seismometers on the
(80) seafloor with instruments on land has provided the most persuasive evidence yet for the existence of a mantle plume extending into the lower mantle beneath Hawaii."

The project involved four oceanographic
(85) research cruises to deploy and recover ocean bottom seismometers at 73 sites, and a concurrent deployment of land seismometers on the main Hawaiian Islands. The large, 1,000-km wide

GO ON TO THE NEXT PAGE →

7

seafloor network yielded unprecedented results in
(90) a remote oceanic region. The seismometers were
used to record the timing of seismic shear waves
from large earthquakes (magnitudes greater than
5.5) around the world. This information was used
to determine whether seismic waves travel more
(95) slowly through hot rock as they pass beneath
Hawaii.

Combining the timing measurements from
earthquakes recorded on many seismometers
allowed scientists to construct a sophisticated 3-
(100) dimensional image of the Hawaiian mantle. In the
upper mantle, the Hawaiian Islands are underlain
by low shear-wave velocities, linked with hotter-
than-average material from an upwelling plume.
Low velocities continue down into the Earth's
(105) transition zone, at 410 to 660 km depth, and
extend even deeper into the Earth's lower mantle
down to at least 1,500 km depth.

The location of the Hawaiian Islands in the
middle of the Pacific Ocean had hampered past
(110) efforts to resolve its deep structure. Seismometer
deployments limited to land sites on the islands
did not provide sufficient coverage for high-
resolution imaging, and Hawaii is also far from
the most active circum-Pacific zones of
(115) earthquakes. As a result, scientists turned to a
more technologically challenging, marine
approach by placing temporary instrumentation
on the seafloor to record seismic waves.

Results of the project make a strong case for
(120) the existence of a deep mantle plume, with
implications not just for Hawaii, but for how
convection in the solid Earth works; the Earth's
composition with depth; and the inner Earth's
evolution.

13. Passage 1 provides information explaining all of
the following EXCEPT

(A) the process by which an island is formed over
a hotspot
(B) the cause of hotspots
(C) why the Hawaiian Island-Emperor Seamount
chain has a linear shape
(D) why volcanic rocks on Kauai are deeply
eroded, whereas those on the Big Island are
not
(E) why the volcanoes of the Hawaiian chain
become progressively older as one moves
north along the chain

14. According to J. Tuzo Wilson's "hotspot" theory,
the fact that volcanic rock is regularly being
formed on the "Big Island" suggests that

(A) the "Big Island" is situated over a hotspot
(B) the reason that the "Big Island" is larger than
the other islands in the Hawaii Island chain is
that it alone was formed as a result of a
hotspot
(C) volcanism is a relatively recent phenomenon
on the "Big Island"
(D) the "Big Island," alone among the Hawaiian
Islands, was created by plate tectonics
(E) the Pacific Plate is much nearer to the ocean
surface in the area of the "Big Island" than it
is in the areas of the other Hawaiian Islands

15. Which of the following is true about J. Tuzo
Wilson's "hotspot" theory?

(A) There is no place in it for the mechanism of
plate tectonics.
(B) It incorporates some features of plate tectonics
but largely supersedes it as a theory explaining
the cause of volcanoes around the world.
(C) It envisions hotspots as occurring only in the
area of the Hawaiian Island-Emperor
Seamounts chain.
(D) It does not claim to explain the origin of all
volcanoes in the world.
(E) It satisfactorily explains why volcanic activity
begins in an area, but it cannot explain why
volcanic activity ceases there.

16. Which of the following sequences best describes
the chronological order of the thought process by
which J. Tuzo Wilson most likely came up with the
"hotspot" theory?

(A) Observation, deduction, formation of
hypothesis
(B) Observation, induction, formation of
hypothesis
(C) Observation, formation of hypothesis, testing
of hypothesis
(D) Formation of hypothesis, deduction,
observation
(E) Induction, deduction, observation, formation
of hypothesis

17. According to the "hotspot" theory, the reason that some Hawaiian islands are older than other Hawaiian islands is that

    (A) hotspots move steadily below Earth's crust, creating island volcanoes at different times
    (B) the smaller, younger volcanoes have not emerged from the ocean to form islands
    (C) the Pacific tectonic plate continuously moves, causing one island volcano to form over a hotspot, then another, and so on
    (D) erosion has worn away much of the material from the older islands, such as Kauai
    (E) there are several hot spots, of varying ages, below the Pacific tectonic plate in the area of the Hawaiian Islands; the oldest islands were created by the oldest hotspots and the youngest island were created by the youngest hotspots

18. In line 68, "window" is used

    (A) hyperbolically
    (B) literally
    (C) ironically
    (D) metaphorically
    (E) humorously

19. In line 86, "concurrent" most nearly means

    (A) subsequent
    (B) up-to-date
    (C) at the same time
    (D) acting in conjunction with another
    (E) timely

20. It can be inferred that the earthquakes mentioned in line 92

    (A) were caused by volcanic activity in many places around the world
    (B) were caused by the eruption of volcanoes in the Hawaiian Islands
    (C) were caused by mid-tectonic hotspots
    (D) were largely or entirely unrelated to geological activity on or near the Hawaiian Islands
    (E) occurred simultaneously

21. In line 94, "seismic waves" refers to

    (A) ocean waves caused by the collision of the Pacific Plate and the Hawaiian Islands
    (B) vibrations caused by upwelling plumes of lava from the base of Earth's lower mantle
    (C) electromagnetic waves generated by sea floor seismometers
    (D) waves caused by volcanic activity
    (E) waves caused by earthquakes

22. In line 110, "resolve" most nearly means

    (A) theorize about
    (B) speculate about
    (C) to render visible and distinct
    (D) scientifically establish the facts about
    (E) solve

23. Both passages are primarily concerned with the question of

    (A) what causes deep mantle plumes
    (B) what causes volcanic islands to form in the middle of tectonic plates
    (C) the mechanism by which heat is transferred from Earth's core to it upper mantle
    (D) what caused volcanism to occur in the area of the Hawaiian Islands
    (E) what caused the "Big Island" of Hawaii to form

GO ON TO THE NEXT PAGE

7

24. Which best describes the relationship between Passage 1 and Passage 2?

   (A) Passage 1 describes a theory in detail and provides some evidence for it; Passage 2 describes two experiments that have been done to test the theory described in Passage 1.

   (B) Passage 1 describes a theory and discusses evidence that has been found both for and against the theory; Passage 2 describes an experiment that has produced evidence supporting one of the theories described in Passage 1.

   (C) Passage 1 describes two competing theories and the evidence for one of them; Passage 2 evaluates the two theories described in Passage 1 and reaches a conclusion about which one is better supported by the evidence.

   (D) Passage 1 describes the main geological processes involved in creating the Hawaiian Islands; Passage 2 describes an experiment done to gather information about these processes.

   (E) Passage 1 describes a theory in considerable detail and provides some evidence for it; Passage 2 describes an experiment that produced good evidence supporting the theory described in Passage 1.

STOP

IN ANY REMAINING TIME YOU MAY REVIEW THE
ANSWERS YOU CHOSE IN THIS SECTION. DO NOT WORK
ON ANY OTHER SECTION OF THE TEST DURING THIS TIME.

SECTION 8

Time—20 Minutes
16 Questions

For each problem in this section determine which of the five choices is correct and blacken the corresponding choice on your answer sheet. You may use any blank space on the page for your work.

Notes:

- You may use a calculator whenever you think it will be helpful.
- Only real numbers are used. No question or answer on this test involves a complex or imaginary number.
- Use the diagrams provided to help you solve the problems. Unless you see the words "Note: Figure not drawn to scale" under a diagram, it has been drawn as accurately as possible. Unless it is stated that a figure is three-dimensional, you may assume it lies in a plane.
- For any function f, the domain, unless specifically restricted, is the set of all real numbers for which $f(x)$ is also a real number.

Reference Information

Area Facts

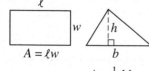

$A = \ell w$

$A = \frac{1}{2} bh$

$A = \pi r^2$
$C = 2\pi r$

Volume Facts

$V = \ell w h$

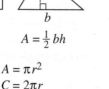

$V = \pi r^2 h$

Triangle Facts

$a^2 + b^2 = c^2$

Angle Facts

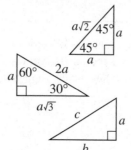

$360°$

$x + y + z = 180$

1. If $a = \frac{1}{3}b$, $b = \frac{3}{5}c$, and $c = \frac{5}{7}d$, what is the value of a if $d = 77$?

(A) 11
(B) 13
(C) 33
(D) 53
(E) 55

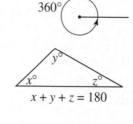

2. In the figure above, if lines ℓ and m are parallel, what is the value of $x + y$?

(A) 110°
(B) 140°
(C) 180°
(D) 220°
(E) 290°

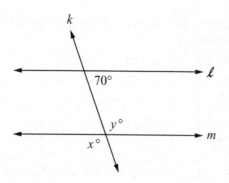

GO ON TO THE NEXT PAGE

8   8   8   8   8   8   8   8   8   8   8

3. A machine shop has nine employees: one supervisor and eight workers. The supervisor's salary is equal to twice the average (arithmetic mean) salary of the workers. The supervisor's salary is what fraction of the total of the salaries of all the employees?

(A) $\dfrac{1}{9}$

(B) $\dfrac{1}{8}$

(C) $\dfrac{1}{5}$

(D) $\dfrac{1}{4}$

(E) $\dfrac{1}{3}$

4. 1 kilometer = 1,000 meters; 1 meter = 100 cm; 5 cm ≈ 2 inches; 12 inches = 1 foot; and 1 yard = 3 feet. To the nearest hundred, how many yards are there in 1 kilometer?

(A)   600
(B) 1,100
(C) 1,200
(D) 1,700
(E) 2,200

5. If n is an integer, which of the following must be an odd integer?

(A) $5n^2 + 3$
(B) $3n^2 + 5$
(C) $4n^2 + 7$
(D) $7n^2 - 4$
(E) $4n^2 - 2$

6. In the xy-plane, lines $\overleftrightarrow{AB}$ and $\overleftrightarrow{CD}$ have slopes of 4 and −4, respectively. Which of the following statements could be true?

I. $\overleftrightarrow{AB}$ and $\overleftrightarrow{CD}$ are parallel.
II. $\overleftrightarrow{AB}$ and $\overleftrightarrow{CD}$ are perpendicular.
III. $\overleftrightarrow{AB}$ and $\overleftrightarrow{CD}$ have the same y-intercept.

(A) None
(B) II only
(C) III only
(D) I and III only
(E) II and III only

7. If $f(x) = 2x + 3$ and $g(x) = 3x + 2$, for how many integers n is $f(3n) = g(2n)$?

(A) None
(B) 1
(C) 2
(D) 3
(E) More than 3

8. Dan and Laurel each drove 180 miles from their house to their summer home. If Dan's average speed was 50 miles per hour and Laurel's average speed was 45 miles per hour, how much longer, in minutes, did it take Laurel to do the drive than Dan?

(A)   5
(B)   6
(C)   10
(D)   24
(E)   40

9. If $0 < a < b < 1$, which of the following must be true?

(A) $0 < (a + b) < 1$
(B) $0 < (a - b) < 1$
(C) $0 < (a^2 - b^2) < 1$

(D) $0 < \dfrac{a}{b} < 1$

(E) $0 < \dfrac{b}{a} < 1$

10. If the circumference of a circle is C inches, and if the area of that circle is A square inches, then which of the following statements could be true?

I. $C = A$
II. $C < A$
III. $C > A$

(A) None
(B) II only
(C) III only
(D) II and III only
(E) I, II, and III

GO ON TO THE NEXT PAGE ⟹

8   8   8   8   8   8   8   8   8   8   8

11. If $n > 10$ and $n - 5$ is prime, which of the following could also be prime?

(A) n
(B) $5n$
(C) n^2
(D) $n + 3$
(E) $n + 4$

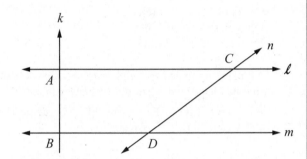

12. In the figure above, lines l and m are parallel and line k is perpendicular to l. If $AB = 10$ and $CD = 20$, how much longer is AC than BD?

(A) 10
(B) 20
(C) $10\sqrt{2}$
(D) $10\sqrt{3}$
(E) It cannot be determined from the given information.

13. A sequence is formed as follows: The first term is $-\dfrac{1}{2}$ and every term after the first one is obtained by multiplying the previous term by -1 and then adding 1. What is the 13th term of this sequence?

(A) $-\dfrac{25}{2}$

(B) $-\dfrac{13}{2}$

(C) $-\dfrac{1}{2}$

(D) $\dfrac{1}{2}$

(E) $\dfrac{3}{2}$

14. The formula that converts temperature measured in degrees Celsius (C) to degrees Fahrenheit (F) is $F = \dfrac{9}{5}C + 32$. (For example, when the temperature is 10°C, it is $\dfrac{9}{5}(10) + 32 = 50$°F.) For what value of x, if any, is x°F = x°C?

(A) −40
(B) −8
(C) 0
(D) 72
(E) There is no value of x for which x°F = x°C.

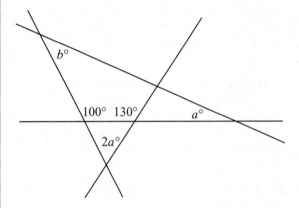

Note: Figure not drawn to scale.

15. In the figure above, four lines intersect as shown. What is the value of b?

(A) 45
(B) 55
(C) 60
(D) 65
(E) 70

16. Let $g(x)$ be defined as $g(x) = \dfrac{\sqrt{x^2 - 4}}{x^2 - 3}$. For how many integers, x, is $g(x)$ *not* defined?

(A) None
(B) 1
(C) 2
(D) 3
(E) More than 3

STOP

IN ANY REMAINING TIME YOU MAY REVIEW THE ANSWERS YOU CHOSE IN THIS SECTION. DO NOT WORK ON ANY OTHER SECTION OF THE TEST DURING THIS TIME.

Practice Test 6

9 9 9 9 9 9 9

SECTION 9 | Time—20 Minutes 19 Questions | Choose the best answer to each of the following questions in this section. Then blacken the appropriate space on your answer sheet.

Each of the following sentences contains one or two blanks, indicating that a word or set of words has been omitted. Beneath each sentence there are five answer choices labeled A to E from which you must select the word or set of words that best fits the meaning of the sentence as a whole.

Example:

Records of colonization can be found as far back as the Phoenicians, but colonization became a major force in world history only when European countries began, in the fifteenth century, to make ---- Asia, the Americas, and Africa.

(A) queries about   (B) incursions into
   (C) tirades against   (D) enemies in
        (E) amends for

 Ⓐ ● Ⓒ Ⓓ Ⓔ

---

1. In order to write ---- one must be able to organize one's thoughts logically.

   (A) creatively   (B) emotionally
      (C) coherently   (D) poetically
         (E) rhapsodically

2. The psychologist assured the concerned parents that it was normal for a child to have some ---- feelings toward his or her parents.

   (A) ambivalent   (B) innocuous   (C) tender
      (D) sympathetic   (E) inconsequential

3. The defense attorneys for the foreign national argued that if he had been ---- he would have fled the country when he had the ---- to do so.

   (A) opportunistic . . misfortune
   (B) innocent . . audacity
   (C) culpable . . opportunity
   (D) fastidious . . wherewithal
   (E) reprehensible . . egotism

4. To gain ---- view of an issue one must not ---- the issue based on one's preconceptions.

   (A) a comprehensive . . reconsider
   (B) a logical . . clarify
   (C) an objective . . prejudge
   (D) a biased . . embellish
   (E) a tentative . . decide

5. The judge reminded the witness to speak ---- about what had happened when giving her testimony.

   (A) equivocally   (B) caustically   (C) demurely
      (D) candidly   (E) tentatively

6. The ---- meaning of a piece of language is its ---- meaning.

   (A) true . . historical
   (B) denotative . . explicit
   (C) figurative . . implied
   (D) metaphorical . . lexical
   (E) dictionary . . abstract

GO ON TO THE NEXT PAGE

9　　9　　9　　9　　9　　9　　9

Below are passages followed by questions on them. Questions on a pair of related passages may be about the relationship between the two passages. For each question, select the best answer based on what is stated or implied in the passage (or passages).

Questions 7–19 are based on the following passage.

I call the "to each his own" quandary the His'er Problem, after a solution originally proposed by Chicago school superintendent Ella
Line Young in 1912: "To each his'er own." I'm sorry.
(5) I just can't. My reactionary self has aesthetic as well as grammatical standards, and *his'er* is hideous. Unlike *Ms.*, *his'er* could never become reflexive. (I might interject here that when I posed the His'er Problem to my brother, who was
(10) raised in the same grammatical hothouse as I, he surprised me by saying, "I won't say *his'er*. That would be a capitulation to barbarism. But I would be willing to consider a more rhythmically acceptable neologism such as *hyr* or *hes*, which
(15) would be preferable to having to avoid *his* by plotting each sentence in advance like a military campaign.")

What about "to each his or her own"? I do resort to that construction occasionally, but I find
(20) the double pronoun an ungainly burden. More frequently I recast the entire sentence in the plural, although "to all their own" is slightly off pitch. Even a phrase that is not stylistically disfigured—for example, "all writers worth their
(25) salt," which is only marginally more lumpish than "every writer worth his salt"—loses its specificity, that fleeting moment in which the reader conjures up an individual writer (Isaiah Berlin in one mind's eye, Robert James Waller in
(30) another) instead of a faceless throng.

But I can't go back. I said "to each his own" until about five years ago, believing what my sixth-grade grammar textbook, *Easy English Exercises*, had told me: that "or her" was
(35) "understood," just as womankind was understood to be lurking somewhere within "mankind." I no longer understand. The other day I came across the following sentence by my beloved role model, E.B. White: "There is one thing the
(40) essayist cannot do—he cannot indulge himself in deceit or concealment, for he will be found out in no time." I felt the door slamming in my face so fast I could feel the wind against my cheek. "But

he meant to include you!" some of you may be
(45) murmuring. "It was understood!"

I don't think so. Long ago, my father wrote something similar: "The best essays [do not] develop original themes. They develop original men, their composers." Since my father, unlike E.
(50) B. White, is still around to testify, I called him up last night and said, "Be honest. What was really in your mind when you wrote those sentences?" He replied, "Males. I was thinking about males. I viewed the world of literature—indeed, the entire
(55) world of artistic creation—as a world of males, and so did most writers. Any writer of fifty years ago who denies that is lying. Any male writer, I mean."

I believe that although my father and E.B.
(60) White were not misogynists, they didn't really see women, and their language reflected and reinforced that blind spot. Our invisibility was brought home to me fifteen years ago, after *Thunder Out of China*, a 1946 best-seller about
(65) China's role in the Second World War, was reissued in paperback. Its co-authors were Theodore H. White and Annalee Jacoby, my mother. In his foreword to the new edition, Harrison Salisbury mentioned White nineteen
(70) times and my mother once. His first sentence was "There is, in the end, no substitute for the right man in the right place at the right moment." I wrote to Salisbury, suggesting that sometimes— for example, in half of *Thunder Out of China*—
(75) there is no substitute for the right woman in the right place at the right moment. To his credit, he responded with the following mea culpa: "Oh, oh, oh! You are totally right. I am entirely guilty. You are the second person who has pointed that
(80) out to me. What can I say? It is just one of those totally dumb things which I do sometimes." I believe that Salisbury was motivated by neither malice nor premeditated sexism; my mother, by

GO ON TO THE NEXT PAGE →

9   9   9   9   9   9   9

being a woman, just happened to be in the wrong
(85) place at the wrong moment.
    For as long as anyone can remember, my
father has called every woman who is more than
ten years his junior a girl. Since he is now ninety-
one, that covers a lot of women. He would never
(90) call a man over the age of eighteen a boy. I have
tried to persuade him to mend his ways, but the
word is ingrained, and he means it gallantly. He
truly believes that inside every stout, white-haired
woman of eighty there is the glimmer of that
(95) fresh and lissome thing, a girl.
    If my father were still writing essays, every
full-grown "girl" would probably be transformed
by an editor's pencil into a "woman." The same
thing would happen to E.B. White. In an essay
(100) called "The Sea and the Wind That Blows,"
White described a small sailing craft as "shaped
less like a box than like a fish or a bird or a girl."
I don't think he meant a ten-year-old girl. I think
he meant a girl old enough to be called a woman.
(105) But if he had compared that boat to a woman, his
slim little craft, as well as his sentence, would
have been forever slowed.
    What I am saying here is very simple. Changing
our language to make men and women equal has a
(110) cost. That doesn't mean it shouldn't be done. High
prices are attached to many things that are on the
whole worth doing. It does mean that the loss of
our heedless grace should be mourned, and then
accepted with all the civility we can muster, by
(115) every writer worth his'er salt.

7. In line 5, "aesthetic" most nearly means

    (A) political
    (B) relating to truth
    (C) relating to beauty
    (D) visual
    (E) objective

8. The author says that she and her brother were
"raised in the same grammatical hothouse" (line
10). By this she most likely means to suggest that

    (A) as children she and her brother continually
        fought with each other about questions of
        grammar
    (B) she and her brother were sent to schools that
        emphasized the importance of correct
        grammar
    (C) she and her brother were brought up to regard
        grammar as merely a flexible tool that good
        writers sometimes ignore in order to write
        well
    (D) she and her brother were brought up by
        parents who were very concerned with correct
        grammar and did everything they could to
        make sure that their children knew and cared
        about correct grammar
    (E) she and her brother were raised in a family
        that placed so much emphasis on grammar
        that it ruined their ability to appreciate
        beautiful prose

9. The most likely reason that the author was
"surprised" (line 11) by her brother's response
when she posed the His'er Problem to him is that

    (A) she did not believe that he would object to
        saying "his'er"
    (B) she thought he was not concerned with the
        issue because it mainly concerns women
    (C) she thought he would object to saying "hyr"
        or "hes" because they sound bad
    (D) she thought he would object to using any new
        word
    (E) she assumed that he was against anything that
        would promote the equality of women

10. In line 14, "neologism" most nearly means

    (A) new word
    (B) contraction
    (C) pronoun
    (D) correct word
    (E) substitute

GO ON TO THE NEXT PAGE →

9 9 9 9 9 9 9

11. In line 61, "see women" most nearly means

(A) regard women as human beings
(B) notice women
(C) take women seriously
(D) appreciate women
(E) have women as friends

12. The author's "reactionary self" (line 5) would most likely write

(A) "her book"
(B) "his book"
(C) "his or her book"
(D) "his'er book"
(E) "hes book"

13. In line 77, "mea culpa" most nearly means

(A) excuse
(B) remark
(C) justification for an action
(D) compulsion to confess
(E) acknowledgement of a personal error

14. The author comments on a sentence E.B. White wrote in an essay: "But if he had compared that boat to a woman, his slim little craft, as well as his sentence, would have been forever slowed" (lines 105–107). The author most likely means to suggest by this comment that if E.B. White had written "woman" instead of "girl"

(A) his sentence would not have demonstrated the age-old bias of the English language toward men
(B) his sentence would have illustrated clearly that he was not sexist
(C) his sentence would have illustrated the truth of the view that although changing language to make it gender neutral has a cost, the cost is worth it
(D) his sentence would not have been as graceful and as effective at conveying its meaning
(E) like the boat in his sentence, his career as a writer would have been slowed

15. In line 113, "heedless grace" refers to

(A) elegant writing that is not concerned with treating women as the equals of men
(B) awkward language
(C) writing that appears to be aesthetically pleasing but that is really ugly
(D) refusal to be concerned with sexist language
(E) writing that is aesthetically pleasing but that has little meaning

16. The phrase "all the civility we can muster" (line 114) suggests that

(A) writers are essentially selfish in that all they really care about is writing well
(B) writers are generally not courteous people
(C) female writers will be able to adapt more easily than male writers to using gender-neutral language
(D) few writers will be able to write well using gender-neutral language
(E) it will not be easy for writers to accept the need to change their writing habits to avoid sexist language

17. The most likely reason that the author uses the expression "his'er" in line 115 is to

(A) use some humor to remind the reader of the ongoing difficulties writers face in deciding how to deal with the His'er Problem
(B) demonstrate that the only solution to the His'er Problem is to use clumsy, unappealing language
(C) show that she agrees with Ella Young's suggestion about how to deal with the His'er Problem after all
(D) show that it doesn't really matter whether we say *he or she* or *his'er* or *hyr* or *hes* or any of the other suggestions that have been made about how to deal with the His'er Problem
(E) demonstrate that the English language is perfectly capable of dealing with the His'er Problem

GO ON TO THE NEXT PAGE

18. Which of the following statements would the author of the passage be most likely to agree with?

    (A) The need to use the English language in a gender-neutral way has imposed an unfair and unnecessary burden on writers.

    (B) The English language should not be used to promote social or political objectives.

    (C) Too much emphasis is put on style as opposed to meaning in the critical evaluation of writing.

    (D) Writers should make some effort to use gender-neutral language, but should not let it significantly affect their style.

    (E) Writers should make every effort to use language that treats men and women equally, even if their writing loses much of its grace as a result.

19. Based on what she says in the passage, the author would be most likely to believe that the best way to change the sentence "Every writer should watch his P's and Q's when referring to male and female human beings" to make it gender neutral would be

    (A) all writers, regardless of his or her gender, should watch his or her P's and Q's when referring to male and female human beings

    (B) all writers should watch their P's and Q's when referring to male and female human beings

    (C) every writer should watch his'er P's and Q's when referring to male and female human beings

    (D) when referring to male human beings or female human beings (the order is not intended to suggest superiority), a writer, irrespective of his/her sex, should watch her (or his) P's and Q's

    (E) every writer should watch her P's and Q's when referring to male and female human beings

STOP

IN ANY REMAINING TIME YOU MAY REVIEW THE ANSWERS YOU CHOSE IN THIS SECTION. DO NOT WORK ON ANY OTHER SECTION OF THE TEST DURING THIS TIME.

10   10   10   10   10   10   10

SECTION **10**   Time—10 Minutes
14 Questions

Choose the best answer to each of the following questions in this section. Then blacken the appropriate space on your answer sheet.

Each sentence below may or may not employ correct or effective expression. If you think that the underlined phrasing makes the most clear and precise sentence, select choice A. If, however, you think that the underlined phrasing makes the meaning of the sentence unclear or awkward, or that it is grammatically incorrect, select another answer from choices B to E.

In choosing your answers, follow the conventions of English as it is used by educated writers. Consider sentence structure, grammar, word choice, and punctuation. Choose the answer that produces the sentence that is the most clear and effective.

Example:

In her comments after the debate the judge said that she had been impressed by the ability of both teams to exploit logical weaknesses and in citing relevant examples.

(A) in citing relevant examples
(B) in that relevant examples had been cited
(C) in the citing of relevant examples
(D) to cite relevant examples
(E) to be able to cite relevant examples

Ⓐ Ⓑ Ⓒ ● Ⓔ

---

1. Returning home to New York City after two years spent teaching in the remote village, the fast pace of city life was something Tom found difficult to get used to.

(A) the fast pace of city life was something Tom found difficult to get used to
(B) getting used to the fast pace of city life was something Tom found difficult
(C) it was found difficult by Tom to get used to the fast pace of city life
(D) Tom, finding the fast pace of city life difficult to get used to
(E) Tom found the fast pace of city life difficult to get used to

2. Some scholars believe that Gautama Buddha was an agnostic, being however no definitive evidence for this, only conjecture based on his statements about other matters.

(A) being however no definitive evidence for this
(B) but there is no definitive evidence for this
(C) there being however no definitive evidence for this
(D) they have no definitive evidence for this
(E) this has no definitive evidence

3. Recent changes to the tax code have made it so complicated for people to figure out their taxes to the point where many people are paying accountants to do it for them.

(A) taxes to the point where
(B) taxes that
(C) taxes,
(D) taxes to where
(E) taxes, therefore

4. There is a considerable body of educational research from a number of countries that suggest that class size does not play a decisive part in student performance.

(A) that suggest that class size does not play a decisive part in student performance
(B) that will suggest that class size does not play a decisive part in the students' performance
(C) that suggest that class size does not play a part that is decisive in student performance
(D) that suggest that class size does not play a decisive role in the performance by students
(E) that suggests that class size does not play a decisive role in student performance

GO ON TO THE NEXT PAGE

10   10   10   10   10   10   10

5. The value of the U.S. dollar on the international currency market varies according to a number of factors, one of these is the interest rate.

(A) factors, one of these is the interest rate
(B) factors; of these the interest rate is one of them
(C) factors; one of these factors is the interest rate
(D) factors, and the interest rate being one of them
(E) factors, for one of these is the interest rate

6. Some people believe that one day humans will establish a permanent base on the Moon and also there will be colonization of Mars.

(A) humans will establish a permanent base on the Moon and also there will be colonization of
(B) humans will establish a permanent base on the Moon and also establish a self-sufficient colony on
(C) humans will establish two things: first, as base that is on the Moon; second, a colony that is self-sufficient on
(D) humans will establish a permanent base on the Moon as well as a self-sufficient colony on
(E) a permanent base will be established on the Moon by humans and also they will establish a self-sufficient colony on

7. Though heavily dependent on foreign investments for capital while overseas countries provide markets for manufactured goods, the Republic of Singapore has become one of the wealthiest countries in the world.

(A) while overseas countries provide markets for manufactured goods,
(B) and at the same time manufactured goods are provided by overseas countries,
(C) and on overseas markets for its manufactured goods,
(D) and on manufactured goods which are provided by overseas countries,
(E) as overseas countries are providing manufactured goods,

8. The founder of Creative Technology, Sim Wong Hoo, once said that entrepreneurship and business schools are an oxymoron; by definition you can't be an entrepreneur if you need to be taught how to be one.

(A) oxymoron; by definition you can't be an entrepreneur if you need to be taught how
(B) oxymoron, by definition you can't be an entrepreneur if you need to be taught how
(C) oxymoron; how you can't be an entrepreneur by definition if you need to be taught
(D) oxymoron; being by definition you can't be an entrepreneur if you need to be taught how
(E) oxymoron; you can't be by definition one if you need to be taught how

9. The former basketball star Bill Walton was a big fan of The Grateful Dead and former vice president Al Gore also was a big fan of theirs.

(A) The former basketball star Bill Walton was a big fan of the Grateful Dead and former vice president Al Gore also was a big fan of theirs.
(B) The former basketball star Bill Walton and former vice president Al Gore were both big fans of The Grateful Dead.
(C) Bill Walton, the former basketball star, and the former vice president, Al Gore, were both of them big fans of The Grateful Dead.
(D) Big fans of The Grateful Dead were both former vice president Al Gore and former basketball star Bill Walton.
(E) The former basketball star Bill Walton, as well as former vice president Al Gore, was a big fan of the Grateful Dead.

10. Some critics believe that the English novel reached perfection in the work of Jane Austen, whereas others believe it wasn't until Henry James that the genre truly achieved perfection.

(A) whereas others believe it wasn't until Henry James that the genre
(B) whereas others believe it was with the novels that Henry James wrote that the genre
(C) whereas it is believed by others that it was with those novels by Henry James that the genre
(D) but there are others who believe Henry James was the one before which the genre had not
(E) others believing it wasn't until Henry James that the genre

GO ON TO THE NEXT PAGE ▶

10　　10　10　10　10　10　10

11. The company, once it dominated its market, is now filing for bankruptcy.

   (A) The company, once it dominated its market,

   (B) The company once dominant in its market

   (C) Once dominant in its market, the company

   (D) Once it was dominant in its market, the company

   (E) The company, at one time which was dominant in its market,

12. The survey of high school students found that the three most important qualities that must be had by a good teacher are knowledge of the subject being taught, fairness in evaluating students' work, and being approachable.

   (A) that must be had by a good teacher are knowledge of the subject being taught, fairness in evaluating students' work, and being approachable

   (B) a teacher must have to be considered a good teacher are she must have knowledge of her subject, she must be fair in evaluating students' work, and she also must be approachable

   (C) that any good teacher must have are approachability, subject matter knowledge, and being fair in evaluating the students' work

   (D) that a person must have to be considered a good teacher are approachability, knowledge of the subject, and fairness in evaluating students' work

   (E) that an individual must have to be considered a good teacher are: approachability, knowledge of subject, and fairness in evaluating students' work

13. A useful tip for students who want to improve their writing: Read what you've written aloud, listening for anything that doesn't sound good.

   (A) A useful tip for students who want to improve their writing: Read what you've written aloud, listening for anything that doesn't sound good.

   (B) A useful tip for students who want to improve their writing is reading aloud what they've written; then, listen for anything that doesn't sound good.

   (C) A useful tip for students who want to improve their writing is: Read what you've written aloud, listening for anything that doesn't sound good.

   (D) Here is a useful tip for students who want to improve their writing: Read what you've written aloud, listening for anything that doesn't sound good.

   (E) Reading what you've written aloud, listening for anything that doesn't sound good: a useful tip for students who want to improve their writing.

14. Because the ability to write clearly and interestingly about a wide range of subjects is rare, top journalists are being competed for by major newspapers and magazines, who pay them high salaries to attract them.

   (A) top journalists are being competed for by major newspapers and magazines, who pay them high salaries to attract them

   (B) major newspapers and magazines are competing for top journalists by paying them high salaries to attract them

   (C) major newspapers and magazines pay top journalists high salaries when competing to attract them

   (D) this means that high salaries are paid to top journalists by major newspapers and magazines to attract them

   (E) in order to attract top journalists for major newspapers and magazines they pay them high salaries

IN ANY REMAINING TIME YOU MAY REVIEW THE ANSWERS YOU CHOSE IN THIS SECTION. DO NOT WORK ON ANY OTHER SECTION OF THE TEST DURING THIS TIME.

Practice Test 6

Answer Key

CRITICAL READING

Section 3

Ans.	Level of Diff.	Ans.	Level of Diff.
1. E	1	13. B	2
2. C	2	14. D	3
3. D	4	15. E	4
4. D	4	16. D	2
5. C	5	17. C	3
6. E	3	18. D	1
7. C	3	19. D	1
8. B	4	20. C	4
9. A	4	21. B	3
10. E	5	22. D	4
11. C	3	23. A	3
12. E	3	24. E	5

Section 7

Ans.	Level of Diff.	Ans.	Level of Diff.
1. E	1	13. B	3
2. D	2	14. A	3
3. B	3	15. D	3
4. C	3	16. A	4
5. B	4	17. C	2
6. A	4	18. D	4
7. D	4	19. C	2
8. D	5	20. D	3
9. C	2	21. E	2
10. C	5	22. C	4
11. E	3	23. B	5
12. D	3	24. E	3

Section 9

Ans.	Level of Diff.	Ans.	Level of Diff.
1. C	1	11. C	3
2. A	2	12. B	4
3. C	3	13. E	3
4. C	3	14. D	4
5. D	4	15. A	3
6. B	5	16. E	3
7. C	3	17. A	3
8. D	3	18. E	3
9. C	5	19. B	5
10. A	3		

MATH

Section 2

Ans.	Level of Diff.	Ans.	Level of Diff.
1. C	1	11. C	3
2. A	1	12. B	3
3. C	1	13. B	3
4. C	1	14. E	4
5. D	2	15. E	3
6. D	3	16. C	4
7. D	2	17. E	4
8. C	2	18. E	4
9. B	3	19. B	5
10. A	3	20. B	5

Section 5

Ans.	Level of Diff.	Ans.	Level of Diff.
1. B	1	11. 1024	3
2. C	1	12. 104	3
3. C	2	13. 2303	3
4. E	2	14. 60	4
5. B	3	15. 15	5
6. C	4	16. 43	4
7. E	5	17. 5/2 or 2.5	4
8. A	4	18. 9/4 or 2.25	5
9. 1/54	1		
10. 2	2		

Section 8

Ans.	Level of Diffx.	Ans.	Level of Diff.
1. A	1	9. D	3
2. D	1	10. E	3
3. C	2	11. D	3
4. B	2	12. D	3
5. C	2	13. C	4
6. C	3	14. A	4
7. A	4	15. B	5
8. D	3	16. D	5

WRITING

Section 6

Ans.	Level of Diff.	Ans.	Level of Diff.	Ans.	Level of Diff.	Ans.	Level of Diff.
1. C	1	10. D	3	19. A	2	28. D	4
2. C	1	11. E	5	20. E	3	29. D	5
3. B	1	12. C	1	21. B	3	30. C	3
4. A	1	13. B	1	22. B	3	31. D	3
5. C	2	14. B	1	23. D	3	32. E	4
6. D	3	15. C	1	24. E	3	33. D	5
7. B	3	16. C	1	25. C	4	34. C	4
8. D	3	17. A	2	26. B	4	35. C	4
9. E	3	18. D	2	27. C	4		

Section 10

Ans.	Level of Diff.	Ans.	Level of Diff.
1. E	2	8. A	3
2. B	2	9. B	3
3. B	2	10. A	3
4. E	2	11. C	4
5. C	2	12. D	4
6. D	3	13. D	5
7. C	3	14. B	5

Score Your Own SAT Essay

Use this table as you rate your performance on the essay-writing section of this Practice Test. Circle the phrase that most accurately describes your work. Enter the numbers in the scoring chart below. Add the numbers together and divide by 6 to determine your total score. The higher your total score, the better you are likely to do on the essay section of the SAT.

Note that on the actual SAT two readers will rate your essay; your essay score will be the sum of their two ratings and could range from 12 (highest) to 2 (lowest). Also, they will grade your essay holistically, rating it on the basis of their overall impression of its effectiveness. They will *not* analyze it piece by piece, giving separate grades for grammar, vocabulary level, and so on. Therefore, you cannot expect the score you give yourself on this Practice Test to predict your eventual score on the SAT with any great degree of accuracy. Use this scoring guide instead to help you assess your writing strengths and weaknesses, so that you can decide which areas to focus on as you prepare for the SAT.

Like most people, you may find it difficult to rate your own writing objectively. Ask a teacher or fellow student to score your essay as well. With his or her help you should gain added insights into writing your 25-minute essay.

	6	5	4	3	2	1
POSITION ON THE TOPIC	Clear, convincing, & insightful	Fundamentally clear & coherent	Fairly clear & coherent	Insufficiently clear	Largely unclear	Extremely unclear
ORGANIZATION OF EVIDENCE	Well organized, with strong, relevant examples	Generally well organized, with apt examples	Adequately organized, with some examples	Sketchily developed, with weak examples	Lacking focus and evidence	Unfocused and disorganized
SENTENCE STRUCTURE	Varied, appealing sentences	Reasonably varied sentences	Some variety in sentences	Little variety in sentences	Errors in sentence structure	Severe errors in sentence structure
LEVEL OF VOCABULARY	Mature & apt word choice	Competent word choice	Adequate word choice	Inappropriate or weak vocabulary	Highly limited vocabulary	Rudimentary
GRAMMAR AND USAGE	Almost entirely free of errors	Relatively free of errors	Some technical errors	Minor errors, and some major ones	Numerous major errors	Extensive severe errors
OVERALL EFFECT	Outstanding	Effective	Adequately competent	Inadequate, but shows some potential	Seriously flawed	Fundamentally deficient

Self-Scoring Chart

For each of the following categories, rate the essay from 1 (lowest) to 6 (highest)

Position on the Topic   _____

Organization of Evidence   _____

Sentence Structure   _____

Level of Vocabulary   _____

Grammar and Usage   _____

Overall Effect   _____

TOTAL   _____

(To get a score, divide the total by 6)   _____

Scoring Chart (Second Reader)

For each of the following categories, rate the essay from 1 (lowest) to 6 (highest)

Position on the Topic   _____

Organization of Evidence   _____

Sentence Structure   _____

Level of Vocabulary   _____

Grammar and Usage   _____

Overall Effect   _____

TOTAL   _____

(To get a score, divide the total by 6)   _____

Scoring Practice Test 6

Refer to the answer key for Practice Test 6 on page 420. Then use the Scoring Worksheet below to determine your raw scores for Critical Reading, Mathematics, and Writing. For each section, give yourself one point for each answer that is correct. Your total raw score is the total number of correct answer points minus $\frac{1}{4}$ of the total number of incorrect answer points. Round off the total raw score to the nearest whole number to get your Rounded Raw Score. Convert your raw scores to scaled scores using the Conversion Tables on pages 424–425.

SCORING WORKSHEET

Critical Reading

Section 3 $\underline{\hspace{3cm}}_{\text{number correct}} - \frac{1}{4}\left(\underline{\hspace{3cm}}_{\text{number incorrect}} \right) = \underline{\hspace{3cm}}$ (A)

Section 7 $\underline{\hspace{3cm}}_{\text{number correct}} - \frac{1}{4}\left(\underline{\hspace{3cm}}_{\text{number incorrect}} \right) = \underline{\hspace{3cm}}$ (B)

Section 9 $\underline{\hspace{3cm}}_{\text{number correct}} - \frac{1}{4}\left(\underline{\hspace{3cm}}_{\text{number incorrect}} \right) = \underline{\hspace{3cm}}$ (C)

Critical Reading Raw Score = (A) + (B) + (C) = $\underline{\hspace{3cm}}$

Critical Reading Scaled Score (See Table 1) = $\underline{\hspace{3cm}}$

Mathematics

Section 2 $\underline{\hspace{3cm}}_{\text{number correct}} - \frac{1}{4}\left(\underline{\hspace{3cm}}_{\text{number incorrect}} \right) = \underline{\hspace{3cm}}$ (D)

Section 5
Part I
(1–8) $\underline{\hspace{3cm}}_{\text{number correct}} - \frac{1}{4}\left(\underline{\hspace{3cm}}_{\text{number incorrect}} \right) = \underline{\hspace{3cm}}$ (E)

Part II
(9–18) $\underline{\hspace{3cm}}_{\text{number correct}}$ $= \underline{\hspace{3cm}}$ (F)

Section 8 $\underline{\hspace{3cm}}_{\text{number correct}} - \frac{1}{4}\left(\underline{\hspace{3cm}}_{\text{number incorrect}} \right) = \underline{\hspace{3cm}}$ (G)

Mathematics Raw Score = (D) + (E) + (F) + (G) = $\underline{\hspace{3cm}}$

Mathematics Scaled Score (See Table 2) = $\underline{\hspace{3cm}}$

Writing Skills

Essay $\dfrac{}{\text{score 1}} + \dfrac{}{\text{score 2}} = \underline{}$ (H)

Section 6 $\dfrac{}{\text{number correct}} - \dfrac{1}{4}\left(\dfrac{}{\text{number incorrect}}\right) = \underline{}$ (I)

Section 10 $\dfrac{}{\text{number correct}} - \dfrac{1}{4}\left(\dfrac{}{\text{number incorrect}}\right) = \underline{}$ (J)

Writing Raw Score = I + J (H is a separate subscore) $= \underline{}$

Writing Scaled Score (See Table 3) $= \underline{}$

TABLE 1: CRITICAL READING CONVERSION TABLE

Raw Score	Scaled Score	Raw Score	Scaled Score	Raw Score	Scaled Score	Raw Score	Scaled Score
67	800	49	630	31	510	14	400
66	790	48	620	30	510	13	400
65	790	47	610	29	500	12	390
64	780	46	610	28	490	11	380
63	770	45	600	27	490	10	370
62	760	44	590	26	480	9	360
61	750	43	590	25	480	8	350
60	740	42	580	24	470	7	340
59	730	41	570	23	460	6	330
58	720	40	570	22	460	5	320
57	710	39	560	21	450	4	310
56	700	38	550	20	440	3	300
55	690	37	550	19	440	2	280
54	680	36	540	18	430	1	270
53	670	35	540	17	420	0	260
52	660	34	530	16	420	−1	230
51	650	33	520	15	410	−2 and below	210
50	640	32	520				

TABLE 2: MATH CONVERSION TABLE

Math Raw Score	Math Scaled Score	Math Raw Score	Math Scaled Score	Math Raw Score	Math Scaled Score	Math Raw Score	Math Scaled Score
54	800	40	630	26	500	12	390
53	790	39	620	25	500	11	380
52	770	38	610	24	490	10	370
51	750	37	600	23	480	9	360
50	730	36	590	22	470	8	340
49	710	35	580	21	460	7	330
48	700	34	570	20	450	6	320
47	690	33	560	19	450	5	300
46	680	32	560	18	440	4	290
45	670	31	550	17	430	3	270
44	660	30	540	16	420	2	250
43	650	29	530	15	410	1	240
42	640	28	520	14	410	0	230
41	640	27	510	13	400	−1 and below	200

TABLE 3: WRITING CONVERSION TABLE

Writing Raw Score	Essay Score					
	6	5	4	3	2	1
49	800	800	770	740	710	680
48	800	790	750	710	680	650
47	790	760	720	690	660	630
46	770	740	700	670	640	610
45	760	730	690	650	620	590
44	740	710	670	640	610	580
43	730	700	660	620	600	570
42	720	690	650	610	580	550
41	710	670	630	600	570	540
40	690	660	620	590	560	530
39	680	650	610	580	550	520
38	670	640	600	570	540	510
37	670	630	590	560	530	500
36	660	630	590	550	520	490
35	650	620	580	540	510	480
34	640	610	570	530	510	480
33	630	600	560	530	500	470
32	620	590	550	520	490	460
31	620	590	550	510	480	450
30	610	580	540	500	480	450
29	600	570	530	500	470	440
28	590	560	520	490	460	430
27	590	560	520	480	450	430
26	580	550	510	480	450	420
25	570	540	500	470	440	410
24	570	540	500	460	440	410
23	560	530	490	460	430	400
22	560	520	480	450	420	390
21	550	520	480	440	420	390
20	540	510	470	440	410	380
19	540	510	470	430	400	370
18	530	500	460	430	400	370
17	520	490	450	420	390	360
16	520	490	450	410	380	350
15	510	480	440	410	380	350
14	500	470	430	400	370	340
13	500	470	430	390	370	340
12	490	460	420	390	360	330
11	480	450	410	380	350	320
10	480	450	410	370	350	320
9	470	440	400	370	340	310
8	460	430	390	360	330	300
7	460	420	390	350	320	290
6	450	420	380	340	310	280
5	440	410	370	330	310	280
4	430	400	360	320	300	270
3	420	390	350	310	280	250
2	400	360	330	300	270	240
1	390	360	320	290	260	230
0	370	340	300	270	240	210

ANSWERS EXPLAINED

Section 2 Mathematics

<u>Note</u>:

1. See page 32 for an explanation of the symbol $\Rightarrow$ that is used in some answer explanations.

2. A calculator icon, , is placed next to the answer explanation of any question for which a calculator *could* be useful. Almost always, the question can be answered easily without using a calculator.

3. If you are unfamiliar with any of the math facts used in the following answer explanations, refer to Barron's *SAT*, which, in addition to having practice tests, has a full review of all the math you need to know.

1. **C**

   • $\dfrac{2}{5} < \dfrac{9}{n} \Rightarrow 2n < 5 \times 9 = 45 \Rightarrow n < 22.5$.

   • $\dfrac{9}{n} < \dfrac{3}{4} \Rightarrow 4 \times 9 < 3n \Rightarrow 36 < 3n \Rightarrow 12 < n$.

   • There are 10 integers that satisfy the inequality $12 < n < 22.5$, namely $13, 14, \ldots, 21, 22$.

2. **A** If a fraction is equal to 1, its numerator and denominator are equal. So,

$$x^2 - a = x^2 + 2 \Rightarrow -a = 2 \Rightarrow a = -2.$$

3. **C** In any quadrilateral, the sum of the measures of the four angles is 360°, so

$$62 + 115 + x + 2x = 360 \Rightarrow 177 + 3x = 360 \Rightarrow 3x = 183 \Rightarrow x = 61.$$

4. **C**

   • The value of 12 nickels is $12 \times 5 = 60$ cents.
   • The value of 8 dimes is $8 \times 10 = 80$ cents.

   So the ratio of the value of Chloe's nickels to the value of her dimes is $60:80 = 3:4$.

5. **D** **Solution 1.** The give condition is: $\dfrac{a+b+c+d}{4} = \dfrac{b+c+d+e}{4} - 2$.

   Multiplying both sides of this equation by 4, we get $a+b+c+d = b+c+d+e-8 \Rightarrow a = e-8$.

   So, e is 8 more than a.

   Solution 2. Pick any four numbers for a, b, c, and d. Say they are each 2. Then their average is 2, and so the average of b, c, d, and e must be 4. So, $\dfrac{2+2+2+e}{4} = 4 \Rightarrow 6 + e = 16 \Rightarrow e = 10$.

   So e is 8 more than a.

6. **D** A number that leaves a remainder of 2 when divided by 7 is 2 more than a multiple of 7. Be careful. Don't forget that 0 is a multiple of 7, and 2 more than 0 is 2 $(2 = 0 \times 7 + 2)$. So, the smallest positive integer less or equal to 100 that leaves a remainder of 2 when divided by 7 is 2 and the largest is 100 $(100 = 14 \times 7 + 2)$. So there are 15 such integers — all integers of the form $7q + 2$, where $0 \le q \le 14$.

7. **D** Draw a diagram and label it, letting ℓ represent the length of the rectangle and d its diagonal. Since the perimeter is 70, we have that $70 = 15 + 15 + \ell + \ell$. So $2\ell = 40$ and $\ell = 20$. Then d is the length of the hypotenuse of a right triangle whose legs are 15 and 20. If you recognize this as a 15-20-25 right triangle (a 3-4-5 triangle in which each side has been multiplied by 5), you're done. Otherwise, use the Pythagorean theorem: $15^2 + 20^2 = d^2 \Rightarrow d^2 = 225 + 400 = 625$. So, $d = 25$.

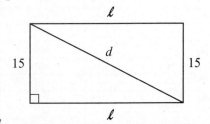

8. **C** Since x and y are integers whose product, xy, is either 6 or -6, x and y are each either ± 1 and ± 6 or ± 2 and ± 3. The greatest value of $x - y$ is 7, when $x = 6$ and $y = -1$.

9. **B** You can calculate the cost of each item, but that's not necessary. The easiest way to answer the question is to add the three given equations. Let r, n, and b represent the prices of the ring, necklace, and bracelet, respectively. Then

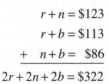

$$r + n = \$123$$
$$r + b = \$113$$
$$\underline{+ \quad n + b = \ \ \$86}$$
$$2r + 2n + 2b = \$322$$

Dividing by 2, we get $r + n + b = \$161$. Since Heather has \$140, she needs $\$161 - \$140 = \$21$ more. Note: $r = \$75$, $n = \$48$, $b = \$38$, but you did *not* need to calculate that.

10. **A** $f(6) = a$ means that $(6, a)$ is a point on the graph of $y = f(x)$. Since the point on the graph whose x-coordinate is 6 is $(6,4)$, $a = 4$, and, therefore, $f(a) = f(4)$. Since $f(4)$ is the y-coordinate of the point on the graph whose x-coordinate is 4, $f(4) = 0$.

11. **C**
- The charge to come to Julie's house was d dollars.
- The charge to hang the first 5 paintings was ${}^{1}\cancel{5}\left(\dfrac{3d}{\cancel{10}_{2}}\right) = \dfrac{3d}{2}$ dollars.
- The charge to hang the next 5 paintings was ${}^{1}\cancel{5}\left(\dfrac{d}{\underset{2}{\cancel{10}}}\right) = \dfrac{d}{2}$ dollars.
- So the total charge was $d + \dfrac{3d}{2} + \dfrac{d}{2} = d + 1.5d + 0.5d = 3d$ dollars.
- Finally, since $3d = 75$, we have $d = 25$.

12. **B** Let C_1 and C_2 represent the circumferences of circles 1 and 2, respectively. Then $C_2 = 2\pi(5281)$ and $C_1 = 2\pi(5280)$. So, $C_2 - C_1 = 2\pi(5281) - 2\pi(5280) = 2\pi(5281 - 5280) = 2\pi(1) = 2\pi$. Since $2\pi \approx 6.28$, the difference between the circumferences lies in the interval from 5 to 10 feet.

13. **B**
- $(a + 2) \blacksquare (b + 2) = (a + 2)^2 - (b + 2) = a^2 + 4a + 4 - b - 2 = a^2 + 4a - b + 2$
- $a \blacksquare b = a^2 - b$
- So, $\cancel{a^2} + 4a - \cancel{b} + 2 = \cancel{a^2} - \cancel{b} \Rightarrow 4a + 2 = 0 \Rightarrow a = \dfrac{-2}{4} = -\dfrac{1}{2}$.

14. **E**
- If p and q are both odd, then $p - q$ is even, and both 4 and 6 are possible values. For example, $11 - 7$ and $17 - 13$ are both equal to 4 and $11 - 5$ and $13 - 7$ are both equal to 6.
- The only even prime is 2, so the only way that $p - q$ could be odd is if p is odd and $q = 2$: $5 - 2 = 3$ and $7 - 2 = 5$, but $p - 2 = 7 \Rightarrow p = 9$, which is not prime. So it is impossible for $p - q$ to equal 7.

15. **E** Since $\overline{EG}$ is a diagonal of square $EFGH$, the area of that square is $\dfrac{6^2}{2} = \dfrac{36}{2} = 18$. NOTE: If you don't know the formula $A = \dfrac{d^2}{2}$, for the area of a square whose diagonal is d, use the formula $A = s^2$, where s is the length of a side. Since the diagonal is 6, each side is $\dfrac{6}{\sqrt{2}}$. Then $A = \left(\dfrac{6}{\sqrt{2}}\right)^2 = 18$. So the area of square $ABCD = 82 + 18 = 100$, and the length of each of its sides is 10.

16. **C Solution 1.** $f\left(\dfrac{1}{2}\sqrt{a}\right) = \left(\dfrac{1}{2}\sqrt{a}\right)^2 + 7 = \dfrac{1}{4}a + 7$.

So, $4f\left(\dfrac{1}{2}\sqrt{a}\right) = 4\left(\dfrac{1}{4}a + 7\right) = a + 28$.

Since $4f\left(\dfrac{1}{2}\sqrt{a}\right) = 30$, we have $a = 2$.

Solution 2. Divide both sides of the equation $4f\left(\frac{1}{2}\sqrt{a}\right) = 30$ by 4.

Then, $f\left(\frac{1}{2}\sqrt{a}\right) = 7.5$. As above, $f\left(\frac{1}{2}\sqrt{a}\right) = \frac{1}{4}a + 7$, so, $\frac{1}{4}a + 7 = 7.5$ and $\frac{1}{4}a = 0.5$. So, $a = 4 \times (0.5) = 2$.

17. **E** If $x^3 < x^2$, then either x is negative or $0 < x < 1$. But if x were between 0 and 1, then x^4 would be less than x^2. So x must be negative. But if x were between -1 and 0, again, x^4 would be less than x^2. Therefore, x must be a negative number less than -1.

 I. If $x^2 < 1$, then $-1 < x < 1$. So I *cannot* be true.
 II. Since x is negative, x^3 is negative. So II *cannot* be true.
 III. If $x^3 < x^5$, then dividing both sides by x^3 and reversing the inequality since x^3 is negative, yields $1 < x^2$, which we already know *cannot* be true.

18. **E** **Solution 1.** The number of elements only in A is $a - c$; the number of elements only in B is $b - c$. So the number of elements in exactly one of the sets A and B is $(a - c) + (b - c) = a + b - 2c$.

 Solution 2. Take two small sets, say $A = \{1, 2, 3, 4, 5\}$ and $B = \{4, 5, 6, 7\}$. Then $C = \{4, 5\}$ and $a = 5$, $b = 4$, and $c = 2$. There are 5 numbers (1, 2, 3, 6, and 7) that are in exactly one of the two sets A and B. The only answer choice that equals 5 when $a = 5$, $b = 4$, and $c = 2$ is choice (E).

19. **B** **Solution 1.** The graph of $y = g(x)$ is simply the graph of $y = f(x)$ shifted 3 units to the right. So $g(x) = f(x - 3)$.

 Solution 2. $g(0) = 0$. Test each of the answer choices to see which one works.
 • (A): $f(0 + 3) = f(3) = 4$. Eliminate (A).
 • (B): $f(0) + 3 = f(-3) = 0$. Choice (B) is possible.
 • (C): $f(0) + 3 = 3 + 3 = 6$. Eliminate (C).
 • (D): $f(0) - 3 = 3 - 3 = 0$. Choice (D) is possible.
 • (E): $f(0 - 3) + 3 = f(-3) + 3 = 0 + 3 + 3$. Eliminate (E).
 So the answer is (B) or (D). If at this point you run out of time, guess. Otherwise, test another number: $g(3) = 3$.
 • (B): $f(3 - 3) = f(0) = 3$. (B) is still possible.
 • (D): $f(3) - 3 = 4 - 3 = 1$. Eliminate (D).
 • The answer is (B).

20. **B** Use the formula $d = rt$ (distance = rate $\times$ time). Let r be Eileen's rate, in miles per hour. Since her time was 2 hours, we have $d = 2r$. Since Bob's rate was 20% faster than Eileen's rate, his rate was $1.2r$. So, letting t represent Bob's time, we have $d = (1.2r)t$. Since their distances were equal, we get

$$2r = (1.2r)t \Rightarrow t = \frac{2r}{1.2r} = \frac{2}{1.2} = \frac{20}{12} = \frac{5}{3} = 1\frac{2}{3}.$$

So the trip took Bob $1\frac{2}{3}$ hours, or 1 hour and 40 minutes—20 minutes less than it took Eileen.

Section 3 Critical Reading

1. **E** The word "planning" signals that *relevant* (pertinent) material is to be selected and organized. The word "generally" signals that this is the most common purpose for planning an essay.

2. **C** "Learn to speak any language" signals that the sentence is about language being *acquired* (learned).

3. **D** It makes sense that pharaohs would require *imposing* (impressive) burial chambers. (A) *grandiose* is also a good choice. However, (A) *pragmatic* (practical) does not make sense in context because a pragmatic meaning would be a "functional one." (D) *arcane* (mysteriously obscure) makes good sense because an arcane meaning would be one other than a "purely functional one."

4. **D** (A) *flood*, (C) *emigration* (leaving a country), and (D) *exodus* (migration) are all good choices for the first answer blank. However, (A) *foreign* and (C) *heterogeneous* (consisting of dissimilar parts) do not make sense, whereas (D) *indigenous* (native) makes good sense because a large number of people coming from overseas could overwhelm local culture.

5. **C** (A) *Postulate* (assume to be true) and (C) *posit* (hypothesize) both are good choices for the first answer blank. However, (A) *initially* (at first) makes little sense because there is not any indication that how the beings would be regarded would change. (C) *arbitrarily* (done in a way that is not based on objective facts) makes good sense because the tradition *posits* that each being has spiritual value, which suggests that any one cannot be seen as superior.

6. **E** In the sentence immediately following the one in which the author mentions "noble deeds" she says, "Idle wishes, vain repinings, loud-sounding declamations can never bring freedom to any human soul" (lines 4–6). It can be inferred from this that she is urging women to take action. The adjective "noble" suggests self-sacrifice and putting the interests of others above one's own interests. We can infer that the author is urging women to help advance the cause of women's freedom and equality because the rest of the passage is about the importance of women having equality with men.

7. **C** The author of Passage 1 says, "No genuine equality, no real freedom . . . can exist on any foundation save that of pecuniary independence" (lines 12–14). The word *pecuniary* means "financial." We can infer from this that the author believes that in most cases such financial independence could best be achieved by taking a salaried job outside the home. The author of Passage 2 argues that women should not be slaves owned by men. It can be inferred from this that the author of Passage 2 would agree that women should take salaried jobs so that they are no longer dependent on men.

8. **B** Passage 1 does not consider a counter argument to its main argument, whereas Passage 2 does: "It is said that as a rule man does sufficiently provide for woman, and that she ought to remain content. The great facts of the world are at war with this assumption" (lines 31–34).

9. **A** In Passage 1 the author "Exhort[s] all women . . . to assert their individuality . . . by the doing of noble deeds" (lines 1–4). The author of Passage 2 says that women are the slaves of men and that "All the wrongs . . . of modern society grow out of this false condition of relations between man and woman" (lines 26–29). The author then mentions "the present agitation" (line 29), a reference to the growing movement for women's rights and equality.

10. **E** The word "catechized" means to "instruct in basic principles of church doctrine," so it makes sense that it is used here to refer to new black members of the Union League being *instructed in important basic principles*.

11. **C** In context "franchise" refers to *the legal right to vote*. "Exercise" means *to put to use*. Thus, "exercise their franchise" means *vote to elect government officials*.

12. **E** The author quotes Elsa Barkey Brown: "'African-American women in Virginia, Mississippi, South Carolina and elsewhere understood themselves to have a vital stake in African-American men's franchise'" (lines 44–47). We can infer that black women were vocal at political meetings because they believed it was a way of helping blacks improve their position.

13. **B** The author says, "With the establishment of Radical Reconstruction, the league became the spearhead for Southern Republicanism. Because blacks were the most numerous enfranchised group in many areas, the league depended on them for the bulk of Republican strength" (lines 27–33).

14. **D** The author says that all of the people and groups mentioned except Union troops in the South strongly supported the Republican Party in the South.

15. **E** The author says, "During most of Reconstruction, the Union League and such smaller organizations as the Lincoln Brotherhood and the Red Strings delivered the black vote to the Republican Party" (lines 63–67).

16. **D** The author says he has liked the novels that have been read to him "if they do not end unhappily" (lines 24–25). He is most likely being *jocular* (humorous) because it is very unlikely that he would believe that a law should be passed against novels ending unhappily.

17. **C** In the paragraph before the one in which he refers to his "loss of the higher aesthetic tastes" (line 30) the author describes how he lost his ability to enjoy and appreciate high quality art, music, and literature. The word "aesthetic" means *concerned with art and beauty*.

18. **D** The author says that he still enjoys "books on history, biographies, and travels . . . and essays on all sorts of subjects" (lines 31–34). It is thus likely that the author would enjoy reading an essay on English history. He says he no longer enjoys (A) and (B), and it is unlikely that he would enjoy (C) *a symphony* because he says in

lines 14–16 that music generally does not give him pleasure. It is unlikely he would enjoy studying advanced mathematics because he says, "My power to follow a long and purely abstract train of thought is very limited . . . and therefore I could never have succeeded with . . . mathematics" (lines 58–61).

19. **D** The author says, "I have no great quickness of apprehension or wit . . . I am therefore a poor critic: a paper or book, when first read, generally excites my admiration, and it is only after considerable reflection that I perceive the weak points" (lines 52–58).

20. **C** Induction is *the process of deriving general principles from particular facts*. The author says, "My mind seems to have become a kind of machine for grinding general laws out of large collections of facts" (lines 35–37). He also says, "I have had the strongest desire to understand or explain whatever I observed,— that is, to grasp all facts under some general laws" (lines 92–95). Finally, he says, "This has naturally led me to distrust greatly deductive reasoning in the mixed sciences" (lines 108–110).

21. **B** The author says, "I am not very skeptical—a frame of mind which I believe to be injurious to the progress of science. A good deal of skepticism in a scientific man is advisable to avoid much loss of time, but [some men] have often been deterred from experiment or observations, which would have proved directly or indirectly serviceable" (lines 111–118).

22. **D** The author is describing his intellectual abilities, so the meaning he intends by the word "apprehension" must be *understanding*.

23. **A** The author's main point in the sentence is that his loss of "the higher aesthetic tastes" is strange in view of the fact that he is still able to appreciate essays on history and so forth. The words in parentheses are thus presumably intended mainly to make it clear that he is interested in such essays for their intrinsic merit and not only for the scientific facts they may contain.

24. **E** The writer is describing his intellectual abilities. He has already discussed his "power of reasoning" (lines 77–78), so it is unlikely that "invention" refers to (C) logical ability. Therefore, the meaning of the word "invention" as it is used in line 78 is *creativity*.

Section 5 Mathematics

<u>Note</u>:

1. See page 32 for an explanation of the symbol $\Rightarrow$ that is used in some answer explanations.

2. A calculator icon, , is placed next to the answer explanation of any question for which a calculator *could* be useful. Almost always, the question can be answered easily without using a calculator.

3. If you are unfamiliar with any of the math facts used in the following answer explanations, refer to Barron's *SAT*, which, in addition to having practice tests, has a full review of all the math you need to know.

1. **B** $\frac{2}{3}(60) = 40$, which is $\frac{40}{100}$ of 100. And $\frac{40}{100} = \frac{4}{10} = \frac{2}{5}$.

2. **C** In any quadrilateral the sum of the measures of the four angles is 360°. So, $90 + 2a + 90 + a = 360 \Rightarrow 3a + 180 = 360 \Rightarrow 3a = 180 \Rightarrow a = 60$. Finally, since $a + b = 180$, we get $b = 120$.

3. **C** $(c + d)^2 = c^2 + 2cd + d^2 = (c^2 + d^2) + 2cd = 20 + 2(10) = 20 + 20 = 40$

4. **E** **Solution 1.** If C represents the number of dolls in Chris's collection, then $C - 40\%C = 90$, the number of dolls that Claire has. So, $90 = C - 40\%C = 60\%C = 0.6C$. Then $C = 90 \div 0.6 = 150$.

Solution 2. Backsolve. Test choice (C), 130. If Chris had 130 dolls, then Claire would have had $130 - 40\%(130) = 130 - 52 = 78$ dolls, which is too small. Eliminate choice (C), as well as choices (A) and (B), which are even smaller. Now test choice (D) or (E). Choice (D) is still too small; choice (E) works: $150 - 40\%(150) = 150 - 60 = 90$.

5. **B** Since 40 of the 50 integers are greater than 19, 10 of them are less than or equal to 19. Then of the 30 integers that are less than 50, 10 of them are less than 20, and the other 20 lie between 20 and 49, inclusive. So 20 of them have a ten's digit of 2, 3, or 4.

Section 7 Critical Reading

1. **E** Immigrants frequently are not easily *assimilated* (integrated into a larger group) into society.

2. **D** The word "languages" signals that the sentence is concerned with *linguistic* (relating to language) universals.

3. **B** (A) *expenditures*, (D) *interference*, and (E) *control* make sense in the first answer blank. However, (A) *minimum*, (D) *selection*, and (E) *modicum* (small amount) do not make sense in the second answer blank. (B) *bureaucracy* (administrative system) makes good sense because a bureaucracy can exercise a lot of control over people. (B) *Myriad* (a great number) makes sense because it is difficult to decrease the size and influence of the bureaucracy because citizens expect it, as an agency of the government, to perform a great number and variety of tasks.

4. **C** The words "which remains one of the greatest stories ever told" in reference to *The Odyssey* signal that the use of a physical journey to symbolize a personal voyage of discovery and transformation reached its *apogee* (highest point) in *The Odyssey*.

5. **B** By definition a *connotation* means *implied additional meanings*.

6. **A** It makes sense that strict pollution control measures would *forestall* (prevent) environmental disaster.

7. **D** By definition a *postulate* is a statement accepted as true for the purpose of argument or *empirical* (based on observation and experiment) investigation.

8. **D** The words "only a" signal that the nucleus of an atom occupies only a *negligible* (tiny) amount of an atom's volume. Other clues are the words *fraction* and *but*.

9. **C** There is no suggestion that countries recruited and trained pirates to harass Roman shipping. The other reasons are all mentioned.

10. **C** In context the word "disaffected" means *no longer loyal to their group*. This makes sense because it is reasonable that some Italians would be unhappy with the Roman Empire and that some of these would become pirates.

11. **E** The phrase "this benign principle" refers to the fact mentioned in the preceding sentence: "Fortunately nature has ways of healing diseases in spite of theories and drugs" (lines 8–10). It thus makes sense that this principle is described as *benign* (beneficial).

12. **D** The author says, "They were hampered with the old Chinese notions about a male principle and a female principle which were conceived to prevail in nature, and with the five elements to which the human organs were supposed to correspond" (lines 4–8).

13. **B** No information about the cause of hotspots is given in Passage 1. The author concentrates on explaining what J. Tuzo Wilson's "hotspot" theory says is caused by hotspots. Information is provided explaining all of the other choices.

14. **A** Wilson's theory predicts that a hotspot exists "beneath the present-day position of the Island of Hawaii" (also called the "Big Island" (lines 26–27). The fact that "new volcanic rock is continually being formed" (lines 54–55) suggests that the "Big Island" is located over a hotspot because it is consistent with the hotspot theory.

15. **D** The author says, "The vast majority of earthquakes and volcanic eruptions occur near tectonic plate boundaries, but there are some exceptions" (lines 1–3). The passage describes how the "hotspot" theory explains at least some of these exceptions. The "hotspot" theory explains how volcanoes form in the interior of tectonic plates.

16. **A** This is the most likely choice because the passage says that Wilson first "*noted that* in certain locations . . . volcanism has been active for very long periods of time" (lines 13–16; italics mine) Wilson then "*reasoned* [that] if . . . hotspots existed below the plates that would provide . . . energy . . . to sustain volcanism" (lines 17–21; italics mine). Finally, he "*hypothesized*" (line 22; italics mine) about how volcanism occurred in a specific area, creating an island volcano, and about how plate movement affects this process. Note that the process of reasoning Wilson used was *deduction*—reasoning that infers something from a general principle.

17. **C** The author describes the "hotspot" theory: "Wilson suggested that continuing plate movement eventually carries the island beyond the hotspot, cutting it off from the magma source, and volcanism ceases. As one island volcano becomes extinct, another develops over the hotspot, and the cycle is repeated" (lines 35–40) The final paragraph describes how the structure and age of the Hawaiian Islands support the hotspot theory.

18. **D** The author says, "They [a team of scientists] deployed a large network of sea-floor seismometers . . . , opening up a window into the Earth" (lines 64–69). The word "window" as it is used here means *a means of observing*.

19. **C** In context the word "concurrent" means *at the same time*. Ocean bottom seismometers and land seismometers were deployed at the same time.

20. **D** It can be inferred that the earthquakes mentioned in line 92 were largely or entirely unrelated to geological activity on or near the Hawaiian Islands because the purpose of recording the seismic waves from the earthquakes was to "determine whether seismic waves travel more slowly through hot rock as they pass beneath Hawaii" (lines 94–96).

21. **E** The phrase "seismic waves" in line 94 refers to *waves generated by earthquakes*.

22. **C** In the sentence following the one in which the word "resolve" (line 110) appears, the author says, "Seismometer deployments limited to land sites on the islands did not provide enough coverage for high-resolution imaging" (lines 110–113). It can be inferred from this that in context the word "resolve" as it is used in line 110 means *to render visible and distinct*.

23. **B** Both passages are concerned mainly with what causes volcanic islands to form in the middle of tectonic plates when both the theory of tectonic plates and observation of volcanic activity show that most volcanic activity occurs near places where two tectonic plates meet. Passage 1 describes a theory to explain this, called the "hotspot" theory, which examines the case of Hawaii as a good example of the phenomenon. Passage 2 describes efforts to confirm this theory, again focusing on the Hawaiian Islands as an example of the phenomenon.

24. **E** Much of Passage 1 describes the hotspot theory in considerable detail. The final paragraph describes the geology of the Hawaiian Islands, providing evidence for the theory. Most of Passage 2 is devoted to describing PLUME, an experiment that produced strong evidence for the hotspot theory described in Passage 1.

Section 8 Mathematics

<u>Note</u>:

1. See page 32 for an explanation of the symbol $\Rightarrow$ that is used in some answer explanations.

2. A calculator icon, 🖩, is placed next to the answer explanation of any question for which a calculator *could* be useful. Almost always, the question can be answered easily without using a calculator.

3. If you are unfamiliar with any of the math facts used in the following answer explanations, refer to Barron's *SAT*, which, in addition to having practice tests, has a full review of all the math you need to know.

1. **A** Solution 1.

- $c = \dfrac{5}{7}d = \dfrac{5}{\cancel{7}}(\overset{11}{\cancel{77}}) = 55$

- $b = \dfrac{3}{5}c = \dfrac{3}{\cancel{5}}(\overset{11}{\cancel{55}}) = 33$

- $a = \dfrac{1}{3}b = \dfrac{1}{\cancel{3}}(\overset{11}{\cancel{33}}) = 11$

Solution 2.

$a = \dfrac{1}{3}b = \dfrac{1}{\cancel{3}}\left(\dfrac{\cancel{3}}{5}c\right) = \dfrac{1}{5}c = \dfrac{1}{\cancel{5}}\left(\dfrac{\cancel{5}}{7}d\right) = \dfrac{1}{7}d$. So, $a = \dfrac{1}{\cancel{7}}(\overset{11}{\cancel{77}}) = 11$.

2. **D**   **Solution 1.** In the diagram to the right, $z = 70°$. Since $z + x = 180$ and $z + y = 180$, x and y are each equal to 110, and $x + y = 220$.

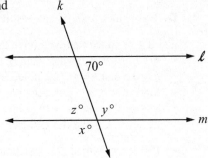

Solution 2. $70 + y = 180 \Rightarrow y = 110$, and since vertical angles are congruent, $x = y$. So, $x = 110$, and $x + y = 220$.

3. **C**   **Solution 1.** Assume that each of the 8 workers earns x dollars. Then clearly their average salary is x dollars, the supervisor's salary is $2x$ dollars, and the total of all the salaries is $10x$ dollars. Finally, $2x$ is $\frac{2}{10} = \frac{1}{5}$ of $10x$.

Solution 2. Do exactly what we did in Solution 1, except instead of using x, assume that each of the 8 workers earns \$1 and the supervisor earns \$2. Then the total of all the salaries is \$10, and the supervisor's salary is $\frac{2}{10} = \frac{1}{5}$ of the total.

Solution 3. Let T be the total of the salaries of the 8 workers. Then their average salary is $\frac{T}{8}$, and the supervisor's salary is $2\left(\frac{T}{8}\right) = \frac{T}{4}$. So the total of the 9 salaries is $T + \frac{T}{4} = \frac{5}{4}T$ and the supervisor's salary of $\frac{1}{4}T$ is $\frac{1}{5}$ of $\frac{5}{4}T$.

4. **B**

    - 1 kilometer = 1,000 meters = 100,000 centimeters
    - $\dfrac{5 \text{ centimeters}}{2 \text{ inches}} = \dfrac{100,000 \text{ centimeters}}{x \text{ inches}} \Rightarrow 5x = 200,000 \Rightarrow x = 40,000$
    - So, 1 kilometer $\approx$ 40,000 inches.
    - 1 yard = 3 feet = 36 inches $\Rightarrow$ 1 inch $= \dfrac{1}{36}$ yard
    - So, 1 kilometer $\approx 40,000 \left(\dfrac{1}{36} \text{ yard}\right) \approx 1,111 \text{ yards}$.
    - To the nearest hundred, 1 kilometer = 1,100 yards.

5. **C**
    - If $n = 1$, then $5n^2 + 3 = 8$, $3n^2 + 5 = 8$, and $4n^2 - 2 = 2$, so eliminate (A), (B), and (E).
    - If $n = 2$, then $7n^2 - 4 = 24$, so eliminate (D).
    - Whether n is even or odd, $4n^2$ is even, and so $4n^2 + 7$ is odd.

6. **C**
    - If two lines are parallel, their slopes are equal. Since $4 \neq -4$, I is false.
    - If two lines are perpendicular, the product of their slopes is -1. Since $4 \times (-4) \neq -1$, II is false.
    - Of course, the two lines don't have to have the same y-intercept, but they could. For example, the lines $y = 4x$ and $y = -4x$ each have y-intercepts of 0 and $y = 4x + 1$ and $y = -4x + 1$ each have y-intercepts of 1.

7. **A**
    - $f(3n) = 2(3n) + 3 = 6n + 3$
    - $g(2n) = 3(2n) + 2 = 6n + 2$.
    There are *no* numbers that satisfy the equation $6n + 3 = 6n + 2$.

8. **D**

    - It took Dan 180 miles ÷ 50 miles per hour = 3.6 hours.
    - It took Laurel 180 miles ÷ 45 miles per hour = 4 hours.
    - So, Laurel took $4 - 3.6 = 0.4$ hours more.
    - Finally, 0.4 hours × 60 minutes per hour = 24 minutes.

9. **D** First, since a and b are positive, $\dfrac{a}{b}$ is positive, and if $0 < a < b$, then $\dfrac{a}{b} < 1$. So clearly, choice (D) is true, and if you notice that, you have the answer. If not, check the choices.

- $a + b$ is surely greater than 0, and although $a + b$ *could be* less than 1, it doesn't have to be (for example, $a = 0.5$ and $b = 0.7$). Choice (A) is false.
- Since $a < b$, $a - b$ is negative. Choice (B) is false.
- $a^2 - b^2 = (a - b)(a + b)$, which is the product of a negative number and a positive number, and so is negative. Choice (C) is false.
- If $0 < a < b$, then $\dfrac{b}{a} > 1$. Choice (E) is false.

10. **E** Let r represent the radius of the circle. Then $C = 2\pi r$ and $A = \pi r^2$.
- Could $C = A$? Could $2\pi r = \pi r^2$? Yes, if $r = 2$.
- Could $C < A$? Could $2\pi r < \pi r^2$? Yes, if $r > 2$.
- Could $C > A$? Could $2\pi r > \pi r^2$? Yes, if $r < 2$.

Note that the question asks which of the statements *could* be true, not which of the statements *must* be true. *None* of the statements must be true, but *all* of them *could* be true.

11. **D** If $n > 10$ then $n - 5 > 5$, and since all primes other than 2 are odd, $n - 5$ must be odd. Therefore, n is even, which means that choices (A), (B), (C), and (E) are all even, and since they are all greater than 2, they cannot be prime. Choice (D), $n + 3$, does not *have* to be prime, but it *could be*. For example, if $n = 16$, then $n - 5 = 11$ and $n + 3 = 19$, both of which are prime.

12. **D** Draw in $\overline{DE}$ perpendicular to line ℓ.

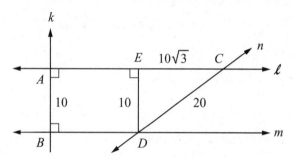

Then $AEDB$ is a rectangle and so $DE = AB = 10$. Since, in right triangle DEC, the hypotenuse is twice as long as a leg, the triangle is a 30-60-90 right triangle and the second leg is $\sqrt{3}$ times the length of the first leg. So, EC is $10\sqrt{3}$, and AC is $10\sqrt{3}$ greater than AE, which equals BD.

13. **C**

- The first term is $-\dfrac{1}{2}$.

- The second term is $\left(-\dfrac{1}{2}\right) \times (-1) + 1 = \dfrac{1}{2} + 1 = \dfrac{3}{2}$.

- The third term is $\left(\dfrac{3}{2}\right) \times (-1) + 1 = -\dfrac{3}{2} + 1 = -\dfrac{1}{2}$.

- The fourth term is $\left(-\dfrac{1}{2}\right) \times (-1) + 1 = \dfrac{1}{2} + 1 = \dfrac{3}{2}$.

So the terms alternate: $-\dfrac{1}{2}, \dfrac{3}{2}, -\dfrac{1}{2}, \dfrac{3}{2}, \ldots$ and the 13th term is $-\dfrac{1}{2}$.

14. **A** If $x°F = x°C$, then $x = \dfrac{9}{5}x + 32 \Rightarrow 5x = 9x + 5(32) \Rightarrow -4x = 160 \Rightarrow x = -40$.

15. **B** In quadrilateral *ABDF* the sum of the four interior angles is 360°.

So, $100 + 130 + b + c = 360 \Rightarrow b + c = 130$. Therefore, in $\triangle ABE$,
$180 = 2a + b + c = 2a + 130 \Rightarrow 2a = 50$ and $a = 25$. Then in $\triangle ACF$,
$a + b + 100 = 180 \Rightarrow b + 125 = 180 \Rightarrow b = 55$.

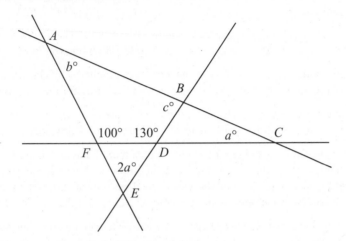

16. **D**
   - $g(x)$ is not defined for any value of x that makes the denominator, $x^2 - 3$, equal to 0 or for any number that makes the quantity, $x^2 - 4$, under the square root sign negative.
   - $x^2 - 3 = 0$ only if $x = \sqrt{3}$ or $x = -\sqrt{3}$, neither of which is an integer.
   - $x^2 - 4$ is negative only if $x^2 < 4$, which means $-2 < x < 2$. There are three integers that satisfy this inequality: -1, 0, and 1.

Section 9 Critical Reading

1. **C** The phrase "organize one's thoughts" signals that *coherently* (logically) is the best choice. In writing that is coherent the ideas are logically organized.

2. **A** The parents are "concerned," so it is reasonable that they are concerned about their child's *ambivalent* (having conflict feelings) feelings toward them.

3. **C** The defense attorneys argued that if the foreign national had been *culpable* (guilty) he would have fled the country when he had the *opportunity* to do so.

4. **C** (C) is the best choice because the resulting sentence makes the best sense. To gain an *objective* (free of bias) view of an issue one must not *prejudge* (judge prematurely) the issue based on one's *preconceptions* (ideas formed in advance).

5. **D** It makes sense that a judge would remind a witness to be *candid* (open and honest) when giving testimony.

6. **B** By definition the *denotative* (referring to the explicit meaning) meaning of a piece of language is its *explicit* (literal) meaning.

7. **C** The word "aesthetic" means *relating to beauty*.

8. **D** A "hothouse" in this context is *an environment conducive to vigorous development*. Thus, a "grammatical hothouse" is an environment in which a great effort is made to teach children about grammar.

9. **C** It can be inferred from the fact that the author's brother "was raised in the same grammatical hothouse" (lines 9–10) as the author that he would, like the author, be unwilling to consider using substitute words for "his."

10. **A** A "neologism" is a *new word*.

11. **C** The author quotes her father to illustrate the fact that in the past men "viewed the world . . . of artistic creation as a world of males" (lines 54–55). She says she doesn't believe her father was a misogynist (a man who hates women), but that he and other men in the past didn't "really see women" (lines 60–61). In context, therefore, "see women" means *take women seriously*. Clues to the meaning are "blind spot" (line 62) and "invisibility" (line 62).

12. **B** In context the word "reactionary" means *extremely conservative*. The author's "reactionary self" would most likely write "his book" because as a conservative she would follow the traditional and accepted practice.

13. **E** In context, a "mea culpa" is an *acknowledgement of a personal error*. Harrison Salisbury admits that he is "guilty" (line 78) of favoring males over females. "Mea culpa" in Latin literally means "through my fault."

14. **D** The author uses the word "slowed" figuratively to mean the sentence would not have been as graceful and effective if E. B. White had used the word "woman" instead of the word "girl."

15. **A** In the last paragraph (lines 109–111) the author argues that although "changing our language to make men and women equal has a cost . . . that doesn't mean it shouldn't be done." In the phrase "heedless grace" the word "grace" refers to *elegant writing* and the word "heedless" means *unconcerned*. The author is saying that we should be sad about losing the opportunity to write elegantly, but that we should accept its necessity.

16. **E** The author is suggesting that we should accept the necessity of changing our language so that it is not sexist, but that doing so will undoubtedly be difficult for some people to do graciously. The word "muster" in context means *summon up* and has a connotation of "exerting great effort to summon up." The author is being somewhat jocular in the last sentence of the passage.

17. **A** As mentioned in the explanation of question 16, the author is being somewhat humorous in the last sentence of the passage. We can infer that she mainly uses the expression "his'er" to remind us that every writer has to deal with the His'er Problem and must decide how to do so. The author's use of "his'er," although humorous, suggests that she might even consider using this expression she thinks is "hideous" (line 7) regularly.

18. **E** The author would almost certainly agree with this statement because she argues, "Changing our language to make men and women equal has a cost. That doesn't mean it shouldn't be done" (lines 109–111).

19. **B** The author would almost certainly change the sentence so that it does not suggest either that all writers are female or that all writers are male. Choice (A) does this but would not generally be considered graceful, a quality valued by the author. She probably would not like choice (C) because it uses "his'er," which she believes is "hideous" (line 7). She would probably reject (D) as unnecessarily wordy. Choice (B) changes the sentence so that the His'er Problem is avoided.

Section 10 Writing

1. **E** Dangling participle. The long participial phrase *returning home to New York City after two years spent teaching in the remote village* refers to *Tom*. Choice (E) improves the sentence by making *Tom* the subject of the independent clause and putting *Tom* at the beginning of the independent clause, immediately after the participial phrase that refers to *Tom*.

2. **B** The given sentence is a run-on sentence. Choice (B) corrects this by the use of the coordinate conjunction *but* at the beginning of the independent clause.

3. **B** Faulty diction. The phrase *have made it so complicated* must be completed with a phrase beginning with the word *that*.

4. **E** Subject–verb agreement. The verb *suggests* must agree in number with the noun *body*, the subject of the independent clause. This is the only answer choice that corrects the error in the given sentence while creating a clear and grammatical sentence. Choice (B) corrects the subject–verb agreement error, but changes the correct present tense (*suggest*) to the incorrect future tense (*will suggest*).

5. **C** Run-on sentence. Two independent clauses cannot be joined by a comma. Choice (C) correctly joins two independent clauses with a semicolon.

6. **D** Faulty parallelism. The noun clause *that one day humans will establish a permanent base on the Moon and also there will be colonization of Mars* is the object of the verb *believe*. Therefore, there is no reason to use different forms to say what people believe. Choice (D) improves the sentence by using one verb, *will establish*, in the clause, complemented by the direct objects, *base* and *colony*.

7. **C** Faulty parallelism. The adverb clause beginning with the subordinating conjunction *though* (consisting of all the words before the comma) mentions two things that Singapore is *heavily dependent on*, so it does not make sense for these to be in different forms. Choice (C) corrects this faulty parallelism.

8. **A** The given sentence is clear and grammatical. Note that a semicolon can be used to connect two independent clauses in a sentence, as it is here. This use of the semicolon is especially useful when the writer wants to emphasize that there is a close connection between what could be two separate sentences.

9. **B** This improves the given sentence so that it is less wordy.

10. **A** The given sentence is clear and grammatical.

11. **C** The given sentence does not make good sense because a company's filing for bankruptcy would not be caused by its starting to dominate its market. Choice (C) improves the sentence so that *once dominant in its market* is a participial phrase referring to the noun *company*, which is the subject of the independent clause.

12. **D** Faulty parallelism. Three qualities of a good teacher are given. The third of these qualities, *being approachable*, is not in the same form as the other two qualities. Choice (D) corrects this. Choice (E) is incorrect because a colon cannot be used to set off a list if the words before the colon do not form a complete sentence.

13. **D** Grammar error. The words before the colon are not an independent clause. Choice (D) corrects this so that there is an independent clause before the colon.

14. **B** The given sentence is grammatical and fairly clear. However, it is unnecessarily wordy, mainly because of the use of the passive voice. Choice (B) makes *major newspapers and magazines* the subject of the main (independent) clause of the sentence and uses a verb in the active voice. This creates a clear and more concise sentence.